BARC

Computer Science Engineering (CS/IT)

Latest Edition
Practice Kit

10 Tests
10 Mock Test

Based On Real Exam Pattern

✓ Thoroughly Revised and Updated

✓ Detailed Analysis of all MCQs

<table>
<tr><td>Title</td><td>: BARC Computer Science Engineering (CS/IT)</td></tr>
<tr><td>Author Name</td><td>: Mr. Rohit Manglik</td></tr>
<tr><td>Published By</td><td>: EduGorilla Community Pvt. Ltd.</td></tr>
<tr><td>Publishers Address</td><td>: 12/651, First Floor Opp. Arvindo Park, Near Jama Masjid,
Indira Nagar, Lucknow, Uttar Pradesh-226016, India</td></tr>
</table>

Copyright EduGorilla

Disclaimer EduGorilla

Compiled and created by EduGorilla Community Pvt. Ltd

Printed By EduGorilla Community Pvt. Ltd.

ROHIT MANGLIK
CEO, EduGorilla

Dear Applicants,

People say *"Success comes to those who work hard."* But I've seen people working hard for their exams day in and day out for marginal success. While others succeed in their examinations by putting in just half the work. So are they God Gifted? No! I believe that it's because they work *smart* and not just *hard*. Similarly, for your exams, you should strategize your preparation so as to increase the likelihood of success. Well with EduGorilla get ready to increase your *chances of selection* in your exam by *16x*.

EduGorilla helps you in not only working *hard* but also working in a *smart and strategic* manner. With EduGorilla's preparation package, you get a chance to make your exam preparation easy, and a fun learning path towards selection. Finding the right path to your preparations can be difficult if you don't know in which direction to head. Don't worry, we have you covered! EduGorilla will be your guide to success in your journey. With our Preparation Package, you can prepare strategically and beat the exam in just one attempt.

EduGorilla's Preparation Package includes-

• **Test Series**   • **Books**

Our preparation package is handcrafted as per the latest changes, expert opinions, and students' discretion. Thus, enabling you to get through each stage of the selection process for your exam.

Our Books are designed by the teachers and experts of the respective exam with a combined 150+ years of experience; to provide you with easy, efficient, and effective learning. Our books are smart, in the sense that not only do they give you the answers to the questions but also provide similar questions for practice.

EduGorilla's competent Test Series gives you real-time experience and confidence through which you can clear your offline or online exam in just one attempt. We currently host 83,000+ mock tests for 1,440+ competitive and academic exams.

Thus, EduGorilla misses no chance to assist you in your preparation and covers all stages of the exam, so that you don't have to look anywhere else.

We provide complete preparation packages for defense, banking, teaching, and other National & State-Level exams. Hence, it doesn't matter which exam you aspire to because you will reach your success.

ALL THE BEST !
Let EduGorilla be your Guide to Success.

Rohit Manglik,
Founder and CEO, EduGorilla

INTRODUCTION

EduGorilla focuses on guiding students to succeed in their examinations. With that in mind, our book, titled "BARC : Computer Science Engineering (CS/IT)", has been drafted through the collective efforts of our distinguished experts with 150+ years of combined experience. This book consists of questions that are created following the latest changes in the syllabus and exam pattern. We compiled the book on the basis of questions that are most likely to appear in the BARC Computer Science Engineering. Through EduGorilla's "BARC : Computer Science Engineering (CS/IT)" your chances of success will increase 16x.

EduGorilla does this through our Complete Preparation Package. This package consists of well-conceptualized and structured content in the form of questions that are tailor-made according to your needs and will help you practice for exams in a smart way by pinpointing all the necessary information. It also provides hints and solutions, along with a smart answer sheet for your self-evaluation. You can assess your shortcomings and work accordingly on areas that may require more of your attention.

EduGorilla promises to help you succeed in your examination and accomplish your dream goals. We believe in our aspirants and see them at the top of the merit list. And the first step towards the top is to start preparing with us. EduGorilla's "BARC : Computer Science Engineering (CS/IT)" includes the following attributes.

➤ Well-Researched Content

➤ Top-Notch Quality

➤ Detailed Answers and Analysis

➤ Smart Answer Sheet

➤ Exam Relevant Questions

Therefore, EduGorilla fortifies your preparation and makes it durable enough to help you stand tall and beat the examination.

BARC Computer Science Engineering
Scan QR code for Eligibility, Exam Pattern, Syllabus and more.

Book ID: 1033

TABLE OF CONTENTS

Q.1 Which among the following comparison sorts are in-place sorts?

A. Bucket sort   **B.** Insertion sort
C. Selection sort   **D.** Both (B) and (C)

Q.2 A max heap can be converted into a min heap in ________.

A. Exponential time   **B.** Quadratic time
C. Linear time   **D.** Logarithmic time

Q.3 To delete a dynamically allocated tree, the most suitable traversal technique is __________.

A. Pre-order   **B.** Post-order
C. In-order   **D.** Level-order

Q.4 Which of the following is true for a sorted list with 'n' elements?

A. Insertion in a sorted array takes constant time.
B. Insertion in a sorted linear linked list takes constant time.
C. Searching for a key in a sorted array can be done in O(log n) time.
D. Searching for a key in a sorted linear linked list can be done in O(log n) time.

Q.5 Consider the following linked list. Which of the following piece of code will insert the node pointed to by q at the end of the list?

A. for (p=list; p!=NULL; p=p→next); p=q;
B. for (p=list; p!=NULL; p=p→next); p→next=q;
C. for (p=list; p→next !=NULL; p=p→next); p=q;
D. for (p=list; p→next !=NULL; p=p→next); p→next=q;

Q.6 Let G be a simple undirected graph, T_D be a DFS tree on G, and T_B be the BFS tree on G.

Consider the following statements:

Statement I: No edge of G is a cross with respect to T_D.

Statement II: For every edge (u, v) of G, if u is at depth i and v is at depth j in T_B then $|i - j| = 1$.

In the light of the above statements, choose the correct answer from the options given below:

A. Both Statement I and Statement II are correct.
B. Both Statement I and Statement II are not correct.
C. Statement I is correct but Statement II is incorrect.
D. Statement I is incorrect but Statement II is correct.

Q.7 Consider the recurrence relation:

$$T(n) = 16T(n/4) + n!$$

The above recurrence relation represents the running time of an algorithm. Which of the following represents the time complexity of the algorithm?

A. $\theta(n)$ **B.** $\theta(\log n)$
C. $\theta(n\log n)$ **D.** $\theta(n!)$

Q.8 Consider the following statements:

$$S_1: f(n) = O\big(g(n)\big) \text{ iff } \lim_{n\to\infty} \frac{f(n)}{g(n)} = \infty$$

$$S_2: f(n) = \Omega\big(g(n)\big) \text{ iff } \lim_{n\to\infty} \frac{f(n)}{g(n)} = 0$$

How many statements are true?

A. 0   **B.** 1   **C.** 2   **D.** 3

Q.9 Consider the following code snippet:

```
int i = 0;
while(i<n)
{
    printf("GATE CS 2022");
    while(i<n)
    {
        printf("GATE CS 2022 SHIFT 1");
        while(i<n3)
        {
            printf("GATE CS 2022 SHIFT 2");
            i++;
        }
        i++;
    }
    i++;
}
```

What will be the time complexity of above code snippet?

A. $\theta(n^5)$ **B.** $\theta(n^6)$ **C.** $\theta(n^4)$ **D.** $\theta(n^3)$

Q.10 In how many ways can an object be passed to a function?

A. 1   **B.** 2   **C.** 3   **D.** 4

Q.11 What is the reason for avoiding the attributes property in the HTML DOM?

A. Found unnecessary
B. Attributes don't have attributes
C. Attributes have attributes
D. Considered irrelevant

Q.12 Which language made up of binary coded instructions?

A. Machine   **B.** C
C. BASIC   **D.** High level

Q.13 Translator which is used to convert codes of assembly language into machine language is termed as:

A. Assembler   **B.** Attember
C. Compiler   **D.** Debugger

Q.14 First element of an array is stored at index ________.

A. 0   **B.** 1   **C.** n **D.** $n-1$

Q.15 What is the complexity of Merge Sort?

A. $O(n^2\log n)$ **B.** $O(n\log n)$
C. $O(n^2)$ **D.** $O(n)$

Q.16 Which of the following sorting algorithms can be used to sort a random linked list with minimum time complexity?

A. Insertion Sort   **B.** Quick Sort
C. Heap Sort   **D.** Merge Sort

Q.17 The topological sorting of any DAG can be done in _______ time.

A. Cubic   **B.** Quadratic
C. Linear   **D.** Logarithmic

Q.18 What is the time complexity of inserting at the end in dynamic arrays?

A. $O(1)$ **B.** $O(n)$
C. $O(\log n)$ **D.** Either (A) or (B)

Q.19 Which of the following terms is just the connection of networks that can be joined together?

A. Internet
B. Virtual private network
C. Intranet
D. Extranet

Q.20 A computer checks the _______ of user names and passwords for a match before granting access.

A. Website   **B.** Network
C. Backup file   **D.** Database

Q.21 Network components are connected to the same cable in the _______ topology.

A. Star   **B.** Ring   **C.** Bus   **D.** Mesh

Q.22 What is backup?

A. Adding more components to your network.
B. Protecting data by copying it from the original source to a different destination.
C. Filtering old data from the new data.
D. All of these

Q.23 WPA 2 is used for security in _______.

A. Internet   **B.** Bluetooth
C. Wi-Fi   **D.** (A) and (B) both

Q.24 Which of the following is false in case of packet switching?

A. Network bandwidth consumption is minimum in packet switching.
B. Packet switching permits better sharing of the links amongst multiple users.
C. Packets need to be given sequence numbers for reordering them at the destination.
D. Packet requires retransmission.

Q.25 What is the main function of the transport layer?

A. Node to node delivery
B. Synchronization
C. Updating and maintenance of routing tables
D. The process to process message delivery

Q.26 A layer- 4 firewall (a device that can look at all protocol headers up to the transport layer) cannot:

A. Block entire HTTP traffic during $9{:}00$ PM and $5{:}00$ AM.
B. Block all ICMP traffic.
C. Stop incoming traffic from a specific IP address but allow outgoing traffic to the same IP address.
D. Block TCP traffic from a specific user on a multi-user system during $9{:}00$ PM and $5{:}00$ AM.

Q.27 Which type of address is $255.255.255.255$ according to IPv 4 addressing?

A. Multicast address
B. Limited broadcast address
C. Loopback address
D. Direct broadcast address

Q.28 The _______ format is usually used to store data.

A. BCD   **B.** Decimal
C. Hexadecimal   **D.** Octal

Q.29 RTN stands for _______.

A. Register Transfer Notation
B. Register Transmission Notation
C. Regular Transmission Notation
D. Regular Transfer Notation

Q.30 The instruction, Add $Loc, R1$ in RTN is _______.

A. AddSet CC $Loc + R1$
B. $R1 = Loc + R1$
C. Not possible to write in RTN
D. $R \leftarrow [Loc] + [R1]$

Q.31 Can you perform an addition on three operands simultaneously in ALN using Add instruction?

A. Yes
B. Not possible using Add, we've to use Add Set CC
C. Not permitted
D. None of these

Q.32 The main virtue for using single bus structure is _______.

A. Fast data transfers.
B. Cost effective connectivity and speed.
C. Cost-effective connectivity and ease of attaching peripheral devices.
D. None of these

Q.33 _______ are used to overcome the difference in data transfer speeds of various devices.

A. Speed enhancing circuitory
B. Bridge circuits
C. Multiple Buses
D. Buffer registers

Q.34 To extend the connectivity of the processor bus we use _______.

A. PCI bus   **B.** SCSI bus
C. Controllers   **D.** Multiple bus

Q.35 The instruction, Add $\#45, R1$ does _______.

A. Adds the value of 45 to the address of $R1$ and stores 45

in that address.

B. Adds 45 to the value of $R1$ and stores it in $R1$.

C. Finds the memory location 45 and adds that content to that of $R1$.

D. None of these

Q.36 In the case of, Zero-address instruction method the operands are stored in __________.

A. Registers

B. Accumulators

C. Push down stack

D. Cache

Q.37 As companies move past the experimental phase with Hadoop, many cite the need for additional capabilities, including ____________.

A. Improved data storage and information retrieval.

B. Improved extract, transform and load features for data integration.

C. Improved data warehousing functionality.

D. Improved security, workload management, and SQL support.

Q.38 Facebook Tackles Big Data With __________ based on Hadoop.

A. 'Project Prism'

B. 'Prism'

C. 'Project Big'

D. 'Project Data'

Q.39 Identify the DBMS among the following:

A. PL/SQL

B. MS-PowerPoint

C. MS-Access

D. MS-Excel

Q.40 What package of MS Office 2007 manages RDBMS?

A. Excel   **B.** Access   **C.** Goove   **D.** OneNote

Q.41 Which of the following do not use a DBMS?

A. Ultimate users

B. Administrators

C. Database designers

D. Hardware support teams

Q.42 What is the difference between DBMS and RDBMS?

A. A DBMS can be manipulated but an RDBMS cannot be.

B. A DBMS is a database of commercial type by an RDBMS is the data of engineers.

C. A DBMS cannot link up various files with one another whereas an RDBMS can.

D. Both (A) and (B)

Q.43 In DBMS, a defined field can have __________.

A. A fixed length

B. An unlimited length

C. A fixed-length defined by data type

D. An unlimited length defined by programmer

Q.44 Which one of the following is an RDBMS?

A. Java Beans

B. Fox Pro

C. Oracle

D. DBase IV

Q.45 Find out the correct option:

A. Documents can contain many different key-value pairs, or key-array pairs, or even nested documents.

B. MongoDB has official drivers for a variety of popular programming languages and development environments.

C. When compared to relational databases, NoSQL databases are more scalable and provide superior performance.

D. All of these

Q.46 The process of transferring data intended for a peripheral device into a disk (or intermediate store) so that it can be transferred to peripheral at a more convenient time or in bulk, is known as:

A. Multi-programming

B. Spooling

C. Caching

D. Virtual programming

Q.47 Block caches or buffer caches are used:

A. To improve disk performance

B. To handle interrupts

C. To increase the capacity of the main memory

D. All of these

Q.48 Which algorithm is defined in time quantum?

A. Shortest job scheduling algorithm

B. Round robin scheduling algorithm

C. Priority scheduling algorithm

D. Multilevel queue scheduling algorithm

Q.49 What is the number of characters contained in the primary name of the file of MS-DOS?

A. Up to 8 characters

B. 3 characters

C. Up to 10 characters

D. 5 characters

Q.50 Which of the following do not belong to queues for processes?

A. Job queue

B. PCB queue

C. Device queue

D. Ready queue

Q.51 When did IBM release the first version of disk operating system DOS version 1.0?

A. 1981   **B.** 1982   **C.** 1983   **D.** 1984

Q.52 Consider the 3 processes, $P1, P2$ and $P3$ shown in the table:

Process	Arrival time	Time unit Required
$P1$	0	5
$P2$	1	7
$P3$	3	4

The completion order of the 3 processes under the policies FCFS and RR 2 (round robin scheduling with CPU quantum of 2 time units) are:

A. FCFS: $P1, P2, P3$
RR 2: $P1, P2, P3$

B. FCFS: $P1, P3, P2$
RR 2: $P1, P3, P2$

C. FCFS: $P1, P2, P3$
RR 2: $P1, P3, P2$

D. FCFS: $P1, P3, P2$
RR 2: $P1, P2, P3$

Q.53 There are 200 tracks on a disk platter and the pending requests have come in the order $36, 69, 167, 76, 42, 51, 126, 12$, and 199. Assume the arm is located at the 100th track and moving towards track

200. If the sequence of disc access is $126, 167, 199, 12, 36, 42, 51, 69,$ and 76 then which disc access scheduling policy is used?

A. Elevator
B. Shorter Seek Time First
C. C-SCAN
D. First Come First Served

Q.54 A system that uses a two-level page has 2^{12} bytes pages and 32-bit virtual addresses. Assume each entry size is 4-byte. The first 10 bits of the address serve as the index into the first-level page. How many entries in a level-two page?

A. 2^8　　B. 2^{10}　　C. 2^{20}　　D. 2^{32}

Q.55 The simultaneous equations on the boolean variables a, b, c and d:

$$a + b + c = 1$$
$$\overline{a} + \overline{d} = 0$$
$$b\overline{c} = 1$$

Will have the following solutions for a, b, c and d respectively?

A. 0001　　B. 1110　　C. 1111　　D. 1101

Q.56 Given the function $f(a, b, c) = a(b + c)$. Which of the following option is/are correct?

A. $f(a, b, c)$ as a minterm expansion is given by $\sum m(0,2,3)$.
B. The complement of $f(a, b, c)$ as a maxterm expression is given by $\Pi M(1,4,5,6,7)$.
C. The complement of $f(a, b, c)$ as a maxterm expression is given by $\sum m(1,4,5,6,7)$.
D. None of these

Q.57 Find the boolean function for the shaded region of the following diagram represented:

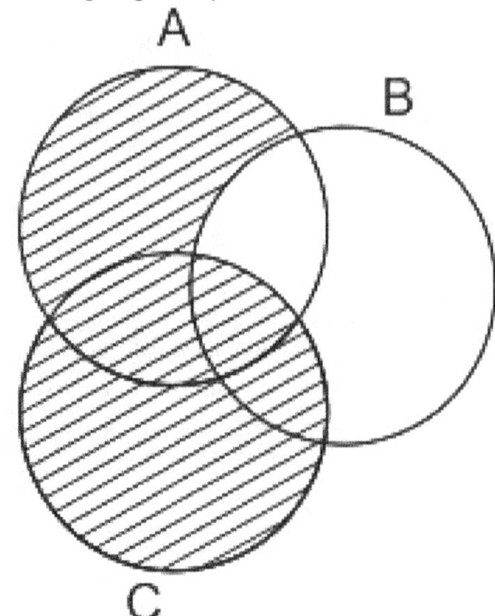

A. (A + C')(B' + C)
B. (A + C)(B' + C)
C. (A + C')(B' + C')
D. (A + C)(A + B')

Q.58 If a, b, c, d are ternary variables, then how many covering functions do a f have?
Where $f(a, b, c, d) = \Sigma(0,1,15,18,20)$:

A. 2^{76}　　B. 3^{76}　　C. 3^{59}　　D. 2^{59}

Q.59 Which boolean expression represents the following statements?
The outcome of three events are as follows. When all or any two events occur then it is 1 and for the remaining it is 0:

A. AB + BC + ABC
B. A'BC + AB + AC
C. AB + BC + AC
D. BC + ABC'

Q.60 What is the probability that the below-given $f(x, y, z)$ will return 1?

$$f(x, y, z) = \overline{x} + \overline{y} + x.z\left(x.(\overline{y} + z)\right)$$

Where $f(x, y, z)$ is a boolean function (answer upto 2 decimal places).

A. 0.75　　B. 1.75　　C. 0.78　　D. 0.85

Q.61 Which one of the following is/are valid identity, where $\odot$ is Ex-NOR and x, y are boolean variables?

S_1:
if $(x == 1 \,\|\, y == 1)$
Then $x \odot y = x.y$

S_2:
$$(x \odot y) \odot z = x \odot (y \odot z)$$

A. Only S_1
B. Only S_2
C. Both S_1 and S_2
D. Neither S_1 nor S_2

Q.62 What is the minimum number of NAND gates needed for the below given?

$$f(X, Y, Z, W) = X\overline{Y}Z\overline{W} + \overline{X}\overline{Y}ZW + X\overline{Y}Z W +$$
$$XYZ\overline{W} + \overline{X}Y\overline{Z}W + \overline{X}YZW + XY\overline{Z}W + XYZW$$

A. 5　　B. 6　　C. 7　　D. 8

Q.63 Consider the Boolean function $z(a, b, c)$.

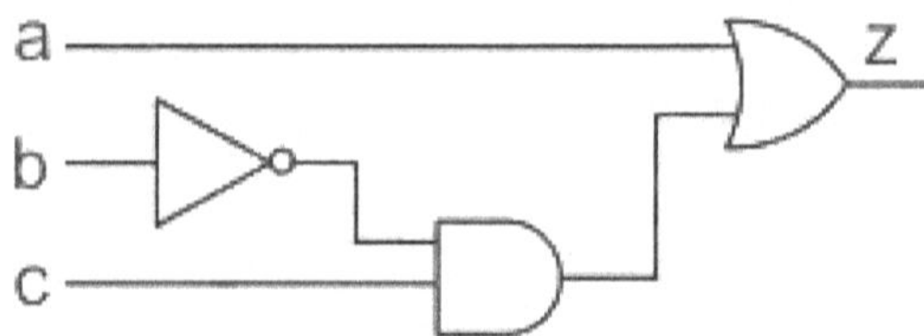

Which one of the following minterm lists represents the circuit given above?

A. $z = \Sigma(0,1,3,7)$
B. $z = \Sigma(1,4,5,6,7)$
C. $z = \Sigma(2,4,5,6,7)$
D. $z = \sum(2,3,5)$

Q.64 According to the given transitions, which among the following are the epsilon closures of $q1$ for the given NFA?

$$\Delta(q1, \varepsilon) = \{q2, q3, q4\}$$
$$\Delta(q4, 1) = q1$$

$$\Delta(q1, \varepsilon) = q1$$

A. $q4, q3, q2$ **B.** $q2, q1, q4$

C. $q3, q2$ **D.** $q1, q2, q3, q4$

Q.65 Statement 1: ε- transition can be called as hidden non-determinism.

Statement 2: δ (q, ε) = p means from q it can jump to p with a shift in read head.

Which among the following options is correct?

A. Statement 1 and 2, both are correct.

B. Statement 1 and 2, both are incorrect.

C. Statement 1 is correct while Statement 2 is incorrect.

D. Statement 1 is incorrect while Statement 2 is correct.

Q.66 The number of eight-bit strings beginning with either 111 or 101 is _________.

A. 64   **B.** 128

C. 265   **D.** None of these

Q.67 Which of the following does not belong to input alphabet if S={a, b}* for any language?

A. a   **B.** b

C. e   **D.** None of these

Q.68 The number of final states we need as per the given language?

Language L: {an| n is even or divisible by 3}

A. 1   **B.** 2   **C.** 3   **D.** 4

Q.69 Which phenomenon happens when the non-terminal on the left side is repeated as the first symbol on the right side?

A. Left-most derivation

B. Left recursion

C. Left factoring

D. Left parsing

Q.70 Which computer program accepts the high-level language and converts it into assembly language?

A. Interpreter   **B.** Linker

C. Assembler   **D.** Compiler

Q.71 Which of the following file is an output of the compiler or assembler?

A. Program file   **B.** Object file

C. Data File   **D.** Task File

Q.72 Which tool is used for grouping of characters in tokens in the compiler?

A. Parser   **B.** Code optimizer

C. Code generator   **D.** Scanner

Q.73 What is the major drawback of the Spiral Model?

A. Higher amount of risk analysis.

B. Doesn't work well for smaller projects.

C. Additional functionalities are added later on.

D. Strong approval and documentation control.

Q.74 Which two models doesn't allow defining requirements early in the cycle?

A. Waterfall and RAD

B. Prototyping and Spiral

C. Prototyping and RAD

D. Waterfall and Spiral

Q.75 Which of the following life cycle model can be chosen if the development team has less experience on similar projects?

A. Spiral

B. Waterfall

C. RAD

D. Iterative Enhancement Model

Q.76 If you were a lead developer of a software company and you are asked to submit a project/product within a stipulated time-frame with no cost barriers, which model would you select?

A. Waterfall   **B.** Spiral

C. RAD   **D.** Incremental

Q.77 Which two of the following models will not be able to give the desired outcome if user's participation is not involved?

A. Waterfall and Spiral

B. RAD and Spiral

C. RAD and Waterfall

D. RAD and Prototyping

Q.78 What does RAD stand for?

A. Rapid Application Document

B. Rapid Application Development

C. Relative Application Development

D. Both (A) and (B)

Q.79 The major drawback of RAD model is:

A. It requires highly skilled developers/designers.

B. It necessitates customer feedbacks.

C. It increases the component reusability.

D. Both (A) and (B)

Q.80 BPR stands for _________.

A. Business Process Re-engineering

B. Business Product Re-engineering

C. Business Process Requirements

D. Business Purpose Requirements

Q.81 The first step in the systems development life cycle (SDLC) is _____________.

A. Analysis

B. Design

C. Problem/Opportunity Identification

D. Development and Documentation

Q.82 A box contains 3 blue caps and 2 black caps. 2 caps are drawn from the box without replacement. Then, find the probability that the drawn caps are in alternate colour:

A. $\frac{2}{5}$ **B.** $\frac{3}{5}$ **C.** $\frac{1}{9}$ **D.** $\frac{1}{8}$

Q.83 A bunch of 10 bulbs contains 4 defective ones. Two bulbs are selected at random from the bunch. Out of $10,6$ are

red colour and 3 are red colour defective bulbs. What is the probability that red colour bulb but no one is defective?

A. $\frac{1}{60}$ B. $\frac{4}{9}$

C. $\frac{2}{25}$ D. None of these

Q.84 Find the degree and order of given equation:

$$\frac{d^3y}{dx^3} = \frac{d^2y}{dx^2} + \sin 60°$$

A. 1,3   B. 3,1

C. 0,1   D. None of these

Q.85 If $xdy = ydx + y^2dy, y > 0$ and $y(1) = 1$, then what is $y(-3)$ equal to?

A. 3 only   B. -1 only

C. Both -1 and 3   D. Neither -1 nor 3

Q.86 Let $f(t) = \sin^2 t$, find the Laplace transform of $f(t)$:

A. $\frac{2}{s^2+4}$ B. $\frac{2}{s(s^2+4)}$ C. $\frac{2s}{s^2+4}$ D. $\frac{2}{s(s^2-4)}$

Q.87 The inverse Laplace transform of $\frac{2s^2-4}{(s-3)(s^2-s-2)}$ is:

A. $(1+t)e^{-t} + \frac{7}{2}e^{-3t}$

B. $\frac{e^t}{3} + te^{-t} + 2t$

C. $\frac{7}{2}e^{3t} - \frac{e^{-t}}{6} - \frac{4}{3}e^{2t}$

D. $\frac{7}{2}e^{-3t} - \frac{e^t}{6} - \frac{4}{3}e^{-2t}$

Q.88 For what value of λ, the simultaneous equation $2x + 3y = 1, 4x + 6y = \lambda$ have infinite solutions?

A. $\lambda = 0$ B. $\lambda = 1$ C. $\lambda \neq 2$ D. $\lambda = 2$

Q.89 The standard ordered basis of R^3 is $\{e_1, e_2, e_3\}$. Let $T: R^3 \to R^3$ be the linear transformation such that:

$T(e_1) = 7e_1 - 5e_3, \ T(e_2) = -2e_2 + 9e_3, T(e_3) = e_1 + e_2 + e_3$

The standard matrix of T is:

A. $\begin{bmatrix} 7 & 0 & 1 \\ 0 & -2 & 1 \\ -5 & 9 & 1 \end{bmatrix}$ B. $\begin{bmatrix} 7 & -2 & 1 \\ -5 & 9 & 1 \\ 0 & 0 & 1 \end{bmatrix}$

C. $\begin{bmatrix} 7 & 0 & -5 \\ 0 & -2 & 9 \\ 1 & 1 & 1 \end{bmatrix}$ D. $\begin{bmatrix} 7 & -5 & 0 \\ -2 & 9 & 1 \\ 1 & 1 & 1 \end{bmatrix}$

Q.90 If $f(x) = x^3 + 3x^2 + 3x - 7$, then find the value of $\frac{df(x)}{dx}$ at $x = 2$:

A. 23   B. 24   C. 27   D. 30

Q.91 If $\int \frac{(x-1)^2}{(x^2+1)^2}dx = \tan^{-1}x + g(x) + k$, then $g(x)$:

A. $\frac{1}{2(x^2-1)}$ B. $\frac{1}{2(x^2+1)}$

C. $\tan^{-1}\frac{x}{2}$ D. None of these

Q.92 Direction: Negate the below-given statement.
Every Indian likes Bollywood movies.

A. Every Indian does not like Bollywood movies.

B. No Indian likes Bollywood movies.

C. There exists an Indian who doesn't like Bollywood movies.

D. There doesn't exists an Indian who like Bollywood movies.

Q.93 Which of the following statement is/are tautology?

A. $P \lor \neg P$ B. $(P \land Q) \Rightarrow P$

C. $(P \Rightarrow Q) \lor P$ D. All of these

Q.94 Any group of order 3 is:

A. Cyclic and abelian

B. Cyclic but not abelian

C. Infinite cyclic group

D. None of these

Q.95 What is the total number of spanning trees of a complete graph of 4 vertices K_4?

A. 15   B. 3   C. 16   D. 17

Q.96 Which one of the following function $f: R \to R$ is injective?

A. $f(x) = |x|, x \in R$ B. $f(x) = -x, x \in R$

C. $f(x) = x^2, x \in R$ D. $f(x) = c, x \in R$

Q.97 How many 3 digit numbers can be formed using the numbers $6,1,2,3$ without repetition?

A. 36   B. 24   C. 18   D. 12

Q.98 How many even 4 digit whole numbers are there?

A. 1358   B. 7250   C. 4500   D. 3600

Q.99 In the principle of mathematical induction, which of the following steps is mandatory?

A. Induction hypothesis

B. Inductive reference

C. Induction set assumption

D. Minimal set representation

Q.100 Consider the recurrence relation $a_1 = 4, a_n = 5n + a_{n-1}$. The value of a_{64} is ________.

A. 10399   B. 23760   C. 75100   D. 53700

// Smart Answer Sheet //

Correct — Percentage of students who answered correctly. **Skipped** — Percentage of students who skipped.

Q.	Ans.	Correct	Skipped	Q.	Ans.	Correct	Skipped	Q.	Ans.	Correct	Skipped	Q.	Ans.	Correct	Skipped	Q.	Ans.	Correct	Skipped	Q.	Ans.	Correct	Skipped
1	D	56.19 %	11.43 %	18	D	22.86 %	23.81 %	35	B	36.19 %	17.14 %	52	C	43.81 %	25.71 %	69	B	49.52 %	24.77 %	86	B	12.38 %	25.72 %
2	C	30.48 %	24.76 %	19	A	66.67 %	3.81 %	36	C	39.05 %	17.14 %	53	C	39.05 %	24.76 %	70	D	45.71 %	11.43 %	87	C	5.71 %	23.81 %
3	B	37.14 %	15.24 %	20	D	61.9 %	16.2 %	37	D	14.29 %	25.71 %	54	C	12.38 %	18.1 %	71	B	58.1 %	16.19 %	88	D	20.0 %	27.62 %
4	C	36.19 %	25.71 %	21	C	61.9 %	13.34 %	38	A	19.05 %	23.81 %	55	D	41.9 %	25.72 %	72	D	30.48 %	24.76 %	89	A	7.62 %	23.81 %
5	D	23.81 %	20.95 %	22	B	44.76 %	24.76 %	39	C	13.33 %	25.72 %	56	A	27.62 %	23.81 %	73	B	29.52 %	23.81 %	90	C	38.1 %	23.8 %
6	C	8.57 %	23.81 %	23	C	52.38 %	10.48 %	40	B	18.1 %	24.76 %	57	B	31.43 %	24.76 %	74	B	22.86 %	23.81 %	91	B	9.52 %	23.81 %
7	D	38.1 %	23.8 %	24	A	16.19 %	22.86 %	41	D	64.76 %	12.38 %	58	B	10.48 %	19.04 %	75	A	8.57 %	21.91 %	92	C	35.24 %	15.24 %
8	A	20.0 %	22.86 %	25	D	24.76 %	23.81 %	42	C	19.05 %	23.81 %	59	C	36.19 %	16.19 %	76	C	22.86 %	24.76 %	93	D	47.62 %	25.71 %
9	D	33.33 %	23.81 %	26	D	10.48 %	24.76 %	43	C	54.29 %	16.19 %	60	A	20.0 %	26.67 %	77	D	20.95 %	23.81 %	94	A	32.38 %	20.95 %
10	C	9.52 %	24.77 %	27	B	35.24 %	11.43 %	44	C	49.52 %	24.77 %	61	C	28.57 %	23.81 %	78	B	70.48 %	11.42 %	95	C	44.76 %	22.86 %
11	B	20.0 %	19.05 %	28	A	41.9 %	25.72 %	45	D	45.71 %	14.29 %	62	A	20.0 %	20.0 %	79	D	41.9 %	16.2 %	96	B	18.1 %	25.71 %
12	A	58.1 %	23.8 %	29	A	27.62 %	14.28 %	46	B	27.62 %	22.86 %	63	B	40.95 %	22.86 %	80	A	22.86 %	12.38 %	97	B	42.86 %	23.81 %
13	A	52.38 %	14.29 %	30	D	11.43 %	22.86 %	47	D	37.14 %	25.72 %	64	D	30.48 %	22.85 %	81	C	30.48 %	24.76 %	98	C	39.05 %	20.95 %
14	A	65.71 %	23.81 %	31	C	15.24 %	18.09 %	48	B	58.1 %	25.71 %	65	C	15.24 %	24.76 %	82	B	35.24 %	22.86 %	99	A	30.48 %	17.14 %
15	B	65.71 %	18.1 %	32	C	47.62 %	18.09 %	49	A	23.81 %	22.86 %	66	A	38.1 %	24.76 %	83	B	12.38 %	23.81 %	100	A	13.33 %	25.72 %
16	D	25.71 %	17.15 %	33	D	42.86 %	11.43 %	50	B	31.43 %	14.28 %	67	C	43.81 %	25.71 %	84	A	5.71 %	24.77 %				
17	C	23.81 %	25.71 %	34	A	13.33 %	24.77 %	51	A	25.71 %	14.29 %	68	B	17.14 %	22.86 %	85	A	3.81 %	23.81 %				

//Hints and Solutions//

1. An in-place sort is one that sorts the input without requiring additional space.

A sort algorithm in which the sorted items occupy the same storage as the original ones. A sorting algorithm that uses a small constant amount of extra space in addition to the original input, usually overwrite the input space, is referred as in-place sorting.

- Insertion Sort is typically done in-place, by iterating up the array, growing the sorted list behind it. At each array-position, it checks the value there against the largest value in the sorted list (which happens to be next to it, in the previous array-position checked).

- The selection sort algorithm finds the smallest (or largest, depending on sorting order) element in the unsorted sub-list, exchanges it with the leftmost unsorted element (putting it in sorted order), and moves the sub-list boundaries one element to the right without any additional space.

Hence, the correct option is (D).

2. Building a min heap on any array will take linear time. Therefore, converting a max heap array into min heal will take the same time.

Min heap is a special binary tree where the value stored in the parent node is less than or equal to the children and max heap is a tree where the parent is larger than or equal to the children.

Hence, the correct option is (C).

3. To delete a dynamically allocated tree, we can delete the child node first and then the parent first. So, the most suitable traversal technique is post-order.

We will traverse the tree by using post-order traversal because we have to delete all child nodes first before deleting root node. If we delete root node first then we cannot traverse child nodes of root without maintaining a separate data store.

Hence, the correct option is (B).

4. Searching for a key in a sorted array can be done in O(log n) time. In a sorted array, the search operation can be performed by using a binary search. Time Complexity of Search Operation: O(log n) [Using Binary Search]. Where n is number of elements.

Hence, the correct option is (C).

5. Piece of code will insert the node pointed to by q at the end of the list in the following linked list is:

for (p=list; p→next !=NULL; p=p→next); p→next=q;

A linked list is a linear collection of data elements whose order is not given by their physical placement in memory. Instead, each element points to the next. It is a data structure consisting of a collection of nodes that together represent a sequence.

Hence, the correct option is (D).

6. Statement I: Correct

Undirected graphs do not have cross edges in Depth First Search. But there can be cross edges in directed graphs. This statement is correct.

Statement II: Incorrect

In Breadth-First Search, an edge can be present between vertices of the same level. So, $|i - j| = 0$. This statement is incorrect.

Hence, the correct option is (C).

7. Given,

$$T(n) = 16T(n/4) + n!$$

On comparing with equation:

$$T(n) = aT\left(\frac{n}{b}\right) + f(n)$$ we get,

$$a = 16, \ b = 4, f(n) = n!$$

$$n^{\log_b a} = n^2$$

Here, $f(n) = \Omega\left(n^{\log_b a}\right)$

$$n! = \Omega(n^2)$$

And $af\left(\frac{n}{b}\right) \leq cf(n)$

$$T(n) = \theta\big(f(n)\big)$$

$$T(n) = \theta(n!)$$

Hence, the correct option is (D).

8. The main idea of asymptotic analysis is to have a measure of the efficiency of algorithms that don't depend on machine-specific constants, mainly because this analysis doesn't require algorithms to be implemented and time taken by programs to be compared.

Big- O is used as a tight upper bound on the growth of an algorithm's effort (this effort is described by the function $f(n)$, even though, as written, it can also be a loose upper-bound. "Little- O " (O) notation is used to describe an upper bound that cannot be tight.

The relationship between Big Omega (Ω) and Little Omega (ω) is similar to that of Big- O and Little o except that now we are looking at the lower bounds. Little Omega (ω) is a rough estimate of the order of the growth whereas Big Omega (Ω) may represent the exact order of growth. We use ω notation to denote a lower bound that is not asymptotically tight.

1. $f(n) = O\big(g(n)\big)$ iff $\lim\limits_{n\to\infty} \dfrac{f(n)}{g(n)} \leq C$

Where, (C is some constant).

2. $f(n) = \Omega\big(g(n)\big)$ iff $\lim\limits_{n\to\infty} \dfrac{f(n)}{g(n)} \geq C$

3. $f(n) = o\big(g(n)\big)$ iff $\lim\limits_{n\to\infty} \dfrac{f(n)}{g(n)} = 0$

4. $f(n) = \omega\big(g(n)\big)$ iff $\lim\limits_{n\to\infty} \dfrac{f(n)}{g(n)} = \infty$

5. $f(n) = \theta\big(g(n)\big)$ iff $\lim\limits_{n\to\infty} \dfrac{f(n)}{g(n)} = C$

Hence, the correct option is (A).

9. We know that, the execution process is:

1. Control enters into the first while ($i < n$) (condition is true).

2. Control also enters into the inner while($i < n$) loop.

3. Control again enter into innermost while $(i < n^3)$ loop and then continues its execution until i is equal to n^3. Then the control cannot go inside any of the while loops because all the 3 conditions will result in false.

So, total iteration is n^3 (inner most while) $+1$ (inner while) $+1$ (outer most while).

So, Time complexity $= O(n^3)$.

Hence, the correct option is (D).

10. The objects can be passed in three ways:

1. Pass by value

2. Pass by reference

3. Pass by address

Pass by value means you are making a copy in memory of the actual parameter's value that is passed in, a copy of the contents of the actual parameter.

Pass by reference of an argument in the calling function to the corresponding formal parameter of the called function. The called function can modify the value of the argument by using its reference passed in.

If you declare a formal parameter of a function as a pointer type, you are passing that parameter by its address. The pointer is copied, but not the data it points to. So, pass by address offers another method of allowing us to change the original argument of a function.

Hence, the correct option is (C).

11. When a web page is loaded, the browser creates a Document Object Model of the page. The reason for avoiding the attributes property in the HTML DOM is because Attributes don't have attributes.

The HTML DOM is a standard object model and programming interface for HTML. It defines:

- The HTML elements as objects
- The properties of all HTML elements
- The methods to access all HTML elements
- The events for all HTML elements.

Hence, the correct option is (B).

12. The language made up of binary coded instructions built into the hardware of a particular computer and used directly by the computer is machine language. Machine language, or machine code, is a low-level language comprised of binary digits (ones and zeros). High-level languages, such as Swift and C++ must be compiled into machine language before the code is run on a computer.

Hence, the correct option is (A).

13. A translator which is used to convert codes of assembly language into machine language is termed as an assembler.

An assembler is a software that converts an assembly language code to machine code. It takes basic Computer commands and converts them into binary codes that a computer's processor can use to perform its basic operations. These instructions are assembler language or assembly language.

Hence, the correct option is (A).

14. An array is a collection of homogeneous (same type) data items stored in contiguous memory locations.

First element of an array is stored at index 0.

Arrays are indexed starting at 0, as opposed to starting at 1.

arr[0]	arr[1]	arr[2]	arr[3]	arr[4]
1	2	3	4	5

Hence, the correct option is (A).

15. Merge sort: Merge sort is based on the divide and conquer approach.

Recurrence relation for Merge sort: Merge sort is based on the divide and conquers approach.

Recurrence relation for merge sort will become:

$$T(n) = 2\,T\left(\frac{n}{2}\right) + \theta(n)$$

Using Master's theorem,

$$T(n) = n \times \log n$$

Therefore, the time complexity of Merge Sort is $O(n\,\log n)$.

Hence, the correct option is (B).

16. Both merge sort and insertion sort can be used for linked lists. The slow random-access performance of a linked list makes other algorithms (such as quicksort) perform poorly, and others (such as heapsort) completely impossible. Since worst case time complexity of merge sort is $O(n\,\log n)$ and insertion sort is $O(n^2)$, merge sort is preferred.

Hence, the correct option is (D).

17. The topological sorting of any DAG can be done in linear time. Topological sorting for Directed Acyclic Graph (DAG) is a linear ordering of vertices such that for every directed edge U V, vertex V comes before V in the ordering. Topological Sorting for a graph is not possible if the graph is not a DAG. Topological sorting can be done in O(V+E), here V and E represent the number of vertices and number of edges respectively.

Hence, the correct option is (C).

18. Depending on whether the array is full or not, the complexity in a dynamic array varies. If you try to insert into an array that is not full, then the element is simply stored at the end, this takes $O(1)$ time. If you try to insert into an array that is full, first you will have to allocate an array with double the size of the current array and then copy all the elements into it and finally insert the new element, this takes $O(n)$ time.

Hence, the correct option is (D).

19. The internet is a globally connected network system that uses TCP/IP to transmit data via various types of media. The internet is a network of global exchanges – including private, public, business, academic and government networks – connected by guided, wireless and fiber-optic technologies.

Hence, the correct option is (A).

20. A computer checks the database of user names and passwords for a match before granting access. A database is an organized collection of data, generally stored and accessed electronically from a computer system. Where databases are more complex they are often developed using formal design and modeling techniques.

Hence, the correct option is (D).

21. Network components are connected to the same cable in the bus topology. A bus topology is a topology for a Local Area Network (LAN) in which all the nodes are connected to a single cable. The cable to which the nodes connect is called a "backbone". If the backbone is broken, the entire segment fails.

Hence, the correct option is (C).

22. In information technology, a backup, or data backup, or the process of backing up, refers to the copying into an archive file of computer data so it may be used to restore the original after a data loss event.

Hence, the correct option is (B).

23. WPA 2 is used for security in Wi-Fi. WPA 2 is a type of encryption used to secure the vast majority of Wi-Fi networks. A WPA 2 network provides unique encryption keys for each wireless client that connects to it. WPA 2 is an updated version of WPA that uses AES encryption and long passwords to create a secured network.

Hence, the correct option is (C).

24. After transmitting over a network, the packets are stored and forwarded at every node. Every packet has the source and destination addresses. In packet switching the overhead/wastage is more because every packet is required to carry the addresses on their header. So, with the user message in a packet, the header is to be transmitted also. From this point of view network

bandwidth consumed is maximum in packet switching and minimum in circuit switching.

Hence, the correct option is (A).

25. The transport layer is a 4th layer from the top. The main role of the transport layer is to provide the communication services directly to the application processes running on different hosts. The transport layer provides logical communication between application processes running on different hosts.

Hence, the correct option is (D).

26. Since it is layer- 4 firewall so, it includes the layers→ Physical Layer, Data Link Layer, Network Layer as well as Transport Layer.

Allow → Transport Layer or those layers who comes below Transport Layer.

Not Allow → Application Layer

Option (A): Transport Layer Specific

It is possible to block entire traffic by blocking all the traffic on port number 80. So, here don't need to check anything that it is application layer specific or not. we only need to block port number 80 for the required time interval.

Option (B): Network Layer Specific

ICMP is a network layer protocol that comes below the transport layer.

Option (C): Network Layer Specific

IP addresses are used in the network layer, which is below the transport layer.

Option (D): Application Layer Specific

In this option given that it is a multi-user system, so many users use the same port for communication because of this we can't block any specific port number. if we block a specific port number, all the users also blocked who is using that port number for communication. while we want to block a specific user, so how to do this. We need application layer-specific information of the user like user_id type of things that can't be checked as it is a 4-layer firewall. So, it is not possible to allow other users and block some specific at the same time using a 4-layer firewall.

Hence, the correct option is (D).

27. A limited broadcast address includes the network or subnet fields. In a limited broadcast packet destined for a local network, the network identifier portion and host identifier portion of the destination address is either all ones $(255.255.255.255)$ or all zeros $(0.0.0.0)$.

- A directed broadcast is a packet is sent to a specific destination address where only the host portion of the IP address is either all ones or all zeros (such as $192.20.255.255$ or $190.20.0.0$).

- A multicast address is a logical identifier for a group of hosts in a computer network that are available to

process datagrams or frames intended to be multicast for a designated network service.

- A loop back address is a special IP address, $127.0.0.1$, reserved by InterNIC for use in testing network cards. This IP address corresponds to the software loop back interface of the network card, which does not have hardware associated with it, and does not require a physical connection to a network.

Hence, the correct option is (B).

28. The BCD format is usually used to store data. The data usually used by computers have to be stored and represented in a particular format for ease of use. Data in memory is stored as zeros and ones. Most commonly known as either binary or machine code or a bit. E.g: 01000001 is A, 01000010 is B and 01000011 is C etc.

Hence, the correct option is (A).

29. RTN stands for Register Transfer Notation. This is the way of writing the assembly language code with the help of register notations. Register Transfer Notation (or RTN) is a way of specifying the behavior of a digital synchronous circuit. An example of high-level RTN is Verilog, and a low-level example is Register Transfer Language.

RTN may be written as either abstract or concrete. Abstract RTN is a generic notation that does not have any specific machine implementation details. In contrast, concrete RTN is a notation that does implement specifics of the machine for which it is designed.

Hence, the correct option is (A).

30. The instruction, Add $Loc, R1$ in RTN is $R1 \leftarrow [Loc] + [R1]$.

The possible locations in which transfer of information occurs are:

- Memory-location
- Processor Register
- Registers in I/O device

Add is an instruction that is used to perform an "Addition".

In some of the instructions, the same operand serves as both the source and destination operand.

$R1$ → It is a Processor Register.

Loc → It is a Memory location.

Add $Loc, R1$

Here the contents of memory location Loc is added with the register $R1$ and the resultant is stored in the register $R1$.

This can be written as $R \leftarrow [Loc] + [R1]$

For example: Consider $Loc = 3, R1 = 5$

Add $Loc, R1$

$$R1 = Loc + R1$$

$$\Rightarrow R1 = 3 + 5$$

$$\Rightarrow R1 = 8$$

The resultant value 8 is stored in the register $R1$.

Hence, the correct option is (D).

31. You cannot perform addition on three operands simultaneously because the third operand is where the result is stored. In RTN the first operand is the destination and the second operand is the source.

Hence, the correct option is (C).

32. The main virtue for using a single bus structure is cost-effective connectivity and ease of attaching peripheral devices.

By using a single bus structure we can minimize the amount of hardware (wire) required and thereby reducing the cost. In a single bus structure, one common bus used to communicate between peripherals and microprocessors. Since the bus can be used for only one transfer at a time, only two units can actively use the bus at any given time. Single bus structure is low cost, very flexible for attaching peripheral devices.

Hence, the correct option is (C).

33. Buffer registers are used to overcome the difference in data transfer speeds of various devices.

By using Buffer registers, the processor sends the data to the I/O device at the processor speed and the data gets stored in the buffer. After that, the data gets sent to or from the buffer to the devices at the device speed.

Hence, the correct option is (D).

34. The PCI bus is used as an extension of the processor bus and devices connected to it, is like connected to the processor itself. The PCI bus basically is used to connect to memory devices. PCI bus is used to connect other peripheral devices that require a direct connection with the processor.

Hence, the correct option is (A).

35. The instruction, Add $\#45, R1$ does add 45 to the value of $R1$ and stores it in $R1$. The instruction is using immediate addressing mode hence the value is stored in the location 45 is added.

In immediate addressing mode, the operand is a part of the instruction. There is no address field as the operand is a part of the instruction. It requires one reference to memory. It does not require any reference to memory.

Hence, the correct option is (B).

36. In the case of, Zero-address instruction method the operands are stored in push down stack. In this case, the operands are implicitly loaded onto the ALU.

Zero-address instruction is a format of machine instruction. It has one opcode and no address fields.

Example:

X = (A + B) $\times$ (C + D)

Now,

LOAD A	AC ← M[A]
PUSH A	TOS ← A
PUSH B	TOS ← B
ADD	TOS ← (A + B)
PUSH C	TOS ← C
PUSH D	TOS ← D
ADD	TOS ← (C + D)
MUL	TOS ← (C + D) × (A + B)
POP X	M[X] ← TOS

Hence, the correct option is (C).

37. As companies move past the experimental phase with Hadoop, many cite the need for additional capabilities, including improved security, workload management, and SQL support. Adding security to Hadoop is challenging because all the interactions do not follow the classic client-server pattern.

Hence, the correct option is (D).

38. Facebook tackles big data with 'Project Prism'based on Hadoop. Prism automatically replicates and moves data wherever it's needed across a vast network of computing facilities.

In an intense big data-themed talk on Facebook's campus, the company revealed its latest infrastructure project. Codenamed Prism, this project aims to solve one of the biggest problems Facebook has faced operating at its uniquely massive scale: how to create server clusters that can operate as a unit even when they're geographically distributed.

Hence, the correct option is (A).

39. MS-Access is a general-purpose database management system (DBMS) is a software system designed to allow the definition, creation, querying, update, and administration of databases. Well-known DBMSs include MySQL, Microsoft SQL Server, Oracle, SAP, etc.

Hence the correct option is (C).

40. Microsoft Access is a database management system (RDBMS) from the Microsoft Office package that combines the relational Microsoft Jet Database Engine with a graphical user interface and software-development tools. Microsoft Access has the look and feel of other Microsoft Office products as far as its layout and navigational aspects are concerned, but MS Access is a database and, more specifically, a relational database.

1. Before MS Access 2007, the file extension was *.mdb, but in MS Access 2007 the extension has been changed to *.accdb extension.

2. Early versions of Access cannot read accdb extensions but MS Access 2007 and later versions can read and change earlier versions of Access.

3. An Access desktop database (.accdb or mdb) is a fully functional RDBMS.

4. It provides all the data definition, data manipulation, and data control features that you need to manage large volumes of data.

5. You can use an Access desktop database (.accdb or mdb) either as a standalone RDBMS on a single workstation or in a shared client/server mode across a network.

6. A desktop database can also act as the data source for data displayed on webpages on your company intranet.

7. When you build an application with an Access desktop database, Access is the RDBMS.

Hence the correct option is (B).

41. Hardware support teams only maintain the hardware in which DBMS works. Rest all, that is ultimate users, administrators, and database designers use DBMS.

- Ultimate users are the users who occasionally use/access the database but each time when they access the database they require new information, for example, a middle or higher-level manager.

- A database administrator (DBA) is a person/team who defines the schema and also controls the 3 levels of the database.

- Database designers are the users who design the structure of the database which includes tables, indexes, views, constraints, triggers, stored procedures.

Hence the correct option is (D).

42. An RDBMS has a key that is common to many database files within an RDBMS. With the help of this common key, the RDBMS program can hop and jump from one file to another in no time and thus gather data with ease. In a DBMS, this utility is not available.

Database Management System (DBMS) is software that is used to define, create and maintain a database and provides controlled access to the data.

A Relational Database Management System (RDBMS) is an advanced version of a DBMS.

Hence the correct option is (C).

43. In DBMS, a defined field can have a fixed length defined by data type. In database systems, a field can have a fixed or a variable length. Fixed length means having a set length that never varies. A variable-length field is one whose length can be different in each record, depending on what data is stored in the field.

Hence the correct option is (C).

44. RDBMS include Oracle Database, MySQL, Microsoft SQL Server, and IBM DB2. Some of these programs support non-relational databases, but they are primarily used for relational database management system. Oracle Database is an RDBMS. An RDBMS that implements object-oriented features such as user-defined types, inheritance, and polymorphism is called an object-relational database management system (ORDBMS). An Oracle Database (aka Oracle RDBMS) is a collection of data organized by type with relationships being maintained between the different types.

Hence, the correct option is (C).

45. MongoDB is an open-source NoSQL database management program. NoSQL is used as an alternative to traditional relational databases. NoSQL databases are quite useful for working with large sets of distributed data. MongoDB is a tool that can manage document-oriented information, store or retrieve information.

When compared to relational databases, NoSQL databases are more scalable and provide superior performance, and their data model addresses several issues that the relational model is not designed to address: Large volumes of rapidly changing structured, semi-structured, and unstructured data.

There are also a large number of unofficial or community-supported drivers for other programming languages and frameworks. Documents can contain many different key-value pairs, or key-array pairs, or even nested documents.

Hence, the correct option is (D).

46. The process of transferring data intended for a peripheral device into a disk (or intermediate store) so that it can be transferred to peripheral at a more convenient time or in bulk, is known as 'spooling'. Spooling is a specialized form of multi-programming for the purpose of copying data between different devices. In contemporary systems, it is usually used for mediating between a computer application.

Hence, the correct option is (B).

47. Block caches or buffer caches are used to improve disk performance to handle interrupts to increase the capacity of the main memory to speed up the main memory.

Reading from a disk is very slow compared to accessing (real) memory. In addition, it is common to read the same part of a disk several times during relatively short periods of time. This is called disk buffering, and the memory used for the purpose is called the buffer cache.

The buffer cache is where data blocks are copied to perform SQL operations. The buffer cache is a shared memory structure and is concurrently accessed by all server processes.

Hence, the correct option is (D).

48. Time quantum is defined in round robin scheduling algorithm.

- The period of time for which a process is allowed to run in a pre-emptive multitasking system is generally called the time slice or quantum.

- Each process is assigned a fixed time (Time Quantum/Time Slice) in cyclic way. It is designed especially for the time-sharing system. The ready queue is treated as a circular queue.

- The CPU scheduler goes around the ready queue, allocating the CPU to each process for a time interval of up to 1-time quantum.

- If time quantum for round robin scheduling is very large, then it behaves same as FCFS scheduling.

Hence, the correct option is (B).

49. MS-DOS operating system uses a file system that supports 8.3 characters. The 8 characters are used to the filename, and 3 characters are used to the extension. the older MS-DOS FAT file system supports a maximum of 8 characters for the base filename and 3 characters for the extension, for a total of 12 characters including the dot separator. This is commonly known as an 8.3 filename.

Hence, the correct option is (A).

50. PCB queue does not belong to queues for processes. PCB is a process control block that contains information related to processing. Each process is represented by PCB. A process control block (PCB) is a data structure used by computer operating systems to store all the information about a process. It is also known as a process descriptor. When a process is created (initialized or installed), the operating system creates a corresponding process control block.

This specifies the process state i.e. new, ready, running, waiting or terminated.

Hence, the correct option is (B).

51. Perhaps the first public mention of the operating system was in July 1981, when Byte discussed rumors of a forthcoming personal computer with "a CP/M-like DOS to be called, simply, IBM Personal Computer DOS." 86-DOS was rebranded IBM PC DOS 1.0 for its August 1981 release with the IBM PC.

Hence, the correct option is (A).

52. FCFS is a scheduling algorithm in which the process that is scheduled first will execute first completely.

FCFS stands for first come first serve.

Round Robin is a scheduling algorithm in which the process executes for a fixed CPU quantum time then the next process gets executed then the next process and goes on.

Now,

The GANTT chart for the FCFS scheduling algorithm is:

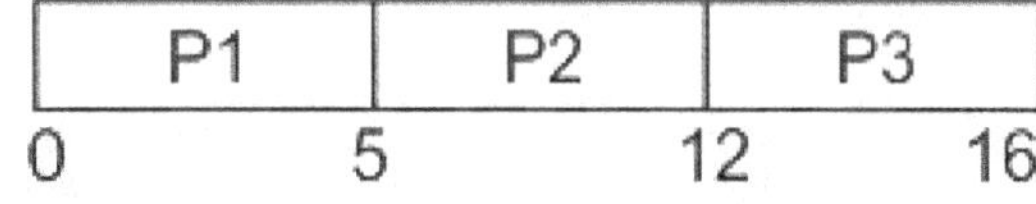

The completion order for the FCFS scheduling algorithm is: $P1, P2, P3$.

The GANTT chart for the RR 2 scheduling algorithm is:

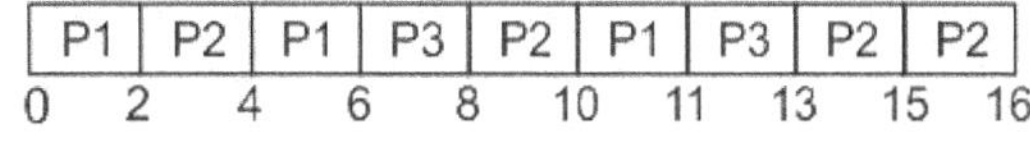

The completion order for the RR 2 scheduling algorithm is $P1, P3, P2$.

Hence, the correct option is (C).

53. Option (A):

The elevator algorithm is also known as the SCAN algorithm.

In this algorithm, the disk moves in a particular direction servicing the requests coming in the way till the end and reverse the direction and service all the requests.

Option (B):

In Shortest Seek Time First (SSTF), the algorithm selects disk I/O which requires the least disk arm movement from the current position

Option (C):

In C-scan i.e. Circular Elevator, the disk moves in a particular direction servicing the requests coming in the way till the end and reverse the direction and again goes to the start point and starts servicing the requests once reach the start point.

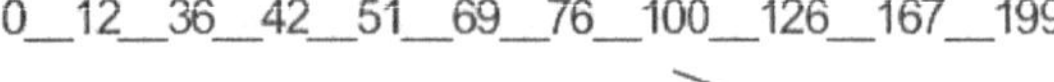

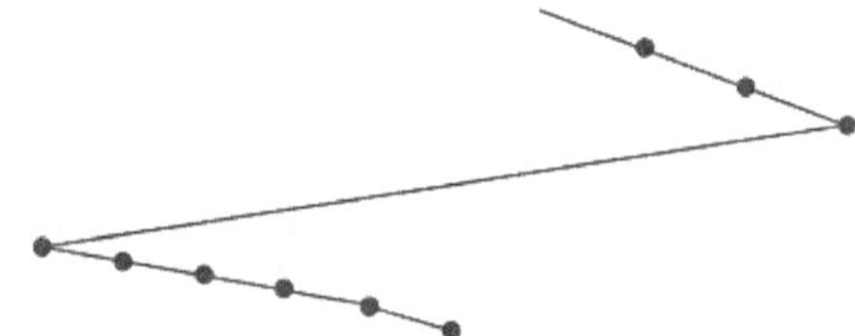

Option (D):

In First Come First Serve (FCFS), the disk service is the request that comes first.

Hence, the correct option is (C).

54. Size of page $= 2^{12}$ byte $=$ Frame Size

So, least significant 12-bits used as offset.

Logical address is 32-bit long.

So, size of logical address space $= 2^{32}$ of pages $\times$ page size (offset).

So, the number of pages $= 2^{20}$

Single level page contain all these page entries, so total number of entry in second label page $= 2^{20}$.

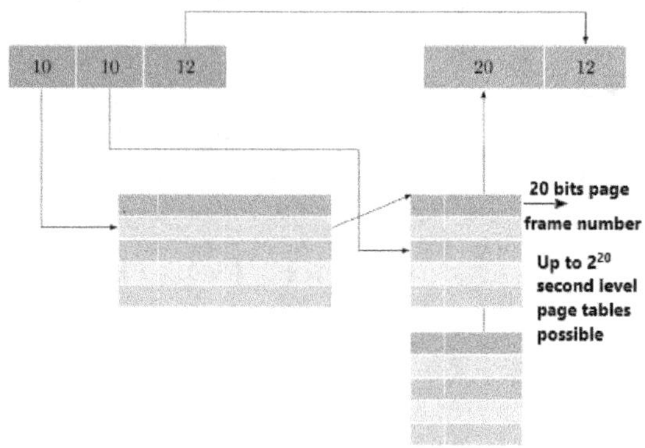

Hence, the correct option is (C).

55. Option (A):

$a + b + c = 0$ (since $a = b = c = 0$)

Option (B):

$\bar{a} + \bar{d} = 1$ $(a = 1, d = 0)$

Option (C):

$b \times \bar{c} = 0 (a = 1, c = 1)$

$\therefore$ Option (A), (B) and (C) are satisfying the expression.

Option (D):

$a = 1, b = 1, c = 0, d = 1$

$a + b + c = 1$ $(a = 1$ or $b = 1)$

$\bar{a} + \bar{d} = 0$ $(a = 1$ and $d = 1)$

$b \times \bar{c} = 1$ $(b = 1$ and $c = 0)$

Hence, the correct option is (D).

56. Given,

$$f(a, b, c) = \bar{a}(b + \bar{c})$$

$$= \bar{a}b + \overline{ac}$$

For the function, we form the K-map as:

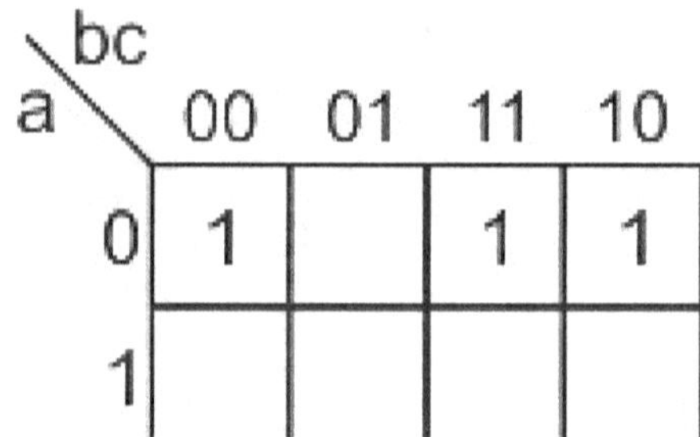

So, the function in the form of minterms is expressed as:

$$f(a, b, c) = \Sigma m(0, 2, 3)$$

Now, we put 0 in each block of the K-map excluding the blocks corresponding to the terms in the above function.

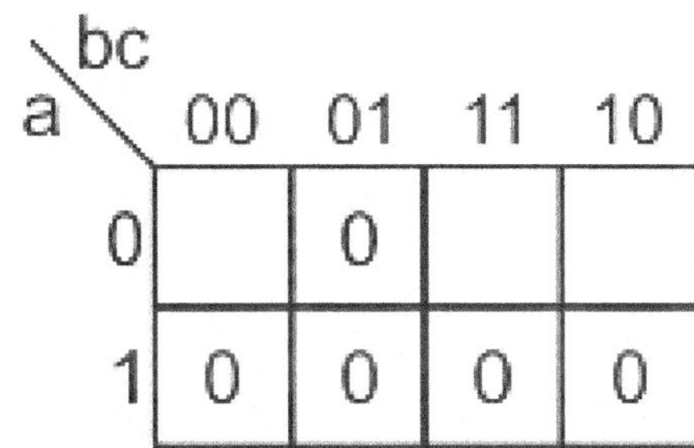

Grouping the 0's in K-map, we obtain the max terms as:

$$f(a, b, c) = \Pi M(1,4,5,6,7)$$

So, the complement of the function will have maxterms that are not present in the present case, i.e.

$$\overline{f}(a, b, c) = \Pi M(0,2,3)$$

Hence, the correct option is (A).

57. A Boolean function is a function that has n variables or entries, so it has $2n$ possible combinations of the variables. These functions will assume only 0 or 1 in its output. An example of a Boolean function is this, $f(a, b, c) = aXb + c$.

By the distributive property we have, the boolean function for shaded regions is:

F(A, B, C) = C + AB'C'

F(A, B, C) = (C + C') · (C + AB')

F(A, B, C) = (A + C) · (B' + C)

F(A, B, C) = (A + C)(B' + C)

Hence, the correct option is (B).

58. No of numbers represented with 4 ternary variables.

$$= 3^4 = 81$$

Function f has 5 minterms.

Case: 1

If the function is binary, then option (A).

No of covering functions are $= 2^{(81-5)}$

$$= 2^{76}$$

Case 2:

If the function is ternary, then option (B).

No of covering functions are $= 3^{(81-5)}$

$$= 3^{76}$$

Hence, the correct option is (B).

59. Let 3 events be A,B,C.

A= 1 means the event occurs.

A= 0 means the event does not occur.

A	B	C	event
0	0	0	0
0	0	1	0
0	1	0	0
0	1	1	1
1	0	0	0
1	0	1	1
1	1	0	1
1	1	1	1

Therefore considering only 1 event occurring case we get the expression;

$\Rightarrow$ A'BC + AB'C + ABC' + ABC

$\Rightarrow$ A'BC + ABC + AB'C + ABC'

$\Rightarrow$ BC + AB'C + ABC'

$\Rightarrow$ C(B + AB') + ABC'

$\Rightarrow$ C(B+B')(B+A) + ABC'

$\Rightarrow$ C(B+A) + ABC'

$\Rightarrow$ BC + AC + ABC'

$\Rightarrow$ BC + A(C + BC')

$\Rightarrow$ BC + A(C+B)(C+C')

$\Rightarrow$ BC + A(C+B)

$\Rightarrow$ BC + AC + AB

Hence, the correct option is (C).

60. Given,

$$f(x, y, z) = \overline{x} + \overline{y} + x \cdot z \left(x \cdot (\overline{y} + z) \right)$$

De Morgan's Law

$$f(x, y, z) = x \cdot \overline{y} + x \cdot z \left(\overline{x} + (\overline{y} + z) \right)$$

We know that,

$$f(x, y, z) = x \cdot \overline{y} + x \cdot z(\overline{x} + (\overline{y} \cdot \overline{z}))$$

$$f(x, y, z) = x \cdot \overline{y} + x \cdot z \cdot \overline{x} + xz \cdot \overline{y} \cdot \overline{z}$$

$$f(x, y, z) = x \cdot \overline{y} + x \cdot z \cdot \overline{x} + x \cdot z \cdot \overline{y} \cdot \overline{z}$$

$$f(x, y, z) = x \cdot \overline{y} + 0 + 0$$

$$f(x, y, z) = x \cdot \overline{y}$$

NAND Gate Truth Table:

x	y	$\overline{x \cdot y}$
0	0	1
0	1	1
1	0	1
1	1	0

Probability of getting $1 = \dfrac{3}{4}$

$= 0.75$

Hence, the correct option is (A).

61.

x	y	$x \odot y$	$x \cdot y$	Condition
0	0	1	0	$x = 0$ and $y = 0$
0	1	0	0	$y = 1$
1	0	0	0	$x = 1$
1	1	1	1	$x = 1$ and $= 1$ in this case $x = 1$ or $y = 1$ hold true

$x \odot y = x \cdot y$, if $x == 1 \parallel y == 1$

Therefore, S_1 is a valid identity.

Exclusive NOR is associative.

x	y	z	$x \odot y$	$(x \odot y) \odot z$	$y \odot z$	$x \odot (y \odot z)$
0	0	0	1	0	1	0
0	0	1	1	1	0	1
0	1	0	0	1	0	1
0	1	1	0	0	1	0
1	0	0	0	1	1	1
1	0	1	0	0	0	0
1	1	0	1	0	0	0
1	1	1	1	1	1	1

$(x \odot y) \odot z = x \odot (y \odot z)$

Therefore S_2 is a valid identity.

Therefore both S_1 and S_2 are valid identity.

Hence, the correct option is (C).

62. As we know that,

$f(X,Y,Z,W) = X\overline{Y}\,\overline{Z}\,\overline{W} + \overline{X}\,\overline{Y}\,\overline{Z}W + X\overline{Y}\,\overline{Z}\,\overline{W} + \overline{X}YZ\overline{W} + \overline{X}Y\overline{Z}W + \overline{X}YZW + XY\overline{Z}W + XYZ\overline{W}$

$f(X,Y,Z,W) = \overline{XY}\,\overline{Z} + \overline{X}\,\overline{Y}\,\overline{Z}\overline{W} + \overline{X}Y\overline{Z}W + \overline{X}YZW + X\overline{Y}\,\overline{Z}\overline{W} + X\overline{Y}Z\overline{W} + XY\overline{Z}W + XYZW$

$f(X,Y,Z,W) = \overline{X}Y\overline{W}(Z + \overline{Z}) + \overline{X}YW(Z + \overline{Z}) + X\overline{Y}\,\overline{W}(Z + \overline{Z}) + XYW(Z + \overline{Z})$

$f(X,Y,Z,W) = \overline{X}\,\overline{Y}\,\overline{W} + \overline{X}Y\overline{W} + X\overline{Y}W + XYW$

$f(X,Y,Z,W) = \left(\overline{X} + X\right)\left(\overline{Y}\,\overline{W}\right) + \left(\overline{X} + X\right)(YW)$

$f(X,Y,Z,W) = \overline{Y}\,\overline{W} + YW$

$f(X,Y,Z,W) = Y \odot W$

XNOR gate with NAND gates:

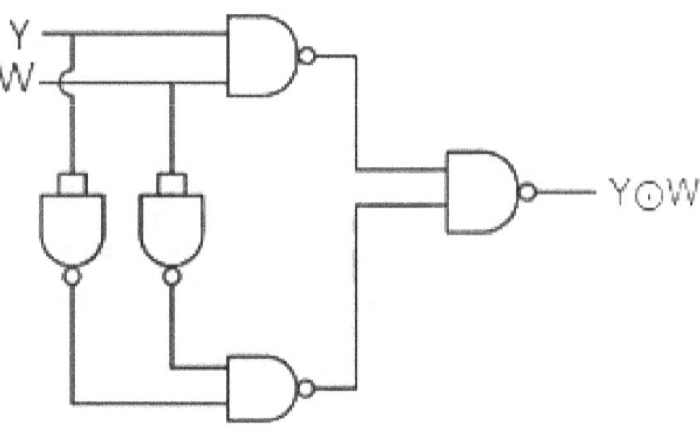

So, 5 NAND gates is needed.

Hence, the correct option is (A).

63. The given circuit gives the output:

$z(a,b,c) = a + \overline{b}c$

Expanding it into canonical form to obtain the minterms

$z(a,b,c) = a\left(b + \overline{b}\right)\left(c + \overline{c}\right) + (a + \overline{a})\overline{b}c$

$= abc + ab\overline{c} + a\overline{b}c + a\overline{b}\,\overline{c} + \overline{a}\,\overline{b}c$

After rearranging the canonical terms, this corresponds to min-terms: $\Sigma(1,4,5,6,7)$.

Alternate solution:

The output of the circuit is $a + \overline{b}c$

K Map for this Boolean expression:

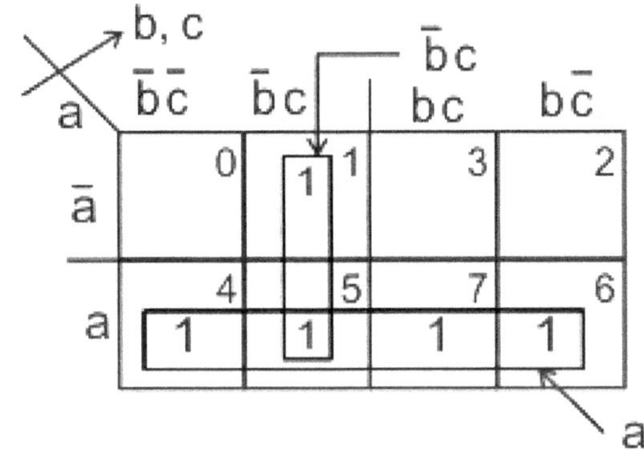

The above K Map corresponds to min-terms: $\sum(1,4,5,6,7)$.

Hence, the correct option is (B).

64. According to the given transitions, $q1, q2, q3, q4$ are the epsilon closures of $q1$ for the given NFA. The set of states which can be reached from q using ε-transitions is called the ε-closure over state q. Epsilon means the present state can go to another state without any input. This can happen only if the present state has an epsilon transition to another state. Epsilon closure is finding all the states which can be reached from the present state on one or more epsilon transitions.

Hence, the correct option is (D).

65. The transition with ε leads to a jump but without any shift in read head. Further, the method can be called one to introduce hidden non-determinism. Therefore, Statement 1 is correct while Statement 2 is incorrect.

Hence, the correct option is (C).

66. The number of 8-bit strings beginning with 111 are 32. First, 3 bits are fixed and the remaining 5 bits can be 0 or 1. So, the total combinations are $2^5 = 32$.

The same is the case with the strings starting with 101. So, the total number of strings is $32 + 32 = 64$.

Hence, the correct option is (A).

67. The automaton may be allowed to change its state without reading the input symbol using epsilon but this does not mean that epsilon has become an input symbol. On the contrary, one assumes that the symbol epsilon does not belong to any alphabet.

Hence, the correct option is (C).

68. According to given language,

L: {an| n is even or divisible by 3}

We have,

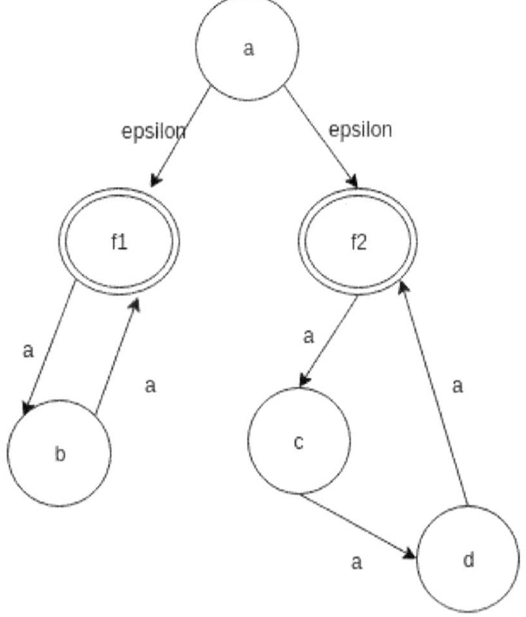

The number of final states we need as per the given language are 2.

Hence, the correct option is (B).

69. A production of grammar is said to have left recursion if the leftmost variable of its RHS is same as variable of its LHS. A grammar containing a production having left recursion is called as Left Recursive Grammar. Left recursion is considered to be a problematic situation for Top down parsers.

Hance, the correct option is (B).

70. A compiler is a translator that converts the high-level language into the low-level language (e.g. assembly language, object code, or machine code) to create an executable program. Compiler is used to show errors to the programmer. The main purpose of compiler is to change the code written in one language without changing the meaning of the program. When you execute a program which is written in HLL programming language then it executes into two parts. In the first part, the source program compiled and translated into the object program (low level language). In the second part, object program translated into the target program through the assembler.

Hence, the correct option is (D).

71. An object file is a computer file containing object code, that is, machine code output of the compiler or assembler. The object code is usually relocatable, and not usually directly executable. There are various formats for object files, and the same machine code can be packaged in different object file formats. An object file may also work like a shared library.

Hence, the correct option is (B).

72. The scanner is a subroutine which is frequently called by an application program like a compiler. The primary function of a scanner is to combine characters from the input stream into recognizable units called tokens. A method has been presented in this paper for designing such a scanner, also frequently referred to as a lexical analyzer in the current literature.

Hence, the correct option is (D).

73. A spiral model is an incremental approach, which is formed as a combination of the waterfall model and prototyping model. The major drawbacks of the Spiral model are as follows:

- Expensive
- Doesn't work well for smaller projects
- Risk analysis requires highly skilled experts.

Hence, the correct option is (B).

74. The prototyping model starts with a requirements analysis phase including techniques like FAST, QFD, Brainstorming. In the case of the Spiral model, the first phase involves activities related to customer communication like determining objectives.

Hence, the correct option is (B).

75. Relying on risk assessment/analysis provides more flexibility than required for many applications which overcomes the criteria of less experienced developers. Spiral model is one of the most important Software Development Life Cycle models, which provides support for Risk Handling. In its diagrammatic representation, it looks like a spiral with many loops.

Hence, the correct option is (A).

76. RAD model is inapplicable to develop cheaper products/software/projects as the cost of modeling, hiring highly skilled developers/designers and automated code generation is very high. But here the cost is not an issue, so one can select this model as it reduces development time.

Hence, the correct option is (C).

77. Active Participation of the user is involved in all four phases of the RAD model and in the case of the prototyping model we need the user's presence/involvement every time a new prototype is a build or design. RAD model refers to Rapid Application Development and it is type of Incremental Model. The components or functions are developed in parallel and it can handle small project as well as medium project. In this model any changes can be made in any stages. It has high productivity due to less number of people. Prototype Model is a software development life cycle model which is used when the customer is not known completely about how the end product should be and its requirements.

Hence, the correct option is (D).

78. RAD stands for Rapid Application Development is categorized as an agile development method, which is meant to accomplish a quick turnaround and high-end outcomes. RAD model is based on prototyping and iterative model with no (or less) specific planning. In general, RAD approach to software development means putting lesser emphasis on planning tasks and more emphasis on development and coming up with a prototype.

Hence, the correct option is (B).

79. The major drawback of RAD model is:

- It needs highly skilled developers.
- It needs user requirement throughout the life cycle of the product.
- It is more complex to manage when compared to other models.
- Only systems which can be modularised can be developed using Rapid application development.
- It cannot work with large teams.

Hence, the correct option is (D).

80. BPR stands for Business Process Re-engineering. Business process re-engineering is the radical redesign of business processes to achieve dramatic improvements in critical aspects like quality, output, cost, service, and speed. Business process re-engineering (BPR) aims at cutting down enterprise costs and process redundancies on a very huge scale.

Hence, the correct option is (A).

81. The first step in the systems development life cycle (SDLC) is Problem/Opportunity Identification. The process of problem identification involves the development of clear, straightforward problem statements that can be linked directly with the specific goals and objectives.

Hence, the correct option is (C).

82. Given:

Total number of caps we have $= 3 + 2 = 5$

Box having blue caps $= 3$

Box having black caps $= 2$

Required probability,

$$P(E) = \frac{\text{Number of favorable outcomes}}{\text{Total number of outcomes}}$$

E_1 : Event that first drawn cap is blue and second is black $= \frac{2}{4}$.

E_2 : Event that first drawn cap is black and second is blue $= \frac{3}{4}$.

$$\Rightarrow P(E_1) = \left(\frac{3}{5}\right) \times \left(\frac{2}{4}\right) = \left(\frac{6}{20}\right)$$

$$\Rightarrow P(E_2) = \left(\frac{2}{5}\right) \times \left(\frac{3}{4}\right) = \left(\frac{6}{20}\right)$$

$$\Rightarrow P(E) = P(E_1) + P(E_2)$$

As we know,

$$= \left(\frac{6}{20}\right) + \left(\frac{6}{20}\right)$$

$$= \frac{12}{20}$$

$$= \frac{3}{5}$$

Hence, the correct option is (B).

83. Given,

Total number of bulbs in the lot $= 10$

Number of defective bulbs $= 4$

Number of red colour bulb $= 6$

Number of defective red colour bulb $= 3$

We know that,

Probability of occurrence of an event in an experiment

$$= \frac{\text{Number of times event occurs}}{\text{Number of sample points in the experiment}}$$

Now,

Number of ways of picking any two bulbs from the 10 bulbs $= {}^{10}C_2$

Number of good condition red bulbs $= 6 - 3 = 3$

Number of ways of selecting red bulbs in good condition $= {}^{6}C_3$

So, the required probability is,

$$\Rightarrow = \frac{{}^{6}C_3}{{}^{10}C_2}$$

$$\Rightarrow \frac{\left(\frac{6!}{3!(6-3)!}\right)}{\left(\frac{10!}{2!(10-2)!}\right)}$$

$$\Rightarrow \frac{\left(\frac{6!}{3!(3)!}\right)}{\left(\frac{10!}{2!(8)!}\right)}$$

$$\Rightarrow \frac{\left(\frac{6\times5\times4\times3!}{3!(3)!}\right)}{\left(\frac{10\times9\times8!}{2!(8)!}\right)}$$

$$\Rightarrow \frac{\left(\frac{6\times5\times4}{3\times2\times1}\right)}{\left(\frac{10\times9}{2\times1}\right)}$$

$$\Rightarrow \frac{(120)}{(90\times3)}$$

$$= \frac{4}{9}$$

$\therefore$ The probability of picking red colour bulb but no one is defective is $\frac{4}{9}$.

Hence, the correct option is (B).

84. Given,

$$\frac{d^3y}{dx^3} = \frac{d^2y}{dx^2} + \sin60° \quad \left(\because \sin60° = \frac{\sqrt{3}}{2}\right)$$

$$\Rightarrow \frac{d^3y}{dx^3} = \frac{d^2y}{dx^2} + \frac{\sqrt{3}}{2}$$

Here, the highest derivative is $\frac{d^3y}{dx^3}$ so the order is 3.

The power of the highest derivative is one so the degree is 1.

$\therefore$ Degree and order is $1,3$.

Hence, the correct option is (A).

85. Given,

$$xdy = ydx + y^2dy$$

$$\Rightarrow xdy - ydx = y^2dy$$

$$\Rightarrow \frac{xdy-ydx}{y^2} = dy$$

$$\left(\because d\left(\frac{x}{y}\right) = \frac{ydx-xdy}{y^2} = \frac{xdy-ydx}{y^2} = -d\left(\frac{x}{y}\right)\right)$$

$$\Rightarrow -d\left(\frac{x}{y}\right) = d(y)$$

Integrating both side,

$$\int -d\left(\frac{x}{y}\right) = \int d(y)$$

$$\Rightarrow -\frac{x}{y} = y + c \dots\dots\text{(i)}$$

Given that $y(1) = 1$

So, by putting $x = 1$ and $y = 1$ in equation (i) we get,

$$\Rightarrow \frac{-1}{1} = 1 + c$$

$$\Rightarrow c = -2$$

$$\Rightarrow -\frac{x}{y} = y - 2$$

$$\Rightarrow y^2 - 2y + x = 0 \text{ (particular solution) } \dots\dots\text{(ii)}$$

Now, the value of $y(-3)$ put $x = -3$ in equation (ii) we get,

$$y^2 - 2y - 3 = 0$$

$$\Rightarrow y^2 - 3y + y - 3 = 0$$

$$\Rightarrow y(y - 3) + 1(y - 3) = 0$$

$$\Rightarrow (y - 3)(y + 1) = 0$$

So, two values of y we will get,

$$y = 3, y = -1$$

But in our question given that $y > 0$. Therefore we will take $y = 3$.

Hence, the correct option is (A).

86. Given,

$$f(t) = \sin^2 t$$

We know that,

$$\sin^2 t = \frac{1-\cos2t}{2} = \frac{1}{2} - \frac{\cos2t}{2}$$

Laplace transform of few functions are mentioned below:

$$L\{1\} = \frac{1}{s}$$

$$L\{cosat\} = \frac{s}{s^2+a^2}$$

Now,

$$\Rightarrow L[\sin^2 t] = L\left[\frac{1-\cos 2t}{2}\right]$$

$$\Rightarrow L[\sin^2 t] = L\left[\frac{1}{2} - \frac{\cos 2t}{2}\right]$$

$$\Rightarrow L[\sin^2 t] = \frac{1}{2}L[1 - \cos 2t]$$

$$\Rightarrow L[\sin^2 t] = \frac{1}{2}\left[\frac{1}{s} - \frac{s}{s^2+4}\right]$$

$$\Rightarrow L[\sin^2 t] = \frac{1}{2}\left[\frac{s^2+4-s^2}{s(s^2+4)}\right]$$

$$= \frac{2}{s(s^2+4)}$$

Hence, the correct option is (B).

87. Given,

$$\frac{2s^2-4}{(s-3)(s^2-s-2)}$$

We know that,

The Laplace transform of a general exponential signal is given by:

$$L[e^{-at}] \leftrightarrow \frac{1}{s+a}$$

where ' a' is any positive integer.

Now,

$$F(s) = \frac{2s^2-4}{(s-3)(s^2-s-2)}$$

$$= \frac{2s^2-4}{(s-3)(s+1)(s-2)}$$

$$= \frac{7}{2(s-3)} - \frac{1}{6(s+1)} - \frac{4}{3(s-2)}$$

Apply Inverse Laplace transform on both sides, we get

$$L^{-1}[F(s)] = f(t) = \frac{7}{2}e^{3t} - \frac{e^{-t}}{6} - \frac{4}{3}e^{2t}$$

Hence, the correct option is (C).

88. Given:

$$2x + 3y = 1$$

$$4x + 6y = \lambda$$

We know that:

Non-homogeneous equation of type $AX = B$ has infinite solutions; if $\rho(A \mid B) = \rho(A) <$ Number of unknowns

Now,

The augmented matrix is given by:

$$(A \mid B) = \begin{bmatrix} 2 & 3 & 1 \\ 4 & 6 & \lambda \end{bmatrix}$$

Applying $R_2 \rightarrow R_2 - 2R_1$

$$(A \mid B) = \begin{bmatrix} 2 & 3 & 1 \\ 0 & 0 & \lambda - 2 \end{bmatrix}$$

For the system to have infinite solutions, the last row must be a fully zero row.

So, if $\lambda = 2$ then the system of equations has infinitely many solutions.

Hence, the correct option is (D).

89. Given linear transformation are:

$$T(e_1) = 7e_1 - 5e_3$$

$$T(e_2) = -2e_2 + 9e_3$$

$$T(e_3) = e_1 + e_2 + e_3$$

Let the standard matrix be A with respect to the basis e_1, e_2, e_3

Now, $T(e_1) = 7e_1 + 0e_2 - 5e_3$

$$T(e_2) = 0e_1 - 2e_2 + 9e_3$$

$$T(e_3) = e_1 + e_2 + e_3$$

The standard matrix will be (transpose of linear combinations).

$$\begin{bmatrix} 7 & 0 & 1 \\ 0 & -2 & 1 \\ -5 & 9 & 1 \end{bmatrix}$$

Hence, the correct option is (A).

90. Given,

$$f(x) = x^3 + 3x^2 + 3x - 7$$

We know that:

$$\frac{d}{dx}(x^n) = nx^{n-1}$$

Derivative of a constant, i.e.,

$$\frac{d(\text{constant})}{dx} = 0$$

Therefore,

$$\frac{df(x)}{dx} = 3x^2 + 6x + 3$$

Putting $x = 2$ in above, we get:

$$\frac{df(2)}{dx} = 3(2)^2 + 6(2) + 3$$

$$= 3(4) + 12 + 3$$

$$= 12 + 12 + 3$$

$$\frac{df(2)}{dx} = 27$$

The value of $\frac{df(x)}{dx}$ at $x = 2$ is 27.

Hence, the correct option is (C).

91. Given,

$$\int \frac{(x-1)^2}{(x^2+1)^2} dx = \tan^{-1}x + g(x) + k$$

$$g(x) = ?$$

C is the arbitrary constant or constant of integration.

$$\int \frac{(x-1)^2}{(x^2+1)^2} dx$$

$$\Rightarrow \int \frac{x^2+1}{(x^2+1)^2} - \frac{2x}{(x^2+1)^2} dx$$

$$\Rightarrow \int \frac{1}{x^2+1} - \frac{2x}{(x^2+1)^2} dx \dots \dots (i)$$

Let $x^2 + 1 = t$

$$\Rightarrow 2x \cdot dx = dt$$

$$\because \int \frac{1}{x^2+1} = \tan^{-1}x + C$$

By putting the above values in equation (i)

$$\Rightarrow \tan^{-1}x - \int \frac{dt}{t^2} + k \quad \text{(where } k \text{ is an arbitrary}$$
constant)

$$\Rightarrow \tan^{-1}x + \frac{1}{t} + k$$

$$\Rightarrow \tan^{-1}x + \frac{1}{x^2+1} + k$$

On comparing it with the given condition i.e.,

$$\int \frac{(x-1)^2}{(x^2+1)^2} dx = \tan^{-1}x + g(x) + k,$$

$$\Rightarrow g(x) = \frac{1}{2(x^2+1)}$$

Hence, the correct option is (B).

92. Let $p(x)$ be x person in India who likes Bollywood movies every Indian likes Bollywood.

$$\forall x p(x)$$

Negate statements:

$$\equiv \neg \forall x p(x)$$

$$\equiv \exists x \neg p(x)$$

There exists an Indian who doesn't like Bollywood.

Hence, the correct option is (C).

93. Option (A): Tautology

P	Q	¬ P	P ∨ ¬p
T	T	F	T
T	F	F	T
F	T	T	T
F	F	T	T

Option (B): Tautology

P	Q	P ∧ Q	P ∧ Q ⇒ P
T	T	T	T
T	F	F	T
F	T	F	T
F	F	F	T

Option (C): Tautology

P	Q	P ⇒ Q	(P ⇒ Q) ∨ P
T	T	T	T
T	F	F	T
F	T	T	T
F	F	T	T

Hence, the correct option is (D).

94. We know that,

Any group of order 3 is cyclic.

Or any group of three elements is an abelian group.

The group has 3 elements: 1, a, and b. ab can't be a or b, because then we'd have b $= 1$ or a $= 1$. So, ab must be 1. The same argument shows ba $= 1$. So, ab=ba, and since that's the only non-trivial case, the group is also abelian.

- Every group of prime orders is cyclic.
- If an abelian group of order 6 contains an element of order 3, then it must be a cyclic group.
- Every subgroup of a cyclic group is itself a cyclic group.
- Every proper subgroup of an infinite cyclic group is infinite.

Hence, the correct option is (A).

95. As we know,

A spanning tree is a subset of Graph G, which has all the vertices covered with the minimum possible number of edges. The spanning tree doesn't have cycles and it cannot be disconnected.

Formula:

Number of spanning trees possible with n nodes $= n^{n-2}$

Now,

Here, a number of vertices are 4.

So, number of spanning trees possible $= 4^{4-2}$

$$= 4^2$$

$$= 16$$

Hence, the correct option is (C).

96. Function: A function is a relation between a set of inputs and a set of permissible outputs with the property that each input is related to exactly one output. Let A and B be any two nonempty sets, mapping from A to B will be a function only when every element in set A has one end only one image in set B.

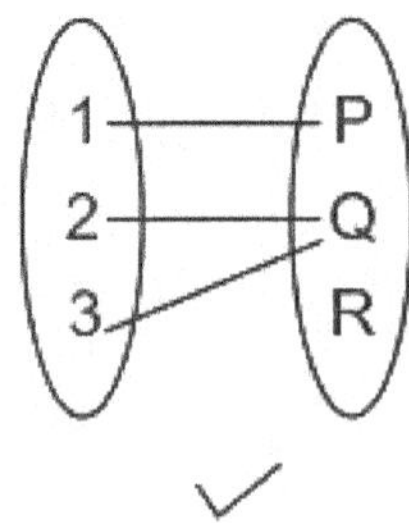 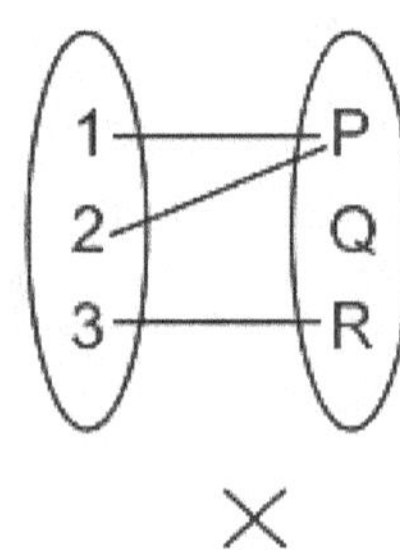

An injective function means one-one.

Consider $f(x) = -x$

Let $f(x) = f(y) \forall x, y \in R$

$\Rightarrow -x = -y \Rightarrow x = y$

For every value of x, we get a different value of f. So, it is injective.

One-One function (Injective function): If each element in the domain of a function has a distinct image in the co-domain, the function is said to be a one-one function.

For example, $f: RR$ given by $f(x) = 3x + 5$ is one - one.

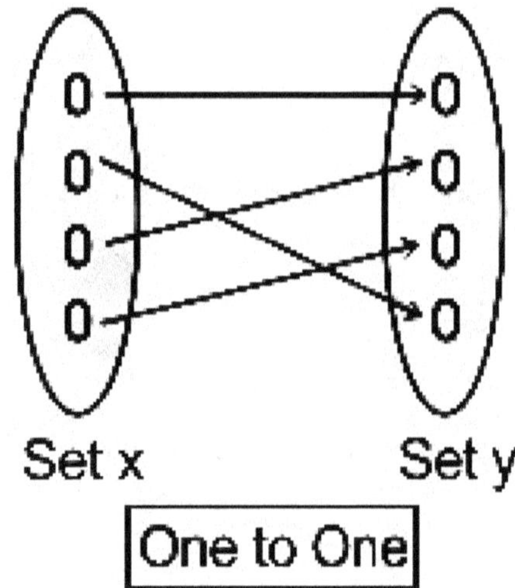

Many-one function: On the other hand, if there are at least two elements in the domain whose images are the same, the function is known as many to one.

For example, $f: RR$ given by $f(x) = x^2 + 1$ is many one.

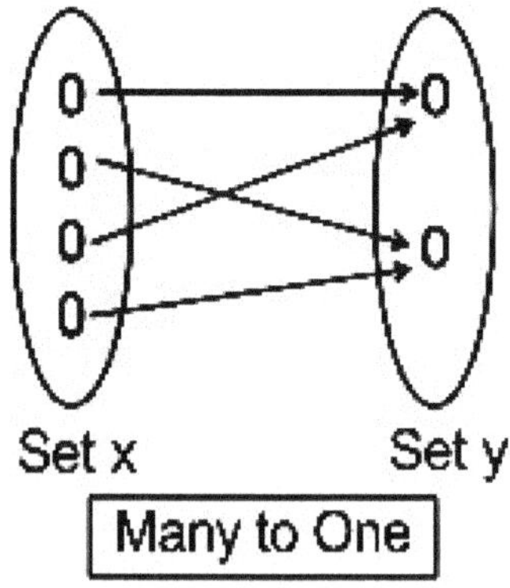

Hence, the correct option is (C).

97. Given,

A number are formed by using $6, 1, 2, 3$

Now,

Number of ways to fill the first position $= 4$

Number of ways to fill second position $= 3$

Number of ways to fill third position $= 2$

Total number of ways $= 4 \times 3 \times 2$

$\Rightarrow$ Total number of ways $= 24$

Hence, the correct option is (B).

98. The thousands digit cannot be zero, so there are 9 choices. There are 10 possibilities for the hundreds digit and 10 possibilities for the tens digit. The units digit can be $0, 2, 4, 6$ or 8, so there are 5 choices. By the basic counting principle, the number of even five-digit whole numbers is $9 \times 10 \times 10 \times 5 = 45,00$.

Hence, the correct option is (C).

99. The hypothesis of step is a must for mathematical induction that is the statement is true for n = k, where n and k are any natural numbers, which is also called induction assumption or induction hypothesis.

Hence, the correct option is (A).

100. Given,

$a_n = 5n + a_{n-1}$

$\Rightarrow 5n + 5(n-1) + \cdots + a_{n-2}$

$\Rightarrow 5n + 5(n-1) + 5(n-2) + \cdots + a_1$

$\Rightarrow 5n + 5(n-1) + 5(n-2) + \cdots + 4 [$ since, $a_1 = 4]$

$\Rightarrow 5n + 5(n-1) + 5(n-2) + \cdots + 5 \times 1 - 1$

$\Rightarrow 5(n + (n-1) + \cdots + 2 + 1) - 1$

$$\Rightarrow 5 \times \frac{n(n+1)}{2} - 1$$

$$a_n = 5 \times \frac{n(n+1)}{2} - 1$$

Now, $n = 64$

$$\Rightarrow a_{64} = 5 \times \frac{64(64+1)}{2} - 1$$

$$\Rightarrow a_{64} = 5 \times \frac{64 \times 65}{2} - 1$$

$$\Rightarrow a_{64} = 5 \times \frac{4160}{2} - 1$$

$$\Rightarrow a_{64} = 5 \times 2080 - 1$$

$$\Rightarrow a_{64} = 10400 - 1$$

$$a_{64} = 10399$$

So, the answer is $a_{64} = 10399$.

Hence, the correct option is (A).

Q.1 Consider a list of recursive algorithms and a list of recurrence relations as shown below. Each recurrence relation corresponds to exactly one algorithm and is used to derive the time complexity of the algorithm.

Recursive Algorithm	Recurrence Relation
(P) Binary search	(I) $T(n) = T(n-k) + T(k) + Cn$
(Q) Merge sort	(II) $T(n) = 2T(n-1) + 1$
(R) Quick sort	(III) $T(n) = 2T\left(\frac{n}{2}\right) + Cn$
(S) Tower of Hanoi	(IV) $T(n) = T\left(\frac{n}{2}\right) + 1$

Which of the following is the correct match between the algorithms and their recurrence relations?

A. P – II, Q – III, R – IV, S – I

B. P – IV, Q – III, R – I, S – II

C. P – III, Q – II, R – IV, S – I

D. P – IV, Q – II, R – I, S – III

Q.2 A recursive algorithm is designed in such a way that it is divided into three sub-problems of size in the ratio $[7:2:9]$ and a non-comparison based sorting algorithm is to be used to merge the results obtained by the subproblems (that the result are of a small range $<$ n). Which of the following describes the time complexity of such an algorithm?

A. O(n ^{2} log n)   **B.** O(n log log n)

C. O(n ^{3} log n)   **D.** O(n log n)

Q.3 All statements, except for the recursive calls $F(n)$, have $O(1)$ time complexity for the below given flow chart. If the worst-case time complexity of this function is $O(n^\lambda)$, then the least possible (accurate up to one decimal position) of λ is ______.

Flowchart for recursive function F(n)

```
              Start
                ↓
             F(n/3)
                ↓
return ← F(n/3) ← F(n/3) ← ◇ → F(n/3) → F(n/3) → return
                               ↓
         return ← F(n/3) ← F(n/3) ← F(n/3)
                               ↓
                              ◇
                               ↓
                            F(n/3)
                               ↓
                            return
```

A. 1.63   **B.** 1.60   **C.** 1.62   **D.** 1.65

Q.4 Consider a person wants to make change for Rs. 1873 and he has infinite supply of denomination i.e.

$1,2,5,10,20,50,100,500,1000$ valued coins. What is the minimum number of coins needed to make the change?

A. 9   **B.** 8   **C.** 10   **D.** 7

Q.5 What is the minimum number of nodes that must be examined in order to find the minimum value in an AVL tree of height 5?

A. 20   **B.** 3   **C.** 12   **D.** 5

Q.6 Consider a perfect binary tree of height h. Which of the following options represents the minimum and the maximum number of nodes in the right sub-tree of the root?

A. $2^h, 2^h$ **B.** $2^h + 1, 2^h - 1$

C. $2^{h-1}, 2^{h-1}$ **D.** $2h - 1, 2h - 1$

Q.7 The height of a tree is the length of the longest root-to-leaf path in it. The maximum and the minimum number of nodes in a binary tree of height 5 are:

A. 63 and 6, respectively

B. 64 and 5, respectively

C. 32 and 6, respectively

D. 31 and 5, respectively

Q.8 Which of the following is an application of depth-first search?

A. Only topological sort.

B. Only strongly connected components.

C. Both topological sort and strongly connected components.

D. Neither topological sort not strongly connected components.

Q.9 Consider product of three matrices M_1, M_2 and M_3 having W rows and X columns, X rows and Y columns, and Y rows and Z columns. Under what condition will it take less time to compute the product as $(M_1 M_2)M_3$ than to compute $M_1(M_2 M_3)$?

A. $\left(\frac{1}{x} + \frac{1}{z}\right) < \left(\frac{1}{w} + \frac{1}{y}\right)$

B. $x > y$

C. $(w + x) > (y + z)$

D. None of these

Q.10 If an object is passed by value, then __________.

A. A new copy of object is created implicitly.

B. The object itself is used.

C. Address of the object is passed.

D. A new object is created with new random values.

Q.11 In HTML, ______ attribute is used for merging of two or more adjacent columns.

A. CELLPADDING   **B.** CELLSPACING

C. ROWSPAN   **D.** COLSPAN

Q.12 A language ______ is supported by MS .Net platform.

A. C   **B.** C++   **C.** Java   **D.** C#

Q.13 Which of the following is not a characteristic of High-level languages?

A. Machine code
B. Platform independent
C. Interactive execution
D. User-friendly

Q.14 Diagram which shows relationship between classes is termed as:

A. Class diagram
B. Sequential diagram
C. Use case diagram
D. Communication diagram

Q.15 Which of the following is false about a doubly linked list?

A. We can navigate in both the directions.
B. It requires more space than a singly linked list.
C. The insertion and deletion of a node take a bit longer.
D. Implementing a doubly linked list is easier than singly linked list.

Q.16 Automatic variables use which data structure for space allocation in memory?

A. Stack   **B.** Queue
C. Priority queue   **D.** List

Q.17 Consider the binary search tree with n elements. The time required to search given element is ______.

A. $\theta(\log n)$ **B.** $\theta(n\log n)$
C. $\theta(n^2)$ **D.** $\theta(n^2\log n)$

Q.18 Which of the following application makes use of a circular linked list?

A. Undo operation in a text editor
B. Recursive function calls
C. Allocating CPU to resources
D. Implement hash tables

Q.19 An IP packet has arrived with the first 8 bits as 01000010. Which of the following is correct?

A. The number of hops this packet can travel is 2.
B. The total number of bytes in the header is 16 bytes.
C. The upper layer protocol is ICMP.
D. The receiver rejects the packet.

Q.20 Which of the following statements is/are correct regarding Http request methods?

A. The GET method requests information about a document from a resource.
B. The post method sends some information to the server from the client.
C. The head method does not have a response body.
D. All of these

Q.21 The message 11001001 is to be transmitted using the CRC polynomial $x^3 + 1$ to protect it from errors. The message that should be transmitted is:

A. 11001001000   **B.** 11001001011
C. 11001010   **D.** 110010010011

Q.22 Match following properties with the corresponding protocol layers:

A: It used to manage/terminate connections.
B: Fragmentation
C: Flow – Control
D: Error – Control
E. : Data Encryption/Decryption
F: It can use almost any network interface available.
G: End-users uses this layer directly
H: It provides end-to-end Communication.
I: Fragmentation

A. Application layer: G, Session layer: A, Presentation Layer: E, Transport layer: C, D, H, Network Layer: B, D, I, Data link layer: F, C, D.
B. Application layer: G, Session layer: A, Presentation Layer: E, Transport layer: C, D, H, Network Layer: B, I, Data link layer: F.
C. Application layer: G, A, E, Session layer: A, Presentation Layer: E, Transport layer: H, Network Layer: B, I, Data link layer: F.
D. Application layer: G, Session layer: A, Presentation Layer: E, Transport layer: C, D, H, Network Layer: B, C, D, I, Data link layer: F, C, D.

Q.23 Complex networks today are made up of hundreds and sometimes thousands of ________.

A. Documents   **B.** Components
C. Servers   **D.** Entities

Q.24 The first Network is ________.
A. CNNET   **B.** NSFNET
C. ASAPNET   **D.** ARPANET

Q.25 A USB communication device that supports data encryption for secure wireless communication for notebook users is called a _____.

A. USB wireless network adapter
B. Wireless switch
C. Wireless hub
D. Router

Q.26 Which of the following is the most common shared resource in a computer network?

A. Keyboard   **B.** Mouse
C. Combo drive   **D.** Printer

Q.27 What is Web Casting?

A. Casting a Mobile TV Star in a role on the web
B. Transmitting the video and audio on the Internet
C. Playing of Music on the Internet
D. Searching on the Web

Q.28 The 8-bit encoding format used to store data in a computer is ______.

A. ASCII   **B.** EBCDIC   **C.** ANCI   **D.** USCII

Q.29 ALU uses ______ to store the intermediate result.

A. accumulators   **B.** registers

C. heap   **D.** stack

Q.30 The Instruction fetch phase ends with _______.

A. Placing the data from the address in MAR into MDR

B. Placing the address of the data into MAR

C. Completing the execution of the data and placing its storage address into MAR

D. Decoding the data in MDR and placing it in IR

Q.31 While using the iterative construct (Branching) in execution ___________ instruction is used to check the condition.

A. Test-And-Set   **B.** Branch

C. TestCondn   **D.** None of these

Q.32 The bus used to connect the monitor to the CPU is _________.

A. PCI bus   **B.** SCSI bus

C. Memory bus   **D.** Rambus

Q.33 _________ register Connected to the Processor bus is a single-way transfer capable.

A. PC   **B.** IR   **C.** Temp   **D.** Z

Q.34 The addressing mode which makes use of in-direction pointers is _____.

A. Indirect addressing mode

B. Index addressing mode

C. Relative addressing mode

D. Offset addressing mode

Q.35 When we use auto increment or auto decrements, which of the following is/are true?

1. In both, the address is used to retrieve the operand and then the address gets altered.

2. In auto increment, the operand is retrieved first and then the address altered.

3. Both of them can be used on general purpose registers as well as memory locations.

A. 1,2,3   **B.** 2,1   **C.** 1,3   **D.** 2,3

Q.36 _______ addressing mode is most suitable to change the normal sequence of execution of instructions.

A. Relative   **B.** Indirect

C. Index with Offset   **D.** Immediate

Q.37 Which of the following is correct statement?

A. HBase is a distributed column-oriented database.

B. HBase is not open source.

C. HBase is horizontally scalable.

D. Both (A) and (C)

Q.38 Find out the correct statement:

A. Hadoop do need specialized hardware to process the data.

B. Hadoop 2.0 allows live stream processing of real-time data.

C. In the Hadoop programming framework output files are divided into lines or records.

D. None of these

Q.39 Entities having a primary key are called:

A. Primary Entities   **B.** Strong Entities

C. Weak Entities   **D.** Primary Key

Q.40 A transparent DBMS _________.

A. Cannot hide sensitive information from users.

B. Keep its logical structure hidden from users.

C. Keeps its physical structure hidden from users.

D. Both (A) and (B)

Q.41 The data stored in a database must be independent of the applications that access the database. This rule is called __________.

A. Logical Data Independence

B. Physical Data Independence

C. Data Dependency

D. None of these

Q.42 Name the data in a database that must be independent of its user's view and any change in logical data must not affect the applications using it:

A. Logical Data Independence

B. Physical Data Independence

C. Data Redundancy

D. Data Logic

Q.43 Name the system in which the end-user must not be able to see that the data is distributed over various locations:

A. Distribution Independence

B. Distribution Dependence

C. Logic Dependence

D. Distribution Logic

Q.44 Name the database that must be independent of the application that uses it:

A. Integrity Rule

B. Logical Rule

C. Logical Relationship

D. Integrity Independence

Q.45 Which of the following is not a NoSQL database?

A. SQL Server   **B.** MongoDB

C. Cassandra   **D.** None of these

Q.46 Processes P_1, P_2, P_3 and P_4 run on a single processor. Arrival time of processes P_1, P_2, P_3 and P_4 are $1,3,3$ and $5ms$ respectively while computation time of P_1, P_2, P_3 and P_4 are $2, X, 5$ and $7ms$ respectively. Algorithm used by processor for processing is Shortest Job First. If the average time turnaround time is $\frac{13}{2} ms$ then the value of X is ___________ ms (computation time of P_2 is less than P_4).

A. 3   **B.** 4   **C.** 5   **D.** 6

Q.47 Consider a fully associative cache with 8 cache blocks and the following sequence of memory block request $(5,4,26,8,20,7,26,8,17,36,46,23,8,4,17,26,9)$. If

LRU replacement policy is used then which cache block will have memory block 17?

A. 5   **B.** 6   **C.** 4   **D.** 7

Q.48 Consider a file system that uses inodes to represent files. Disk blocks are 10 KB in size, and a pointer to a disk block requires 40 bytes. This file system has 6 direct disk blocks, as well as single, double and triple indirect disk blocks. What is the maximum size in GB (up to two decimal) of a file that can be stored in this file system?

A. $160.62 - 160.63$ **B.** $160.62 - 160.60$

C. $150.62 - 160.63$ **D.** $140.62 - 160.63$

Q.49 Most of the microcomputer's operating systems like Apple DOS, MS-DOS and PC DOS etc. are called disk operating systems because:

A. They are memory resident.

B. They are initially stored on disk.

C. They are available on magnetic tapes.

D. They are partly in primary memory and partly on disk.

Q.50 What is Address Binding?

A. Going to an address in memory.

B. Locating an address with the help of another address.

C. Binding two addresses together to form a new address in a different memory space.

D. A mapping from one address space to another.

Q.51 What is the name of the technique in which the operating system of a computer executes several programs concurrently by switching back and forth between them?

A. Partitioning   **B.** Multitasking

C. Windowing   **D.** Paging

Q.52 Binding of instructions and data to memory addresses can be done at __________.

A. Compile-time   **B.** Load time

C. Execution time   **D.** All of these

Q.53 Description of all external symbols and transfer structure (transfer list or map) is provided to the linker by?

A. Macro processor   **B.** Translator

C. Loader   **D.** Editor

Q.54 Which of the following is not true with respect to deadlock prevention and deadlock avoidance schemes?

A. In deadlock prevention, the request for resources is always granted if resulting state is safe.

B. In deadlock avoidance, the request for resources is always granted, if the resulting state is safe.

C. Deadlock avoidance requires knowledge of resource requirements a priori.

D. Deadlock prevention is more restrictive than deadlock avoidance.

Q.55 If $f(x,y) = x + \overline{y}$, then find the value of $f(f(a+b,b),b)$?

A. ab **B.** $\overline{a}b$ **C.** $b\overline{a}$ **D.** $\overline{a}\overline{b}$

Q.56 A boolean algebraic expression F is given as:

$$F = (A + B)(A + \overline{A} + \overline{B})C + \overline{A}(B + \overline{C}) + \overline{A}B + ABC$$

Where A, B and C are logical variables. The most simplified expression for F is:

A. $C(A + B) + \overline{A}\left(B + \overline{C}\right)$

B. $(C + AB)\left(A + B\overline{C}\right)$

C. $\overline{C}A + A\overline{B}$

D. $CAB + \overline{A}\overline{B} + \overline{B}\overline{C}$

Q.57 Consider the below given boolean function:

$$f(a,b,c) = \left(a + \overline{b} + c\right) \cdot \overline{a} + \left(\overline{b} + c\right)$$

What is the number of literal in the simplified expression of $f(a,b,c)$?

A. 3   **B.** 2   **C.** 1   **D.** 0

Q.58 If w, x, y, z Boolean variables, then which one of the following is incorrect?

A. $wx + w(x + y) + x(x + y) = x + wy$

B. $w\overline{x}(y + \overline{z}) + \overline{w}x = \overline{w} + x + \overline{y}z$

C. $(w\overline{x}(y + x\overline{z}) + \overline{wx})y = x\overline{y}$

D. $(w + y)(wxy + wyz) = wxy + wyz$

Q.59 Consider W, Y, A and B be the Boolean variable and $\$$ operator defined as:

$$A\$B = \overline{A} + B \text{ where, } Y = \overline{W} \ \$A \text{ and } W = A + \overline{B}.$$

Find Y?

A. A **B.** $\overline{B}$ **C.** 0   **D.** 1

Q.60 Consider the following function:

$$f(A, B, C, D) = \Pi_m(0,2,7,8,15) + \Sigma_d(5,10,13)$$

Where d represents the don't-care condition in Karnaugh maps.

Which of the following is a minimum product-of-sums (POS) form of $f(A, B, C, D)$?

A. $(B + D) \times \left(\overline{B} + \overline{D}\right)$

B. $\left(\overline{B} + D\right) \times \left(B + \overline{D}\right)$

C. $\left(B + \overline{D}\right) \times \left(\overline{B} + D\right)$

D. $\left(B + \overline{D}\right) \times \left(\overline{B} + \overline{D}\right)$

Q.61 Consider the Karnaugh map given below. Where X represents "don't care condition":

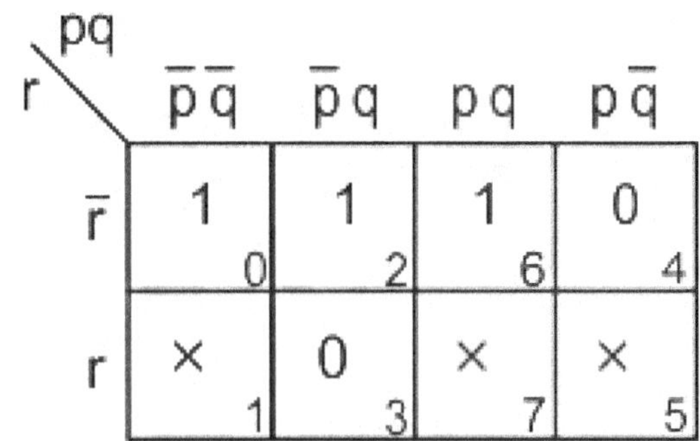

Assume for all inputs $(p, q, r,)$, the respective complements $(\bar{p}, \bar{q}, \bar{r})$ are also available. The above logic is implemented using 2-input NOR gates only. The minimum number of gates required is __________.

A. 2　　　**B.** 3　　　**C.** 4　　　**D.** 5

Q.62 Consider the following logic circuit whose inputs are functions $f1, f2, f3, f4$ and find the output f?

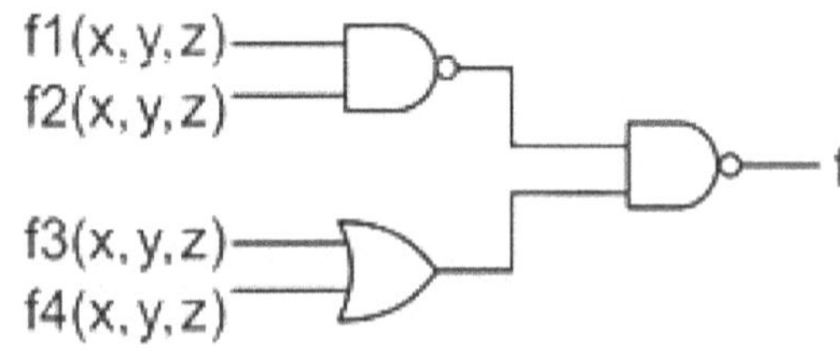

$$f1(x,y,z) = \Sigma(0,2,5)$$
$$f2(x,y,z) = \Sigma(1,5,7)$$
$$f3(x,y,z) = \Sigma(1,5)$$
$$f4(x,y,z) = \Sigma(3,6)$$

A. $\Sigma(0,2,4,5,15)$　　　**B.** $\Sigma(0,3,4,5,7)$
C. $\Sigma(0,2,4,5,7)$　　　**D.** $\Sigma(0,2,4,6,7)$

Q.63 Consider the following boolean expression for F:

$$F(P, Q, R, S) = PQ + \bar{P}QR + \bar{P}Q\bar{R}S$$

The minimal sum-of-products form of F is:

A. $PQ + QR + QS$　　　**B.** $P + Q + R + S$
C. $\bar{P} + \bar{Q} + \bar{R} + \bar{S}$　　　**D.** $\bar{P}R + \bar{P}RS + P$

Q.64 Which of the following belongs to the epsilon closure set of a?

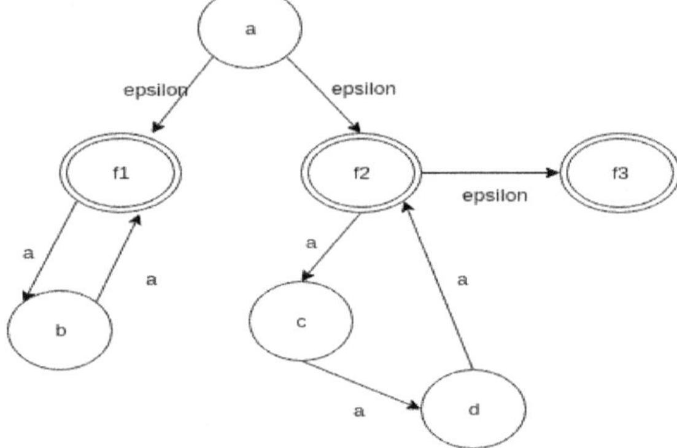

A. $\{f1, f2, f3\}$　　　**B.** $\{a, f1, f2, f3\}$
C. $\{f1, f2, \}$　　　**D.** None of these

Q.65 On translating the expression given below into quadruple representation, how many operations are required?

$$(i*j)+(e+f)*(a*b+c)$$

A. 5　　　**B.** 6　　　**C.** 3　　　**D.** 7

Q.66 Which among the following is false?
ε-closure of a subset S of Q is:

A.　Every element of S ϵ Q.
B.　For any q ϵ ε(S), every element of δ (q, ε) is in ε(S).
C.　No other element is in ε(S).
D.　None of these

Q.67 The automaton which allows transformation to a new state without consuming any input symbols is:

A. NFA　　　**B.** DFA
C. NFA-I　　　**D.** All of these

Q.68 The e-NFA recognizable languages are not closed under:

A. Union　　　**B.** Negation
C. Kleene Closure　　　**D.** None of these

Q.69 Parsing is categorized into how many types?

A. three types　　　**B.** four types
C. two types　　　**D.** five types

Q.70 In which parsing, the parser constructs the parse tree from the start symbol and transforms it into the input symbol?

A.　Bottom-up parsing
B.　Top-down parsing
C.　Operator precedence parser
D.　LR parser

Q.71 Which derivation is generated by the top-down parser?

A.　Right-most derivation in reverse
B.　Left-most derivation in reverse
C.　Right-most derivation
D.　Left-most derivation

Q.72 Which derivation is generated by the bottom-up parser?

A.　Right-most derivation in reverse
B.　Left-most derivation in reverse
C.　Right-most derivation
D.　Left-most derivation

Q.73 Expression $(\neg p \wedge \neg q) \vee (p \wedge q)$ is logically equivalent to:

A. $p \to q$ **B.** $p \leftrightarrow q$ **C.** $\neg p \wedge q$ **D.** $p \wedge q$

Q.74 Which of the following is false for the sets A, B and C?

A. $(A - B) - C = (A - C) - B$

B. $(A - B) - C = (A - C) - (B - C)$

C. $A \oplus (B \cup C) = (A \oplus B) \cup (A \oplus C)$

D. $A - (B \cup C) = (A - B) \cap (A - C)$

Q.75 Every subgroup of a cyclic group is itself a:

A. Group   **B.** Abelian group

C. Finite group   **D.** Cyclic group

Q.76 For which of the following Euler circuit is never possible if the number of vertices is greater than 2:

A. K_n **B.** Q_n **C.** W_n **D.** C_n

Q.77 Which of the following statement is incorrect?

A. A graph of 6 vertices can be 1-chromatic.

B. Every tree with 2 or more vertices is 2-chromatic.

C. A wheel graph of n-vertices is $\left(\left[\frac{n}{2}\right] + 1\right)$ chromatic.

D. A graph which has no circuit of odd-length and has atleast 1 edge is 2-chromatic.

Q.78 How many words with seven letters are there that start with a vowel and end with an A? Note that they don't have to be real words and letters can be repeated.

A. 45087902   **B.** 64387659

C. 12765800   **D.** 59406880

Q.79 For $m = 1, 2, \ldots, 4m + 2$ is a multiple of ______.

A. 3   **B.** 5   **C.** 6   **D.** 2

Q.80 Which of the following complete bipartite graphs will have hamiltonian cycle?

A. $K_{3,5}$ **B.** $K_{3,4}$ **C.** $K_{3,3}$ **D.** $K_{2,4}$

Q.81 What is the sequence depicted by the generating series?

$$4 + 15x^2 + 10x^3 + 25x^5 + 16x^6 + \cdots$$

A. 10,4,0,16,25, …

B. 0,4,15,10,16,25, …

C. 4,0,15,10,25,16, …

D. 4,10,15,25, …

Q.82 The user system requirements are the parts of which document?

A. SDD   **B.** SRS   **C.** DDD   **D.** SRD

Q.83 The reason for software bugs and failures is due to ______.

A. Software Developers

B. Software companies

C. Software platforms

D. Both (A) and (B)

Q.84 Which one of the following is a functional requirement?

A. Maintainability   **B.** Portability

C. Robustness   **D.** None of these

Q.85 Model selection is based on ______.

A. Requirements

B. Development team & users

C. Project type & associated risk

D. All of these

Q.86 The Unified Modeling Language (UML) has become an effective standard for software modelling. How many different notations does it have?

A. Three   **B.** Four   **C.** Six   **D.** Nine

Q.87 Which model in system modelling depicts the dynamic behaviour of the system?

A. Context Model   **B.** Behavioral Model

C. Data Model   **D.** Object Model

Q.88 Which model in system modelling depicts the static nature of the system?

A. Behavioral Model   **B.** Context Model

C. Data Model   **D.** Structural Model

Q.89 Which perspective in system modelling shows the system or data architecture?

A. Structural perspective

B. Behavioral perspective

C. External perspective

D. Both (A) and (B)

Q.90 The UML supports event-based modeling using ______ diagrams.

A. Deployment   **B.** Collaboration

C. State chart   **D.** All of these

Q.91 A bag contains black and white balls, such that the probability of picking a black ball is $\frac{4}{7}$. If the probability of picking two black balls without replacing the first is $\frac{4}{13}$, how many black balls are there in the bag?

A. 5   **B.** 6   **C.** 7   **D.** 8

Q.92 A small spherical substance was accidently dropped into a cylindrical vessel of height 42 cm and radius 30 cm filled with water. A small cylindrical glass of height 7 cm and radius 5 cm was used to take some water from it. What is the probability that the small spherical substance gets transferred to the glass?

A. $\frac{1}{6}$ **B.** $\frac{1}{36}$ **C.** $\frac{1}{216}$ **D.** $\frac{1}{24}$

Q.93 Find the general solution of the differential equation:

$$\frac{y^2}{x^2} = \frac{dy}{dx}$$

A. $\frac{1}{y} = \frac{1}{x} + C$ **B.** $y = x + C$

C. $\frac{y^2}{2} = \frac{x^2}{2} + C$ **D.** $y^2 = x^2 + C$

Q.94 If $\frac{dy}{dx} = e^{-3y}, y = 0$ when $x = 5$, value of x for $y = 5$ is:

A. $\frac{e^{15}+14}{3}$ **B.** $\frac{e^{15}-14}{3}$ **C.** 0   **D.** $e - \frac{3y}{5}$

Q.95 The Laplace transform of $\sinh(at)$ is:

A. $\frac{s}{s^2-a^2}$ **B.** $\frac{s}{s^2+a^2}$ **C.** $\frac{a}{s^2-a^2}$ **D.** $\frac{a}{s^2+a^2}$

Q.96 $F(s)$ is the Laplace transform of the function $f(t) = 2t^2e^{-t}$:

What is $F(1)$ is (correct to two decimal places)?

A. $0.59 - 0.62$ **B.** $0.48 - 0.52$

C. $0.38 - 0.49$ **D.** $0.68 - 0.72$

Q.97 If $A = \begin{bmatrix} 8 & 5 \\ 7 & 6 \end{bmatrix}$ then the value of $|A^{121} - A^{120}|$.

A. 0   **B.** 1   **C.** 120   **D.** 121

Q.98 Differentiate the following expression:

$$y = x^{\frac{2}{5}} - 2x^3 + 2x + 16$$

A. $\frac{2}{5x^{\frac{3}{3}}} + 6x^2 + 18$ **B.** $\frac{2}{5x^{\frac{3}{5}}} - 6x^2$

C. $\frac{2}{5x^{\frac{3}{5}}} - 6x^2 + 2$ **D.** $\frac{2}{5x^{\frac{3}{5}}} + 6x^2 + 14$

Q.99 What is $\int_{-a}^{a}(x^2 + \sin x)\,dx$ equal to?

A. a **B.** 0   **C.** $\frac{2a^2}{3}$ **D.** $\frac{2a^3}{3}$

Q.100 Consider the following statements:

(a) A lattice with 4 or fewer elements is distributive.

(b) Every sublattice of a distributive lattice is also a distributive lattice.

(c) Every totally ordered set is a distributive lattice.

(d) Every distributive lattice is a bounded lattice.

Which of the above statement are not true?

A. (a) and (b) only   **B.** (d) only

C. (a), (c) and (d) only   **D.** (a) and (d) only

// Smart Answer Sheet //

Correct	Percentage of students who answered correctly.	Skipped	Percentage of students who skipped.

Q.	Ans.	Correct / Skipped	Q.	Ans.	Correct / Skipped	Q.	Ans.	Correct / Skipped	Q.	Ans.	Correct / Skipped	Q.	Ans.	Correct / Skipped	Q.	Ans.	Correct / Skipped	Q.	Ans.	Correct / Skipped
1	B	63.43 % / 35.63 %	18	C	13.65 % / 71.77 %	35	D	89.19 % / 10.34 %	52	D	46.59 % / 37.85 %	69	C	84.16 % / 12.78 %	86	D	43.65 % / 47.39 %
2	A	68.18 % / 30.38 %	19	A	53.12 % / 35.9 %	36	A	45.41 % / 49.42 %	53	B	76.06 % / 23.24 %	70	B	62.14 % / 31.61 %	87	B	68.55 % / 30.82 %
3	A	28.18 % / 69.6 %	20	D	62.79 % / 30.57 %	37	D	43.69 % / 45.32 %	54	A	21.35 % / 71.26 %	71	D	50.85 % / 48.75 %	88	D	50.06 % / 48.97 %
4	A	60.25 % / 34.15 %	21	B	65.67 % / 32.45 %	38	B	41.06 % / 40.41 %	55	C	49.64 % / 47.59 %	72	A	59.58 % / 39.55 %	89	A	80.69 % / 10.45 %
5	B	67.72 % / 31.91 %	22	A	44.18 % / 55.03 %	39	B	83.29 % / 16.12 %	56	A	64.21 % / 30.78 %	73	B	49.47 % / 45.89 %	90	C	48.31 % / 46.67 %
6	B	27.96 % / 67.63 %	23	B	44.62 % / 34.2 %	40	C	42.78 % / 40.63 %	57	C	46.46 % / 52.99 %	74	C	25.8 % / 69.16 %	91	D	40.1 % / 57.05 %
7	A	84.35 % / 11.8 %	24	D	44.49 % / 43.85 %	41	B	48.36 % / 37.88 %	58	C	17.39 % / 67.54 %	75	D	79.23 % / 12.07 %	92	C	53.84 % / 34.78 %
8	C	25.95 % / 67.82 %	25	A	45.26 % / 34.66 %	42	A	77.38 % / 11.05 %	59	D	67.52 % / 32.09 %	76	A	49.47 % / 39.22 %	93	A	76.82 % / 15.94 %
9	A	43.33 % / 44.17 %	26	D	56.35 % / 41.11 %	43	A	65.5 % / 31.31 %	60	A	19.58 % / 67.63 %	77	C	28.45 % / 69.51 %	94	A	13.93 % / 81.39 %
10	A	83.51 % / 12.29 %	27	B	10.15 % / 70.29 %	44	D	46.49 % / 47.71 %	61	A	40.27 % / 47.23 %	78	D	69.47 % / 30.45 %	95	C	59.92 % / 32.08 %
11	D	64.31 % / 33.25 %	28	B	67.06 % / 31.16 %	45	A	83.93 % / 12.04 %	62	C	77.31 % / 16.93 %	79	D	29.01 % / 68.56 %	96	B	49.35 % / 41.07 %
12	D	54.56 % / 36.68 %	29	A	80.53 % / 10.95 %	46	A	29.93 % / 67.76 %	63	A	58.56 % / 36.64 %	80	C	22.9 % / 73.19 %	97	A	50.74 % / 31.04 %
13	A	58.8 % / 37.35 %	30	D	61.97 % / 37.19 %	47	B	53.34 % / 41.29 %	64	B	57.32 % / 36.48 %	81	C	82.74 % / 14.73 %	98	C	13.72 % / 80.43 %
14	A	80.89 % / 12.37 %	31	B	44.36 % / 37.17 %	48	A	59.35 % / 30.1 %	65	B	29.99 % / 68.1 %	82	B	55.43 % / 42.41 %	99	D	10.56 % / 80.76 %
15	D	77.82 % / 17.38 %	32	B	83.0 % / 11.48 %	49	B	49.81 % / 38.22 %	66	D	88.76 % / 10.66 %	83	D	50.76 % / 47.84 %	100	B	42.91 % / 54.51 %
16	A	56.24 % / 42.9 %	33	D	44.25 % / 48.53 %	50	D	55.72 % / 39.24 %	67	C	58.1 % / 33.37 %	84	D	76.18 % / 15.67 %			
17	A	55.3 % / 44.15 %	34	A	81.04 % / 10.78 %	51	B	59.67 % / 39.7 %	68	D	89.49 % / 10.27 %	85	D	58.26 % / 30.64 %			

//Hints and Solutions//

1. Binary search: Binary search is a fast search algorithm with run-time complexity of $O(\log n)$. This search algorithm works on the principle of divide and conquer. For this algorithm to work properly, the data collection should be in sorted form.

Merge sort: Merge Sort is a Divide and Conquer algorithm. It divides the input array into two halves, calls itself for the two halves, and then merges the two sorted halves. Once the size becomes 1, the merge processes come into action and start merging arrays back till the complete array is merged.

Quicksort: Quicksort is an in-place sorting algorithm. Quicksort is a divide-and-conquer algorithm. It works by selecting a 'pivot' element from the array and partitioning the other elements into two sub-arrays, according to whether they are less than or greater than the pivot.

Tower of Hanoi: A solution to the Towers of Hanoi problem points to the recursive nature of divide and conquer. We solve the bigger problem by first solving a smaller version of the same kind of problem. The recursive nature of the solution to the Towers of Hanoi is made obvious if we write a pseudocode algorithm for moving the disks.

(P) Binary search $\rightarrow T\left(\dfrac{n}{2}\right) + 1$

(Q) Merge sort $\rightarrow T(n) = 2T\left(\dfrac{n}{2}\right) + Cn$

(R) Quick sort $\rightarrow T(n) = T(n-k) + T(k) + Cn$

(S) Tower of Hanoi $\rightarrow T(n) = 2\,T(n-1) + 1$

So, the correct match is P - IV, Q - III, R - I, S - II.

Hence, the correct option is (B).

2. Given,

The problem is divided into 3 sub-problems in the ratio $7:2:9$.

The problem of size n is divided into sub-problems of size:

- $\dfrac{7n}{18}$
- $\dfrac{2n}{18}$
- $\dfrac{9n}{18}$

Also, it is given that it makes use of a non-comparison based sorting algorithm also it is given that the numbers are of a small range, therefore, we can take time complexity as O(n).

If we solved by "Recursion Tree Method" the work done at each level is O(n) and therefore the time taken by each level is O(n) and the tree is of height O(log n) , therefore the total time taken is O(n log n).

Hence, the correct option is (A).

3. The worst-case happens for the recursive calls on the longer route.

There are 6 such recursive calls to $A\left(\dfrac{n}{3}\right)$ in the worst case.

So, recurrence relation will become like this:

$$F(n) = 6F\left(\frac{n}{3}\right) + O(1)$$

Where $O(1)$ is constant.

By using master's theorem,

$$a = 6, b = 3$$

$$O\left(n^{\log_3 6}\right) = O(n^{1.63})$$

$$O\left(n^{\lambda}\right) = O(n^{1.63})$$

$$\lambda = 1.63$$

Hence, the correct option is (A).

4. Find the largest denomination which is smaller than given amount i.e. 1000.

New value $= 1873 - 1000 = 873$

Find the largest denomination which is smaller than given amount i.e. 500.

New value $= 873 - 500 = 373$

Find the largest denomination which is smaller than given amount i.e. 100.

New value $= 373 - 100 = 273$

Find the largest denomination which is smaller than given amount i.e. 100.

New value $= 273 - 100 = 173$

Find the largest denomination which is smaller than given amount i.e. 100.

New value $= 173 - 100 = 73$

Find the largest denomination which is smaller than given amount i.e. 50.

New value $= 73 - 50 = 23$

Find the largest denomination which is smaller than given amount i.e. 20.

New value $= 23 - 20 = 3$

Find the largest denomination which is smaller than given amount i.e. 2.

New value $= 3 - 2 = 1$

Find the largest denomination which is smaller than given amount i.e. 1.

New value $= 1 - 1 = 0$

So, coins required $1,2,20,50,100,100,100,500,1000$.

Hence, the correct option is (A).

5. The minimum number of nodes in an AVL tree can be calculated as follows:

Minimum number of nodes of height h, $N(h) = N(h-1) + N(h-2) + 1$

Where, $N(0) = 1$ and $N(1) = 2$

So,

$N(2) = N(1) + N(0) + 1 = 2 + 1 + 1 = 4,$

$N(3) = N(2) + N(1) + 1 = 4 + 2 + 1 = 7,$

$N(4) = N(3) + N(2) + 1 = 7 + 4 + 1 = 12,$

$N(5) = N(4) + N(3) + 1 = 12 + 7 + 1 = 20.$

Therefore, to find the minimum number of nodes of an AVL tree of height 5, the values of $N(2)$, $N(3)$ and $N(4)$ must be found. So, the values of 3 nodes have to be found.

Hence, the correct option is (B).

6. A perfect binary tree is a binary tree in which all interior nodes have two children and all leaves have the same depth or same level. In this tree each level contains the maximum number of nodes, ie., every level is completely full of nodes.

The number of nodes in a perfect binary tree $= 2^{h+1} - 1$

As per the question, we need to find the number of nodes in the right sub-tree alone. Also, the right sub-tree is at a height less than that of the original tree. So, the number of nodes $= 2^h - 1$

For a perfect binary tree, the minimum and the maximum number of nodes will be $2^h + 1, 2^h - 1$. Therefore, for the right sub-tree alone, they are $2^h - 1$.

Hence, the correct option is (B).

7. Calculating minimum and the maximum number of nodes from height.

If the binary search tree has height h, the minimum number of nodes is $h + 1$.

If the binary search tree has height h, the maximum number of nodes will be when all levels are completely full. Total number of nodes will be $= 2^{(h+1)} - 1$.

Now,

Maximum number of nodes $= 2^{(h+1)} - 1 = 2^6 - 1 = 63$.

Minimum number of nodes $= h + 1 = 5 + 1 = 6$.

The maximum and the minimum number of nodes in a binary tree of height 5 are 63 and 6, respectively.

Hence, the correct option is (A).

8. Depth first search:

Depth first search algorithm is used to traverse the vertices of a graph. It uses the concept of back tracking. Depth first search uses a data structure for its implementation which is known as stack.

Application of depth first search:

1. It is used to find the strongly connected components.
2. It helps in topological sorting.
3. To check the bipartiteness of a graph.
4. It helps in detecting cycles in a graph.
5. To find articulation points in a graph.

Example:

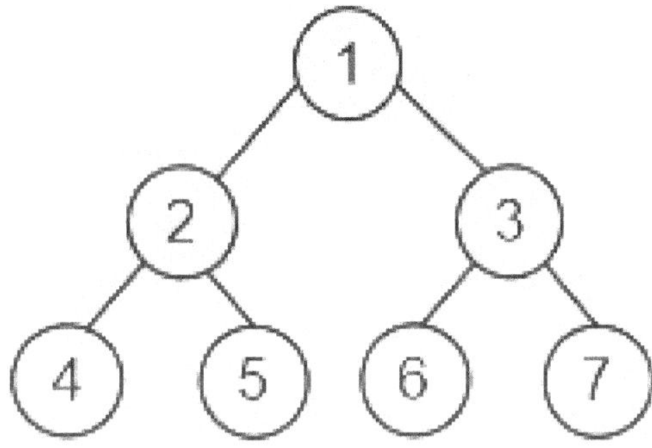

DFS traversal for this: $1,2,4,5,3,6,7$.

Hence, the correct option is (C).

9. Order of $M_1 = w \times x$

Order of $M_2 = x \times y$

Order of $M_3 = y \times z$

For cost of $(M_1 M_2)M_3 = wxy + wyz$. Detailed steps below.

- Cost of $M_1 M_2 = w \times x \times y$
- This gives us a new matrix. Let the new matrix be M.
- Order of M is $w \times y$
- Cost of $MM_3 = w \times y \times z$
- Total cost $= M_1 M_2$ cost $+ MM_3$ cost

Similarly, cost of $M_1(M_2 M_3) = xyz + wxz$

For $(M_1 M_2)M_3$ to take less time than $M_1(M_2 M_3)$

$(wxy + wyz) < (xyz + wxz)$

Dividing both the sides of above equation, we get

$\left(\frac{1}{x} + \frac{1}{z}\right) < \left(\frac{1}{w} + \frac{1}{y}\right)$

Hence, the correct option is (B).

10. When an object is passed by value, a new object is created implicitly. This new object uses the assignment of the implicit value, the same as that of the object being passed. Pass by value means you are making a copy in memory of the actual parameter's value that is passed in, a copy of the contents of the actual parameter. Use pass by value when when you are only "using" the parameter for some computation, not changing it for the client program.

Hence, the correct option is (A).

11. COLSPAN is the attribute of HTML language which defines the number of columns a table cell should span. It can be applied to <td> and <th>. HTML is a language that is used to create web pages and web applications. There are numbers of attributes in HTML language and COLSPAN is one of them.

Syntax:

<td colspan = "value">table content...</td>

Hence, the correct option is (D).

12. C# is a language supported by the MS .Net platform. C# is a general-purpose, multi-paradigm programming language encompassing static typing, strong typing, lexically scoped, imperative, declarative, functional, generic, object-oriented (class-based), and component-oriented programming disciplines.

Programming Languages which are designed and developed by Microsoft are:

- C#.NET
- VB.NET
- C++.NET
- J#.NET
- F#.NET
- JSCRIPT.NET
- WINDOWS POWERSHELL
- IRON RUBY
- IRON PYTHON
- C OMEGA
- ASML(Abstract State Machine Language)

Hence, the correct option is (D).

13. Machine code is not a characteristic of high-level languages. It is converted to machine language for further processing. A high-level language (HLL) is a programming language such as C, Fortran, or Pascal that enables a programmer to write programs that are more or less independent of a particular type of computer. Such languages are considered high-level because they are closer to human languages and further from machine languages.

Hence, the correct option is (A).

14. The diagram which shows the relationship between classes is termed as Class diagram. Class diagrams are the main building block in object-oriented modeling. They are used to show the different objects in a system, their attributes, their operations and the relationships among them.

The following figure is an example of a simple class:

Loan Account
type: String accountName:String dateReleased:Date loanAmount: Number
renew() extend()

Hence, the correct option is (A).

15. A doubly linked list has two pointers 'left' and 'right' which enable it to traverse in either direction. Compared to singly liked list which has only a 'next' pointer, doubly linked list requires extra space to store this extra pointer. Every insertion and deletion requires manipulation of two pointers, hence it takes a bit longer time. Implementing doubly linked list involves setting both left and right pointers to correct nodes and takes more time than singly linked list.

Hence, the correct option is (D).

16. Memory of a computer is organized for running program into three segments: the text segment, stack segment, heap segment.

Stack and heap is where storage is allocated for data storage. Stack is where memory is allocated for automatic variables within functions.

Hence, the correct option is (A).

17. The time required to search a given n elements in a binary $\theta(\log n)$.

In a Binary search tree, searching a given element depends on the height of BST.

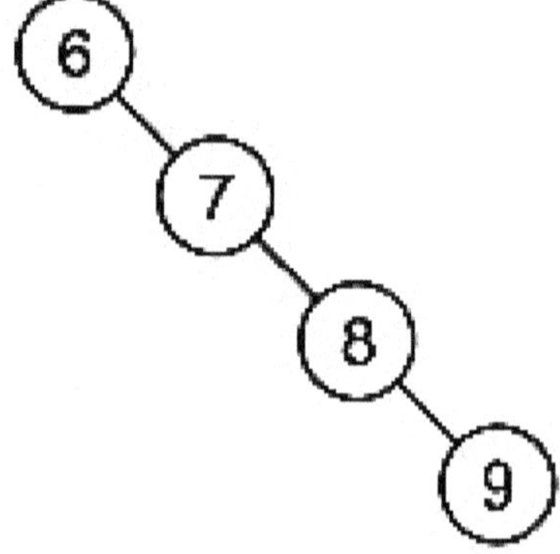

Height of BST in Worst case: $O(n)$.

Best case

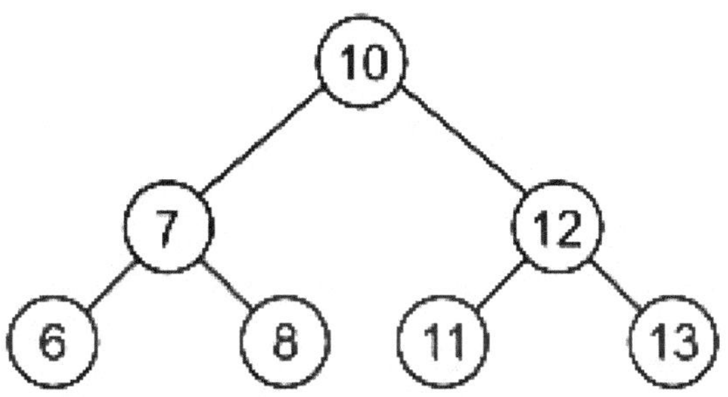

Height of BST in Best case: $\Omega(\log n)$

Height of BST in Average case: $\theta(\log n)$

Hence, the correct option is (A).

18. Generally, round robin fashion is employed to allocate CPU time to resources which makes use of the circular linked list data structure. Recursive function calls use stack data structure. Undo Operation in text editor uses doubly linked lists. Hash tables uses singly linked lists.

Hence, the correct option is (C).

19. Minimum header size of IPv $4 = 20$ byte

Maximum header size of IPv $4 = 60$ byte

Header length field in the IPv 4 header is 4 bits.

Maximum possible value $(1111) = 15$

The scaling factor of $\dfrac{60}{15} = 4$ is introduced.

IP header:

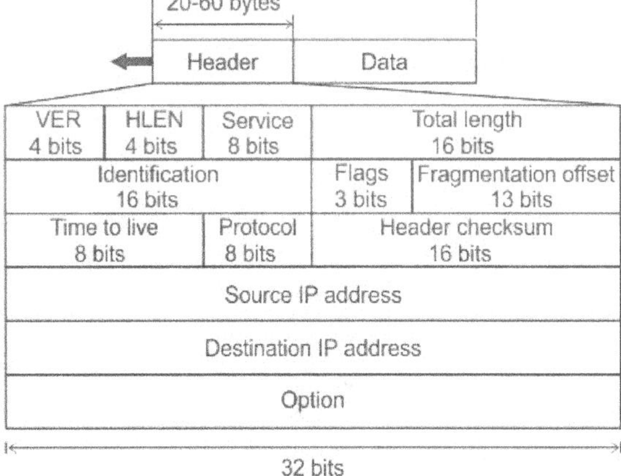

But the first 8 bits in the Question are 01000010.

The first 4 bits indicate the version which is IPv $4(0100)$.

Now, the next four bit indicates Header length (bits decimal value $\times 4$) which is $2 \times 4 = 8$ bytes which are not possible since the minimum header length for IPv 4 is 20 bytes.

So, the receiver will reject the packet.

Hence, the correct option is (A).

20. The GET method requests information about a document from a resource. This is the true statement. The GET method is used to request data from the server.

The post method sends some information to the server from the client. This is also a true statement. since The post method is used to send some information/data to the server.

The head method does not have a response body. This is the true statement, since the head method almost the same as the GET method except for the response body for head.

Hence, the correct option is (D).

21. Message: 11001001

CRC polynomial: $x^3 + 1 = 1x^3 + 0x^2 + 0x^1 + 1 \cdot x^0$

CRC generator: 1001

Since polynomial is of order 3 append 3 0's at the end of the message.

Message: 11001001000

	11001001000
	$\oplus\ 1001$
	———
	01011
	$\oplus\ 1001$
	———
	001000
	$\oplus\ 1001$
	———
	0001100
	$\oplus\ 1001$
	———
	01010
	$\oplus\ 1001$
	———
	011

Transmitted Message: 11001001011

Hence, the correct option is (B).

22. A: It is used to manage/terminate connections.

It is the functionality of the Session layer.

B: Fragmentation

It is the functionality of the Network layer.

C: Flow – Control

D: Error – Control

These two are provided by both the Transport layer and the Data link layer.

The network layer also provides Error control. (though only for Header)

E: Data Encryption/Decryption

It is the functionality of the Presentation layer.

F: It can use almost any network interface available.

it is the Data Link layer.

G: End-users uses this layer directly.

End-users interact with the application layer.

H: It provides end-to-end Communication.

It is the functionality of the Transport layer.

I: Fragmentation

It is the functionality of the Network layer.

Hence, the correct option is (A).

23. Nowadays, complex networks are made up of hundreds and sometimes thousands of components. For the effective functioning of these thousands of components, good network management is essential. Computer network components are the major parts that are needed to install the software. Some important network components are NIC, switch, cable, hub, router, and modem.

Hence, the correct option is (B).

24. The Advanced Research Projects Agency Network (ARPANET) was an early packet-switching network and the first network to implement the protocol suite TCP/IP. Both technologies became the technical foundation of the Internet. The Advanced Research Projects Agency Network (ARPANET) was the first wide-area packet-switched network with distributed control and one of the first networks to implement the TCP/IP protocol suite. The ARPANET was established by the Advanced Research Projects Agency (ARPA) of the United States Department of Defense.

Hence, the correct option is (D).

25. USB wireless network adapter is a communication device that plugs into a USB port and usually provides an intuitive graphical user interface (GUI) for easy configuration. It supports data encryption for secure wireless communication and is perfect for the traveler and notebook user.

Hence, the correct option is (A).

26. Printer is the most common shared resource in a computer network. A combo drive is a type of optical drive that combines CD-R/CD-RW recording capability with an ability to read (but not write) DVD media; some manufacturers refer this as CD-RW/DVD-ROM drive.

Hence, the correct option is (D).

27. Web Casting is Transmitting the video and audio on the Internet. Webcasting is the process of video broadcasting live over the internet. This technology operates in real-time and allows for active conversations among and between the webcaster and their viewers.

Hence, the correct option is (B).

28. EBCDIC, in full extended binary-coded decimal interchange code, data-encoding system, developed by IBM and used mostly on its computers, that uses a unique 8-bit binary code for each number and alphabetic character as well as punctuation marks and accented letters and nonalphabetic characters. The data to be stored in the computers have to be encoded in a particular way so as to provide secure processing of the data.

Hence, the correct option is (B).

29. ALU uses accumulators to store intermediate results. It holds the data or results of an operation during the processing cycles. The accumulator can hold one of the two operands during any ALU operation. The ALU is the computational center of the CPU. It performs all mathematical and logical operations. For better performance, it uses some internal memory space to store the immediate result.

Hence, the correct option is (A).

30. The Instruction fetch phase ends with decoding the data in MDR and placing it in IR. The Control Unit generates the control signals that copy an instruction byte from the memory into the Instruction Register, IR. The address of this instruction is in the Program Counter, PC. The fetch ends with the instruction getting decoded and being placed in the IR and the PC getting incremented.

Hence, the correct option is (D).

31. While using the iterative construct (Branching) in execution branch instruction is used to check the condition. A branch is an instruction in a computer program that may, when executed by a computer, cause the computer to begin execution of a different instruction sequence. Branch instruction is used to check the test condition and to perform the memory jump with the help of offset.

Hence, the correct option is (B).

32. SCSI BUS is usually used to connect video devices to the processor. A small computer systems interface (SCSI) is a standard interface for connecting peripheral devices to a PC. Depending on the standard generally, it can connect up to 16 peripheral devices using a single bus including one host adapter. This number is called a SCSI ID.

Hence, the correct option is (B).

33. The Z register is a special register that can interact with the processor BUS only. Z register is an 8-bit temporary register of 8085 microprocessor, which is not accessible to the user. This register is used either to store 8-bit information in Z registers. Z register pairs with lower-order 8-bits in Z.

Hence, the correct option is (D).

34. In Indirect addressing mode, the value of the register serves as another memory location and so we use pointers to get the

data. Indirect addressing is a scheme in which the address specifies which memory word or register contains not the operand but the address of the operand. For example, LOAD R $1, @100$ Load the content of memory address stored at memory address 100 to the register R 1.

Hence, the correct option is (A).

35. In the case of, auto-increment the increment is done afterward and in auto decrement, the decrement is done first.

Auto Indexed (increment mode): Effective address of the operand is the contents of a register specified in the instruction. After accessing the operand, the contents of this register are automatically incremented to point to the next consecutive memory location (R 1)+.

Auto Indexed (decrement mode): Effective address of the operand is the contents of a register specified in the instruction. Before accessing the operand, the contents of this register are automatically decremented to point to the previous consecutive memory location –(R 1).

Hence, the correct option is (D).

36. Relative addressing mode is most suitable to change the normal sequence of execution of instructions. The relative addressing mode is used for this since it directly updates the PC. In this mode, the Effective Address (EA) of the operand is calculated by adding the content of the CPU register and the address part of the instruction word. The effective address is calculated by adding displacement (immediate value given in the instruction) and the register value. The address part of the instruction is usually a signed number, either positive or negative. The effective address thus calculated is relative to the address of the next instruction.

Hence, the correct option is (A).

37. HBase is a data model that is similar to Google's big table designed to provide quick random access to huge amounts of structured data. HBase is a distributed column-oriented database built on top of the Hadoop file system. It is an open-source project and is horizontally scalable.

Hence, the correct option is (D).

38. Hadoop batch processes data distributed over a number of computers ranging in 100s and 1000s. Hadoop 2.0 allows live stream processing of real-time data. Apache Hadoop 2 (Hadoop 2.0) is the second iteration of the Hadoop framework for distributed data processing. Short for yet another resource negotiator, YARN puts resource management and job scheduling functions in a separate layer beneath the data processing one, enabling Hadoop 2 to run a variety of applications.

Hence, the correct option is (B).

39. The strong entities have a primary key. Weak entities are dependent on strong entities. Its existence is not dependent on any other entity. An entity set that does not possess sufficient attributes to form a primary key is called a weak entity set. One that does have a primary key is called the strong entities set. A strong entity is represented by a single rectangle.

Hence, the correct option is (B).

40. A DBMS that keeps its physical structure hidden from the user is known as a transparent DBMS. A DBMS may provide a various· levels of transparency. However, they all participate in the same overall objective: to make the use of the distributed database, equivalent to that of a centralized database.

We can identify four main types of transparency in a DBMS:

- Distribution transparency
- Transaction transparency
- Performance transparency;
- DBMS transparency.

Hence, the correct option is (C).

41. The data stored in a database must be independent of the applications that access the database. Any change in the physical structure of a database must not have any impact on how the data is being accessed by external applications. This rule is called Physical Data Independence. This is the first major rule of DBMS.

Hence, the correct option is (B).

42. The logical data in a database must be independent of its user's view level (application level). Any change in logical data must not affect the applications using it. This rule is called Logical Data Independence. For example, if two tables are merged or one is split into two different tables, there should be no impact or change on the user application. This is one of the most difficult rules to apply. This is the second major rule of DBMS.

Hence, the correct option is (A).

43. In Distribution Independence, the end-user must not be able to see that the data is distributed over various locations. Users should always get the impression that the data is located at one site only. This rule has been regarded as the foundation of distributed database systems. This is the third major rule of DBMS.

Hence, the correct option is (A).

44. A database must be independent of the application that uses its integrity independence. Integrity independence is the ability to change integrity constraints without changing updated transactions and application programs (Codd, 1990). Thus in relational DBMSs integrity independence is either missing or restricted. All its integrity constraints can be independently modified without the need for any change in the application. This rule makes a database-independent of the front-end application and its interface.

Hence, the correct option is (D).

45. SQL Server is not a NoSQL database. Microsoft SQL Server is a relational database management system developed by Microsoft. Microsoft SQL Server is one of the database technology market leaders. It is a relational database management system that supports many applications including business intelligence, transaction processing and analytics.

Hence, the correct option is (A).

46. Let the computation time of P_2 is less than or equal to computation time of P_3.

Gantt chart:

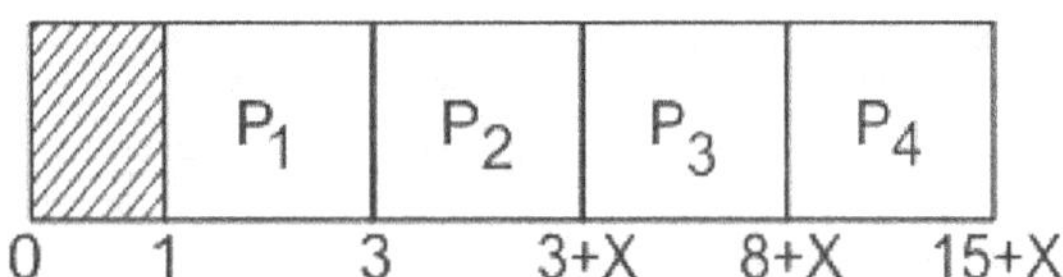

Process Table:

Process	Arrival Time (AT)	Computation Time (BT)	Completion Time (CT)	Turn Around Time (TAT)
P_1	1	2	3	2
P_2	3	X	$3 + X$	X
P_3	3	5	$8 + X$	$5 + X$
P_4	5	7	$15 + X$	$10 + X$

As we know,

$$\text{TAT} = \text{CT} - \text{AT}$$

Average Turnaround time $= \dfrac{13}{2}$

$$\Rightarrow \frac{2 + X + 5 + X + 10 + X}{4} = \frac{13}{2}$$

$$\Rightarrow \frac{3X + 17}{4} = \frac{13}{2}$$

$$\Rightarrow 2(3X + 17) = 13 \times 4$$

$$\Rightarrow 6X + 34 = 52$$

$$\Rightarrow 6X = 52 - 34$$

$$\Rightarrow 6X = 18$$

$$\Rightarrow X = \frac{18}{6}$$

$$\therefore X = 3 \text{ ms}$$

Important points:

$ms \rightarrow$ milliseconds

Explore: If computation time of P_2 is more than computation time of P_3.

Hence, the correct option is (A).

47. Fully associative mapping: In this type of mapping, a block of memory can be mapped to any cache line available that time.

Given,

Memory block requests are:

$5, 4, 26, 8, 20, 7, 26, 8, 17, 36, 46, 23, 8, 4, 17, 26, 9$.

0	$\frac{5}{46}$
1	$\frac{4}{23}$
2	26
3	8
4	$\frac{20}{4}$
5	$\frac{7}{9}$
6	17
7	36

So, at the end of mapping with LRU replacement policy, memory block 17 maps to cache line 6.

Hence, the correct option is (B).

48. 10 KB $= 10 \times 2^{10}$ bytes $= 10240$ bytes.

We can allocate an entire 10240-byte block of pointers to a block of 40 bytes; we can fit total $\dfrac{10240}{40} = 256$ pointers.

For direct disk block:

Size of file $= 10 \times 6 = 60$ KB

For single indirect disk block:

Size of file $= 256 \times 10 = 2560$ KB

For double indirect disk block:

Size of file $= 256 \times 256 \times 10 = 655360$ KB

For triple indirect disk block:

Size of file $= 256 \times 256 \times 256 \times 10 = 167772160$ KB

Maximum size of a file that can be stored in this file system $= 160.63$ GB.

Hence, the correct option is (A).

49. A disk operating system (DOS) is a computer operating system that resides on and can use a disk storage device, such as a floppy disk, hard disk drive, or optical disc. A disk operating system must provide a file system for organizing, reading, and writing files on the storage disk.

Hence, the correct option is (B).

50. Address binding is the process of mapping the program's logical or virtual addresses to corresponding physical or main memory addresses. In other words, a given logical address is mapped by the MMU (Memory Management Unit) to a physical address.

Hence, the correct option is (D).

51. In a multitasking system, a computer executes several programs simultaneously by switching them back and forth to increase user interactivity. Processes share the CPU and execute in an interleaving manner. This allows the user to run more than one program at a time.

Hence, the correct option is (B).

52. Binding of instructions and data to memory addresses can happen at three stages:

- **Compile-time:** If memory location knew a priori, absolute code can be generated; must recompile code if starting location changes.

- **Load time:** Must generate relocatable code if memory location is not known at compile time.

- **Execution time:** The execution time or CPU time of a given task is defined as the time spent by the system executing that task, including the time spent executing run-time or system services on its behalf.

Hence, the correct option is (D).

53. Details of all external symbols and transfer structure (transfer list or map) are provided by the translator to the linker. Any program written in a high-level language is known as source code. However, computers cannot understand source code. Before it can be run, the source code must first be translated into a form that the computer understands - this form is called object code.

Hence, the correct option is (B).

54. Deadlock prevention can be done by eliminating any of the below conditions:

- Mutual Exclusion

- Hold and wait

- No preemption

- Circular Wait

In deadlock prevention, the request for resources is not always granted if the resulting state is safe.

Deadlock avoidance can be done with Banker's Algorithm.

Banker's Algorithm:

Banker's Algorithm is resource allocation and deadlock avoidance algorithm which test all the request made by processes for resources, it checks for the safe state, if after granting request system remains in the safe state it allows the request and if there is no safe state it doesn't allow the request made by the process. Deadlock avoidance requires knowledge of resource requirements a priori.

Comparison:

Deadlock prevention is more restrictive than deadlock avoidance.

Hence, the correct option is (A).

55. Given,

$$f(x, y) = x \overline{+} y$$

Now,

$$f(a + b, b)$$

$$\Rightarrow a + \overline{b} + b$$

$$\Rightarrow \overline{a + b}$$

Then we have,

$$f(f(a + b, b), b)$$

$$\Rightarrow f\left(\overline{a + b}, b\right)$$

$$\Rightarrow \overline{\overline{a + b} + b}$$

$$\Rightarrow (a + b) \cdot \overline{b}$$

$$\Rightarrow a\overline{b} = \overline{b}a$$

So, the value of $f(f(a + b, b), b)$ is $\overline{b}a$.

Hence, the correct option is (C).

56. Given,

$$F = (A + B)(A + \overline{A} + \overline{B})C + \overline{A}(B + \overline{C}) + \overline{A}B + ABC$$

Now, the most simplified expression for F is:

$$F = (A + B)(A + \overline{A} + \overline{B})C + \overline{A}(B + \overline{C}) + \overline{A}B + ABC$$

$$F = (A + B)C + \overline{A}B + \overline{A}\,\overline{C} + \overline{A}B + ABC$$

$$F = AC + BC + \overline{A}B + \overline{A}\,\overline{C} + ABC$$

$$F = AC + BC + \overline{A}B + \overline{A}\,\overline{C}$$

$$F = C(A + B) + \overline{A}\left(B + \overline{C}\right)$$

Hence, the correct option is (A).

57. A literal is any boolean variable x or its complement x'.

De Morgan's Law:

$$\overline{a + b} = \overline{a} \cdot \overline{b}$$

Given,

$$f(a, b, c) = \left(a \overline{+} b + c\right) \cdot \overline{a} + \left(\overline{b} + c\right)$$

Now,

$$f(a, b, c) = \left(a \overline{+} b + c\right) \cdot \overline{a} + \left(\overline{b} + c\right)$$

$$f(a, b, c) = \overline{a} \overline{+} b + c + a + \overline{b} + c$$

$$f(a, b, c) = (a + b) \cdot \overline{c} + a + \overline{b} + c$$

$$f(a, b, c) = a\overline{c} + b\overline{c} + a + \overline{b} + c$$

$$f(a, b, c) = a\left(\overline{c} + 1\right) + \left(\overline{b} + b\right)\left(\overline{b} + \overline{c}\right) + c$$

$$f(a, b, c) = a + \overline{b} + \overline{c} + c$$

$$f(a, b, c) = a + \overline{b} + 1$$

$$f(a, b, c) = 1$$

Hence, the correct option is (C).

58. Formula:

$$A + A = A; A \cdot A = A; A + A \cdot B = A;$$

$$1 + A = 1; 1 \cdot A = A$$

Consider all the options,

Option (A):

$$wx + w(x + y) + x(x + y) = x + wy$$

$$wx + wx + wy + xx + xy = x + wy$$

$$wx + wy + x + xy = x + wy$$

$$x + wy = x + wy$$

Option (B):

$$w\overline{x}(\overline{y} + \overline{z}) + \overline{w}x = \overline{w} + x + \overline{y}z$$

$$\overline{w} + \overline{x} + y\overline{z} + x - 2w + x + yz$$

$$\overline{w} + \overline{x} + \overline{y\overline{z}} + \overline{w}x = \overline{w} + x + \overline{y}z$$

$$\overline{w} + x + \overline{y}z + \overline{w}x = \overline{w} + x + \overline{y}z$$

$$\overline{w} + x + \overline{y}z = \overline{w} + x + \overline{y}z$$

Opation (C):

$$(w\overline{x}(y + x\overline{z}) + \overline{wx})y = x\overline{y}$$

$$(w\overline{x}y + w\overline{z} + \overline{wx})y = x\overline{y}$$

$$(w\overline{x}y + w\overline{z}y + \overline{wx} \quad y) = x\overline{y}$$

$$(\overline{x}y + w\overline{z}y) = \overline{xy}$$

$$\therefore (\overline{x}y + w\overline{z}y) \neq \overline{xy}$$

Opation (D):

$$(w + y)(wxy + wyz) = wxy + wyz$$

$$wxy + wyz + wxy + wyz = wxy + wyz$$

$$wxy + wyz = wxy + wy$$

Hence, the correct option is (C).

59. Given,

$$A\$B = \overline{A} + B \cdots (1)$$

$$W = A + \overline{B} \cdots (2)$$

$$Y = \overline{W}\$\overline{A}$$

From 1 we get,

$$Y = W + \overline{A}$$

From 2 we get,

$$Y = A + \overline{B} + \overline{A}$$

$$Y = 1 + \overline{B} = 1$$

Hence, the correct option is (D).

60. Canonical form: Any boolean function that expressed as a sum of minterms or as a product of max terms is said to be in its canonical form.

There are two types of canonical forms:

1. **SOP:** Sum of products or sum of minterms. In SOP (sum of product) form, a minterm is represented by 1.

Example of SOP: $XY + X'Y'$

2. **POS:** Product of sums or product of max terms. In POS (product of sum) form, a maxterm is represented by 0.

Example of POS: $(X + Y)(X' + Y')$

K-Map:

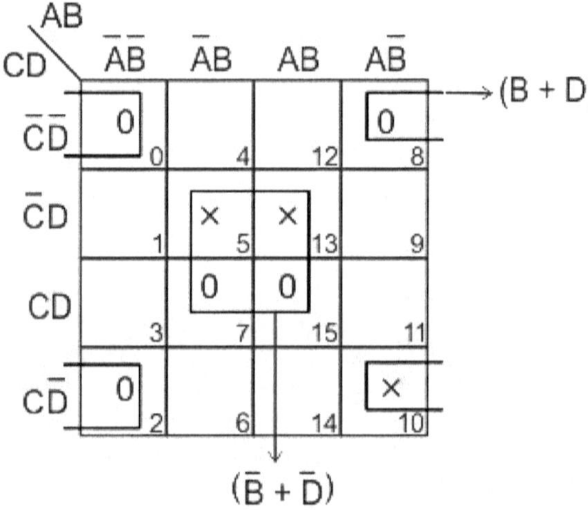

$$f(A, B, C, D) = (B + D) \times \left(\overline{B} + \overline{D}\right)$$

Hence, the correct option is (A).

61. K-Map:

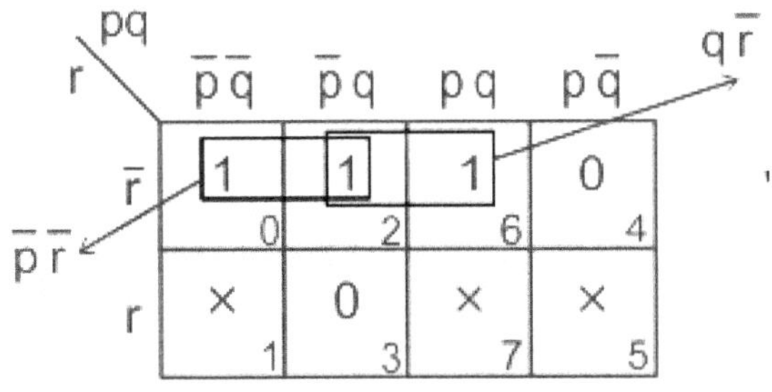

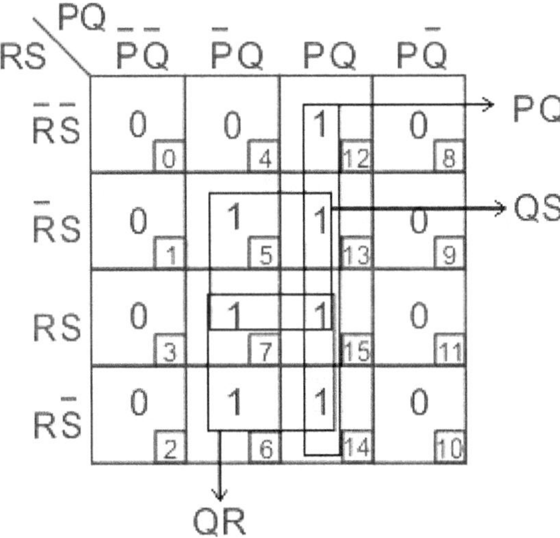

$$F(p, q, r) = \bar{p} + q + \bar{r}$$
$$= (\bar{p} + q)\bar{r} = \bar{p}\bar{r} + q\bar{r}$$

∴ The correct representation using only NOR gate will be:

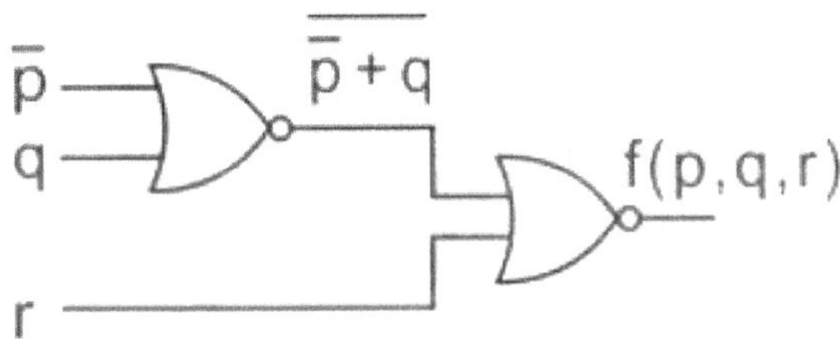

Therefore, 2 NOR gate is needed.

Hence, the correct option is (A).

62. $f = \Sigma\left(\overline{f1}.f2 \cdot (f3 + f4)\right)$

$$f = \Sigma\left((f1.f2) + \overline{f3 + f4}\right)$$

$$f = \Sigma\left((0,2,5) \cdot (1,5,7) + \overline{(1,5) + (3,6)}\right)$$

$$f = \Sigma(5 + (\overline{(1,3,5,6)})$$
$$f = \Sigma(5 + (0,2,4,7)$$
$$f = \Sigma(0,2,4,5,7)$$

Hence, the correct option is (C).

63. As we know, it is given that

$$F(P, Q, R, S) = PQ + \bar{P}QR + \bar{P}QRS$$

$$F(P, Q, R, S) = PQ(R + \bar{R})(S + \bar{S}) + \bar{P}QR(S + \bar{S}) + \bar{P}QRS$$

$$F(P, Q, R, S) = PQRS + PQR\bar{S} + PQ\bar{R}S + PQ\bar{R}S + \bar{P}QRS + \bar{P}QR\bar{S} + \bar{P}QRS$$

$$F(P, Q, R, S) = \Sigma(15 + 14 + 13 + 12 + 7 + 6 + 5)$$

K-Map:

$$F(P, Q, R, S) = PQ + QR + QS$$

Hence, the correct option is (A).

64. The epsilon closure of the set a is the set that contains a, together with all the states which can be reached starting at a by following only epsilon transitions. Therefore, the epsilon closure of the set a will be $\{a, f1, f2, f3\}$.

Hence, the correct option is (B).

65. Quadruple representation is the three-address code representation. In this, each instruction is spitted into four fields which are operator, argument 1, argument 2, and result.

Now,

Given Expression:

(i*j)+(e+f)*(a*b+c)

T1 = (i * j)

T2 = (e + f)

T3 = (a * b)

T4 = T3 + c

T5 = T2 * T4

T6 = T1 + T5

Table Form:

	Operator	Argument 1	Argument 2	Result
1	*	i	j	T1
2	+	e	f	T2
3	*	a	b	T3
4	+	T3	c	T4
5	+	T1	T2	T5
6	*	T5	T4	T6

So, total 6 operations are required.

Hence, the correct option is (B).

66. All the given are the closure properties of ε and encircles all the elements if it satisfies the following options:

(a) Every element of S ε Q.

(b) For any q ε ε(S), every element of δ (q, ε) is in ε(S).

(c) No other element is in ε(S).

Hence, the correct option is (D).

67. The automaton which allows transformation to a new state without consuming any input symbols is NFA-I. NFA-I or e-NFA is an extension of Non-deterministic Finite Automata which are usually called NFA with epsilon moves or lambda transitions.

In the automata theory, a non-deterministic finite automaton with ε-moves (NFA-ε)(also known as NFA-λ) is an extension of a non-deterministic finite automaton(NFA), which allows a transformation to a new state without consuming any input symbols. The transitions without consuming an input symbol are called ε-transitions or λ-transitions. In the state diagrams, they are usually labeled with the Greek letter ε or λ.

Hence, the correct option is (C).

68. The languages which are recognized by epsilon as non-deterministic automata are closed under the following operations:

(a) Union

(b) Intersection

(c) Concatenation

(d) Negation

(e) Star

(f) Kleene closure

Hence, the correct option is (D).

69. The parser is mainly classified into two types: Top-down Parser, and Bottom-up Parser.

Top-Down Parsing: Involves searching a parse tree to find the left-most derivations of an input stream by using a top-down expansion. Parsing begins with the start symbol which is transformed into the input symbol until all symbols are translated and a parse tree for an input string is constructed. Examples include LL parsers and recursive-descent parsers. Top-down parsing is also called predictive parsing or recursive parsing.

Bottom-Up Parsing: Involves rewriting the input back to the start symbol. It acts in reverse by tracing out the rightmost derivation of a string until the parse tree is constructed up to the start symbol This type of parsing is also known as shift-reduce parsing. One example is an LR parser.

Hence, the correct option is (C).

70. Top-down parsing is a technique which constructs the parse tree from the start symbol and transforms it to the input symbol. It involves searching a parse tree to find the left-most derivations of an input stream by using a top-down expansion. Top-down parsing is also called predictive parsing or recursive parsing.

Hence, the correct option is (B).

71. Top-down parsing can be viewed as an attempt to find left-most derivations of an input-stream by searching for parse-trees using a top-down expansion of the given formal grammar rules. Inclusive choice is used to accommodate ambiguity by expanding all alternative right-hand-sides of grammar rules.

Hence, the correct option is (D).

72. Bottom-up parser generates the right-most derivation in reverse. In the bottom up parsing, the parsing starts with the input symbol and construct the parse tree up to the start symbol by tracing out the rightmost derivations of string in reverse. Bottom-up parsing is also known as shift-reduce parsing.

Hence, the correct option is (A).

73. The given expression is:

$$(\neg p \wedge \neg q) \vee (p \wedge q)$$

Truth Table:

p	q	$p \leftrightarrow q$
T	T	T
F	T	F
T	F	F
F	F	T

So, the logically equivalent expression is:

$$p \leftrightarrow q \equiv (p \wedge q) \vee (\neg p \wedge \neg q) \equiv (\neg p \wedge \neg q) \vee (p \wedge q)$$

Hence, the correct option is (B).

74. Consider the sets in the form of Venn diagram as:

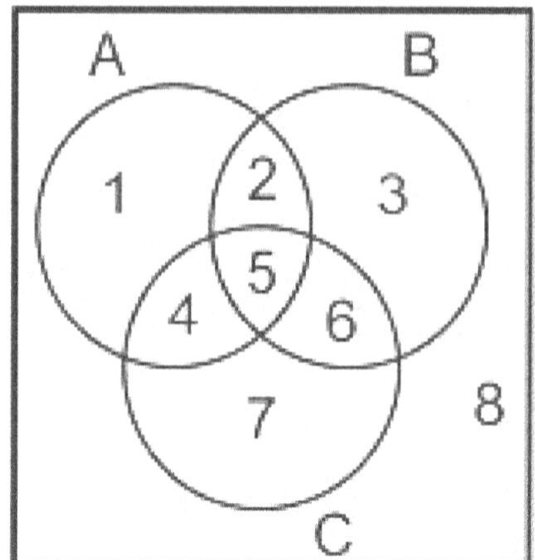

1. $(A - B) - C = (A - C) - B$

Take L.H.S $(A - B) - C = \{1,4\} - \{4,5,6,7\} = \{1\}$

Take R.H.S $(A - C) - B = \{1,2\} - \{2,3,5,6\} = \{1\}$

So, L.H.S = R.H.S

2. $(A - B) - C = (A - C) - (B - C)$

L.H.S $(A - B) - C = \{1\}$

R.H.S. $(A - C) - (B - C) = \{1,2\} - \{2,3\} = \{1\}$

L.HS. $=$ R.H.S

3. $A \oplus (B \cup C) = (A \oplus B) \cup (A \oplus C)$

L.H.S. $= A \oplus (B \cup C) = \{1,2,4,5\} \oplus \{2,3,4,5,6,7\}$
$= \{1,3,6,7\}$

R.H.S $= (A \oplus B) \cup (A \oplus C) = \{1,4,3,6\} \cup \{1,2,6,7\}$
$= \{1,2,3,4,6,7\}$

Here, L.H.S is not equal to R.H.S.

4. $A - (B \cup C) = (A - B) \cap (A - C)$

L.H.S $= A - (B \cup C) = \{1,2,4,5\} - \{2,3,4,5,6,7\} = \{1\}$

R.H.S $= (A - B) \cap (A - C) = \{1,4\} - \{1,2\} = \{1\}$

L.H.S = R.H.S

Hence, the correct option is (C).

75. Theorems on the subgroup of a cyclic group:

- Every subgroup of a cyclic group is itself a cyclic group.
- Every proper subgroup of an infinite cyclic group is finite.
- If G={a} be a finite cyclic group of order n, then for any divisor d of n, there is a unique subgroup of G of order d.

Hence, the correct option is (D).

76. A graph G is an Eulerian circuit, if and only if it has at most one non-trivial component and its vertices all have an even degree.

For the complete graph (K_n):

Every vertex has $(n - 1)$ degree.

If n is even then Euler circuit is not possible.

For Cycle graph (C_n):

Every vertex has 2 degrees, therefore it always has an Euler circuit.

For Wheel graph (W_n):

Every vertex has 3 degrees, therefore the Euler circuit is not possible.

For n-dimensional cube (Q_n):

Every vertex has (n) degree.

If n is odd then Euler circuit is not possible.

Therefore, none of this is the correct answer.

Result:

K_n is Euler iff n is odd.

Q_n is Euler iff n is even.

Important Points:

Generally, n is the number of vertices in a graph.

For wheel $(W_n) = (n + 1)$ is the number of vertices in a graph.

For Hypercube $(Q_n) = 2^n$ is the number of vertices in a graph.

Hence, the correct option is (A).

77. Consider each options:

(A) Null graph of 6 vertices is 1-chromatic so it is correct.

(B) It is correct because tree with 2 or more vertices is always bichromatic.

(C) It is incorrect. Consider a wheel graph of 7 vertices.

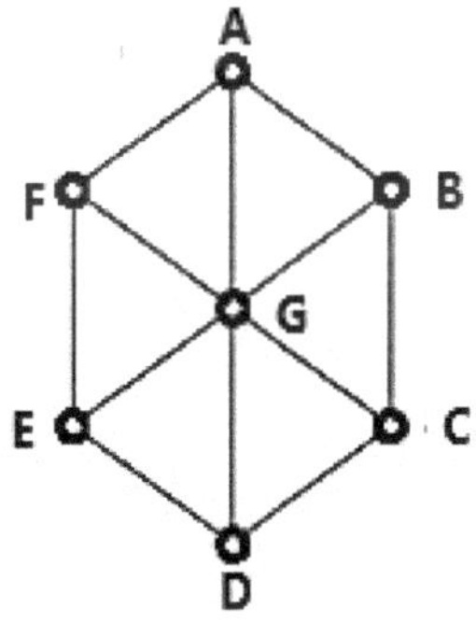

The chromatic number of graph is 3.

- Color 1 for G
- Color 2 for A, E, C
- Color 3 for F, B, D
- A wheel graph is 3-chromatic when n-vertices are odd and 4-chromatic when n-vertices is even.
- So, here $n = 7, \left(\left[\frac{n}{2} \right] + 1 \right) = \left(\left[\frac{7}{2} \right] + 1 \right) = 4$ which is incorrect because only 3 colors are required to color the above wheel graph.

(D) This statement is correct because graph without odd length cycle having atleast 1 edge is bichromatic.

Hence, the correct option is (C).

78. The first letter must be a vowel, so there are 5 choices. The second letter can be any one of 26, the third letter can be any one of 26, the fourth letter can be any one of 26 and fifth and sixth letters can be any of 26 choices. The last letter must be an A, so there is only 1 choice. By the basic counting principle, the number of 'words' is $5 \times 26 \times 26 \times 26 \times 26 \times 26 \times 1 = 59406880$.

Hence, the correct option is (D).

79. For $m = 1$, we have $(4 \times 1 + 2) = 6$, which is a multiple of 2.

Assume that $4m + 2$ is true for $m = k$ and so, $4k + 2$ is true based on the assumption. Now, to prove that $4k + 2$ is also a multiple of 2.

Now,

$$4(k + 1) + 2$$

$$\Rightarrow 2 \times 4k - 4k + 6$$

$$\Rightarrow 2 \times 4k + 4 - 4k + 2$$

$$\Rightarrow 2(4k + 2) - 2(2k + 1)$$

Here, the first term $2(4k + 2)$ is true as per assumption and the second term $2(4k + 2)$ is must to be a multiple of 2. Thus, $4(k + 1) + 2$ is a multiple of 2. So, by induction hypothesis, $(4m + 2)$ is a multiple of 2, for $m = 1, 2, 3, \dots$

Hence, the correct option is (D).

80. Dirac's theorem states that min degree(s) should be $\geq \left\lfloor \dfrac{n}{2} \right\rfloor$.

This is satisfied by only $K_{3,3}$ and $K_{3,4}$.

As we know,

Minimum degree for $K_{m,n} = \min(m, n)$.

Every cycle in a bipartite graph is even and alternates between vertices from V_1 and V_2.

Since a Hamilton cycle uses all the vertices in V_1 and V_2, we have $m = |V_1| = |V_2| = n$.

This condition is satisfied by $K_{3,3}$ only.

Therefore, only $K_{3,3}$ will have a hamiltonian cycle.

Hence, the correct option is (C).

81. Consider the coefficients of each x^n term.

So, $a_0 = 4$, since the coefficient of x_0 is 4 ($x_0 = 1$ so, this is the constant term). Since 15 is the coefficient of x^2, so, 15 is the term a_2 of the sequence. To find a_1 check the coefficient of x_1 which in this case is 0. So, $a_1 = 0$. Continuing with these we have $a_2 = 15, a_3 = 10, a_4 = 25$, and $a_5 = 16$. So, we have the sequence $4,0,15,10,25,16, \dots$

Hence, the correct option is (C).

82. The user system requirements are the parts of SRS document. SRS is stands for Software requirements specification (SRS). It is a complete description of the behaviour of a system to be developed and may include a set of use cases that describe interactions the users will have with the software.

Hence, the correct option is (B).

83. Software companies are responsible for making policies and providing working atmosphere for the software development, so in turn these companies become a part of software development process. Bugs from developers side is no new thing, even the slightest mistake in the program causes a bug.

Hence, the correct option is (D).

84. All are non-functional requirements representing quality of the system such as security, reliability, performance, maintainability, scalability, and usability.
Functional requirements describe what the software has to do. Here are the most common functional requirement types:

- Transaction Handling
- Business Rules
- Certification Requirements
- Reporting Requirements
- Administrative functions
- Authorization levels
- Audit Tracking
- External Interfaces
- Historical Data management
- Legal and Regulatory Requirements

Hence, the correct option is (D).

85. Model selection is based on requirements, a team of developers, users as well as the risk involved in developing a project. Model selection is the task of selecting a statistical model from a set of candidate models, given data. In the simplest cases, a pre-existing set of data is considered.

Hence, the correct option is (D).

86. The different notations of UML includes the nine UML diagrams namely class, object, sequence, collaboration, activity, state-chart, component, deployment and use case diagrams.

1. **Class diagrams** consists of classes, interfaces, associations, and collaboration. Class diagrams basically represent the object-oriented view of a system, which is static in nature.

2. **Object diagrams** can be described as an instance of class diagram. Thus, these diagrams are more close to real-life scenarios where we implement a system.

3. **A sequence diagrams** is an interaction diagram. From the name, it is clear that the diagram deals with some sequences, which are the sequence of messages flowing from one object to another.

4. **Collaboration diagrams** is another form of interaction diagram. It represents the structural organization of a system and the messages sent/received. Structural organization consists of objects and links.

5. **Activity diagrams** describes the flow of control in a system. It consists of activities and links. The flow can be sequential, concurrent, or branched.

6. **State-chart diagram** is used to represent the event driven state change of a system. It basically describes the state change of a class, interface, etc.

7. **Component diagrams** represent a set of components and their relationships. These components consist of classes, interfaces, or collaborations. Component diagrams represent the implementation view of a system.

8. **Deployment diagrams** are a set of nodes and their relationships. These nodes are physical entities where the components are deployed.

9. **Use case diagrams** are a set of use cases, actors, and their relationships. They represent the use case view of a system.

Hence, the correct option is (D).

87. Behavioral models are used to describe the dynamic behavior of an executing system. This can be modeled from the perspective of the data processed by the system or by the events that stimulate responses from a system. Behavioral model is specially designed to make us understand behavior and factors that influence behavior of a system.

Hence, the correct option is (B).

88. Structural models show the organization and architecture of a system. These are used to define the static structure of classes in a system and their associations. A structural model is an architectural map for a large software system or family of systems. The structural model used in a domain represents the point of convergence for trade-offs between maintainability and performance, quality and efficiency.

Hence, the correct option is (D).

89. Structural perspective is used to define the static structure of classes in a system and their associations. A structural perspective of software display the organization of a system in terms of the components that make up that system and their relationships.

Hence, the correct option is (A).

90. The UML supports event-based modeling using State chart diagrams. State chart diagram is used to describe the states of different objects in its life cycle. Emphasis is placed on the state changes upon some internal or external events. These states of objects are important to analyze and implement them accurately.

Hence, the correct option is (C).

91. Let the bag contain 'x' black and 'y' white balls.

Total number of balls $= x + y$

Probability of picking a black ball $= \dfrac{4}{7}$

$\Rightarrow \dfrac{x}{(x+y)} = \dfrac{4}{7}$

$\Rightarrow 7x = 4x + 4y$

$\Rightarrow 3x = 4y$

$\Rightarrow y = \dfrac{3x}{4}$

$\Rightarrow$ Total number of balls $= x + \dfrac{3x}{4} = \dfrac{7x}{4}$

Now, probability of picking two black balls without replacement

$= \dfrac{4}{13}$

$\Rightarrow \left[\dfrac{x}{(x+y)}\right] \times \left(\dfrac{(x-1)}{(x+y-1)}\right) = \dfrac{4}{13}$

$\Rightarrow \dfrac{4}{7} \times \left[\dfrac{(x-1)}{\left(\frac{7x}{4}-1\right)}\right] = \dfrac{4}{13}$

$\Rightarrow \dfrac{4(x-1)}{(7x-4)} = \dfrac{7}{13}$

$\Rightarrow 52(x - 1) = 7(7x - 4)$

$\Rightarrow 52x - 52 = 49x - 28$

$\Rightarrow 52x - 49x = 52 - 28$

$\Rightarrow 3x = 24$

$\Rightarrow x = \dfrac{24}{3}$

$\Rightarrow x = 8$

$\therefore$ There are 8 black balls in the bag.

Hence, the correct option is (D).

92. Given,

Height of cylindrical vessel $= 42$ cm
Radius of cylindrical vessel $= 30$ cm
Height of cylindrical glass $= 7$ cm
Radius of cylindrical glass $= 5$ cm
$\because$ Volume of the cylinder $= \pi r^2 h$
Probability of the small spherical substance getting transferred to

the glass $= \dfrac{\text{Volume of glass}}{\text{Volume of vessel}}$

$= \left(\dfrac{\text{Radius of glass}}{\text{Radius of vessel}}\right)^2 \times \left(\dfrac{\text{Height of the glass}}{\text{Height of vessel}}\right)$

$= \left(\dfrac{5}{30}\right)^2 \times \left(\dfrac{7}{42}\right)$

$= \dfrac{1}{36} \times \dfrac{1}{6}$

$= \dfrac{1}{216}$

$\therefore$ Probability of the small spherical substance getting transferred

to the glass $= \dfrac{1}{216}$

Hence, the correct option is (C).

93. Given,

$\dfrac{y^2}{x^2} = \dfrac{dy}{dx}$

Separate the variables,

$$\frac{dx}{x^2} = \frac{dy}{y^2}$$

On integrating both side we get,

$$\int \frac{dx}{x^2} = \int \frac{dy}{y^2} \quad \left(\because \int \frac{1}{x^2} dx = \frac{-1}{x} \right)$$

$$\Rightarrow -\frac{1}{x} + C = -\frac{1}{y}$$

$$\Rightarrow \frac{1}{y} = \frac{1}{x} + C$$

Hence, the correct option is (A).

94. Given,

$$\frac{dy}{dx} = e^{-3y}$$

$$\Rightarrow \frac{dy}{e^{-3y}} = dx$$

$$\Rightarrow e^{3y} dy = dx$$

On integrating both side we get,

$$\int e^{3y} dy = \int dx$$

$$\Rightarrow \frac{e^{3y}}{3} = x + C \dots \dots (i)$$

$$\Rightarrow \frac{e^{2(0)}}{3} = 5 + C \quad (\because e^0 = 1)$$

$$\Rightarrow C + 5 = \frac{1}{3}$$

$$\Rightarrow C = \frac{1}{3} - 5$$

$$\Rightarrow C = \frac{-14}{3}$$

Substituting $y = 5$ and $C = \frac{-14}{5}$ in equation (i), we get,

$$\frac{e^{15}}{3} = x - \frac{14}{3}$$

$$\Rightarrow x = \frac{e^{15} + 14}{3}$$

Hence, the correct option is (A).

95. The Laplace transform is defined by:

$$F(s) = \int_0^\infty e^{-st} f(t) dt$$

Where,

$F(t)$, the function that varies with time t is,

$F(s), f(t)$ is the Laplace transform.

$$\sinh(at) = \frac{e^{at} - e^{-at}}{2}$$

$$F(s) = \int_0^\infty e^{-st} \left[\frac{e^{at} - e^{-at}}{2} \right] dt$$

On solving the above equation:

$$F\{\sinh(at)\} = \int_0^\infty e^{-st} \sinh(at) dt$$

from, $\sinh(x) = \frac{e^x - e^{-x}}{2}; x = at$

$$F\{\sinh(at)\} = \int_0^\infty e^{-st} \left(\frac{e^{et} - e^{-at}}{2} \right) dt$$

$$F\{\sinh(at)\} = \frac{1}{2} \int_0^\infty e^{-(s-a)t} dt - \frac{1}{2} \int_0^\infty e^{-(s+a)t} dt$$

$$F\{\sinh(at)\} = \frac{1}{2[-(s-a)]} \left[e^{-(s-a)t} \right]_0^\infty - \frac{1}{2[-(s+a)]} \left[e^{-(s+a)t} \right]_0^\infty$$

$$F\{\sinh(at)\} = -\frac{1}{2(s-a)} [0 - 1] + \frac{1}{2(s+a)} [0 - 1]$$

$$F\{\sinh(at)\} = \frac{1}{2(s-a)} - \frac{1}{2(s+a)}$$

$$F\{\sinh(at)\} = \frac{s+a-s+a}{2(s^2 - a^2)}$$

$$F\{\sinh(at)\} = \frac{a}{s^2 - a^2}$$

Hence the correct option is (C).

96. As we know,

$$L(t^n) = \frac{n!}{s^{n+1}}$$

$$L(e^{at}) = \frac{1}{s-a}$$

$$L(t^n e^{at}) = \frac{n!}{(s-a)^{n+1}}$$

$$f(t) = 2t^2 e^{-t}$$

$$F(s) = L(f(t))$$

$$= 2L(t^2 e^{-t})$$

$$= 2 \times \frac{2!}{(s+1)^{2+1}}$$

$$= \frac{4}{(s+1)^3}$$

$$F(1) = \frac{4}{(1+1)^3}$$

$$= \frac{1}{2}$$

$$= 0.5$$

Hence, the correct option is (B).

97. Let, $B = |A^{121} - A^{120}|$

$$B = |A^{120} \times (A - 1)|$$

$$B = |A^{120}| \times |A - 1|$$

$$A = \begin{bmatrix} 8 & 5 \\ 7 & 6 \end{bmatrix}$$

Now, calculating matrix $[A - 1]$

$$[A - 1] = \begin{bmatrix} 8 & 5 \\ 7 & 6 \end{bmatrix} - \begin{bmatrix} 1 & 0 \\ 0 & 1 \end{bmatrix}$$

$$[A - 1] = \begin{bmatrix} 7 & 5 \\ 7 & 5 \end{bmatrix}$$

Now, determinant of $|A - 1|$,

$$[A - 1] = \begin{bmatrix} 7 & 5 \\ 7 & 5 \end{bmatrix}$$

$$|A - 1| = 0$$

(Since two rows are repeated, therefore determinant $= 0$)

So, $|A^{121} - A^{120}| = 0$

Hence, the correct option is (A).

98. Given,

$$y = x^{\frac{2}{5}} - 2x^3 + 2x + 16$$

Differentiating with respect to x, we get:

$$\frac{d}{dx}(y) = \frac{d}{dx}\left(x^{\frac{2}{5}} - 2x^3 + 2x + 16\right)$$

$$\frac{dy}{dx} = \frac{d}{dx}x^{\frac{2}{5}} - 2\frac{d}{dx}x^3 + 2\frac{d}{dx}x + 16\frac{d}{dx}1$$

$$\frac{dy}{dx} = \frac{2}{5}x^{\frac{2}{5}-1} - 2 \times 3x^2 + 2 \times 1 + 16 \times 0$$

$$\frac{dy}{dx} = \frac{2}{5}x^{\frac{2-5}{5}} - 6x^2 + 2$$

$$\frac{dy}{dx} = \frac{2}{5}x^{-\frac{3}{5}} - 6x^2 + 2$$

$$\frac{dy}{dx} = \frac{2}{5x^{\frac{3}{5}}} - 6x^2 + 2$$

Hence, the correct option is (C).

99. Given:

$$I = \int_{-a}^{a}(x^2 + \sin x)\, dx$$

$$= \int_{-a}^{a} x^2\, dx + \int_{-a}^{a} \sin x dx$$

$$= I_1 + I_2$$

Now,

$$I_1 = \int_{-a}^{a} x^2\, dx$$

Here $f(x) = x^2$

Replace x by $-x$, we get

$$\Rightarrow f(-x) = (-x)^2 = x^2$$

$$\Rightarrow f(-x) = f(x)$$

So, $f(x)$ is even function.

As we know,

If $f(x)$ even function then,

$$\int_{-a}^{a} f(x)dx = 2\int_{0}^{a} f(x)dx$$

Therefore, $I_1 = 2\int_{0}^{a} x^2\, dx$

$$\Rightarrow 2 \times \left[\frac{x^3}{3}\right]_0^a$$

$$\Rightarrow 2 \times \left[\frac{a^3}{3} - 0\right] = \frac{2a^3}{3}$$

Now,

$$I_2 = \int_{-a}^{a} \sin x dx$$

Here $f(x) = \sin x$

Replace x by $-x$, we get:

$$\Rightarrow f(-x) = \sin(-x) = -\sin x \quad (\because \sin(-\theta) = -\sin\theta)$$

$$\Rightarrow f(-x) = -f(x)$$

So, $f(x)$ is odd function.

As we know, If $f(x)$ even function then $\int_{-a}^{a} f(x)dx = 0$

$$I = I_1 + I_2$$

$$= \frac{2a^3}{3} + 0$$

$$= \frac{2a^3}{3}$$

Hence, the correct option is (D).

100. A distributed lattice can't have kite and pentagonal shape lattice as a sublattice.

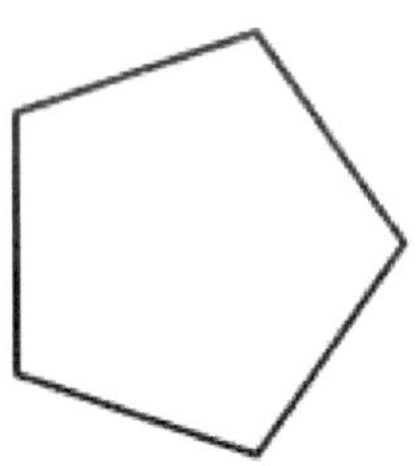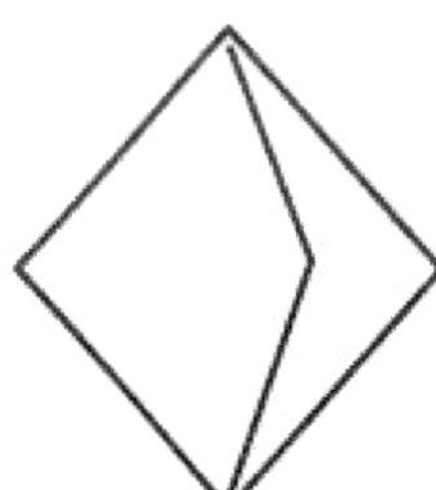

So, first option is true as with 4 element we can't have these two lattices as a sublattice.

Second option is also true and can be easily proofed by "proof by contradiction method".

A totally order set has a straight line in hasse diagram therefore it can't have pentagonal and kite shape lattice as a sublattice, therefore it is true.

Option (D), is false, because the poset [N; <=] is unbounded distributive lattice.

Hence, the correct option is (B).

Q.1 The complexity of recurrence relation: $T(n) = 2T(sqrt(n)) + \lg(n)$ is:

A. $O(\lg(n)\lg(n))$
B. $O(\lg(n))$
C. $O(n\lg(n))$
D. $O\left(\lg(n)\lg(\lg(n))\right)$

Q.2 Consider the equality $\sum_{i=0}^{n} i^3 = X$ and the following choices for X.

I. $\theta(n^4)$

II. $\theta(n^5)$

III. $O(n^5)$

IV. $\Omega(n^3)$

The equality above remains correct if X is replaced by:

A. I, II, IV
B. II, III, IV
C. I, II, III
D. I, III, IV

Q.3 Consider the following statements:

Statement 1: Greedy technique solves the problem correctly and always provides an optimized solution to the problem.

Statement 2: Bellman ford, Floyd-warshal, and Prim's algorithms use the Dynamic Programming technique to solve the Path problems.

Which of the following is true?

A. Statement 1 is true only.
B. Statement 2 is false only
C. Statement 1 and Statement 2 both are false.
D. Statement 1 and Statement 2 both are true.

Q.4 With reference to implementation of different association mining algorithms, identify the correct statement:

A. The FP growth method was usually better than the best implementation of the apriori algorithm.
B. Apriori algorithm is usually better than CHARM.
C. Apriori algorithm is good when the support required is low.
D. At very low support the number of frequent items becomes less.

Q.5 The maximum number of nodes in a binary tree of depth 10 is:

A. 1024
B. 1023
C. 1000
D. None of these

Q.6 The time required to find shortest path in a graph with n vertices and e edges is:

A. $O(e)$
B. $O(n)$
C. $O(e^2)$
D. $O(n^2)$

Q.7 Preorder is also known as:

A. Depth first order
B. Breadth first order
C. Topological order
D. Linear order

Q.8 Data abstraction means:

A. Objects of one class acquire properties of object of another class.
B. Insulation of data from direct access by programs.
C. Code associated with a procedure call is not known until run time.
D. Putting together essential features without including background details.

Q.9 Pass by address passes the address of object _______ and pass by reference passes the address of the object _______.

A. Explicitly, explicitly
B. Implicitly, implicitly
C. Explicitly, implicitly
D. Implicitly, explicitly

Q.10 Which of the following is a back-end language?

A. HTML
B. CSS
C. JavaScript
D. Python

Q.11 Which is interpreted language?

A. C++
B. C
C. MATLAB
D. FORTRAN

Q.12 If Programmer wants to open a file in C programming, In which mode it should not be opened if we want to retain the old content of the file:

A. w
B. a+
C. a
D. r

Q.13 Higher-order functions are not built into the:

A. Structural language
B. Object oriented programming
C. JAVA
D. C++

Q.14 Which of the following highly uses the concept of an array?

A. Binary Search tree
B. Caching
C. Spatial locality
D. Scheduling of Processes

Q.15 Which one of the following is the size of int arr $[9]$ assuming that int is of 4 bytes?

A. 9
B. 13
C. 17
D. 36

Q.16 If the size of the stack is 10 and we try to add the 11th element in the stack then the condition is known as _______.

A. Underflow
B. Garbage collection
C. Overflow
D. Insertion

Q.17 The minimum number of stacks required to implement a queue is _______.

A. 1
B. 2
C. 3
D. 4

Q.18 Consider the following statements regarding switching networks:

Statement 1: The packet switching technique is preferred when the data to be sent must be ordered and transmitted in less time.

Statement 2: In-Circuit Switching, the resources needed along a path between end systems are reserved for the duration of the communication.

Which of the following is/are true or false regarding the above statements?

A. Statement 1 is true.   **B.** Statement 2 is true.

C. Statement 1 is false.   **D.** Both (B) and (C)

Q.19 What is the Hamming distance between 1101 and 110?

A. 2   **B.** 0   **C.** 4   **D.** 3

Q.20 Which of the following is/are true about Ethernet networks?

A. Ethernet frames have a maximum data size of 1500B to ensure the good throughput of the network.

B. A bridge will forward a broadcast, but a switch will not.

C. A hub does not have filtering capacity.

D. Both (A) and (B)

Q.21 Match the following:

List I	List II
I) Attenuation	P) Loss of energy
II) Shannon	Q) Changes in shape of the signal
III) Nyquist bit rate	R) Noisy channel
IV) Distortion	S) Noiseless channel

A. I – Q, II – P, III – S, IV - R

B. I – P, II – Q, III – R, IV - S

C. I – S, II – R, III – Q, IV - P

D. I – P, II – R, III – S, IV - Q

Q.22 Which NetWare protocol works on layer 3 which is the network layer of the OSI model?

A. IPX   **B.** NCP

C. SPX   **D.** NetBIOS

Q.23 What is the full form of ISP?

A. Internet Service Provider

B. Internet Segregation Principle

C. Informal Segregation Principle

D. None of these

Q.24 In which method we can connect to internet?

A. Dial-up   **B.** SLIP

C. PPP   **D.** All of these

Q.25 The three types of IP addresses are:

A. 1. Network Address 2. Host Address 3. Local Address

B. 1. Network Address 2. Host Address 3. Broad Cast Address

C. 1. Network Address 2. Host Address 3. Packet Address

D. 1. Network Address 2. Host Address 3. Frame Address

Q.26 A network that needs human beings to manually route signals is called:

A. Fiber Optic Network

B. Bus Network

C. T-switched network

D. Ring network

Q.27 When can input devices send information to the processor?

A. When the SIN status flag is set.

B. When the data arrives regardless of the SIN flag.

C. When the data is on the external SIN flag.

D. None of these

Q.28 _____ structure is usually used to connect the I/O devices.

A. Single bus   **B.** Multiple bus

C. Star bus   **D.** Ram bus

Q.29 The I/O interface required to connect the I/O device to the bus consists of _____.

A. Address decoder and Registers

B. Control circuits

C. Both (A) and (B)

D. None of these

Q.30 _____ directive is used to specify and assign the memory required for the block of code.

A. Allocate   **B.** Assign   **C.** Set   **D.** Reserve

Q.31 When dealing with the branching code the assembler _____.

A. Replaces the target with its address.

B. Does not replace until the test condition is satisfied.

C. Finds the branch offset and replaces the branch target with it.

D. Replaces the target with the value specified by the dataword directive.

Q.32 The assembler stores all the names and their corresponding values in _____.

A. Special purpose register

B. Symbol table

C. Value map set

D. None of these

Q.33 Which representation is most efficient to perform arithmetic operations on the numbers?

A. Sign-magnitude   **B.** 1's complement

C. 2's complement   **D.** None of these

Q.34 The computer architecture aimed at reducing the time of execution of instructions is _____.

A. CISC   **B.** RISC   **C.** ISA   **D.** ANNA

Q.35 In CISC architecture most of the complex instructions are stored in _____.

A. Register   **B.** Diodes

C. CMOS   **D.** Transistors

Q.36 All of the following accurately describe Hadoop, except _____.

A. Open-source
B. Real-time
C. Java-based
D. Distributed computing approach

Q.37 ________ can best be described as a programming model used to develop Hadoop-based applications that can process massive amounts of data.
A. MapReduce
B. Mahout
C. Oozie
D. All of these

Q.38 Related fields in a database are grouped to form a ________.

A. Data File
B. Data Record
C. Menu
D. Bank

Q.39 An expression builder is an access tool that controls an expression ________ for entering an expression.
A. Table
B. Box
C. Cell
D. Palette

Q.40 Consider the attributes ID, CITY and NAME. Which one of these can be considered as a super key?
A. NAME
B. ID
C. CITY
D. Both (A) and (B)

Q.41 The purpose of the primary key in a database is to ________.

A. Unlock the database
B. Provide a map of the data
C. Uniquely identify a record
D. Establish constraints on database operations

Q.42 Name the database object in MS Access that stores a question about the data in the database?
A. Table
B. Form
C. Query
D. Report

Q.43 What will be the normal form of a table after normalization in which all determinants are candidate key?
A. $BCNF$
B. $2NF$
C. $5NF$
D. $4NF$

Q.44 Find out the wrong statement:
A. Non Relational databases require that schemas be defined before you can add data.
B. NoSQL databases are built to allow the insertion of data without a predefined schema.
C. NewSQL databases are built to allow the insertion of data without a predefined schema.
D. All of these

Q.45 Consider a non-negative counting semaphore S. The operation $P(S)$ decrements S, and $V(S)$ increments S. During an execution, $20\ P(S)$ operations and $12\ V(S)$ operations are issued in some order. The largest initial value of S for which at least one $P(S)$ operation will remain blocked is ________.
A. 7
B. 9
C. 10
D. 11

Q.46 Consider a machine with byte addressable memory and 32 bits virtual address space, physical memory is 4 GB and 4 KB page size. If page table occupies one page and page table

entries is 4 B each, then the memory overhead for this machine is ________ KB.
A. 4100
B. 4200
C. 4000
D. 4300

Q.47 Suppose that a system is in unsafe state. Is it possible for the processes to complete their execution without entering a deadlock state?
A. Yes, it is possible that a system in an unsafe state may still allow all processes to complete without deadlock occurring.
B. It is not possible since only one process can be in the critical section at any time.
C. Yes, it is possible that some of the processes can complete their execution.
D. Both (A) and (C)

Q.48 Which module gives control of the CPU to the process selected by the short-term scheduler?
A. Dispatcher
B. Interrupt
C. Scheduler
D. None of these

Q.49 What problem is solved by Dijkstra's banker's algorithm?
A. Mutual exclusion
B. Deadlock recovery
C. Deadlock avoidance
D. Cache coherence

Q.50 Which of the following option is correct about the dispatcher?
A. Actually schedules the tasks into the processor.
B. Puts tasks in I/O wait.
C. Is always small and simple.
D. Never changes task priorities.

Q.51 When the process issues an I/O request ________.
A. It is placed in an I/O queue.
B. It is placed in a waiting queue.
C. It is placed in the ready queue.
D. It is placed in the job queue.

Q.52 The processes that are residing in main memory and are ready and waiting to execute are kept on a list called ________.

A. Job queue
B. Ready queue
C. Execution queue
D. Process queue

Q.53 If the number of bits in a virtual address of a program is 16 and the page size is 0.5 KB, the number of pages in the virtual address space is:
A. 16
B. 32
C. 64
D. 128

Q.54 Consider the circuit figure which has three-bit binary number $a_2a_1a_0$ as input and a four-bit binary bit binary number $O_3O_2O_1O_0$ as output. The circuit implements:

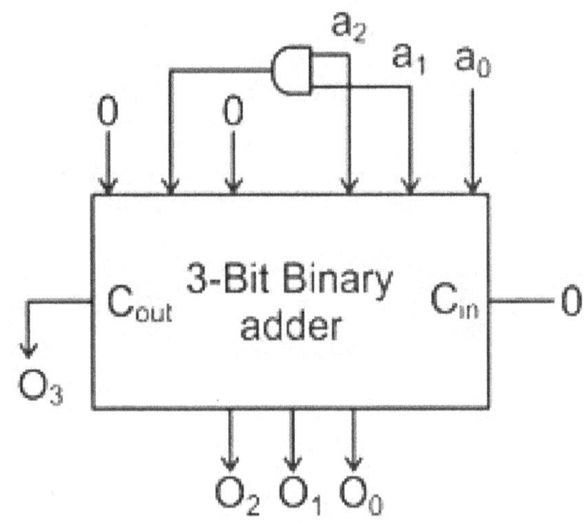

A. Binary to Hex conversion
B. Binary to Octal conversion
C. Binary to radix- 6 conversion
D. Binary to excess- 3 conversion

Q.55 Consider $X = 11111011$ and $Y = 00001010$ be two 8 bit two's compliment number. What is the value of their product in two's complement?

A. 10101000
B. 11001110
C. 11011010
D. 00101000

Q.56 The output of the following combinational circuit is F.

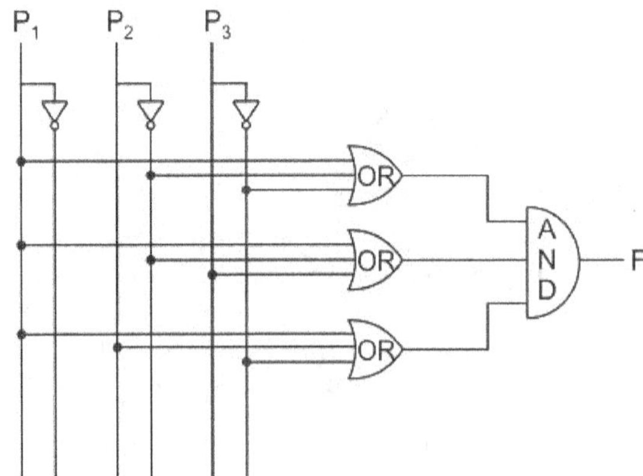

The value of F is:

A. $P_1 + P_2 P_3$
B. $P_1 + P_2' P_3'$
C. $P_1 + P_2 P_3'$
D. $P'_1 + P_2 P_3$

Q.57 If there are m input lines and n output lines for a decoder that is used to uniquely address a byte-addressable 4 KB RAM, then the minimum value of $m + n$ is __________.

A. 4108
B. 4109
C. 4110
D. 4118

Q.58 If the input to the digital circuit of the below figure consisting of a cascade of $20 XOR$ gates is X, then what is the output Y?

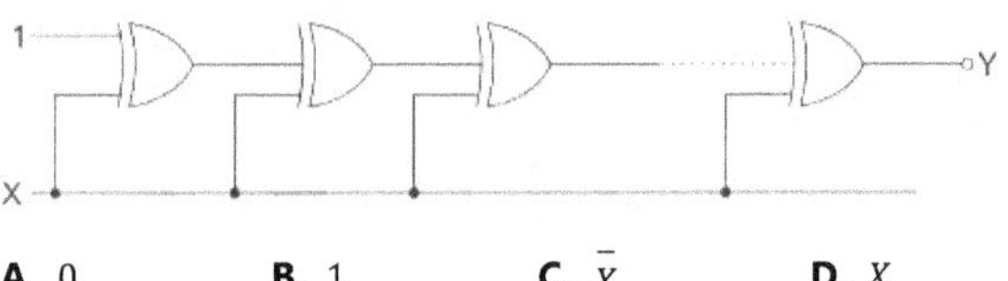

A. 0
B. 1
C. $\bar{X}$
D. X

Q.59 Consider the following multiplexer where $0,1,2,3$ are four data input lines selected by two address line combination of $CB = 00,01,10,11$ respectively and f is the output of the multiplexer.

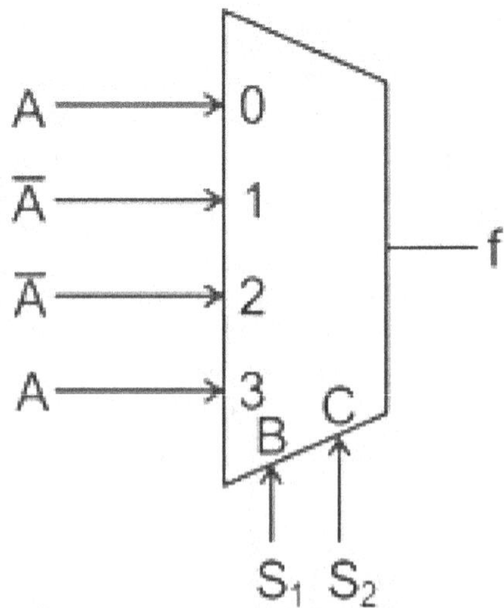

The function $f(S_2, S_1, A)$ implemented by the above circuit is?

A. $S_2 \odot S_1 \odot A$
B. $S_2 \odot S_1 \oplus A$
C. $S_2 \oplus S_1 \oplus A$
D. Both (A) and (C)

Q.60 The following circuit compares two 2-bit binary numbers, X and Y represented by $X_1 X_0$ and $Y_1 Y_0$ respectively. $(X_0$ and Y_0 represent Least Significant Bits.)

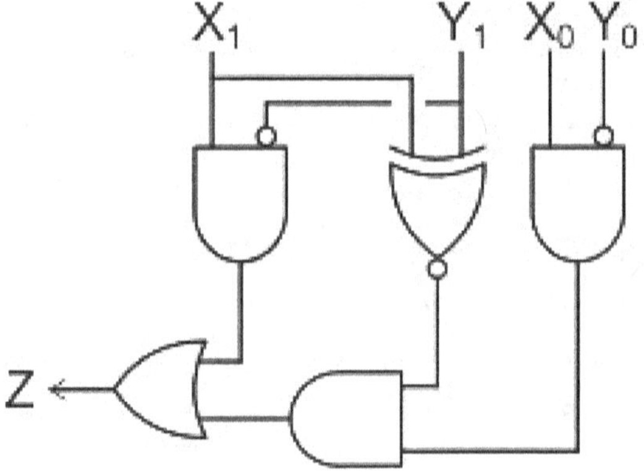

Under what condition Z will be 1?

A. $X > Y$
B. $X < Y$
C. $X = Y$
D. None of these

Q.61 In the two-bit full adder/subtractor unit shown in the figure, when the switch is in position 1 then which operation is performed provided that operands are in $2's$ complement representation.

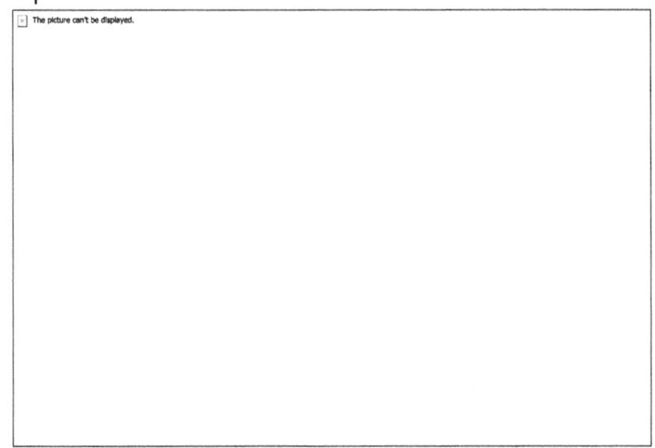

A. $A - B$ **B.** $A + B$
C. $B - A$ **D.** $A + B + 1$

Q.62 What is the minimum number of 2 input NAND gates needed to implement $F(p, q, r, s, t)$ where $F(p, q, r, s, t) = (\overline{p} + \overline{q})(r + s + t)$?
A. 7   **B.** 8   **C.** 9   **D.** 10

Q.63 Regular sets are closed under union, concatenation and kleene closure. Is it true or false?
A. True
B. False
C. Depends on regular set
D. Can't say

Q.64 Complement of a DFA can be obtained by:
A. Making starting state as final state
B. No trival method
C. Making final states non-final and non-final to final
D. Make final as a starting state

Q.65 Reverse of $(0 + 1)^*$ will be:
A. Phi   **B.** Null   **C.** $(0 + 1)^*$ **D.** $(0 + 1)$

Q.66 Recursive languages are ___________.
A. A proper superset of CFL.
B. Always recognized by PDA.
C. Are also called type 0 languages.
D. Always recognized by FSA.

Q.67 Which of the following regular expression identity is true?
A. $r(^*) = r^*$ **B.** $(r^*s^*)^* = (r + s)^*$
C. $(r + s)^* = r^* + s^*$ **D.** $r^*s^* = r^* + s^*$

Q.68 Which parser is most powerful in the following parsers?
A. Operator Precedence
B. SLR
C. Canonical LR
D. LALR

Q.69 The output of the lexical analyzer is ______.
A. String character   **B.** A syntax tree
C. A set of RE   **D.** A set of tokens

Q.70 Which grammar gives multiple parse trees for the same string?
A. Unambiguous   **B.** Regular
C. Ambiguous   **D.** None of these

Q.71 In compiler, lexical analyzer is used for:
A. Removing comments
B. Removing whitespace
C. Breaking the syntaxes in the set of tokens
D. All of these

Q.72 Consider P and Q be the two propositions. Which of the following is/are equivalent to ¬ (P ↔ Q)?
A. P ↔ ¬ Q   **B.** ¬ P ↔ ¬ Q
C. ¬ P ↔ Q   **D.** Both (A) and (C)

Q.73 Which of the following is an equivalence relation on the set of all functions from Z to Z?
A. $\{(f, g) \mid f(x) - g(x) = 1x \in Z\}$
B. $\{(f, g) \mid f(0) = g(0)$ or $f(1) = g(1)\}$
C. $\{(f, g) \mid f(0) = g(1)$ and $f(1) = g(0)\}$
D. $\{(f, g) \mid f(x) - g(x) = k$ for some $k \in Z\}$

Q.74 Consider the given statements:
Statement A: All cyclic groups are an abelian group.
Statement B: The order of the cyclic group is the same as the order of its generator.
Which of these are true/false?
A. A and B are false
B. A is true, B is false
C. B is true, A is false
D. A and B both are true

Q.75 K 4 and Q 3 are graphs with the following structures:

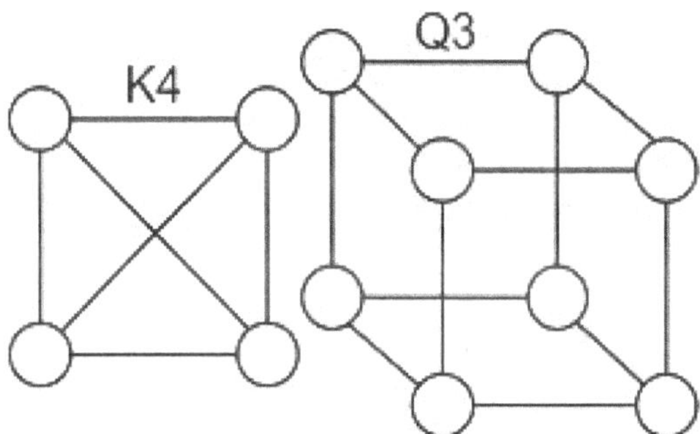

Which one of the following statements is TRUE in relation to these graphs?
A. K 4 is planar while Q 3 is not.
B. Both K4 and Q 3 are planar.
C. Q 3 is planar while K 3 is not.
D. Neither K 4 nor Q 3 is planar.

Q.76 In how many ways we can wear 4 distinct rings in 3 particular fingers?
A. 360   **B.** 362   **C.** 420   **D.** 365

Q.77 Neela has twelve different skirts, ten different tops, eight different pairs of shoes, three different necklaces and five different bracelets. In how many ways can Neela dress up?

A. 50057 **B.** 14400 **C.** 34870 **D.** 56732

Q.78 For any integer $m \geq 3$, the series $2 + 4 + 6 + \cdots + (4m)$ can be equivalent to _______.

A. $m^2 + 3$ **B.** $m + 1$ **C.** m^m **D.** $3m^2 + 4$

Q.79 PCNF is also called __________.

A. Sum of product canonical form
B. Product of sum canonical form
C. Sum canonical form
D. Product canonical form

Q.80 What is the generating function for the generating sequence $A = 1,9,25,49, ...$?

A. $1 + (A - x^2)$
B. $(1 - A) - \frac{1}{x}$
C. $(1 - A) + \frac{1}{x^2}$
D. $\frac{(A-x)}{x^3}$

Q.81 Which tool is used for structured designing?

A. Program flowchart **B.** Structure chart
C. Data-flow diagram **D.** Module

Q.82 Efficiency in a software product does not include _______.

A. Licensing **B.** Processing time
C. Responsiveness **D.** Memory utilization

Q.83 Actual programming of software code is done during the __________ step in the SDLC.

A. Maintenance and Evaluation
B. Design
C. Analysis
D. Development and Documentation

Q.84 Which of the following models doesn't necessitate defining requirements at the earliest in the lifecycle?

A. RAD and Waterfall
B. Prototyping and Waterfall
C. Spiral and Prototyping
D. Spiral and RAD

Q.85 What are attributes of good software?

A. Software maintainability
B. Software functionality
C. Software development
D. Both (A) and (B)

Q.86 In Design phase, which is the primary area of concern?

A. Architectural **B.** Detailed
C. Interface **D.** All of these

Q.87 The importance of software design can be summarized in a single word which is:

A. Efficiency **B.** Accuracy
C. Quality **D.** Complexity

Q.88 Where is a need of a software engineering?

A. For large software

B. To reduce cost
C. Software quality management
D. All of these

Q.89 Coupling is a qualitative indication of the degree to which a module __________.

A. Can be written more compactly
B. Focuses on just one thing
C. Is able to complete its function in a timely manner
D. Is connected to other modules and the outside world

Q.90 A speaks truth in 75% cases and B speaks truth in 25% cases. A car accident takes place on the highway. What is the probability that they will report this event truly or both of them will not speak the truth?

A. $\frac{3}{16}$ **B.** $\frac{3}{8}$ **C.** $\frac{5}{8}$ **D.** $\frac{5}{16}$

Q.91 There are 49 cards in a box numbered from 1 to 49. Every card is numbered with only 1 number. Probability of picking up a card, the number printed on which is a multiple of 5 but not that of 10 or 15 is:

A. $\frac{2}{49}$ **B.** $\frac{3}{49}$ **C.** $\frac{4}{49}$ **D.** $\frac{5}{49}$

Q.92 The differential equation of the family of curves $y = c_1 e^x + c_2 e^{-x}$ is:

A. $\frac{d^2y}{dx^2} + y = 0$ **B.** $\frac{d^2y}{dx^2} - y = 0$
C. $\frac{d^3y}{dx^3} + y = 0$ **D.** $\frac{d^4y}{dx^4} - 1 = 0$

Q.93 The differential equation of all parabolas whose axis is y-axis is:

A. $x\frac{d^2y}{dx^2} - \frac{dy}{dx} = 0$ **B.** $x\frac{d^2y}{dx^2} + \frac{dy}{dx} = 0$
C. $\frac{d^2y}{dx^2} - y = 0$ **D.** $\frac{d^2y}{dx^2} - \frac{dy}{dx} = 0$

Q.94 The solution of $\frac{d^2y}{dt^2} - y = 1$, which additionally satisfies $y\big|_{t=0} = \frac{dy}{dt}\big|_{t=0} = 0$ in the Laplace s-domain is:

[GATE Mechanical Engineering ME, 2020]

A. $\frac{1}{s(s+1)(s-1)}$ **B.** $\frac{1}{s(s+1)}$
C. $\frac{1}{s(s-1)}$ **D.** $\frac{1}{s-1}$

Q.95 The Laplace transform of $e^{at}\cos\omega t$:

A. $\frac{(s-a)}{(s-a)^2+\omega^2}$ **B.** $\frac{\omega}{(s-a)^2+\omega^2}$
C. $\frac{a}{(s-a)^2+\omega^2}$ **D.** $\frac{s}{(s-a)^2+\omega^2}$

Q.96 A matrix X has a dimension of 2×2. If the eigenvalues of this matrix is 5 and 6, what would be the eigenvalues of X^2?

A. 2.5 and 3 **B.** 5 and 6
C. 10 and 12 **D.** 25 and 36

Q.97 The approximate solution of the system of simultaneous equations by applying Gauss-Seidel method one time (using initial approximation as $x = 0, y = 0, z = 0$) will be:

$$2x - 5y + 3z = 7$$
$$x + 4y - 2z = 3$$
$$2x + 3y + z = 2$$

A. $x = 2.32, y = 1.245, z = -3.157$
B. $x = 1.25, y = -2.573, z = -3.135$
C. $x = 2.45, y = -1.725, z = -3.565$
D. $x = 3.5, y = -0.125, z = -4.625$

Q.98 Differentiate the following:

$$x^8 + 12x^5 - 4x^4 + 10x^3 - 6x + 5$$

A. $8x^7 + 60x^4 - 16x^3 + 30x^2$
B. $8x^7 + 60x^4 - 16x^3 + 30x^2 - 6$
C. $8x^7 + 60x^4 + 30x^2 - 6$
D. None of these

Q.99 What is $\int \dfrac{dx}{\sec^2(\tan^{-1}x)}$ equal to?

A. $\sin^{-1}x + C$
B. $\tan^{-1}x + C$
C. $\sec^{-1}x + C$
D. $\cos^{-1}x + C$

Q.100 A hash table has space for 100 records. Then the probability of collision before the table is 10% full is:

A. 0.45
B. 0.5
C. 0.37
D. 0.34

// Smart Answer Sheet //

Correct — Percentage of students who answered correctly.　　**Skipped** — Percentage of students who skipped.

Q.	Ans.	Correct / Skipped	Q.	Ans.	Correct / Skipped	Q.	Ans.	Correct / Skipped	Q.	Ans.	Correct / Skipped	Q.	Ans.	Correct / Skipped	Q.	Ans.	Correct / Skipped
1	D	53.41 % / 40.12 %	18	D	52.8 % / 45.8 %	35	D	49.86 % / 38.82 %	52	B	57.75 % / 38.27 %	69	D	80.07 % / 14.81 %	86	D	63.03 % / 34.77 %
2	D	13.78 % / 84.09 %	19	D	24.26 % / 68.37 %	36	B	87.28 % / 12.28 %	53	D	47.21 % / 50.89 %	70	C	43.57 % / 47.26 %	87	C	46.21 % / 51.88 %
3	C	56.72 % / 30.33 %	20	D	60.38 % / 39.26 %	37	A	66.73 % / 30.85 %	54	C	32.86 % / 67.05 %	71	D	47.96 % / 37.12 %	88	D	66.06 % / 30.14 %
4	A	48.98 % / 31.76 %	21	D	11.82 % / 73.91 %	38	B	68.35 % / 31.2 %	55	B	58.2 % / 31.32 %	72	D	51.89 % / 47.22 %	89	D	58.87 % / 35.51 %
5	B	79.98 % / 13.77 %	22	A	56.56 % / 42.13 %	39	B	30.15 % / 69.12 %	56	B	22.88 % / 74.64 %	73	D	62.93 % / 35.47 %	90	B	62.77 % / 34.17 %
6	D	22.14 % / 70.16 %	23	A	63.69 % / 31.38 %	40	B	56.95 % / 32.52 %	57	A	61.95 % / 37.07 %	74	D	88.94 % / 10.71 %	91	B	41.72 % / 58.02 %
7	A	60.07 % / 39.09 %	24	D	44.94 % / 50.86 %	41	C	76.68 % / 14.09 %	58	B	53.68 % / 39.82 %	75	B	67.98 % / 31.6 %	92	B	69.75 % / 30.01 %
8	D	81.51 % / 11.08 %	25	B	60.22 % / 33.66 %	42	C	83.9 % / 10.38 %	59	D	23.97 % / 71.07 %	76	A	57.37 % / 35.02 %	93	A	50.74 % / 34.18 %
9	C	61.47 % / 33.24 %	26	C	46.44 % / 41.32 %	43	A	40.34 % / 43.19 %	60	A	67.09 % / 32.33 %	77	B	55.89 % / 36.66 %	94	A	58.43 % / 34.49 %
10	D	79.76 % / 17.14 %	27	A	53.24 % / 30.34 %	44	A	21.65 % / 77.0 %	61	B	68.52 % / 30.63 %	78	A	47.51 % / 36.35 %	95	A	82.54 % / 13.53 %
11	C	47.57 % / 43.43 %	28	A	82.77 % / 14.63 %	45	A	63.63 % / 30.93 %	62	A	66.18 % / 31.78 %	79	B	17.2 % / 68.27 %	96	D	47.56 % / 50.89 %
12	A	52.14 % / 31.13 %	29	C	41.94 % / 53.14 %	46	A	49.29 % / 46.41 %	63	A	53.35 % / 35.43 %	80	B	53.42 % / 45.88 %	97	D	41.51 % / 44.33 %
13	A	88.37 % / 10.99 %	30	D	69.66 % / 30.32 %	47	D	52.11 % / 46.89 %	64	C	57.08 % / 41.47 %	81	B	80.35 % / 10.65 %	98	B	53.26 % / 36.35 %
14	C	54.7 % / 31.17 %	31	C	51.68 % / 35.57 %	48	A	64.07 % / 34.93 %	65	C	58.72 % / 31.12 %	82	A	52.61 % / 40.3 %	99	B	61.46 % / 37.74 %
15	D	69.97 % / 30.01 %	32	B	81.7 % / 11.78 %	49	C	59.96 % / 34.43 %	66	A	84.0 % / 14.18 %	83	D	69.92 % / 30.04 %	100	C	42.72 % / 30.41 %
16	C	42.83 % / 39.44 %	33	C	61.02 % / 35.09 %	50	A	28.88 % / 68.03 %	67	B	29.54 % / 67.13 %	84	C	67.68 % / 30.51 %			
17	B	85.22 % / 10.69 %	34	B	59.29 % / 37.35 %	51	A	55.77 % / 39.28 %	68	C	52.76 % / 40.76 %	85	D	32.9 % / 67.03 %			

//Hints and Solutions//

1. Given, recurrence relation:

$$T(n) = 2T(sqrt(n)) + \lg(n) \quad \dots (1)$$

Now,

Put $n = 2^m$

Taking logarithm both sides, we get $\log n = m$

Put value of n in (1),

$$T(2^m) = 2\,T\left(2^{\frac{m}{2}}\right) + m$$

Let $S(m) = T(2^m)$

So, $S(m) = 2S\left(\dfrac{m}{2}\right) + m$

Using master's theorem:

Here $a = 2, b = 2$

$$m^{\log_b a}$$

$$= m^{\log_2 2}$$

$$= m$$

Now, both the $m^{\log a}$ and value of function are equal. So, time complexity will be $O(m \log m)$.

Put the value of m in terms of n.

So, time complexity of given recurrence relation will be:

$$O\left(\lg(n)\lg\big(\lg(n)\big)\right)$$

Hence, the correct option is (D).

2. Given,

$$\sum_{i=0}^{n} i^3 = X$$

As we know that,

$$\Rightarrow X = \frac{n^2(n+1)^2}{4}$$

Now,

$$\sum_{i=0}^{n} i^3 = \frac{n^2(n+1)^2}{4}$$

In choice (III),

$$\frac{n^2(n+1)^2}{4} = O(n^5)$$

In choice (IV),

$$\frac{n^2(n+1)^2}{4} = \Omega(n^3)$$

In choice (I),

$$\frac{n^2(n+1)^2}{4} = \theta(n^4)$$

In choice (II),

$$\frac{n^2(n+1)^2}{4} \neq \theta(n^5)$$

So, the equality above remains correct if X is replaced by (I, III, IV).

Hence, the correct option is (D).

3. Statement 1: Greedy technique solves the problem correctly and always provides an optimized solution to the problem.

This statement is false. Since the Greedy technique does not always solve a problem correctly.

Statement 2: Bellman ford, Floyd-warshal, and Prim's algorithms use the Dynamic Programming technique to solve the Path problems.

This statement is also false. Since Prim's algorithm does not use the Dynamic Programming technique.

Hence, the correct option is (C).

4. The FP growth method was usually better than the best implementation of the apriori algorithm. Apriori is an algorithm for frequent item set mining and association rule learning over relational databases. It proceeds by identifying the frequent individual items in the database and extending them to larger and larger item sets as long as those item sets appear sufficiently often in the database.

Hence, the correct option is (A).

5. The maximum number of nodes in a binary tree of depth K is $2^K - 1$.

Where, K is the depth of binary tree, $K > 1$.

Given, $K = 10$

So, maximum number of nodes $= 2^{10} - 1 = 1023$

Hence, the correct option is (B).

6. The time required to find shortest path in a graph with n vertices and e edges is $O(n^2)$.

Dijkstra's algorithm's time complexity is:

$$V \times \log\,(V) + E \text{ (using fibonacci heaps)}$$

They have given # edges as e. Now, e can be equal to $V \times V$. Also, the notation being used is big- O.

Hence, the correct option is (D).

7. Preorder is also known as depth first order. Preorder traversal is another variant of DFS. Where atomic operations in a recursive function, are as same as inorder traversal but with a different order.

We visit the current node first and then goes to the left sub-tree. After covering every node of the left sub-tree, we will move towards the right sub-tree and visit in a similar fashion.

The order of the steps will be like:

- Visit Node.
- Go to left-subtree.
- Go to right-subtree.

Hence, the correct option is (A).

8. Data abstraction is one of the most essential and important feature of object-oriented programming in C++. Data abstraction means displaying only essential information and hiding the details. Data abstraction refers to providing only essential information about the data to the outside world, hiding the background details or implementation.

Hence, the correct option is (D).

9. Pass by address uses the explicitly address passing to the function whereas pass by reference implicitly passes the address of the object. When an object is passed by reference, its address is passed implicitly. This will make changes to the main function whenever any modification is done. Explicit means were done by the programmer. Implicit means were done by the JVM or the tool, not the Programmer. For example, Java will provide us, default constructor, implicitly. Even if the programmer didn't write code for the constructor, he can call the default constructor.

Hence, the correct option is (C).

10. Python is a back-end language.

- Python is an interpreted, high-level, general-purpose programming language.

- Python can be used on a server to create web applications.

- Python lets user work quickly and integrate systems more efficiently.

Therefore, python is treated as a back-end language.

Hence, the correct option is (D).

11. MATLAB is an interpreted language. All the other languages are compiled languages. In the case of Interpreted language, the translation to machine-language is performed incrementally at run-time. MATLAB is a proprietary multi-paradigm programming language and numeric computing environment developed by MathWorks. MATLAB allows matrix manipulations, plotting of functions and data, implementation of algorithms, creation of user interfaces, and interfacing with programs written in other languages.

Hence, the correct option is (C).

12. We can open a file or create a file in C programming using the function fopen().

It takes two arguments:

- filename or path to file (including file name.
- mode: which mode we want to open the file.

There are various modes in C programming for opening a file:

$1.$ 'r': This indicates that the file will be opened in read-only mode. (no write operation will be permitted.)

$2.$ 'w': This indicates that the file will be opened in write mode and all the data that previously have been written to the file will be overwritten. the file will be created if not exists in the specified path or directory.

$3.$ 'a': This indicates that the file will be open in append mode. means from now on data will be appended to the file content.

$4.$ 'r+': This indicates the file will be opened in reading and write mode.

$5.$ 'a+': This indicates the file will be opened in append and write mode, If the file doesn't exist, a new file is created.

Hence, the correct option is (A).

13. Higher-order functions are not built into the structural language. A higher-order function is a function that either takes a function as an argument or returns a function. This type of function has implementations in many programming languages including Go, JavaScript, Python, etc.

Hence, the correct option is (A).

14. Spatial locality is highly uses the concept of an array. Spatial locality means that the instruction accessed recently, then the nearby memory location would be accessed in the next iteration. As we know that in an array, all the elements are stored in a contiguous block of memory, so spatial locality is accessed quickly.

Hence, the correct option is (C).

15. Given,

The size of int type data is 4 bytes.

The array stores 9 elements.

Now,

The size of the array will be $9 \times 4 = 36$ bytes.

Hence, the correct option is (D).

16. If the size of the stack is 10 and we try to add the 11th element in the stack then the condition is known as overflow. A stack overflow occurs if the call stack pointer exceeds the stack bound. The call stack may consist of a limited amount of address space, often determined at the start of the program. The size of the call stack depends on many factors, including the programming language, machine architecture, multi-threading, and amount of available memory.

Hence, the correct option is (C).

17. The minimum number of stacks required to implement a queue is 2. In Queue, one stack is required for the enqueue operation, and another stack will be used for the dequeue operation. The first stack is considered as the input stack whereas the second stack is considered as the output stack.

Hence, the correct option is (B).

18. Given,

Statement 1:

"The packet switching technique is preferred when the data to be sent must be ordered and transmitted in less time".

This statement is false. Since packet switching does not reserve the resources need along the path, it just encapsulates the data in packets and throws them into the network. So, packets may arrive in a different order at the source.

Statement 2:

"In-Circuit Switching, the resources needed along a path between end systems are reserved for the duration of the communication".

This statement is true. Since in-circuit switching resources needed along a path already reserved before the transmission and then the data transmitted so, it will take less time and data will arrive in the same order as sent by the host.

Hence, the correct option is (D).

19. Hamming distance: Hamming distance between two binary strings is equal to the number of bit changes between those two strings.

For example:

1. Consider two binary strings as 11011001 and 10011101.

1	1	0	1	1	0	0	1
1	0	0	1	1	1	0	1
No change	Change	No change	No change	No change	Change	No change	No change

So, in the above two binary strings, there are two positions where bit changes. So, Hamming distance $= 2$.

Now,

Given, binary strings 1101 and 0110.

1	1	0	1
0	1	1	0
Change	No Change	Change	Change

So, here the Hamming distance $= 3$

Instead of checking for each bit, we can simply perform an XOR operation between two strings, and the number of 1's in the result indicates the Hamming distance between the strings.

So, we get

$$1101 \oplus 0110 \equiv 1011$$

The number of 1's is 3 so, Hamming distance $= 3$.

Hence, the correct option is (D).

20. Ethernet frames have a minimum size of 1500B to ensure good utilization of the network (i.e., senders could otherwise have a large overhead to send a small piece of data).

Both bridges and switches will forward broadcast and multicast traffic, assuming that the traffic remains in the same VLAN.

Hub doesn't have filtering capacity; it does not have the intelligence to find that from which port it should send the packet.

Hence, the correct option is (D).

21. Attenuation: Attenuation is the loss of communication signal strength. It means loss of energy. When a signal travels through a medium, it loses some of its energy in overcoming the resistance of the medium.

Distortion: It means that the signal changes its form or shape. Distortion can occur in a composite signal made up of different frequencies. Signal components at the receiver have phases different from what they has at the sender. The shape of the signal is not the same.

Nquist bit rate: Nquist bit rate is used for noiseless channels. It defines the bit rate as:

Bit rate $= 2 \times$ bandwidth $\times \log_2$ L, where L is the number of signal levels.

Shannon capacity: Shannon capacity is used for noisy channels. Bit rate in this case.

Bit rate $=$ bandwidth $\times \log_2(1 + \text{SNR})$, where SNR is signal to noise ratio.

Hence, the correct option is (D).

22. IPX (Internetwork Packet Exchange) is the NetWare network layer 3 protocol used for transferring information on LANs that use Novell's NetWare.

IPX is the network layer and SPX is the transport layer of the IPX/SPX network protocol. IPX and IP protocol have similar functions and this defines how data is sent and received between devices. The transport layer protocol or SPX protocol is used to establish and maintain a connection between devices.

Hence, the correct option is (A).

23. The full form of ISP is Internet Service Provider. Internet Service Provider is a term used to refer to a company that provides internet access to people who pay the company or subscribe to the company for the same. For their services, the customers have to pay the internet service provider a nominal fee which varies according to the amount of data they actually use or the data plan which they purchase. An Internet Service Provider is also known as an Internet Access Provider or an online service provider. An Internet Service Provider is a must if one wants to connect to the internet.

Hence, the correct option is (A).

24. Dial-up Internet access is a form of Internet access that uses the facilities of the public switched telephone network to establish a connection to an Internet service provider by dialing a telephone number on a conventional telephone line. SLIP (Serial Line Internet Protocol) is the result of the integration of modem protocols prior to the suite of TCP/IP protocols. Point-to-Point Protocol (PPP) is a data link layer communications protocol used to establish a direct connection between two nodes.

Hence, the correct option is (D).

25. Host address is the portion of the address used to identify hosts and network address is an identifier for a node or network interface of a telecommunications network. The broadcast address represents all devices of the network. If an IP packet is sent on a broadcast address, it is intended for all devices of that network.

Hence, the correct option is (B).

26. A network that needs human beings to manually route signals is called a T-switched network. A network switch (also called switching hub, bridging hub, officially MAC bridge) is a computer networking device.

Switches are key building blocks for any network. They connect multiple devices, such as computers, wireless access points, printers, and servers; on the same network within a building or campus. A switch enables connected devices to share information and talk to each other.

Hence, the correct option is (C).

27. The Input devices can send information to the processor When the SIN status flag is set. The input devices use buffers to store the data received and when the buffer has some data it sends it to the processor. The flag register is a special purpose register.

Hence, the correct option is (A).

28. Single bus structure is usually used to connect the I/O devices. Bus is a bunch of wires which carry addresses, control signals and data. It is used to connect various components of the computer. In a single bus structure, one common bus is used to communicate between peripherals and microprocessors.

Hence, the correct option is (A).

29. The I/O interface required to connect the I/O device to the bus consists of Address decoder, Registers and Control circuits. The I/O devices are connected to the CPU via BUS and to interact with the BUS they have an interface. The main purpose of the I/O interfaces is to transmit and receive data. I/O Interface provides a method for transferring information between internal storage and external I/O devices. Peripherals connected to a computer need special communication links for interfacing them with the central processing unit.

Hence, the correct option is (C).

30. Reserve directive is used to specify and assign the memory required for the block of code. This instruction is used to allocate a block of memory and to store the object code of the program there. The reserve directives are used for reserving space for uninitialized data. The reserve directives take a single operand that specifies the number of units of space to be reserved. Each define directive has a related reserve directive.

Hence, the correct option is (D).

31. When dealing with the branching code the assembler finds the branch offset and replaces the branch target with it. The table where the assembler stores the variable names along with their corresponding memory locations and values. These instructions are accessed through assembly programming and are also referred to as "jump" instructions.

Hence, the correct option is (C).

32. The table where the assembler stores the variable names along with their corresponding memory locations and values in symbol table. The symbol table contains information to locate and relocate symbolic definitions and references. The assembler creates the symbol table section for the object file. It makes an entry in the symbol table for each symbol that is defined or referenced in the input file and is needed during linking.

Hence, the correct option is (B).

33. The two's complement form is more suitable to perform arithmetic operations as there is no need to involve the sign of the number into consideration. 2's complement is used for representing signed numbers and performing arithmetic operations such as subtraction, addition, etc. The positive number is simply represented as a magnitude form. So, there is nothing to do for representing positive numbers. But if we represent the negative number, then we have to choose either 1's complement or 2's complement technique. 1's complement is an ambiguous technique, and 2's complement is an unambiguous technique.

Hence, the correct option is (C).

34. The computer architecture aimed at reducing the time of execution of instructions is RISC. The RISC stands for Reduced Instruction Set Computer. A Reduced Instruction Set Computer is a type of microprocessor architecture that utilizes a small, highly-optimized set of instructions rather than the highly-specialized set of instructions typically found in other architectures. RISC processors can be designed more quickly than CISC processors due to its simple architecture.

Hence, the correct option is (B).

35. In CISC architecture more emphasis is given on the instruction set and the instructions take over a cycle to complete. CISC are larger as they require more transistors. CISC was developed to make compiler development easier and simpler. The full form of CISC is Complex Instruction Set Computer. They are chips that are easy to program that makes efficient use of memory.

Hence, the correct option is (D).

36. All of the above accurately describe Hadoop, except real-time. Hadoop was initially designed for batch processing. That means, take a large dataset in input all at once, process it, and write a large output. The very concept of MapReduce is geared towards batch and not real-time. Apache Hadoop is an open-source software framework for distributed storage and distributed processing of Big Data on clusters of commodity hardware.

Hence, the correct option is (B).

37. MapReduce can best be described as a programming model used to develop Hadoop-based applications that can process massive amounts of data. It is a programming model and an associated implementation for processing and generating large data sets with a parallel, distributed algorithm. MapReduce facilitates concurrent processing by splitting petabytes of data into smaller chunks, and processing them in parallel on Hadoop commodity servers. In the end, it aggregates all the data from multiple servers to return a consolidated output back to the application.

Hence, the correct option is (A).

38. Related fields in a database are grouped to form a data record. A record is a collection of fields, possibly of different data types, typically in fixed number and sequence. In the structure of a database, the part consisting of several uniquely named components called data fields. Several data records make up a data file, and several data files make up a database.

Hence, the correct option is (B).

39. An expression is any legal combination of symbols and characters that results a value. An expression builder is an access tool that controls an expression box for entering an expression.

The expression builder is a general-purpose tool that helps you construct WEAP's expressions by dragging and dropping the functions and WEAP branches into an editing box.

Hence, the correct option is (B).

40. We can define a super key as a set of those keys that identify a row or a tuple uniquely. The word super denotes the superiority of a key. Thus, a super key is the superset of a key known as a Candidate key. Here the "ID" is the only attribute that can be taken as a key. Other attributes are not uniquely identified.

Hence, the correct option is (B).

41. A primary key is a special relational database table column (or combination of columns) designated to uniquely identify all table records. A primary key's main feature is that it must contain a unique value for each row of data and it cannot contain null values.

Hence, the correct option is (C).

42. Databases in MS Access are composed of four objects that is tables, queries, forms, and reports. Together, these objects allow you to enter, store, analyze, and compile your data however you want. Query in the database object in MS Access stores a question about the data in the database.

Hence, the correct option is (C).

43. In which all the determinant are candidates 'key', the normal form will be $BCNF$ of that table after normalization. A relation is in $BCNF$ if, and only if, all determinant is a candidate key. Boyce-Codd's normal form is a special case of $3NF$.

Hence, the correct option is (A).

44. There's also no way, using a relational database, to effectively address data that's completely unstructured or unknown in advance. Non-relational databases (often called NoSQL databases) are different from traditional relational databases in that they store their data in a non-tabular form. Instead, non-relational databases might be based on data structures like documents. A document can be highly detailed while containing a range of different types of information in different formats. This ability to digest and organize various types of information side-by-side makes non-relational databases much more flexible than relational databases.

Hence, the correct option is (A).

45. $V(S)$: Signal will increment the semaphore variable, that is, $S + +.$

$P(S)$: Signal will decrement the semaphore variable., that is, $S - -.$

Given,

Initial counting semaphore $= x$

Signal operation $= 12\ V$

Wait operation $= 20\ P$

Since at least 1 process in blocked state.

Final counting semaphore $(F) = -1$

As we know,

$$F \geq x + 20\ P + 12\ V$$

Now,

$$-1 \geq x + 20(-1) + 12(+1)$$

$$\therefore x \leq 7$$

Therefore, largest value of initial semaphore count is 7.

Hence, the correct option is (A).

46. Given,

Virtual address space VAS $= 32$ bits

Virtual memory VA $= 2^{32}$ Byte

Physical Memory PA $= 4$ GB $= 2^{32}$ B

Page size PS $= 4$ KB $= 2^{12}$ B

Page Table Entry (PTE) $= 4$ byte

As we know that,

$$\text{Page table size } = \frac{VA}{PS} \times PTE$$

$$\text{Number of entries in the page table } = \frac{PS}{PTE}$$

Now,

Level 1: page table size $= \frac{2^{32}}{2^{12}} \times 4$ byte $= 2^{22}$ byte $>$ PTS

Level 2: page table size $= \frac{2^{22}}{2^{12}} \times 4$ byte $= 2^{12}$ byte $=$ PTS

$\therefore$ level needed $= 2$

Number of entries in a page $= \frac{2^{12}}{4} = 2^{10}$

Overhead $=$ Outer page size $+$ Inner page size

$= 4$ KB $+ 2^{10} \times 4$ KB

$= 4100$ KB

Hence, the correct option is (A).

47. An unsafe state may not necessarily lead to deadlock, it just means that we cannot guarantee that deadlock will not occur. Thus, it is possible that a system in an unsafe state may still allow all processes to complete without deadlock occurring.

It is possible if a process releases its resources before requesting any further, thereby, providing any other process to execute and complete.

Hence, the correct option is (D).

48. Dispatcher is the module that gives control of the CPU to the process selected by the short-term scheduler. It receives control in kernel mode as the result of an interrupt or system call. The functions of a dispatcher mop the following:

- Context switches, in which the dispatcher saves the state (also known as context) of the process or thread that was previously running; the dispatcher then loads the initial or previously saved state of the new process.

- Switching to user mode.

- Jumping to the proper location in the user program to restart that program indicated by its new state.

Hence, the correct option is (A).

49. Deadlock avoidance problem is solved by Dijkstra's banker's algorithm. Banker's algorithm pretends to have allocated te required resources to the processes, and if the system doesn't lead to deadlock, it actually allocates the resources. The Banker's algorithm is a resource allocation and deadlock avoidance algorithm developed by Edsger Dijkstra.

Hence, the correct option is (C).

50. The dispatcher actually schedules the tasks into the processor. The dispatcher is the module that gives process control over the CPU after it has been selected by the short-term scheduler. This function involves the following:

- Switching context.

- Switching to user mode.

- A dispatcher is a special program which comes into play after the scheduler.

Hence, the correct option is (A).

51. When the process issues an I/O request it is placed in an I/O queue. I/O is a resource and it should be used effectively and every process should get access to it. There might be multiple processes which requested for I/O. Depending on scheduling algorithm I/O is allocated to any particular process and after completing I/O operation, I/O access is returned to the OS.

Hence, the correct option is (A).

52. The processes that are residing in main memory and are ready and waiting to execute are kept on a list called ready queue. The ready queue is a simplified version of a kernel data structure consisting of a queue with one entry per priority. Each entry in turn consists of another queue of the threads that are READY at the priority. Any threads that aren't READY aren't in any of the queues but they will be when they become READY.

Hence, the correct option is (B).

53. If the number of bits in a virtual address of a program is 16 and the page size is 0.5 KB.

A 16-bit address can locate up to $2^{16} = 65536$ locations (bytes).

Given, page size is 0.5 KB $= 512$ bytes

As we know that,

1 KB $= 1024$ bytes

Therefore,

Total pages $= \dfrac{65536}{512}$

$= 128$ pages

Then, the number of pages in the virtual address space is 128.

Hence, the correct option is (D).

54. If $a_2 a_1 = 11$ then $010(2)$ is added:

a_2	a_1	a_0	O_2	O_1	O_0	Decimal value of Output
0	0	0	0	0	0	0
0	0	1	0	0	1	1
0	1	0	0	1	0	2
0	1	1	0	1	1	3
1	0	0	1	0	0	4
1	0	1	1	0	1	5
1	1	0	0	0	0	0
1	1	1	0	0	1	1

Range is only (0 to 5)

$\therefore$ It is a binary to radix- 6 conversion.

Important points:

Carry $= C_{\text{out}} = O_3$ is discarded.

Hence, the correct option is (C).

55. Since 8 bit number is in 2's complement, weight of the last bit will be negative:

$(11111011)_2$

$\Rightarrow -1 \times 2^7 + 1 \times 2^6 + 1 \times 2^5 + 1 \times 2^4 + 1 \times 2^3 + 0 \times 2^2 + 1 \times 2^1 + 1 \times 2^0$

$= -5$

$(00001010)_2$

$= -0 \times 2^7 + 0 \times 2^6 + 0 \times 2^5 + 0 \times 2^4 + 1 \times 2^3 + 0 \times 2^2 + 1 \times 2^1 + 0 \times 2^0$

$= 10$

Now, we get

$(11111011)_2 \times (00001010)_2$

$$= -5 \times 10$$

$$= -50$$

$$11001110 = -1 \times 2^7 + 1 \times 2^6 + 0 \times 2^5 + 0 \times 2^4 + 1 \times 2^3 + 1 \times 2^2 + 1 \times 2^1 + 0 \times 2^0$$

$$11001110 = -128 + 64 + 8 + 4 + 2 = -50$$

So, the value of their product in two's complement is 11001110.

Hence, the correct option is (B).

56. The combinational circuit is the circuit whose output depends only on an input value present at that particular instant.

In other words, a combinational circuit depends on the current input value.

According to the figure given in question,

Output of 1st OR gate:

$$P_1 + P_2' + P_3' \{P' -\text{complement of } P\}$$

Output of 2nd OR gate:

$$P_1 + P_2' + P_3$$

Output of 3rd OR gate:

$$P_1 + P_2 + P_3'$$

$$F = (P_1 + P_2' + P_3') \cdot (P_1 + P_2' + P_3) \cdot (P_1 + P_2 + P_3')$$

We know that,

$$(A + B)(A + C) = A + BC$$

Here, $A - P_1 + P_2', B - P_3', C - P_3$

$$(P_1 + P_2' + P_3') \cdot (P_1 + P_2' + P_3) = P_1 + P_2' + P_3' \cdot P_3$$

$$= P_1 + P_2'$$

$$F = (P_1 + P_2') \cdot (P_1 + P_2 + P_3')$$

Here, $A - P_1, B - P_2', C - P_2 + P_3'$

$$F = (P_1 + P_2') \cdot (P_1 + P_2 + P_3')$$

$$F = P1 + \left(P_2' \cdot (P_2 + P_3')\right)$$

$$F = P_1 + P_2' \cdot P_2 + P_2' \cdot P_3'$$

Complement law: $P_2' \cdot P_2 = 0$

$$F = P_1 + P_2' P_3'$$

So, the output of the combinational circuit is $P_1 + P_2' P_3'$.

Hence, the correct option is (B).

57. A decoder with k input lines has 2^k output lines.

Now,

The memory is byte addressable.

So, 4 KB $= 2^{12}$ bytes.

Then, 12×2^{10} decoder.

Therefore, the number of input lines $(m) = 12$

Number of output lines $(n) = 2^m$

$$= 2^{12}$$

$$= 4096$$

So, $(m + n)$

$$= 12 + 4096$$

$$= 4108$$

Therefore, if there are m input lines and n output lines for a decoder that is used to uniquely address a byte-addressable 4 KB RAM, then the minimum value of $m + n$ is 4108.

Hence, the correct option is (A).

58. The truth table for an XOR gate is:

A	X	Y
0	0	0
0	1	1
1	0	1
1	1	0

We know that,

When one of the input to an XOR Gate is 1, the output is simply the inverted value of the other input.

Application:
The output of the first XOR gate will be:

$$1 \oplus X = \overline{X}$$

Now, the output of second XOR gate will be:

$$\overline{X} \oplus X = 1$$

For 20 such XOR gates in cascade, the final output will be 1.

Hence, the correct option is (B).

59.

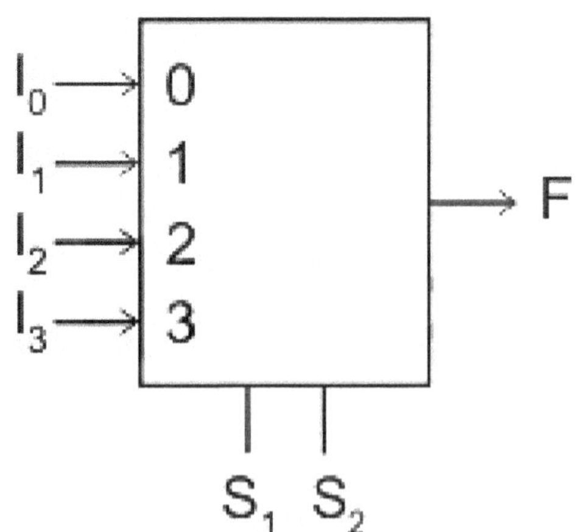

For a general 4 to 1 multiplier as shown, with S_1 as MSB and S_2 as LSB, the output expression is written as:

$$F = \bar{S}_2\bar{S}_1 I_0 + \bar{S}_2 S_1 I_1 + S_2\bar{S}_1 I_2 + S_2 S_1 I_3$$

i.e. I will be the output when the select inputs are 00, I_1 will be the output when the select inputs are 01, and so on.

Analysis:

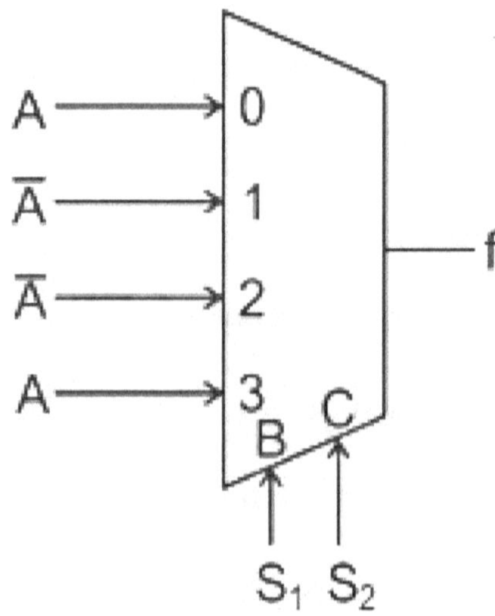

$$f = \bar{S}_2\bar{S}_1 A + \bar{S}_2 S_1\bar{A} + S_2\bar{S}_1\bar{A} + S_2 S_1 A$$

$$f = \bar{S}_2\left(\bar{S}_1 A + S_1\bar{A}\right) + S_2\left(\bar{S}_1\bar{A} + S_1 A\right)$$

$$f = \bar{S}_2(\bar{S}_1 A + S_1\bar{A}) + S_2(\bar{S}_1\bar{A}$$

$$f = \bar{S}_2(S_1 \oplus A) + S_2(S_1 \oplus A)$$

$$f = \bar{S}_2 \oplus S_1 \oplus A$$

OR

$$f = \bar{S}_2\left(\bar{S}_1 A + S_1\bar{A}\right) + S_2\left(\bar{S}_1\bar{A} + S_1 A\right)$$

$$f = \bar{S}_2\left(S_1 \odot A\right) + S_2(S_1 \odot A)$$

$$f = S_2 \odot S_1 \odot A$$

Hence, the correct option is (D).

60. Let's name the circuit for our convenience.

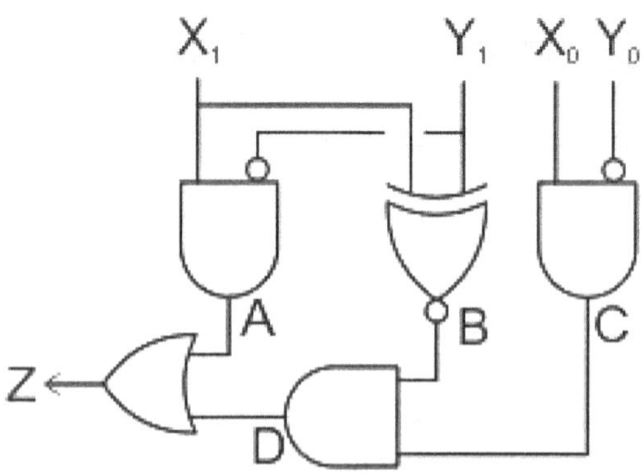

A, B, C and D are assumed output of the above given gates:

$$A = X_1 \times \bar{Y}_1$$

$$B = X_1 \odot Y_1$$

$$C = X_0 \times \bar{Y}_0$$

$$D = B \times C$$

$$Z = A + D$$

Truth table:

X_1	X_0	X_1	X_0	A	B	C	D	Z
0	0	0	0	0	1	0	0	0
0	0	0	1	0	1	0	0	0
0	0	1	0	0	0	0	0	0
0	0	1	1	0	0	0	0	0
0	1	0	0	0	1	1	1	1
0	1	0	1	0	1	0	0	0
0	1	1	0	0	0	1	0	0
0	1	1	1	0	0	0	0	0
1	0	0	0	1	0	0	0	1
1	0	0	1	1	0	0	0	1
1	0	1	0	0	1	0	0	0
1	0	1	1	0	1	0	0	0
1	1	0	0	1	0	1	0	1
1	1	0	1	1	0	0	0	1
1	1	1	0	0	1	1	1	1
1	1	1	1	0	1	0	0	0

As it can be seen, wherever $X > Y, Z = 1$.

Hence, the correct option is (A).

61. According to the given figure,

In position 1 ground is connected:

$C_{in} = 0$ (Ground is used)

$$B_{in} = \left(B_1 \overline{C_{in}} + \overline{B_1} C_{in} \right)\left(B_0 \overline{C_{in}} + \overline{B_0} C_{in} \right)$$

$$B_{in} = \left(B_1 \overline{0} + \overline{B_1} 0 \right)\left(B_0 \overline{0} + \overline{B_0} 0 \right)$$

$$B_{in} = B_1 B_0 = B \quad (B_0 \text{ is LSB})$$

Similiarly, A_{in}

$$A_{in} = A_1 A_0 = A$$

Since it is a full adder, we have

$$S = A_{in} + B_{in} + C_{in}$$

$$= A + B + 0$$

$$\therefore S = A + B$$

Hence, the correct option is (B).

62. Circuit:

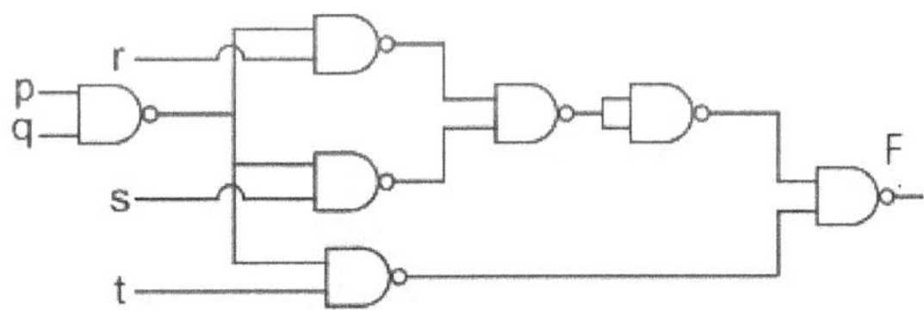

$$F(p,q,r,s,t) = (\overline{p} + \overline{q})(r + s + t)$$

Let, $X = (\overline{p} + \overline{q})$

$$F(p,q,r,s,t) = Xr + Xs + Xt$$

Therefore, 7 NAND gates in needed.

Hence, the correct option is (A).

63. Regular sets are closed under these three operations. The set of regular languages is closed under concatenation, union and kleene closure.

It follows from the definition of the operators of concatenation,* and | that the set of regular languages is closed under concatenation, union and kleene closure:

- If r is a regular expression and L is the regular language it denotes, then L* is denoted by the regular expression r* and it is also regular.

- If r 1 and r 2 are regular expressions denoting L 1 and L 2 respectively, then L 1 U L 2 is denoted by the regular expression r1|r2 and it is also regular.

- If r 1 and r 2 are regular expressions denoting L1 and L 2 respectively, then L 1L 2 is denoted by the regular expression r 1r 2 and itself regular.

Hence, the correct option is (A).

64. Complement of a DFA can be obtained by making final states non-final and non-final to final. String accepted in previous DFA will not be accepted and the non-accepting string will be accepted. The language accepted by the complemented DFA $L2$ is the complement of the language $L1$.

Example 1:

$L1$: Set of all strings over {a, b} of even length.

$L1 =$ {epsilon, ab, aa, abaa, aaba, ...}

$L2$: Set of all strings over {a, b} of odd length.

$L2 =$ { a, b, aab, aaa, bba, bbb, ...}

So, we can see that $L2 = \overline{L1}$.

Hence, the correct option is (C).

65. Reverse of $(0 + 1)^*$ will be $(0 + 1)^*$. There is only one state which is start and final state of DFA so interchanging starting start and final state doesn't change DFA. Reversing a language means reversing each string in the language. Reversal process goes like this:

Steps to Reversal:

- Draw the states as it is.

- Make final state as initial state and initial states as a final state.

- Reverse the edges.

- Loop will remain the same.

- Remove the inappropriate transition state.

Hence, the correct option is (C).

66. Recursive languages are a proper superset of CFL. When we come to recursive language it always halt whether it is accepted by the machine or not. if it is accepted it reaches at (q accept) and halt. and if not accepted by the machine it directly reach (q halt). We know CFL is a proper subset to Recursive language, this means Recursive language is a proper superset to CFL.

Hence, the correct option is (A).

67. The regular expression identity which is true is:

$$(r^* s^*)^* = (r + s)^*$$

r and s are regular expressions, which represent regular sets. If r and s are regular expressions that represent sets R and S, then the regular expression $r + s$ denotes the set $R \cup S$. Yes, 01 can be generated by $(0 + 1)^*$; $0 \in R$ and $1 \in S$, so, $01 \in (R \cup S)^*$. And yes, it's not generated by $0^* + 1^*$, but

not because 0^* and 1^* generate the empty string: the empty string is generated by $(0 + 1)^*$.

$01 \notin R^* \cup S^*$ because the R^* contains only strings of 0's (including the empty string), and S^* contains only strings of 1's (including the empty string), and 01 is neither.

Hence, the correct option is (B).

68. The CLR parser stands for canonical LR parser. It is a more powerful LR parser. It makes use of lookahead symbols. This method uses a large set of items called LR(1) items. The main difference between LR(0) and LR(1) items is that, in LR(1) items, it's possible to carry more information in a state, which will rule out useless reduction states. This extra information is incorporated into the state by the lookahead symbol. The general syntax becomes $[A \rightarrow \propto.B, a\ ]$.

Where A $\rightarrow \propto$

B is the production and a is a terminal or right end marker.

LR(1) items $=$ LR(0) items $+$ look ahead.

Hence, the correct option is (C).

69. The output of the lexical analyzer is a set of tokens. Lexical analysis is the first phase of the compiler also known as a scanner. It converts the high level input program into a sequence of tokens. Lexical analysis can be implemented with the deterministic finite automata. The output is a sequence of tokens that is sent to the parser for syntax analysis.

Hence, the correct option is (D).

70. Ambiguous grammar is a context-free grammar which gives more than one leftmost or rightmost derivation for the same specified sentence. An ambiguous grammar is one for which there is more than one parse tree for a single sentence. Since each parse tree corresponds to exactly one leftmost (or rightmost) derivation, an ambiguous grammar is one for which there is more than one leftmost (or rightmost) derivation of a given sentence.

Hence, the correct option is (C).

71. Lexical analysis is the first phase of a compiler. It takes the modified source code from language preprocessors that are written in the form of sentences. The lexical analyzer breaks these syntaxes into a series of tokens, by removing any whitespace or comments in the source code.

Hence, the correct option is (D).

72. As we know,

¬ (P ↔ Q) = (¬P ↔ Q) = (P ↔ ¬Q)

(P ↔ Q) ≡ p ⊙ q

¬ (P ↔ Q) ≡ p ⊕ q

Truth Table:

P	¬P	Q	¬Q	¬(P ↔	P ↔	P ↔	¬P ↔	Q →

			Q)	¬Q	¬Q	¬Q	P
F	T	F	T	F	F	F	T	T
F	T	T	F	T	T	T	F	F
T	F	F	T	T	T	T	F	T
T	F	T	F	F	F	F	T	T

Therefore, ¬ (P ↔ Q) is equivalent to (¬P ↔ Q) and (P ↔ ¬Q)

Hence, the correct option is (D).

73. Equivalence relation: A relation is said to be an equivalence relation if it is a reflexive, symmetric, and transitive relation.

- **Reflexive relation:** A relation in which every element maps to itself.
- **Symmetric relation:** A relation is symmetric if there exists (a, b), then (b, a) should also be in relation.
- **Transitive relation:** A relation is transitive if there exists (a, b) and (b, c) then there must also exist (a, c) in the relation.

Now,

Option (A):

$$\{(f, g) \mid f(x) - g(x) = 1\, x \in Z\}$$

It is not reflexive. As $f(x) - f(x) = 0$ it is not 1. It is also not transitive. So, it cannot be an equivalence relation.

Option (B):

$$\{(f, g) \mid f(0) = g(0) \text{ or } f(1) = g(1)\}$$

This relation is not transitive. Suppose $f(x) = 0, g(x) = x$ and $h(x) = 1$. Here f is not related to h. Only we have a relation given between f and g, g and h but not between f and h. So, it cannot be an equivalence relation.

Option (C):

$$\{(f, g) \mid f(0) = g(1) \text{ and } f(1) = g(0)\}$$

It is not always true $f(0) = f(1)$ for reflexive case. So, it is not reflexive. So, no equivalence relation.

Option (D):

$$\{(f, g) \mid f(x) - g(x) = k \text{ for some } k \in Z\}$$

It is reflexive relation, consider constant as 0. It is also symmetric because the difference will be equal to a constant value. It is also transitive. So, it is an equivalence relation.

Hence, the correct option is (D).

74. Abelian Group: Let {G=e, a, b} where e is identity. The operation 'o' is defined by the following composition table. Then(G, o) is called Abelian if it follows the following property:

1. Closure Property
2. Associativity
3. Existence of Identity

4. Existence of Inverse

5. Commutativity

Cyclic Group: A group a is said to be cyclic if it contains an element 'a' such that every element of G can be represented as some integral power of 'a'. The element 'a' is then called a generator of G, and G is denoted by <a> (or [a]).

Theorem:

(i) All cyclic groups are Abelian, but an Abelian group is not necessarily cyclic.

(ii) The order of a cyclic group is the same as the order of its generator.

Thus it is clear that A and B both are true.

Hence, the correct option is (D).

75. A planar graph is a graph in which no two edges cross each other. A vertex coloring of a graph is an assignment of colors to the vertices of a graph such that adjacent vertices have different colors.

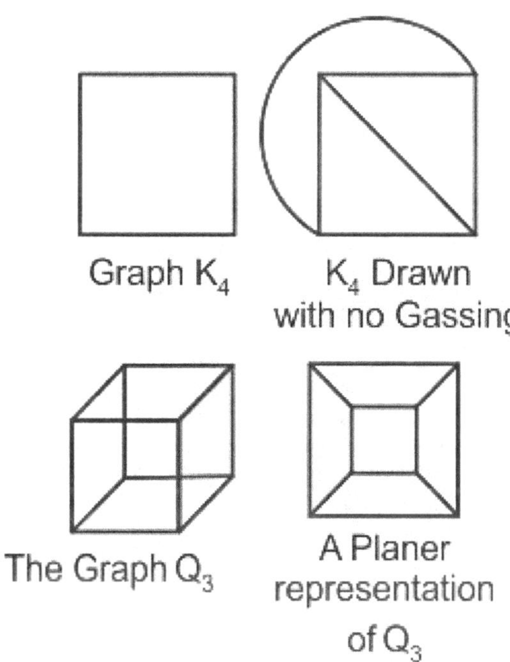

Graph K_4

K_4 Drawn with no Gassing

The Graph Q_3

A Planer representation of Q_3

Hence, the correct option is (B).

76.

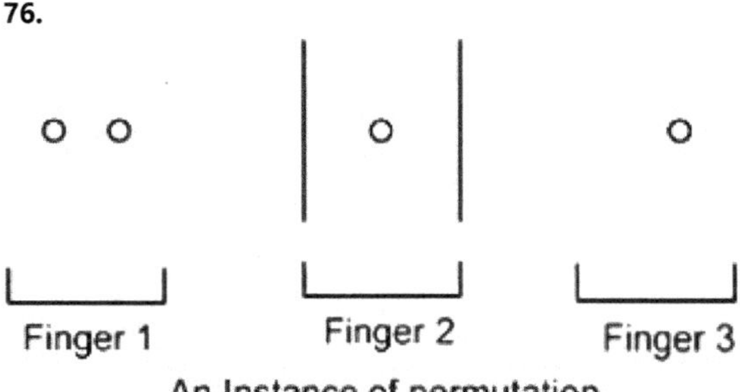

Finger 1   Finger 2   Finger 3

An Instance of permutation

The first ring can be worn in 3 different ways:

The second ring can be worn in 4 different ways (as it can go on any of three fingers - 3 ways; plus it can go below/above the first one - 1).

The third ring can be worn in 5 different ways (as it can go on any of three fingers - 3 ways; plus it can go below/above the first and second one - 2).

The fourth ring can be worn in 6 different ways (as it can go on any of three fingers - 3 ways; plus it can go below/above the first, second and third one - 3).

Total no. of ways $= 3 \times 4 \times 5 \times 6 = 360$

Hence, the correct option is (A).

77. Given,

Number of different skirts Neela has $= 12$

Number of different tops Neela has $= 10$

Number of different pairs of shoes Neela has $= 8$

Number of different necklaces Neela has $= 3$

Number of different bracelets Neela has $= 5$

By the basic counting principle,

The number of different ways in which Neela can be dressed $= 12 \times 10 \times 8 \times 3 \times 5$

$= 14400$ ways

Note that shoes come in pairs. So, she must choose one pair of shoes from ten pairs, not one shoe from twenty.

Hence, the correct option is (B).

78. The simplest application of proof by induction is to prove that a statement $P(n)$ is true for all $n = 1,2,3, ...$ For example, "The number $n^3 - n$ is divisible by 6". "The number a_n is equal to $f(n)$ " and "There are $n!$ permutations of n elements" are such statements. Induction usually amounts to proving that $P(1)$ is true, and then that the implication $P(n) \Rightarrow P(n + 1)$. The principle of mathematical induction can formally be stated as:

$$P(1) \text{ and } P(n) \Rightarrow P(n + 1) \text{ for all } n \geq 1$$

Implies that $P(n)$ is true for all $n \geq 1$.

Strong induction is similar, but where we instead prove the implication

$$(1)\ P(1) \wedge P(2) \wedge \cdots \wedge P(n) \Rightarrow P(n + 1).$$

However, if we define introduce the new statement $Q(n)$ as

$$Q(n) := P(1) \wedge P(2) \wedge \cdots \wedge P(n),$$

then (1) is equivalent to $Q(n) \Rightarrow Q(n+1)$. Thus, strong induction is not really different from usual induction, other than that the inductive hypothesis has a particular form.

This is a pedagogical tool that is used to make the structure clearer. However, proofs by induction "in the wild" do not explicitly use the notation $P(n)$, the statement is simply written out. In my experience, it is easy to confuse the statement $P(n)$ with the formula one is asked to prove. For example,

"The equality $a_n = f(n)$ holds."

is the statement $P(n)$, and $f(n)$ is the actual formula.

First 2 can be taken commonly from the given sequence, we get

$$2(1 + 2 + 3 + \cdots + 2m)$$

Then it becomes,

$2(2m)(2m+1)/2$..two will be removed, therefore it becomes,

$$2m(2m+1)..$$

The minimum value of this sequence is:

$$2 \times 3(2 \times 3 + 1)$$

$= 42$ it's minimum value at $m = 3$

Now, by induction assumption, we have to prove:

$2 + 4 + 6 + \cdots + 4(k+1) = (k+1)^2 + 3$ also can be true,

$$= 2 + 4 + 6 + \cdots + 4(k+1)$$

$$2 + 4 + 6 + \cdots + (4k + 4)$$

And by the subsequent steps, we can prove that:

$m^2 + 3$ also holds for $m = k$

So, it is proved.

Hence, the correct option is (A).

79. PCNF is also called product of sum canonical form. It stands for Principal Conjunctive Normal Form. It refers to the Product of Sums, i.e., POS. For eg. : If P, Q, R are the variables then (P + Q' + R).(P' + Q + R).(P + Q + R') is an example of an expression in PCNF. Here '.' i.e. product is the main operator.

Here also, the Key difference between PCNF and CNF is that in case of CNF, it is not necessary that the length of all the variables in the expression is same .

For example:

- (P + Q' + R).(P' + Q + R).(P + Q) is an example of an expression in CNF but not in PCNF.
- (P + Q' + R).(P' + Q + R).(P + Q + R') is an example of an expression which is both in PCNF and CNF.

Hence, the correct option is (B).

80. Given,

The generating function for the sequence A:

$$1, 9, 25, 49, \ldots$$

Using differencing:

$$A = 1 + 9x + 25x^2 + 49x^3 + \cdots (1)$$

$$-xA = 0 + x + 9x^2 + 25x^3 + 49x^4 + \cdots (2)$$

From (1) and (2), we get

$$(1 - x)A = 1 + 8x + 16x^2 + 24x^3 + \cdots$$

Since, $8x + 16x^2 + 24x^3 + \cdots = (1 - x)A - 1$

$$\Rightarrow 8 + 16x + 24x^2 + \cdots = (1 - A) - \frac{1}{x}$$

Hence, the correct option is (B).

81. A structure chart (SC) is used for structured designing. Structure chart represent hierarchical structure of modules. It breaks down the entire system into lowest functional modules, describe functions and sub-functions of each module of a system to a greater detail. Structure chart partitions the system into black boxes.

Hence, the correct option is (B).

82. Efficiency in a software product does not include licensing. Licensing of a software product comes under corporate part of the software company. Efficiency, in software development, is simply the amount of software developed or requirement meant divided by the amount of resources used like processing time, responsiveness and memory utilization.

Hence, the correct option is (A).

83. The actual programming of software code is done during the development and documentation step in the SDLC. The presence of documentation helps keep track of all aspects of an application and it improves on the quality of a software product. Development documentation comprises documents created in course of software engineering process.

Hence, the correct option is (D).

84. Spiral and Prototyping models doesn't necessitate defining requirements at the earliest in the lifecycle. In the Prototyping model, the first phase is the requirement analysis phase, which involves Brainstorming, QFD, and FAST, whereas the Spiral model encompasses customer communication activities such as defining objectives.

Hence, the correct option is (C).

85. The attributes of good software are software maintainability and functionality. Good software should deliver the required functionality and performance to the user and should be maintainable, dependable, and usable. Software should be written in such a way so that it can evolve to meet the changing needs of customers. Maintainability is a critical attribute because software change is an inevitable requirement of a changing business environment. Software should not make wasteful use of system resources such as memory and processor cycles. Efficiency

therefore includes responsiveness, processing time, memory utilization, etc.

Hence, the correct option is (D).

86. The software design process can be divided into the following three levels of phases of design which is the primary area of concern interface design, architectural design, design.

- Interface design is the specification of the interaction between a system and its environment. this phase proceeds at a high level of abstraction with respect to the inner workings of the system i.e, during interface design, the internal of the systems are completely ignored and the system is treated as a black box.

- Architectural design is the specification of the major components of a system, their responsibilities, properties, interfaces, and the relationships and interactions between them.

- Design is the specification of the internal elements of all major system components, their properties, relationships, processing, and often their algorithms and the data structures.

Hence, the correct option is (D).

87. The importance of software design can be summarized in a single word which is quality. The quality of functional software, functional depicts how well it can conform with or adapts to a given design based on functional requirements or specifications.

Hence, the correct option is (C).

88. The necessity of software engineering appears because of a higher rate of progress in user requirements and the environment on which the program is working.

For large software: It is simpler to manufacture a wall than to a house or building, similarly, as the measure of programming become extensive engineering has to step to give it a scientific process.

Adaptability: If the software procedure were not based on scientific and engineering ideas, it would be simpler to re-create new software than to scale an existing one.

To reduce cost: As the hardware industry has demonstrated its skills and huge manufacturing has let down the cost of computer and electronic hardware. But the cost of programming remains high if the proper process is not adapted.

Dynamic nature: The continually growing and adapting nature of programming hugely depends upon the environment in which the client works. If the quality of the software is continually changing, new upgrades need to be done in the existing one.

Software quality management: Better procedure of software development provides a better and quality software product.

Hence, the correct option is (D).

89. Coupling is a qualitative indication of the degree to which a module is connected to other modules and the outside world . It is the degree of interdependence between software modules, which is a measure of how closely two routines or modules are connected, the strength of the relationship between modules.

Coupling is usually contrasted with cohesion. Low coupling often correlates with high cohesion and vice versa.

Hence, the correct option is (D).

90. Given,

A speaks truth in 75% cases.

B speaks truth in 25% cases.

$$P(A) = \frac{75}{100} = \frac{3}{4}$$

$$P(B) = \frac{25}{100} = \frac{1}{4}$$

$$\therefore P(\overline{A}) = 1 - \frac{3}{4} = \frac{1}{4}$$

$$\therefore P(\overline{B}) = 1 - \frac{1}{4} = \frac{3}{4}$$

The probability that both of them speak the same thing $=$

$$P[(A \cap B) \cup (\overline{A} \cap \overline{B})]$$

$$= P(A \cap B) + P(\overline{A} \cap \overline{B})$$

$$= P(A) \times P(B) + P(\overline{A}) \times P(\overline{B})$$

$$= \left(\frac{3}{4} \times \frac{1}{4}\right) + \left(\frac{1}{4} \times \frac{3}{4}\right)$$

$$= \frac{3}{8}$$

Hence, the correct option is (B).

91. Given,

In a box there are 49 card from number 1 to 49.

According to the qustion,

Card numbers which are multiples of 5 are
$5, 10, 15, 20, 25, 30, 35, 40, 45$

Card numbers which are multiples of 10 or 15 are
$10, 15, 20, 30, 40, 45$

The latter ones are to be ruled out from the former ones.

So, the only card numbers we are left with are $5, 25, 35$.

$\therefore$ Probability of picking up a card, the number on which is a multiple of 5 but not that of 10 and $15 = \frac{3}{49}$

Hence, the correct option is (B).

92. Given,

$$y = c_1 e^x + c_2 e^{-x}$$

Differentiating with respect to x we get,

$$\frac{dy}{dx} = \frac{d}{dx} c_1 e^x + \frac{d}{dx} c_2 e^{-x}$$

$$\Rightarrow \frac{dy}{dx} = c_1 e^x - c_2 e^{-x}$$

$$\Rightarrow \frac{d}{dx}\left(\frac{dy}{dx}\right) = \frac{d}{dx}(c_1 e^x - c_2 e^{-x})$$

$$\Rightarrow \frac{d^2y}{dx^2} = c_1 e^x + c_2 e^{-x}$$

$$\Rightarrow \frac{d^2y}{dx^2} = y$$

$$\Rightarrow \frac{d^2y}{dx^2} - y = 0$$

Hence, the correct option is (B).

93. Given,

The general equation of a parabola is:

$$y = a(x - h)^2 + k\,(\text{regular})$$

$$x = a(y - k)^2 + h\,(\text{sideways})$$

where,

$|h, k| = $ vertex of the parabola

The standard equation of a regular parabola is $y^2 = 4ax$.

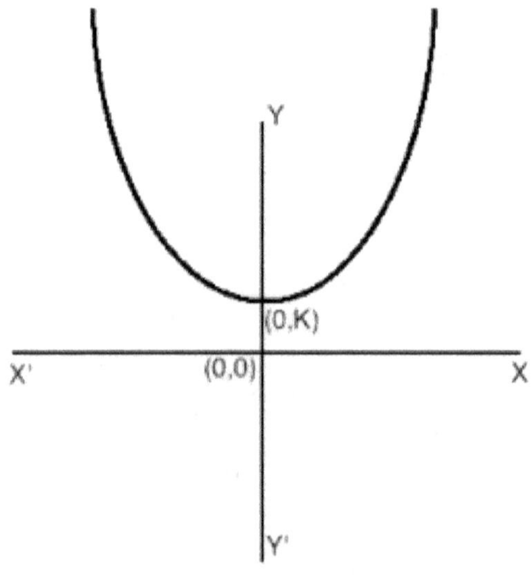

Now,

Equation of parabola with y-axis and vertex $(0, k)$ is:

$$(x - 0)^2 = 4a(y - k)$$

$$\Rightarrow x^2 = 4ay - 4ak$$

Taking derivative on both side, we get,

$$\frac{d}{dx}(x^2) = \frac{d}{dx}(4ay - 4ak)$$

$$\Rightarrow 2x = 4a\frac{dy}{dx}$$

$$\Rightarrow \frac{1}{x}\frac{dy}{dx} = \frac{1}{2a}$$

Again taking derivative on both side, we get,

$$\Rightarrow \frac{d}{dx}\left(\frac{1}{x}\frac{dy}{dx}\right) = \frac{d}{dx}\left(\frac{1}{2a}\right)$$

$$\Rightarrow \frac{1}{x}\frac{d^2y}{dx^2} + \frac{dy}{dx}\left(\frac{-1}{x^2}\right) = 0$$

$$\Rightarrow x\frac{d^2y}{dx^2} - \frac{dy}{dx} = 0$$

Hence, the correct option is (A).

94. Few necessary Laplace transform properties are given below:

- $L[f''(t)] = s^2\, L[f(t)] - sf(0) - f'(0)$
- $L[f'(t)] = sL[f(t)] - f(0)$

Here, the given equation is:

$$\frac{d^2y}{dt^2} - y = 1$$

$$\Rightarrow L(y'' - y) = L(y'') - L(y) = L$$

$$\frac{d^2y}{dt^2} - y = 1,$$

The above equation can be written as:

$$f''(y) - y = 1$$

Now, for calculation the Laplace domain of the above equation:

$$L(y'' - y)$$

$$\therefore L(y'') - L(y) = L(1)$$

$$[s^2 L(y) - sy(0) - y'(0)] - [L(y)] = L(1)$$

$$\Rightarrow s^2[L(y)] - L(y)] = \frac{1}{s}$$

$$\Rightarrow L(y)[s^2 - 1] = \frac{1}{s}$$

$$\Rightarrow L(y) = \frac{1}{s(s^2 - 1)}$$

$$\therefore L(y) = \frac{1}{s(s+1)(s-1)}$$

Hence, the correct option is (A).

95. Shifting property:

$$L\{e^{at}f(t)\} = F(s - a)$$

Laplace transformation of $\cos\omega t = \frac{s}{s^2 + \omega^2}$

From first shifting property:

$$L\{e^{at}f(t)\} = F(s - a)$$

Laplace transformation of $e^{at}\cos\omega t = \frac{(s-a)}{(s-a)^2 + \omega^2}$

Hence, the correct option is (A).

96. As we know that,

If A is any square matrix of order n, we can form the matrix $[A - \lambda I]$, where I is the nth order unit matrix. The determinant of this matrix equated to zero i.e., $|A - \lambda I| = 0$ is called the characteristic equation of A.

The roots of the characteristic equation are called Eigenvalues or latent roots or characteristic roots of matrix A.

Properties of Eigenvalues:

(1). If λ is an eigenvalue of a matrix A, then λ^n will be an eigenvalue of a matrix A^n.

(2). If λ is an eigenvalue of a matrix A, then $k\lambda$ will be an eigenvalue of a matrix kA where k is a scalar.

(3). Sum of eigenvalues is equal to the trace of that matrix.

(4). The product of Eigenvalues of a matrix A is equal to the determinant of that matrix A.

(5). If λ is an Eigenvalue of matrix A, then λ^2 will be an Eigenvalue of matrix A^2.

(6). If λ_1 is an Eigenvalue of matrix A, then $(\lambda_1 + 1)$ will be an Eigenvalue of the matrix $(A + I)$.

(7). Eigenvalues of a matrix and its transpose are the same because the transpose matrix will also have the same characteristic equation.

Now,

If $\lambda_1, \lambda_2, \lambda_3 \dots \lambda_4$ are the given values of A, then eigenvalues of A^m will be $\lambda_1^m, \lambda_2^m, \lambda_3^m, \cdots$

$'X'$ matrix has eigenvalues 5 and 6.

X^2 matrix has eigenvalues 5^2 and 6^2.

i.e., 25 and 36.

Hence, the correct option is (D).

97. Gauss-Seidel Method:

In Gauss-Seidel method, the value of x calculated is used in next calculation putting another variable as 0.

Putting $y = 0, z = 0$

$2x - 5y + 3z = 7$

$2x - 0 + 0 = 7$

$\Rightarrow x = 3.5$

Putting $x = 3.5, z = 0$

$x + 4y - 2z = 3$

$3.5 + 4y - 0 = 3$

$4y = -0.5$

$\Rightarrow y = -0.125$

Putting $x = 3.5, y = -0.125$

$2x + 3y + z = 2$

$z = 2 - 3(-0.125) - 2(3.5)$

$z = -4.625$

Hence, the correct option is (D).

98. Given,

$x^8 + 12x^5 - 4x^4 + 10x^3 - 6x + 5$

If f and g are both differentiable, then

$\dfrac{d}{dx}[f(x) - g(x)] = \dfrac{d}{dx}f(x) - \dfrac{d}{dx}g(x)$

As we know,

$\dfrac{d}{dx}(x^n) = nx^{n-1}$

Differentiating with respect to x, we get

$\dfrac{d}{dx}(x^8 + 12x^5 - 4x^4 + 10x^3 - 6x + 5)$

$= \frac{d}{dx}\left(x^8\right) + 12\frac{d}{dx}\left(x^5\right) - 4\frac{d}{dx}\left(x^4\right) + 10\frac{d}{dx}\left(x^3\right) - 6\frac{d}{dx}\left(x\right) + \frac{d}{dx}\left(5\right)$

$= 8x^7 + 12(5x^4) - 4(4x^3) + 10(3x^2) - 6(1) + 0$

$= 8x^7 + 60x^4 - 16x^3 + 30x^2 - 6$

Hence, the correct option is (B).

99. Given,

$I = \int \dfrac{dx}{\sec^2(\tan^{-1}x)}$

As we know,

$\sec^2 x - \tan^2 x = 1$

$I = \int \dfrac{dx}{1+\tan^2(\tan^{-1}x)}$

$\Rightarrow I = \int \dfrac{dx}{1+[\tan(\tan^{-1}x)]^2}$

$\Rightarrow I = \int \dfrac{dx}{1+x^2}$

We know that,

$\int \dfrac{dx}{1+x^2} = \tan^{-1}x + C$

Where, C is constant.

$I = \int \dfrac{dx}{\sec^2(\tan^{-1}x)}$

$= \tan^{-1}x + C$

Hence, the correct option is (B).

100. Given,

Hash Table Size: 100

Probability of collision before 10% full $\left(100 \times \dfrac{10}{100} = 10\right)$

At first insertion, a collision can not happen so, the collision can happen from 2nd insertion.

So, probability for 1st collision $= \dfrac{100 \times 1}{100 \times 100}$

Probability for 2nd collision $= \dfrac{100 \times 99 \times 2}{100^3}$

Probability for 3rd collision $= \dfrac{100 \times 99 \times 98 \times 3}{100^4}$

Table has 100 slots. So, for 10% filling it must take 10 slots. Now, the question is like this- collision before 10% full. This should mean the first collision happened before the 10th entry is made. So, the first collision can happen from 2nd entry (for 1st entry there won't be a collision) to 10th entry. So, required probability

$$= \frac{100 \times 1}{100^2} + \frac{100 \times 99 \times 2}{100^3} + \frac{100 \times 99 \times 98 \times 3}{100^4} + \cdots + \frac{100 \times 99 \times 98 \dots 92 \times 9}{100^{10}}$$

$$\approx 0.37$$

The probability will be the sum of all those probabilities ~ 0.37.

Hence, the correct option is (C).

Q.1 Solve the following recurrence relation and pick out the correct option:

$T(n) = T(n-1) \times n$ when $n > 1$

$T(n) = 1$ when $n = 1$

A. $O(n^n)$
B. $O(2^n)$
C. $\Omega(2^n)$
D. Both (A) and (C)

Q.2 What will be the worst-case time complexity of an efficient algorithm for putting exactly one specified element of an unsorted array on same index as in sorted array?

A. O(log n)
B. O(n)
C. O(n log n)
D. None of these

Q.3 Consider a 13 element hash table for which f(key)= key mod 13 is used with integer keys. Assuming linear probing is used for collision resolution, at which location would the key 103 be inserted, if the keys $661,182,24$ and 103 are inserted in that order?

A. 0
B. 1
C. 11
D. 12

Q.4 Direction: Consider the following postfix expression with single digit operands:

$623 * / 42 * + 68 * -$

The top two elements of the stack after the second $*$ is evaluated, are:

A. 8,2
B. 8,1
C. 6,2
D. 6,3

Q.5 Direction: A binary search tree is constructed by inserting the following numbers in order:

$60,25,72,15,30,68,101,13,18,47,70,34$

The number of nodes in the left subtree is:

A. 5
B. 6
C. 7
D. 3

Q.6 What is the correct output of the breadth first traversal of the following graph?

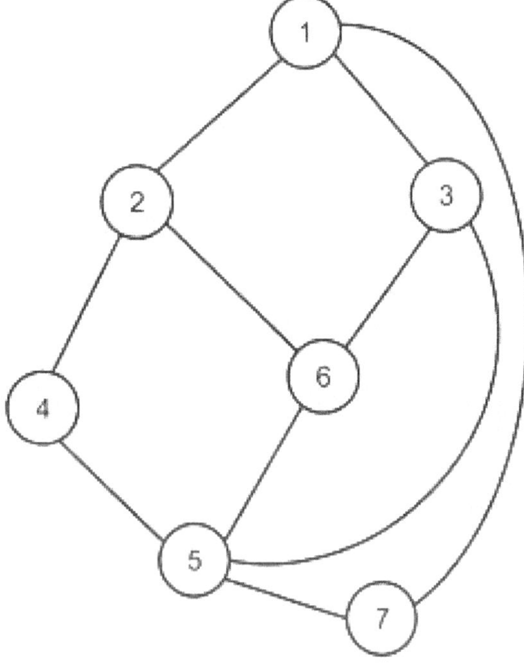

I. $1,2,3,7,4,6,5$

II. $1,3,2,7,6,4,5$

III. $1,7,3,2,5,6,4$

A. I only
B. II and III only
C. I and III only
D. I, II and III

Q.7 Heap allocation is required for languages that:

A. Use dynamic scope rules
B. Support dynamic data structures
C. Support recursion
D. Both (B) and (C)

Q.8 Number of bits saved using Huffman encoding:

A networking company uses a compression technique to encode the message before transmitting over the network. Suppose the message contains the following characters with their frequency:

Character	Frequency
a	5
b	9
c	12
d	13
e	16
f	45

Note that each character in input message takes 1 byte. If the compression technique used is Huffman Coding, how many bits will be saved in the message?

A. 224   **B.** 800   **C.** 576   **D.** 324

Q.9 Which of the following option is/are false?

A. The Reverse Kruskal's algorithm that selects maximum element first from a graph with distinct edge weights, produces the incorrect Minimum cost spanning tree.

B. For a dynamic programming algorithm, computing all values in a bottom-up fashion is asymptotically faster than using recursion.

C. In Dynamic programming, among top-down approach and bottom-up approach; the top-down approach is not memory efficient.

D. Both (A) and (B)

Q.10 If an object is passed by reference, the changes made in the function __________.

A. Are reflected to the main object of caller function too.

B. Are reflected only in local scope of the called function.

C. Are reflected to the copy of the object that is made during pass.

D. Are reflected to caller function object and called function object also.

Q.11 What is the output of the following program?

```c
#include<stdio.h>
void main()
{
char *s = "C++";
printf("%s ", s);
s++;
printf("%s", s);
}
```

A. C++ C++   **B.** C++ ++

C. ++ ++   **D.** Compile error

Q.12 A text file that contains our program is called as __________.

A. Exe file   **B.** Doc file

C. Obj file   **D.** Source file

Q.13 First statement in a fortran code is __________.

A. include statement   **B.** import statement

C. program statement   **D.** data statement

Q.14 Animations and interactivity with the user on web pages can be done by:

A. PHP   **B.** Java script

C. Visual Basic   **D.** Visual C#

Q.15 What is another name for the circular queue among the following options?

A. Square buffer   **B.** Rectangle buffer

C. Ring buffer   **D.** Round buffer

Q.16 A list of elements in which enqueue operation takes place from one end, and dequeue operation takes place from one end is __________.

A. Binary tree   **B.** Stack

C. Queue   **D.** Linked list

Q.17 Backtracking uses ______ node generation ______ bounding functions.

A. Breadth first, with

B. Breadth first, without

C. Depth-first, with

D. Depth-first, without

Q.18 ______ sorting algorithms has the lowest worst-case complexity.

A. Selection Sort   **B.** Bubble Sort

C. Merge Sort   **D.** Quick Sort

Q.19 Consider the following Statements regarding switching networks:

Statement 1: The packet switching technique is preferred when the data to be sent must be ordered and transmitted in less time.

Statement 2: In-Circuit Switching, the resources needed along a path between end systems are reserved for the duration of the communication.

Which of the following is/are true and false regarding the above statements?

A. Statement 1 is true.   **B.** Statement 1 is false.

C. Statement 2 is true.   **D.** Both (B) and (C)

Q.20 A and B are 2 stations on an Ethernet, each having steady queue of frames to send. Both A and B attempt to transmit a frame, collides and A wins the first back off race. At the end of the successful transmission by A, both A & B attempt to transmit and again collide. What is the probability B wins the 2nd back off race.

A. 0.5   **B.** 0.25   **C.** 0.125   **D.** 0.625

Q.21 Consider a LAN with five nodes. Time is divided into fixed-size slots. A node can begin its transmission only at the beginning of a slot. A collision occurs if more than two nodes transmits in the same slot. The probabilities of generation of a frame in a time slot by these LAN are $0.2, 0.3, 0.25, 0.16$ and 0.09, respectively. The probability of transmission in the first slot without any collision by any of these five stations is __________. (Compute the answer up to 2 decimal places.)

A. $0.41 - 0.42$ **B.** $0.41 - 0.48$

C. $0.41 - 0.47$ **D.** $0.41 - 0.49$

Q.22 Consider the following set of statements:

$S1: FF:FF:FF:FF:FF:FF$ is a broadcast MAC address.

$S2: 45:20:1B:2E:08:EE$ is a unicast MAC address.

$S3:$ If the signal propagates at $2 \times 10^8 \ m/s$, the maximum length of the network is $5120 \ m$ if the slot time is $51.2 \mu s$.

Which of the above statements is false?

A. Only $S2$ **B.** Both $S2$ and $S3$

C. Only $S1$ **D.** Both $S1$ and $S3$

Q.23 ______ is generally used to increase the apparent size of physical memory.

A. Secondary memory   **B.** Virtual memory
C. Hard-disk   **D.** Disks

Q.24 MFC stands for _________.
A. Memory Format Caches
B. Memory Function Complete
C. Memory Find Command
D. Mass Format Command

Q.25 The time delay between two successive initiations of memory operation is _________.
A. Memory access time
B. Memory search time
C. Memory cycle time
D. Instruction delay

Q.26 The assembler stores the object code in _________.
A. Main memory   **B.** Cache
C. RAM   **D.** Magnetic disk

Q.27 The utility program used to bring the object code into memory for execution is _________.
A. Loader   **B.** Fetcher
C. Extractor   **D.** Linker

Q.28 To overcome the problems of the assembler in dealing with branching code we use _________.
A. Interpreter   **B.** Debugger
C. Op-Assembler   **D.** Two-pass assembler

Q.29 The type of memory assignment used in Intel processors is _______.
A. Little-Endian   **B.** Big-Endian
C. Medium Endian   **D.** None of these

Q.30 To get the physical address from the logical address generated by CPU we use _________.
A. MAR   **B.** MMU   **C.** Overlay   **D.** TLB

Q.31 _______ method is used to map logical addresses of variable length onto physical memory.
A. Paging
B. Overlay
C. Segmentation
D. Paging with segmentation

Q.32 _______ is a platform for constructing data flows for extract, transform, and load (ETL) processing and analysis of large datasets.
A. Pig Latin   **B.** Oozie
C. Pig   **D.** Hive

Q.33 Find out the correct option.
A. Hive is not a relational database, but a query engine that supports the parts of SQL specific to querying data.
B. Hive is a relational database with SQL support.
C. Pig is a relational database with SQL support.
D. All of these

Q.34 _______ hides the limitations of Java behind a powerful and concise Clojure API for Cascading.

A. Scalding   **B.** HCatalog
C. Cascalog   **D.** All of these

Q.35 Hive also support custom extensions written in _________.
A. C#   **B.** Java   **C.** C   **D.** C++

Q.36 Find out the wrong option.
A. Elastic MapReduce (EMR) is Facebook's packaged Hadoop offering.
B. Amazon Web Service Elastic MapReduce (EMR) is Amazon's packaged Hadoop offering.
C. Scalding is a Scala API on top of Cascading that removes most Java boilerplate.
D. All of these

Q.37 DML language is used to _________.
A. Define schema
B. Define internal level
C. Access Data
D. None of these

Q.38 The view of total database content is _________.
A. Conceptual view   **B.** Internal view
C. External view   **D.** Physical View

Q.39 Which of the following is the reference to the tuples in a relation?
A. Index   **B.** Reference
C. Assertion   **D.** Timestamp

Q.40 What type of relationship exists between a teacher table and a class table?
A. One to many   **B.** Many to many
C. One to one   **D.** Many to one

Q.41 What is the maximum number of processes that can be in the running state with eight CPU and thirty-two processes in the ready state for a computer system?
A. 32   **B.** 8
C. 8×32 **D.** Independent of n

Q.42 The following C program is executed on a Unix/Linux system:

```
#include <unistd.h>
int main ( )
{
int p;
for (p = 0; p <= 21; p++)
if (p % 3 == 0)
fork ( );
return 0;
}
```

The total number of child processes created is _______.
A. 255   **B.** 245   **C.** 235   **D.** 225

Q.43 Match the following:

List - 1	List- 2
A. Moves suspended process to	I. Short-Term

secondary storage	Scheduler
B. Loads the processes into memory for execution	II. dispatcher
C. Moves one of the processes to Running state	III. Medium-Term Scheduler
D. Allocates CPU to a process	IV. Long-Term Scheduler

A. A – III, B – IV, C – I, D - II
B. A – III, B – I, C – II, D - IV
C. A – II, B – I, C – IV, D – III
D. A – II, B – IV, C – I, D – III

Q.44 What will happen when a process terminates?
A. It is removed from all queues.
B. It is removed from all, but the job queue.
C. Its process control block is de-allocated.
D. Its process control block is never de-allocated.

Q.45 The characteristic of Feed back queue is:
A. Are very easy to implement.
B. Dispatch tasks according to execution characteristics.
C. Are used to favor real-time tasks.
D. Require manual intervention to implement properly.

Q.46 Which program runs first after booting the computer and loading the GUI?
A. Desktop Manager   **B.** File Manager
C. Windows Explorer   **D.** Authentication

Q.47 The interval from the time of submission of a process to the time of completion is termed as __________.
A. Waiting time   **B.** Turnaround time
C. Response time   **D.** Throughput

Q.48 Which scheduling algorithm allocates the CPU first to the process that requests the CPU first?
A. First-come first-served scheduling
B. Shortest job scheduling
C. Priority scheduling
D. Shortest-Job-First (SJF) Scheduling

Q.49 What is Dynamic loading?
A. loading multiple routines dynamically
B. loading a routine only when it is called
C. loading multiple routines randomly
D. None of the above

Q.50 In a 8-bit ripple carry adder using identical full adders, each full adder takes $34\ ns$ for computing sum. If the time taken for 8-bit addition is $90\ ns$, find time taken by each full adder to find carry:
A. $6\ ns$ **B.** $7\ ns$ **C.** $10\ ns$ **D.** $8\ ns$

Q.51

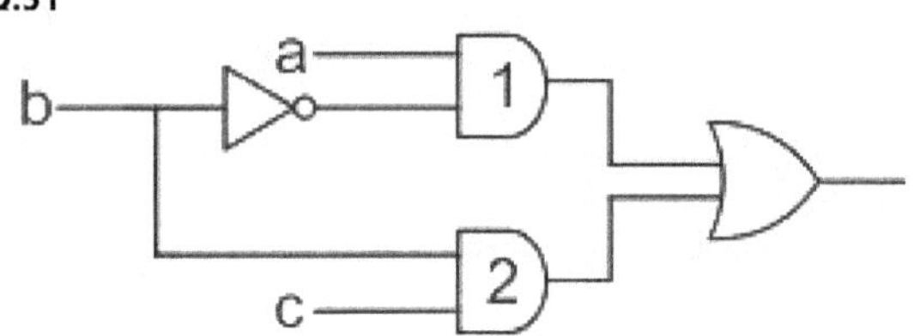

In the diagram above, the inverter (NOT gate) and the AND-gates labelled 1 and 2 have delays of $9, 10$ and $12\ ns$, respectively. Wire delays are negligible. For certain values of a and c, together with certain transition of b, a glitch (spurious output) is generated for a short time, after which the output assumes its correct value. The duration of the glitch is:
A. $7\ ns$ **B.** $9\ ns$ **C.** $11\ ns$ **D.** $13\ ns$

Q.52 All the output of the chip will not be high when $G_1 G_2 G_3$ is ________.

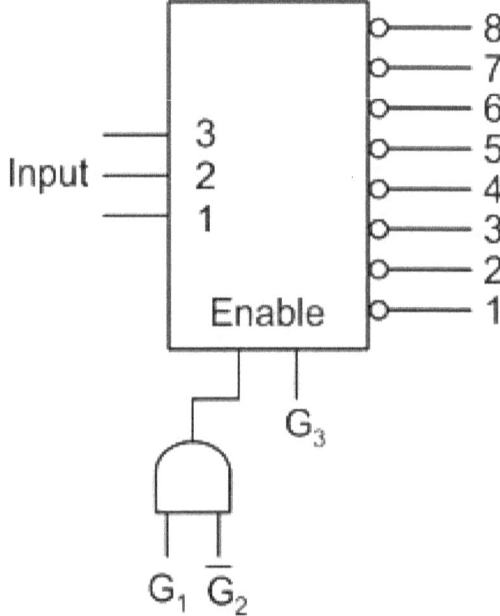

A. 010   **B.** 111   **C.** 101   **D.** 001

Q.53 The next state table of a 2-bit saturating up-counter is given below:

Q_1	Q_0	Q_1^+	Q_0^+
0	0	1	0
0	1	0	1
1	0	1	0
1	1	0	1

The counter is built as an asynchronous sequential circuit using T flip-flops. The expressions for T_1 and T_0 are:
A. $T_0 = 0,\ T_1 = Q_1 \oplus Q_0$
B. $T_0 = 1,\ T_1 = \overline{Q_1} Q_0$
C. $T_0 = 0,\ T_1 = Q_1 \odot Q_0$
D. $T_0 = 1,\ T_1 = Q_1 Q_0$

Q.54 How many pulses are needed to change the contents of a n-bit up-counter from x_{10} to y_{10} if $x > y$ and x is less than 2^n?

A. $2^n + x - y$　　　　B. $2^n - 1 + y - x$
C. $2^n + y - x$　　　　D. $2^n - 1 + x - y$

Q.55 The minimum number of JK flip-flops required to construct a synchronous counter with the count sequence of $(0,0,1,1,2,2,3,3,0,0 \dots)$ is ______.

A. 3　　　　B. 4　　　　C. 5　　　　D. 6

Q.56 In an SR latch by cross-coupling two NOR gates if $S = 1$ and $R = 0$, then it will result in:

Note: For 1st NOR gate input is S and output is Q.

A. $Q = 1$ and $\bar{Q} = 0$　　　　B. $Q = 0$ and $\bar{Q} = 0$
C. $Q = 0$ and $\bar{Q} = 1$　　　　D. Indeterminate state

Q.57 A counter is constructed with three D flip-flops. The input-output pairs are named (D_0, Q_0), (D_1, Q_1), and (D_2, Q_2), where the subscript 0 denotes the least significant bit. The output sequence is desired to be the Gray-code sequence $000, 001, 011, 010, 110, 111, 101$, and 100, repeating periodically. Note that the bits are listed in the $Q_2 Q_1 Q_0$ format. The combinational logic expression for D_1 is:

A. $Q_2 Q_0 + Q_1 \bar{Q_0}$　　　　B. $Q_2 Q_1 + \bar{Q_2}\bar{Q_1}$
C. $Q_2 Q_1 Q_0$　　　　D. $\bar{Q_2} Q_0 + Q_1 \bar{Q_0}$

Q.58 For the multistage counter arrangement of the given figure, determine the frequency of the output signal in Hz:

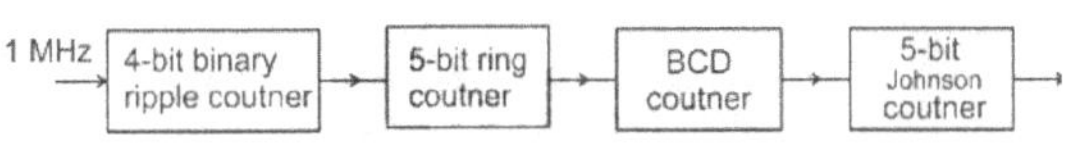

A. 125　　　　B. 135　　　　C. 145　　　　D. 155

Q.59 Let R 1 and R 2 be regular sets defined over the alphabet, then:

A. R 1 ∩ R 2 is not regular
B. R 1 ∪ R 2 is not regular
C. $\Sigma^* -$ R 1 is regular
D. R 1 * is not regular

Q.60 Design a NFA for the language:

L: {an| n is even or divisible by 3}

Which of the following methods can be used to simulate the same.

A. e-NFA
B. Power Construction Method
C. Both (A) and (B)
D. None of these

Q.61 A ________ is a substitution such that h(a) contains a string for each a.

A. Closure
B. Interchange
C. Homomorphism
D. Inverse Homomorphism

Q.62 Homomorphism of a regular set is ________.

A. Universal set　　　　B. Null set
C. Regular set　　　　D. Non regular set

Q.63 Which of the following is type 3 language?

A. Strings of $0's$ whose length is a perfect square
B. Palindromes string
C. Strings of $0's$ having length prime number
D. A string of odd numbers of $0's$

Q.64 Which is considered as the sequence of characters in a token?

A. Mexeme　　B. Lexeme　　C. Texeme　　D. Pattern

Q.65 Which part of the compiler highly used the grammar concept?

A. Code optimization　　　　B. Code generation
C. Parser　　　　D. Lexical Analysis

Q.66 Which phase of the compiler checks the grammar of the programming?

A. Code Optimization　　　　B. Semantic Analysis
C. Code Generation　　　　D. Syntax Analysis

Q.67 Which of the following component is important for semantic analysis?

A. Yacc　　　　B. Lex
C. Symbol Table　　　　D. Type Checking

Q.68 Choose the correct choice regarding the following propositional logic assertion X :

$$X : \big((P \wedge Q) \to R\big) \to \big((P \wedge Q) \to (Q \to R)\big)$$

A. X is a contradiction.
B. X is neither a tautology nor a contradiction.
C. The antecedent of X is not logically equivalent to the consequent of X.
D. X is a tautology.

Q.69 Consider a relation ' R ' on a set ' X ' is given as $R = \{(a, b) \in X \times X$ and $b > a)\}$ then X is/are not:

A. Reflexive　　　　B. Irreflexive
C. Symmetric　　　　D. None of these

Q.70 Which of the following statement is not correct?

A. The union of any two subgroups of a group G is also a subgroup of G.
B. The intersection of any two subgroups of a group G is also subgroup of G.
C. The union of two subgroups $H1$ and $H2$ of a group $(G, *)$ is also subgroup of G.
D. Every subgroup of an abelian group is also an abelian group.

Q.71 Consider a graph G to be a connected planar graph with 10 vertices. Which of the following can be the number of edges in graph G order to G be connected?

A. 22　　　　B. 23

C. 24   **D.** All of these

Q.72 Find a closed form for the generating function for the given sequences:

$$0,1,0,0,0,1,0,0,0,1,0,0,0,1 \ldots?$$

A. $\dfrac{1}{(1-x^4)}$ **B.** $\dfrac{x}{(1-x^3)}$ **C.** $\dfrac{x^2}{(1-x^4)}$ **D.** $\dfrac{x}{(1-x^4)}$

Q.73 There are two different Geography books, five different Natural Sciences books, three different History books and four different Mathematics books on a shelf. In how many different ways can they be arranged if all the books of the same subjects stand together?

A. 353450   **B.** 638364   **C.** 829440   **D.** 768700

Q.74 For every natural number k, which of the following is true?

A. $(mn)^k = m^k n^k$ **B.** $m * k = n + 1$

C. $(m+n)^k = k+1$ **D.** $m^k n = mn^k$

Q.75 Determine the solution for the recurrence relation $b_n = 8b_{n-1} - 12b_{n-2}$ with $b_0 = 3$ and $b_1 = 4$.

A. $\frac{7}{2} \times 2^n - \frac{1}{2} \times 6^n$ **B.** $\frac{2}{3} \times 7^n - 5 \times 4^n$

C. $4! \times 6^n$ **D.** $\frac{2^n}{8}$

Q.76 How many cards must be selected from a standard deck of 52 cards to guarantee that at least three cards of the same suit are chosen ____________.

A. 9   **B.** 10   **C.** 8   **D.** 7

Q.77 ____________ can be defined as the duplication of another creator's or developer's product trailing a thorough examination of its production or development.

A. Reverse hacking

B. Cracking

C. Social engineering

D. Reverse engineering

Q.78 Which of the following is the best type of module coupling?

A. Control Coupling   **B.** Stamp Coupling

C. Data Coupling   **D.** Content Coupling

Q.79 The core of reverse engineering is an activity called:

A. Restructure code   **B.** Directionality

C. Extract abstractions   **D.** Interactivity

Q.80 The open source movement has meant that there is a huge reusable code base available at ___________.

A. Free of cost   **B.** Low cost

C. High cost   **D.** Short period of time

Q.81 Forward engineering is also known as:

A. Extract abstractions

B. Renovation

C. Reclamation

D. Both renovation and reclamation

Q.82 Source code translation is a part of which re-engineering technique?

A. Data re-engineering   **B.** Refactoring

C. Restructuring   **D.** None of these

Q.83 Which of the following model has a major downfall to a software development life cycle in terms of the coding phase?

A. 4GT Model   **B.** Waterfall Model

C. RAD Model   **D.** Spiral Model

Q.84 Which of these are not among the eight principles followed by Software Engineering Code of Ethics and Professional Practice?

A. Public   **B.** Profession

C. Product   **D.** Environment

Q.85 CASE stands for__________.

A. Cost Aided Software Engineering

B. Computer Aided Software Engineering

C. Control Aided Software Engineering

D. None of the above

Q.86 What is the probability of solving a given problem if three students $(A, B$ and $C)$, try it independently, with respective probabilities $\frac{4}{7}, \frac{3}{8}$ and $\frac{1}{2}$?

A. $\frac{97}{112}$ **B.** $\frac{95}{112}$ **C.** $\frac{97}{111}$ **D.** $\frac{97}{125}$

Q.87 A dice is rolled three times and the sum of three numbers appearing on the uppermost face is 15. What is the chance that the first roll was four?

A. $\frac{1}{216}$ **B.** $\frac{2}{69}$ **C.** $\frac{1}{5}$ **D.** $\frac{3}{71}$

Q.88 Form the differential equation of $y = ae^{3x}\cos(x+b)$ where $y' = \dfrac{dy}{dx}$ and $y^n = \dfrac{d^2y}{dx^2}$?

A. $y'' - 6y' + 10y = 0$ **B.** $y'' - 6y' - 10y = 0$

C. $y'' + 6y' - 10y = 0$ **D.** $y'' + 6y' + 10y = 0$

Q.89 The differential equation representing the family of curves $y = a\sin(\lambda x + a)$ is:

A. $\dfrac{d^2y}{dx^2} + \lambda^2 y = 0$ **B.** $\dfrac{d^2y}{dx^2} - \lambda^2 y = 0$

C. $\dfrac{d^2y}{dx^2} + \lambda y = 0$ **D.** None of these

Q.90 Laplace transform of $\cos(\omega t)$ is:

A. $\dfrac{s}{s^2+w^2}$ **B.** $\dfrac{w}{s^2+w^2}$ **C.** $\dfrac{s}{s^2-\omega^2}$ **D.** $\dfrac{\omega}{s^2-\omega^2}$

Q.91 The Laplace transform of $f(t) = \begin{cases} \dfrac{t}{T}, & 0 < t < T \\ 1, & t > T \end{cases}$ is:

A. $-\dfrac{(1-e^{-\alpha T})}{s^2 T}$ **B.** $\dfrac{(1-e^{-sT})}{s^2 T}$

C. $\dfrac{(1+e^{-8T})}{s^2 T}$ **D.** $\dfrac{(1-e^{<T})}{s^2 T}$

Q.92 Which of the following is the inverse of the matrix $A = \begin{bmatrix} 3 & 0 \\ 1 & 2 \end{bmatrix}$

A. $\begin{bmatrix} \frac{1}{3} & 0 \\ -\frac{1}{6} & \frac{1}{2} \end{bmatrix}$ **B.** $\begin{bmatrix} 0 & \frac{1}{6} \\ -\frac{1}{6} & \frac{1}{2} \end{bmatrix}$

C. $\begin{bmatrix} \frac{1}{3} & -\frac{1}{6} \\ \frac{1}{3} & \frac{1}{2} \end{bmatrix}$ **D.** $\begin{bmatrix} \frac{1}{3} & 0 \\ 0 & \frac{1}{2} \end{bmatrix}$

Q.93 Find the Eigen values of matrix $A = \begin{bmatrix} 2 & 1 & 0 \\ 1 & 2 & 1 \\ 0 & 1 & 2 \end{bmatrix}$.

A. $2+\sqrt{2}, 2-\sqrt{2}, 2$ **B.** $2,1,2$
C. $2,2,0$ **D.** $2,2,2$

Q.94 If $f(x) = \tan^{-1}\left[\dfrac{\sin x}{1+\cos x}\right]$, then what is first term derivative of $f(x)$?

A. $\dfrac{1}{2}$ **B.** $-\dfrac{1}{2}$ **C.** 2 **D.** -2

Q.95 The improper integral $\int_0^\infty e^{-2t}\, dt$ converges to:

A. 0 **B.** 1 **C.** 0.5 **D.** 2

Q.96 DNS can obtain the _________ of host if its domain name is known and vice versa.

A. Station address   **B.** IP address
C. Port address   **D.** Checksum

Q.97 A network, which is used for sharing data, software and hardware among several users of microcomputers, is called:

A. Wide Area Network
B. Metropolitan Area Network
C. Local Area Network
D. Value Added Network

Q.98 A VLAN equals to _________.

A. Router   **B.** Subnet
C. Firewall   **D.** Host/Client ID

Q.99 An example of a medium speed, switched communications service is:

A. Series 1000   **B.** Data phone 50
C. DDD   **D.** None of these

Q.100 Wide area networks (WANs) always require:

A. High bandwidth communication source link
B. High speed processors
C. Both (A) and (B)
D. None of these

// Smart Answer Sheet //

Correct Percentage of students who answered correctly.   **Skipped** Percentage of students who skipped.

Q.	Ans.	Correct / Skipped	Q.	Ans.	Correct / Skipped	Q.	Ans.	Correct / Skipped	Q.	Ans.	Correct / Skipped	Q.	Ans.	Correct / Skipped	Q.	Ans.	Correct / Skipped
1	D	66.34 % / 31.25 %	18	C	76.75 % / 15.31 %	35	B	65.74 % / 33.94 %	52	C	51.4 % / 39.09 %	69	A	44.65 % / 46.41 %	86	A	25.13 % / 72.17 %
2	B	68.68 % / 30.2 %	19	D	52.49 % / 41.94 %	36	A	27.01 % / 69.32 %	53	C	40.94 % / 36.32 %	70	A	29.85 % / 68.02 %	87	C	46.09 % / 38.96 %
3	B	16.25 % / 75.9 %	20	C	45.14 % / 54.6 %	37	C	48.59 % / 33.0 %	54	C	59.99 % / 33.2 %	71	C	67.15 % / 30.7 %	88	C	56.95 % / 39.18 %
4	B	16.12 % / 83.14 %	21	A	32.34 % / 67.12 %	38	A	45.6 % / 48.81 %	55	A	68.36 % / 30.34 %	72	D	23.46 % / 74.97 %	89	A	11.59 % / 84.94 %
5	C	26.23 % / 67.28 %	22	A	58.68 % / 33.14 %	39	A	63.6 % / 31.89 %	56	C	62.52 % / 32.2 %	73	C	53.12 % / 36.88 %	90	A	58.2 % / 36.45 %
6	C	83.6 % / 10.74 %	23	B	80.41 % / 16.84 %	40	B	49.84 % / 30.16 %	57	D	12.0 % / 87.89 %	74	A	78.38 % / 15.9 %	91	B	19.31 % / 69.45 %
7	B	59.47 % / 39.84 %	24	B	63.3 % / 35.35 %	41	D	40.37 % / 37.28 %	58	A	49.87 % / 38.63 %	75	A	19.59 % / 78.59 %	92	A	43.15 % / 44.07 %
8	C	15.93 % / 81.15 %	25	C	53.46 % / 40.67 %	42	A	15.33 % / 83.66 %	59	C	55.4 % / 35.71 %	76	A	68.3 % / 30.05 %	93	A	59.92 % / 36.66 %
9	D	63.71 % / 35.96 %	26	D	83.08 % / 15.46 %	43	A	53.45 % / 31.62 %	60	C	24.55 % / 69.54 %	77	D	56.62 % / 38.42 %	94	A	40.17 % / 35.33 %
10	A	78.18 % / 21.5 %	27	A	58.23 % / 32.14 %	44	A	54.8 % / 44.16 %	61	C	89.53 % / 10.45 %	78	C	52.36 % / 33.96 %	95	C	59.7 % / 31.0 %
11	B	81.5 % / 15.6 %	28	D	62.12 % / 36.85 %	45	B	69.16 % / 30.2 %	62	C	79.73 % / 17.93 %	79	C	40.24 % / 53.33 %	96	B	69.23 % / 30.02 %
12	D	40.07 % / 32.99 %	29	A	13.29 % / 77.4 %	46	D	47.19 % / 39.87 %	63	D	52.15 % / 42.62 %	80	B	69.47 % / 30.06 %	97	C	63.52 % / 34.6 %
13	C	28.74 % / 70.79 %	30	B	68.63 % / 30.76 %	47	B	47.08 % / 31.31 %	64	B	66.61 % / 31.84 %	81	D	66.9 % / 30.41 %	98	B	66.52 % / 31.94 %
14	B	62.03 % / 30.03 %	31	C	76.21 % / 17.5 %	48	A	57.08 % / 33.45 %	65	C	66.82 % / 32.51 %	82	C	52.6 % / 37.35 %	99	C	65.7 % / 30.89 %
15	C	69.15 % / 30.83 %	32	C	43.57 % / 49.6 %	49	B	60.2 % / 31.09 %	66	D	66.01 % / 30.3 %	83	A	53.32 % / 39.78 %	100	D	61.94 % / 30.49 %
16	C	64.64 % / 32.57 %	33	A	14.35 % / 75.46 %	50	D	56.45 % / 41.84 %	67	D	10.8 % / 73.04 %	84	D	40.22 % / 56.51 %			
17	C	58.85 % / 30.7 %	34	C	85.56 % / 13.1 %	51	A	49.8 % / 47.48 %	68	D	55.52 % / 36.67 %	85	B	88.24 % / 10.44 %			

//Hints and Solutions//

1. Given, recurrence relation:

$$T(n) = T(n-1) \times n \text{ when } n > 1$$

$$T(n) = 1 \text{ when } n = 1$$

Using substitution method to solve recurrences,

$$T(n) = T(n-1) \times n$$

$$T(n) = T(n-2) \times (n-1) \times n$$

$$T(n) = T(n-3) \times (n-2) \times (n-1) \times n$$

Substituting k times.

$$T(n) = T(n-k) \times (n-k-1) \times (n-k-2) \times \times (n-1) \times n \cdots (1)$$

Using termination,

$$n - k = 1$$

$$k = n - 1$$

Put value of k in equation (1),

$$T(n) = T(1) \times 2 \times 3 \times n$$

$$(T(n) = 1 \times 2 \times 3 \times 4 \times 5 \dots n)$$

$$T(n) = n!$$

Increasing order of complexity class is $2^n < n! < n^n$

So,

$$T(n) = O(n^n)$$

$$T(n) = \Omega(2^n)$$

Hence, the correct option is (D).

2. "An efficient algorithm for putting exactly one specified element of an unsorted array on the same index as in a sorted array."
This is what the partition algorithm does following algorithm for partition algorithm:

```
partition (arr[], low, high)
{
// pivot - Element at right most position
pivot = arr[low];
i = low ;
// Index of smaller element
for (j = low; j<= high-1; j++)
{
// If the current element is smaller than the pivot, swap the element
if (arr[j]<= pivot)
{
swap(arr[i+1], arr[j]);
i++; // increment index of smaller element
}
}
```

```
swap(arr[i], arr[low]);
return (i);
}
```

Hence, the correct option is (B).

3. Now,

We insert the keys $661, 182, 24, 103$ into the index slot in the given order using linear probing.

Hash function: h(key)=key mod 13.

Step (1):

h $(661) = 661\%13$

h $(661) = 11$

So, we insert 661 into the 11th index slot.

Step (2):

h $(182) = 182\%13$

h $(182) = 0$

So, we insert 182 into the 0th index slot.

Step (3):

h $(24) = 24\%13$

h $(24) = 11$

But index slot 11 is already full then we go to check for next slot.

h $(24) = (24 + 1)\%13$

h $(24) = 12$

So, we insert 24 into the 12th index slot.

Step 4:

h $(103) = 103\%13$

h $(103) = 12$

But index slot 12 is already full then we go to check for next slot,

h $(103) = (103 + 1)\%13$

h $(103) = 0$

But index slot 0 is already full then we go to check for next slot,

h $(103) = (103 + 2)\%13$

h $(103) = 1$

So, we insert 103 into the 1st index slot.

Index	Value
0	182

1	103
2	
3	
4	
5	
6	
7	
8	
9	
10	
11	661
12	24

Hence, the correct option is (B).

4. Given,

$$623 * /42 * +68 * -$$

The procedure is:

1. Push 6 into the stack.

2. Push 2 into the stack.

3. Push 3 into the stack.

4. Now, we encounter an operator. So, pop top 2 elements and apply the operator between them, it should be like:

(second_pop operator first_pop) $\Rightarrow 2 * 3$ but not $3 * 2$

result is $6 \Rightarrow$ push into the stack.

5. Now, we encounter an operator. So, pop top 2 elements and apply the operator between them, it should be like:

(second_pop operator first_pop) $\Rightarrow \dfrac{6}{6}$

result is $1 \Rightarrow$ push into the stack.

6. Push 4 into the stack, Push 2 into the stack.

7. Now, we encounter an operator. So, pop top 2 elements and apply the operator between them, it should be like:

(second_pop operator first_pop) $\Rightarrow 4 * 2$

result is $8 \Rightarrow$ push into the stack.

According to the question evaluate up to 2nd $*$ evaluated, $\Rightarrow$ our task complete.

The top of the two elements of our stacks is $8,1$ in the order from top to bottom.

Hence, the correct option is (B).

5. Given, numbers to be inserted is:

$$60,25,72,15,30,68,101,13,18,47,70,34$$

Algorithm for the construction of a binary tree:

If root is NULL

then create root node

return

If root exists then

compare the data with node.data

while until insertion position is located

 If data is greater than node

data goto right subtree

else

goto left subtree

end while

insert data

end if

According to the given numbers and the algorithm, we construct a binary tree i.e.,

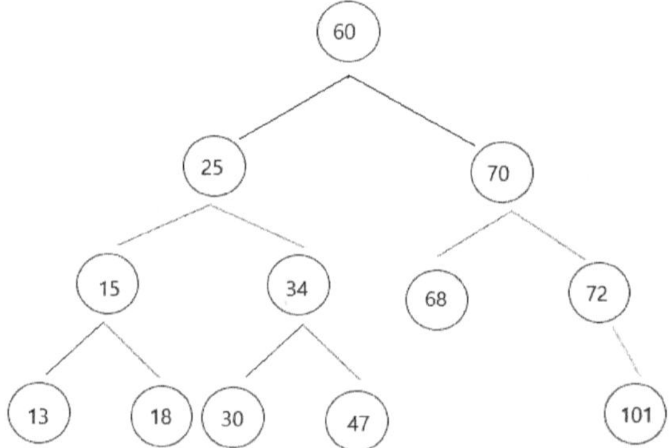

So, the number of nodes in the left subtree is 7 i.e., $13,15,18,25,30,34,47$.

Hence, the correct option is (C).

6. Breadth-First Search (BFS) is an algorithm for traversing or searching tree or graph data structures.

Breadth-First Search (BFS) algorithm traverses a graph in a breadthwise manner and uses a queue to remember to get the next vertex to start a search when a dead end occurs in any iteration.

Now,

From Root $1 \to$ Options $(2,3,7)$ nodes can be traversed in any order.

From node $2 \to$ Options $(4,6)$ nodes can be traversed in any order.

From node $3 \to$ Options $(6,5)$ nodes can be traversed in any order.

From node $7 \to$ Options (5) nodes will be traversed.

Statement I: $1,2,3,7,4,6,5$

Choose node 1 (Root) $\rightarrow 2 \rightarrow 3 \rightarrow 7$ (Level 1)

Choose node 2:

$\rightarrow 4 \rightarrow 6$

Choose node 3:

$\rightarrow 5$

This is the correct order for traversal.

Statement III: $1,7,3,2,5,6,4$

Choose node 1 (Root) $\rightarrow 7 \rightarrow 3 \rightarrow 2$ (Level 1)

Chose node 3:

$\rightarrow 5 \rightarrow 6$

Chose node 2:

$\rightarrow 4$

This is also the correct order for traversal.

Hence, the correct option is (C).

7. In many situations, it is not possible to allocate data in a LIFO fashion with a stack. In this case, data is dynamically allocated from a pool of memory commonly called the heap. Heap allocation is considerably slower and more complex than stack allocation and may also result in allocations scattered all over memory. Such scattered allocations can lead to a loss of coherence and a reduction in memory access efficiency. A parallelized heap allocator should be used when writing parallel programs that use dynamic data structures.

Hence, the correct option is (B).

8. Finding number of bits without using Huffman,

Total number of characters $=$ sum of frequencies $= 100$

Size of 1 character $= 1$ byte $= 8$ bits

Total number of bits $= 8{*}100 = 800$

Using Huffman Encoding, total number of bits needed can be calculated as:

$5{*}4 + 9{*}4 + 12{*}3 + 13{*}3 + 16{*}3 + 45{*}1 = 224$

Bits saved $= 800 - 224 = 576$.

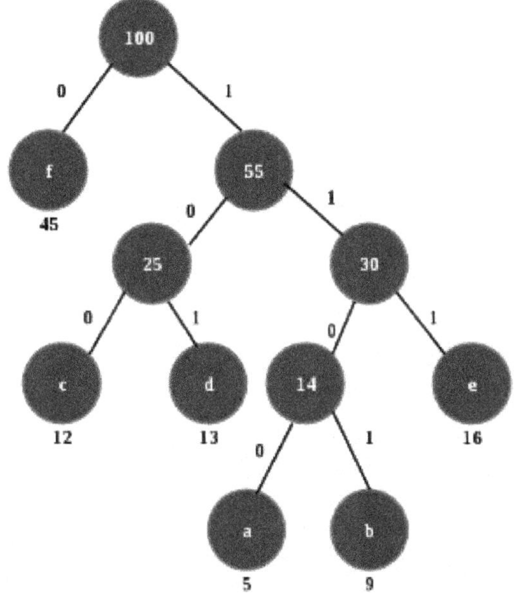

Hence, the correct option is (C).

9. Given,

Option (A):

"The Reverse Kruskal's algorithm that selects maximum element first from a graph with distinct edge weights, produces the incorrect Minimum cost spanning tree".

This option is false as:

Consider the following Reverse Kruskal's Algorithm:

$1.$ Sort the edges in decreasing order of their edge weights.

$2.$ For each edge e, if this edge is part of a cycle delete it.

This algorithm produces the correct minimum spanning tree.

Option (B):

"For a dynamic programming algorithm, computing all values in a bottom-up fashion is asymptotically faster than using recursion".

This is also false since in DP; memoization and bottom-up approaches have the same Asymptotic time complexity.

Option (C):

"In Dynamic programming, among top-down approach and bottom-up approach; the top-down approach is not memory efficient".

This option is true since in the top-down approach recursion is required which will make use of the stack. So, the bottom-up approach is more memory efficient as compared to the top-down.

Hence, the correct option is (D).

10. If an object is passed by reference, the changes made in the function are reflected to the main object of caller function too. When an object is passed by reference, its address is passed implicitly. This will make changes to the main function whenever any modification is done. The objects can be passed by reference if required to use the same object. The values can be passed so that the main objective remains the same.

Hence, the correct option is (A).

11. C programming has two operators increment ++ and decrement -- to change the value of an operand (constant or variable) by 1. Increment ++ increases the value by 1 whereas decrement -- decreases the value by 1. These two operators are unary operators, meaning they only operate on a single operand.

After s++, s points the string "++".

Thus the output will be: C++ ++.

Hence, the correct option is (B).

12. A text file that contains our program is called as source file. A source file is a glorified text file with program instructions written in a specific programming language like, C or Java or Python. You can compile or interpret this file to run the program. When the source file has been compiled it's basically transformed/translated into a lower level language like Assembly.

Hence, the correct option is (D).

13. First statement in a fortran code is program statement. The first statement of this program begins with the word program. It is a non-executable statement that specifies the name of the program to the fortran compiler. Its name can be up to 31 characters long and can be any combination of alphabetic characters, digits, and underscores.

Hence, the correct option is (C).

14. Animations and interactivity with the user on web pages can be done by Java script. Java script is a scripting language that enables you to create dynamically updating content, control multimedia, animate images, and pretty much everything else. Java script is a text-based programming language used both on the client-side and server-side that allows you to make web pages interactive. Where HTML and CSS are languages that give structure and style to web pages, Java script gives web pages interactive elements that engage a user.

Hence, the correct option is (B).

15. The circular queue is also known as a ring buffer. A circular queue is similar to a linear queue as it is also based on the FIFO (First In First Out) principle except that the last position is connected to the first position in a circular queue that forms a circle. Therefore, the structure of a circular queue is also known as a ring structure.

Hence, the correct option is (C).

16. A list of elements in which enqueue operation takes place from one end, and dequeue operation takes place from one end is Queue. Queue is an abstract data structure, somewhat similar to Stacks. Unlike stacks, a queue is open at both its ends. One end is always used to insert data (enqueue) and the other is used to remove data (dequeue). Queue follows First-In-First-Out methodology, i.e., the data item stored first will be accessed first.

Hence, the correct option is (C).

17. Backtracking uses depth-first node generation with bounding functions. It traverses all the nodes by starting from the root node and covers the nodes possible before backtracking. Backtrack means when you are moving forward and find no more nodes in that path then start moving in a backward direction to traverse the remaining nodes.

The depth-first search uses the stack to implement this process.

Algorithm:

1. Pick the root node.

2. Push all the adjacent nodes to the stack.

3. Pop the node from the stack to select the next node to visit.

4. Go to step 2.

5. Terminate when all nodes are visited.

Hence, the correct option is (C).

18. Merge Sort sorting algorithms has the lowest worst-case complexity. It is based on the divide and conquers approach. It divides the complete array into small sub-arrays until each sub-array contains an element and then sorts them and merges them. Time complexity, in this case, is O(n log n).

The complexity of other sorts:

Algorithm	Time complexity: Worst
Quicksort	$O(n^2)$
Merge sort	$O(n \log(n))$
Heapsort	$O(n \log(n))$
Smooth sort	$O(n \log(n))$
Bubble sort	$O(n^2)$
Insertion sort	$O(n^2)$
Selection sort	$O(n^2)$
Bogo sort	$O(\infty)$

Hence, the correct option is (C).

19. Statement 1**:** The packet switching technique is preferred when the data to be sent must be ordered and transmitted in less time.

This statement is false. Since packet switching does not reserve the resources needed along the path, it just encapsulates the data in packets and throws them into the network. So, packets may arrive in a different order at the source.

Statement 2**:** In-Circuit Switching, the resources needed along a path between end systems are reserved for the duration of the communication.

This statement is true. Since In-Circuit Switching resources are needed along a path already reserved before the transmission and then the data transmitted so it will take less time and data will arrive in the same order as sent by the host.

Hence, the correct option is (D).

20. During the 2nd back off race, A & B will be given following timestamps:

A B

[0,1] [0,1,2,3]

Now, the only case where B wins the back off race is:

A B

1   0

$\therefore$ The winning probability of B $= \dfrac{1}{8}$

$= 0.125$

Hence, the correct option is (C).

21. Probability of transmission on the first slot by 1st node:

$\Rightarrow 0.2 \times (1 - 0.3) \times (1 - 0.25) \times (1 - 0.16) \times (1 - 0.09)$

$\Rightarrow 0.2 \times 0.7 \times 0.75 \times 0.84 \times 0.91$

$= 0.080262$

Probability of transmission on the first slot by 2nd node:

$\Rightarrow (1 - 0.2) \times 0.3 \times (1 - 0.25) \times (1 - 0.16) \times (1 - 0.09)$

$\Rightarrow 0.8 \times 0.3 \times 0.75 \times 0.84 \times 0.91$

$= 0.137592$

Probability of transmission on the first slot by 3rd node:

$\Rightarrow (1 - 0.2) \times (1 - 0.3) \times 0.25 \times (1 - 0.16) \times (1 - 0.09)$

$\Rightarrow 0.8 \times 0.7 \times 0.25 \times 0.84 \times 0.91$

$= 0.107016$

Probability of transmission on the first slot by 4th node:

$\Rightarrow (1 - 0.2) \times (1 - 0.3) \times (1 - 0.25) \times 0.16 \times (1 - 0.09)$

$\Rightarrow 0.8 \times 0.7 \times 0.75 \times 0.16 \times 0.91$

$= 0.061152$

Probability of transmission on the first slot by 5th node:

$\Rightarrow (1 - 0.2) \times (1 - 0.3) \times (1 - 0.25) \times (1 - 0.16) \times 0.09$

$\Rightarrow 0.8 \times 0.7 \times 0.75 \times 0.84 \times 0.09$

$= 0.031752$

Probability
$= 0.080262 + 0.137592 + 0.107016 + 0.061152 + 0.031752$

$= 0.4177$

Hence, the correct option is (A).

22. As we know,

The micrometer (international spelling as used by the International Bureau of Weights and Measures or micrometer (American spelling), also commonly known as a micron, is an SI derived unit of length equalling 1×10^{-6} meter (SI standard prefix "micro-" = 10^{-6}); that is, one-millionth of a meter.

To find the type of the address, we look at the second hexadecimal digit from the left. If it is even, the address is unicast. If it is odd, the address is multicast. If all digits are $F's$, the address is broadcast.

Therefore, $S1$ is true because all digits are $F's$.

$S2$ is false because 5 in binary is 0101 (odd). It means $45:20:1B:2E:08:EE$ is a multicast MAC address.

$S3$ is true. It can be calculated as:

$$\text{Max Length} = \text{Propogation Speed} \times \dfrac{\text{SlotTime}}{2}$$

$$\dfrac{\left(2\times10^{8}\right)\times\left(51.2\times10^{-6}\right)}{2}$$

$$= 5120\ m$$

Hence, the correct option is (A).

23. Virtual memory is like an extension to the existing memory. Virtual memory is generally used to increase the apparent size of physical memory. Virtual memory is a feature of an operating system that enables a computer to be able to compensate for shortages of physical memory by transferring pages of data from random access memory to disk storage. This process is done temporarily and is designed to work as a combination of RAM and space on the hard disk.

Hence, the correct option is (B).

24. MFC stands for Memory Function Complete. Memory function complete or MFC is just a signal that tells the CPU that the current operation involving the memory is complete and by that definition, it is obvious that MFC signal will be generated in case of write operation also as in the case of read operation. This is a system command enabled when a memory function is completed by a process.

Hence, the correct option is (B).

25. The time delay between two successive initiations of memory operation is memory cycle time. The time is taken to finish one task and to start another. It is the time that is measured in nanoseconds, the time between one Ram access of time when the next Random Access Memory (RAM) access starts. That Cycle Time finds the right place for the memory to take place in the memory and transfer time of that information/process. So, one should not get confused while thinking about the Clock Cycle or Clock Speed which have to do with the number of cycles/second to which a processor is paced.

Hence, the correct option is (C).

26. The assembler stores the object code in magnetic disk. After compiling the object code, the assembler stores it in the magnetic disk and waits for further execution. A magnetic disk is a storage device that uses a magnetization process to write, rewrite and access data. It is covered with a magnetic coating and stores data in the form of tracks, spots and sectors. Hard disks, zip disks and floppy disks are common examples of magnetic disks.

Hence, the correct option is (D).

27. The utility program used to bring the object code into memory for execution is loader. The program is used to load the program into memory. In computer systems, a loader is the part of an operating system that is responsible for loading programs and libraries. It is one of the essential stages in the process of starting a program, as it places programs into memory and prepares them for execution. The different types of loaders are absolute loader, bootstrap loader, relocating loader (relative loader), direct linking loader.

Hence, the correct option is (A).

28. To overcome the problems of the assembler in dealing with branching code we use a two-pass assembler. This creates entries into the symbol table first and then creates the object code. Basically, the assembler goes through the program one line at a time and generates machine code for that instruction. Then the assembler proceeds to the next instruction. In this way, the entire machine code program is created.

Hence, the correct option is (D).

29. The type of memory assignment used in Intel processors is little-endian. The method of address allocation to data to be stored is called memory assignment. Specifically, little-endian is when the least significant bytes are stored before the more significant bytes, and big-endian is when the most significant bytes are stored before the less significant bytes. When we write a number (in hex), i.e., 0×12345678, we write it with the most significant byte first (the 12 part).

Hence, the correct option is (A).

30. To get the physical address from the logical address generated by CPU we use MMU. Memory Management Unit is used to add the offset to the logical address generated by the CPU to get the physical address. A memory management unit (MMU), sometimes called paged memory management unit (PMMU), is a computer hardware unit having all memory references passed through itself, primarily performing the translation of virtual memory addresses to physical addresses.

Hence, the correct option is (B).

31. Segmentation method is used to map logical addresses of variable length onto physical memory. Segmentation is a process in which memory is divided into groups of variable length called segments. A process is divided into Segments. The chunks that a program is divided into which are not necessarily all of the same sizes are called segments. Segmentation gives user's view of the process which paging does not give. Here the user's view is mapped to physical memory. There is no simple relationship between logical addresses and physical addresses in segmentation.

Hence, the correct option is (C).

32. Pig is a platform for constructing data flows for extract, transform, and load (ETL) processing and analysis of large datasets. Apache Pig is a platform for analyzing large data sets that consists of a high-level language for expressing data analysis programs.

Apache Pig is an abstraction over MapReduce. It is a tool/platform which is used to analyze larger sets of data representing them as data flows. Pig is generally used with Hadoop; we can perform all the data manipulation operations in Hadoop using Pig.

Hence, the correct option is (C).

33. Hive is a SQL-based data warehouse system for Hadoop that facilitates data summarization, ad hoc queries, and the analysis of large datasets stored in Hadoop-compatible file systems.

Hive is an ETL and data warehouse tool on top of the Hadoop ecosystem and used for processing structured and semi-structured data. Hive is a database present in the Hadoop ecosystem that performs DDL and DML operations, and it provides flexible query language such as HQL for better querying and processing of data.

Hence, the correct option is (A).

34. Cascalog hides the limitations of Java behind a powerful and concise Clojure API for Cascading. Cascalog also adds Logic Programming concepts inspired by Datalog. So, the name "Cascalog" is a contraction of Cascading and Datalog. Cascalog is a Clojure-based query language for Hadoop inspired by Datalog.

Hence, the correct option is (C).

35. Hive also supports custom extensions written in Java, including user-defined functions (UDFs) and serializer-deserializers for reading and optionally writing custom formats. Hive allows users to read, write, and manage petabytes of data using SQL. Hive is built on top of Apache Hadoop, which is an open-source framework used to efficiently store and process large datasets. As a result, Hive is closely integrated with Hadoop and is designed to work quickly on petabytes of data.

Hence, the correct option is (B).

36. Rather than building Hadoop deployments manually on EC 2 (Elastic Compute Cloud) clusters, users can spin up fully configured Hadoop installations using simple invocation commands, either through the AWS Web Console or through command-line tools. Elastic MapReduce (EMR) is a web service that makes it easy to quickly and cost-effectively process vast amounts of data. EMR uses Hadoop, an open-source framework, to distribute your data and processing across a resizable cluster of Amazon EC 2 instances.

Hence, the correct option is (A).

37. DML refers to the tools used to add, update and access the data within a database, including things like artists, albums, and so on in our music database example. DML is a categorization of existing SQL commands. DML commands include SELECT, INSERT, UPDATE, and DELETE.

Hence, the correct option is (C).

38. The view of total database content is conceptual view. The conceptual view is where it describes what data are actually stored in the database. It contains information about the entire

database in terms of small and simple structures. The conceptual view is at a higher level than the physical level. It is also known as the logical level. It describes how the database appears to the users conceptually and the relationships between various data tables. The conceptual level does not care for how the data in the database is actually stored.

Hence, the correct option is (A).

39. An index of an attribute of a relation is a data structure that allows the database management system to find those tuples in the relation that have a specified value for that attribute efficiently, without scanning through all the tuples of the relation.

Hence, the correct option is (A).

40. A many-to-many relationship occurs when multiple records in a table are associated with multiple records in another table. For example, a relationship exists between a teacher table and a class table.

Hence, the correct option is (B).

41. There can be more than one process in the ready state, and more than one process in the blocked state, but as there is only one CPU, there can only be one process in the running state. On multiprocessor systems, there can be up to one running process per CPU.

The maximum number of processes in the running state is not equal to the number of CPU.

Number of CPU's $= n = 8$

The size of the ready queue doesn't depend on the number of processes. A single processor system may have a large number of processes waiting in a ready queue.

Transition Diagram (for single CPU):

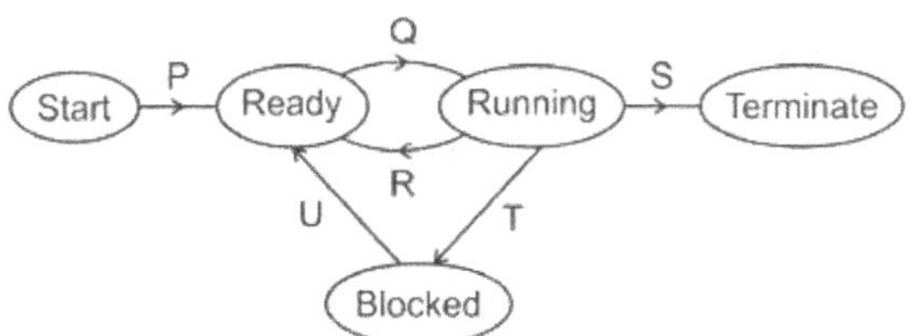

Hence, the correct option is (D).

42. There is always only one parent process of these processes and the remaining will be child processes.

Condition "if" will be satisfy for i $= 0,3,6,9,12,15,18,21$ only. So, "fork()" will call for 8 times.

Value of p	fork calling
0	called
3	called
6	called
9	called
12	called
15	called
18	called
21	called

From the table, it is clear that the fork() is called 8 times.

If n times fork is called the number of child processes created
$= 2^n - 1$
Since $n = 8$ in the given code then the number of child processes created $= 2^8 - 1$

$\Rightarrow 256 - 1$
$= 255$

Hence, the correct option is (A).

43. Process scheduling is the activity of selecting one process from ready state for scheduling it on the running state. Process scheduling process:

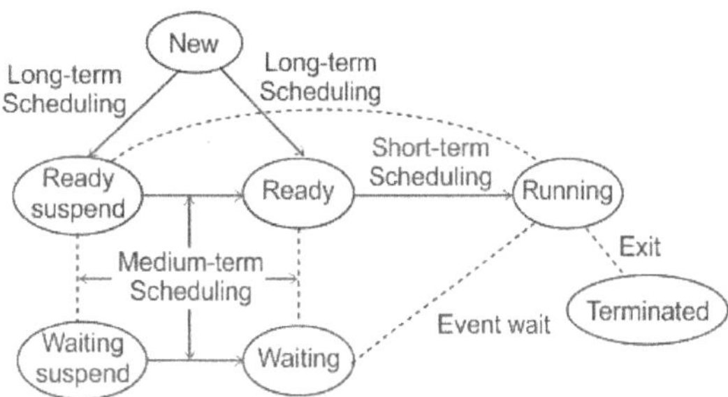

Three types of schedulers are there in this process:

- Short-term scheduler: It changes the state of processes from ready to run. It moves one of the processes from the ready state to running state.

- Long-term scheduler: It selects processes from the queue and loads them into memory for execution.

- Mid-term scheduler: It is the process of swapping. It removes processes from memory that need I/O and makes space for other processes.

Dispatcher: The dispatcher helps in the allocation of CPU to the processes i.e. restoring the state of a process and storing the state of another process in memory.

Hence, the correct option is (A).

44. When a process terminates, it removes from all queues. All allocated resources to that particular process are deallocated and all those resources are returned back to OS. The process eventually switches from the waiting state to the ready state and is then put back in the ready queue. A process continues this cycle until it terminates, at which time it is removed from all queues and has its PCB and resources deallocated.

Hence, the correct option is (A).

45. Feed back queue dispatch tasks according to execution characteristics. Multilevel Feedback Queue Scheduling (MLFQ) keep analyzing the behaviour (time of execution) of processes and according to which it changes its priority. In the last queue, processes are scheduled in FCFS manner. A process in a lower priority queue can only execute only when higher priority queues are empty.

Hence, the correct option is (B).

46. The authentication program is run first after booting the computer and loading the GUI. Authentication is the process of verifying the person or device. For example, when you log in to Facebook, you enter a username and password.

Hence, the correct option is (D).

47. The interval from the time of submission of a process to the time of completion is the turnaround time. It can also be considered as the sum of the time periods spent waiting to get into memory or ready queue, execution on CPU and executing input/output. Turnaround time is an important metric in evaluating the scheduling algorithms of an operating system.

Hence, the correct option is (B).

48. The first-come-first-served scheduling (FCFS) algorithm allocates the CPU first to the process that requests the CPU first. The implementation of the FCFS policy is easily managed with a First In, First Out (FIFO) queue such as customers waiting in line at the bank or the post office.

Hence, the correct option is (A).

49. Dynamic loading is a mechanism by which a computer program can, at run time, load a library (or other binary) into memory, retrieve the addresses of functions and variables contained in the library, execute those functions or access those variables, and unload the library from memory.

Hence, the correct option is (B)

50. As we know,

The total time taken by the for ' n ' bit ripple carry adder is
$t_d = (n-1)t_c + \text{Maximum } (t_c, t_s)$

t_c = Delay for carry through a single flip flop

$t_s = $ Delay for sum

Given,

Each full adder takes $34\ ns$ for computing.

From this, Maximum $(t_c, t_s) = t_s = 34\ ns$

$t_d = 90\ ns.$

$n = 8$

Now,

$t_d = (n-1)t_c + \text{Maximum } (t_c, t_s)$

$90 = (8-1)t_c + 34$

$7t_c = 56\ ns$

$\therefore t_c = 8\ ns$

Time taken by each full adder to find carry is $8\ ns$.

Important Point:

If Maximum($t_c, t_s) = t_c$ then answer is 11.25 which is not in option.

$\therefore$ Maximum (t_c, t_s) has to be t_s.

Hence, the correct option is (D).

51. To perform an operation:

Inverter and first AND gate will take total time $= 9 + 10 = 19\ ns$

To produce the output:

Second AND gate will take time $= 12\ ns$

This glitch is generated for some time just before the final output.

So, before operating OR gate glitch takes the time of $19 - 12 = 7\ ns$

Then the OR will operate normally and produced the correct value.

Hence, the correct option is (A).

52. All the output lines will not be high when the chip will be enabled, i.e. when the two enable inputs are 11.

Option (A): 010

The enable input will be 00.

$\therefore$ Not enabled

Option (B): 111

The enable input will be 01.

$\therefore$ Not enabled

Option (C): 101

The enable input will be 11.

$\therefore$ Enabled

Option (D): 001

The enable input will be 01.

$\therefore$ Not enabled

Hence, the correct option is (C).

53. As we know,

The output of T flip flop will change when $T = 1$ and remain same when $T = 0$.

Excitation table for T flip flop:

Q_1	Q_0	Q_1^+	Q_1^+	T_1	T_0
0	0	1	0	1	0
0	1	0	1	0	0

1	0	1	0	0	0
1	1	0	1	1	0

From this table,

$$T_0 = 0$$
$$T_1 = \overline{Q_1}Q_0 + Q_1\overline{Q_0} = Q_1 \odot Q_0$$

Hence, the correct option is (C).

54. Up-counter: An up-counter is a counter that counts occurrences in ascending order. A down-counter counts objects in decreasing order. A combination of an up-counter and a down-counter is an up-down counter. It has the ability to count in both directions, growing and decreasing.

Important points:

n bit Up-counter counts from 0 to $2^n - 1$.

$$x > y$$

Here, already x pulses are completed then, from x to $2^n - 1$ number of pulses needed $= (2^n - 1) - x$

From $2^n - 1$ to 0 number of pulses needed $= 1$

From 0 to y umber of pulses needed $= y - 0 = y$

Total number of pulses needed $= 2^n - 1 - x + 1 + y$

$$= 2^n + y - x$$

So, the correct answer is $2^n + y - x$.

Hence, the correct option is (C).

55. Design: Count sequence they are saying is :

$$(00,00,01,01,10,10,11,11)$$

We can see the repeated sequence above. So two bits will not be sufficient, we need atleast three flip flops.

A	B	C	Ignore A in output to get desired output
0	0	0	0
0	0	1	1
1	0	0	0
1	0	1	1
0	1	0	2
0	1	1	3
1	1	0	2
1	1	1	3

From the table, it is clear that at least 3 Flip-flop is needed to implement the given sequence count.

Hence, the correct option is (A).

56. When both R and S are set as 0, we will get both Q and Q' as 1 (these must be ideally mutually complementary). This output will be permanent and is not dependent on any sequence of events but just the input values (so, no race condition). But after this state if we enter both R and S as 1, the output will be indeterminate depending on which NAND gate processes first (either Q or Q' will become 0 but we can't determine which (race condition) and it will lead to an indeterminate state.

$R = 0, S = 0$ in an SR latch made by cross-coupling 2 NAND gates will lead to a forbidden state. A forbidden state means, this state is invalid and must not be entered. This is different from an indeterminate state which means a state where we are not sure of the output. Again this is different from a toggling state where the output changes continuously.

Circuit:

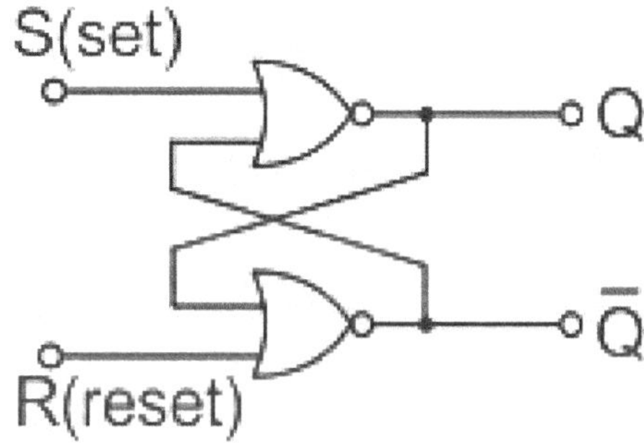

Truth table of SR Latch:

S	R	Q	$\overline{Q}$
0	0	No change	
0	1	1	0
1	0	0	1
1	1	X	X

Where X is don't care.

When $S1$ and $R = 0$ then $Q = 0$ and $\overline{Q} = 1$
Hence, the correct option is (C).

57. Excitation Table/Transition Table:

D **Flip-Flop:**

The single input is called the 'DATA' input. If this data input is held HIGH, the flip flop would be 'SET' and when it is LOW the flip flop would change and become 'RESET'.

Present State Q	Next State $Q+$	D
0	0	0
0	1	1
1	0	0
1	1	1

Given,
$$000 \rightarrow 001 \rightarrow 011 \rightarrow 010 \rightarrow 110 \rightarrow 111 \rightarrow 101 \rightarrow 100 \rightarrow 000 \ldots\ldots\ldots$$

Table for the given condition will be:

Present State	Next State			

Q_2	Q_1	Q_0	Q_1^+	Q_2^+	Q_0^+	D_2	D_1	D_0
0	0	0	0	0	1	0	0	1
0	0	1	0	1	1	0	1	1
0	1	1	0	1	0	0	1	0
0	1	0	1	1	0	1	1	0
1	1	0	1	1	1	1	1	1
1	1	1	1	0	1	1	0	1
1	0	1	1	0	0	1	0	0
1	0	0	0	0	0	0	0	0

D_1 will have high logic at $(1,3,2,6) \Rightarrow D_1 = \sum m(1,3,2,6)$

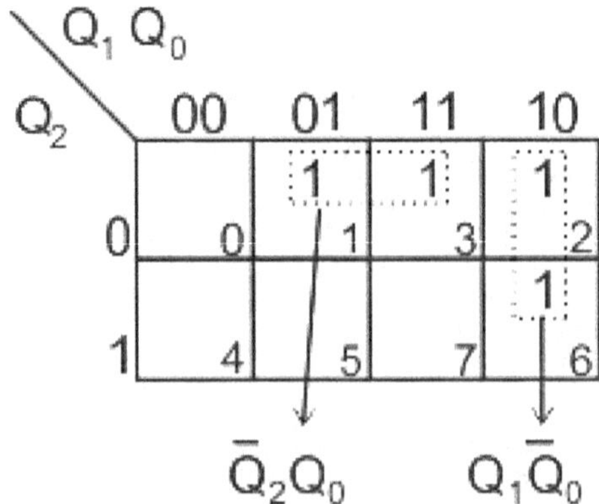

$$\therefore D_1 = \overline{Q_2}Q_0 + Q_1\overline{Q_0}$$

Hence, the correct option is (D).

58. Given,

Input frequency $= 1 MHz = 1 \times 10^6 Hz$

4-bit binary ripple counter has $2^4 = 16$ states.

Now,

The frequency $= \dfrac{1 \times 10^6}{16} = 62.5 \times 10^3\ Hz$

5-bit ring counter has 5 states.

Now, the frequency $= \dfrac{62.5 \times 10^3}{5} = 12.5\ kHz$

BCD counter has 10 states.

Now, the frequency $= \dfrac{12.5 \times 10^3}{10} = 1250\ Hz$

5-bit Johnson counter has $2 \times 5 = 10$ states.

The output frequency $= \dfrac{1250}{10} = 125\ Hz$

Hence, the correct option is (A).

59. Regular languages are closed under Union ($\cup$), Intersection ($\cap$) and Kleene Closure (*), which make options (A), (B) and (D) incorrect.

Option (C): $\Sigma^* - R1 = \Sigma^* \cap R1' =$ Regular languages are closed under complement operation, it is regular.

Hence, the correct option is (C).

60. It is more convenient to simulate a machine using e-NFA else the method of Power Construction is used from the union-closure of DFA's.

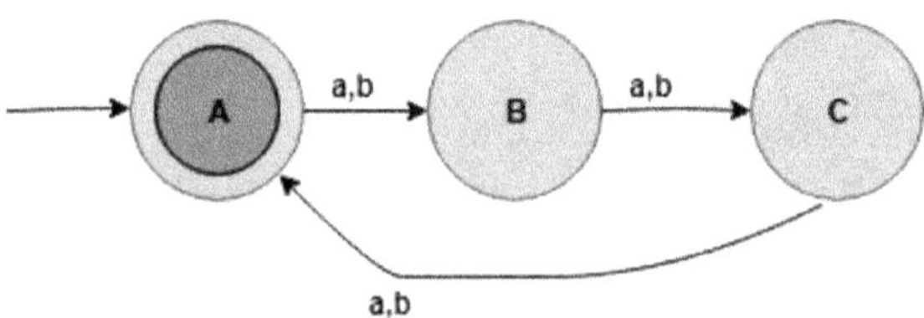

The desired language will be like this:

L $= \{$?, aaa, aab, aba, abb, aaaaaa, bbbbbb, ... $\}$

Here, state A represents set for which string's length is divided by 3 then the remainder is zero (0), state B represents set for which string's length is divided by 3 then the remainder is one (1), and state C represents set for which string's length divided by 3 then the remainder is two (2).

Number of states: n

If |W| mod n $= 0$

The above automata will accept all the strings having the length of the string divisible by 3. When the length of the string is 1, then it will go from state A to B. When the length of the string is 2, then it will go from state B to C and When the length of the string is 3, then it will go from state C to A (final state). State A is the final state i.e, it accepts all the strings having the length divisible by 3.

Hence, the correct option is (C).

61. A Homomorphism is a substitution such that h(a) contains a string for each a. A homomorphism is a mapping h with domain $\Sigma *$ for some alphabet Σ which preserves concatenation: h(v $\cdot$ w) $=$ h(v) $\cdot$ h(w). Simply speaking in homomorphism we replace each letter in a language with another letter in some other language. This operation replaces using a function.

Hence, the correct option is (C).

62. Any set that represents the value of the Regular Expression is called a Regular set. Regular set are closed under homomorphism. If L is a regular language, and h is a homomorphism on its alphabet, then h(L) $=$ {h(w) | w is in L} is also a regular language.

Proof: Let E be a regular expression for L. Apply h to each symbol in E. Language of resulting R, E is h(L).

Hence, the correct option is (C).

63. A string of an odd number of $0's$ is the type 3 language. Type 3 Grammar is known as regular grammar. Regular languages are those languages that can be described using regular expressions. These languages can be modeled by NFA or DFA. Type- 3 grammars must have a single non-terminal on the left-hand side and a right-hand side consisting of a single terminal or single terminal followed by a single non-terminal.

Hence, the correct option is (D).

64. A lexeme is a sequence of alphanumeric characters in a token. The term is used in both the study of language and in the lexical analysis of computer program compilation. In the context of computer programming, lexemes are part of the input stream from which tokens are identified.

Hence, the correct option is (B).

65. The concept of grammar is much used in the parser phase of the compiler. The parser phase is next to the lexical analysis phase in the compiler. Parser generated the parse tree using the predefined grammar. The parser has two different techniques for creating a different parse tree.

Hence, the correct option is (C).

66. Syntax Analysis is a second phase of the compiler design process in which the given input string is checked for the confirmation of rules and structure of the formal grammar. It analyses the syntactical structure and checks if the given input is in the correct syntax of the programming language or not.

Hence, the correct option is (D).

67. In the semantic analysis, type checking is an important component because it verifies the program's operations from the semantic conventions. Type checking is the process of verifying that each operation executed in a program respects the type system of the language. This generally means that all operands in any expression are of appropriate types and number. Much of what we do in the semantic analysis phase is type checking.

Hence, the correct option is (D).

68. We know that,

An antecedent is the first half of a hypothetical proposition, whenever the if-clause precedes the then-clause.

A consequent is the second half of a hypothetical proposition.

Symbol:

$\wedge = $ AND $= \cdot$

$\vee = $ OR $= +$

$\neg = $ NOT $= ^{-}$

$1 = $ TRUE

Formula:

$$A \rightarrow B = \neg A \vee B = \neg A + B$$

$$\neg(A.B) = \overline{A} + \overline{B}$$

Calculation:

Antecedent of X:

$$(P \wedge Q) \rightarrow R \equiv \neg(P.Q) + R \equiv \overline{P} + \overline{Q} + R$$

Consequent of X:

$$(P \wedge Q) \rightarrow (Q \rightarrow R) \equiv \neg(P.Q) + (\neg Q + R)$$

$$= \overline{P} + \overline{Q} + \overline{Q} + R \equiv \overline{P} + \overline{Q} + R$$

So, the antecedent of X is logically equivalent to the consequent of X.

$$X = \big((P \wedge Q) \rightarrow R\big) \rightarrow \big((P \wedge Q) \rightarrow (Q \rightarrow R)\big)$$

$$X = \neg(\neg(P \cdot Q) + R) + \big(\neg(P \cdot Q) + (\neg Q + R)\big)$$

$$X = P \cdot Q \cdot \neg R + \neg P + \neg Q \cdot + (\neg Q + R)$$

$$X = P \cdot Q \cdot \overline{R} + \overline{P} + \overline{Q} + \overline{Q} + R$$

$$X = P \cdot Q \cdot \overline{R} + \overline{P} + \overline{Q} + R$$

$$X = (\overline{P} + P)(\overline{P} + Q \cdot \overline{R}) + \overline{Q} + R \qquad (A + \overline{A}B = A + B)$$

$$X = \overline{P} + Q \cdot \overline{R} + \overline{Q} + R$$

$$X = \overline{P} + \overline{Q} + \overline{R} + R$$

$$X = 1 = \text{TRUE} \qquad (A + \overline{A} = 1)$$

X is a tautology.

Hence, the correct option is (D).

69. Let $X = \{1,2,3\}$

$$X \times X = \{(1,1),(1,2),(1,3),(2,1),(2,2),(2,3),(3,1),(3,2),(3,3)\}$$

$$R = \{(1,2),(1,3),(2,3)\}$$

In Relation R, $(1,1)$, $(2,2)$ and $(3,3)$ is not present therefore it is not reflexive.

In Relation R, $(1,2)$ is present but $(2,1)$ is not present therefore it is not symmetric.

In Relation R, $(1,1)$ OR $(2,2)$ OR $(3,3)$ is not present therefore it is irreflexive.

Hence, the correct option is (A).

70. (A) The union of any two subgroups of a group G is also a subgroup of G.

Consider group $G = \{1,3,5,7\}$ w.r.t multiplicative (8)

$$H1 = \{1,3\}$$

$H2 = \{1,5\}$

$H1 \cup H2 = \{1,3,5\}$

This is not a subgroup of G. As $(3*5)\mathrm{mod}8 = 7$ which is not in $H1UH2$.

(B) The intersection of any two subgroups of a group G is also subgroup of G.

From above example, it is correct. As $H1 \cap H2 = \{1\}$.

(C) The union of two subgroups $H1$ and $H2$ of a group $(G, {}^*)$ is also subgroup of G.

This statement is correct when either $H1$ is a subset of $H2$ or $H2$ is a subset of $H1$.

(D) Every subgroup of an abelian group is also an abelian group

Real numbers are abelian group under addition. Every subgroup of abelian group is normal so, each subgroup rise to a quotient group and subgroups, quotients of abelian group are abelian.

So, given statement is correct.

Hence, the correct option is (A).

71. For any connected simple planner graph, the following condition holds true.

$e \leq 3n - 6$

By Euler formula for connected planar graph,

$\Rightarrow n - e + f = 2$

$\Rightarrow 10 - \frac{3f}{2} + f = 2$ (An edge is part of two faces)

$\Rightarrow \frac{f}{2} = 8$

$f = 16$

$\therefore e = \frac{3f}{2}$

$= 24$

So, the minimum number of edges in such a graph is $e \leq 24$.

Hence, the correct option is (C).

72. Sequence:

$0,1,0,0,0,1,0,0,0,1,0,0,0,1$

$G(x) = 0x^0 + 1x^1 + 0x^2 + 0x^3 + 0x^4 + 1x^5 + 0x^6 + 0x^7 + 0x^8 + 1x^9 + 0x^{10} + 0x^{11} + 0x^{12} + 1x^{13}$

$G(x) = 0 \cdot x^0 + 1 \cdot x^1 + 0 \cdot x^2 + 0 \cdot x^3 + 0 \cdot x^4 + 1 \cdot x^5 \ldots$

$G(x) = x + x^5 + x^9 + x^{13} + x^{17} + \cdots$

$G(x) = x + x^5(1 + x^4 + x^8 + x^{12} + \cdots)$

It's just an index shift.

Since

$\frac{1}{1-x} = \sum_{n=0}^{\infty} x^n$

is generating for $1,1,1, \ldots$, and you want to make the first three into zeros, you multiply by x^3 resulting in an index shift:

$\frac{x^3}{1-x} = \sum_{n=0}^{\infty} x^{n+3}$

So that you get the same sequence with three zeroes introduced at the beginning. If this is still not explicit enough, you can see this is:

$\sum_{n=3}^{\infty} x^n$

By making the index shift $n + 3 \mapsto n$.

So, we have

$G(x) = x + \frac{x^5}{(1-x^4)}$

$G(x) = \frac{x}{(1-x^4)}$

Hence, the correct option is (D).

73. There are four groups of books which can be arranged in $4!$ different ways. Among those books, two are Geography books, five are Natural Sciences books, three are History books and four are Mathematics books.

Therefore, there are $4! \times 2! \times 5! \times 3! \times 4! = 829440$ ways to arrange the books.

Hence, the correct option is (C).

74. In the first step, for $k = 1, (mn)^1 = m^1 n^1 = mn$, thus it is true.

Let us assume the statement is true for $k = 1$.

Now, by induction assumption, $(mn)^1 = m^1 n^1$ is true. So, to prove,

$(mn)^{1+1} = m^{1+1} + n^{1+1}$

We have $(mn)^1 = m^1 n^1$ and multiplying both sides by (mn)

$\Rightarrow (mn)^1(mn) = (m^1 n^1)(mn)$

$\Rightarrow (mn)^{1+1} = (mm^1)(nn^1)$

$\Rightarrow (mn)^{1+1} = (m^{1+1} n^{1+1})$.

Therefore, it is proved. So, $(mn)^k = m^k n^k$ is true for every natural number k.

Hence, the correct option is (A).

75. Given, the recurrence relation:

$b_n - 8b_{n-1} + 12b_{n-2} = 0$

Now, from the characteristic equation:

$x^2 - 8x + 12 = 0$ we have,

$x: (x - 2)(x - 6) = 0$

So, $x = 2$ and $x = 6$ are the characteristic roots.

Therefore the solution to the recurrence relation will have the form:

$b_n = b2^n + c6^n$

To find b and c, we set $n = 0$ and $n = 1$ to get a system of two equations with two unknowns:

$3 = b2^0 + c6^0 = b + c \cdots (1)$

$4 = b2^1 + c6^1 = 2b + 6c \cdots (2)$

Solving system of equations (1) and (2) gives,

$c = -\dfrac{1}{2}$ and $b = \dfrac{7}{2}$

So, the solution to the recurrence relation is:

$b_n = \dfrac{7}{2} \times 2^n - \dfrac{1}{2} \times 6^n.$

Hence, the correct option is (A).

76. Suppose there are four boxes, one for each suit, and as cards are selected, they are placed in the box reserved for cards of that suit. Using the generalized pigeonhole principle, we see that if N cards are selected, there is at least one box containing at least $\lfloor \frac{N}{4} \rfloor$ cards. Consequently, we know that at least three cards of one suit are selected if $\lfloor \frac{N}{4} \rfloor \geq 3$.

The smallest integer N such that $\lfloor \frac{N}{4} \rfloor \geq 3$ is $N = 2 \cdot 4 + 1 = 9$.

So, nine cards suffice.

Note: that if eight cards are selected, it is possible to have two cards of each suit, so more than eight cards are needed. Consequently, nine cards must be selected to guarantee that at least three cards of one suit is chosen. One good way to think about this is to note that after the eighth card is chosen, there is no way to avoid having a third card of same suit.

Hence, the correct option is (A).

77. Reverse engineering can be made functional to diverse aspects of software development and hardware improvement activities. This practice absorbs how the system or the application works and what concepts have to implement in order to crack or duplicate it.

Hence, the correct option is (D).

78. Data coupling is the best type of module coupling because in this type of coupling has low coupling. If the dependency between the modules is based on the fact that they communicate by passing only data, then the modules are said to be data coupled. In data coupling, the components are independent to each other and communicating through data. Module communications don't contain tramp data.

Hence, the correct option is (C).

79. The core to reverse engineering is an activity called extract abstractions. In abstraction activity, the engineer must evaluate older program and extract information about procedures, interface, data structure or database used. The engineer must evaluate the old program and from the source code, extract a meaningful specification of the processing that is performed, the user interface that is applied, and the program data structures or database that is used.

Hence, the correct option is (C).

80. The open-source movement has meant that there is a huge reusable code base available at a low cost. This may be in the form of program libraries or entire applications. Open source is a term that originally referred to open source software (OSS). Open-source software is code that is designed to be publicly accessible i.e., anyone can see, modify, and distribute the code as they see fit. The term "open source" requires that no one can discriminate against a group in not sharing the edited code or hinder others from editing their already-edited work. This approach to software development allows anyone to obtain and modify open-source code.

Hence, the correct option is (B).

81. Forward engineering, also called renovation or reclamation, not only recovers design information from existing software, but uses this information to alter or reconstitute the existing system in an effort to improve its overall quality.

Hence, the correct option is (D).

82. Restructuring involves automatic conversion from unstructured to structured code. Software restructuring is a form of perfective maintenance that modifies the structure of a program's source code. Its goal is increased maintainability to better facilitate other maintenance activities, such as adding new functionality to, or correcting previously undetected errors within a software system.

Hence, the correct option is (C).

83. Much more expertise is needed in the 4GT model for analyzing, designing, and testing activities as it eliminates the coding phase. The term fourth-generation technique 4GT encompasses a broad array of software tools that have one thing in common: each enables the software engineer to specify some characteristics of software at a high level. The tool then automatically generates the source code based on the developer's specification. Therefore in this model, there is a major downfall in the software development life-cycle in terms of the coding phase.

Hence, the correct option is (A).

84. Environment are not among the eight principles followed by Software Engineering Code of Ethics and Professional Practice. Rest all are clauses for software ethics, environment does not focus on specific clause nor its of importance related to question.

Hence, the correct option is (D).

85. CASE stands for Computer-Aided Software Engineering. CASE is the domain of software tools used to design and implement applications. CASE software is often associated with methods for the development of information systems together with automated tools that can be used in the software development process.

Hence, the correct option is (B).

86. Given,

$$P(A) = \frac{4}{7}, P(B) = \frac{3}{8} \text{ and } P(C) = \frac{1}{2}$$

We know that,

$$P(A \cup B \cup C) = P(A) + P(B) + P(C) - P(A \cap B) - P(B \cap C) - P(C \cap A) + P(A \cap B \cap C)$$

$$\Rightarrow P(A \cap B) = P(A) \times P(B)$$

So, the probability of the question getting solved is:

$$P(A \cup B \cup C) = \frac{4}{7} + \frac{3}{8} + \frac{1}{2} - \left(\frac{4}{7} \times \frac{3}{8}\right) - \left(\frac{3}{8} \times \frac{1}{2}\right) - \left(\frac{1}{2} \times \frac{4}{7}\right) + \left(\frac{4}{7} \times \frac{3}{8} \times \frac{1}{2}\right)$$

$$\Rightarrow P(A \cup B \cup C) = \frac{4}{7} + \frac{3}{8} + \frac{1}{2} - \left(\frac{3}{14}\right) - \left(\frac{3}{16}\right) - \left(\frac{2}{7}\right) + \left(\frac{3}{28}\right)$$

$$\Rightarrow P(A \cup B \cup C) = \frac{81}{56} - \left(\frac{3}{14}\right) - \left(\frac{3}{16}\right) - \left(\frac{2}{7}\right) + \left(\frac{3}{28}\right)$$

$$\Rightarrow P(A \cup B \cup C) = \frac{81}{56} + \frac{3}{28} - \left(\frac{24+21+32}{112}\right)$$

$$\Rightarrow P(A \cup B \cup C) = \frac{87}{56} - \frac{77}{112}$$

$$\Rightarrow P(A \cup B \cup C) = \frac{174-77}{112}$$

$$\Rightarrow P(A \cup B \cup C) = \frac{97}{112}$$

Hence, the correct option is (A).

87. Given,

The sum of three numbers appearing on the uppermost face is 15.

According to the question,

All the combinations of outcomes for getting a sum of 15 on the uppermost face are:

$(4,5,6), (5,4,6), (6,5,4), (5,6,4), (4,6,5), (6,4,5),$
$(5,5,5), (6,6,3), (6,3,6), (3,6,6)$

$$\Rightarrow n(S) = 10$$

Now, outcomes on which first roll was four are:

$$n(E) = (4,5,6), (4,6,5)$$

$$\Rightarrow n(E) = 2$$

Therefore required probability $P(E)$:

$$P(E) = \frac{n(E)}{n(S)}$$

$$= \frac{2}{10}$$

$$= \frac{1}{5}$$

Hence, the correct option is (C).

88. Given equation is:

$$y = ae^{3x}\cos(x + b)$$

There are two constants a and b so, differentiate two times.

Differentiating with respect to x, we get,

$$\Rightarrow y' = 3ae^{3x}\cos(x + b) - ae^{3x}\sin(x + b)$$

$$\Rightarrow y' = 3y - ae^{3x}\sin(x + b)$$

$$\Rightarrow ae^{3x}\sin(x + b) = 3y - y'$$

Differentiating again with respect to x, we get,

$$\Rightarrow 3ae^{3x}\sin(x + b) + ae^{3x}\cos(x + b) = 3y' - y''$$

$$\Rightarrow 3(3y - y') + y - 3y' - y'' = 0$$

$$\Rightarrow 9y - 3y' + y - 3y' - y'' = 0$$

$$\Rightarrow y'' + 6y' - 10y = 0$$

Hence, the correct option is (C).

89. Given,

$$y = a\sin(\lambda x + a) \dots \text{(i)}$$

Now differentiating both sides equation (i) we get,

$$\Rightarrow \frac{dy}{dx} = \frac{d}{dx}\left(a\sin(\lambda x + a)\right)$$

$$\Rightarrow \frac{dy}{dx} = a \cdot \cos(\lambda x + \alpha) \times \frac{d}{dx}(\lambda x + \alpha)$$

$$\Rightarrow \frac{dy}{dx} = a\lambda\cos(\lambda x + \alpha)$$

Again differentiating both sides we get,

$$\Rightarrow \frac{d^2y}{dx^2} = -a\lambda^2\sin(\lambda x + a)$$

From equation (i) we get,

$$\Rightarrow \frac{d^2y}{dx^4} = -\lambda^2 y$$

$$\therefore \frac{d^2y}{dx^2} + \lambda^2 y = 0$$

Hence, the correct option is (A).

90. Some important Laplace transforms are:

$$L(t^n) = \frac{n!}{s^{n+1}}$$

$$L(t^n) = \frac{n!}{s^{n+1}}$$

$$L(t^n e^{at}) = \frac{n!}{(s-a)^{n+1}}$$

$$L\{\cos\omega t\} = \frac{s}{s^2+\omega^2}$$

$$L\{\sin(\omega t)\} = \frac{\omega}{s^2+\omega^2}$$

Hence, the correct option is (A).

91. Given,

$$f(t) = \begin{cases} \frac{t}{T}, & 0 < t < T \\ 1, & t > T \end{cases}$$

$$L\{f(t)\} = \int_0^T e^{-st}\left(\frac{t}{T}\right) dt + \int_T^\infty e^{-st} dt$$

$$\Rightarrow \frac{1}{T}\int_0^T t\, e^{-st} dt + \int_T^\infty e^{-st} dt$$

$$\Rightarrow \frac{1}{T}\left[t\int e^{-st} dt - \int 1 \cdot \int e^{-st} dt dt\right]_0^T + \int_T^\infty e^{-st} dt$$

$$\Rightarrow \frac{1}{T}\left[\frac{te^{-st}}{-s} - \int \frac{e^{-st}}{-s} dt\right]_0^T + \int_T^\infty e^{-st} dt$$

$$\Rightarrow \frac{1}{T}\left[\frac{te^{-st}}{-s} - \frac{e^{-st}}{s^2}\right]_0^T + \left[\frac{e^{-st}}{-s}\right]_T^\infty$$

$$\Rightarrow \frac{1}{T}\left[\frac{Te^{-sT}}{-s} - \frac{e^{-sT}}{s^2} + \frac{1}{s^2}\right] + \left[0 + \frac{e^{-sT}}{s}\right]$$

$$= \frac{(1-e^{-sT})}{s^2 T}$$

Hence, the correct option is (B).

92. The inverse of a matrix A is defined by the following formula.

$$A^{-1} = \frac{Adj(A)}{|A|}$$

Where, $Adj(A) = [cofactor(A)]^{\mathsf{T}}$

For a 2×2 matrix there is a formula for obtaining the inverse:

$$\Rightarrow \begin{bmatrix} a_{11} & a_{12} \\ a_{21} & a_{22} \end{bmatrix}^{-1} = \frac{1}{a_{11}a_{22}-a_{12}a_{21}}\begin{bmatrix} a_{22} & -a_{12} \\ -a_{21} & a_{11} \end{bmatrix}$$

Given,

$$A = \begin{bmatrix} 3 & 0 \\ 1 & 2 \end{bmatrix}$$

$$\Rightarrow A^{-1} = \frac{1}{6-0}\begin{bmatrix} 2 & 0 \\ -1 & 3 \end{bmatrix}$$

$$= \begin{bmatrix} \frac{1}{3} & 0 \\ -\frac{1}{6} & \frac{1}{2} \end{bmatrix}$$

Hence, the correct option is (A).

93. To find the Eigen values it satisfy the condition,

$$|A - \lambda I| = 0$$

$$|A - \lambda I| = \begin{bmatrix} 2 & 1 & 0 \\ 1 & 2 & 1 \\ 0 & 1 & 2 \end{bmatrix} - \lambda\begin{bmatrix} 1 & 0 & 0 \\ 0 & 1 & 0 \\ 0 & 0 & 1 \end{bmatrix}$$

$$= \begin{bmatrix} 2-\lambda & 1 & 0 \\ 1 & 2-\lambda & 1 \\ 0 & 1 & 2-\lambda \end{bmatrix}$$

$$= (2-\lambda)((2-\lambda)^2 - 1) - 1((2-\lambda) - 0) + 0$$

$$= (2-\lambda)(4 + \lambda^2 - 4\lambda - 1) - 2 + \lambda$$

$$= (2-\lambda)(\lambda^2 - 4\lambda + 3) - 2 + \lambda$$

$$= (-\lambda^3 + 6\lambda^2 - 11\lambda + 6) - 2 + \lambda$$

$$= -\lambda^3 + 6\lambda^2 - 10\lambda + 4$$

$$= -\lambda^3 + 2\lambda^2 + 4\lambda^2 - 8\lambda - 2\lambda + 4$$

$$= -\lambda^2(\lambda - 2) + 4\lambda(\lambda - 2) - 2(\lambda - 2)$$

$$= (\lambda - 2)(-\lambda^2 + 4\lambda - 2) \dots \text{(i)}$$

By using Shri Dronacharya's formula for quadratic equation, we get,

$$x = \frac{-b \pm \sqrt{b^2 - 4ac}}{2a}$$

So,

$$\Rightarrow \lambda = \frac{-4 \pm \sqrt{16 - 4 \times (-1) \times (-2)}}{2 \times (-1)}$$

$$\Rightarrow \lambda = \frac{-4 \pm \sqrt{16 - 8}}{-2}$$

$$\Rightarrow \lambda = 2 \pm \sqrt{2}$$

And from equation (i) we get,

$$\Rightarrow x = 2$$

By solving the above equation, we get,

$$\therefore \lambda = 2 + \sqrt{2}, 2 - \sqrt{2}, 2$$

Hence, the correct option is (A).

94. Given,

$$f(x) = \tan^{-1}\left[\frac{\sin x}{1+\cos x}\right]$$

As we know,

$$\sin x = 2\sin\frac{x}{2}\cos\frac{x}{2}$$

$$\cos x = \cos^2\frac{x}{2} - \sin^2\frac{x}{2}$$

$$\cos^2\frac{x}{2} + \sin^2\frac{x}{2} = 1$$

$$\frac{\sin x}{1+\cos x} = \frac{2\sin\frac{x}{2}\cos\frac{x}{2}}{\left(\cos^2\frac{x}{2}+\sin^2\frac{x}{2}\right)+\left(\cos^2\frac{x}{2}-\sin^2\frac{x}{2}\right)}$$

$$= \frac{2\sin\frac{x}{2}\cos\frac{x}{2}}{2\cos^2\frac{x}{2}}$$

$$= \frac{\sin\frac{x}{2}}{\cos\frac{x}{2}}$$

$$= \tan\frac{x}{2}$$

$$\therefore f(x) = \tan^{-1}\left[\frac{\sin x}{1+\cos x}\right]$$

$$= \tan^{-1}\left(\tan\frac{x}{2}\right) = \frac{x}{2}$$

For first term derivative, we have to put $x = 1$.

The first derivative of $f(x) = \frac{1}{2}$

Hence, the correct option is (A).

95. Given improper integral $\int_0^{\infty} e^{-2t}\, dt$

Applying limit by the value a tends to ∞

$$\int_0^{\infty} e^{-2t}\, dt = \lim_{a \to \infty} \int_0^{a} e^{-2t}\, dt$$

$$\Rightarrow \int_0^{\infty} e^{-2t}\, dt = \lim_{a \to \infty}\left[\frac{e^{-2t}}{-2}\right]_0^{a}$$

$$\Rightarrow \int_0^{\infty} e^{-2t}\, dt = \left[-\frac{1}{2} \times e^{-2\times\infty} + \frac{1}{2} \times e^{-2\times 0}\right]$$

$$\Rightarrow \int_0^{\infty} e^{-2t}\, dt = 0.5$$

$\therefore$ The improper integral $\int_0^{\infty} e^{-2t}\, dt$ converges to 0.5

Hence, the correct option is (C).

96. DNS can obtain the IP address of the host if its domain name is known and vice versa. DNS automatically converts between the names we type in our Web browser address bar to the IP addresses of Web servers hosting.

Hence, the correct option is (B).

97. A local area network is a group of computers and associated devices that share a common communications line or wireless link to a server. A local area network is a computer network that interconnects computers within a limited area such as a residence, school, laboratory, university campus or office building.

Hence, the correct option is (C).

98. VLAN and Subnet are both developed to deal with segmenting or partitioning a portion of the network. And they also share such similarities as restricting broadcast domains or ensuring security through isolation of different sub-networks.

Hence, the correct option is (B).

99. The domain-driven design (DDD) approach enables the development of software that is focused on the complex requirements of those that need it and doesn't waste effort on anything unneeded. The clients of domain-driven design are often enterprise-level businesses.

Hence, the correct option is (C).

100. A WAN is a communications network that spans a large geographic area such as across cities, states, or countries. They can be private to connect parts of a business or they can be more public to connect smaller networks together.

Hence, the correct option is (D).

Q.1 Which of the following sorting algorithms has the minimum running time complexity in the best and average case?

A. Insertion sort, Quicksort
B. Quicksort, Quicksort
C. Quicksort, Insertion sort
D. Insertion sort, Insertion sort

Q.2 Which of the following sorting algorithms is/are stable?

A. Merge Sort
B. Selection Sort
C. Bubble Sort
D. Both (A) and (C)

Q.3 How many comparisons are required to sort an array of length 5 if the straight selection sort is used and the array is already sorted in the opposite order?

A. 1
B. 20
C. 10
D. 5

Q.4 Consider the following undirected, weighted graph:

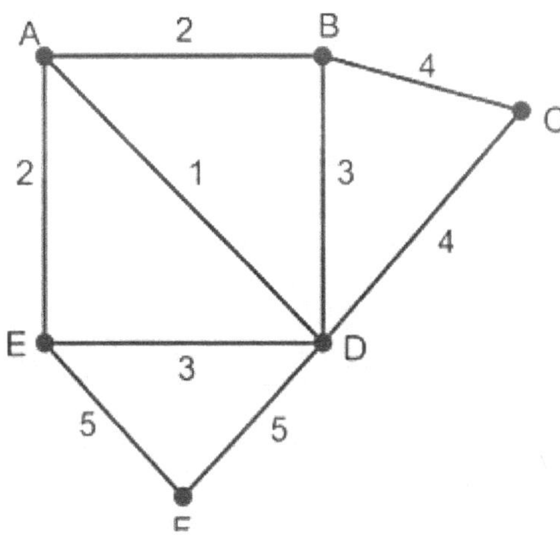

The number of distinct MSTs for the above graph are:

A. 4
B. 8
C. 6
D. 2

Q.5 For parameters a and b, both of which are $\omega(1)$, $T(n) = T\left(n^{\frac{1}{a}}\right) + 1$, and $T(b) = 1$. Then $T(n)$ is:

A. $\theta(\log_a \log_b n)$
B. $\theta(\log_{ab} n)$
C. $\theta(\log_b \log_a n)$
D. $\theta(\log_2 \log_2 n)$

Q.6 Suppose we have a $O(n)$ time algorithm that finds the median of an unsorted array. Now consider a quicksort implementation where we first find the median using the above algorithm, then use the median as a pivot. What will be the worst-case time complexity of this modified quicksort:

A. $O(n^2 \log n)$
B. $O(n^2)$
C. $O(n \log n \log n)$
D. $O(n \log n)$

Q.7 Given an unsorted array. The array has this property that every element in array is at most k distance from its position in sorted array where k is a positive integer smaller than size of array. Which sorting algorithm can be easily modified for sorting this array and what is the obtainable time complexity?

A. Insertion Sort with time complexity $O(kn)$
B. Heap Sort with time complexity $O(n \log k)$
C. Quick Sort with time complexity $O(k \log k)$
D. Merge Sort with time complexity $O(k \log k)$

Q.8 What is time complexity of fun()?

```
int fun(int n)
{
int count = 0;
for (int i = n; i >0; i /= 2)
for (int j = 0; j< i; j++)
count += 1;
return count;
}
```

A. O(n²)
B. O(nLogn)
C. O(n)
D. O(nLognLogn)

Q.9 What is the time complexity of fun()?

```
int fun(int n)
{
int count = 0;
for (int i = 0; i< n; i++)
for (int j = i; j >0; j--)
count = count + 1;
return count;
}
```

A. Theta (n)
B. Theta (n²)
C. Theta (n log n)
D. Theta (n log n log n)

Q.10 Which of the following feature is also known as run-time binding or late binding?

A. Dynamic typing
B. Dynamic loading
C. Dynamic binding
D. Data hiding

Q.11 Which component of MVC architecture deals the database?

A. View
B. Model
C. Controller
D. Storage

Q.12 A Fortran is not _________ language.

A. System supported
B. Source supported
C. Case Sensitive
D. Programmer supported

Q.13 The delimiter in a Fortran code is _______.

A. Semicolon
B. Blank space
C. Colon
D. Comma

Q.14 What error would be following function given on compilation?

```
f (int a, int b)
{
int a;
a = 20;
return a;
}
```

A. Missing parentheses is return statement.
B. Function should be defined as int f(int a, int b).
C. Redeclaration of a.
D. None of these

Q.15 The post-order traversal of a binary tree is OPQRST. Then possible pre-order traversal will be ________.

A. TQRSOP
B. TOQRPS
C. TQOPSR
D. TQOSPR

Q.16 A full binary tree can be generated using ________.

A. Post-order traversal
B. Pre-order traversal
C. Inorder traversal
D. Both (A) and (B)

Q.17 Which one of the following is not the type of the queue?

A. Linear Queue
B. Circular Queue
C. Double-ended Queue
D. Single-ended Queue

Q.18 Which of the following determines the need for the circular queue?

A. Avoid wastage of memory
B. Access the queue using priority
C. Follows the FIFO principle
D. None of these

Q.19 A layer- 4 firewall (a device that can look at all protocol headers up to the transport layer) Cannot:

A. Block entire HTTP traffic during $9{:}00$ PM and $5{:}00$ AM.
B. Block all ICMP traffic.
C. Stop incoming traffic from a specific IP address but allow outgoing traffic to the same IP address.
D. Block TCP traffic from a specific user on a multi-user system during $9{:}00$ PM and $5{:}00$ AM.

Q.20 While transmitting odd-parity coded symbols, the number of zeros in each symbol is:

A. Odd
B. Even
C. Unknown
D. None of these

Q.21 Which of the following transmission systems provides the highest data rate to an individual device?

A. Digital PBX
B. Computer Bus
C. LAN
D. Voiceband modem

Q.22 One important characteristic of LAN is _____.

A. Parallel transmission
B. Low cast access for low bandwidth channel
C. Unlimited expansion
D. Application independent interfaces

Q.23 The Sharing of a medium and its path by two or more devices is called:

A. Modulation
B. Encoding
C. Multiplexing
D. Line discipline

Q.24 Which of the following option is true?

A. TCP/IP Model developed before OSI model.
B. TCP/IP model developed after the OSI model.
C. TCP/IP model developed simaltaneousaly to the Model OSI model.
D. TCP/IP model developed to overcome the shortcomings of OSI Model.

Q.25 What is the use of FTP?

A. To view a file on a remote computer.
B. To identify the name of the domain.
C. To identify the name of the host.
D. To send the file to the network.

Q.26 Which of the following wire-network remains within an office?

A. LAN
B. WAN
C. Cellular network
D. MAN

Q.27 How many TCP connections does FTP use?

A. One
B. Two
C. Three
D. Four

Q.28 The main difference between the VLIW and the other approaches to improve performance is ________.

A. Cost-effectiveness
B. Increase in performance
C. Lack of complex hardware design
D. None of these

Q.29 The processor keeps track of the results of its operations using flags called ________.

A. Conditional code flags
B. Test output flags
C. Type flags
D. None of these

Q.30 The Flag 'V' is set to 1 indicates that __________.

A. The operation is valid.
B. The operation is invalid.
C. The operation has resulted in an overflow.
D. None of these

Q.31 In a normal n-bit adder, to find out if an overflow has occurred we make use of ________.

A. And gate
B. Nand gate
C. Nor gate
D. Xor gate

Q.32 In the implementation of a multiplier circuit in the system we make use of ________.

A. Counter
B. Flip flop
C. Shift register
D. Push down stack

Q.33 Does the load instruction do the following operations?

A. Loads the contents of a disc onto a memory location.

B. Loads the contents of a location onto the register.
C. Load the contents of the PCB onto the register.
D. None of these

Q.34 A RAM chip has a capacity of 1024 words of 8 bits each $(1k \times 8)$. The number of 2×4 decoders with enable line needed to construct a $16k \times 16$ RAM from $1k \times 8$ RAM is:

A. 4   **B.** 5   **C.** 6   **D.** 7

Q.35 During the transfer of data between the processor and memory, we use _______.

A. Cache   **B.** TLB
C. Buffers   **D.** Registers

Q.36 The parallel execution of operations in VLIW is done according to the schedule determined by _______.

A. Task scheduler   **B.** Interpreter
C. Compiler   **D.** Encoder

Q.37 Find out the wrong option:

A. Hadoop processing capabilities are huge and its real advantage lies in the ability to process terabytes and petabytes of data.
B. Hadoop uses a programming model called "MapReduce", all the programs should conform to this model in order to work on the Hadoop platform.
C. The programming model, MapReduce, used by Hadoop is difficult to write and test.
D. All of these

Q.38 Assume that a B tree has been built with data pointers of size 5 bytes and key size 10 bytes and tree pointers of size 6 bytes. The size of each page in the system is 512 bytes. What is the branching factor of the B-tree?

A. 25   **B.** 30   **C.** 35   **D.** 40

Q.39 ZooKeeper is especially fast in _______ workloads.

A. Write   **B.** Read-dominant
C. Read-write   **D.** None of these

Q.40 The language used in application programs to request data from the DBMS is referred to as _______.

A. DML   **B.** DDL   **C.** VDL   **D.** SDL

Q.41 Arrange the following according to the size in ascending order:

A. Record, field, byte, bit
B. Bit, field, byte, record
C. Field, byte, record, bit
D. Bit, byte, field, record

Q.42 Aggregate functions are functions that take a _______ as input and return a single value.

A. Collection of values   **B.** Single value
C. Aggregate value   **D.** None of these

Q.43 What field type is best to store serial numbers?

A. Number   **B.** AutoNumber
C. Text   **D.** Memo

Q.44 What is part of a database that holds only one type of information?

A. Report   **B.** Field   **C.** Record   **D.** File

Q.45 In DBMS, all the data is stored at a _______.

A. Central   **B.** Multiple
C. RDBMS   **D.** None of these

Q.46 Locality of reference implies that the page reference being made by a process:

A. Will always be to the page used in the previous page reference.
B. Is likely to be the one of the pages used in the last few page references.
C. Will always be to one of the pages existing in memory.
D. Will always lead to a page fault.

Q.47 Block caches or buffer caches are used:

A. To improve disk performance.
B. To handle interrupts.
C. To increase the capacity of the main memory.
D. To speed up the main memory read operation.

Q.48 In mass storage devices _______ is process of rearranging/relocating many small non-contiguous blocks of data, into fewer contiguous big-sized blocks.

[HTET PGT - Computer Science, 2019]

A. Defragmentation   **B.** Paging
C. Booting   **D.** Restoring

Q.49 What is a Multiprogramming?

A. Is a method of memory allocation by which the program is subdivided into equal portions, or pages and core is subdivided into equal portions or blocks.
B. Consists of those addresses that may be generated by a processor during execution of a computation.
C. Is a method of allocating processor time.
D. Allows multiple programs to reside in separate areas of the core at the time.

Q.50 What is the advantage of dynamic loading?

A. A used routine is used multiple times
B. An unused routine is never loaded
C. CPU utilization increases
D. None of these

Q.51 The SJF algorithm executes first the job:

A. That last entered the queue
B. That first entered the queue
C. That has been in the queue the longest
D. With the least processor needs

Q.52 The working set theory of programming behavior of processes running within an operating system involves:

A. The collection of pages that a process accesses
B. Disk scheduling mechanisms
C. Coalescing holes in memory
D. Assigning the CPU to processes

Q.53 What is the name of a memory buffer used to accommodate a speed differential?

A. Cache
B. Stack Pointer
C. Accumulator
D. Disc

Q.54 If all processes I/O bound, the ready queue will almost always be _____ and the Short term Scheduler will have a _____ to do.

A. Full, little
B. Full, lot
C. Empty, little
D. Empty, lot

Q.55 A language can be generated from simple primitive language in a simple way if and only if:

A. It is recognized by a device of infinite states
B. It takes no auxiliary memory
C. Both (A) and (B)
D. None of these

Q.56 Which of the following does not represents the given language?

Language: $\{0,01\}$

A. $0 + 01$
B. $\{0\} \cup \{01\}$
C. $\{0\} \cup \{0\}\{1\}$
D. $\{0\}^\wedge\{01\}$

Q.57 According to the given language, which among the following expressions does it corresponds to?

Language $L = \{X \in \{0,1\} \mid X$ is of length 4 or less $\}$

A. $(0 + 1 + 0 + 1 + 0 + 1 + 0 + 1)^4$
B. $(0 + 1)^4$
C. $(01)^4$
D. $(0 + 1 + \varepsilon)^4$

Q.58 If R represents a regular language, which of the following represents the Venn-diagram most correctly?

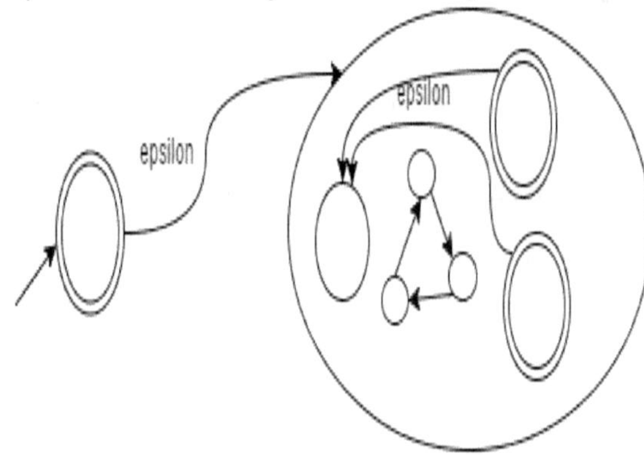

A. An Irregular Set
B. R*
C. R complement
D. R reverse

Q.59 The given NFA corresponds to which of the following Regular expressions:

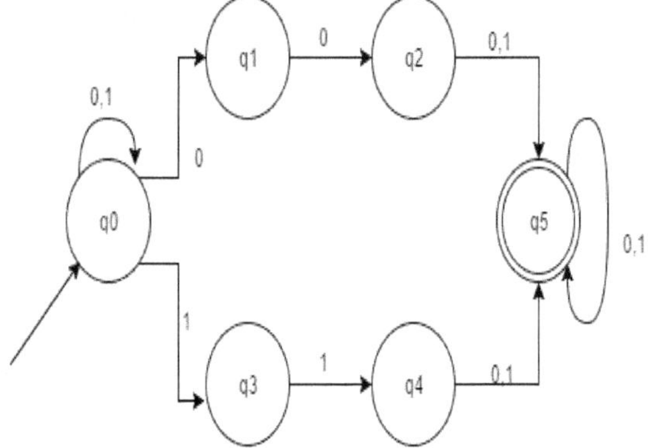

A. $(0 + 1)^*(00 + 11)(0 + 1)^*$
B. $(0 + 1)^*(00 + 11)^*(0 + 1)^*$
C. $(0 + 1) * (00 + 11)(0 + 1)$
D. $(0 + 1)(00 + 11)(0 + 1)^*$

Q.60 NFA is an abbreviation of _____.

A. Non Deterministic Finite set Automata
B. Non Finite set Automata
C. Non Deterministic Finite Automata
D. Non Finite Automata

Q.61 Which of the following parser is a top-down parser?

A. LALR parser
B. LR parser
C. Operator precedence parser
D. Recursive descent parser

Q.62 A series of statements explaining how the data is to be processed is called _____.

A. Assembly
B. Machine
C. COBOL
D. Program

Q.63 Which graph describes the basic block and successor relationship?

A. Control graph
B. DAG
C. Flow graph
D. Hamilton graph

Q.64 The document listing all procedures and regulations that generally govern an organization is the:

A. Procedures log
B. Organization manual
C. Personal policy book
D. Administrative policy manual

Q.65 What is developed by utilizing the historical cost function?

A. Parkinson's Law
B. Expert judgment
C. Algorithmic cost modeling
D. Estimation by analogy

Q.66 Which of the following is used to predict the effort as a function of LOC or FP?

A. COCOMO
B. FP-based estimation
C. Process-based estimation

D. Both (A) and (B)

Q.67 Which is a software configuration management concept that helps us to control change without seriously impeding justifiable change?

A. Baselines   **B.** Source code
C. Data model   **D.** None of these

Q.68 Which of the following is an incorrect activity for the configuration management of a software system?

A. Change management
B. System management
C. Internship management
D. Version management

Q.69 Which of the following interface design principles reduces the user's memory load?

A. Define intuitive shortcuts
B. Disclose information in a progressive fashion
C. Establish meaningful defaults
D. All of these

Q.70 Verification has a __________ activities.

A. Dynamic   **B.** Subjective
C. Static   **D.** Objective

Q.71 Which of the following is most abstract development artifact that can be reused?

A. Requirement specification
B. Design
C. Code
D. Knowledge

Q.72 What is the main intent of project metrics?

A. For strategic purposes.
B. To minimize the development schedule.
C. To evaluate the ongoing project's quality on a daily basis.
D. To minimize the development schedule and evaluate the ongoing project's quality on a daily basis.

Q.73 A problem is given to three persons and their chances of solving it are $\frac{1}{3}, \frac{1}{4}, \frac{1}{5}$ respectively. This probability that none will solve it is:

A. $\frac{1}{3} \times \frac{1}{4} \times \frac{1}{5}$ **B.** $\frac{2}{3} \times \frac{3}{4} \times \frac{4}{5}$
C. $1 - \frac{2}{3} \times \frac{3}{4} \times \frac{4}{5}$ **D.** $\frac{1}{3} + \frac{1}{4} + \frac{1}{5}$

Q.74 In a box, 4 coins of ten rupees, 2 coins of five rupees, 2 coins of two rupees and 2 coins of one rupee are put. Now, three coins are taken out randomly. What is the probability that the amount drawn is 12 rupees?

A. $\frac{1}{5}$ **B.** $\frac{1}{6}$ **C.** $\frac{6}{16}$ **D.** $\frac{1}{20}$

Q.75 Find the value of $y\left(\frac{1}{2}\right)$ for the differential equation $dy = x\sec\frac{y}{x}dx + \frac{y}{x}dx$ with initial condition $y(1) = \frac{\pi}{2}$?

A. $\frac{\pi}{12}$ **B.** $\frac{\pi}{6}$ **C.** 0 **D.** $\frac{\pi}{2}$

Q.76 The solution of the differential equation $\frac{dy}{dx} = \sec\left(\frac{y}{x}\right) + \frac{y}{x}$ is:

A. $\cos\left(\frac{y}{x}\right) = \log(cx)$ **B.** $\sin\left(\frac{x}{y}\right) = \log(cx)$
C. $\sin\left(\frac{y}{x}\right) = \log(cx)$ **D.** None of these

Q.77 The solution of the differential equation $f(t) + f''(t) = 0$ with initial conditions $f'(0) = 1$ and $f(0) = 1$, for $t \geq 0$ is:

A. $-\cos t + \sin t$ **B.** $\cos t - \sin t$
C. $-\cos t - \sin t$ **D.** $\cos t + \sin t$

Q.78 If the Laplace transform of $f(t)$ which is given below is $F(s) = \frac{a - 5e^{-2s} + be^{-c8}}{'}$, then the value of $a + b + c$ is:

$$f(t) = \begin{cases} 2 & ; & 0 < t < 2 \\ -3 & ; & 2 < t < 5 \\ 4 & ; & t > 5 \end{cases}$$

A. 12 **B.** $\frac{3}{4}$ **C.** 14 **D.** 10

Q.79 Find the value of determinant:

$$\begin{vmatrix} 1 & a & b+c \\ 1 & b & c+a \\ 1 & c & a+b \end{vmatrix}$$

A. 0 **B.** 1
C. $a+b+c$ **D.** 2

Q.80 For the matrix $A = \begin{bmatrix} 1 & 4 \\ 2 & 3 \end{bmatrix}$ the expression $A^5 - 4A^4 - 7A^3 + 11A^2 - A - 10I$ is equivalent to:

A. $A^2 + A + 5I$ **B.** $A + 5I$
C. $A^2 + 5I$ **D.** $A^2 + 2A + 6I$

Q.81 Find the value of $\frac{d}{dx}\left(\frac{x^2+x-2}{x^3+6}\right)$:

A. $\frac{-2x^3+6x^2+12x+6}{(x^3+6)^2}$ **B.** $\frac{x^4-2x^3+6x^2+12x+6}{(x^3+6)^2}$
C. $\frac{-x^4-2x^3+6x^2+12x+6}{(x^3+6)^2}$ **D.** $2e^2$

Q.82 The value of $\int_0^\pi \sin^6 x \cdot \cos^5 x \, dx$ is:

A. 0 **B.** -1 **C.** 1 **D.** 2

Q.83 Consider a 4-bit Johnson counter with an initial value of 1000. The counting sequence of this counter is/are:

Note: MSB and LSB are not fixed for initial value.

I. $8,12,14,7,15,3,1,0,8$

II. $8,0,1,3,7,15,14,12,8$

III. $8,10,12,14,0,2,4,6,8$

IV. $8,12,14,15,7,3,1,0,8$

A. Only I and II   **B.** Only I and IV
C. Only II and III   **D.** Only II and IV

Q.84 A 4-bit, serial-in, parallel-out right shift, shift register is loaded with an initial bit pattern $b_3 b_2 b_1 b_0 = 1100$. The clock is applied to the shift register and bits b_0 and b_1 are connected to the serial input through an EXOR gate. After how many clock cycles will the initial pattern 1100 return:

A. 12   **B.** 13   **C.** 15   **D.** 18

Q.85 Consider the following sequential circuit:

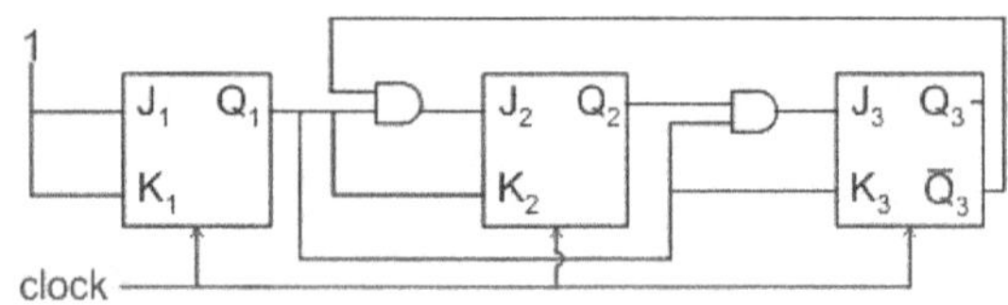

Assume initially $Q_1 Q_2 Q_3 = 000$, which of the following statement is correct about this circuit?

A. $Q_1 Q_2 Q_3$ after 4 clock pulse $= 001$
B.   It is a mod - 5 counter
C.   It is a mod - 6 counter
D. $Q_1 Q_2 Q_3$ after 4 clock pulse $= 101$

Q.86 A J-K flip-flop has $t_{pd} = 15\ ns$, the largest MOD counter that can be constructed from cascading these FF_s and still operating upto $10MHz$ is:

A. 64   **B.** 46   **C.** 68   **D.** 70

Q.87 If $(1235)_x = (3033)_y$, where x and y indicate the bases of the corresponding numbers, then:

A. $x = 9$ and $y = 7$ **B.** $x = 8$ and $y = 6$
C. $x = 7$ and $y = 5$ **D.** $x = 6$ and $y = 4$

Q.88 Consider an signed number system in which an integer $N = A_7 A_6 A_5 A_4 A_3 A_2 A_1$ is transformed as $M = A_7\ A_6\ A_5\ A_4\ A_3\ A_2\ A_1 1$.
Which of the following is/are true?

A. $M = 2N$ **B.** $M = 2^*N + 1$
C. M might overflow   **D.** Both (B) and (C)

Q.89 Consider the following equation:

$$(x^2 - 10x + 31)_r = [(x - 5)(x - 8)]_{10}$$

What should be the value of 'r' to satisfy the given equation?

A. 13   **B.** 14   **C.** 16   **D.** 18

Q.90 Consider the following IEEE- 754 single precision number:

1	10101010	01010100........0

Value represented by above number is ______________.

A. -170×2^{36} **B.** -170×2^{43}
C. -126×2^{170} **D.** -85×2^{36}

Q.91 An 8085 microprocessor executes the following instructions:

Two numbers are represented in signed 2's complement form as:

$$P = 11101101 \text{ and } Q = 11100110$$

If Q is subtracted from P, the value obtained in signed 2's complement form is:

A. 100000111   **B.** 00000111
C. 11111001   **D.** 011111001

Q.92 Consider the following expression:

I. A ∧ B

II. A ∨ B

III. ¬ (A ∨ B)

IV. TRUE

V. FALSE

The expressions given above are logically implied by (A ∧ B) ∧ (¬ A → B) is:

A. I, II and IV   **B.** I and III
C. III, II and IV   **D.** III, V and IV

Q.93 Let S denote the set of all functions $f : \{0,1\}^4 \to \{0,1\}$. Denote by N the number of functions from S to the set $\{0,1\}$. The value of $\log_2 \log_2 N$ is ________.

A. 16   **B.** 18   **C.** 20   **D.** 22

Q.94 Which of the following is/are correct regarding lattice?

A. $[\{1,2,3,6,9,18\}]$ is a bounded lattice.
B. $[I, \le]$ is not a bounded lattice, where I is the set of integers.
C. $[[0,1], \le]$ is bounded lattice.
D.   All of these

Q.95 Consider n-dimensional cube and its complement graph represented by ' G ' and ' H ' respectively. $y \times 2^{10}$ edges are present in graph ' H ' if ' n ' is equal to 11. Find the value of y ?

A. 2036   **B.** 2022   **C.** 2018   **D.** 2000

Q.96 Let G be a complete undirected graph on 8 vertices. If vertices of G are labelled the number of distinct cycles of length 5 in G is equal to ______.

A. 672   **B.** 670   **C.** 671   **D.** 665

Q.97 Determine the solution for the recurrence relation $a_n = 6a_{n-1} - 8a_{n-2}$ provided initial conditions $a_0 = 3$ and $a_1 = 5$:

A. $a_n = 4 \times 2^n - 3^n$
B. $a_n = 3 \times 7^n - 5 \times 3^n$
C. $a_n = 5 \times 7^n$
D. $a_n = 3! \times 5^n$

Q.98 The number of words of 4 consonants and 3 vowels can be made from 15 consonants and 5 vowels, if all the letters are different is ________.

A. $3! \times {}^{12}C_5$ **B.** ${}^{16}C_4 \times {}^4C_4$
C. $15! \times 4$ **D.** ${}^{15}C_4 \times {}^5C_3 \times 7!$

Q.99 Let a set $S = \{2,4,8,16,32\}$ and $\le$ be the partial order defined by $S \le R$ if a divides b. Number of edges in the Hasse diagram is ________.

A. 6 **B.** 5 **C.** 8 **D.** 4

Q.100 By induction hypothesis, the series $1^2 + 2^2 + 3^2 + \cdots + p^2$ can be proved equivalent to _________.

A. $\dfrac{p^2+2}{7}$

B. $\dfrac{p \times (p+1) \times (2p+1)}{6}$

C. $\dfrac{p \times (p+1)}{4}$

D. $p + p^2$

// Smart Answer Sheet //

Correct — Percentage of students who answered correctly. **Skipped** — Percentage of students who skipped.

Q.	Ans.	Correct / Skipped	Q.	Ans.	Correct / Skipped	Q.	Ans.	Correct / Skipped	Q.	Ans.	Correct / Skipped	Q.	Ans.	Correct / Skipped	Q.	Ans.	Correct / Skipped
1	A	41.23 % / 42.4 %	18	A	84.41 % / 12.32 %	35	D	57.18 % / 33.99 %	52	A	57.53 % / 40.31 %	69	D	13.62 % / 71.32 %	86	A	14.39 % / 71.61 %
2	D	89.87 % / 10.12 %	19	D	55.38 % / 30.83 %	36	C	51.46 % / 38.28 %	53	A	85.72 % / 12.35 %	70	C	79.75 % / 16.31 %	87	B	52.74 % / 33.36 %
3	C	60.8 % / 33.49 %	20	C	56.43 % / 38.19 %	37	C	21.48 % / 76.37 %	54	C	17.02 % / 81.88 %	71	D	52.69 % / 33.6 %	88	D	80.55 % / 19.32 %
4	A	41.33 % / 48.1 %	21	B	77.37 % / 17.96 %	38	A	54.11 % / 33.79 %	55	B	47.49 % / 45.81 %	72	D	65.85 % / 32.86 %	89	A	48.93 % / 38.74 %
5	A	67.3 % / 31.3 %	22	D	80.25 % / 14.82 %	39	B	43.46 % / 44.92 %	56	D	57.71 % / 38.8 %	73	B	58.93 % / 34.1 %	90	A	82.01 % / 14.27 %
6	D	83.86 % / 16.02 %	23	C	56.74 % / 35.62 %	40	A	67.97 % / 31.38 %	57	D	53.0 % / 35.55 %	74	D	12.43 % / 69.22 %	91	B	61.66 % / 37.61 %
7	B	69.42 % / 30.34 %	24	A	51.68 % / 32.42 %	41	D	83.18 % / 10.58 %	58	B	26.55 % / 70.76 %	75	A	48.96 % / 40.07 %	92	A	52.04 % / 32.41 %
8	C	62.75 % / 33.23 %	25	D	86.44 % / 11.36 %	42	A	50.04 % / 34.81 %	59	A	20.06 % / 77.08 %	76	C	27.57 % / 67.15 %	93	A	47.31 % / 30.89 %
9	B	54.56 % / 42.26 %	26	A	49.23 % / 49.41 %	43	B	49.53 % / 44.32 %	60	C	82.33 % / 14.45 %	77	D	63.33 % / 31.79 %	94	D	54.41 % / 42.81 %
10	C	50.19 % / 46.68 %	27	B	52.71 % / 30.85 %	44	B	88.76 % / 10.26 %	61	D	68.71 % / 30.89 %	78	C	10.78 % / 73.15 %	95	A	29.07 % / 69.64 %
11	B	65.82 % / 33.25 %	28	C	56.33 % / 35.26 %	45	A	69.62 % / 30.01 %	62	D	42.32 % / 38.11 %	79	A	69.3 % / 30.06 %	96	A	84.56 % / 11.27 %
12	C	81.08 % / 16.93 %	29	A	43.45 % / 56.32 %	46	B	53.3 % / 35.51 %	63	C	80.93 % / 17.64 %	80	B	13.91 % / 71.37 %	97	B	55.24 % / 35.89 %
13	B	89.02 % / 10.83 %	30	C	15.95 % / 72.25 %	47	A	40.98 % / 55.51 %	64	B	46.63 % / 46.77 %	81	C	47.67 % / 38.63 %	98	D	77.68 % / 21.26 %
14	C	64.41 % / 35.37 %	31	D	30.47 % / 68.93 %	48	A	47.56 % / 39.8 %	65	C	20.6 % / 67.22 %	82	A	89.11 % / 10.67 %	99	D	57.87 % / 40.93 %
15	C	66.29 % / 33.6 %	32	C	83.02 % / 10.13 %	49	D	58.8 % / 40.07 %	66	D	44.22 % / 40.39 %	83	D	53.22 % / 37.7 %	100	B	44.68 % / 40.13 %
16	D	61.45 % / 31.34 %	33	B	41.89 % / 55.47 %	50	B	45.23 % / 40.01 %	67	A	67.36 % / 32.32 %	84	C	42.21 % / 32.11 %			
17	D	23.42 % / 67.48 %	34	B	24.72 % / 68.57 %	51	D	46.02 % / 42.15 %	68	C	69.11 % / 30.82 %	85	A	68.62 % / 31.27 %			

//Hints and Solutions//

1. Quicksort: Quicksort is an efficient sorting algorithm. It is also called partition-exchange sort which follows the divide and conquers technique. In quicksort, worst case, the first or the last element is selected at the pivot element.

For a quicksort, in worst case recurrence relation will become

$$T(n) = T(n-1) + T(1) + n$$

Recurrence relation gives: $T(n) = O(n^2)$. So, option (B) is correct.

Therefore, the worst-case time complexity of the quicksort is $O(n^2)$.

Insertion sort: In Insertion sort, the worst-case takes $\Theta(n^2)$ time, the worst case of insertion sort is when elements are sorted in reverse order. In that case the number of comparisons will be like:

$$\sum_{p=1}^{n-1} p = 1 + 2 + 3 + \cdots + n - 1 = \frac{n(n-1)}{2} - 1$$

This will give $\Theta(n^2)$ time complexity.

The best-case complexity for insertion sort will be $O(n)$, and for quicksort will be $O(n \log n)$, so insertion sort has minimum best case time complexity.

The average time complexity for insertion sort is $O(n^2)$, and for quicksort is $O(n\log n)$, so quicksort has the minimum average-case time complexity.

Hence, the correct option is (A).

2. The stable property of the sorting algorithm is that a stable sort is one that conserves the original order of the input set.

Stable sorting algorithms:

1. Insertion sort
2. Merge sort
3. Bubble sort etc

Sorted the value:

Unsorted List: (value, key)

7,3	2,4	2,1	5,2	4,7	1,6	1,5

Stable Array:

1,6	1,5	2,4	2,1	4,7	5,2	7,3

Unstable Array:

1,5	1,6	2,1	2,4	4,7	5,2	7,3

The selection sort is not stable.
Hence, the correct option is (D).

3. In the selection sorting algorithm, none of the loops depend on the data in the array. Using selection sort first select the lowest element to require scanning through all elements (it takes $n-1$ comparisons) and then swap with the first position and finding the next lowest element requires scanning the remaining $n-1$ elements and so on,

$$(n-1) + (n-2) + (n-3) + \ldots\ldots\ldots + 2 + 1 = \frac{n(n-1)}{2}$$

comparisons.

Pseudo code of selection sort:

for(i=0;i<n-1;i++)
{min_idx=i;for(j=i+i; j<n; j++){f(a[j] < a[min_idx])
//comparisonmin_idx=j;}swap(a[i],a[min_idx]); // only 1 swap each iteration for a total of n-1 iterations

}

Given, $n = 5$

So, total comparison required $= \frac{5 \times 4}{2} = 10$

Hence, the correct option is (C).

4. A Minimum Spanning Tree (MST) is a subset of edges of a connected weighted undirected graph that connects all the vertices together with the minimum possible total edge weight.

According to the question, if you observe carefully, there is only one way to choose edge weights $1, 2, 2$.

But for selecting edge weights 4 and 5, there are 2 possibilities for each.

So, the total number of MSTs possible is $2 \times 2 = 4$.

Hence, the correct option is (A).

5. Recurrence relation:

$$\Rightarrow T(n) = T\left(n^{\frac{1}{a}}\right) + 1, T(b) = 1$$

Where ' a' and ' b' are parameters of order $\omega(1)$.

Using substitution method to solve recurrences,

$$T(n) = T\left(n^{\frac{1}{a}}\right) + 1$$

$$= T\left(\left(n^{\frac{1}{a^2}}\right) + 1\right) + 1$$

$$= T\left(n^{\frac{1}{a^2}}\right) + 2$$

$$= \left(T\left(n^{\frac{1}{n^3}}\right) + 1\right) + 2$$

$$= T\left(n^{\frac{1}{a^3}}\right) + 3$$

Continuing this for ' m' iterations, we get,

$$T(n) = T\left(n^{\frac{1}{a^m}}\right) + m$$

Put $\left(n^{\frac{1}{a^m}}\right) = b$

Taking log on both sides,

$$\Rightarrow \frac{1}{a^m}\log n = \log b$$

$$\Rightarrow a^m = \frac{\log n}{\log b}$$

$$\Rightarrow m = \log_a \log_b n$$

Now,

$$\Rightarrow T(n) = T\left(n^{\frac{1}{a^m}}\right) + m$$

$$\Rightarrow T(n) = b + \log_a \log_b n$$

So, the asymptotic order of $T(n)$ is $\Theta(\log_a \log_b n)$.

Hence, the correct option is (A).

6. If we use median as a pivot element, then for each iteration it takes $O(n)$ time to find median from given function and every time the array partitions in 2 subparts.

So, the recurrence equation becomes:

$$T(n) = 2T\left(\frac{n}{2}\right) + O(n)$$

The above recurrence can be solved using the "Master Method". It falls in case 2 of the master method.

The results in complexity is $O\,(n \log n)$.

Hence, the correct option is (D).

7. Steps to sort the array:

1. Firstly create a min-heap with first $k+1$ elements and a separate array as a resultant array.

2. Because elements are at most k distance apart from an original position, it is guaranteed that the smallest element will be in this $k+1$ elements.

3. Remove the smallest element from the min-heap (extract min) and put it in the result array.

4. Now, insert another element from the unsorted array into the mean-heap, now, the second smallest element will be in this, perform extract min and continue this process until no more elements are in the unsorted array.

5. Finally, use simple heap sort for the remaining element's time complexity.

Now, we have

- $O(k)$ to build the initial min-heap.
- $O(n-k)(\log k)$ for remaining elements.
- $O(1)$ for extract min so overall $O(k) + O\big((n-k)\log k\big) + O(1) = O(n \log k)$.

Hence, the correct option is (B).

8. For a input integer n, the innermost statement of fun() is executed following times n + n/2 + n/4 + ... 1. So, time complexity T(n) can be written as:

T(n) = O(n + n/2 + n/4 + ... 1) = O(n)

The value of count is also n + n/2 + n/4 + .. + 1.

Hence, the correct option is (C).

9. The time complexity can be calculated by counting number of times the expression "count = count + 1;" is executed. The expression is executed 0 + 1 + 2 + 3 + 4 + ... + (n-1) times. Time complexity = Theta (0 + 1 + 2 + 3 + .. + n-1) = Theta (n*(n-1)/2) = Theta (n²).

Hence, the correct option is (B).

10. Dynamic binding or run-time binding or late binding is that type of binding which happens at the execution time of the program or code. Function or method overriding is the perfect example of this type of binding. Virtual functions are used to achieve the concept of function overriding.

Hence, the correct option is (C).

11. Model–view–controller (MVC) is a software design pattern commonly used for developing user interfaces that divide the related program logic into three interconnected elements Model, View and Controller. But the Model element is deal with the database. Model is the central component of the architecture. It is the application's dynamic data structure, independent of the user interface. It directly manages the data, logic and rules of the application.

Hence, the correct option is (B).

12. Fortran is not a case sensitive language. For e.g. Program xyz also works. Also multiple consecutive blank spaces are ignored. Fortran is a general-purpose, compiled imperative programming language that is especially suited to numeric computation and scientific computing. It is a popular language for high-performance computing and is used for programs that benchmark and rank the world's fastest supercomputers.

Hence, the correct option is (C).

13. The delimiter in a Fortran code is blank space. Delimiter separates the tokens we use in our code. In a Fortran code, single blank space serves as a delimiter. Though, multiple blank spaces are ignored. In computer programming, a delimiter is a character that identifies the beginning or the end of a character string (a contiguous sequence of characters). Delimiters can also be used to separate the data items in a database (the columns in the database table) when transporting the database to another application.

Hence, the correct option is (B).

14. Given,

f (int a, int b)

{

int a;

a = 20;

return a;

}

Option (A): Missing parentheses in the return statement.

This would not cause an error since parentheses in the return statement is not mandatory.

Option (B): Function should be defined as int f(int a, int b).

This would not cause an error since the function is returning int only because it will have the default return type assigned as int.

Option (C): Redeclaration of a.

This would cause an error since variable a has been already declared in the argument list of the function so declaring again will cause a syntax error.

Hence, the correct option is (C).

15. Given, the post order traversal of a binary tree is OPQRST. The method is used in post-order traversing is- Left, Right, Root.

So, the binary tree is:

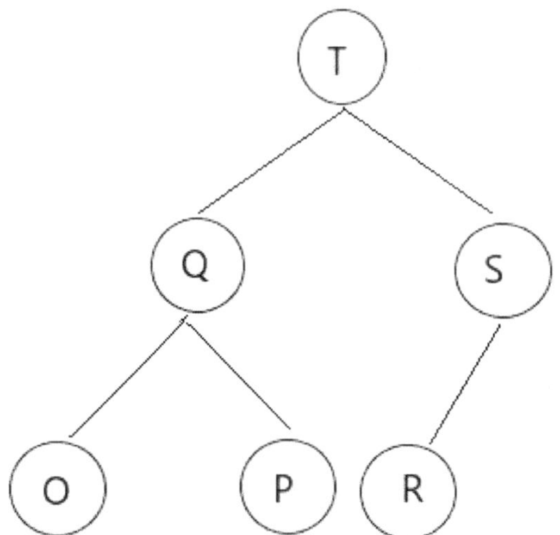

Now, the pre-order traversal,

Method- Root, Left, Right.

So, traversal is TQOPSR.

Hence, the correct option is (C).

16. Every node in a full binary tree has either 0 or 2 children. A binary tree can be generated by two traversals if one of them is inorder traversal. But, we can generate a full binary tree using post-order and pre-order traversals.

Hence, the correct option is (D).

17. A single-ended queue is not a type of queue. A queue has two ends in which one end is used for the insertion and another end is used for the deletion. Therefore, it is not possible for the Queue to have a single-ended queue.

The type of queue:

- Linear Queue

- Input restricted Queue

- Double-ended Queue

- Circular Queue

- Output-restricted Queue

- Priority Queue

Hence, the correct option is (D).

18. In a linear queue, there are chances of wastage of memory because if the rear is pointing to the last element whereas the front is pointing to the element other than the first element; it means that spaces allocated before the front are free, but it cannot be reused as rear cannot be incremented. In contrast, the last element is connected to the first element in a circular queue; if initial spaces are vacant, then the rear can be incremented by using the statement (rear $+1$) mod max where max is the size of the array. Therefore, we conclude that the circular queue avoids wastage of memory.

Hence, the correct option is (A).

19. Since it is Layer- 4 Firewall so it includes the layers $\rightarrow$ Physical Llayer, Data link layer, Network layer as well as Transport laye.r

Allow $\rightarrow$ Transport layer or those layers who comes below transport layer.

Not Allow $\rightarrow$ Application layer.

Option (A): Transport layer specific.

It is possible to block entire traffic by blocking all the traffic on port number 80.

So, here don't need to check anything that it is application layer specific or not. we only need to block port number 80 for the required time interval.

Option (B): Network layer specific.

ICMP is a network layer protocol that comes below the transport layer.

Option (C): Network layer specific.

IP addresses are used in the network layer, which below the transport layer.

Option (D): Application layer specific.

In this option given that it is a multi-user system, so many users use the same port for communication because of this we can't block any specific port number. if we block a specific port number, all the users also blocked who is using that port number for communication. while we want to block a specific user, so how to do this. We need application layer-specific information of the user like userid type of things that can't be checked as it is a 4-layer firewall. so it is not possible to allow other users and block some specific at the same time using a 4-layer firewall.

Hence, the correct option is (D).

20. The parity bit ensures that the total number of 1-bits in the string is even or odd. Accordingly, there are two variants of parity bits: even parity bit and odd parity bit. If that count is odd, the parity bit value is set to 1, making the total count of occurrences of 1s in the whole set (including the parity bit) an even number. In the case of odd parity, the coding is reversed. For a given set of bits, if the count of bits with a value of 1 is even, the parity bit value is set to 1 making the total count of 1s in the whole set (including the parity bit) an odd number. If the count of bits with a value of 1 is odd, the count is already odd so the parity bit's value is 0.

Hence, the correct option is (C).

21. Computer Bus provides the highest data rate to an individual device. The Computer Bus is a communication link used in a computer system to send the data, addresses, control signals, and power to various components in a computer system. The computer buses are used to connect the various hardware components that are part of the computer system.

Hence, the correct option is (B).

22. An application independent interface is one of the main characteristics of LAN. GUI is an example of an application independent interface. It acts as an intermediary between internal software functions and external ones, creating an exchange of information so, seamless that it often goes unnoticed by the end-user. LAN is used for the school environments, offices, hospitals, etc. as it allows sharing of resources like sharing data, scanners, printing and the internet. LAN serves users at home to access the internet.

Hence, the correct option is (D).

23. Multiplexing is a method by which multiple analog or digital signals are combined into one signal over a shared medium. The multiplexed signal is transmitted over a communication channel such as a cable. Multiplexing divides the capacity of the communication channel into several logical changes.

Hence, the correct option is (C).

24. The TCP/IP model, which is realistically the Internet Model, came into existence about 10 years before the OSI model. The four-layer Internet model defines the Internet protocol suite, better known as the TCP/IP suite.

Hence, the correct option is (A).

25. FTP stands for File transfer protocol. FTP is a standard internet protocol provided by TCP/IP used for transmitting the files from one host to another. It is mainly used for transferring the web page files from their creator to the computer that acts as a server for other computers on the internet. The use of FTP is to send the file to the network. FTP is used to transfer files between computers on a network. FTP is to exchange files between computer accounts, transfer files between an account and a desktop computer, or access online software archives.

Hence, the correct option is (D).

26. Local Area Network (LAN) might connect together devices over a distance measured in tens of metres. At office or school, the LAN might connect devices over hundreds of metres. A Wide Area Network operates over a much larger area, as they interconnect LAN to allow them to exchange data

Hence, the correct option is (A).

27. FTP uses two TCP connections for communication. One to pass control information and is not used to send files on port 21, only control information. And the other, a data connection on port 20 to send the data files between the client and the server.

Hence, the correct option is (B).

28. The main difference between the VLIW and the other approaches to improve performance is the lack of complex hardware design. The pipe-lining and super-scalar architectures involved the usage of complex hardware circuits for the implementation. In VLIW the decision for the order of execution of the instructions depends on the program itself. VLIW is used for static scheduling. Superscalar is used for dynamic scheduling.

Hence, the correct option is (C).

29. The processor keeps track of the results of its operations using flags called conditional code flags. These flags are used to indicate if there is an overflow or carry or zero result occurrence. Condition codes are extra bits kept by a processor that summarize the results of an operation and that affect the execution of later instructions. These bits are often collected together in a single condition or indicator register (CR/IR) or grouped with other status bits into a status register (PSW/PSR).

Hence, the correct option is (A).

30. The Flag 'V' is set to 1 indicates the overflow that occurs in the operation. In computer processors, the overflow flag (sometimes called the V flag) is usually a single bit in a system status register used to indicate when an arithmetic overflow has occurred in an operation, indicating that the signed two's-complement result would not fit in the number of bits used for the result. Some architectures may be configured to automatically generate an exception on an operation resulting in overflow.

Hence, the correct option is (C).

31. So, overflow can be detected by checking the Most Significant Bit(MSB) of two operands and answers. But Instead of using 3-bit Comparator Overflow can also be detected using 2 Bit Comparator just by checking Carry-in(C-in) and Carry-Out(C-out) from MSBs. Consider N-Bit Addition of 2's Complement number.

MSB

$$\begin{array}{l} \text{C-in} \\ A_{n-1} \quad A_{n-2} \quad A_{n-3} \quad A_{n-4} \quad A_{n-5} \quad A \ldots \ldots A_0 \\ \qquad B_{n-1} \quad B_{n-2} \quad B_{n-3} \quad B_{n-4} \quad B_{n-5} \quad B \ldots \\ \ldots B_0 \\ \hline S_{n-1} \quad S_{n-2} \quad S_{n-3} \quad S_{n-4} \quad S_{n-5} \quad S \ldots \ldots S_0 \end{array}$$

C-out

Overflow Occurs when C-in is not equal to C-out. The above expression for overflow can be explained from the below Analysis.

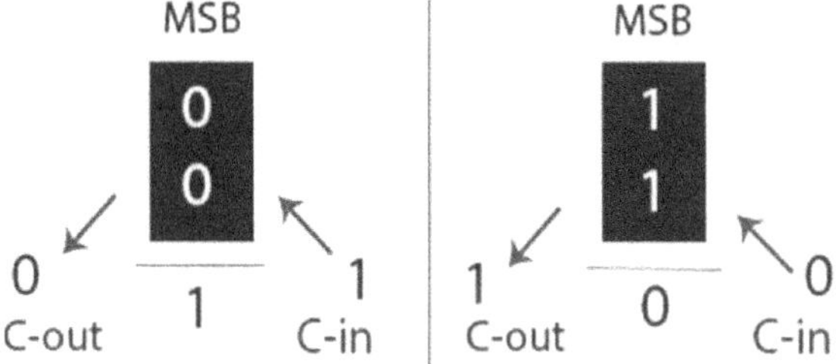

In the first Figure, the MSB of the two numbers is 0 which means they are positive. Here if C-in is 1 we get the answer's MSB as 1 means the answer is negative (Overflow) and C-out as 0. C-in is not equal to C-out So, overflow.

In the second Figure, the MSB of two numbers is 1 which means they are negative. Here if C-in is 0 we get the answer MSB as 0 means the answer is positive(Overflow) and C-out as 1. C-in is not equal to C-out. So, overflow.

Readers can also try out other combinations of C-in C-out and MSBs to check overflow.

So, Carry-in and Carry-out at MSBs are enough to detect overflow.

Above XOR Gate can be used to detect overflow.

Hence, the correct option is (D).

32. In the implementation of a multiplier circuit in the system we make use of a shift register. The shift registers are used to store the multiplied answer. A shift register is a group of flip flops used to store multiple bits of data. The bits stored in such registers can be made to move within the registers and in/out of the registers by applying clock pulses. An n-bit shift register can be formed by connecting n flip flops where each flip flop stores a single bit of data.

Hence, the correct option is (C).

33. The load instruction is basically used to load the contents of a memory location onto a register. Load instructions move data from memory into a register. The address for the load is the sum of a register specified in the instruction and a constant value that is coded into the instruction. LOAD is used to load data from memory to the accumulator. STORE is used to store the accumulator result in memory.

Hence, the correct option is (B).

34. Given,

RAM chip size $= 1k \times 8 [1024$ words of 8 bits each]

RAM to construct $= 16k \times 16$

Now,

Number of chips required $= \dfrac{(16k \times 16)}{(1k \times 8)} = (16 \times 2)$

[16 chips vertically with each having 2 chips horizontally]

So, to select one chip out of 16 vertical chips, we need 4×16 decoder.

Available decoder is 2×4 decoder.

To be constructed is 4×16 decoder.

So, $4 + 1 = 5$ decoders are required to construct a $16k \times 16$ RAM from $1k \times 8$ RAM.

Hence, the correct option is (B).

35. During the transfer of data between the processor and memory, we use registers. Registers are a type of computer memory used to quickly accept, store, and transfer data and instructions that are being used immediately by the CPU. The registers used by the CPU are often termed Processor registers. A processor register may hold an instruction, a storage address, or any data (such as bit sequence or individual characters).

Hence, the correct option is (D).

36. The parallel execution of operations in VLIW is done according to the schedule determined by the compiler. The compiler first checks the code for interdependencies and then determines the schedule for its execution. VLIW Architecture deals with it by depending on the compiler. The compiler checks for dependencies before scheduling the parallel execution of the instructions.

Hence, the correct option is (C).

37. The programming model, MapReduce, used by Hadoop is simple to write and test. MapReduce is a programming model and an associated implementation for processing and generating big data sets with a parallel, distributed algorithm on a cluster. The model is a specialization of the split-apply-combine strategy for data analysis.

Hence, the correct option is (C).

38. Given,

Data pointer size $= 5$ bytes

Key size $= 10$ bytes

Tree pointers size $= 6$ bytes

Page/block size $= 512$ bytes

Assume that branching factor/order of the B-tree is P.

$$P(6) + (P - 1)(5 + 10) \le 512$$

$$6P + 15P \le 512 + 15$$

$21P \leq 527$

$P \leq 25.09$

$P = 25$

Hence, the correct option is (A).

39. ZooKeeper applications run on thousands of machines, and it performs best where reads are more common than writes, at ratios of around $10:1$. ZooKeeper is replicated over a set of hosts (called an ensemble) and the servers are aware of each other. ZooKeeper in Hadoop can be viewed as a centralized repository where distributed applications can put data and get data out of it. It is used to keep the distributed system functioning together as a single unit, using its synchronization, serialization and coordination goals.

Hence, the correct option is (B).

40. A data manipulation language (DML) is a computer programming language used for adding (inserting), deleting, and modifying (updating) data in a database. And, it is the language used in application programs to request data from the DBMS. A DML is often a sub-language of a broader database language such as SQL, with the DML comprising some of the operators in the language.

Hence, the correct option is (A).

41. The ascending order or correct order among the following is:

Bit (Character): A bit is the smallest unit of data representation (value of a bit may be a 0 or 1). Eight bits make a byte which can represent a character or a special symbol in a character code.

Field: A field consists of a grouping of characters. A data field represents an attribute (a characteristic or quality) of some entity (object, person, place, or event).

Record: A record represents a collection of attributes that describe a real-world entity. A record consists of fields, with each field describing an attribute of the entity.

Hence, the correct option is (D).

42. An aggregate function receives a set or collection of values for each argument (such as the values of a column) and returns a single-value result for the set of input values. In database management, an aggregate function is a function where the values of multiple rows are grouped together as input on certain criteria to form a single value of more significant meaning.

Count(): Count(*) it returns total number of records.

Hence, the correct option is (A).

43. AutoNumber field type is best to store serial numbers. AutoNumber is a type of data used in Microsoft Access tables to generate an automatically incremented numeric counter. The serial data type stores a sequential integer, of the int data type, that is automatically assigned by the database server when a new row is inserted. The default serial starting number is 1, but you can assign an initial value, n when you create or alter the table.

Hence, the correct option is (B).

44. The field is part of a database that holds only one type of information. Field (also called data member or member variable) is the data encapsulated within a class or object. The field is the lowest level of the database. The field stores the information as the base level of the database management system or DBMS. The combination of one or more than one field is known as a record.

Hence, the correct option is (B).

45. In DBMS, all the data is stored at a central. A central database is a database that is located, stored, and maintained in a single location. This location is most often a central computer or database system, for example, a desktop or server CPU, or a mainframe computer.

Hence, the correct option is (A).

46. In computer science, locality of reference, also known as the principle of locality is the tendency of a processor to access the same set of memory locations repetitively over a short period of time. The spatial aspect of locality of reference tells that the nearby instruction is more likely to be executed in future. When the cache location is updated in order to signal to the processor this bit is used.

Hence, the correct option is (B).

47. Block caches or buffer caches are used to improve disk performance to handle interrupts to increase the capacity of the main memory to speed up the main memory.

Reading from a disk is very slow compared to accessing (real) memory. In addition, it is common to read the same part of a disk several times during relatively short periods of time. This is called disk buffering, and the memory used for the purpose is called the buffer cache.

The buffer cache is where data blocks are copied to perform SQL operations. The buffer cache is a shared memory structure and is concurrently accessed by all server processes.

Hence, the correct option is (A).

48. Defragmentation:

It is a process that reduces the degree of fragmentation. It does this by physically organizing the contents of the mass storage device used to store files into the smallest number of contiguous regions.

Paging:

It is a memory management scheme by which a computer stores and retrieves data from secondary storage for use in the main memory.

Booting:

It is a startup sequence that starts the operating system of a computer when it is turned on. A boot sequence is the initial set of operations that the computer performs when it is switched on. Every computer has a boot sequence.

Restoring:

It is the process of copying backup data from secondary storage and restoring it to its original location or a new location. A restore is performed to return data that has been lost, stolen, or

damaged to its original condition or to move data to a new location.

Hence, the correct option is (A).

49. Multiprogramming allows multiple programs to reside in separate areas of the core at the time. Multiprogramming is a rudimentary form of parallel processing in which several programs are run at the same time on a uniprocessor. Instead, the operating system executes part of one program, then part of another, and so on. To the user, it appears that all programs are executing at the same time.

Hence, the correct option is (D).

50. The advantage of dynamic loading is that an unused routine is never loaded. Dynamic loading does not require special support from the OS. Operating systems may help the programmer, however, by providing library routines to implement dynamic loading.

Hence, the correct option is (B).

51. Shortest job first (SJF) or micro job, the process that is active for a particular task. The SJF algorithm first executes the task with the least processor requirement. Shortest Job First (SJF) is an algorithm in which the process having the smallest execution time is chosen for the next execution. It significantly reduces the average waiting time for other processes awaiting execution.

Hence, the correct option is (D).

52. The working set theory of programming behaviour of processes running within an operating system involves the collection of pages that a process accesses. The process control block in the Linux operating system is represented by the C structure task struct.

Hence, the correct option is (A).

53. The memory buffer used to accommodate a speed differential is called cache. It is a hardware or software component that stores data so future requests for that data can be served faster. Cache serves to add fast memory between the CPU and main memory.

Hence, the correct option is (A).

54. If all processes are I/O bound, the ready queue will almost empty and the short-term scheduler will have a little to do. I/O bound processes spend more time doing I/O than computation. When a process issues an input/output request then it goes from running state to blocked state. When a process terminates itself it goes from running state to terminate state.

Hence, the correct option is (C).

55. A language is regular if and only if it can be accepted by a finite automaton. Secondly, it supports no concept of auxiliary memory as it loses the data as soon as the device is shut down. A regular language satisfies the following equivalent properties:

- It is the language of a regular expression.
- It is the language accepted by a non-deterministic finite automaton (NFA).

- It is the language accepted by a deterministic finite automaton (DFA).

Hence, the correct option is (B).

56. The $\{0\}^\wedge\{01\}$ represents $\{0,01\}$ in different forms using set operations and regular expressions. The operator like $^\wedge$,V, etc. are logical operation and they form invalid regular expressions when used. Regular expressions are a formal notation for generating patterns. This notation is used extensively in programming language manuals (used to describe legal patterns of input) and in command languages (such as the Unix shell, where it is used to describe patterns for naming files, etc.).

Hence, the correct option is (D).

57. The extended notation would be $(0+1)^4$ but however, we may allow some or all the factors to be ε. Thus ε needs to be included in the given regular expression.

Expression (E)= Length 4 or less means, length 0 or length (1) or length (2) or length (3) or length 4.

$$= \varepsilon + (0+1)^1 + (0+1)^2 + (0+1)^3 + (0+1)^4 = (\varepsilon + 0 + 1)^4$$

Hence, the correct option is (D).

58. If R represents a regular language, R* represents the Venn-diagram most correctly. The given diagram in the question represents the Kleene operation over the Regular Language (R) in which the final states become the initial and the initial state becomes final. The equivalence of regular expressions and finite automata is known as Kleene's theorem (after American mathematician Stephen Cole Kleene). In the Chomsky hierarchy, regular languages are the languages generated by Type- 3 grammars.

Hence, the correct option is (B).

59. The transition states shown are the result of breaking down the given regular expression in fragments. For dot operation, we change a state, for union (plus) operation, we diverge into two transitions and for Kleene Operation, we apply a loop.

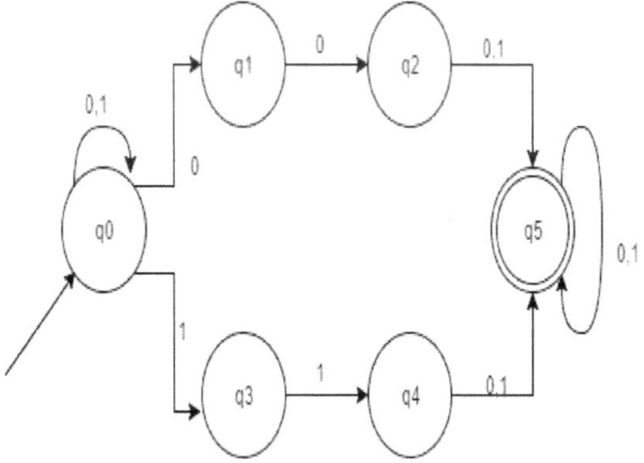

So, value of $q0 = (0+1)^*$

$$q1, q2, q3, q4 = (00+11)$$

And, $q5 = (0+1)^*$

Therefore, the final result is $= (0 + 1)^*(00 + 11)(0 + 1)^*$.

Hence, the correct option is (A).

60. The full form of NFA is Non-Deterministic Finite Automata. It is also known as a Non-Deterministic Finite State-machine. In NFA, for a particular input symbol, the machine can move to any combination of the states in the machine. In other words, the exact state to which the machine moves cannot be determined.

Hence, the correct option is (C).

61. Recursive descent parser is a kind of top-down parser built from a set of mutually recursive procedures (or a non-recursive equivalent) where each such procedure implements one of the nonterminal of the grammar. Thus the structure of the resulting program closely mirrors that of the grammar it recognizes.

Hence, the correct option is (D).

62. A series of statements explaining how the data is to be processed is called program. A program is a sequence of instructions, written to perform a task by computer. It requires programs to function, typically executing the program's instructions in a central processor. A program is usually written by a computer programmer in a programming language. From the program in its human-readable form of source code, a compiler or assembler can derive machine code a form consisting of instructions that the computer can directly execute.

Hence, the correct option is (D).

63. The graph that shows the basic blocks and their successor relationship is called flow graph. A flow graph is a graph of the compiler which describes the basic blocks and how the program control is passed between the blocks. Basic block is a set of statements that always executes in a sequence one after the other. A flow graph is a directed graph with flow control information added to the basic blocks.

Hence, the correct option is (C).

64. The document listing all procedures and regulations that generally govern an organization is the organization manual. This manual gives a detailed account of the organization. The authority and responsibility of every person is given in detail. It avoids confusion and conflicts among various persons. The extent of authority and the relationship of executives is explained in this manual. The extent of span of management and delegation of authority are facilitated by a properly drawn manual.

Hence, the correct option is (B).

65. The algorithmic cost modeling utilizes the basic regression formula with such parameters that have been derived from the data of a historical project and current as well as characteristics of a future project. Algorithmic cost modelling uses a mathematical formula to predict project costs based on estimates of the project size, the number of software engineers, and other process and product factors.

Hence, the correct option is (C).

66. Both COCOMO and FP-based estimation is used to calculate the effort by utilizing the empirically derived formulas. COCOMO is one of the most generally used software estimation models in the world. COCOMO predicts the efforts and schedule of a software product based on the size of the software. A Function Point (FP) is a unit of measurement to express the amount of business functionality, an information system (as a product) provides to a user. FPs measure software size. They are widely accepted as an industry standard for functional sizing.

Hence, the correct option is (D).

67. Baselines is a software configuration management concept that helps us to control change without seriously impeding justifiable change. A baseline is a milestone and reference point in software development that is marked by completion or delivery of one or more software configuration items and formal approval of a set of predefined products is obtained through formal technical review. Baseline is a shared project database.

Hence, the correct option is (A).

68. Internship management is an incorrect activity for the configuration management of a software system. Configuration management policies and processes define how to record, and process proposed system changes, how to decide what system components to change, how to manage different versions of the system and its components, and how to distribute changes to customers.

Hence, the correct option is (C).

69. Reducing memory load means that users should not be required to memorize (or recall out of their heads) a great deal of information to carry out tasks. Memory load reduces users' capacity to perform the main task. There are many instances where a user's memory load can be reduced, such as:

- Disclose information in a progressive fashion
- Define intuitive shortcuts
- Recognition rather than recall
- Externalize information through visualization
- Hierarchical structure
- Default values
- Concrete examples
- Generic rules and actions
- Establish meaningful defaults.

Hence, the correct option is (D).

70. Verification has a static activities. Static verification is the process of checking that software meets requirements by inspecting the code before it runs. For example:

- Code conventions verification
- Bad practices (anti-pattern) detection
- Software metrics calculation
- Formal verification

Hence, the correct option is (C).

71. Knowledge is most abstract development artifact that can be reused. Out of all the reuse artifacts, reuse of knowledge occurs automatically without any conscious effort in this direction. Two

major difficulties with unplanned reuse of knowledge is that a developer experienced in one type of product might be included in a team developing a different type of software. Also, it is difficult to remember details of the potentially reusable development knowledge. A planned reuse of knowledge can increase the effectiveness of reuse. For this, the reusable knowledge should be systematically extracted and documented.

Hence, the correct option is (D).

72. The main intent of project metrics is to minimize the development schedule and evaluate the ongoing project's quality on a daily basis. A project metric refers to a quantifiable measure of the degree to which a system, component, or process owns a certain trait. A metric is simply a measurement of something. When managing a project, you can choose to use project metrics to track progress. Metrics are selected based on the goals of the project and critical factors for success.

Hence, the correct option is (D).

73. Given,

Probability of Solving the problem by first-person $= \dfrac{1}{3}$

Probability of Solving the problem by second person $= \dfrac{1}{4}$

Probability of Solving the problem by third-person $= \dfrac{1}{5}$

Probability of not solving the problem by first-person $= 1 - \left(\dfrac{1}{3}\right)$

$= \dfrac{2}{3}$

Probability of not solving the problem by second person $= 1 - \left(\dfrac{1}{4}\right)$

$= \dfrac{3}{4}$

Probability of not solving the problem by third-person $= 1 - \left(\dfrac{1}{5}\right)$

$= \dfrac{4}{5}$

So, the probability of none of the person solving the problem $= \dfrac{2}{3} \times \dfrac{3}{4} \times \dfrac{4}{5}$

Hence, the correct option is (B).

74. Given,

There are 4 coins of ten rupees, 2 coins of five rupees, 2 coins of two rupees and 2 coins of one rupee.

Total coins $= 4 + 2 + 2 + 2$

$= 10$

Total number of ways in which 3 coins can be taken out $= {}^{10}C_3 = 120$

Amount drawn can be 12 rupees in the following cases:

i. 1 coin of ten rupees and 2 coins of 1 rupee.

This can be done in ${}^{4}C_1 \times {}^{2}C_2$ ways, i.e. $4 \times 1 = 4$ ways.

ii. 2 coins of five rupees and 1 coin of 2 rupees.

This can be done in ${}^{2}C_2 \times {}^{2}C_1$ ways, i.e. $1 \times 2 = 2$ ways.

Total number of ways in which 12 rupees can be drawn $= 4 + 2 = 6$

$\therefore$ Probability of drawing 12 rupees

$= \dfrac{\text{Total number of ways in which 12 rupees can be drawn in three coins}}{\text{Total number of ways in which 3 coins can be drawn}}$

$= \dfrac{6}{120}$

$= \dfrac{1}{20}$

Hence, the correct option is (D).

75. Given,

$$dy = x\sec\dfrac{y}{x}\,dx + \dfrac{y}{x}\,dx$$

Put $y = vx$, and $\dfrac{dy}{dx} = v + x\dfrac{dv}{dx}$

$$v + x\dfrac{dv}{dx} = x\sec v + v \quad \dfrac{dv}{dx} = \sec v \quad \cos v\,dv = dx$$

By integrating both sides we get,

$$\int \cos v\,dv = \int dx \quad \sin v = x + c$$

Now, by putting $v = \dfrac{y}{x}$ in the above equation we get,

$$\sin\dfrac{y}{x} = x + c$$

Put $y(1) = \dfrac{\pi}{2}$ in the above equation we get $c = 0$

$$y = x\sin^{-1}x$$

Put $x = \dfrac{1}{2}$ in the above equation we get,

$$y = \dfrac{1}{2}\sin^{-1}\dfrac{1}{2}$$

$$= \dfrac{\pi}{12}$$

Hence, the correct option is (A).

76. Given,

$$\dfrac{dy}{dx} = \sec\left(\dfrac{y}{x}\right) + \dfrac{y}{x}$$

Let $\dfrac{y}{x} = t$

$\Rightarrow y = xt$

Differentiating with respect to x, we get

$\Rightarrow \dfrac{dy}{dx} = x\dfrac{dt}{dx} + t$

Now,

$x\dfrac{dt}{dx} + t = \sec t + t$

$\Rightarrow x\dfrac{dt}{dx} = \sec t$

$\Rightarrow \dfrac{dt}{\sec t} = \dfrac{dx}{x}$

Integrating both sides, we get

$\Rightarrow \int \dfrac{dt}{\sec t} = \int \dfrac{dx}{x}$

$\Rightarrow \int \cos t\, dt = \int \dfrac{dx}{x}$

$\Rightarrow \sin t = \log x + \log c$

$\Rightarrow \sin t = \log(cx) \quad (\because \log m + \log n = \log(mn))$

$\therefore \sin\left(\dfrac{y}{x}\right) = \log(cx)$

Hence, the correct option is (C).

77. If $L\{f(t)\} = f(s)$

To solve the differential equation we have:

If $f(t)$ is a function of independent variable ' t' then

$L\{f'(t)\} = sL\{f(t)\} - f(0)$

$L\{f''(t)\} = s^2 L\{f(t)\} - sf(0) - f'(0)$

$L\{\sin(at)\} = \dfrac{a}{s^2+a^2}$

$L\{\cos(at)\} = \dfrac{s}{s^2+a^2}$

Now,

Given,

$f(t) + f''(t) = 0$ and $f(0) = f'(0) = 1$

We know that:

$L\{f''(t)\} = s^2 L\{f(t)\} - sf(0) - f'(0)$

$\therefore s^2 f(s) - sf(0) - f(0) + f(s) = 0$

$\therefore f(s)[s^2 + 1] - (s + 1) = 0 \quad [\because f(0) = f'(0) = 1]$

$\therefore f(s) = \dfrac{s+1}{s^2+1}$

$\dfrac{s+1}{s^2+1} = \dfrac{s}{s^2+1} + \dfrac{1}{s+1}$

$\because L^{-1}f(s) = f(t)$

$\therefore L^{-1}\left(\dfrac{s+1}{s^2+1}\right) = L^{-1}\left(\dfrac{s}{s^2+1} + \dfrac{1}{s+1}\right)$

$\therefore f(t) = \cos t + \sin t$

Hence, the correct option is (D).

78. Given,

$F(s) = \dfrac{a - 5e^{-2s} + be^{-\alpha}}{s} \cdots (1)$

$f(t) = 2u(t) - 5u(t-2) + 7u(t-5)$

$\Rightarrow F(s) = \dfrac{2}{s} - \dfrac{5e^{-2s}}{s} + \dfrac{7e^{-5s}}{s}$

$= \dfrac{2 - 5e^{-2s} + 7e^{5s}}{s} \cdots (2)$

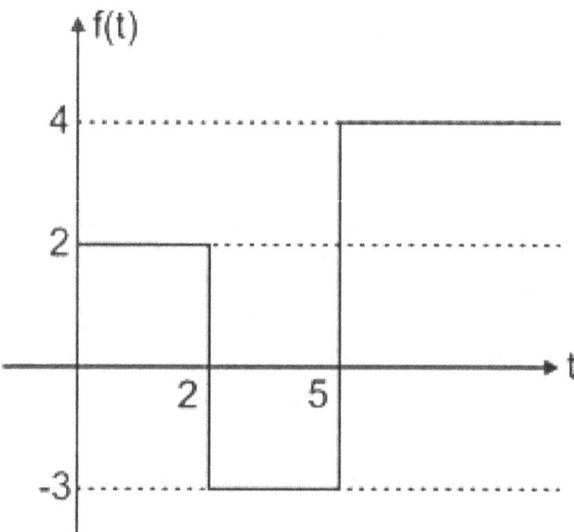

By comparing both equations (1) and (2) we get,

$a = 2, b = 7, c = 5$

$\Rightarrow a + b + c$

$= 14$

Hence, the correct option is (C).

79. Properties of the determinant of a matrix:

- If each entry in any row or column of a determinant is 0, then the value of the determinant is zero.
- For any square matrix say $A, |A| = |A^{\mathsf{T}}|$.
- If we interchange any two rows (columns) of a matrix, the determinant is multiplied by -1.
- If any two rows (columns) of a matrix are same then the value of the determinant is zero.

Now,

$\begin{vmatrix} 1 & a & b+c \\ 1 & b & c+a \\ 1 & c & a+b \end{vmatrix}$

Apply $C_2 \to C_2 + C_3$

$$= \begin{vmatrix} 1 & a+b+c & b+c \\ 1 & a+b+c & c+a \\ 1 & a+b+c & a+b \end{vmatrix}$$

Taking common $(a+b+c)$ from column 2, we get

$$= (a+b+c)\begin{vmatrix} 1 & 1 & b+c \\ 1 & 1 & c+a \\ 1 & 1 & a+b \end{vmatrix}$$

As we can see that the first and the second column of the given matrix are equal.

We know that, if any two rows (columns) of a matrix are same then the value of the determinant is zero.

$$\therefore \begin{vmatrix} 1 & a & b+c \\ 1 & b & c+a \\ 1 & c & a+b \end{vmatrix}$$

$$= 0$$

Hence, the correct option is (A).

80. Cayley-Hamilton theorem: According to the Cayley-Hamilton theorem, every matrix A satisfies its own characteristic equation.

Characteristic equation: If A is any square matrix of order n, we can form the matrix $[A - \lambda I]$, where I **is the** n^{th} **order unit matrix.** The determinant of this matrix equated to zero i.e. $|A - \lambda I| = 0$ is called the characteristic equation of A.

Now,

Characteristic equation: $|A - \lambda I| = 0$

Now,

$$\Rightarrow A - \lambda I = \begin{bmatrix} 1 & 4 \\ 2 & 3 \end{bmatrix} - \begin{bmatrix} \lambda & 0 \\ 0 & \lambda \end{bmatrix} = \begin{bmatrix} 1-\lambda & 4 \\ 2 & 3-\lambda \end{bmatrix}$$

$$\Rightarrow |A - \lambda I| = \begin{vmatrix} 1-\lambda & 4 \\ 2 & 3-\lambda \end{vmatrix} = 0$$

$$\Rightarrow (1-\lambda)(3-\lambda) - 8 = 0$$

$$\Rightarrow \lambda^2 - 4\lambda - 5 = 0$$

From Cayley-Hamilton theorem, we get

$$\Rightarrow A^2 - 4A - 5I = 0$$

$$\Rightarrow A^2 = 4A + 5I \cdots (1)$$

By multiplying equation (1) with A, we get

$$\Rightarrow A^3 = 4A^2 + 5A = 4(4A + 5I) + 5A = 21A + 20I \cdots (2)$$

By multiplying equation (2) with A, we get

$$\Rightarrow A^4 = 21A^2 + 20A = 104A + 105I \cdots (3)$$

By multiplying equation (3) with A, we get

$$\Rightarrow A^5 = 104A^2 + 105A = 521A + 520I$$

Now, consider the given expression:

$$A^5 - 4A^4 - 7A^3 + 11A^2 - A - 10I$$

$$= 521A + 520I - 4(104A + 105I) - 7(21A + 20I) + 11(4A + 5I) - A - 10I$$

$$= A + 5I$$

Hence, the correct option is (B).

81. Given,

$$\frac{d}{dx}\left(\frac{x^2 + x - 2}{x^3 + 6}\right)$$

As we know,

$$\frac{d}{dx}\left[\frac{f(x)}{g(x)}\right] = \frac{g(x)\frac{d}{dx}[f(x)] - f(x)\frac{d}{dx}[g(x)]}{[g(x)]^2}$$

$$\frac{d}{dx}(x^n) = nx^{n-1}$$

Differentiating with respect to x, we get

$$= \frac{(x^3+6)\frac{d}{dx}(x^2+x-2) - (x^2+x-2)\frac{d}{dx}(x^3+6)}{(x^3+6)^2}$$

$$= \frac{(x^3+6)(2x+1) - (x^2+x-2)(3x^2)}{(x^3+6)^2}$$

$$= \frac{(2x^4+x^3+12x+6) - (3x^4+3x^3-6x^2)}{(x^3+6)^2}$$

$$= \frac{-x^4-2x^3+6x^2+12x+6}{(x^3+6)^2}$$

Hence, the correct option is (C).

82. Given,

$$I = \int_0^\pi \sin^6 x \cdot \cos^5 x\, dx \,\dots (1)$$

By the properties of definite integral,

$$\int_0^\pi f(x)dx = \int_0^a f(a-x)dx$$

$$I = \int_0^\pi [\sin(\pi - x)]^6 \cdot [\cos(\pi - x)]^5 dx$$

$$\Rightarrow I = -\int_0^\pi \sin^6 x \cdot \cos^5 x\, dx \,\dots (2)$$

Adding equation (1) and (2) we get,

$$2I = \int_0^\pi \sin^6 x \cdot \cos^5 x\, dx - \int_0^\pi \sin^6 x \cdot \cos^5 x\, dx$$

$$\Rightarrow 2I = 0$$

$$\Rightarrow I = 0$$

Hence, the correct option is (A).

83. Circuit for Johnson counter:

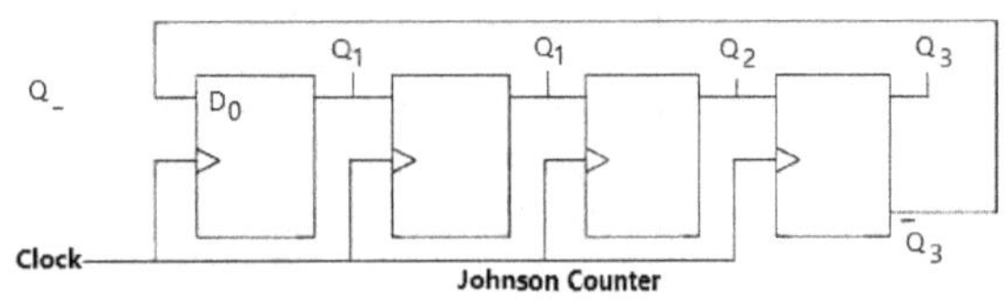

Johnson Counter

If Q_0 is MSB and Q_3 is LSB.

CLK	Q_0	Q_1	Q_2	Q_3	Decimal
0(initial)	1	0	0	0	8
1	1	1	0	0	12
2	1	1	1	0	14
3	1	1	1	1	15
4	0	1	1	1	7
5	0	0	1	1	3
6	0	0	0	1	1
7	0	0	0	0	0
8	1	0	0	0	8

Count sequence of $8 \rightarrow 12 \rightarrow 14 \rightarrow 15 \rightarrow 7 \rightarrow 3 \rightarrow 1 \rightarrow 0 \rightarrow 8 \rightarrow$ (repeat) If Q_3 is MSB and Q_0 is LSB.

CLK	Q_3	Q_2	Q_1	Q_0	Decimal
0(initial)	1	0	0	0	8
1	0	0	0	0	0
2	0	0	0	1	1
3	0	0	1	1	3
4	0	1	1	1	7
5	1	1	1	1	15
6	1	1	1	0	14
7	1	1	0	0	12
8	1	0	0	0	8

Count sequence of $8 \rightarrow 0 \rightarrow 1 \rightarrow 3 \rightarrow 7 \rightarrow 15 \rightarrow 14 \rightarrow 12 \rightarrow 8 \rightarrow$ (repeat)

Since the least significant bits and the most significant bit is not signified. Therefore statement II and statement IV both are correct.

Hence, the correct option is (D).

84.

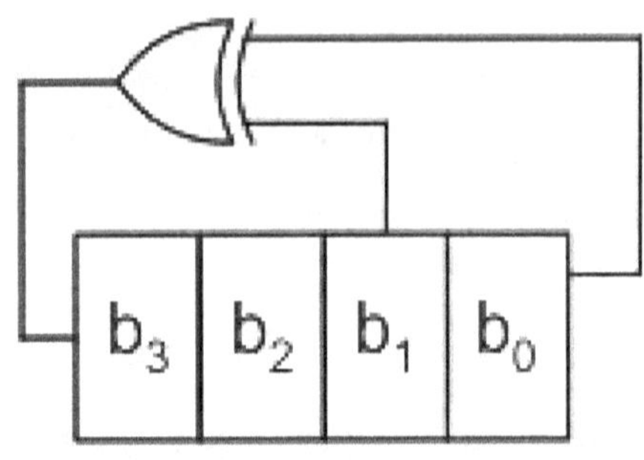

Clock pulse	Output $(b_3 b_2 b_1 b_0)$

Initial	1100
1	0110
2	1011
3	0101
4	1010
5	1101
6	1110
7	1111
8	0111
9	0011
10	0001
11	1000
12	0100
13	0010
14	1001
15	1100

Therefore, the shift register need 15 clock pulses to reach the given initial position.

Hence, the correct option is (C).

85. From the given $J-K$ flip flop circuit, it is clear that,

$J_1 = 1$ and $K_1 = 1$

$J_2 = Q_1 Q_3'$ and $K_2 = Q_1$

$J_3 = Q_2 Q_1$ and $K_3 = Q_1$

$J-K$ flip flop table:

J	K	Q_{n+1}
0	0	Q_n
0	1	0
1	0	1
1	1	Q_n

Now, according to the above conditions, clock cycles with the sequences are represented as:

Clock	J_1	K_1	J_2	K_2	J_3	K_3	Q_1	Q_2	Q_3
0							0	0	0
1	1	1	0	0	0	0	1	0	0
2	1	1	1	1	0	1	0	1	0
3	1	1	0	0	0	0	1	1	0
4	1	1	1	1	1	1	0	0	1
5	1	1	0	0	0	0	1	0	1
6	1	1	0	1	0	1	0	0	0

Initial state is repeating itself after 6th clock cycle. So, it is a mod - 6 counter. $Q_1 Q_2 Q_3$ after 4 clock pulses is 001.

Hence, the correct option is (A).

86. The MOD number of a counter is equal to the number of complete states that a counter goes through before it recycles back to its starting state. To construct a counter with MOD X, it requires a minimum number of N flip-flops.

Such that, $2^N \geq$ MOD.

Now,

The time period of the clock pulse $= \dfrac{1}{10MHz} = 10^{-7}\,\text{sec}$

Propagation delay of each flip-flops $= 15 \times 10^{-9}\,\text{sec}$

Number of flip-flops required $= \dfrac{t_{clk}}{t_{pd}} = \dfrac{10^{-7}}{15 \times 10^{-9}} = 6.67$

$\therefore$ Number of flip-flops required $= 6$

Modulus of counter $= 2^6 = 64$.

Precautions:

We should not take $N = 7$.

If we take $N = 7$, Using 7 flip-flops with delay $15\,ns$. The total delay becomes $105\,ns$, which is greater than the time period of the clock $(100\,ns)$, is not a desirable operation.

Using 6 flip-flops allows us to keep a delay under $100\,ns$ ($90\,ns$).

Hence, the correct option is (A).

87. Given,

$$(1235)_x = (3033)_y$$

Converting both the RHS and LHS into its decimal equivalent, we get:

$$(x^3 + 2x^2 + 3x + 5)_{10} = (3y^3 + 0y^2 + 3y + 3)_{10}$$

Substituting the values given in the options in the above equation, we get:

$x = 8$ and $y = 6$

As we know,

Putting $x = 8$ in $x^3 + 2x^2 + 3x + 5$

$= (8)^3 + 2(8)^2 + 3(8) + 5$

$= (699)_{10}$

Putting $y = 6$ in $3y^3 + 0y^2 + 3y + 3$

$= 3(6)^3 + 3(6) + 3$

$= 3(216) + 18 + 3$

$= (699)_{10}$

Hence, the correct option is (B).

88. Option (B): Correct

$$N = A_7\, A_6\, A_5\, A_4\, A_3\, A_2\, A_1$$

Bitwise Shift left (x by 2)

$$2\,N = A_7\, A_6\, A_5\, A_4\, A_3\, A_2\, A_1 0$$

Addind 1, we get

$$2\,N + 1 = A_7\, A_6\, A_5\, A_4\, A_3\, A_2\, A_1 1$$

Option (C): Correct

While multiplying and adding 1 numbers might overflow as in M.

Hence, the correct option is (D).

89. Given,

$$(x^2 - 10x + 31)_r = [(x - 5)(x - 8)]_{10}$$

After simplifying it, we get:

$$(x^2 - 10x + 31)_r = (x^2 - 13x + 40)_{10}$$

By comparing the terms:

$$(10)_r = (13)_{10}$$

$$r.1 + r^0.0 = 13$$

$$r = 13$$

Also, $(31)_r = (40)_{10}$

If $r = 13$

$$3 \times 13 + 1 = (40)_{10}$$

So, the value of 'r' to satisfy the given equation is 13.

Hence, the correct option is (A).

90. IEEE format:

1 bit (signed)	8 bits (Exponent)	23 bits (Mantissa)

Signed bit $= 5 = 1$
Exponent $= E = 10101010 = 170$
Mantissa $= M = 01010100000000000000000$
$= (-1)^S (1.M) \times 2^{E-127}$
$= -1 \times (1.010101) \times 2^{170-127}$
$= -1 \times (1010101)_2 \times 2^{-6} \times 2^{43}$
$= -1 \times 85 \times 2^{37}$
$= -170 \times 2^{36}$

Thus, the value represented by the above number is -170×2^{36}.

Hence, the correct option is (A).

91. Given,

$$P = 11101101$$

$$Q = 11100110$$

Take the 2's complement of Q and add it to P.

Using 2's complement addition $P + (-Q)$ we get,

2's compliment of Q is:

$Q = 00011010$

11101101

$+00011010$
<hr>

100000111
<hr>

After neglecting the carry we'll get;

000000111

Hence, the correct option is (B).

92. Given,

$(A \wedge B) \wedge (\neg A \rightarrow B)$

As we know,

$(A \wedge B) \wedge (\neg A \rightarrow B) \equiv A.B.(A' + B) \equiv A.B \equiv A \wedge B$

. $\equiv \wedge$

$+ \equiv \vee$

$' \equiv \neg$

Statement I: A ∧ B ≡ A.B

$(A \wedge B) \rightarrow (A \wedge B) \equiv \neg (A \wedge B) \vee (A \wedge B) \equiv X' + X \equiv 1 \equiv$ TRUE

$(A \wedge B) \rightarrow (A \wedge B) \equiv \neg (A \wedge B) \vee (A \wedge B) \equiv X' + X \equiv 1 \equiv$ TRUE

A	B	(A ∧ B) → (A ∧ B)
0	0	1
0	1	1
1	0	1
1	1	1

Statement II: A ∨ B ≡ A + B

$(A \wedge B) \rightarrow (A \vee B) \equiv (A.B)' + (A + B) \equiv (A' + B') + (A + B) \equiv A' + A + B' + B \equiv 1 \equiv$ TRUE

A	B	(A ∧ B) → (A ∨ B)
0	0	1
0	1	1
1	0	1
1	1	1

Statement III: ¬ (A ∨ B) ≡ A'.B'

$(A \wedge B) \rightarrow (\neg (A \vee B)) \equiv (A.B)' + A'.B' \equiv (A' + B') + A'.B'$

$\equiv A' + B' \equiv (A.B)' \equiv$ FALSE (if A = TRUE and B = TRUE)

A	B	(A ∧ B) →(¬A ∨ B))
0	0	1
0	1	1

Statement IV: TRUE

(A ∧ B) → TRUE ≡ ¬(A ∧ B) ∨ 1 ≡ 1 ≡ TRUE

A	B	(A ∧ B) → TRUE
0	0	1
0	1	1
1	0	1
1	1	1

Statement V: FALSE

(A ∧ B) → FALSE ≡ ¬(A ∧ B) ∨ 0 ≡ ¬(A ∧ B) ≡ FALSE (if A = TRUE and B = TRUE)

A	B	(A ∧ B) → FALSE
0	0	1
0	1	1
1	0	1
1	1	0

So, the statements I, II and IV are logically implied by (A ∧ B) ∧ (¬ A → B).

Hence, the correct option is (A).

93. Let A and B are two sets having m and n elements respectively.

In $f : A \rightarrow B$, total number of functions will be n^m.

Now,

$S \rightarrow f : 2^4 \rightarrow 2$ gives total number of functions to be $2^{2 \wedge 4} = 2^{16}$

N is defined by $f : S > \{0,1\}$.

Therefore, total number of functions will be 2^S.

So, $\log_2 \log_2 N$

$= \log_2 \log_2 2^S$

$= \log_2 \log_2 2^{2 \wedge 16}$

$= \log_2 2^{16}$

$= 16$

Hence, the correct option is (A).

94. A bounded lattice is a lattice where both the upper bound and lower bound exist.

Every finite lattice is a bounded lattice because, for any finite lattice, there exists a unique least as well as the unique greatest element.

Every finite lattice is a bounded lattice but the converse is not true. i.e. A bounded lattice may or may not be finite. For example,

$[[0,1], \leq]$ is a bounded lattice but not finite. Here, the least element is 0 and the greatest element is 1.

Note that $[(0,1), \leq]$ is not a bounded lattice because there is no least or greatest element.

Hence, the correct option is (D).

95. Given,

$$|H| = |G| = n = 11$$

Number of edges in $H = |E| = y \times 2^{10}$

As we know,

By Handshaking Lemma:

$$\Sigma d_i = 2 \times |E|$$

Where, d_i is the degree of ith vertex.

$|E|$ is the number of edges in a graph.

Now,

For n-dimensional cube:

Degree of vertices $= n = 11$

Number of vertices $= 2^n = 2^{11}$

$$11 \times 2^{11} = 2 \times |E_1|$$

$$|E_1| = 11 \times 2^{10}$$

For complete graph:

Degree of each vertex:

$$\Rightarrow 2^{11} - 1$$

$$\Rightarrow (2^{11} - 1) \times 2^{11} = 2 \times |E_2|$$

$$\Rightarrow |E_2| = 2047 \times 2^{10}$$

$$\Rightarrow E = |E_2| - |E_1|$$

$$\Rightarrow y \times 2^{10} = 2047 \times 2^{10} - 11 \times 2^{10}$$

$$= y = 2036$$

Hence, the correct option is (A).

96. Given,

Vertices $= v = 8$

Length of cycle $= c = 5$

As we know,

Number of cycles $= {}^v C_c \times \dfrac{(c-1)!}{2}$

Now,

Number of cycles $= {}^8 C_5 \times \dfrac{(5-1)!}{2}$

$$= 672$$

Hence, the correct option is (A).

97. The characteristic polynomial is $x^2 - 6x + 8$.

By solving the characteristic equation, $x^2 - 6x + 8 = 0$ we get $x = 2$ and $x = 4$, these are the characteristic roots.

Therefore we know that the solution to the recurrence relation has the form $a_n = a \times 2^n + b \times 4^n$, for some constants a and b.

Now, by using the initial conditions a_0 and a_1 we have: $a = \dfrac{7}{2}$ and $b = -\dfrac{1}{2}$. Therefore the solution to the recurrence relation is: $a_n = 4 \times 2^n - 1 \times 3^n = \dfrac{7}{2} \times 2^n - \dfrac{1}{2} \times 3^n$.

Hence, the correct option is (B).

98. There are 4 consonants out of 15 can be selected in ${}^{15}C_4$ ways and 3 vowels can be selected in ${}^5C_3$ ways. Therefore, the total number of groups each containing 4 consonants and 3 vowels $= {}^{15}C_4 \times {}^4C_3$. Each group contains 7 letters which can be arranged in $7!$ ways. So, required number of words $= {}^{15}C_4 \times {}^5C_3 \times 7!$.

Hence, the correct option is (D).

99. A Hasse diagram is a graphical representation of the relation of elements of a partially ordered set (poset) with an implied upward orientation.

Hasse Diagram is:

$$32$$
$$|$$
$$16$$
$$|$$
$$8$$
$$\bigwedge$$
$$2 \quad 4$$

So, the number of edges should be 4.

Hence, the correct option is (D).

100. By the principle of mathematical induction,

We now assume that $p(b)$ is true $1^2 + 2^2 + 3^2 + \cdots + b^2$

$$\Rightarrow \dfrac{b(b+1)(2b+1)}{6}$$

So, to prove $p(b+1)$:

$$\Rightarrow 1^2 + 2^2 + 3^2 + \cdots + b^2 + (b+1)^2$$

$$\Rightarrow \frac{b(b+1)(2b+1)}{6} + (b+1)^2$$

By induction assumption it is shown that $1^2 + 2^2 + 3^2 +$
$\ldots + b^2 + (b+1)^2$

$$\Rightarrow \frac{(b+1)[(b+2)(2b+3)]}{6}.$$

So, it is proved that $1^2 + 2^2 + 3^2 + \cdots + p^2$

$$= \frac{p \times (p+1) \times (2p+1)}{6}$$

Hence, the correct option is (B).

$$\Rightarrow \frac{b(b+1)(2b+1)}{6} + (b+1)^2$$

By induction assumption it is shown that $1^2 + 2^2 + 3^2 +$

Q.1 When an object is returned by a function, a ______________ is automatically created to hold the return value.

A. Temporary object   **B.** Virtual object

C. New object   **D.** Data member

Q.2 What are <a> and </a> tags used for?

A. For adding Image

B. For aligning text

C. For audio-voiced text

D. For adding links to your page

Q.3 A program that reads the source code and converts it to a form usable by the computer, is known as __________.

A. Interpreter   **B.** Compiler

C. Linker   **D.** Assembler

Q.4 Prolog comes under __________.

A. Logic Programming

B. Procedural Programming

C. OOP

D. Functional

Q.5 The method that can be used to create new properties and also to modify the attributes of existing properties is _________.

A. Object.defineProperty()

B. Object.defineProperties()

C. Object.inherit()

D. Both (A) and (B)

Q.6 Which data structure is the best for implementing a priority queue?

A. Stack   **B.** Linked list

C. Array   **D.** Heap

Q.7 A linear data structure in which insertion and deletion operations can be performed from both the ends is _______.

A. Queue   **B.** Deque

C. Priority queue   **D.** Circular queue

Q.8 What is a full binary tree?

A. Each node has exactly zero or two children.

B. Each node has exactly two children.

C. All the leaves are at the same level.

D. Each node has exactly one or two children.

Q.9 In a circular queue implementation using array of size 5, the array index starts with 0 where front and rear values are 3 and 4 respectively. Determine the array index at which the insertion of the next element will take place?

A. 5   **B.** 0   **C.** 1   **D.** 2

Q.10 Which of the following is not a characteristic of the hub architecture of Arc net?

A. Directionalized transmission

B. Alternative routing

C. Zero insertion loss amplifier

D. RIM port isolation

Q.11 A group of packets from a source through an X. 25 packet system to sink:

A. Arrive in the same order sent for VC, but not for PVC

B. Arrive in the same order sent for PVC, but not for VC

C. Arrive in the same order sent for both VC and PVC

D. None of these

Q.12 How many OSI layers are covered in the X. 25 standard?

A. Three   **B.** Four   **C.** Two   **D.** Seven

Q.13 A protocol is a rule governing a time sequence of events that must take place:

A. Between peers   **B.** Across an interface

C. Between non-peers   **D.** None of these

Q.14 What do we call a network whose elements may be separated by some distance, it usually involves two or more small networks and dedicated high speed telephone lines?

A. URL   **B.** LAN   **C.** WAN   **D.** WWW

Q.15 What is the maximum data capacity for optical fiber cable?

A. 10 Mbps   **B.** 100 Mbps

C. 1000 Mbps   **D.** 10000 Mbps

Q.16 If a computer on the network shares, resources for other to use, it is called _______.

A. Server   **B.** Client

C. Mainframe   **D.** All of these

Q.17 What is work of TDM?

A. Several signals are sent in a time-slotted mode on a channel.

B. Several signals are sent on separate channels at a time.

C. One signal is sent to several users.

D. All of these

Q.18 What is the full form of MODEM?

A. Modulator/Demodulator

B. Modulation/Rough modulation

C. Modulation/Rough demodulation

D. All of these

Q.19 What is subroutine nesting?

A. Having multiple subroutines in a program.

B. Using a linking nest statement to put many subroutines under the same name.

C. Having one routine call the other.

D. None of these

Q.20 In case of nested subroutines the return addresses are stored in _________.

A. System heap
B. Special memory buffers
C. Processor stack
D. Registers

Q.21 The _______ circuit enables the generation of the ASCII code when the key is pressed.
A. Generator
B. Debouncing
C. Encoder
D. Logger

Q.22 To overcome multiple signals being generated upon a single press of the button, we make use of _______.
A. Generator circuit
B. Debouncing circuit
C. Multiplexer
D. XOR circuit

Q.23 The best mode of connection between devices which need to send or receive large amounts of data over a short distance is ______.
A. BUS
B. Serial port
C. Parallel port
D. Isochronous port

Q.24 _____ serves as an intermediary between the device and the buses.
A. Interface circuits
B. Device drivers
C. Buffers
D. None of these

Q.25 The side of the interface circuits, that has the data path and the control signals to transfer data between interface and device is _______.
A. Bus side
B. Port side
C. Hardwell side
D. Software side

Q.26 The contention for the usage of a hardware device is called _______.
A. Structural hazard
B. Stalk
C. Deadlock
D. None of these

Q.27 _________ method is used in centralized systems to perform out of order execution.
A. Scorecard
B. Score boarding
C. Optimizing
D. Redundancy

Q.28 The computational technique used to compute the disk storage address of individual records is called:
A. Bubble memory
B. Key fielding
C. Dynamic reallocation
D. Hashing

Q.29 The Database Management Query language is generally designed for the _________.
A. Support end-users who use English-like commands.
B. Specifying the structure of the database.
C. Support in the development of complex applications software.
D. All of these

Q.30 Find out the wrong option:
A. Distributed applications use SQL to store important configuration information.
B. The service maintains a record of all transactions, which can be used for higher-level abstractions, like synchronization primitives.
C. ZooKeeper maintains a standard hierarchical name space, similar to files and directories.
D. ZooKeeper provides superior reliability through redundant services.

Q.31 Find out the correct option:
A. Ambari provides a dashboard for monitoring the health and status of the Hadoop cluster.
B. Ambari provides a step-by-step wizard for installing Hadoop services across any number of hosts.
C. Ambari handles configuration of Hadoop services for the cluster.
D. All of these

Q.32 Which of the following keys is generally used to represents the relationships between the tables?
A. Primary key
B. Foreign key
C. Secondary key
D. Super Key

Q.33 Which of the following levels is considered as the level closed to the end-users?
A. Internal Level
B. External Level
C. Conceptual Level
D. Physical Level

Q.34 Suppliers(Sid: integer, sname:string, city:string, street:string)
Parts(pid:integer, pname:string, color:string)
Catalog(sid:integer, pid:integer, cost:real)
Consider the following relational query on the above database:
SELECT S.sname
FROM Suppliers S
WHERE S.sid NOT IN (SELECT C.sid
FROM Catalog C
WHERE C.pid NOT IN (SELECT P.pid
FROM Parts P
WHERE P.color < > 'blue'))
Assume that relations corresponding to the above schema are not empty. Which of the following is the correct interpretation of the above query?
A. Find the names of all suppliers who have supplied a non-blue part.
B. Find the names of all suppliers who have not supplied a non-blue part.
C. Find the names of all suppliers who have supplied only blue parts.
D. Find the names of all suppliers who have not supplied only blue parts.

Q.35 Which of the following are a collaborative data analytics and visualization tool?
A. ACE
B. Abdera
C. Zeppelin
D. Accumulo

Q.36 Which one of the following keywords is used to find out the number of values inside a column?
A. TOTAL
B. COUNT
C. SUM
D. ADD

Q.37 Which of the following commands creates an emergency repair disk for Windows NT 4.0?
A. BAT
B. EXE
C. EXE/S
D. ADD/REMOVE program

Q.38 Four necessary conditions for deadlock to exist are mutual exclusion, no-preemption, circular wait and:
A. Hold and wait
B. Deadlock avoidance
C. Race around condition
D. Buffer overflow

Q.39 A partitioned data set is most used for:
A. A program or source library
B. Storing program data
C. Storing backup information
D. Storing ISAM files

Q.40 What is the correct way the segmentation program address is stored?
A. name and offset
B. start and stop
C. access and rights
D. offset and rights

Q.41 What does the linker program do?
A. Places the program in the memory for the purpose of execution.
B. Relocates the program to execute from the specific memory area allocated to it.
C. Links the program with other programs needed for its execution.
D. Interfaces the program with the entities generating its input data.

Q.42 Which scheduling policy is most suitable for a time-shared operating system?
A. Shortest-job First
B. Elevator
C. Round-Robin
D. First-Come-First-Serve

Q.43 A critical section is a program segment:
A. Which should run in a certain specified amount of time.
B. Which avoids deadlocks.
C. Where shared resources are accessed.
D. Which must be enclosed by a pair of semaphore operations, P and V.

Q.44 An operating system contains 3 user processes each requiring 2 units of resource R. The minimum number of units of R such that no deadlocks will ever arise is:
A. 4
B. 3
C. 5
D. 6

Q.45 The main function of the dispatcher (the portion of the process scheduler) is _________.
A. Swapping a process to the disk.
B. Assigning ready process to the CPU.
C. Suspending some of the processes when the CPU load is high.
D. Bring processes from the disk to the main memory.

Q.46 Concatenation operation refers to which of the following set operations?
A. Union
B. Dot
C. Kleene
D. None of these

Q.47 Which of the following can be used to prove a language is not context free?
A. Ardens theorem
B. Power construction method
C. Regular closure
D. None of these

Q.48 Which of the following is not an example of bounded information?
A. Fan switch outputs {on, off}
B. Electricity meter reading
C. Colour of the traffic light at the moment
D. None of these

Q.49 A language for which no DFA exist is a _______.
A. Regular Language
B. Non-Regular Language
C. May be Regular
D. Cannot be said

Q.50 A DFA cannot be represented in which of the following format:
A. Transition graph
B. Transition table
C. C code
D. None of these

Q.51 Which language is accepted by the push-down automata?
A. Type 0 language
B. Type 1 language
C. Type 2 language
D. Type 3 language

Q.52 The most general phase of structured grammar is __________.
A. Context-sensitive grammar
B. Context-free grammar
C. Regular grammar
D. None of these

Q.53 In the compiler, the function of using intermediate code is:
A. To improve the register allocation.
B. To increase the error reporting & recovery.
C. To make semantic analysis easier.
D. To increase the chances of reusing the machine-independent code optimizer in other compilers.

Q.54 In how many types of code optimization can be divided?
A. Two types
B. Three types
C. Four types
D. Five types

Q.55 Which of the following tools is not used for process descriptions?
A. Structured
B. Pseudocodes
C. Decision tables
D. Data Dictionary

Q.56 Which of the following is not a factor in the failure of a systems development project?

A. Size of the company

B. Inadequate user involvement

C. Failure of systems integration

D. Continuation of a project that should have been cancelled

Q.57 Software Configuration Management can be administered in several ways. These include:

A. A single software configuration management team for the whole organization.

B. A separate configuration management team for each project.

C. Software Configuration Management distributed among the project members.

D. All of these

Q.58 What combines procedures and tools to manage different versions of configuration objects that are created during the software process?

A. Change control

B. Version control

C. SCI

D. None of these

Q.59 Interface consistency implies that:

A. Each application should have its own distinctive look and feel.

B. Input mechanisms remain the same throughout the application.

C. Visual information is organized according to a design standard.

D. Both (B) and (C)

Q.60 Which model depicts the image of a system that an end-user creates in his or her head?

A. Design model

B. User model

C. System model

D. System perception model

Q.61 Which testing includes testing a software manually, i.e. without using any automated tool or any script?

A. Automation Testing

B. Client Testing

C. Manual Testing

D. All of these

Q.62 Which testing comes under manual testing?

A. Unit Testing

B. Integration Testing

C. System Testing

D. All of these

Q.63 Model that translates design classes into software components is:

A. Analysis model

B. Implementation model

C. Design model

D. Use case model

Q.64 Five letters are sent to different persons and addresses on the five envelopes are written at random. The probability that all the letters do not reach the correct destiny is:

A. $\frac{44}{120}$ **B.** $\frac{1}{120}$ **C.** $\frac{1}{5}$ **D.** $\frac{5}{120}$

Q.65 A box contains 4 tennis balls, 6 season balls and 8 dues balls. 3 balls are randomly drawn from the box. What is the probability that the balls are different?

A. $\frac{4}{17}$ **B.** $\frac{3}{11}$ **C.** $\frac{2}{13}$ **D.** $\frac{5}{17}$

Q.66 Find the general solution of given differential equation:
$$\frac{xdy}{dx} + 3y = 4x^3?$$

A. $x^3 \cdot y = \frac{2}{3} \cdot x^5 + c$ **B.** $x^3 \cdot y = 3x^6 + c$

C. $x^3 \cdot y = \frac{2}{3} \cdot x^6 + c$ **D.** None of these

Q.67 Solve $x\frac{dy}{dx} - y = x^2$ for $y(2)$, given $y(1) = 1$:

A. 1   **B.** 2   **C.** 3   **D.** 4

Q.68 Using Laplace transform evaluate:
$$\int_0^\infty \frac{\sin 2t}{t}\, dt$$

A. 2π **B.** π **C.** $\frac{\pi}{2}$ **D.** $\frac{\pi}{4}$

Q.69 Find the Laplace transform of the periodic function:
$$f(t) = \begin{cases} t, & 0 < t < \pi \\ \pi - t, & \pi < t < 2\pi \end{cases}$$

A. $\frac{1}{1-e^{-2\pi s}}\left\{\frac{\pi}{s}(e^{-2\pi s} - e^{-\pi s}) - \frac{1}{s^2}(1 - e^{-2\pi s} - 2e^{-\pi s})\right\}$

B. $\frac{1}{1-e^{-2\pi s}}\left\{\frac{\pi}{s}(e^{-2\pi s} - e^{-\pi s}) + \frac{1}{s^2}(1 + e^{-2\pi s} - 2e^{-\pi s})\right\}$

C. $\frac{1}{1-e^{-2\pi s}}\left\{\frac{\pi}{s}(e^{-2\pi s} - e^{-\pi s}) + \frac{1}{s^2}(1 - e^{-2\pi s} + 2e^{-\pi s})\right\}$

D. $\frac{1}{1-e^{-2\pi x}}\left\{\frac{\pi}{s}(e^{-2\pi s} - e^{-\pi s}) - \frac{1}{s^2}(1 + e^{-2\pi s} - 2e^{-\pi s})\right\}$

Q.70 For the matrix $A = \begin{bmatrix} 5 & 3 \\ 1 & 3 \end{bmatrix}$, one of the normalized eigen vectors is given as:

A. $\begin{bmatrix} \frac{1}{2} \\ \frac{\sqrt{3}}{2} \end{bmatrix}$ **B.** $\begin{bmatrix} 1 \\ -1 \end{bmatrix}$ **C.** $\begin{bmatrix} \frac{3}{\sqrt{10}} \\ \frac{-1}{\sqrt{10}} \end{bmatrix}$ **D.** $\begin{bmatrix} \frac{1}{\sqrt{5}} \\ \frac{2}{\sqrt{5}} \end{bmatrix}$

Q.71 If the product of eigenvalues of the matrix $A = \begin{bmatrix} 1 & 2 & -1 \\ 3 & 5 & 2 \\ 1 & k & 2 \end{bmatrix}$ is -8 then the value of k will be:

A. 3   **B.** 2   **C.** -2 **D.** -3

Q.72 Find $f'(x)$ if $f(x) = (6x^3)(7x^4)$:

A. $294x^6$ **B.** $294x^5$ **C.** $29x^6$ **D.** $294x^2$

Q.73 If $\int \frac{xe^x}{\sqrt{1+e^x}}\, dx = f(x)\sqrt{1+e^x} - 2\log\frac{\sqrt{1+e^x}-1}{\sqrt{1+e^x}+1} + C$, then $f(x)$ is:

A. $2x - 1$ **B.** $2x - 4$ **C.** $x + 4$ **D.** $x - 4$

Q.74 Consider column A and column B:

Column A represents algorithms.

Column B represents the resources/operations which is optimized by corresponding column A row among its competitor.

A	B

A_1	Selection Sort	B_1	Comparison
A_2	Quick sort	B_2	Time
A_3	Binary Search	B_3	Swaps
A_4	Counting Sort	B_4	Memory

- **A.** $A_1 - B_3, A_2 - B_4, A_3 - B_1, A_4 - B_1$
- **B.** $A_1 - B_3, A_2 - B_1, A_3 - B_2, A_4 - B_2$
- **C.** $A_1 - B_3, A_2 - B_4, A_3 - B_2, A_4 - B_2$
- **D.** Both (A) and (B)

Q.75 In a hash table with 40 slots 60 records are inserted with collisions being resolved by chaining. What is the expected number of key comparisons in an unsuccessful search assuming uniform hashing?

- **A.** 1.5
- **B.** 2
- **C.** 2.5
- **D.** 1

Q.76 What is the content of the array after two delete operations?

- **A.** 14,13,12,10,8
- **B.** 14,12,13,8,10
- **C.** 14,13,8,12,10
- **D.** 14,13,12,8,10

Q.77 Consider the following statements:

Statement 1: G is an undirected graph with vertices $\{P, Q, R, S, T\}$. Every edge has a distinct weight. RS is the edge with minimum edge weight and ST is an edge with maximum edge weight. ST is in the minimum Spanning tree if and only if it is a cut edge.

Statement 2: If we run Prim's Algorithm and Kruskal's algorithm on a graph G then the Minimum cost tree produced, can be different.

Statement 3: If we run Bellman ford algorithm on a weighted graph G with V vertices, It is been observed that even in $V + 1$ iteration distance decreased then there exists a negative weight cycle in G.

Which of the following is/are true?

- **A.** Statement 1 is true
- **B.** Statement 2 is true
- **C.** Statement 3 is false
- **D.** All of these

Q.78 The recurrence relation capturing the optimal time of the Tower of Hanoi problem with n discs is:

- **A.** $T(n) = 2T(n - 2) + 2$
- **B.** $T(n) = 2T(n - 1) + n$
- **C.** $T(n) = 2T\left(\frac{n}{2}\right) + 1$
- **D.** $T(n) = 2T(n - 1) + 1$

Q.79 Let $W(n)$ and $A(n)$ denote respectively, the worst case and average case running time of an algorithm executed on an input of size n. Which of the following is always true?

1. $A(n) = \Omega\big(W(n)\big)$
2. $A(n) = \Theta\big(W(n)\big)$
3. $A(n) = O\big(W(n)\big)$
4. $A(n) = o\big(W(n)\big)$

- **A.** 1
- **B.** 2
- **C.** 3
- **D.** 4

Q.80 Which of the following is not $O(n^2)$?

- **A.** $(15^{10}) \times n + 12099$
- **B.** $n^{1.98}$
- **C.** $\frac{n^3}{\sqrt{(n)}}$
- **D.** $(2^{20}) \times n$

Q.81 Which of the given options provides the increasing order of asymptotic complexity of functions f_1, f_2, f_3 and f_4?

- $f_1(n) = 2^n$
- $f_2(n) = n^{\left(\frac{3}{2}\right)}$
- $f_3(n) = n\log n$
- $f_4(n) = n^{(\log n)}$

- **A.** f_3, f_2, f_4, f_1
- **B.** f_3, f_2, f_1, f_4
- **C.** f_2, f_3, f_1, f_4
- **D.** f_2, f_3, f_4, f_1

Q.82 Consider the following program fragment for reversing the digits in a given integer to obtain a new integer. Let n = D1D2...Dm:

```
int n, rev;
rev = 0;
while (n >0)
{
rev = rev*10 + n%10;
n = n/10;
}
```

The loop invariant condition at the end of the ith iteration is:

- **A.** n = D1D2....Dm-i and rev = DmDm-1...Dm-i+1
- **B.** n = Dm-i+1...Dm-1Dm and rev = Dm-1....D2D1
- **C.** n != rev
- **D.** n = D1D2....Dm and rev = DmDm-1...D2D1

Q.83 If $f(x) = x$ is my friend, and $p(x) = x$ is perfect. Then correct logical translation of the "some of my friends are not perfect" is __________.

- **A.** $\forall_x \big(f(x) \wedge \neg p(x)\big)$
- **B.** $\exists_x \big(f(x) \wedge \neg p(x)\big)$
- **C.** $\neg \big(f(x) \wedge \neg p(x)\big)$
- **D.** $\exists_x \big(\neg f(x) \wedge \neg p(x)\big)$

Q.84 Consider the following statements:

(I) If the binary relation itself is transitive, then the transitive closure is that same binary relation.

(II) An asymmetric relation is always anti-symmetric.

(III) An empty relation on a nonempty set is always symmetric.

Which of the above statements is/are true?

- **A.** (II) and (III) only
- **B.** (II) only
- **C.** (I) and (III) only
- **D.** (I), (II) and (III)

Q.85 Consider the poset $\{3,5,9,15,24,45\}$.

Which of the following is correct for the given poset?

- **A.** There exists a greatest element and a least element.
- **B.** There exists a greatest element but not a least element.
- **C.** There exists a least element but not a greatest element.
- **D.** There does not exist a greatest element and a least element.

Q.86 If a graph (G) has no loops or parallel edges and if the number of vertices (n) in the graph is $n \geq 3$, then the graph G is Hamiltonian if:

(i) $deg(v) \geq \dfrac{n}{3}$ for each vertex v.

(ii) $deg(v) + deg(w) \geq n$ whenever v and w are not connected by an edge.

(iii) $E(G) \geq \dfrac{1}{3}(n-1)(n-2) + 2$.

A. (i) and (iii) only   **B.** (ii) and (iii) only
C. (iii) only   **D.** (ii) only

Q.87 How many distinguishable permutations of the letters in the word $BANANA$ are there?

A. 720   **B.** 120   **C.** 60   **D.** 360

Q.88 $P(n): 2 \times 7^n + 3 \times 5^n - 5$ is divisible by:

A. $24, \forall n \in N$ **B.** $21, \forall n \in N$
C. $32, \forall n \in N$ **D.** $50, \forall n \in N$

Q.89 How many ways are there to arrange 7 chocolate biscuits and 12 cheesecake biscuits into a row of 19 biscuits?

A. 52347   **B.** 50388   **C.** 87658   **D.** 24976

Q.90 The less-than relation, <, on a set of real numbers is ________.

A. Not a partial ordering because it is not asymmetric and irreflexive equals antisymmetric.
B. A partial ordering since it is asymmetric and reflexive.
C. A partial ordering since it is antisymmetric and reflexive.
D. Not a partial ordering because it is not antisymmetric and reflexive.

Q.91 ______ and ______ are the two binary operations defined for lattices.

A. Join, meet
B. Addition, subtraction
C. Union, intersection
D. Multiplication, modulo division

Q.92 Let the N and M be the two hexadecimal number in $IEEE - 754$ format: $0 \times 3E6D0000$ and $0 \times C1200000$ respectively.

The value of $N_{10} + M_{10}$ is ________ (correct answer upto 1 decimal place).

A. $-9.8 - -9.7$ **B.** $-9.8 - -9.1$
C. $-9.8 - -9.6$ **D.** $-9.9 - -9.7$

Q.93 When two numbers are added in excess - 3 code and the sum is less than 9, then in order to get the correct answer it is necessary to:

A. Subtract 0011 from the sum
B. Add 0011 to the sum
C. Subtract 0110 from the sum
D. Add 0110 to the sum

Q.94 Consider the unsigned 8-bit point binary number representation below:

$$N_7 \ N_6 \ N_5 \ N_4 \ N_3 \cdot N_2 \ N_1 \ N_0$$

where the position of the binary point is between N_3 and N_2. Assume N_7 is the MSB. Which of the decimal numbers can be represented exactly in the above representation?

A. 11.375   **B.** 33.0
C. 29.625   **D.** Both (A) and (C)

Q.95 In Boolean algebra, $\left(A.\overline{A}\right) + A =?$

A. A **B.** 0 **C.** $\overline{A}$ **D.** 1

Q.96 Which among following is not a logic gate?

A. AND   **B.** OR   **C.** XR   **D.** NOT

Q.97 D flip flop can be made from a $J - K$ flip flop by making:

A. $J = K$ **B.** $J = K = 1$
C. $J = 0, K = 1$ **D.** $J = \overline{K}$

Q.98 Original ASCII coding scheme uses ______ bits for coding 128 different characters.

A. 6   **B.** 7   **C.** 8   **D.** 16

Q.99 What is the 2's complement of $0011010110011100?$

A. 1100101011001011
B. 1100101001100011
C. 1100101001100100
D. 1100101011111111

Q.100 If there are m input lines and n output lines for a decoder that is used to uniquely address a byte addressable $1\ KB$ RAM, then the minimum value of $m + n$ is ________.

A. 1034   **B.** 1024   **C.** 995   **D.** 1022

// Smart Answer Sheet //

Correct Percentage of students who answered correctly.　　**Skipped** Percentage of students who skipped.

Q.	Ans.	Correct / Skipped	Q.	Ans.	Correct / Skipped	Q.	Ans.	Correct / Skipped	Q.	Ans.	Correct / Skipped	Q.	Ans.	Correct / Skipped	Q.	Ans.	Correct / Skipped
1	A	58.99 % / 30.39 %	18	A	66.71 % / 31.79 %	35	C	13.6 % / 79.95 %	52	A	50.72 % / 39.78 %	69	B	22.21 % / 70.59 %	86	D	40.56 % / 49.31 %
2	D	85.26 % / 11.7 %	19	C	80.42 % / 14.09 %	36	B	68.87 % / 30.78 %	53	D	32.97 % / 67.01 %	70	B	50.75 % / 47.14 %	87	C	29.82 % / 67.86 %
3	B	58.95 % / 34.23 %	20	C	42.55 % / 47.37 %	37	B	15.47 % / 73.95 %	54	A	41.27 % / 40.27 %	71	A	61.95 % / 30.65 %	88	A	40.54 % / 39.52 %
4	A	85.99 % / 10.17 %	21	C	57.81 % / 30.8 %	38	A	46.99 % / 42.57 %	55	D	60.11 % / 36.03 %	72	A	88.58 % / 10.55 %	89	B	51.75 % / 42.21 %
5	D	53.4 % / 38.1 %	22	B	48.49 % / 34.03 %	39	A	76.97 % / 12.17 %	56	A	63.34 % / 33.81 %	73	B	27.75 % / 70.3 %	90	A	45.95 % / 44.06 %
6	D	41.12 % / 45.3 %	23	C	53.5 % / 40.58 %	40	A	54.51 % / 39.24 %	57	A	13.89 % / 70.12 %	74	D	26.47 % / 73.51 %	91	A	57.48 % / 40.9 %
7	B	66.18 % / 33.76 %	24	A	86.68 % / 11.87 %	41	C	50.92 % / 43.36 %	58	B	49.57 % / 38.43 %	75	A	69.63 % / 30.21 %	92	A	17.12 % / 79.49 %
8	A	85.19 % / 14.74 %	25	B	84.44 % / 10.44 %	42	C	63.74 % / 35.47 %	59	D	78.9 % / 15.14 %	76	D	69.77 % / 30.14 %	93	A	57.0 % / 33.77 %
9	B	59.75 % / 35.25 %	26	A	40.48 % / 46.23 %	43	C	62.73 % / 32.76 %	60	D	40.82 % / 48.42 %	77	D	40.75 % / 40.92 %	94	D	41.22 % / 49.01 %
10	B	15.61 % / 67.37 %	27	B	64.72 % / 32.37 %	44	A	47.62 % / 33.7 %	61	C	54.77 % / 43.54 %	78	D	29.27 % / 68.08 %	95	A	85.31 % / 11.99 %
11	C	19.55 % / 73.88 %	28	D	68.78 % / 30.95 %	45	B	42.5 % / 43.39 %	62	D	32.77 % / 67.18 %	79	C	69.41 % / 30.05 %	96	C	65.03 % / 30.3 %
12	A	42.88 % / 34.21 %	29	D	22.7 % / 68.18 %	46	B	51.23 % / 42.45 %	63	B	43.18 % / 48.78 %	80	C	19.21 % / 70.7 %	97	D	10.49 % / 74.17 %
13	A	63.6 % / 34.92 %	30	D	22.13 % / 68.39 %	47	C	65.36 % / 31.67 %	64	A	21.12 % / 69.13 %	81	A	13.69 % / 82.38 %	98	B	60.28 % / 34.93 %
14	C	41.17 % / 32.19 %	31	A	18.05 % / 79.29 %	48	B	63.36 % / 31.82 %	65	A	56.69 % / 43.3 %	82	A	52.89 % / 46.27 %	99	C	52.48 % / 37.61 %
15	D	51.45 % / 40.6 %	32	B	64.09 % / 31.51 %	49	B	53.78 % / 41.78 %	66	C	67.72 % / 30.98 %	83	B	47.47 % / 40.2 %	100	A	51.66 % / 45.36 %
16	A	67.18 % / 32.6 %	33	B	78.53 % / 20.45 %	50	D	18.68 % / 67.61 %	67	D	42.43 % / 33.04 %	84	D	20.03 % / 68.41 %			
17	A	20.41 % / 73.16 %	34	D	15.17 % / 83.29 %	51	C	44.84 % / 43.31 %	68	C	65.14 % / 34.63 %	85	D	67.69 % / 31.86 %			

//Hints and Solutions//

1. When an object is returned by a function, a temporary object is automatically created to hold the return value. The values get assigned as required, and the temporary object gets destroyed. The temporary object is used to copy the values to another object or to be used in some way. The object holds all the values of the data members of the object.

Hence, the correct option is (A).

2. <a> tag is used to add links to the webpage.

The </a> tag defines a hyperlink, which is used to link from one page to another.

Attribute 'href' indicates the link's destination.

Example:

How to link to an email address:

<a href="mailto:someone@example.com">Send email</a>

Hence, the correct option is (D).

3. A program that reads the source code and converts it to a form usable by the computer, is known as a compiler. A compiler is a computer program that translates computer code written in one programming language (the source language) into another language (the target language). The name "compiler" is primarily used for programs that translate source code from a high-level programming language to a lower level language (e.g. assembly language, object code, or machine code) to create an executable program.

Hence, the correct option is (B).

4. Prolog stands for Programming in Logic. Prolog differs from the most common programming languages because it is a declarative language. This means that the programmer must specify in detail how to solve a problem. Prolog is a type of logic programming. The four options mentioned are the four categories of programming.

Hence, the correct option is (A).

5. The method that can be used to create new properties and also to modify the attributes of existing properties is both Object.defineProperty() and Object.defineProperties(). The method Object.defineProperty() defines a new property directly on an object, or modifies an existing property on an object, and returns the object. Both Object.defineProperty() and Object.defineProperties() can be used to define new properties.

Hence, the correct option is (D).

6. All the data structures that are given in the above options can be used to implement a priority queue but the most efficient way of implementing a priority queue is heap data structure. Heaps are tree-based data structures constrained by a heap property. Heaps are used in many famous algorithms such as Dijkstra's algorithm for finding the shortest path, the heap sort sorting algorithm, implementing priority queues, and more.

Hence, the correct option is (D).

7. A linear data structure in which insertion and deletion operations can be performed from both the ends is Deque. The deque is a data structure in which both insertion and deletion can be performed from both the ends whereas, in Queue, insertion can be done from one end and deletion can be performed from another end.

Hence, the correct option is (B).

8. A full binary tree is a tree in which each node has exactly zero or two children. The full binary tree is also known as a strict binary tree. The full binary tree can also be defined as the tree in which each node must contain 2 children except the leaf nodes.

Hence, the correct option is (A).

9. As it is mentioned in the question that the size of the array is 5. Therefore, the range would be from 0 to 4. In a circular queue, the last element is connected to the first element; the value of rear is 4 so when we increment the value then it will point to the 0th position of the array.

Hence, the correct option is (B).

10. Alternative routing is not a characteristic of the hub architecture of Arc net. Alternative routing provides two different cables from the local exchange to your site, so you can protect against cable failure as your service will be maintained on the alternative route.

Hence, the correct option is (B).

11. X. 25 is an International Telecommunication Union Telecommunication Standardization Sector (ITU-T) protocol standard simply for Wide Area Network (WAN) communications that basically describes how the connections among user devices and network devices are established and maintained. It supports two types of virtual circuits as given below:

Switched Virtual Circuit (SVC): This virtual circuit Is established among a computer and network when the computer transfers a packet or data to the network that is requesting to make a call to another computer. VCs are simply implemented and established in connection-oriented systems like analog telephone networks and ATM networks.

Permanent Virtual Circuit (PVC): It is a permanent association among two DTE's that is established only when a user subscribes to a public network. PVCs are more costly than SVC's. This is also similar to the leased line that is used to link all of the data devices.

Hence, the correct option is (C).

12. The X. 25 protocol is divided into 3 layers (or Levels):

X. 25 Physical Layer: The Physical Layer used for X. 25 can also be employed by a number of other protocols, such as PPP, Cisco HDLC (cHDLC) or Frame Relay.

X. 25 Data Link Layer: The purpose of the link layer is essential to provide a reliable mechanism to exchange data between one end of the link and the other. The link-layer protocol, therefore, provides a procedure for error detection and correction.

X. 25 **Packet Layer Protocol (PLP):** The X. 25 Packet Layer Protocol is the network layer (level 3) of X. 25, and handles the virtual circuits, providing the multiplexing capability.

Hence, the correct option is (A).

13. A protocol is a rule governing a time sequence of events that must take place between peers. Peer-to-peer (P 2P) computing or networking is a distributed application architecture that partitions tasks or workloads between peers. Peers are equally privileged, equipotent participants in the application. They are said to form a peer-to-peer network of nodes.

Hence, the correct option is (A).

14. WAN networks may be separated by some distance, it usually involves two or more small networks and dedicated high speed telephone lines.TCP/IP is used for a WAN in combination with devices such as routers, switches, firewalls and modems.

Hence, the correct option is (C).

15. The maximum data capacity for optical fiber cable is 10000 Mbps. 10000 Enabled Capabilities Enabled to be enabled in particular applicable conditions, when enabled to charge, is changed as being capable of communication with the camera. It is said to be the fastest among the other kinds of cables like STP cables and co-axial cables. People are now using optical fiber cables instead of STP cables for LANs due to their fast data transfer capability.

Hence, the correct option is (D).

16. Server gives the permission to sharing the resources of the computer in the network that is used by the client which is connected to that server. The client gives the request to the server for the services according to her request the server response and shared the resources and providing the services to the client in the network. The processor of the server is more powerful as compare to the client computer because it handles lots of requests. If the server is crash then nothing can be done.

Hence, the correct option is (A).

17. Time-division multiplexing (TDM) is a method of transmitting and receiving independent signals over a common signal path by means of synchronized switches at each end of the transmission line so that each signal appears on the line, only a fraction of time in an alternating pattern.

Hence, the correct option is (A).

18. The full form of MODEM is "Modulator/Demodulator" which allows a computer or other devices, such as a router or switch, to connect to the Internet. It converts or "modulates" an analog signal from a telephone or cable wire to a digital signal that a computer can recognize. Similarly, it converts outgoing digital data from a computer or other device to an analog signal.

Hence, the correct option is (A).

19. Subroutine nesting is a common programming practice In which one Subroutine call another Subroutine. A nested subroutine is a subroutine that is called from within some other subroutine. Now a nested subroutine can invoke itself some other subroutine(s). These are subroutines that call themselves from within their own code. With these kinds of subroutines, nesting can reach enormous depths.

Hence, the correct option is (C).

20. In the case of nested subroutines, there will be more number of return addresses it is stored in the processor stack. The subroutine carries out its task. The end of the task is often marked by a 'RETURN' statement within the subroutine. The return operation will POP the calling address from the stack and if required will PUSH a return value onto the stack. Control now jumps back to the instruction at the calling address.

Hence, the correct option is (C).

21. The signal generated upon the pressing of a button is encoded by the encoder circuit into the corresponding ASCII value. An encoder can also be described as a combinational circuit that performs the inverse operation of a decoder. An encoder has a maximum of 2^n (or less) input lines and n output lines. In an encoder, the output lines generate the binary code corresponding to the input value.

Hence, the correct option is (C).

22. When the button is pressed, the contact surfaces bounce and so, it might lead to the generation of multiple signals. In order to overcome this, we use debouncing circuits. Electrical contacts in mechanical pushbutton switches often make and break contact several times when the button is first pushed. A debouncing circuit removes the resulting ripple signal and provides a clean transition at its output.

Hence, the correct option is (B).

23. The best mode of connection between devices that need to send or receive large amounts of data over a short distance is a parallel port. The parallel port transfers around 8 to 16 bits of data simultaneously over the lines, therefore, increasing transfer rates. On PCs, the parallel port uses a 25-pin connector (type DB- 25) and is used to connect printers, computers and other devices that need relatively high bandwidth. It is often called a Centronics interface after the company that designed the original standard for parallel communication between a computer and printer.

Hence, the correct option is (C).

24. The interface circuits act as a hardware interface between the device and the buses. An Input/output (I/O) interface consists of the circuitry required to connect an I/O device to a computer bus. On one side of the interface, we have the bus signals for address, data, and control. An interface circuit is a signal conditioning circuit used to bring signals from the sensor up to the format that is compatible with the load device.

Hence, the correct option is (A).

25. A port side is basically a physical docking point which is basically used to connect the external devices to the computer, or we can say that a port act as an interface between the computer and the external devices, e.g., we can connect hard drives, printers to the computer with the help of ports. Port side connects the device to the motherboard.

Hence, the correct option is (B).

26. The contention for the usage of a hardware device is called structural hazard. The processor contends for the usage of the hardware and might enter into a deadlock state. A structural hazard occurs when two (or more) instructions that are already in pipeline need the same resource. The result is that instruction must be executed in series rather than parallel for a portion of the pipeline. Hardware cannot support certain combinations of instructions (two instructions in the pipeline require the same resource).

Hence, the correct option is (A).

27. Score boarding method is used in centralized systems to perform out of order execution. In a scoreboard, the data dependencies of every instruction are logged. Instructions are released only when the scoreboard determines that there are no conflicts with previously issued and incomplete instructions.

Hence, the correct option is (B).

28. The computational technique used to compute the disk storage address of individual records is called hashing. Hashing is simply passing some data through a formula that produces a result, called a hash. Hashing is the process of transforming any given key or a string of characters into another value. This is usually represented by a shorter, fixed-length value or key that represents and makes it easier to find or employ the original string. The most popular use for hashing is the implementation of hash tables.

Hence, the correct option is (D).

29. The database management query language is generally designed by keeping in mind that it must support the end-users who are familiar with the English-like commands. It should also boost the process of development of the complex applications software and helps in specifying the structure of the database.

Hence, the correct option is (D).

30. Distributed applications use Zookeeper to store and mediate updates to important configuration information. ZooKeeper provides superior reliability through redundant services. Availability of data even when one or a few nodes are down. ZooKeeper is itself a distributed application providing services for writing a distributed application.

Hence, the correct option is (D).

31. Ambari provides central management for starting and stopping Hadoop services across the entire cluster. Ambari provides a dashboard for monitoring the health and status of the Hadoop cluster. Ambari will send emails when your attention is needed (e.g., a node goes down, remaining disk space is low, etc). This simplification is done by providing an easy-to-use web UI and REST API.

Hence, the correct option is (A).

32. A foreign key is generally used to represent the relationships between the tables. This unique key communicates one or more interrelationships in a relational database between two or more tables. A Foreign Key is a database key that is used to link two tables together. The Foreign Key constraint identifies the relationships between the database tables by referencing a column or set of columns, in the child table that contains the foreign key, to the primary key column or set of columns, in the parent table.

Hence, the correct option is (B).

33. The database's external level is the one and only level that is considered the closest level to the end-users. This is the highest level in the three level architecture and closest to the user. It is also known as the view level. The external level only shows the relevant database content to the users in the form of views and hides the rest of the data.

Hence, the correct option is (B).

34. The above query will return the Name of all suppliers who will not supply blue parts, which means it can include non-Blue parts and Null values.

Consider the following table:

Name	ID	Color
A	1	Blue
B	2	Blue
C	3	Blue
D	4	Blue
E	5	Red
F	6	Red
G	7	Red
H	8	Red
I	9	Null
J	10	Null

The QUERY "SELECT P.pid FROM Parts P where P.color < > 'blue' " will give:

Name	ID	Color
E	5	red
F	6	Red
G	7	Red
H	8	Red
I	9	Null
J	10	Null

The Query "SELECT C.sid FROM Catalog C where C.pid NOT IN (SELECT P.pid FROM Parts P where P.color < > 'blue')" will give:

Name	ID	Color
A	1	Blue
B	2	Blue
C	3	Blue
D	4	Blue

The query " SELECT S.sname FROM Suppliers S where S.sid NOT IN (SELECT C.sid FROM Catalog C where C.pid NOT IN (SELECT P.pid FROM Parts P where P.color < > 'blue')) " will give:

Name	ID	Color
E	5	Red

F	6	Red
G	7	Red
H	8	Red
I	9	Null
J	10	Null

Option (A): FALSE

The non-blue part does not include the Null values.

Option (B): FALSE

It will include both Null values and Blue parts.

Option (C): FALSE

It will include only Blue parts.

Option (D): TRUE

It will include Non-Blue parts and Null values.

Hence, the correct option is (D).

35. Zeppelin is used for general-purpose data processing systems such as Apache Spark, Apache Flink, etc. Apache Zeppelin is a new and upcoming web-based notebook that brings data exploration, visualization, sharing and collaboration features to Spark. It supports Python, but also a growing list of programming languages such as Scala, Hive, SparkSQL, Shell and Markdown.

Hence, the correct option is (C).

36. The "COUNT" keyword is used to find the total number of values inside a column. So, whenever a user wants to find the total values in a column, he can use the keyword "COUNT". To count the number of different values that are stored in a given column, you simply need to designate the column you pass into the COUNT function as DISTINCT. When given a column, COUNT returns the number of values in that column. Combining this with DISTINCT returns only the number of unique (and non-NULL) values.

Hence, the correct option is (B).

37. EXE is the command which creates an emergency repair disk for Windows NT 4.0. There are the following steps to repair disk in windows NT 4.0:

Step 1: Go to the search button in windows NT 4.0, then type Command Prompt.

Step 2: Then type "RDISK.EXE" and press enter.

Step 3: Then open a pop-up window. This pop-up window will update the emergency repair disk.

Hence, the correct option is (B).

38. Four necessary conditions for deadlock to exist are mutual exclusion, no-preemption, circular wait and hold and wait.

A deadlock in OS is a condition where two or more processes get blocked. The four essential conditions, mutual exclusion, no-preemption, circular weight, and hold and wait, must be together for a deadlock to occur.

Mutual Exclusion: At least one process must be held in a non-sharable mode.

Hold and Wait: There must be a process holding one resource and waiting for another.

No preemption: Resources cannot be preempted.

Circular wait: There must exist a set of processes.

Hence, the correct option is (A).

39. A partitioned data set is most used for a program or source library.

A partitioned data set (PDS) is a data set containing multiple members, each of which holds a separate sub-data set, similar to a directory in other types of file systems. A partitioned data set or PDS consists of a directory and members. The directory holds the address of each member and thus makes it possible for programs or the operating system to access each member directly. Each member, however, consists of sequentially stored records.

Hence, the correct option is (A).

40. OS can retrieve the real address via looking for the table then making a simple calculation: address of the name and offset. Segmentation is a memory-management scheme that supports the programmer's view of memory. A logical address space is a collection of segments. Each segment has a name and a length. The programmer therefore specifies each address by two quantities: a segment name and an offset. For simplicity of implementation, segments are numbered and are referred to by a segment number, rather than by a segment name.

Hence, the correct option is (A).

41. The linker program links the program with other programs needed for its execution. The linker is a program in a system that helps to link object modules of the program into a single object file. It performs the process of linking. The linker is also called a link editor. Linking is the process of collecting and maintaining pieces of code and data into a single file.

Hence, the correct option is (C).

42. Round-Robin (RR) is one of the algorithms employed by process and network schedulers in computing. As the term is generally used, time slices (also known as time quanta) are assigned to each process in equal portions and in circular order, handling all processes without priority (also known as cyclic executive). Round-robin scheduling is simple, easy to implement, and starvation-free. Round-robin scheduling can be applied to other scheduling problems, such as data packet scheduling in computer networks. It is an operating system concept.

Hence, the correct option is (C).

43. A critical section is a program segment where shared resources are accessed. A critical section is a section of code belonging to a process in a. concurrent program that accesses a shared resource, e.g., a shared variable, shared. communication channel, shared file, etc. and for correct behavior of the program, only one process may access the.

Hence, the correct option is (C).

44. In worst case,

The number of units that each process holds $=$ One less than its maximum demand

So,

Process P_1 holds 1 unit of resource R.

Process P_2 holds 1 unit of resource R.

Process P_3 holds 1 unit of resource R.

Thus,

Maximum number of units of resource R that ensures deadlock $= 1 + 1 + 1 = 3$.

The minimum number of units of resource R that ensures no deadlock $= 3 + 1 = 4$.

Hence, the correct option is (A).

45. The main function of the dispatcher is assigning the ready processes to the CPU. CPU scheduler selects a process among the processes that are ready to execute and allocates CPU to one of them. Short-term schedulers, also known as dispatchers, make the decision of which process to execute next.

Hence, the correct option is (B).

46. Concatenation operation refers to dot operations. The concatenation operator is a binary operator, whose syntax is shown in the general diagram for an SQL expression. You can use the concatenation operator ($\parallel$) to concatenate two expressions that evaluate to character data types or to numeric data types. The second example concatenates the suffix.

Two operands are said to be performing concatenation operation $AB = A \cdot B = \{xy: x \in A \;\&\; y \in B\}$.

Hence, the correct option is (B).

47. Regular closure can be used to prove a language is not context-free. We can use the properties of regular closure to prove that a language is not a context-free language. Example: Intersection of context-free language and regular language is a context-free language. Closure properties on regular languages are defined as certain operations on regular language which are guaranteed to produce regular language. Closure refers to some operation on a language, resulting in a new language that is of the same "type" as originally operated on i.e., regular.

Hence, the correct option is (C).

48. Bounded information refers to one whose output is limited and it cannot be said what were the recorded outputs previously until memorized. Strings such as $\{1101,101,10101\}$ are being accepted while $\{1001,11001\}$ are not. So, the electricity meter reading is not an example of bounded information.

Hence, the correct option is (B).

49. A language for which there is no existence of deterministic finite automata is always a non-regular language. There is a well-established theorem to identify if a language is regular or not,

based on Pigeon Hole Principle, called as Pumping Lemma. if a language doesn't satisfy pumping lemma, then we can definitely say that it is not regular, but if it satisfies, then the language may or may not be regular.

Hence, the correct option is (B).

50. A DFA can be represented in the following formats:

Transition Graph:

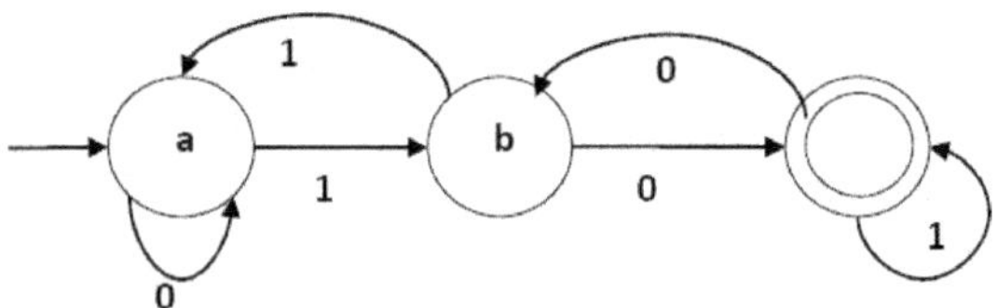

Transition Table:

Present State	Next State for Input 0	Next State for Input 1
a	a	b
b	c	a
c	b	c

Any Programming Language:

Let a deterministic finite automaton be:

- $Q = \{a, b, c\}$,
- $\Sigma = \{0, 1\}$,
- $q_0 = \{a\}$,
- $F = \{c\}$

Hence, the correct option is (D).

51. According to the Chomsky hierarchy, push-down automata accepts the Type 2 language, which is used for context-free language. Pushdown Automata is a finite automaton with extra memory called stack which helps push-down automata to recognize context Free languages.

Hence, the correct option is (C).

52. Context-sensitive grammar is the most general phase of structured grammar. A context-sensitive grammar (CSG) is a formal grammar in which the left-hand sides and right-hand sides of any production rules may be surrounded by a context of terminal and nonterminal symbols. CSG are positioned between context-free and unrestricted grammars in the Chomsky hierarchy.

Hence, the correct option is (A).

53. After semantic analysis, the code is converted into intermediate code which is platform(OS + hardware) independent, the advantage of converting into intermediate code is to improve the performance of code generation and to increase the chances of reusing the machine-independent code optimizer in other compilers.

Hence, the correct option is (D).

54. The code optimization technique is divided into two types machine-independent optimization and machine-dependent optimization types.

1. **Machine-Independent Optimization:** This code optimization phase attempts to improve the intermediate code to get a better target code as the output. The part of the intermediate code which is transformed here does not involve any CPU registers or absolute memory locations.

2. **Machine-Dependent Optimization:** Machine-dependent optimization is done after the target code has been generated and when the code is transformed according to the target machine architecture. It involves CPU registers and may have absolute memory references rather than relative references. Machine-dependent optimizers put efforts to take maximum advantage of the memory hierarchy.

Hence, the correct option is (A).

55. The data dictionary is the major component in the structured analysis model of the system. A data dictionary in software engineering means a file or a set of files that includes a database's metadata (hold records about other objects in the database), like data ownership, relationships of the data to another object, and some other data. So, it is a tool that is not used for process descriptions.

Hence, the correct option is (D).

56. Most systems development projects fail because such basic management principles as planning and control are violated. Measures the project manager can take to minimize the risks of failure are also included. A successful project is one that produces a user-effective system on time and within budget. Therefore, size of the company is not a factor in the failure of a systems development project.

Hence, the correct option is (A).

57. In Software Engineering, Software Configuration Management(SCM) is a process to systematically manage, organize, and control the changes in the documents, codes, and other entities during the Software Development Life Cycle. The primary goal is to increase productivity with minimal mistakes. Software Configuration Management can be administered by a single software configuration management team for the whole organization.

Hence, the correct option is (A).

58. Version control is the process by which different drafts and versions of a document or record are managed. It is a tool that tracks a series of draft documents, culminating in a final version. It provides an audit trail for the revision and update of these finalized versions. For the examples in this book, you will use software source code as the files being version controlled, though, in reality, you can do this with nearly any type of file on a computer.

Hence, the correct option is (B).

59. The interface should present and acquire information in a consistent fashion. This implies that:

- All visual information is organized according to a design standard that is maintained throughout all-screen displays.

- Input mechanisms are constrained to a limited set that are used consistently throughout the application.

- Mechanisms for navigating from task to task are consistently defined and implemented.

Hence, the correct option is (D).

60. System perception model is also known as the Mental model.

Mental model (system perception): The user's mental image of what the interface is. The user's mental model shapes how the user perceives the interface and whether the UI meets the user's needs and depicts the image of a system that an end-user creates in his or her head.

Hence, the correct option is (D).

61. Manual testing is a software testing process in which test cases are executed manually without using any automated tool. All test cases are executed by the tester manually according to the end user's perspective. Manual testing is one of the most fundamental testing processes as it can find both visible and hidden defects of the software.

Hence, the correct option is (C).

62. Unit Testing: Unit testing is defined as a type of software testing where individual components of the software are tested. Unit testing is typically performed by the developer.

Integration Testing: So, you can run integration tests manually without any software. If you consider automating integration, here is a list of popular tools and frameworks with brief overviews.

System Testing: System testing is defined as the testing of a complete and fully integrated software product. This testing falls in black-box testing wherein knowledge of the inner design of the code is not a pre-requisite and is done by the testing team.

Following are the testing techniques that are performed manually during the test life cycle:

- Acceptance Testing
- White Box Testing
- Black Box Testing
- Unit Testing
- System Testing
- Integration Testing

Hence, the correct option is (D).

63. A model that translates design classes into software components is an implementation model. An implementation model is a representation of how a system (application, service, interface, etc.) actually works. It's often described with system diagrams and pseudocode and later translated into real code. They have their own ideas about what is happening when they interact with the system.

Hence, the correct option is (B).

64. We know that,

$$\text{Probability} = \left[\frac{\text{Number of Favorable Outcomes}}{\text{Number of Total Outcomes}} \right]$$

Number of total outcomes $=$ Total Number of ways in which 5 envelopes can be sent to 5 persons $= 5! = 120$

Number of Favorable Outcomes $=$ When none of the letters reaches correct destiny.

Unfavorable cases $=$ When all the five envelope reaches their destiny $+$ When one of them reaches its correct destiny $+$ Two of them reaches its correct destiny $+$ Three of them reaches their correct place.

$${}^5C_1 \times$$
$$[4! - {}^4C_1 \times \{3! - ({}^3C_1 \times 1 + 1)\} + {}^4C_2 \times 1 + 1]$$
$$+ {}^5C_2 \times \{3! - ({}^3C_1 \times 1 + 1)\} + {}^5C_3 \times 1 + 1$$

Number of Favorable Outcomes $=$ Total Outcomes $-$ Unfavorable Outcomes $= 120 - [5 \times 9 + 10 \times 2 + 10 + 1]$

$$= 120 - 45 - 20 - 11$$

$$= 44$$

$\therefore$ Probability $= \dfrac{44}{120}$

Hence, the correct option is (A).

65. Given,

A box contains 4 tennis balls, 6 season balls and 8 dues balls.

We know that,

Probability $= \dfrac{\text{Favourable outcomes}}{\text{Total outcomes}}$

Let us assume that all balls are unique.

There are a total of 18 balls.

Number of all combinations of n things, taken r at a time, is given by ${}^nC_r = \dfrac{n!}{(r)!(n-r)!}$

Total ways $= 3$ balls can be chosen in ${}^{18}C_3$ ways

$$= \dfrac{18!}{3! \times 15!}$$

$$= \dfrac{18 \times 17 \times 16}{3 \times 2 \times 1}$$

$$= 816$$

There are 4 tennis balls, 6 season balls and 8 dues balls, 1 tennis ball, 1 season ball and 1 dues ball drawn.

Therefore, favorable ways $= 4 \times 6 \times 8$

$$= 192$$

Probability $= \dfrac{192}{816}$

$$= \dfrac{4}{17}$$

Hence, the correct option is (A).

66. Given,

$$\dfrac{x\,dy}{dx} + 3y = 4x^3 \ \text{... (i)}$$

$$\Rightarrow \dfrac{dy}{dx} + \dfrac{3y}{x} = 4x^2$$

By comparing equation (i) with $\dfrac{dy}{dx} + Py = Q$ we get,

$$P = \dfrac{3}{x} \text{ and } Q = 4x^2$$

$$\Rightarrow I.F = e^{\int P\,dx} = e^{\int \frac{3}{x} dx} \quad \left(\because \int \dfrac{1}{x} = \log x \right)$$

$$\Rightarrow I.F. = e^{3\log x}$$

$$\Rightarrow I.F. = e^{\log x^3}$$

$$\Rightarrow I.F. = x^3 \left(\because e^{\log x} = x \right)$$

Now general solution will be,

$$y \cdot (I.F.) = \int \left(Q \cdot (I.F') \right) dx + c$$

$$\Rightarrow y \cdot (x^3) = \int \left(4x^2 \times (x^3) \right) dx + c$$

$$\Rightarrow x^3 \cdot y = \int 4x^5 dx + c$$

$$\Rightarrow x^3 \cdot y = \dfrac{4x^6}{6} + c$$

$$\therefore x^3 \cdot y = \dfrac{2}{3} \cdot x^6 + c$$

Hence, the correct option is (C).

67. As we know,

x is a function of y.

Given,

$$x \dfrac{dy}{dx} - y = x^2$$

$$\Rightarrow \dfrac{dy}{dx} - \dfrac{y}{x} = x$$

It is linear differential equation is of first order.

$$I.F. = e^{\frac{-1}{x} dx}$$

$$\Rightarrow I.F. = e^{-\ln x}$$

$$\Rightarrow I.F. = \dfrac{1}{x}$$

Now,

$$y \times (I.F.) = \int Q (I.F.) dx$$

$$\Rightarrow y \times \dfrac{1}{x} = \int x \times \dfrac{1}{x} dx$$

$$\Rightarrow \dfrac{y}{x} = \int dx$$

Integrating,

$\Rightarrow \dfrac{y}{x} = x + c$ (where c is integration constant)

$\Rightarrow y(1) = 1$

$\Rightarrow \dfrac{1}{1} = 1 + c$

$\Rightarrow c = 0$

$\dfrac{y}{x} = x$ OR $y = x^2$

For $y(2)$

$y = 2^2$

$\therefore y = 4$

Hence, the correct option is (D).

68. We know,

$L(\sin mt) = \dfrac{m}{s^2 + m^2} = f(s)$

$\therefore \left(\dfrac{\sin mt}{t}\right) = \int_s^\infty f(s)\,ds$

$\int_s^\infty \dfrac{m\,ds}{s^2 + m^2} = \left|\tan^{-1}\dfrac{s}{m}\right|_s^\infty$

$= \dfrac{\pi}{2} - \tan^{-1}\left(\dfrac{s}{m}\right)$

Now,

$L\left(\dfrac{\sin mt}{t}\right) = \int_0^\infty e^{-st}\dfrac{\sin mt}{t}\,dt$

$\int_0^\infty \dfrac{\sin mt}{t}\,dt = \dfrac{\pi}{2} - \lim_{s\to 0}\tan^{-1}\left(\dfrac{s}{m}\right)$

Taking limit as $s \to 0$, we get

$\int_0^\infty \dfrac{\sin mt}{t}\,dt = \dfrac{\pi}{2} - \lim_{s\to 0}\tan^{-1}\left(\dfrac{s}{m}\right)$

If $m > 0$

$\lim_{s\to 0}\tan^{-1}\left(\dfrac{s}{m}\right) = 0$

If $m < 0$

$\lim_{s\to 0}\tan^{-1}\left(\dfrac{s}{m}\right) = \pi$

According to the question, $m = 2$

$\int_0^\infty \dfrac{\sin 2t}{t}\,dt = \dfrac{\pi}{2}$

Hence, the correct option is (C).

69. If $f(t)$ is a periodic function with period T,

i.e. $f(t + T) = f(t)$, then

$L\{f(t)\} = \dfrac{\int_0^T e^{-st} f(t)\,dt}{1 - e^{-ST}}$

Here the period of $f(t) = 2\pi$

$Lf(t) = \dfrac{1}{1 - e^{-2\pi s}}\left\{\int_0^\pi e^{-st}\,t\,dt + \int_\pi^{2\pi} e^{-st}(\pi - t)\,dt\right\}$

$= \dfrac{1}{1 - e^{-2\pi ms}}\left\{\left[t\left(\dfrac{e^{-st}}{-s}\right) - 1\left(\dfrac{e^{-st}}{s^2}\right)\right]_0^\pi + \left[(\pi - t)\left(\dfrac{e^{-\alpha t}}{-s}\right) - (-1)\left(\dfrac{e^{2\pi s}}{s^2}\right)\right]_\pi^{2\pi}\right\}$

$= \dfrac{1}{1 - e^{-2\pi s}}\left\{\dfrac{-\pi e^{-\pi s}}{s} - \dfrac{e^{-\pi s}}{s^2} + \dfrac{1}{s^2} + \dfrac{\pi e^{-2\pi s}}{s} + \dfrac{e^{-2\pi s}}{s^2} - \dfrac{e^{\frac{-\pi}{s^2}}}{s}\right\}$

$= \dfrac{1}{1 - e^{-2\pi s}}\left\{\dfrac{\pi}{s}\left(e^{-2\pi s} - e^{-\pi s}\right) + \dfrac{1}{s^2}\left(1 + e^{-2\pi s} - 2e^{-\pi s}\right)\right\}$

Hence, the correct option is (B).

70. Characteristic equation:

$|A - \lambda I| = 0$

$\Rightarrow \begin{vmatrix} 5 - \lambda & 3 \\ 1 & 3 - \lambda \end{vmatrix} = 0$

$\Rightarrow (5 - \lambda)(3 - \lambda) - 3 = 0$

$\Rightarrow \lambda^2 - 8\lambda + 15 - 3 = 0$

$\Rightarrow \lambda^2 - 8\lambda + 12 = 0$

$\Rightarrow \lambda = 2, \lambda = 6$

Eigenvector for $\lambda = 2$,

$|A - 2I| \times X = 0$

$\begin{bmatrix} 3 & 3 \\ 1 & 1 \end{bmatrix}\begin{bmatrix} x_1 \\ x_2 \end{bmatrix} = \begin{bmatrix} 0 \\ 0 \end{bmatrix}$

$\Rightarrow 3x_1 + 3x_2 = 0$

$\Rightarrow x_1 = -x_2$

The eigenvector will be $\begin{bmatrix} 1 \\ -1 \end{bmatrix}$

Hence, the correct option is (B).

71. As we know,

Sum of elements along principle diagonal $=$ Trace $= \sum$ Eigen values

Product of eigen values $=$ determinant $= Det(A)$

Given,

$$A = \begin{bmatrix} 1 & 2 & -1 \\ 3 & 5 & 2 \\ 1 & k & 2 \end{bmatrix}$$

We know that;

Det (A) = Product of eigen values

$\Rightarrow 1 \times (10 - 2 \times k) - 2 \times (6 - 2) - (3 \times k - 5) = -8$

$\Rightarrow 10 - 2k - 8 - 3k + 5 = -8$

$\Rightarrow 7 - 5k = -8$

$\Rightarrow 15 = 5k$

$k = 3$

Hence, the correct option is (A).

72. Given,

$$f(x) = (6x^3)(7x^4)$$

The Product Rule is,

$\frac{d}{dx}[f(x)g(x)]$ is $f(x)\frac{d}{dx}[g(x)] + g(x)\frac{d}{dx}[f(x)]$

$$\frac{d}{dx}(x^n) = nx^{n-1}$$

By the Product Rule, we have

$$f'(x) = (6x^3)\frac{d}{dx}(7x^4) + (7x^4)\frac{d}{dx}(6x^3)$$

$$= (6x^3)(28x^3) + (7x^4)(18x^2)$$

$$= 168x^6 + 126x^6$$

$$= 294x^6$$

Hence, the correct option is (A).

73. Given,

$$I = \int \frac{xe^x}{\sqrt{1+e^x}}dx \ldots (A)$$

Take $1 + e^x = t^2 \quad \ldots(1)$

Differentiating with respect to x, we get $e^x dx = 2t\, dt$

From equation (1), we get

$$e^x = t^2 - 1$$

So, $x = \log(t^2 - 1)$

Now, put the above values in (A)

$$I = \int \frac{\log(t^2-1)}{\sqrt{t^2}} 2t\, dt$$

$$\Rightarrow 2 \times \int \frac{\log(t^2-1)}{t} \times t\, dt$$

$$\Rightarrow 2\int \log(t^2 - 1)dt$$

Using integration by parts rule, we get

Integration by parts:

$$\int uvdx = u\int vdx - \int \left(\frac{du}{dx} \times \int vdx\right)dx + c$$

$$\Rightarrow 2\left[\log(t^2 - 1) \times t - 2\int \frac{t^2}{t^2-1}dt\right]$$

$$\Rightarrow 2t\log(t^2 - 1) - 4\int \left[1 + \frac{1}{t^2-1}\right]dt$$

$$\Rightarrow 2t\log(t^2 - 1) - 4t - 4 \times \frac{1}{2}\log\left(\frac{t-1}{t+1}\right) + c$$

$$\Rightarrow 2t\log(t^2 - 1) - 4t - 2\log\left(\frac{t-1}{t+1}\right) + c$$

$$\Rightarrow 2t(\log(t^2 - 1) - 2) - 2\log\left(\frac{t-1}{t+1}\right) + c$$

Resubstitute the value of t, we get

$$\Rightarrow 2(x - 2)\sqrt{1 + e^x} - 2\log\frac{\sqrt{1+e^x}-1}{\sqrt{1+e^x}+1} + c$$

$$\Rightarrow (2x - 4)\sqrt{1 + e^x} - 2\log\frac{\sqrt{1+e^x}-1}{\sqrt{1+e^x}+1} + c \ldots\ldots (2)$$

On comparing equation (2) with question, we get.

$$\therefore f(x) = 2x - 4$$

Hence, the correct option is (B).

74. A_1. Selection Sort:

Selection sort algorithms minimize only the number swap required to sort the array.

A_2. Sedgewick Quicksort:

Sedgewick's modification to quick sort optimizes the space required by the quick sort algorithm by simply solving the smaller partition side first.

A_3. Binary Search:

Binary search provides efficient search in a sorted array by simply dividing the array space into 2 parts. it saves time and the number of comparisons as compared to sequential or linear search.

A_4. Counting Sort:

Counting sort is a non-comparison-based sorting algorithm that improves the number of comparisons required and also O(n) time.

So, counting sort optimizes time, number of comparisons.

Hence, the correct option is (D).

75. A Hash table is a data structure that stores data in an associative manner. In a hash table, data is stored in an array format, where each data value has its own unique index value. Access to data becomes very fast if we know the index of the desired data.

As we know,

In a hash-table with chaining and uniform hashing, the expected number of comparisons in an unsuccessful search is given by:

α, where α is the load factor.

$$\alpha = \frac{m}{n}$$

$$= \frac{60}{40}$$

$$= 1.5$$

So, we have

Number of comparisons for an unsuccessful search $= 1.5$

Hence, the correct option is (A).

76. For heap trees, deletion of a node includes following two operations.

1. Replace the root with last element on the last level.

2. Starting from root, heapify the complete tree from top to bottom

Let us delete the two nodes one by one:

1. Deletion of 25:

Replace 25 with 12.

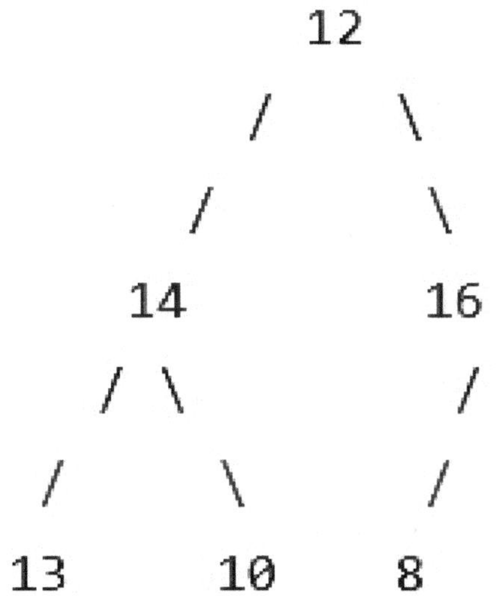

Since heap property is violated for root (16 is greater than 12), make 16 as root of the tree.

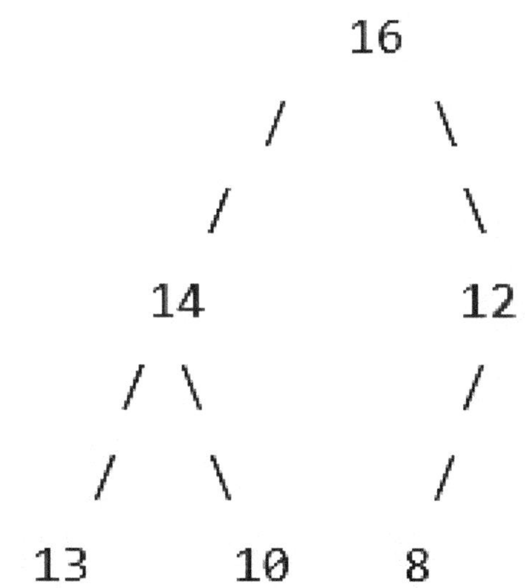

2. Deletion of 16:

Replace 16 with 8.

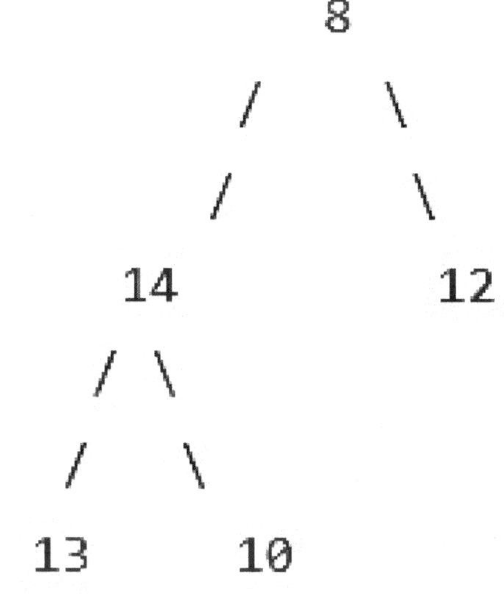

Heapify from root to bottom.

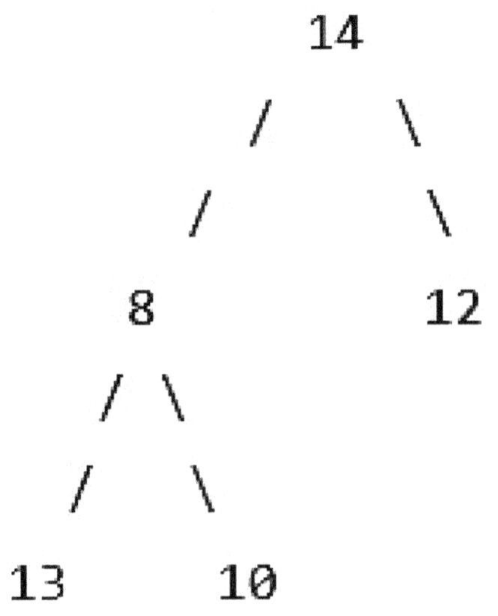

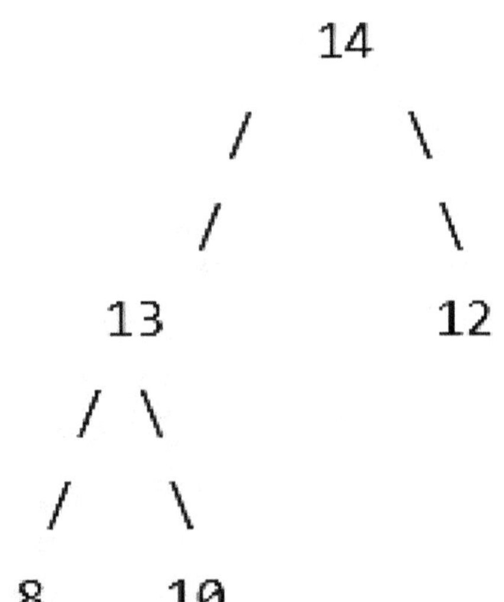

The content of the array after two delete operations is $14,13,12,8,10$.

Hence, the correct option is (D).

77. Given,

Statement 1: G is an undirected graph with vertices $\{P, Q, R, S, T\}$. Every edge has a distinct weight. RS is the edge with minimum edge weight and ST is an edge with maximum edge weight. ST is in the minimum spanning tree if it is a cut edge.

This statement is true. Since maximum edge can only be present in MST if and only if its removal can cause the graph to be disconnected.

Statement 2: If we run Prim's Algorithm and Kruskal's algorithm on a graph G then the minimum cost tree produced, can be different.

This statement is true. Since if edges weights are distinct then the MST produced will be the same for both the algorithms. But if edge weights are not distinct then there is the possibility that the MST produced may differ only in non-unique edge weights.

Statement 3: If we run the Bellman ford algorithm on a weighted graph G with V vertices, It is been observed that even in the $V + 1$ iteration distance decreased then there exists a negative weight cycle in G.

This statement is false. Since even if the $V + 1$ iteration distance decreased it is not guaranteed that a negative weight cycle is present in the graph.

But yes you can say that negative edge weight present in the graph.

Hence, the correct option is (D).

78. Following are the steps to follow to solve the Tower of Hanoi problem recursively:

Let the three pegs be A, B and C. The goal is to move n pegs from A to C.

To move n discs from peg A to peg C:

Move $n - 1$ discs from A to B. This leaves disc n alone on peg A.

Move disc n from A to C.

Move $n - 1$ discs from B to C so they sit on disc n.

The recurrence function $T(n)$ for time complexity of the above recursive solution can be written as following:

$$T(n) = 2T(n - 1) + 1$$

Hence, the correct option is (D).

79. The worst-case time complexity is always greater than or the same as the average case time complexity. There are three types of complexities:

$1.$ Worst case: It is the maximum running time taken by any algorithm.

$2.$ Average case: It is the average running time taken by any algorithm.

$3.$ Best case: It is the minimum running time taken by any algorithm.

So, $A(n)$ would be the upper bound case by $W(n)$.

Also, it will not be a strict upper bound as it can be the same as an average case like merge sort.

Therefore,

$$A(n) = O\big(W(n)\big)$$

Hence, the correct option is (C).

80. An upper bound means that $f(n) = n$ can be expressed as:

$O(n)$, $O(n^2)$, $O(n^3)$, and others but not in other functions like $O(1)$, $O(\log n)$

So, we can examine the all options:

Option (C): $\dfrac{n^3}{\sqrt{(n)}} = n^{\frac{5}{2}} > n^2$ for all $n > 1$. So, $\neq O(n^2)$

Option (A): $15^{10} \times n + 12099 < c \times n^2$, for some $n > \sqrt{12100}$ i.e. $n > 110$. Therefore, $= O(n^2)$

Option (B): $n^{1.98} < n^2$, for all $n > 1$. So, $= O(n^2)$

Option (D): $2^{20} \times n = 1024 \times 1024 \times n < c \times n^2$ for all $n > 1$, where $c = 1024 \times 1024$

So, $O(n^2)$

Hence, the correct option is (C).

81. Given,

$$f_1(n) = 2^n$$

$$f_2(n) = n^{\left(\frac{3}{2}\right)}$$

$$f_3(n) = n\log n$$

$$f_4(n) = n^{(\log n)}$$

Except f_3, all other are exponential. So, f_3 is definitely first in output. Among remaining, $n^{\left(\frac{3}{2}\right)}$ is next.

One way to compare f_1 and f_4 is to take log of both functions. Order of growth of $\log\big(f_1(n)\big)$ is $\Theta(n)$ and order of growth of $\log\big(f_4(n)\big)$ is $(\log n \times \log n)$.

Since $\Theta(n)$ has higher growth than $\Theta(\log n \times \log n)$, $f_1(n)$ grows faster than $f_4(n)$.

Following is another way to compare f_1 and f_4. Let us compare f_4 and f_1.

Let us take few values to compare:

$$n = 32, f_1 = 2^{32}, f_4 = 32^5 = 2^{25}$$

$$n = 64, f_1 = 2^{64}, f_4 = 64^6 = 2^{36}$$

Hence, the correct option is (A).

82. We can get it by taking an example like n = 54321. After 2 iterations, rev would be 12 and n would be 543. A loop invariant is something that holds at the start of a loop, across each iteration (inside an iteration it can change but before the iteration ends original condition must be true) and at the end also. So, we

can check for the satisfiability of the condition at the loop header for the start of the loop, for each iteration and also at the exit. Here, in each iteration, the rightmost digit of n is moving to the right end of rev. The 2 conditions given in (A) choice are true on entry to the loop, after each iteration (not necessarily during an iteration), and at end of the loop.

Hence, the correct option is (A).

83. Given,

$$f(x) = x \text{ is my friend.}$$

$$p(x) = x \text{ is perfect.}$$

So, they are asking about "SOME". Finally, outer most parentheses will get "SOME" $\exists_x$.

They are given conditions like NOT perfect. So,we get $\neg p(x)$.

The final condition is $\exists_x\big(f(x) \wedge \neg p(x)\big)$.

Hence, the correct option is (B).

84. Given,

Statement (I):

If the binary relation itself is transitive, then the transitive closure is that same binary relation, otherwise, it will be different.

Statement (II):

An asymmetric relation is always anti-symmetric, as anti-symmetric relation allows self-loops in digraph but asymmetric does not. So asymmetric condition is more strict.

Statement (III):

An empty relation on a nonempty set is always symmetric, but not reflexive.

So, all the given three statements are true.

Hence, the correct option is (D).

85. Greatest element: It is the maximum element i.e. element succeeding all other elements.

Least element: It is the minimum element i.e. element preceding all other elements.

Poset: $\{3,5,9,15,24,45\}$

Hasse diagram for the given poset is:

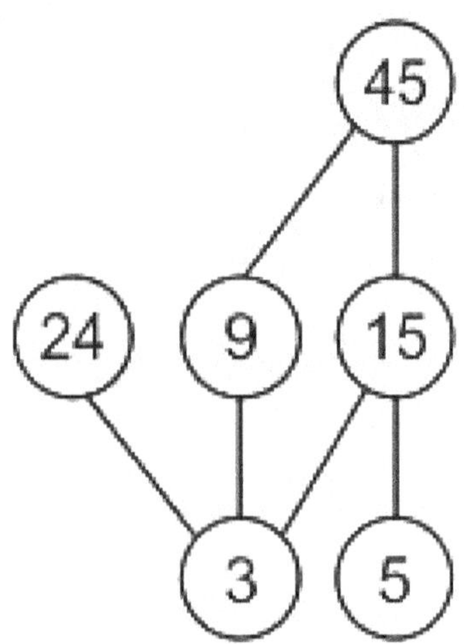

There are two maximal elements in this Hasse diagram: 24 and 45.

Also, there are two minimal elements: 3 and 5

Both the maximal elements are at the same level. They are not dividing each other.

So, there is no maximum or greatest element here.

Also, both the minimal elements are at the same level.

There is no minimum element.

Hence, the correct option is (D).

86. Hamiltonian graph:

A Hamiltonian graph is one which contains a Hamiltonian cycle. A Hamiltonian cycle is a cycle in which each vertex is visited exactly once.

Properties of Hamiltonian graph:

- A graph has a Hamiltonian circuit if each vertex has degree ≥ 3.
- If $G = (V, E)$ has $n \geq 3$ vertices and every vertex has degree $\geq \frac{n}{2}$, then G has a Hamilton circuit.
- If G is a graph with n vertices and $n \geq 3$, also $deg(u) + deg(v) \geq n$, if u and v are not connected by an edge, then G has a hamiltonion circuit.
- $E(G) = \frac{1}{2}(n-1)(n-2) + 2.$

Hence, the correct option is (D).

87. Given,

Word: " $BANANA$"

Let's first assume that all letters are distinct then the no. of permutation will be $6!$.

Now, assume $2\ N's$ in the word $= \{N_a, N_b\}$ and $3\ A's$ in the Word as $\{A_a, A_b, A_c\}$.

These $2\ A's$ and $3\ N$'s are indistinguishable we using this Notation just to differentiate between permutations.

Now,

Lets take example of the two words- " $BA_aN_aA_bN_bA_c$" and " $BA_aN_bA_bN_aA_c$".

In these 2 strings we have swapped $N(N_a$ with N_b). But, these two strings are indistinguishable if we ignore the subscript (because we are using subscripts just to explain this indistinguishable part).

But in $6!$ we also considering these indistinguishable strings so, we need to subtract/remove these strings to calculate the distinguishable no. of strings.

For every permutation of $2\ A's$ and $3\ N's$ respectively, we will have only 1 distinguishable string.

So, total no. of distinguishable strings become $\frac{6!}{(3!2!)} = 60$

General Formula:

Distinguishable permutation of n length string in which $r_1, r_2, r_3, \ldots, r_k$ are k repeating letters $= \dfrac{n!}{r_1! r_2! \ldots r_k!}$

Hence, the correct option is (C).

88. Suppose there is a given statement $P(n)$ involving the natural number n such that:

- The statement is true for $n = 1$, i.e., $P(1)$ is true.
- If the statement is true for $n = k$ (where k is some positive integer), then the statement is also true for $n = k + 1$, i.e., truth of $P(k)$ implies the truth of $P(k + 1)$.

Then, $P(n)$ is true for all natural numbers n.

Given,

$$P(n) = 2 \times 7^n + 3 \times 5^n - 5$$

Put $n = 1$

$$P(1) = 2 \times 7^1 + 3 \times 5^1 - 5 = 24,$$ which is divisible by 24.

Assume $P(k)$ is true.

$$P(k) = 2 \times 7^k + 3 \times 5^k - 5 = 24q,$$ where $q \in N$ ... (1)

Now,

$$\mathrm{T}(k+1) = 2 \times 7^{k+1} + 3 \times 5^{k+1} - 5 = 2 \times 7^k \times 7 + 3 \times 5^k \times 5 - 5$$

$$\Rightarrow 7\left\{2 \times 7^k + 3 \times 5^k - 5 - 3 \times 5^k + 5\right\} + 3 \times 5^k \times 5 - 5$$

$$\Rightarrow 7\{24q - 3 \times 5^k + 5\} + 15 \times 5^k - 5$$

$$\Rightarrow (7 \times 24q) - 21 \times 5^k + 35 + 15 \times 5^k - 5$$

$$\Rightarrow (7 \times 24q) - 6 \times 5^k + 30 = (7 \times 24q) - 6\left(5^k - 5\right)$$

$$\Rightarrow (7 \times 24q) - 6 \times (4p)\{\text{As } \left(5^k - 5\right) \text{ is a multiple of } 4\}$$

$$\Rightarrow (7 \times 24q) - 24p = 24(7q - p)$$

$$\Rightarrow 24 \times r, r = 7q - p, \text{ is some natural number } \dots (2)$$

Thus, $P(k + 1)$ is true whenever $P(k)$ is true.

So, by the principle of mathematical induction $P(n)$ is true for all $n \in N$.

Hence, the correct option is (A).

89. Consider the situation as having 19 spots and filling them with 7 chocolate biscuits and 19 cheesecake biscuits. Then we just choose 7 spots for the chocolate biscuits and let the other 10 spots have cheesecake biscuits. The number of ways to do this job is $^{19}C_7 = 50388$.

Hence, the correct option is (B).

90. Relation less than a set of real numbers is not antisymmetric and reflexive. Relation is not POSET because it is irreflexive. Again, aRb != bRa unless a=b and so it is antisymmetric. A relation may be 'not asymmetric and not reflexive but still antisymmetric, as $\{(1,1)(1,2)\}$.

So, the relation is not a partial ordering because it is not asymmetric and irreflexive equals antisymmetric.

Hence, the correct option is (A).

91. Join and meet are the binary operations reserved for lattices. The join of two elements is their least upper bound. It is denoted by V, not to be confused with disjunction. The meet of two elements is their greatest lower bound. It is denoted by ∧ and not to be confused with a conjunction.

Hence, the correct option is (A).

92. 32-bit floating-point representation of a binary number in $IEEE - 754$ is:

Sign (1 bit)	Exponent (8 bits)	Mantissa bit (23 bits)

Now,

Given,

Hexadecimal number: N_{16}

0x3E6D0000 = ($0011111001101101000000000000000)_2$

Here, sign bit is 0. So, number is positive.

0	01111100	1101101000000000000000000

Exponent bits $= E = 01111100 = 124$ (in decimal)

Mantissa bits $M = 11011010000000000000000$

In $IEEE - 754$ format, 32-bit (single precision)

$$(-1)^s \times 1.M \times 2^{E-127}$$
$$= (-1)^0 \times 1.1101101 \times 2^{124-127}$$
$$= 1.1101101 \times 2^{-3}$$
$$= (1 + 2^{-1} + 2^{-2} + 2^{-4} + 2^{-5} + 2^{-7})$$
$$N_{10} = 0.231$$

$0xC1200000$. After converting into binary, it can be represented in $IEEE - 754$ format as:

1	10000010	01000000000000000000000

Sign bit is 1 i.e. the number is negative:

Biased Exponent $(E') = 10000010 = 130$

Normalized Mantissa $(M) = 01000000000000000000000$

$$(-1)^1 \times 1.01 \times 2^{130-127}$$
$$= -(1 + 2^{-2}) \times 2^3$$
$$M_{10} = -(8 + 2) = -10$$
$$N_{10} + M_{10} = -10 + 0.231$$
$$= -9.769$$

Hence, the correct option is (A).

93.

Binary				Excess - 3			
A	B	C	D	A	B	C	D
0	0	0	0	0	0	1	1
0	0	0	1	0	1	0	0
0	0	1	0	0	1	0	1
0	0	1	1	0	1	1	0
0	1	0	0	0	1	1	1
0	1	0	1	1	0	0	0
0	1	1	0	1	0	0	1
0	1	1	1	1	0	1	0
1	0	0	0	1	0	1	1
1	0	0	1	1	1	0	0

Now if two excess- 3 is added then the result obtained is excess-6 if sum is less than 9, that is, why 3 is subtracted from the sum.

Example:

In binary
$$0010 + 001 = 0011$$
$$2 + 1 = 3 \text{ and } 3$$

In Excess- $3,3$ is equal at $(6)_{10}$ or $(0110)_2$

Add the Excess- 3 of the binary corresponded number.
$$0101 + 0100 = 1001$$

$$5 + 4 = 9$$
$$(2 + 3) + (1 + 3) = (6 + 3)$$

Subtract $3 (0011)$ from the sum:

$$1001 - 0011 = 0110$$
$$\therefore (6 + 3) - 3 = 6$$

Hence, the correct option is (A).

94. Numbers exactly represented in decimal:

$$01011.011 = 11.375$$

$$11101.101 = 29.625$$

Numbers that cannot be represented in decimal:

Maximum value possible is 31.875

$33.0 \rightarrow 33$ is out of range.

$8.325 \rightarrow .325$ cannot be represented with 3 bits.

Hence, the correct option is (D).

95. Given,

$$\left(A \cdot \bar{A} \right) + A$$

As we know, from the identity law, we get

$$= 0 + A = A$$

All Boolean algebra laws are shown below:

Name	AND Form	OR Form
Identity law	$1 . A = A$	$0 + A = A$
Null Law	$0 . A = 0$	$1 + A = 1$
Idempotent Law	$A . A = A$	$A + A = A$
Inverse Law	$A\bar{A} = 0$	$A + \bar{A} = 1$
Commutative Law	$AB = BA$	$A + B = B + A$
Associative Law	$(AB)C$	$(A + B) + C = A + (B + C)$
Distributive Law	$A + BC = (A + B)(A + C)$	$A(B + C) = AB + AC$
Absorption Law	$A(A + B) = A$	$A + AB = A$
De Morgan's Law	$\left(\overline{AB} \right) = \bar{A} + \bar{B}$	$\left(\overline{A + B} \right) = \bar{A}\bar{B}$

Hence, the correct option is (A).

96. XR is not an example of logic gates. Logic gates are the electronic circuit performing logical operations having one or more than one input and only one output. They work on the principle of a Boolean function. The various examples of logic gates are AND Gate, OR Gate, NAND Gate, NOR Gate, XOR Gate, NOT Gate, etc.

Hence, the correct option is (C).

97. D flip flop:

D flip flop has only one input terminal. The output of the D flip flop will be the same as the input. So, it is used in delay circuits.

The circuit is as shown below.

Logic symbol:

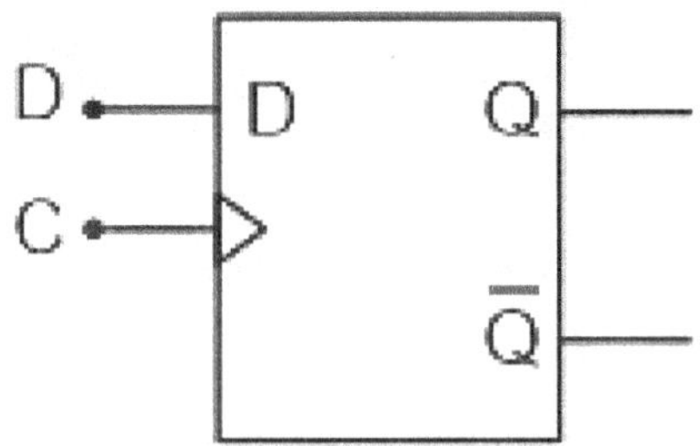

Truth table:

D	Q_n (Present state)	Q_{n+1} (Next state)
0	0	0
0	1	0
1	0	1
1	1	1

Characteristic equation: $Q_{n+1} = D$

The D flip flop may be obtained from an $S - R$ flip flop by just putting one inverter between the S and R as shown in the figure below.

$$S = \bar{R}$$

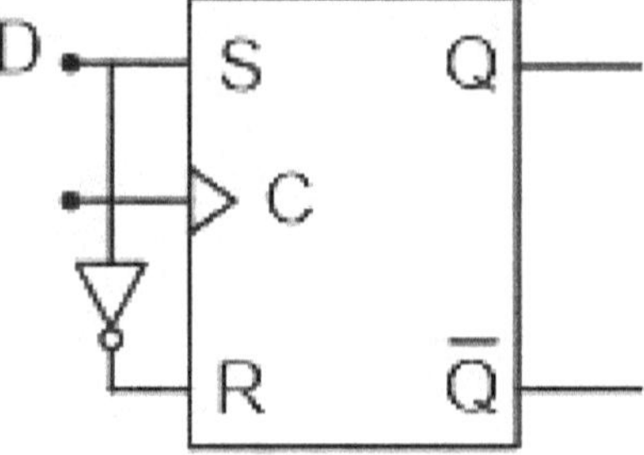

The **D** flip flop may be obtained from a $J - K$ flip flop by just putting one inverter between the J and K as shown in the figure below.

$$K = \bar{J}$$

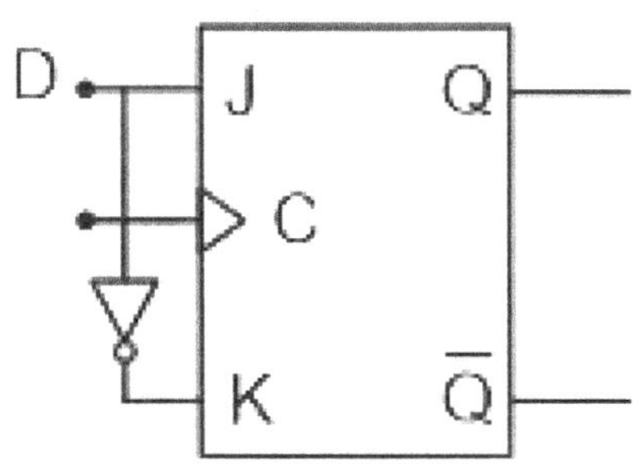

T flip flop:

T flip flop has only one input terminal. The output of the T flip flop will be toggled when the input is high on every new clock pulse. The output will be the same as the previous state when the input is low.

The circuit is as shown below.

Logic symbol:

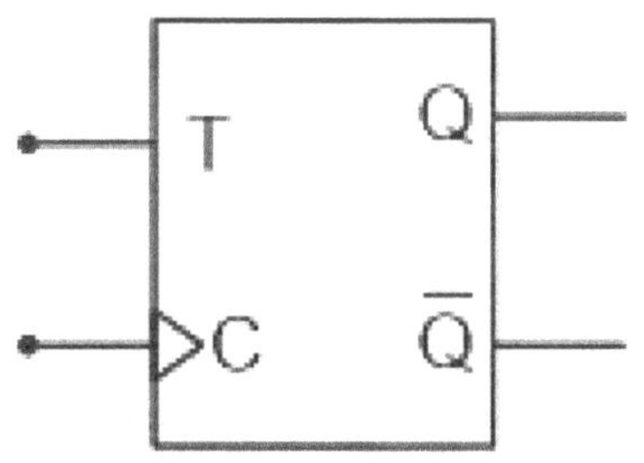

Truth table:

T	Q_n (Present state)	Q_{n+1} (Next state)
0	0	0
0	1	0
1	0	1
1	1	1

Characteristic equation: $Q_{n+1} = T\bar{Q}_n + \bar{T}Q_n$

The T flip flop may be obtained from a $J-K$ flip flop by making both the inputs are the same i.e. $J = \bar{K}$

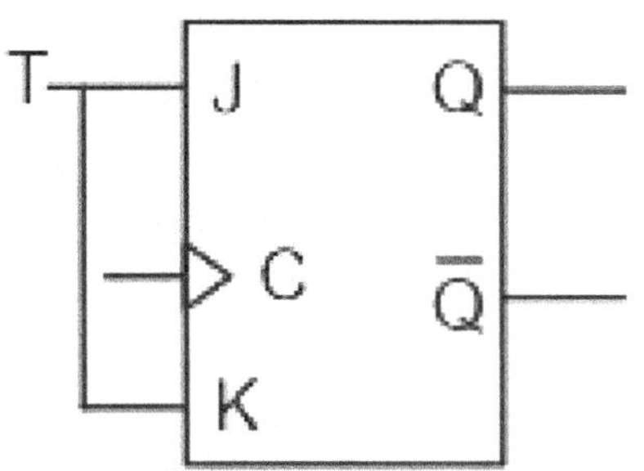

Hence, the correct option is (D).

98. ASCII stands for American Standard Code for Information Interchange is a character encoding standard for electronic communication.

ASCII characters are represented by seven bits. ASCII codes are of two types- ASCII- 7 and ASCII- 8. The standard ASCII character has 7 bits and the basic set ranges from 0 to 127.

The extended ASCII character has 8 bits and the basic set ranges from 0 to 255.

Hence, the correct option is (B).

99. 1's complement of Binary: 1's complement of a Binary number is defined by the value obtained by inverting all the bit, i.e, 0 as 1 and 1 as 0.

$\therefore$ 1's complement of $11000110 = 00111001$

2's complement of Binary: It is the sum of 1's complement of Binary number and 1 to the least significant bit (LSB).

$\therefore$ 2's complement $= 1$'s complement $+1$ (LSB)

Now,

Given Binary Number,

0011010110011100

1's complement $= 1100101001100011$

2's complement $= 1$'s complement $+1$ (LSB)

1100 1010 0110 0011

$+$ 1

1100 1010 0110 0100

As we know a shortcut method of forming the 2's complement of a binary number is to copy bits from the right until a one-bit has been copied, then invert the remaining bits i.e, 0 as 1 and 1 as 0.

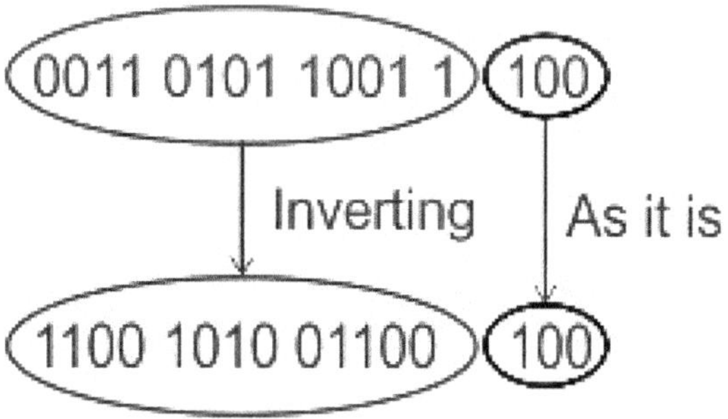

Hence, the correct option is (C).

100. A decoder with k input lines has 2^k output lines.

Now,

The memory is byte-addressable. So $1\ KB = 2^{10}\ B$ i.e.,a 10×2^{10} decoders.

So, the number of input lines $(m) = 10$

Number of output lines $(n) = 2^m = 2^{10} = 1024$

So, $(m + n) = 10 + 1024 = 1034$

Hence, the correct option is (A).

Q.1 Which of the following is/are false?

A. Time complexity of memory efficient merge sort is $O(n^2)$.

B. The recurrence relation for worst case of quick sort algorithm is $T(n) = T(n-2) + T\left(n^{\frac{1}{\log n}}\right) + O(n)$.

C. Let C be the number of comparisons performed in the overall execution of the partition procedure of quick sort algorithm then time complexity is $O(n + C)$.

D. The space complexity of heap sort is $O(\log n)$.

Q.2 Consider a random binary tree on which Breadth-First Search is applied starting from the root node. There exist a node A and B at the distance six from the root. If A is the nth node with a maximum possible value of n and B is the nth node with a minimum possible value of n in the Breadth-First Search traversal. The value of $A + B$ is ______ (Root node is 1st node).

A. 255   **B.** 190   **C.** 180   **D.** 181

Q.3 Consider the table given below consisting of 5 items with their profit and weight associated with it:

Items	1	2	3	4	5
Profit	90	130	60	110	42
Weight	20	60	20	50	15

The weight of the knapsack is 90. Find the maximum profit gain by applying fractional knapsack?

A. 269   **B.** 270   **C.** 268   **D.** 192

Q.4 What is a Rabin and Karp Algorithm?

A. String matching algorithm

B. Shortest path algorithm

C. Minimum spanning tree algorithm

D. Approximation algorithm

Q.5 What is the pre-processing time of the Rabin and Karp algorithm?

A. $\theta(m^2)$ **B.** $\theta(m \log n)$

C. $\theta(m)$ **D.** $O(n)$

Q.6 What is the worst-case running time of the Rabin Karp Algorithm?

A. $\theta(n)$ **B.** $\theta(n - m)$

C. $\theta((n - m + 1)m)$ **D.** $\theta(n \log m)$

Q.7 Which of the following is the fastest algorithm in string matching field?

A. Boyer-Moore's algorithm

B. String matching algorithm

C. Quick search algorithm

D. Linear search algorithm

Q.8 Which of the following algorithms formed the basis for the quick search algorithm?

A. Boyer-Moore's algorithm

B. Parallel string matching algorithm

C. Binary Search algorithm

D. Linear Search algorithm

Q.9 Consider an undirected graph G with 150 vertices and 10 components. Which of the following is/are true regarding G?

A. The Minimum number of edges in G is 75.

B. The Minimum number of edges in G is 140.

C. The Minimum number of edges in G is 149.

D. The Minimum number of edges in G is 148.

Q.10 Which among the following is not a member of the class?

A. Virtual function   **B.** Const function

C. Static function   **D.** Friend function

Q.11 How to overcome the problem arising due to the destruction of the temporary objects?

A. Overloading insertion operator.

B. Overriding functions can be used.

C. Overloading parenthesis or returning object.

D. Overloading assignment operator and defining copy constructor.

Q.12 Which is the correct HTML to left-align the contents inside a cell?

A. <tdleft>   **B.** <td ralign = "left">

C. <td align = "left">   **D.** <td leftalign>

Q.13 Which of the following is/are true about proxy server?

I. HTTP doesn't support proxy server.

II. Proxy sever increases the load on original server.

A. Only I   **B.** Only II

C. Both I and II   **D.** Neither I nor II

Q.14 A program that can execute high-level language programs, are known as __________.

A. Compiler   **B.** Interpreter

C. Sensor   **D.** Circuitry

Q.15 The following function reverse() is supposed to reverse a singly linked list. There is one line missing at the end of the function.

```
/* Link list node */
struct node
{
int data;
struct node* next;
};
/* head_ref is a double pointer that points to the head (or start)
pointer
of linked list */
static void reverse(struct node** head_ref)
{
```

```
struct node* prev = NULL;
struct node* current = *head_ref;
struct node* next;
while (current != NULL)
{
next = current->next;
current->next = prev;
prev = current;
current = next;
}
/*ADD A STATEMENT HERE*/

}
```

What should be added in place of "/*ADD A STATEMENT HERE*/", so that the function correctly reverses a linked list?

A. *head_ref = prev;
B. *head_ref = current;
C. *head_ref = next;
D. *head_ref = NULL;

Q.16 What is the output of following function for start pointing to first node of following linked list?

```
1->2->3->4->5->6
void fun(struct node* start)
{
if(start == NULL)
return;
printf("%d ", start->data);
if(start->next != NULL )
fun(start->next->next);
printf("%d ", start->data);
}
```

A. 1 4 6 6 4 1
B. 1 3 5 1 3 5
C. 1 2 3 5
D. 1 3 5 5 3 1

Q.17 A Double-ended queue supports operations such as adding and removing items from both the sides of the queue. They support four operations like addFront(adding item to top of the queue), addRear(adding item to the bottom of the queue), removeFront(removing item from the top of the queue) and removeRear(removing item from the bottom of the queue). You are given only stacks to implement this data structure. You can implement only push and pop operations. What are the total number of stacks required for this operation? (you can reuse the stack).

A. 1   **B.** 2   **C.** 3   **D.** 4

Q.18 You are asked to perform a queue operation using a stack. Assume the size of the stack is some value 'n' and there are 'm' number of variables in this stack. The time complexity of performing deQueue operation is (Using only stack operations like push and pop)(Tightly bound):

A. O(m)
B. O(n)
C. O(mn)
D. Data is insufficient

Q.19 SD satellite in geosynchronous orbit __________.

A. Remains in a fixed position relative to points on earth.
B. Can cover about 80.
C. Moves faster than the earth's rotation so that it can cover a larger portion of the earth.
D. Remains in a fixed position so as the earth rotates it can fully cover the earth.

Q.20 Protocol converters are _______.
A. Same as multiplexers
B. Same as TDMs
C. Usually not operated in pairs
D. Usually operated in pairs

Q.21 Which of the following is a 16-bit field used for checking errors in header and data?
A. Data offset   **B.** Source port
C. Window   **D.** Checksum

Q.22 What are the roles of frequencies in Satellite transponders?

A. Use a higher frequency for reception of radiation from earth stations and lower frequency for transmission to earth stations.
B. Use lower frequency reception of radiation from earth stations and higher frequency for transmission to earth stations.
C. Use a single frequency for reception and transmission from one point on earth to another.
D. Are devices that echo the radiation without change from one point on earth to another.

Q.23 DHCP uses UDP port _______ for sending data to the server.
A. 66   **B.** 67   **C.** 68   **D.** 69

Q.24 What are the short messages sent by UDP protocol that may arrive out of order in the destination computer called?
A. Tokens   **B.** Synchronization
C. Datagrams   **D.** Database

Q.25 The DHCP server can provide the _____ of the IP addresses.
A. Dynamic allocation
B. Automatic allocation
C. Static allocation
D. All of these

Q.26 _______ is a 1-byte field and is used to indicate the start of a frame.
A. SFD   **B.** Preamble field
C. Address field   **D.** Length

Q.27 In a star network configuration:
A. a central computer connects to a host of nodes
B. a node connects to many computers
C. there is one main computer and one node
D. All of these

Q.28 The less space consideration as lead to the development of ______ (for large memories).
A. SIMM   **B.** DIMM
C. SRAM   **D.** Both (A) and (B)

Q.29 The controller multiplexes the addresses after getting the _______ signal.
A. INTR   **B.** ACK
C. RESET   **D.** REQUEST

Q.30 A main memory unit with a capacity of 4 megabytes is built using $1M \times 1$-bit DRAM chips. Each DRAM chip has $1K$ rows of cells with $1K$ cells in each row. The time taken for a single refresh operation is 100 nanoseconds. The time required to perform one refresh operation on all the cells in the memory unit is:

1. 100 nanoseconds
2. 100×2^{10} nanoseconds
3. 100×2^{20} nanoseconds
4. 3200×20 nanoseconds

A. 1   **B.** 2   **C.** 3   **D.** 4

Q.31 Which of the following is not an addressing mode of 8051?
A. Register instructions
B. Register specific instructions
C. Indexed addressing
D. None of these

Q.32 The iconic feature of the RISC machine among the following is ________.
A. Reduced number of addressing modes
B. Increased memory size
C. Having a branch delay slot
D. All of these

Q.33 The symbol, 'addr 16' represents the 16-bit address which is used by the instructions to specify the __________.
A. Destination address of CALL
B. Source address of JUMP
C. Destination address of call or jump
D. Source address of call or jump

Q.34 Which of the architecture is power efficient?
A. CISC   **B.** RISC   **C.** ISA   **D.** IANA

Q.35 The DMA differs from the interrupt mode by ________.
A. The involvement of the processor for the operation
B. The method of accessing the I/O devices
C. The amount of data transfer possible
D. None of these

Q.36 The DMA controller has ______ registers.
A. 4   **B.** 2   **C.** 3   **D.** 1

Q.37 ________ facilitates installation of Hadoop across any number of hosts.
A. API-driven installations
B. Wizard-driven interface
C. Extensible framework
D. All of these

Q.38 __________ is a Java library for writing, testing, and running pipelines of MapReduce jobs on Apache Hadoop.
A. cTAKES   **B.** Crunch
C. CouchDB   **D.** None of these

Q.39 Which of the following is generally used for performing tasks like creating the structure of the relations, deleting relation?
A. DML(Data Manipulation Language)
B. Query
C. Relational Schema
D. DDL(Data Definition Language)

Q.40 A clustering index is defined on the fields which are of type ________.
A. Non-key and ordering
B. Non-key and non-ordering
C. Key and ordering
D. Key and non-ordering

Q.41 The given query can also be replaced with ________.
SELECT name, course_id
FROM instructor, teaches
WHERE instructor_ID= teaches_ID;
A. Select name,course_id from teaches,instructor where instructor_id=course_id;
B. Select name, course_id from instructor natural join teaches;
C. Select name, course_id from the instructor;
D. Select course_id from instructor join teaches;

Q.42 Which one of the following given statements possibly contains the error?
A. Select * from emp where empid = 10003;
B. Select empid from emp where empid = 10006;
C. Select empid from emp;
D. Select empid where empid = 1009 and Lastname = 'GELLER';

Q.43 Complete the following query:
SELECT emp_name
FROM department
WHERE dept_name LIKE ' ____ Computer Science';
In the above-given Query, which of the following can be placed in the Query's blank portion to select the "dept_name" that also contains Computer Science as its ending string?
A. &   **B.** _   **C.** %   **D.** $

Q.44 In the following Query, which of the following can be placed in the Query's blank portion to display the salary from highest to lowest amount, and sorting the employs name alphabetically?
SELECT *
FROM instructor
ORDER BY salary ___, name ___.
A. Ascending, Descending
B. Asc, Desc
C. Desc, Asc
D. Descending, Ascending

Q.45 The given query can be replaced with _________.
SELECT name
FROM instructor 1

WHERE salary ≤ 100000 AND salary $\geq 90000;$

A. SELECT name
   FROM instructor 1
   WHERE salary BETWEEN 100000 AND 90000

B. SELECT name
   FROM instructor
   WHERE salary BETWEEN 90000 AND 100000;

C. SELECT name
   FROM instructor 1
   WHERE salary BETWEEN 90000 AND 100000;

D. SELECT name
   FROM instructor!
   WHERE salary ≤ 90000 AND salary $\geq 100000;$

Q.46 What is an Address Binding?

A. Going to an address in memory.

B. Locating an address with the help of another address.

C. Binding two addresses together to form a new address in a different memory space.

D. A mapping from one address space to another.

Q.47 Consider the following page reference string:

1,2,3,2,4,1,3,2,4,1

Assume that there are three-page frames that are initially empty. Let LRU, FIFO, OPTIMAL denote the number of page faults under the corresponding page replacement strategy. Then, which of the following is true?

A. LRU = FIFO = OPTIMAL

B. LRU = OPTIMAL

C. FIFO < OPTIMAL < LRU

D. OPTIMAL < FIFO < LRU

Q.48 In which addressing mode the operand is given explicitly in the instruction?

A. Absolute mode
B. Immediate mode
C. Indirect mode
D. Index mode

Q.49 Which of the following method is used to prevent threads or processes from accessing a single resource?

A. PCB
B. Semaphore
C. Job Scheduler
D. None of these

Q.50 What type of commands are required to perform various tasks in DOS?

A. Internal commands
B. External commands
C. Valuable commands
D. Primary commands

Q.51 To access the services of the operating system, the interface is provided by the _________.

A. Library
B. System calls
C. Assembly instructions
D. API

Q.52 Which of the following locates a parameter block by using an address pointer?

A. Operating system
B. Kernel
C. System
D. Memory

Q.53 If you want to execute more than one program at a time, the systems software you are using must be capable of:

A. Word processing
B. Virtual memory
C. Compiling
D. Multitasking

Q.54 What type of scheduling is round-robin scheduling?

A. Linear data scheduling
B. Non-linear data scheduling
C. Preemptive scheduling
D. Non-preemptive scheduling

Q.55 The number of essential prime implicants for the function, Y = A'B'C'D + A'BCD' + ABC'D' is given by _________.

A. 1
B. 2
C. 3
D. 4

Q.56 A 4×1 Multiplexer is shown in the figure below. The output Z is:

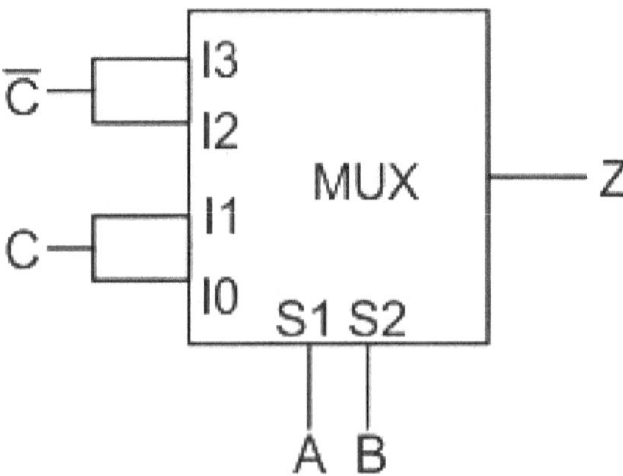

A. A NOR C
B. B NOR C
C. B XOR C
D. A XOR C

Q.57 Addition of the hexadecimal numbers $(DEF.12)_{16}$ and $(12EF.C)_{16}$ gives:

A. $(20DE.E2)_{16}$
B. $(20DE.D2)_{16}$
C. $(20DE \cdot C2)_{16}$
D. $(20DE.B2)_{16}$

Q.58 When two asynchronous active low inputs PRESET and CLEAR are applied to a $J - K$ flip flop the output will be:

A. 0
B. Undefined
C. Previous state
D. 1

Q.59 Consider the following circuit:

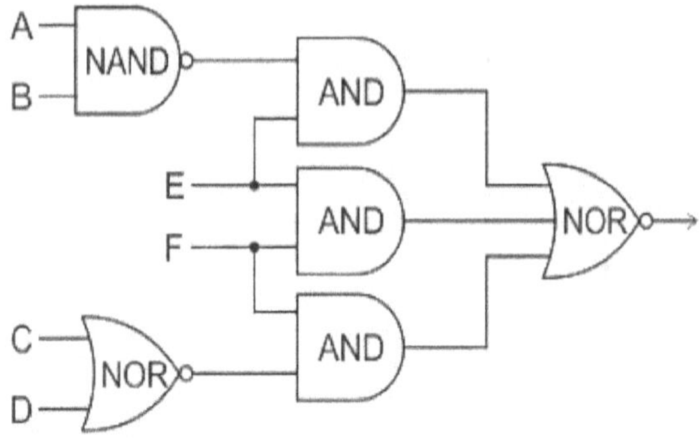

The function by the network above is:

A. $\bar{A}BE + EF + \bar{C}DF$

B. $\left(\bar{E} + AB\bar{F}\right)\left(C + D + \bar{F}\right)$

C. $\left(\bar{AB} + E\right)\left(\bar{E} + \bar{F}\right)\left(C + D + \bar{F}\right)$

D. $(A + B)\bar{E} + E\bar{F} + CD\bar{F}$

Q.60 A 16-bit synchronous binary up-counter is clocked with a frequency f_{CLK}. The two most significant bits are OR-ed together to form an output Y. Measurements show that Y is periodic, and the duration for which Y remains high in each period is $24\ ms$. The clock frequency f_{CLK} is __________ MHz. (Round off 2 decimal places.)

A. $2.00 - 2.10$ **B.** $2.00 - 2.20$

C. $2.10 - 2.15$ **D.** $2.02 - 2.10$

Q.61 In JK flip-flop, which combination will toggle the output?

A. $J = 0, K = 0$ **B.** $J = 1, K = 1$

C. $J = 1, K = 0$ **D.** $J = 0, K = 1$

Q.62 Excess $-3-$ code is also known as:

A. Weighted code

B. Cyclic redundancy code

C. Self-complementing code

D. Algebraic code

Q.63 Let $m = (313)_4$ and $n = (322)_4$. Find the base 4 expansion of $m + n$:

A. $(635)_4$ **B.** $(32312)_4$

C. $(21323)_4$ **D.** $(1301)_4$

Q.64 Which of the given are correct?

A. Moore machine has 6-tuples

B. The mealy machine has 6-tuples

C. Both (A) and (B)

D. None of these

Q.65 State whether the statement is true or false:

I. For every language L accepted by an NFA, there exists a DFA that also accepts L.

II. For every alphabet Σ, every regular language over Σ can be accepted by a finite automaton.

A. I – True, II - True   **B.** I – True, II – False

C. I – False, II – True   **D.** I – False, II – False

Q.66 Let P be a non-deterministic pushdown automaton (NPDA) with exactly one state, q and exactly one symbol Z, in its stack alphabet. State q is both the starting as well as the accepting state of the PDA. The stack is initialized with one Z before the start of the operation of the PDA. Let the input alphabet of the PDA be S. Let L(P) be the language accepted by the PDA by reading a string and reaching its accepting state. Let N(P) be the language accepted by the PDA by reading a string and emptying its stack.

Which of the following statement is true?

A. L(P) is necessarily Σ* but N(P) is not necessary Σ*

B. N(P) is necessarily Σ* but L(P) is not necessarily Σ*

C. Both L(P) and N(P) is necessary Σ*

D. Neither L(P) nor N(P) is necessary Σ*

Q.67 The number of elements present in the e-closure ($f2$) in the given diagram:

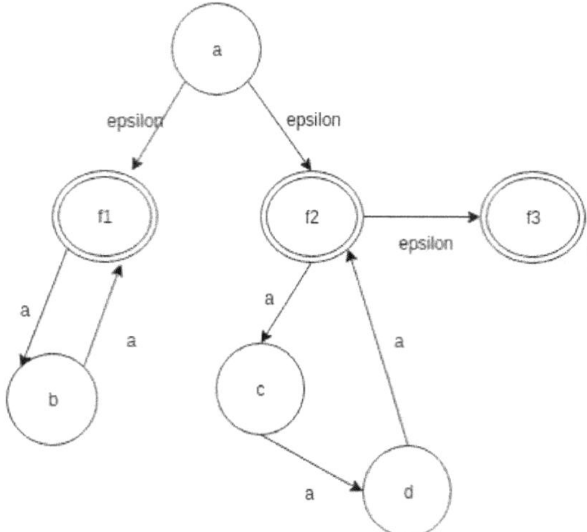

A. 0   **B.** 1   **C.** 2   **D.** 3

Q.68 Let L be the set of all binary strings whose last two symbols are the same. The number of states in the minimum state deterministic finite state automation accepting language is ______.

A. 2   **B.** 5   **C.** 3   **D.** 8

Q.69 A binary string is divisible by 4 if and only if it ends with:

A. 100   **B.** 1000   **C.** 1100   **D.** 0011

Q.70 If $L1$ and $L2$ are regular languages, which among the following is an exception?

A. $L1 \cup L2$ **B.** $L1 - L2$

C. $L1 \cap L2$ **D.** All of these

Q.71 If L is a language, the reversal of the language can be represented as:

A. L' **B.** L^C

C. L^r **D.** None of these

Q.72 If L is a regular language, ______ is also regular.

A. L^r **B.** L'

C. L^* **D.** All of these

Q.73 Which of the following pairs of propositions are not logically equivalent?

A. $\left((p \to r) \wedge (q \to r)\right)$ and $\left((p \vee q) \to r\right)$

B. $p \leftrightarrow q$ and $(\neg p \leftrightarrow \neg q)$

C. $(p \to q) \wedge (q \to p)$ and $p \leftrightarrow q$

D. $\left((p \wedge q) \to r\right)$ and $\left((p \to r) \wedge (q \to r)\right)$

Q.74 What is the number of generators in the group $\left(\{1, \omega, \omega^2\}, *\right)$ where ω and ω^2 are cube root of unity and $*$ is multiplication?

A. 2   **B.** 4   **C.** 6   **D.** 8

Q.75 Consider the following statements:

S_1: If a group $(G, *)$ is of order n, and $a \in G$ is such that $a^m = e$ for some integer $m \leq n$, then m must divide n.

S_2: If a group $(G, *)$ is of even order, then there must be an element $a \in G$ such that $a \neq e$ and $a^* a = e$.

Which of the statements is/are correct?

A. Only S_1
B. Only S_2
C. Both (A) and (B)
D. None of these

Q.76 Consider the following options state whether it is true or false:

A. Any two simple connected graphs with z vertices, where all vertices have degree two, are isomorphic.

B. The maximum vertex connectivity possible is $\frac{3e}{n}$.

C. If G is a simple graph that has a Hamiltonian circuit, then $\deg(u) + \deg(v) \geq n$ for every pair of vertices for $n \geq 5$.

D. The number of the edge-disjoint Hamiltonian circuits in a complete graph with n vertices is $\frac{n-1}{2}$.

Q.77 If $f(z) = \dfrac{1}{(1-z)^2}$ then the coefficient of z^{13} is ________.

A. 14 **B.** 15 **C.** 18 **D.** 16

Q.78 According to principle of mathematical induction, if $P(k + 1) = m^{(k+1)} + 5$ is true then must be true:

A. $P(k) = 3m^{(k)}$
B. $P(k) = m^{(k)} + 5$
C. $P(k) = m^{(k+2)} + 5$
D. $P(k) = m^{(k)}$

Q.79 Match the List 1 and List 2 and choose the correct answer from the code given below:

List 1	List 2
a) Equivalence	i) p ⇒ q
b) Contrapositive	ii) p ⇒ q : q ⇒ p
c) Converse	iii) p ⇒ q : ¬ q ⇒ ¬ p
d) Implication	iv) p ⇔ q

A. (a)-(i), (b)-(ii), (c)-(iii), (d)-(iv)
B. (a)-(ii), (b)-(i), (c)-(iii), (d)-(iv)
C. (a)-(iv), (b)-(iii), (c)-(ii), (d)-(i)
D. (a)-(iii), (b)-(iv), (c)-(ii), (d)-(i)

Q.80 Consider the expression F(p, q, r) ≡ (¬ p ∨ ¬ q) ∧ (p ∧ q ∨ r) → p ∧ (q ∨ r). Which of the following is/are logically equivalent to F(p, q, r)?

A. r → p
B. p → q
C. p ∨ ¬ r
D. Both (A) and (C)

Q.81 A ________ has a greatest element and a least element which satisfy $0 \leq a \leq 1$ for every a in the lattice (say, L).

A. semilattice
B. join semilattice
C. meet semilattice
D. bounded lattice

Q.82 ________ is done in the development phase by the debuggers.

A. Coding
B. Testing
C. Debugging
D. Implementation

Q.83 Who writes the Software Requirement Specifications Document(SRS)?

A. System Developer
B. System Tester
C. System Analyst
D. Systems flowchart

Q.84 In which testing strategy that test the application as a whole?

A. Requirement Gathering
B. Verification testing
C. Validation testing
D. System testing

Q.85 Which of the following is a myth in testing?

A. Tester can find bugs
B. Any user can test software
C. Missed defects are not due to testers
D. Complete testing is not possible

Q.86 Which of the following statements about SRS is/are true?

i. SRS is written by a customer.

ii. SRS is written by a developer.

iii. SRS serves as a contract between customer and developer.

A. Only i is true
B. Both ii and iii are true
C. All are true
D. None of these

Q.87 Which of the following is a desirable property of module?

A. Independency
B. Low cohesiveness
C. High coupling
D. Multifunctional

Q.88 What part of documentation offers both a pictorial and written description of system?

A. System abstract
B. System narrative
C. System overview
D. Problem definition

Q.89 Generally, the top management of an organization is more interested in:

A. Tactical decisions
B. Strategic decisions
C. Day-to-day operations
D. All of these

Q.90 Back-up procedures help in:

A. Restoring the operation whenever there is a disk failure.
B. Restoring the data files whenever there is a system crash.
C. Restoring both application and system software whenever there is a disk corruption.
D. All of these

Q.91 In a room there are eight couples. Out of them if 4 people are selected at random, the probability that they may be couples is:

A. $\dfrac{{}^8C_4}{{}^{16}C_4}$ **B.** $\dfrac{{}^8C_2}{{}^{16}C_8}$ **C.** $\dfrac{{}^8C_2}{{}^8C_4}$ **D.** $\dfrac{{}^8C_2}{{}^{16}C_4}$

Q.92 The odds against an event A are $5:3$ and odds in favor of another independent event B and $6:5$. The chances that neither A nor B occurs is:

A. $\frac{52}{88}$ **B.** $\frac{25}{88}$ **C.** $\frac{10}{88}$ **D.** $\frac{12}{88}$

Q.93 Evaluate: $\displaystyle\int \frac{\sin^{-1}x}{(1-x^2)^{\frac{3}{2}}}\,dx$

A. $\dfrac{x\cdot(\sin^{-1}x)}{\sqrt{1-x^2}} + \dfrac{1}{2}\log|(1+x^2)| + C$

B. $\dfrac{x\cdot(\sin^{-1}x)}{\sqrt{1-x^2}} - \dfrac{1}{2}\log|(1-x^2)| + C$

C. $\dfrac{x\cdot(\sin^{-1}x)}{\sqrt{1-x^2}} + \dfrac{1}{2}\log|(1-x^2)| + C$

D. None of these

Q.94 The degree of the differential equation:

$$\frac{d^2y}{dx^2} + 3\left(\frac{dy}{dx}\right)^2 = x^2\log\left(\frac{d^2y}{dx^2}\right)$$

A. 1   **B.** 2

C. 3   **D.** Not defined

Q.95 The inverse Laplace transform of the function $F(s) = \dfrac{1}{s(s+1)}$ is given by:

A. $f(t) = \sin t$ **B.** $f(t) = e^{-t}\sin t$

C. $f(t) = e^{-t}$ **D.** $f(t) = 1 - e^{-t}$

Q.96 The inverse Laplace transform of $H(s) = \dfrac{s+3}{s^2+2s+1}$ for $t \geq 0$ is:

A. $3te^{-t} + e^{-t}$ **B.** $3e^{-t}$

C. $t^2e^{-t} + e^{-t}$ **D.** $4te^{-t} + e^{-t}$

Q.97 If the system,

$$2x - y + 3z = 2$$
$$x + y + 2z = 2$$
$$5x - y + az = b$$

Has infinitely many solutions, then the values of a and b, respectively, are:

A. -8 and 6 **B.** 8 and 6

C. -8 and -6 **D.** 8 and -6

Q.98 Eigen values of a real symmetric matrix are always __________.

A. Positive   **B.** Negative   **C.** Real   **D.** Complex

Q.99 If $y = 2\sin x - 3x^4 + 8$, then $\dfrac{dy}{dx}$ is:

A. $2\sin x - 12x^3$ **B.** $2\cos x - 12x^3$

C. $2\cos x + 12x^3$ **D.** $2\sin x + 12x^3$

Q.100 $\displaystyle\int \left\{\frac{(\log x - 1)}{1+(\log x)^2}\right\}^2 dx$ is equal to:

A. $\dfrac{xe^x}{1+x^2} + C$ **B.** $\dfrac{x}{(\log x)^2+1} + C$

C. $\dfrac{\log x}{(\log x)^2+1} + C$ **D.** $\dfrac{x}{x^2+1} + C$

// Smart Answer Sheet //

Correct Percentage of students who answered correctly. **Skipped** Percentage of students who skipped.

Q.	Ans.	Correct / Skipped	Q.	Ans.	Correct / Skipped	Q.	Ans.	Correct / Skipped	Q.	Ans.	Correct / Skipped	Q.	Ans.	Correct / Skipped	Q.	Ans.	Correct / Skipped
1	D	16.44 % / 71.17 %	18	A	62.42 % / 37.39 %	35	D	49.28 % / 40.39 %	52	B	68.77 % / 31.09 %	69	A	60.59 % / 35.28 %	86	C	15.54 % / 80.98 %
2	A	67.57 % / 30.21 %	19	D	26.71 % / 67.94 %	36	C	40.1 % / 47.82 %	53	D	46.41 % / 40.21 %	70	D	43.15 % / 38.11 %	87	A	49.15 % / 37.91 %
3	A	55.2 % / 35.25 %	20	C	43.62 % / 37.96 %	37	B	60.64 % / 30.99 %	54	C	52.11 % / 38.14 %	71	C	46.45 % / 42.47 %	88	C	51.65 % / 46.79 %
4	A	44.2 % / 47.69 %	21	D	48.18 % / 48.23 %	38	A	30.3 % / 67.71 %	55	C	52.29 % / 45.56 %	72	D	67.39 % / 31.57 %	89	B	79.19 % / 14.78 %
5	C	64.8 % / 33.03 %	22	A	22.22 % / 70.74 %	39	D	63.53 % / 32.19 %	56	D	47.11 % / 50.91 %	73	D	31.58 % / 67.63 %	90	D	81.13 % / 17.15 %
6	C	58.58 % / 38.26 %	23	B	17.68 % / 71.37 %	40	A	55.35 % / 41.48 %	57	C	45.76 % / 32.4 %	74	A	67.8 % / 30.34 %	91	D	40.51 % / 59.43 %
7	C	51.01 % / 44.58 %	24	C	77.05 % / 16.71 %	41	B	66.09 % / 31.73 %	58	B	13.12 % / 84.77 %	75	C	50.15 % / 47.79 %	92	B	23.82 % / 67.37 %
8	A	65.92 % / 31.78 %	25	D	23.43 % / 71.89 %	42	D	64.07 % / 33.93 %	59	B	30.4 % / 68.09 %	76	D	44.76 % / 33.16 %	93	C	32.06 % / 67.6 %
9	B	69.9 % / 30.07 %	26	A	69.93 % / 30.0 %	43	C	40.92 % / 39.45 %	60	A	40.08 % / 53.31 %	77	A	43.51 % / 54.49 %	94	D	64.43 % / 33.22 %
10	D	79.24 % / 16.84 %	27	A	63.14 % / 31.55 %	44	C	42.09 % / 32.56 %	61	B	66.12 % / 30.31 %	78	B	41.29 % / 54.82 %	95	D	48.31 % / 44.78 %
11	D	11.42 % / 78.69 %	28	D	40.05 % / 57.84 %	45	C	14.01 % / 67.26 %	62	C	68.07 % / 31.78 %	79	C	51.04 % / 38.14 %	96	C	43.89 % / 34.63 %
12	C	24.43 % / 67.67 %	29	D	28.98 % / 68.31 %	46	D	60.8 % / 37.0 %	63	D	59.63 % / 38.16 %	80	D	53.94 % / 42.04 %	97	B	81.22 % / 12.82 %
13	D	68.13 % / 31.43 %	30	B	18.78 % / 76.72 %	47	D	18.5 % / 75.53 %	64	C	31.59 % / 67.35 %	81	D	65.72 % / 32.43 %	98	C	61.55 % / 30.35 %
14	B	84.54 % / 11.24 %	31	D	61.07 % / 34.48 %	48	B	59.56 % / 36.16 %	65	A	55.27 % / 34.55 %	82	C	77.86 % / 20.93 %	99	B	83.05 % / 11.15 %
15	A	20.5 % / 68.37 %	32	C	60.67 % / 34.86 %	49	B	62.11 % / 35.91 %	66	D	48.28 % / 31.63 %	83	A	53.9 % / 38.32 %	100	B	41.11 % / 47.51 %
16	D	65.31 % / 32.95 %	33	C	10.37 % / 84.14 %	50	B	80.2 % / 19.6 %	67	C	41.74 % / 56.2 %	84	D	15.35 % / 83.26 %			
17	B	41.88 % / 39.53 %	34	B	46.17 % / 42.91 %	51	B	41.2 % / 30.12 %	68	B	25.63 % / 68.1 %	85	B	46.2 % / 30.41 %			

//Hints and Solutions//

1. Option (A): Time complexity of memory-efficient merge sort is $O(n^2)$.

This is a true statement. The memory-efficient merge sort is the same as in place merge sort and the recurrence relation will be:

$$T(n) = 2T\left(\frac{n}{2}\right) + n^2 \equiv O(n^2)$$

Option (B): The recurrence relation for worst case of quick sort algorithm is:

$$T(n) = T(n-2) + T\left(n^{\frac{1}{\log n}}\right) + O(n)$$

This is also a true statement. So,

$$T(n) = T(n-2) + T\left(n^{\frac{1}{\log n}}\right) + O(n)$$

$$n^{\frac{1}{\log n}} \equiv n\log_n 2 \equiv 2$$

Option (C): Let C be the number of comparisons performed in the overall execution of the partition procedure of the quick sort algorithm then time complexity is $O(n + C)$.

This is also a true statement. Since all the comparisons are performed by partition algorithm only except base cases.

$$TC = O(n + C)$$

Option (D): The space complexity of heap sort is $O(\log n)$.

This a false statement. Since space complexity for heap sort algorithm is $O(1)$.

HEAPIFY (A, i)

1. $l = $ LEFT (i)

2. $r = $ RIGHT (i)

3. if $l \leq A.$ heap-size and $A[l] > A[i]$

4. largest $= l$

5. else largest $= i$

6. if $r \leq A.$ heap-size and $[r] > A[$ largest $]$

7. largest $= r$

8. if largest $! = i$

9. exchange $A[i]$ with $A[$ largest $]$

10. MAX-HEAPIFY (A, largest)

Hence, the correct option is (D).

2. Given,

A is the nth node with a maximum possible value of n and B is the nth node with a minimum possible value of n in the Breadth-First Search traversal.

Consider that vertex is at distance 3 from the root, that is, height $= 3$ Traverse using Breadth-First Search algorithm, number the node accordingly.

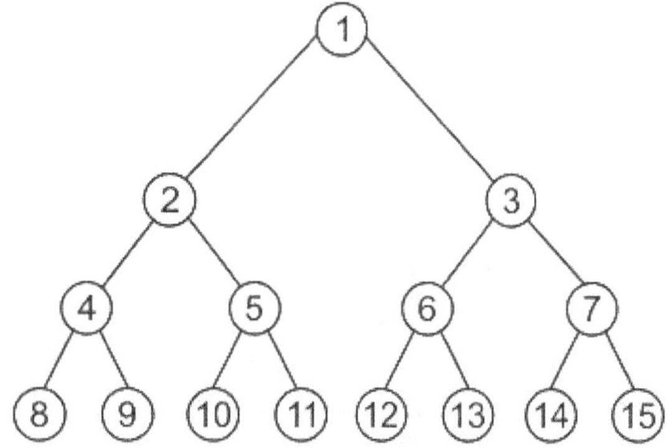

Maximum value $= A = 15$

Minimum value $= B = 8$

$\therefore A - B = 15 - 8$

$\Rightarrow (2^{3+1} - 1) - 2^3$

$\Rightarrow 15 - 8$

$= 7$

According to question, height $= 6$,

$\Rightarrow (2^{6+1} - 1) + 2^6$

$\Rightarrow (2^7 - 1) + 2^6$

$= 255$

Hence, the correct option is (A).

3. Fractional knapsack uses Greedy approach:

An item with maximum profit/weight is selected first.

Now,

Items	1	2	3	4	5
Profit	90	130	60	110	42
Weight	20	60	20	50	15
$\dfrac{Profit}{Weight}$	4.5	2.16	3	2.2	2.8

Profit $=$ Item $1 +$ Item $3 +$ Item $5 +$ fraction part of 4

Profit $= 90 + 60 + 42 + 35 \times \dfrac{110}{50}$

$= 269$

Hence, the correct option is (A).

4. Generalizes to other algorithms and for two-dimensional pattern matching problems. The Rabin–Karp algorithm or Karp–Rabin algorithm is a string-matching algorithm created by Richard M. Karp and Michael O. Rabin (1987) that uses hashing to find an exact match of a pattern string in a text. A practical application of the algorithm is detecting plagiarism.

Hence, the correct option is (A).

5. The for loop in the pre-processing algorithm runs for m (length of the pattern) times. So, the pre-processing time is $\theta(m)$. If the expected number of strong shifts is small $O(1)$ and prime q is chosen to be quite large, then the Rabin-Karp algorithm can be expected to run in time $O(n + m)$ plus the time required to process spurious hits.

Hence, the correct option is (C).

6. The worst-case running time of the Rabin Karp Algorithm is $\theta\big((n - m + 1)m\big)$. We write $\theta(n - m + 1)$ instead of $\theta(n - m)$ because there are $n - m + 1$ different values that the given text takes on. This would occur with an extremely awful hash function that resulted in a false positive at each step.

Hence, the correct option is (C).

7. A quick search algorithm is the fastest algorithm in the·string matching field whereas a Linear search algorithm searches for an element in an array of elements. Quick search is the fastest known searching algorithm because of its highly optimized inner loop. The Boyer-Moore string-search algorithm is an efficient string searching algorithm that is the standard benchmark for practical string-search literature. The algorithm preprocesses the string being searched for (the pattern), but not the string being searched in (the text).

Hence, the correct option is (C).

8. A quick search algorithm was originally formed to overcome the drawbacks of Boyer-Moore's algorithm and also for increased speed and efficiency. Robert Boyer and J Strother Moore established it in 1977. Boyer-Moore's string search algorithm is a particularly efficient algorithm and has served as a standard benchmark for string search algorithms ever since.

Hence, the correct option is (A).

9. Given,

Vertices $V = 150$

Number of components $= 10$

As we know, edges will be minimum if all components are a tree and suppose we have 9 components containing only 1 vertex and we are left with 141 vertices so making a tree using 141 vertices required 140 edges.

So, total number of edges $= 0 + 140$ (9 one vertex components $+1 - 141$ vertex component).

Thus, the minimum number of edges in G is 140.

Hence, the correct option is (B).

10. The public member functions of a class can easily access the private data members of the same class. This is achieved by the "friend", which is a non-member function to the class. Its private data can be accessed. That's why the friend function is not a member of the class.

Hence, the correct option is (D).

11. The problem arising due to the destruction of the temporary objects can be solved by overloading the assignment operator to get the values that might be getting returned while the destructor free the dynamic memory. Defining copy constructors can help us to do this in an even simpler way.

Hence, the correct option is (D).

12. The align attribute in HTML which specifies the horizontal alignment of the content in a cell.

Syntax:

<td align="left ">

Attribute value left is default for <td>. It left-aligns content.

Hence, the correct option is (C).

13. Both statements are false.

- HTTP supports proxy servers.

- A proxy server is a computer that keeps copies of responses to recent requests. The HTTP client sends a request to the proxy server. The proxy server checks its cache. If the response is not stored in the cache, the proxy server sends the request to the corresponding server. Incoming responses are sent to the proxy server and stored for future requests from other clients.

- The proxy server reduces the load on the original server, decreases traffic, and improves latency. However, to use the proxy server, the client must be configured to access the proxy instead of the target server.

Hence, the correct option is (D).

14. Interpreter is a program that can execute high-level language programs "directly," without first being translated into machine language. An Interpreter directly executes instructions written in a programming or scripting language without previously converting them to an object code or machine code. Examples of interpreted languages are Perl, Python and Matlab.

Hence, the correct option is (B).

15. The *head_ref = prev; at the end of the while loop, the prev pointer points to the last node of the original linked list.

We need to change *head_ref so, that the head pointer now starts pointing to the last node.

Hence, the correct option is (A).

16. The fun() prints alternate nodes of the given linked list, first from head to end, and then from end to the head.

If the linked list has an even number of nodes, then skip the last node. Its a case of recursion.and recursive funcion stores data in a stack like fashion. So, after execution, it returns them like poping from a stack.

Hence, the correct option is (D).

17. The addFront and removeFront operations can be performed using one stack itself as push and pop are supported (adding and removing element from top of the stack) but to perform addRear and removeRear you need to pop each element from the current stack and push it into another stack, push or pop the element as per the asked operation from this stack and in the end pop elements from this stack to the first stack.

Hence, the correct option is (B).

18. To perform the deQueue operation you need to pop each element from the first stack and push it into the second stack. In this case, you need to pop 'm' times and need to perform push operations also 'm' times. Then you pop the first element from this second stack (constant time) and pass all the elements to the first stack (as done in the beginning) ('m -1' times). Therefore, the time complexity is O(m).

Hence, the correct option is (A).

19. A special case of geosynchronous orbit is the geostationary orbit, which is a circular geosynchronous orbit in Earth's equatorial plane. A satellite in a geostationary orbit remains in the same position in the sky to observers on the surface. Communications satellites are often given geostationary or close to geostationary orbits so, that the satellite antennas that communicate with them do not have to move, but can be pointed permanently at the fixed location in the sky where the satellite appears.

Hence, the correct option is (D).

20. A protocol converter is a device used to convert the standard or proprietary protocol of one device to the protocol suitable for the other device or tools to achieve the desired interoperability. Protocol converters are usually not operated in pairs. A protocol converter works by utilizing an internal master protocol for communicating with the external devices.

Hence, the correct option is (C).

21. The checksum field is the 16-bit one's complement of the one's complement sum of all 16-bit words in the header. If there is no corruption, the result of summing the entire IP header, including checksum, should be zero. At each hop, the checksum is verified.

Hence, the correct option is (D).

22. Satellite transponders use a higher frequency for reception of radiation from earth stations and lower frequency for transmission to earth stations. The term "satellite transponder" refers collectively to a transmitter-receiver subsystem onboard the satellite that processes, amplifies, and retransmits a range of frequencies (the transponder bandwidth) to another location/terminal/antenna on the earth.

Hence, the correct option is (A).

23. DHCP uses User Datagram Protocol (UDP), RFC 768, as its transport protocol. DHCP messages that a client sends to a server

are sent to well-known port 67 (UDP—Bootstrap Protocol and DHCP). DHCP Messages that a server sends to a client are sent to port 68.

Hence, the correct option is (B).

24. A datagram is primarily used for wireless communication and is self-contained with source and destination addresses written in the header. It is similar to a packet, which is a small piece of data transmitted through a connectionless protocol; but a datagram cannot handle prior or subsequent data communication.

Hence, the correct option is (C).

25. When a host acquires multiple offers of IP addresses from different DHCP servers, the host will broadcast a DHCP request identifying the server whose offer has been accepted.

- **Automatic allocation:** The DHCP server assigns a permanent IP address to a client from its IP Pools. On the firewall, a Lease specified as Unlimited means the allocation is permanent.

- **Dynamic allocation:** The DHCP server assigns a reusable IP address from IP Pools of addresses to a client for a maximum period of time, known as a lease. This method of address allocation is useful when the customer has a limited number of IP addresses; they can be assigned to clients who need only temporary access to the network.

- **Static allocation:** The network administrator chooses the IP address to assign to the client and the DHCP server sends it to the client. A static DHCP allocation is permanent; it is done by configuring a DHCP server and choosing a Reserved Address to correspond to the MAC Address of the client device. The DHCP assignment remains in place even if the client logs off, reboots have a power outage, etc.

Hence, the correct option is (D).

26. Start of frame delimiter (SFD): SFD is a 1-byte field and is used to indicate the start of a frame. This is a 1-byte field which is always set to 10101011. SFD indicates that upcoming bits are starting of the frame, which is the destination address. Sometimes SFD is considered the part of PRE, this is the reason Preamble is described as 8 bytes in many places. The SFD warns stations or stations that this is the last chance for synchronization.

Hence, the correct option is (A).

27. The star topology has one central computer and six or seven nodes connected to it directly. In a star network, every host is connected to a central hub. In its simplest form, one central hub acts as a conduit to transmit messages.

Hence, the correct option is (A).

28. The SIMM (single inline memory module) or DIMM (dual inline memory module) occupy less space while providing greater memory space. DIMM and SIMM are two major types of random-access memory standards for personal computers. The naming of each type of RAM refers to the specific way in which the memory is packaged.

Hence, the correct option is (D).

29. The controller gets the request from the device needing the memory read or write operation and then it multiplexes the address. The multiplexed signal of the controller is split into RAS and CAS. The request controller calls a procedure running in the transaction server, which ACMS calls the procedure server. Since the transaction server is single-threaded, it is typically deployed as a server class consisting of multiple server processes.

Hence, the correct option is (D).

30. Number of chips required for $4\ MB$ is:

$$MM = \frac{(4 \times 2^{20} \times 8)}{(1 \times 2^{20})} = 32 \text{ chips.}$$

In a refresh cycle, a whole row of a memory chip is refreshed at once. This implies the given time of $100\ ns$ for one refresh operation refreshes one row of the memory chip. Since there are $1\ K = 2^{10}$ such rows.

Time for refreshing a whole chip would be $2^{10} \times 100\ ns$.

These chips as there can be many possible arrangements. There is a logical arrangement provided in the problem statement itself as " $1M \times 1$ bit chip". This indicates that to make a " $1M \times 32$ bits" MM, we need to arrange all 32 chips in a line. It is to be noted that a row in all chips in a series can be refreshed in one refresh cycle. This makes the total time to refresh the $4\ MB$ of memory as same as that of one chip.

So, time required to refresh $MM = 100 \times 2^{10}\ ns$.

Hence, the correct option is (B).

31. Given option (A), (B) and (C) are the types of addressing mode of 8051.

In 8051 there are six types of addressing modes are:

1. Direct addressing
2. Indirect addressing
3. Register instructions
4. Register specific(Register Implicit) instructions
5. Immediate mode
6. Indexed addressing

Hence, the correct option is (D).

32. A branch delay slot is an instruction space immediately following a jump or branch. When a branch instruction is involved, the location of the following delay slot instruction in the pipeline may be called a branch delay slot. Branch delay slots are found mainly in DSP architectures and older RISC architectures. The goal of a pipelined architecture is to complete an instruction every clock cycle. It is the iconic feature of the RISC machine.

Hence, the correct option is (C).

33. The symbol, 'addr 16' represents the 16-bit destination address which is used by the LCALL or LJMP instruction to specify the call or jump destination address, within 64 Kbytes program memory. Only internal data RAM and SFRS can be directly addressed indirect addressing mode.

Hence, the correct option is (C).

34. The RISC architecture is followed in the design of mobile devices. In very small devices, RISC is more power efficient because the extra instruction decode logic in a CISC processor has a cost. But this is true only at the very low end. This is where ARM's initial dominance came from. But in high-performance CPUs, the instruction decode logic is tiny.

Hence, the correct option is (B).

35. The DMA differs from the interrupt mode by the involvement of the processor in the operation. The method of accessing the I/O devices. The amount of data transfer possible. DMA is an approach of performing data transfers in bulk between memory and the external device without the intervention of the processor.

Hence, the correct option is (D).

36. The Controller uses the registers to store the starting address, word count, and the status of the operation. The DMA controller has three registers as follows:

- **Address register:** It contains the address to specify the desired location in memory.
- **Word count register:** It contains the number of words to be transferred.
- **Control register:** It specifies the transfer mode.

Hence, the correct option is (C).

37. A Wizard-driven interface or setup assistant is a user interface type that presents a user with a sequence of dialog boxes that lead the user through a series of well-defined steps. It facilitates the installation of Hadoop across any number of hosts.

Hence, the correct option is (B).

38. cTAKES is a Java library for writing, testing, and running pipelines of MapReduce jobs on Apache Hadoop. cTAKES (clinical Text Analysis and Knowledge Extraction System) is a natural language processing tool for information extraction from electronic medical records clinical free-text.

Hence, the correct option is (A).

39. DDL is short name of Data Definition Language, which deals with database schemas and descriptions, of how the data should reside in the database. Data Definition Language, used to perform all other essential tasks such as deleting relation and related schemas in defining the structure relation.

Hence, the correct option is (D).

40. Indexing is a data structure technique to efficiently retrieve records from database files based on some attributes on which the indexing has been done. It is used to optimize the performance of database.

The index structure typically provides secondary access path i.e. alternate way of accessing the records without affecting the physical placement of records on disk.

There are several types of ordered indexes. A primary index is specified on the ordering key field of an ordered file of records. If ordering field is non-key then it is known as the clustering index. Non-key and ordered means if numerous records in the file can have the same value for ordering field. Clustering index is also known as non-dense index.

- First field is of same type as clustering of data file.
- Second field is a block pointer.

Hence, the correct option is (A).

41. Join clause joins two tables by matching the common column.

Therefore, we can also use to the following code for join.

Select name, course_id from instructor natural join teaches;

Hence, the correct option is (B).

42. The statement Select empid where empid $= 1009$ and Lastname $=$ 'GELLER'; does not contain the "from" clause, which specifies the relation from which the values have to be selected or fetched. So, the following given statements possibly contains the error.

Hence, the correct option is (D).

43. In the above-given Query, the "%" (like) operator will be used, which is generally used while searching for a certain pattern in the strings. It represents the single and multiple characters. In this case, it used with "Where "louse to select the "dept_name" that contains the Computer Since as its ending string. To understand it more clearly, consider the following syntax:

Syntax:

SELECT column 1, column 2, ...

FROM table_name

WHERE column LIKE pattern;

Hence, the correct option is (C).

44. To sort the salary from highest to lowest amount and display the employee's name alphabetically, one can use the "Desc and Asc" in the above-given Query.

- For sorting the result in ascending order, use the ASC keyword. This is the default and returns the result from lowest to highest. For example, sorting the Employee Name column alphabetically (A to Z).
- To sort the results from highest to lowest e.g. Z to A or 100 to 1 etc., use the DESC clause with ORDER BY.
- You may specify one or more columns in the ORDER BY Clause.

Hence, the correct option is (C).

45. The "SQL" contains a comparison known as the "BETWEEN," which is also used in one of the given queries, as you can see. The "BETWEEN" operator is generally used to simplify the "WHERE" clause that is used to specify that the value is greater than one value or greater than some values, less than one or more values.

Hence, the correct option is (C).

46. Address binding is the process of mapping the program's logical or virtual addresses to corresponding physical or main memory addresses. In other words, a given logical address is mapped by the MMU (Memory Management Unit) to a physical address.

Hence, the correct option is (D).

47. Reference string: $1,2,3,2,4,1,3,2,4,1$

FIFO:

String	1,2,3	4	1	2
	1	2	3	4
	2	3	4	1
	3	4	1	2
Number of Page Fault	3	1	1	1

Total page fault in FIFO $= 3 + 1 + 1 + 1 = 6$

Reference string: $1,2,3,2,4,1,3,2,4,1$

LRU:

String	1,2,3	4	1	3	2	4	1
	1	2	2	4	1	3	2
	2	3	4	1	3	2	4
	3	4	1	3	2	4	1
Number of Page Fault	3	1	1	1	1	1	1

Total Page fault in LRU $= 3 + 1 + 1 + 1 + 1 + 1 + 1 = 9$

Reference string: $1,2,3,2,4,1,3,2,4,1$

OPTIMAL:

String	1,2,3	4	2
	1	1	1
	2	3	4
	3	4	2
Number of Page Fault	3	1	1

Total page fault with optimal $= 3 + 1 + 1 = 5$

Therefore, OPTIMAL $<$ FIFO $<$ LRU is correct.

Hence, the correct option is (D).

48. In an immediate addressing mode, the operand is a part of the instruction. There is no address field as the operand is a part of the instruction. In direct address mode, the effective address of the operand is equal to the address part of the instruction, that is, the address part of the instruction points to the memory location containing the operand.

Hence, the correct option is (B).

49. Semaphore is an integer variable that is used to prevent threads or processes from accessing a single resource. Semaphore is simply a variable that is non-negative and shared between threads. A semaphore is a signaling mechanism, and a thread that is waiting on a semaphore can be signaled by another thread. It uses two atomic operations, wait, and signal for the process synchronization.

Hence, the correct option is (B).

50. External commands are required to perform various tasks in DOS. They help fix problems, improve performance, and perform other actions as well. External commands usually have higher resource requirements than internal commands. Keeping them in separate files, separated from internal commands, helps to reduce the load on Windows. They can also be added to Windows whenever needed by copying the external command's file to the computer.

Hence, the correct option is (B).

51. To access services of the operating system the interface is provided by the system calls. Generally, these are functions written in C and C++. Open, Close, Read, Write are some of most prominently used system calls. System call provides the services of the operating system to the user programs via Application Program Interface(API). It provides an interface between a process and an operating system to allow user-level processes to request services of the operating system. System calls are the only entry points into the kernel system.

Hence, the correct option is (B).

52. The kernel is the heart of the operating system which can control the hardware and can deal with the interrupts, I/O systems, memory, etc. It can also locate the parameter block by using an address pointer which is stored in the pre-determined address register.

Hence, the correct option is (B).

53. If you want to execute more than one program at a time, the systems software you are using must be capable of multitasking. Multitasking, in an operating system, is allowing a user to perform more than one computer task (such as the operation of an application program) at a time.

Hence, the correct option is (D).

54. Round-robin scheduling is a preemptive scheduling algorithm in which a specific time is provided to execute each process. This specific time is called time-slice. Round-robin is one of the algorithms employed by process and network schedulers in computing. As the term is generally used, time slices are assigned to each process in equal portions and in circular order, handling all processes without priority.

Hence, the correct option is (C).

55. Implicants: Every min-term in SOP form or max-term in POS form in a Boolean function is termed as an implicant.
For example,
F = AB + AC
AB and AC are called implicants.

Prime Implicants: All pairs that cannot be a part of any quad or all quads that cannot be a part of any octet in a K-map are termed as prime implicants.

Essential Prime Implicants: Those prime implicants that cover at least one min-term that can't be covered by any other prime implicant are called essential prime implicants.

Now,

Given the Boolean function,

F (A, B, C, D) = A'B'C'D + A'BCD' + ABC'D'

For the above Boolean function, the K – map representation is:

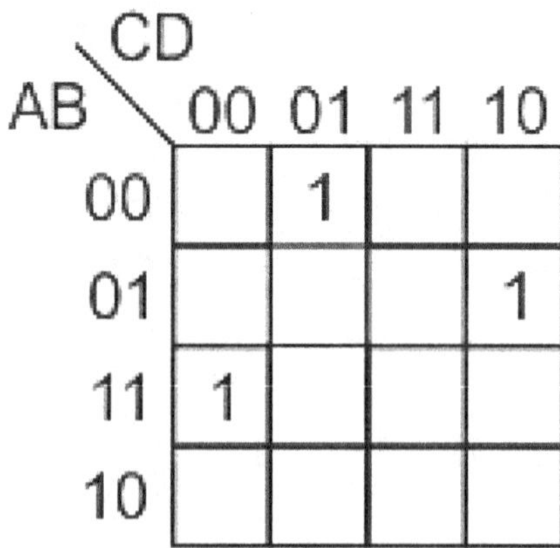

So, we can see there are three minterms in the given function.

Essential prime implicants are also three as they are not covered by any other prime implicant.

Hence, the correct option is (C).

56. In a 4×1 MUX:

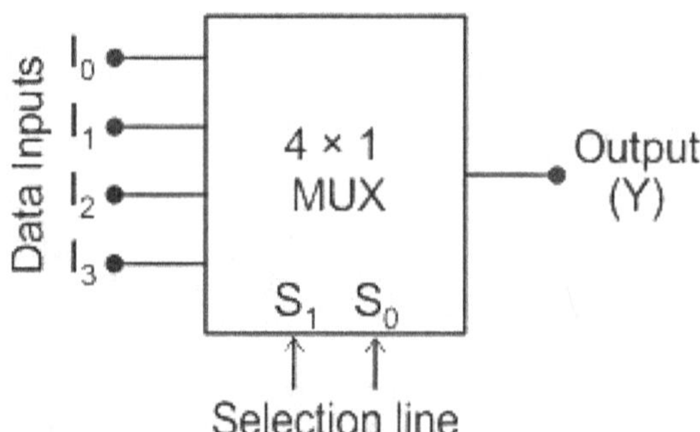

Truth-Table is given as:

S_1	S_0	V
0	0	I_0
0	1	I_1
1	0	I_2
1	1	I_3

$$Y = \text{Output} = \bar{S_1}\bar{S_0}I_0 + \bar{S_1}S_0I_1 + S_1\bar{S_0}I_2 + S_1S_0I_3$$

MUX contains AND gate followed by OR gate.
Now,

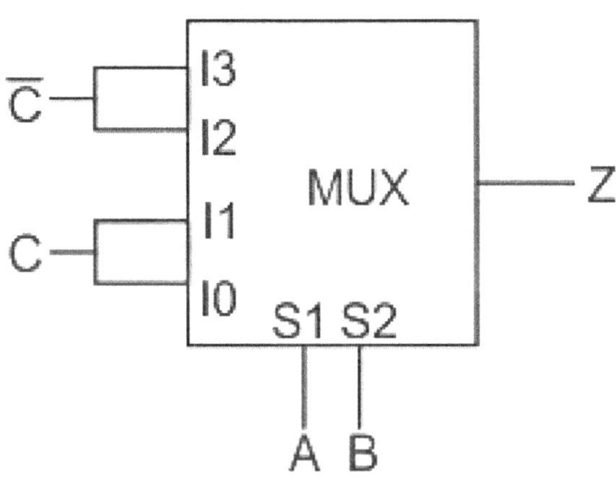

$$Z = \text{Output} = \bar{A}\bar{B}C + \bar{A}BC + A\bar{B}\bar{C} + AB\bar{C}$$

$$Z = \bar{A}C\left(\bar{B} + B\right) + A\bar{C}\left(\bar{B} + B\right)$$

$$Z = \bar{A}C + A\bar{C}$$

$$Z = A \text{ XOR } C$$

Hence, the correct option is (D).

57. For the addition of two hexadecimal numbers, there are two methods:

- In the 1st method, we first convert the hexadecimal number to decimal then add both numbers. After that, we convert that decimal number to a hexadecimal number. But it is a time-consuming method and also calculation becomes bulky.
- In the 2nd method, we directly add both hexadecimal numbers as shown below.

$$a \quad b \quad c \quad d \quad e \quad f$$

$$(1) \ (1) \quad (1)$$

$$O \quad D \quad E \quad F \quad . \quad 1 \quad 2$$

$$+1 \quad 2 \quad E \quad \underline{F} \quad . \quad C \quad O$$

$$2 \quad O \quad D \quad \underline{E} \quad . \quad C \quad 2$$

Hence, the correct option is (C).

58. The PRESET and CLEAR inputs of the JK Flip-Flop are asynchronous, which means that they will have an immediate effect on the Q and Q' outputs regardless of the state of the clock and/or the J and K:

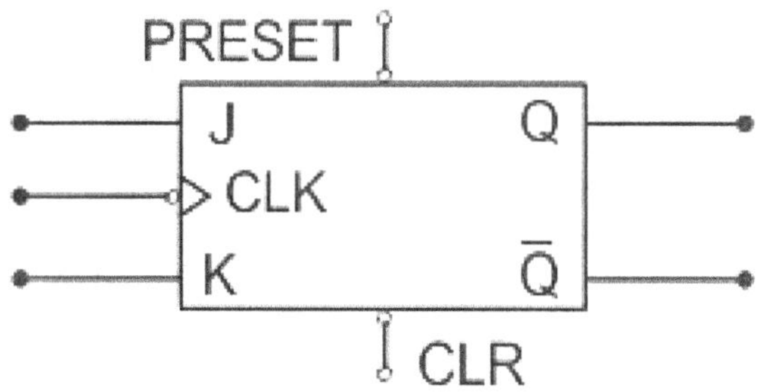

Inputs are:

1. When the preset input is activated, the flip-flop will be set ($Q = 1$, not- $Q = 0$) regardless of any of the synchronous inputs or the clock.

2. When the clear input is activated, the flip-flop will be reset ($Q = 0$, not- $Q = 1$), regardless of any of the synchronous inputs or the clock.

3. When PRESET and CLEAR inputs are activated we get an invalid state on the output, where Q and not- Q go to the same state.

As we know,

JK **Flip-Flop Truth Table:** From truth table it can be seen that the CLEAR (CLR) and PRESET inputs are active at a low logic level and put on the Q output of the flip-flop, a high logic level regardless of the state of the clock and/or the state of the J and K inputs.

	Input					Output	
	PRESET	CLEAR	CLK	J	K	Q	$\bar{Q}$
Invalid	0	0	×	×	×	1*	1*
PRESET	0	1	×	×	×	1	0
CLEAR	1	0	×	×	×	0	1
No change	1	1	×	×	×	Q_0	$\bar{Q}_0$
No change	1	1	↓	0	0	Q_0	$\bar{Q}_0$
Reset	1	1	↓	0	1	0	1
Set	1	1	↓	1	0	1	0
Toggle	1	1	↓	1	1	$\bar{Q}_0$	Q_0

Hence, the correct option is (B).

59. The function by the network given can be found by the following level operations are:

Level 1:

Output of NAND is $\bar{A}B$

Output of NOR is $\overline{C + D}$

Level 2:

Output of 1st AND is $\overline{AB}.E$

Output of 2nd AND is EF

Output of 3rd AND is $\left(\overline{C + D}\right) F$

Level 3:

The final output is 'NOR' all the AND outputs obtained above is:

$$\overline{\overline{AB} \cdot E + EF + (\overline{C + D})\, F}$$

Distributing the bar separately, we get

$$\overline{\overline{A}\,\overline{B} \cdot E} \cdot \overline{EF} \cdot \overline{\left(\overline{C + D}\right)} \cdot \overline{F}$$

Using De Morgan's law, we get

$$\left(AB + \overline{E}\right)\left(\overline{E} + \overline{F}\right)\left(C + D + \overline{F}\right)$$

$$\left(AB\overline{E} + AB\overline{F} + \overline{E} + \overline{E} \cdot \overline{F}\right)\left(C + D + \overline{F}\right)$$

$$\left(\overline{E}\left(AB + 1 + \overline{F}\right) + AB\overline{F}\right)\left(C + D + \overline{F}\right)$$

$$\left(\overline{E} + AB\overline{F}\right)(C + D + \overline{F})$$

Hence, the correct option is (B).

60. Given,

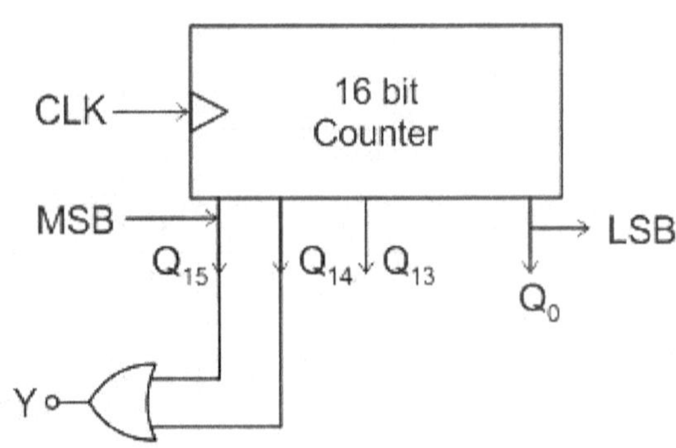

Output (Y) is high (1) for the time period of $24\ ms$.

	Q_{15}	Q_{14}	Q_{13}	....	Q_0
$Y = 1$ begins at:	010	000	000	....	000
$Y = 1$ end at:	111	111	111	....	111

Number of states in which Y is low $(0) = 2^{14}$

Total number of states $= 2^{16}$

Number of states in which Y is high $(1) = 2^{16} - 2^{14}$

Time when Y is high (1) in $2^{16} - 2^{14} = 24 \times 10^{-3}\ s$

Total time $(T) = \dfrac{24 \times 10^{-3}}{2^{16} - 2^{14}}$

Frequency $= \dfrac{1}{T} = \dfrac{2^{16} - 2^{14}}{24 \times 10^{-3}}$

$= 2.048$ MHz.

Hence, the correct option is (A).

61. Analysis:

Truth table for $J - K$ flip flop:

J	K	Q_{n+1}
0	0	Q_n
0	1	0
1	0	1
1	1	$\overline{Q_n}$

So, the output will toggle when both the inputs are 1, i.e. $J = K = 1$

Master-slave flip-flop is a cascade combination of two flip-flops as shown:

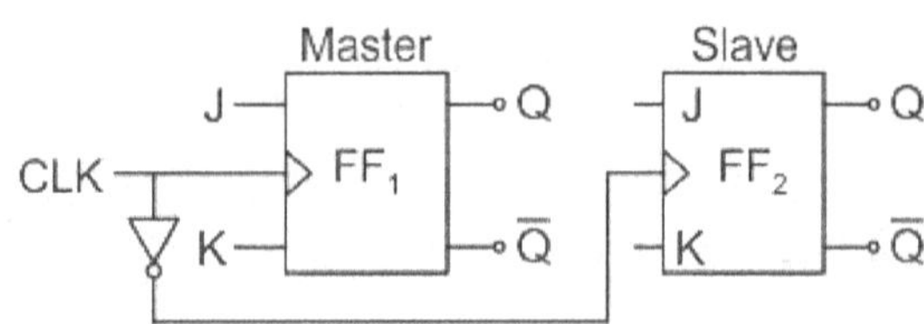

- The first flip flop is called the master flip-flop and the next is called the slave flip-flop.

- Master is triggered by external clock pulse while the slave is activated at its inversion

- If the master is positive edge-triggered, then the slave is negative edge triggered, and vice-versa.

- This means that the data is entered into the flip-flop at the leading/trailing edge of the clock-pulse while its output is obtained at the output pins during the trailing/leading edge of the output pulse.

- So, a master-slave flip-flop completes its operation only after the appearance of one full clock-pulse for which they are also known as Pulse-triggered flip-flops.

Hence, the correct option is (B).

62. Excess $-3 -$ code is also known as self-complementing code which means 1's complement of an excess -3 number is the excess -3 code for the 9's complement of the corresponding decimal number.

Example:

1 in binary is 0001

Excess 3 code is $0001 + 0011 = 0100$

1's complement of the above code is 1011 which is 11.

11 is excess 3 code for 8

9's complement of 1 is 8

Decimal	Excess – 3 code	Binary	Gray code	Octal
0	0011	0000	0000	000
1	0100	0001	0001	001
2	0101	0010	0011	010
3	0110	0011	0010	011
4	0111	0100	0110	100
5	1000	0101	0111	101
6	1001	0110	0101	110
7	1010	0111	0100	111
8	1011	1000	1100	001000

Hence, the correct option is (C).

63. Given,

$m = (313)_4$ and $n = (322)_4$

Now, convert m and n into decimal:

$m = 3 \times 4^2 + 1 \times 4^1 + 3 \times 4^0$

$m = 48 + 4 + 3$

$m = 55$

Now,

$n = 3 \times 4^2 + 2 \times 4^1 + 2 \times 4^0$

$n = 48 + 8 + 2$

$n = 58$

$\therefore m + n = 55 + 58$

$\Rightarrow m + n = 113$

Now, we have to convert 113 into base 4:

Step 1: $113 \% 4 = 1$

$\Rightarrow \dfrac{113}{4} = 28$

Step 2: $28 \% 4 = 0$

$\Rightarrow \dfrac{28}{4} = 7$

Step 3: $7 \% 4 = 3$

$\Rightarrow \dfrac{7}{4} = 1$

Step 4: $1 \% 4 = 1$

$\Rightarrow \dfrac{1}{4} \rightarrow$ will not divide it in quant.

So, we have to stop here the procedure.

The answer will be residue from step 4 to step 1 inorder 1301.

$= (1301)_4$

Hence, the correct option is (D).

64. The six tuples are (Q, Σ, O, δ, X, q0)

It can be described by a 6 tuple (Q, Σ, O, δ, X, q0) where:

- Q is a finite set of states.
- Σ is a finite set of symbols called the input alphabet.
- O is a finite set of symbols called the output alphabet.
- δ is the input transition function.
- X is the output transition function.
- q0 is the initial state from where any input is processed (q0 $\in$ Q).

So, both the machine Moore machine and Mealy machine have 6-tuples.

Hence, the correct option is (C).

65. Non-Deterministic Finite Automata (NFA) and Deterministic Finite Automata (DFA) are equal in power that means, every NFA can be converted into its equivalent DFA and vice versa. So, the statement I is true.

For every alphabet Σ.

Every regular language over Σ can be accepted by a finite automaton.

Therefore, both the statement is true.

Hence, the correct option is (A).

66. Acceptance by accepting start L(P).

Acceptance by empty stack N(P).

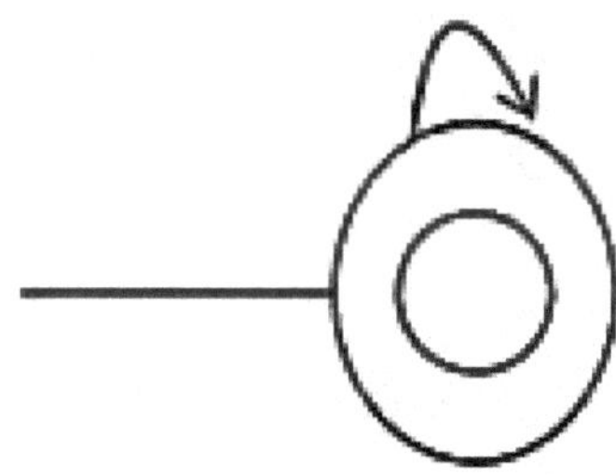

Initial = final

Given,

So, N(P) $\neq \Sigma$ *

L(P) $\neq \Sigma$* not necessarily Σ *

Depending upon the transitions in PDA if any state transaction is absent(dead state) of any input then the string is rejected. So, both L(P) and N(P) are necessarily Σ*.

Hence, the correct option is (D).

67. The epsilon closure set of $f2$ consists of the elements: $f2, f3$. Thus, the count of the element in the closure set is 2. e-closure is defined as the set of states being reached through e-transitions from a starting state. Epsilon means the present state can go to other states without any input. This can happen only if the present state has an epsilon transition to other states. Epsilon closure is finding all the states which can be reached from the present state on one or more epsilon transitions.

Hence, the correct option is (C).

68. Regular expression for the set of all binary strings whose last two symbols are the same will be,

$$(0 + 1) * (00 + 11)$$

Steps:

- Construct NFA
- Convert that NFA into equivalent minimal DFA

NFA for the above expression,

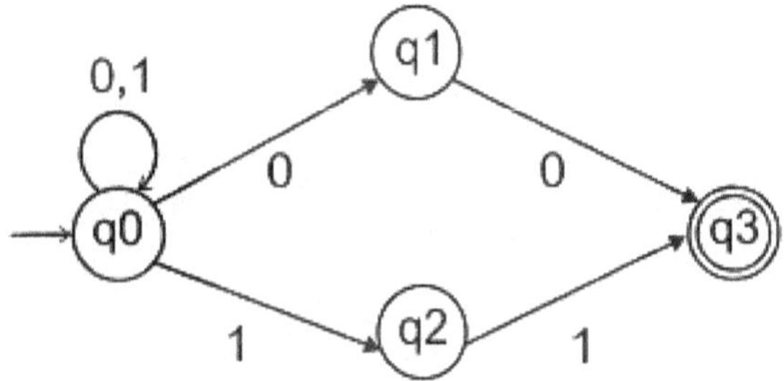

Converting the above NFA into minimal DFA. Note that any state being superset of $q3$ will be our final state:

State	Input – 0	Input – 1
$\rightarrow q0$	$q0, q1 = q01$	$q0, q2 = q02$
$q01$	$q0, q1, q3 = q013$	$q02$
$q02$	$q01$	$q0, q2, q3 = q023$
$q013 *$	$q013$	$q02$
$q023 *$	$q01$	$q023$

So, it is clear that the minimal DFA will have 5 states as shown – $q0, q01, q02, q013, q023$

These states can be renamed as:

$q0 = q0, q01 = q1, q013 = q2, q02 = q3, q023 = q4$. The DFA will look like,

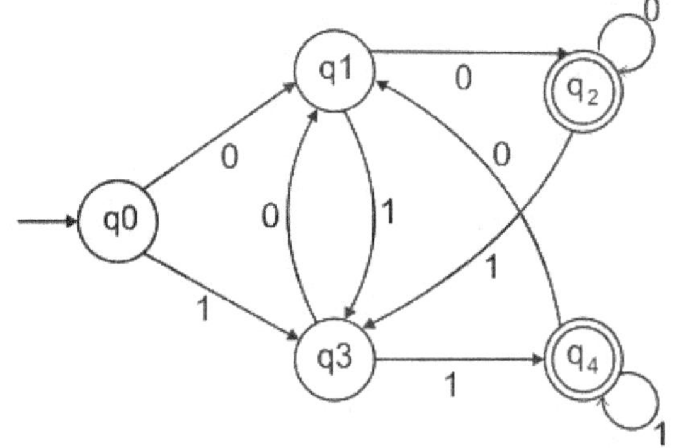

The number of states in the minimum state deterministic finite-state automation accepting language is 5.

Hence, the correct option is (B).

69. If the string is divisible by four, it surely ends with the substring ' 100' while a binary string divisible by 2 would surely end with the substring ' 10'. We have to find out which of the given binary numbers are divisible by ' 4'. For this, we divide each of the given numbers by 4 and the number whose remainder is zero will be the one that is divisible by 4.

Hence, the correct option is (A).

70. Closure properties on regular languages are defined as certain operations on regular language which are guaranteed to produce regular language. Closure refers to some operation on a language, resulting in a new language that is of the same "type" as originally operated on i.e., regular.

It is the closure property of regular language which lays down the following statement:

If $L1, L2$ are two regular languages, then $L1 \cup L2, L1 \cap L2, L1^C, L1 - L2$ are regular languages.

Hence, the correct option is (D).

71. L^r is defined as the reversal of a language. L^r is a set of strings whose reversal is in L.

Example: $L = \{0, 01, 100\}$

$$L^r = \{0, 10, 001\}$$

Let E be a regular expression for L. We show how to reverse E, to provide a regular expression E^r for L^r.

Hence, the correct option is (C).

72. L^r, L', L^* i.e. reversal, complementation and kleene all are the closure properties of regular language. Closure properties on regular languages are defined as certain operations on regular language which are guaranteed to produce regular language. Closure refers to some operation on a language, resulting in a new language that is of the same "type" as originally operated on i.e., regular.

Hence, the correct option is (D).

73. Option A: $\big((p \to r) \wedge (q \to r)\big)$ and $\big((p \vee q) \to r\big)$

Both are equal and it gives the same truth table. So, it is logically equivalent.

Option B: $p \leftrightarrow q$ and $(\neg p \leftrightarrow \neg q)$

$(p \to q)(q \to p)$ and $(\neg p \to q)(\neg q \to p)$

$(p + \overline{q})(q + \overline{p})$ and $(p + \overline{q})(q + \overline{p})$

Both are equal and it gives the same truth table. So, it is logically equivalent.

Option C: $(p \to q) \wedge (q \to p)$ and $p \leftrightarrow q$

Both tables give equal values. So, it is logically equivalent.

Option D: $\big((p \wedge q) \to r\big)$ and $\big((p \to r) \wedge (q \to r)\big)$

P	Q	R	$\neg P$	$\neg Q$	$P \Rightarrow R$	$Q \Rightarrow R$	$(P \Rightarrow R) \wedge (Q \Rightarrow R)$	$P \wedge Q$	$P \wedge Q \Rightarrow R$
T	T	T	F	F	T	T	T	T	T
T	T	F	F	F	F	F	F	T	F
T	F	T	F	T	T	T	T	F	T
T	F	F	F	T	F	T	F	F	T
F	T	T	T	F	T	T	T	F	T
F	T	F	T	F	T	F	F	F	T
F	F	T	T	T	T	T	T	F	T
F	F	F	T	T	T	T	T	F	T

The above truth table is not equivalent. So, the above statement is true, logically not equivalent.

Hence, the correct option is (D

74. Identity $(e) = 1$

From 1 we cannot generate ω and ω^2.

$\therefore$ It is not a generator.

$(\omega)^1 = \omega, (\omega)^2 = \omega^2$ and $(\omega)^3 = 1$

$\therefore$ It is a generator.

$(\omega^2)^1 = \omega^2, (\omega^2)^2 = \omega$ and $(\omega^2)^3 = 1$

It is generator.

There are two generators.

As we know,

$(\{1, \omega, \omega^2\}, *\,)$ is a cyclic group.

Number of generator $= \phi(3) = 3 - 1 = 2$

Hence, the correct option is (A).

75. S_1: If a group $(G, *)$ is of order n, and $a \in G$ is such that $a^m = e$ for some integer $m \leq n$, then m must divide n.

The given statement is correct.

As $a \in G$, is such that $a^m = e$ for some integer $m \leq n$, then it means it is a subgroup of G and m is the order of a. Where order of given group is n. By the property of subgroup or Lagrange's theorem, a order of subgroup divides the order of a group. So, here m must divide n is true.

S_2: If a group $(G, *\,)$ is of even order, then there must be an element $a \in G$ such that $a \neq e$ and $a^* a = e$.

This statement is correct.

Consider an example for this:

Consider G is of order $2n$. There exists $a \in G$ such that $a^p = e$ and p divides $2n$. Let $n = pq$.

So, $(a^n)^2 = (a^{pq})^2 = ((a^p)^q)^2 = (e^q)^2 = e$. It means a^n is an element which satisfy the condition and $a = !\, e$. Here, a is non trivial subgroup of G.

Hence, the correct option is (C).

76. Edge-disjoint Hamiltonian circuit: A Hamiltonian circuit that doesn't have any common edge with other Hamiltonian circuits in the same graph.

In complete graph for $n = 3$. We have only one Hamiltonian circuit $\dfrac{(3-1)}{2} = 1$.

For $n = 4$. We have 6 edges in the complete graph. Suppose in one Hamiltonian cycle you include $e1, e2, e3, e4$ edges. Now we have $e5$ and $e6$ edge left we can't for another Hamiltonian cycle with this edge. So again one $\dfrac{(4-1)}{2} = 1$.

Hence, the correct option is (D).

77. $\dfrac{1}{1-z} = 1 + z + z^2 + z^3 + z^4 \cdots$

Differentiating with respect to x.

$\dfrac{1}{(1-z)^2} = 1 + 2z + 3z^2 + 4z^3 + 5z^4 + 6z^5 \ldots$

$\dfrac{1}{(1-z)^2} = \sum_{k=0}^{k=\infty}(k + 1)\, z^k$

Coefficient of $z^{13} = 13 + 1 = 14$

Hence, the correct option is (A).

78. The principle of mathematical induction is then: If the integer 0 belongs to the class F and F are hereditary, every non-negative integer belongs to F. Alternatively, if the integer 1 belongs to the class F and F is hereditary, then every positive integer belongs to F.

By the principle of mathematical induction, if a statement is true for any number $m = k$, then for its successor $m = k + 1$, the statement also satisfies, provided the statement is true for $m = 1$. So, the required answer is $P(k) = m^{(k)} + 5$.

Hence, the correct option is (B).

79. As we know,

$p \Rightarrow q \equiv \neg q \Rightarrow \neg p$

By the Truth Table:

p	q	p ⇒ q	p ⇔ q	q ⇒ p	¬ p	¬ q	¬ q ⇒ ¬ p
T	T	T	T	T	F	F	T
T	F	F	F	T	F	T	F
F	T	T	F	F	T	F	T
F	F	T	T	T	T	T	T

By the Truth Table, we get,

Equivalence means $p \Leftrightarrow q$

Contrapositive means $p \Rightarrow q$: $\neg q \Rightarrow \neg p$

Converse means $p \Rightarrow q$: $q \Rightarrow p$

Implication means $p \Rightarrow q$

So, the correct match is (a)-(iv), (b)-(iii), (c)-(ii), (d)-(i).

Hence, the correct option is (C).

80. Logically equivalent:

Two expressions are logically equivalent provided that they have the same truth value for all possible combinations of truth values for all variables appearing in the two expressions. In this case, we write X≡Y and say that X and Y are logically equivalent.

Here logical operators are the same meaning as digital operators like,

$\neg$ = not = '

V = or = +

∧ = and = .

$p \rightarrow q$ = implies = ¬pVq = p'+q

The given F(p, q, r) ≡ (¬ p V ¬ q) ∧ (p ∧ q V r) → p ∧ (q V r)

L.H.S:

= (p'+q').(p.q)+r → p.(q+r)   (Here p'.p =0=p.p'= false)

= 0+0+r→ p.(q+r)

= r→(p.q+p.r)   (Here p→q =implies = ¬pVq = p'+q)

= ¬ r+pq+pr

= ¬ r+p+ pq   (Here p+p'q = p+q)

= ¬ r+p   (Here p+p q = p)

Option (A): r → p

True, (¬ p V ¬ q) ∧ (p ∧ q V r)→ p ∧ (q V r) ≡ r → p

R.H.S:

= r → p (Here p→q =implies = ¬pVq = p'+q)

= r'+ p

So, the L.H.S is equal to R.H.S.

Option (B): p → q

False, (¬ p V ¬ q) ∧ (p ∧ q V r) → p ∧ (q V r) ≡ p → q

R.H.S: p → q

= ¬ p+ q

= p'+q

So, the L.H.S is not equal to R.H.S.

Option (C): p V ¬ r

True, (¬ p V ¬ q) ∧ (p ∧ q V r)→ p ∧ (q V r) ≡p V ¬ r

R.H.S:

= p V ¬ r

= p+r'

So, the L.H.S is equal to R.H.S.

Hence, the correct option is (D).

81. A lattice that has additionally a supremum element and an infimum element which satisfy $0 \leq a \leq 1$, for every an in the lattice is called a bounded lattice. A partially ordered set is a bounded lattice if and only if every finite set (including the empty set) of elements has a join and a meet.

Hence, the correct option is (D).

82. Coding is done by the developers. In debugging, the developer fixes the bug in the development phase. Testing is conducted by the testers. Debugging tactics can involve interactive debugging, control flow analysis, unit testing, integration testing, log file analysis, monitoring at the application or system level, memory dumps, and profiling.

Hence, the correct option is (C).

83. System Developer wrote the Software Requirement Specifications Document(SRS). A software requirements specification (SRS) is a document that describes what the software will do and how it will be expected to perform. It also describes the functionality the product needs to fulfill all stakeholders (business, users) needs.

Hence, the correct option is (A).

84. System Testing is a type of software testing that is performed on a complete integrated system to evaluate the compliance of the system with the corresponding requirements. In system testing, integration testing passed components are taken as input.

Hence, the correct option is (D).

85. People outside the IT industry think and even believe that any user can test software and testing is not a creative job. However, testers know very well that this is a myth. Thinking alternative scenarios, try to crash a software with the intent to explore potential bugs is not possible for the person who developed it.

Hence, the correct option is (B).

86. The SRS acts as a communication media between the Customer, Analyst, system developers, maintainers, etc. Thus it is a contract between Purchaser and Supplier. It is essentially written by a developer on the basis of the customer's need but in some cases, it may be written by a customer as well.

Hence, the correct option is (C).

87. We know that,

A design solution is said to be highly modular if the different modules in the solution have high cohesion and their inter-module couplings are low.

A modular program is one that is decomposed into a set of modules such that the modules should have low interdependency among each other.

Weak coupling or Low coupling: Since objects do not directly change each other's internal data, they are weakly coupled. Weak coupling among objects enhances the understandability of the design since each object can be studied and understood in isolation from other objects. Therefore it is one of the desirable properties of a good module.

Independency: Modules should be as independent as possible from another module so that changes to the module don't heavily impact other modules. This is one desirable property of a good module.

High cohesion: The cohesiveness of methods within a class is desirable since it promotes encapsulation of the objects so high cohesion is a desirable property for the module. Therefore, for a good module, we need high cohesion, low coupling and independence.

Hence, the correct option is (A).

88. System Overview is a Dashboard widget that provides various system information including stats, graphs, and recent users. The System Overview clearly identifies the electrical system architecture, electrical equipment items, and circuits required. This document identifies all substantial elements of the system and lists them as a bill of materials.

Hence, the correct option is (C).

89. Generally, the top management of an organization is more interested in Strategic decisions. Strategic decisions are those decisions that have an influence over years, decades, and even beyond the lifetime of the project. Once a strategic decision is made, it is very unlikely to be altered in the short term.

Hence, the correct option is (B).

90. Backup is the process of creating a copy of the data on your system that you use for recovery in case your original data is lost or corrupted. You can also use the backup to recover copies of older files if you have deleted them from your system.

Hence, the correct option is (D).

91. $1.$ Combination:

Selecting r objects from given n objects.

- The number of selections of r objects from the given n objects is denoted by ^nC_r.

- $^nC_r = \dfrac{n!}{r!(n-r)!}$

$2.$ Probability of an event happening $= \dfrac{\text{Number of ways it can happen}}{\text{Total number of outcomes}}$

Note: Use combinations if a problem calls for the number of ways of selecting objects.

Given,

In a room, there are eight couples.

Eight couples $= 16$ peoples.

We have to select four people out of 16 people.

Total possible cases $= {}^{16}C_4$

Now, we have to select four people- they may be couples.

So, we have to select two couples from eight couples.

Favourable cases $= {}^8C_2$

So, Required Probability $= \dfrac{{}^8C_2}{{}^{16}C_4}$

Hence, the correct option is (D).

92. Given,

The odds against an event A are $5:3$.

Probability of not occurring the individual event $A = \dfrac{5}{8}$

Probability of occurring the individual event $A = \dfrac{3}{8}$

Again,

Odds in favor of another independent event B and $6:5$.

Probability of occurring the individual event $B = \dfrac{6}{(6+5)}$

$= \dfrac{6}{11}$

Probability of not occurring the individual event $B = \dfrac{5}{(6+5)}$

$= \dfrac{5}{11}$

The chances that neither A nor B occurs is $=$ Probability of not occurring event $A \times$ probability of not occurring event B [As the two events are independent therefore multiplication will occur]

$= \dfrac{5}{8} \times \dfrac{5}{11}$

$= \dfrac{25}{88}$

Hence, the correct option is (B).

93. $\int \sec^2 x\, dx = \tan x + C$ where C is a constant.

$\int \tan x\, dx = \log|\sec x| + C = -\log|\cos x| + C$ where C is a constant.

Integration by parts:

The formula for integrating by parts is given by;

$$\int u\, v\, dx = u\int v\, dx - \int \left(\frac{du}{dx}\int v\, dx\right) dx$$

Where u is the function $u(x)$ and v is the function $v(x)$

ILATE Rule: Usually, the preference order of this rule is based on some functions such as Inverse, Logarithm, Algebraic, Trigonometric and Exponent.

If the integrand contains a logarithmic or an inverse trigonometric function, we take it as the first function. In all such cases, if the second function is not given, we take it as 1.

Now,

Here we have to find the value of $\int \dfrac{\sin^{-1}x}{(1-x^2)^{\frac{3}{2}}}\, dx$

Let $x = \sin t \Rightarrow t = \sin^{-1}x$

Now, by differentiating $x = \sin t$ with respect to t we get,

$\Rightarrow dx = \cos t\, dt$

$\Rightarrow \int \dfrac{\sin^{-1}x}{(1-x^2)^{\frac{3}{2}}}\, dx = \int \dfrac{t\cos t}{(1-\sin^2 t)^{\frac{3}{2}}}\, dt$

As we know that,

$\cos^2 x = 1 - \sin^2 x$

$\Rightarrow \int \dfrac{t\cos t}{(1-\sin^2 t)^{\frac{3}{2}}}\, dt = \int \dfrac{t\cos t}{\cos^3 t}\, dt = \int t \cdot \sec^2 t\, dt$

According to the integration by parts (ILATE Rule) we have t as our first function and $\sec^2 t$ as our second function.

i.e $u(t) = t$ and $v(t) = \sec^2 t$

As we know that $\int uv\, dx = u\int v\, dx -$
$\int \left(\frac{du}{dx}\int v\, dx\right) dx$

$\Rightarrow \int t \cdot \sec^2 t\, dt = t \cdot \int \sec^2 t\, dt - \int \left\{\frac{d(t)}{dt} \cdot \int \sec^2 t\, dt\right\} dt$

As we know that,
$\int \sec^2 x\, dx = \tan x + C$ where C is a constant.

$\Rightarrow \int t \cdot \sec^2 t\, dt = t \cdot \tan t - \int \tan t\, dt$

$\int \tan x\, dx = \log|\sec x| + C = -\log|\cos x| + C$ where C is a constant

$\Rightarrow \int t \cdot \sec^2 t\, dt = t \cdot \tan t + \log|\cos t| + C$

Now by substituting $t = \sin^{-1}x$ in the above equation.

$\because x = \sin t \Rightarrow \cos t = \sqrt{1-x^2}$ and $\tan t = \dfrac{x}{\sqrt{1-x^2}}$

$\Rightarrow \int \dfrac{\sin^{-1}x}{(1-x^2)^{\frac{3}{2}}}\, dx$

$= \dfrac{x \cdot (\sin^{-1}x)}{\sqrt{1-x^2}} + \dfrac{1}{2}\log|(1-x^2)| + C$ where C is a constant.

Hence, the correct option is (C).

94. Given,

$$\frac{d^2y}{dx^2} + 3\left(\frac{dy}{dx}\right)^2 = x^2 \log\left(\frac{d^2y}{dx^2}\right)$$

For the given differential equation the highest order derivative is 2. The given differential equation is not a polynomial equation because it involved a logarithmic term in its derivatives so, its degree is not defined.

Hence, the correct option is (D).

95. We know that,

If $L^{-1}\{F(s)\} = f(t)$

Then,

$L^{-1}F(s-a) = e^{at} \cdot f(t)$ and $L^{-1}\{F(s+a)\} = e^{-at} \cdot f(t)$

Now,

$F(s) = \dfrac{1}{s(s+1)} = \dfrac{A}{s} + \dfrac{B}{(s+1)}$

$\dfrac{1}{s(s+1)} = \dfrac{A(s+1)+B(s)}{s(s+1)}$

$A(s+1) + B(s) = 1$

Put $s = 0$, we get $A = 1$

Put $s = -1$, we get $B = -1$

$F(s) = \dfrac{1}{s(s+1)} = \dfrac{1}{s} + \dfrac{-1}{(s+1)}$

$f(t) = L^{-1}(s)$

$f(t) = L^{-1}\left(\dfrac{1}{s} - \dfrac{1}{s+1}\right)$

$f(t) = e^{0t} - e^{-t} \quad \left\{\because L^{-1}\left(\dfrac{1}{s}\right) = 1\right\}$

$f(t) = 1 - e^{-t}$

Hence, the correct option is (D).

96. Some pairs of Laplace transforms are given below.

$e^{-at} \leftrightarrow \dfrac{1}{s+a}$

$$t^n e^{-at} \leftrightarrow \frac{n!}{(s+a)^{n+1}}$$

Given:

$$H(s) = \frac{s+3}{s^2+2s+1}$$

$$\Rightarrow \frac{s+3}{(s+1)^2} = \frac{s+1}{(s+1)^2} + \frac{2}{(s+1)^2}$$

$$= \frac{1}{(s+1)} + \frac{2}{(s+1)^2}$$

By applying inverse Laplace transform,

$$\Rightarrow H(t) = e^{-t} + t^2 e^{-t}$$

Hence, the correct option is (C).

97. Given linear system is:

$$2x - y + 3z = 2$$

$$x + y + 2z = 2$$

$$5x - y + az = b$$

Then augmented matrix form is written below;

$$[A \mid B] \equiv \begin{bmatrix} 2 & -1 & 3 & 2 \\ 1 & 1 & 2 & 2 \\ 5 & -1 & a & b \end{bmatrix}$$

$$R_2 \to R_2 + 2R_1$$

$$= \begin{bmatrix} 2 & -1 & 3 & 2 \\ 5 & -1 & 8 & 6 \\ 5 & -1 & a & b \end{bmatrix}$$

$$R_3 \to R_3 - R_2$$

$$= \begin{bmatrix} 2 & -1 & 3 & 2 \\ 5 & -1 & 8 & 6 \\ 0 & 0 & a-8 & b-6 \end{bmatrix}$$

For $rank(A) < n = 3$

'a' must be $= 8$

For rank $[A \mid B] < 3, b = 6$

Therefore $a = 8$ and $b = 6$

Hence, the correct option is (B).

98. Eigen values of a real symmetric matrix are always real.

Eigen values and Eigen vector of a square matrix.

λ is called eigen value and x is called eigen vector of a square matrix A, if

$$Ax = \lambda x.$$

Characteristics of eigen values:

- $Tr(A) =$ Summation of eigen values

- $|A| =$ Product of eigen values
- If $A =$ Upper triangular matrix or lower triangular matrix or diagonal matrix, then its eigen values will be diagonal elements.
- Eigen values of the hermitian matrix and real symmetric matrix are always real.
- Eigen values of the skew-symmetric and skew hermitian matrix are either zero or purely imaginary.
- Eigen values of the orthogonal matrix and unitary matrix have unit modulus.

Hence, the correct option is (C).

99. Given,

$$y = 2\sin x - 3x^4 + 8$$

As we know,

$$\frac{d}{dx}\sin x = \cos x$$

$$\frac{d}{dx}(x^n) = nx^{n-1}$$

Differentiating with respect to x, we get

$$\Rightarrow \frac{dy}{dx} = 2\cos x - 3\left(4x^{(4-1)}\right) + 0$$

$$\Rightarrow \frac{dy}{dx} = 2\cos x - 12x^3$$

Hence, the correct option is (B).

100. Given:

$$I = \int \left(\frac{(\log x - 1)}{1 + (\log x)^2}\right)^2 dx$$

Let $\log x = t \Leftrightarrow x = e^t$

Differentiating with respect to x, we get

$$\frac{1}{x}dx = dt$$

$$\Rightarrow dx = x dt$$

$$\Rightarrow dx = e^t dt$$

Now,

$$I = \int \left(\frac{(t-1)}{1+t^2}\right)^2 e^t dt$$

$$= \int \frac{(t^2+1-2t)}{(1+t^2)^2} e^t dt$$

$$= \int \left[\frac{t^2+1}{(t^2+1)^2} - \frac{2t}{(t^2+1)^2}\right] e^t dt$$

$$= \int e^t \left[\frac{1}{(t^2+1)} - \frac{2t}{(t^2+1)^2}\right] dt$$

Let $f(t) = \frac{1}{(t^2+1)}$

Differentiating with respect to t, we get

$$f'(t) = \frac{-2t}{(t^2+1)^2}$$

$$I = \int e^t [f(t) + f'(t)]dt$$

$$= e^t f(t) + C$$

$$= e^t \frac{1}{(t^2+1)} + C$$

Resubstitute the value of t and e^t, we get

$$I = \frac{x}{(\log x)^2 + 1} + C$$

Hence, the correct option is (B).

Q.1 The characters 'a' to 'e' have the following frequencies. A Huffman code is used to represent the message. A message is made up of characters given below. What is the corresponding Huffman code for message 'ace'? (Consider 0 for left leaf node and 1 for right leaf node.)

Character	Frequency
a	2
b	5
c	1
d	4
e	8

A. 11010101
B. 101001001
C. 11010100
D. 110111000

Q.2 Let us consider that the capacity of the knapsack W $= 80$ and the list of provided items are shown in the following table:

Items	1	2	3	4
Profit (P)	120	60	60	100
Weight (W)	30	60	20	50

Find the maximum profit gain by applying fractional knapsack:

A. 220   **B.** 160   **C.** 240   **D.** 280

Q.3 Consider the following graph g:

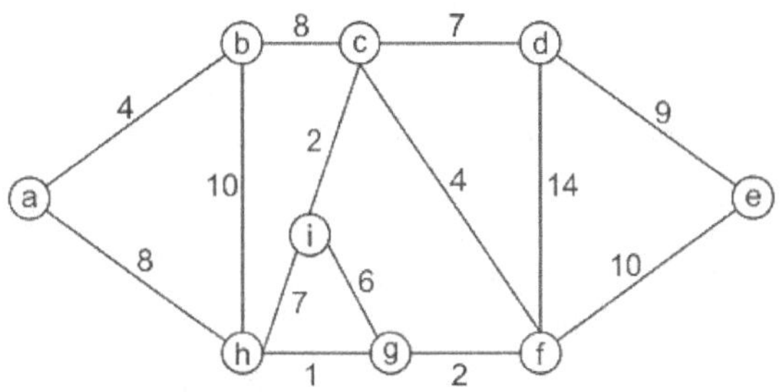

The weight of minimum Spanning tree is _______.

A. 37   **B.** 38   **C.** 39   **D.** 36

Q.4 What is the basic principle in the Rabin-Karp algorithm?

A. Hashing
B. Sorting
C. Augmenting
D. Dynamic Programming

Q.5 If n is the length of text(T) and m is the length of the pattern(P) identify the correct pre-processing algorithm (where q is a suitable modulus to reduce the complexity).

```
p=0; t0=0;
    for i=1 to n
A.  do t0=(dt0 + P[i])mod q
    p=(dp+T[i])mod q
    for i=1 to n
B.  do p=(dp + P[i])mod q
```

```
t0=(dt0+T[i])mod q
    for i=1 to m
C.  do t0=(dp + P[i])mod q
    p=(dt0+T[i])mod q
    for i=1 to m
D.  do p=(dp + P[i])mod q
    t0=(dt0+T[i])mod q
```

Q.6 Given a set of n distinct integers. It is desired to determine the three smallest of these integers using comparisons. Which is true?

A. $n + O(1)$ comparisons are needed.
B. $n + O(\log n)$ comparisons are needed.
C. $O(n)$ comparisons are needed.
D. $O(2n)$ comparisons are needed.

Q.7 Consider the following representation of an adjacency representation of an undirected graph. A graph contains 7 vertices 8 edges.

$$P \to Q \to T \to U$$
$$Q \to P \to R$$
$$R \to Q \to S$$
$$S \to R \to V \to T$$
$$T \to P \to S$$
$$U \to P \to V$$
$$V \to S \to U$$

A depth-first is started at node P. Which one of the following is a possible order of visiting the nodes in the graph if it follows lexicographic ordering?

A. $P\,Q\,R\,S\,T\,V\,U$ **B.** $P\,Q\,S\,T\,U\,R\,V$
C. $P\,T\,S\,R\,Q\,U\,V$ **D.** $P\,Q\,R\,S\,V\,U\,T$

Q.8 During solution of $T(n)$ recurrence relation we find the following series, solve it and find the value for $T(n)$:

$$T(n) = 1 \times 2^1 + 2 \times 2^2 + 3 \times 2^3 + 4 \times 2^4 + 5 \times 2^5 + 6 \times 2^6 + 7 \times 2^7 + \dots n \times 2^n$$

A. $O(2^n)$ **B.** $O(n^2)$
C. $O(n \times 2^n)$ **D.** $O(n^2 \times 2^n)$

Q.9 What is the value of the postfix expression $2\ 3\ +$ $4\ 5\ 6\ -\ -*$:

A. 19   **B.** 21   **C.** -4 **D.** 25

Q.10 The prefix expression of the postfix expression AB+CD-* is _______.

A. (A+B)*(C-D)   **B.** +AB*-CD
C. A+*BCD-   **D.** *+AB-CD

Q.11 Consider you have an array of some random size. You need to perform dequeue operation. You can perform it using stack operation (push and pop) or using queue operations itself (enQueue and Dequeue). The output is guaranteed to be same. Find some differences?

A. They will have different time complexities.

B. The memory used will not be different.

C. There are chances that output might be different.

D. None of these

Q.12 Consider you have a stack whose elements in it are as follows.

5 4 3 2 << top

Where the top element is 2.

You need to get the following stack:

6 5 4 3 2 << top

The operations that needed to be performed are (You can perform only push and pop):

A. Push(pop()), push(6), push(pop())

B. Push(pop()), push(6)

C. Push(pop()), push(pop()), push(6)

D. Push(6)

Q.13 The following C function takes a simply-linked list as an input argument. It modifies the list by moving the last element to the front of the list and returns the modified list. Some part of the code is left blank. Choose the correct alternative to replace the blank line.

```
typedef struct node
{
int value;
struct node *next;
}Node;
Node *move_to_front(Node *head)
{
Node *p, *q;
if head == NULL: || (head->next == NULL)
return head;
q = NULL; p = head;
while (p->next !=NULL)
{
q = p;
p = p->next;
}
________________________________

return head;
}
```

A. q = NULL; p->next = head; head = p;

B. q->next = NULL; head = p; p->next = head;

C. head = p; p->next = q; q->next = NULL;

D. q->next = NULL; p->next = head; head = p;

Q.14 In OSI network architecture, the routing is performed by ______.

A. A data link layer

B. Network layer

C. Transport layer

D. Session layer

Q.15 In OSI network architecture, the dialogue control, and token management are responsibilities of ________.

A. Data link layer

B. Network layer

C. Transport layer

D. Session layer

Q.16 Which of the following is not an example of data communication?

A. A teletype printing news bulletins.

B. A computer transmitting files to another computer.

C. An automatic teller machine checking account balance with the bank's computer.

D. A salesman telephoning orders to the office.

Q.17 The standard ASCII ________.

A. Is version II of the ASC standard.

B. Has 128 characters, including 32 control characters.

C. Is a subset of the 8-bit EBCDIC code.

D. Is used only in the United States and Canada.

Q.18 What kind of transmission medium is most appropriate to carry data in a computer network that is exposed to electrical interferences?

A. Unshielded twisted pair

B. Optical fiber

C. Coaxial cable

D. Microwave

Q.19 Which device is required for the Internet connection?

A. Joystick

B. Modem

C. CD Drive

D. NIC Card

Q.20 DHCP client and servers on the same subnet communicate via ________.

A. UDP broadcast

B. UDP unicast

C. TCP broadcast

D. TCP unicast

Q.21 The location of a resource on the internet is given by its:

A. Protocol

B. URL

C. E-mail address

D. ICQ

Q.22 How a proxy server is used as the computer?

A. With external access

B. Acting as a backup

C. Performing file handling

D. Accessing user permissions

Q.23 The special communication used in RAMBUS are ________.

A. RAMBUS channel

B. D-link

C. Dial-up

D. None of these

Q.24 The RAMBUS requires specially designed memory chips similar to ______.

A. SRAM

B. SDRAM

C. DRAM

D. DDRRAM

Q.25 Which of the following processor possess memory management?

A. 8086

B. 8088

C. 80286

D. 8051

Q.26 The situation wherein the data of operands are not available is called ________.

A. Data hazard

B. Stock

C. Deadlock

D. Structural hazard

Q.27 The stalling of the processor due to the unavailability of the instructions is called as ________.

A. Control hazard   **B.** Structural hazard
C. Input hazard   **D.** None of these

Q.28 The time lost due to the branch instruction is often referred to as __________.
A. Latency   **B.** Delay
C. Branch penalty   **D.** None of these

Q.29 The original design of the RAMBUS required for ______ data lines.
A. 4   **B.** 6   **C.** 8   **D.** 9

Q.30 P is a 16-bit signed integer. The 2's complement representation of P is $(F87B)_{16}$. The 2's complement representation of $8 * P$ is __________.
A. $(C3D8)_{16}$ **B.** $(187B)_{16}$
C. $(F878)_{16}$ **D.** $(987B)_{16}$

Q.31 The device which is allowed to initiate data transfers on the BUS at any time is called ________.
A. BUS master   **B.** Processor
C. BUS arbitrator   **D.** Controller

Q.32 Knox integrates with prevalent identity management and ______ systems.
A. SSL   **B.** SSO   **C.** SSH   **D.** Kerberos

Q.33 The easiest way to have an HDP cluster is to download the __________.
A. Hadoop   **B.** Sandbox
C. Dashboard   **D.** None of these

Q.34 There are similarities between the instructor entity set and the secretary entity set in the sense that they have several attributes that are conceptually the same across the two entity sets: namely, the identifier, name, and salary attributes. This process is called:
A. Commonality   **B.** Specialization
C. Generalization   **D.** Similarity

Q.35 Functional dependencies are a generalization of:
A. Key dependencies
B. Relation dependencies
C. Database dependencies
D. External dependencies

Q.36 Consider the relations Student(name, Marks) and Teacher(ID, name, Salary) in which name is the primary key of the relation Student and ID is the primary of the relation Teacher. Tuples in Student relation is 300 and tuples in teacher is 100. The maximum size of student $\bowtie$ teacher is __________ ($\bowtie$ is natural join).
A. 200   **B.** 100   **C.** 150   **D.** 300

Q.37 Which of the following refers to the level of data abstraction that describes exactly how the data actually stored?
A. Conceptual Level   **B.** Physical Level
C. File Level   **D.** Logical Level

Q.38 Which one of the following refers to the copies of the same data (or information) occupying the memory space at multiple places?
A. Data Repository   **B.** Data Inconsistency
C. Data Mining   **D.** Data Redundancy

Q.39 In general, a file is basically a collection of all related __________.
A. Rows and Columns   **B.** Fields
C. Database   **D.** Records

Q.40 Is Apache Sqoop is an open-source tool?
A. True   **B.** False
C. Can be true or false   **D.** Cannot say

Q.41 A set of overlapping divisions in the main memory are called:
A. Partitions   **B.** Blocks
C. Divisions   **D.** Modules

Q.42 An aid to determine the deadlock occurrence is:
A. Resource allocation graph
B. Starvation graph
C. Inversion graph
D. Dependency graph

Q.43 The dispatcher ________.
A. Actually schedules the tasks into the processor.
B. Puts tasks in I/O wait.
C. Is always small and simple.
D. Never changes task priorities.

Q.44 If a computer system completes n processes in t seconds, then its throughput is ______ processes per second during that interval.
A. $\frac{t}{n}$ **B.** $n + t$ **C.** $\frac{n}{t}$ **D.** $n \times t$

Q.45 Four necessary conditions for deadlock to exist are: mutual exclusion, no-preemption, circular wait and:
A. hold and wait
B. deadlock avoidance
C. race around condition
D. buffer overflow

Q.46 If you do not know which version of MS-DOS you are working with, which command will you use after having booted your operating system?
A. FORMAT command
B. DIR command
C. VER command
D. DISK command

Q.47 The solution to Critical Section Problem is:
A. Mutual Exclusion   **B.** Progress
C. Bounded Waiting   **D.** All of these

Q.48 What is Page-map table?
A. It is a data file.
B. It is a directory.
C. It is used for address translation.

D. None of these

Q.49 The main function of the dispatcher (the portion of the process scheduler) is _________.

A. swapping a process to the disk.

B. assigning ready process to the CPU.

C. suspending some of the processes when the CPU load is high.

D. bring processes from the disk to the main memory.

Q.50 The hexadecimal equivalent of the decimal number 4096 is _______.

A. 1000 **B.** $F100$ **C.** $F0$ **D.** $1F0$

Q.51 In 16 −bit 2's complement representation, the decimal number -28 is:

A. 1111111100011100

B. 0000000011100100

C. 1111111111100100

D. 1000000011100100

Q.52 The number of 1's in the binary representation of $(3 \times 4096 + 15 \times 256 + 5 \times 16 + 3)$ are:

A. 8 **B.** 9 **C.** 10 **D.** 12

Q.53 Race around condition is associated with _______.

A. Combinational circuits

B. Sequential circuits with level triggered clock

C. Sequential circuits

D. Both (A) and (C)

Q.54 A $1\,MHz$ clock is applied to a $J - K = 1$. What is the frequency of the flip-flop output signal?

A. $2\,MHz$ **B.** $500\,kHz$

C. $250\,kHz$ **D.** $500\,MHz$

Q.55 In which of the following gates, the output is 1, if and only if at least one input is 1?

A. NOR   **B.** AND   **C.** OR   **D.** NAND

Q.56 The time required for a gate or inverter to change its state is called:

A. Rise time   **B.** Decay time

C. Propagation time   **D.** Charging time

Q.57 The time required for a pulse to change from 10 to 90 percent of its maximum value is called:

A. Rise time   **B.** Decay time

C. Propagation time   **D.** Operating speed

Q.58 The maximum frequency at which digital data can be applied to the gate is called:

A. Operating speed

B. Propagation speed

C. Binary level transaction period

D. Charging time

Q.59 What is the minimum number of two-input NAND gates used to perform the function of two input OR gate?

A. One   **B.** Two   **C.** Three   **D.** Four

Q.60 How many objects can be returned at once?

A. Only one   **B.** Only two

C. Only three   **D.** Only four

Q.61 Which of the following language was developed as the first purely object programming language?

A. SmallTalk   **B.** C++

C. Kotlin   **D.** Java

Q.62 Which of the following is used to retrieve the information through URL (e.g. http://XYZ.com) on the world wide web?

A. Web server   **B.** Client

C. Web browser   **D.** Cookie

Q.63 What is required in each C program?

A. The program must have at least one function

B. The program does not require any function

C. Input data

D. Output data

Q.64 Statement 1: NFA computes the string along parallel paths.

Statement 2: An input can be accepted at more than one place in an NFA.

Which among the following options are most appropriate?

A. Statement 1 is true while 2 is not.

B. Statement 1 is false while 2 is not.

C. Statement 1 and 2, both are true.

D. Statement 1 and 2, both are false.

Q.65 While proving Inverse Homomorphism, which of the following steps are needed?

A. Start with a DFA A in L.

B. Construct a DFA B for h- 1(L).

C. The set of states, initial and final states should be the same.

D. All of these

Q.66 Which of the following obey the closure properties of regular language?

A. Homomorphism

B. Inverse Homomorphism

C. Reversal

D. All of these

Q.67 Let h(L) be a language of regular expression abe*+e(ab)*. Simplify the h(L):

A. (ab)*+eab*   **B.** abe*+ea*b*

C. (ab)*   **D.** None of these

Q.68 How many languages are over the alphabet R?

A. Countably infinite   **B.** Uncountable finite

C. Both (A) and (B)   **D.** None of these

Q.69 The number of tuples in an extended Non Deterministic Finite Automaton:

A. 5 **B.** 6 **C.** 7 **D.** 4

Q.70 Consider the language L given by the regular expression $(0+1)^*0(0+1)1$ over the alphabet $\{0,1\}$. The smallest number of states needed in a deterministic finite-state automaton (DFA) accepting L is __________.

A. 6   **B.** 8   **C.** 10   **D.** 12

Q.71 In which of the following backtracking is allowed?

A. NDFA
B. DFA
C. Both (A) and (B)
D. None of these

Q.72 The automaton which allows transformation to a new state without consuming any input symbols:

A. NFA
B. DFA
C. NFA-I
D. All of these

Q.73 Amongst which of the following is/are true in terms of design concepts in software engineering. Software design encompasses:

A. Set of principles
B. Concepts and practices
C. Development of a high-quality system or product
D. All of these

Q.74 Design develops a representation or __________.

A. Model
B. Testing
C. Requirements Analysis
D. None of these

Q.75 Generally the software design done by __________.

A. Software engineers
B. Mechanical engineers
C. Architect
D. None of these

Q.76 Amongst which of the following is/are shows the key significances of software designs:

A. Design allows us to build the blue print of the system or product.
B. The model gives clarity of proposed system and can be improved before code is generated.
C. Tests can be carried out, and end users involves during the process.
D. All of these

Q.77 Amongst which of the following is/are the key steps of software designs?

A. Representation of architecture of the system or product.
B. Representation of the interfaces that connect the software to end users.
C. Construction and representation of the software components.
D. All of these

Q.78 The primary work product produced during software design is/are:

A. Architectural design
B. Interface design
C. Creation of components and deployment
D. All of these

Q.79 The design model is assessed by the software team to determine and that have been established in __________.

A. Errors, inconsistencies, or omissions
B. Alternatives existence
C. Implementation of model within the constraints, schedule, and cost
D. All of these

Q.80 Amongst which of the following is/are the key aspects of interface design:

A. Smooth communication between the system and the users who use it.
B. This implies a flow of information.
C. Both (A) and (B)
D. None of these

Q.81 Component design is prepared with the information obtained from __________.

A. The class-based models
B. Behavioral models
C. Both (A) and (B)
D. None of these

Q.82 A basket contains 2 white, 3 red and 4 black balls. Two balls are drawn at random. Find the probability of not any ball being drawn is black?

A. $\frac{10}{21}$ **B.** $\frac{5}{18}$ **C.** $\frac{9}{11}$ **D.** $\frac{7}{11}$

Q.83 Two integers are selected from the first 10 natural numbers. If the sum is even find the probability that both numbers are odd:

A. $\frac{1}{2}$ **B.** $\frac{3}{5}$ **C.** $\frac{2}{5}$ **D.** $\frac{1}{5}$

Q.84 If $f(x) = A\cos\left(\frac{2\pi x}{5}\right) + C, f'\left(\frac{15}{4}\right) = \frac{1}{2}$ and $\int_0^5 f(x)dx = \frac{A\pi}{2}$ then, the value of A and C are respectively:

A. $\frac{5}{4\pi}$ and $\frac{3}{8}$
B. $\frac{5}{4\pi}$ and $\frac{1}{8}$
C. $\frac{5\pi}{4}$ and $\frac{3}{8}$
D. $\frac{5\pi}{4}$ and $\frac{1}{8}$

Q.85 General solution of differential equation $\frac{dy}{dx} + y = 1, (y \neq 1)$, is:

A. $\log\left|\frac{1}{1-y}\right| = x + C$
B. $\log|1 - y| = x + C$
C. $\log|1 + y| = x + C$
D. $\log\left|\frac{1}{1-y}\right| = -x + C$

Q.86 If the Laplace transform of $y(t)$ is given by $Y(s) = L(y(t)) = \frac{5}{2(s-1)} - \frac{2}{s-2} + \frac{1}{2(s-3)}$, then $y(0) + y'(0) = $ __________.

A. 2   **B.** 1   **C.** 4   **D.** 3

Q.87 If the Laplace transform of function $f(t)$ is given by $\frac{s+3}{(s+1)(s+2)}$, then $f(0)$ is:

A. $\frac{3}{2}$ **B.** $\frac{1}{2}$ **C.** 0 **D.** 1

Q.88 Given that the determinant of the matrix $\begin{bmatrix} 1 & 3 & 0 \\ 2 & 6 & 4 \\ -1 & 0 & 2 \end{bmatrix}$ is -12, the determinant of the matrix $\begin{bmatrix} 2 & 6 & 0 \\ 4 & 12 & 8 \\ -2 & 0 & 4 \end{bmatrix}$ is:

A. -96 **B.** -24 **C.** 24 **D.** 96

Q.89 The condition for which the eigenvalues of the matrix $A = \begin{bmatrix} 2 & 1 \\ 1 & k \end{bmatrix}$ are positive is:

A. $k > \frac{1}{2}$ **B.** $k > -2$ **C.** $k > 0$ **D.** $k < \frac{-1}{2}$

Q.90 Derivative of $\log x^{\cos x}$ with respect to x is:

A. $\log x^{\cos x}\left[\frac{\cos x}{x \log x} - \sin x \log(\log x)\right]$

B. $\log x^{\cos x}\left[\frac{\cos x}{x \log x} - \cos x \log(\log x)\right]$

C. $\log x^{\sin x}\left[\frac{\sin x}{x \log x} - \cos x \log(\log x)\right]$

D. None of these

Q.91 What is $\int \dfrac{dx}{\sec x + \tan x}$ equal to?

A. $\ln(\sec x) + \ln|\sec x + \tan x| + C$

B. $\ln(\sec x) - \ln|\sec x + \tan x| + C$

C. $\sec x \tan x - \ln|\sec x - \tan x| + C$

D. $\ln|\sec x + \tan x| - \ln|\sec x| + C$

Q.92 Let G be an undirected graph. Let $P(x, y)$ mean that there is a path from vertex x to vertex y.

$\exists x, y, z \neg P(x, y) \wedge \neg P(x, z) \wedge \neg P(y, z)$ represents that:

A. G has at least three connected components.

B. G has at exactly three connected components.

C. G has at most three connected components.

D. None of these

Q.93 What is the maximum cardinality of a relation R on a set $S = \{a, b, c, d\}$ such that relation R is anti-symmetric?

A. 10 **B.** 12 **C.** 14 **D.** 16

Q.94 Let H be a group with 42 elements. Let K be a subgroup of H. It is known that $K \neq H$ and that the size of K is at least 15. The size of K is ________.

A. 21 **B.** 19 **C.** 23 **D.** 22

Q.95 Which of the following statements is/are true?

A. K_{50} is the Euler graph.

B. Even cycles are bipartite.

C. Edges in n-cube graph is $n \times 2^{n-1}$.

D. Both (B) and (C)

Q.96 Among 150 people, how many people are there atleast who were born in the same month?

A. 13 **B.** 15 **C.** 16 **D.** 17

Q.97 There are 15 people in a committee. How many ways are there to group these 15 people into $3, 5$ and 4?

A. 846 **B.** 2468 **C.** 658 **D.** 1317

Q.98 The inclusion of sets into
$R = \{\{1, 2\}, \{1, 2, 3\}, \{1, 3, 5\}, \{1, 2, 4\}, \{1, 2, 3, 4, 5\}\}$ is necessary and sufficient to make R a complete lattice under the partial order defined by set containment:

A. $\{1\}, \{2,4\}$

B. $\{1\}, \{1,2,3\}$

C. $\{1\}$

D. $\{1\}, \{1,3\}, \{1,2,3,4\}, \{1,2,3,5\}$

Q.99 The graph is the smallest non-modular lattice N_5. A lattice is ______ if and only if it does not have a ______ isomorphic to N_5.

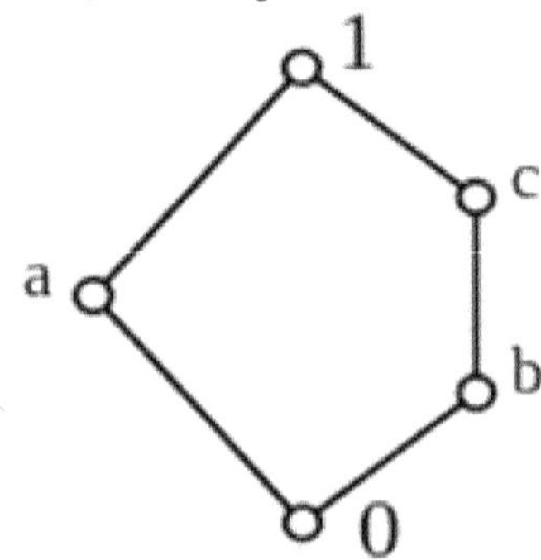

A. Non-modular, Complete lattice

B. Moduler, Semilattice

C. Non-modular, Sublattice

D. Modular, Sublattice

Q.100 If G is the forest with 54 vertices and 17 connected components, G has ______ total number of edges.

A. 38 **B.** 37 **C.** $\frac{17}{54}$ **D.** $\frac{17}{53}$

// Smart Answer Sheet //

Correct — Percentage of students who answered correctly. **Skipped** — Percentage of students who skipped.

Q.	Ans.	Correct	Skipped	Q.	Ans.	Correct	Skipped	Q.	Ans.	Correct	Skipped	Q.	Ans.	Correct	Skipped	Q.	Ans.	Correct	Skipped	Q.	Ans.	Correct	Skipped
1	D	49.16 %	31.71 %	18	B	40.82 %	36.94 %	35	A	49.76 %	49.67 %	52	C	40.08 %	36.72 %	69	A	42.21 %	46.17 %	86	B	26.41 %	68.56 %
2	C	60.61 %	30.91 %	19	B	48.55 %	43.95 %	36	B	63.61 %	36.25 %	53	B	19.76 %	78.96 %	70	A	58.42 %	34.67 %	87	D	65.69 %	32.55 %
3	A	64.74 %	30.04 %	20	A	32.38 %	67.41 %	37	B	54.71 %	32.79 %	54	B	13.5 %	81.04 %	71	B	63.96 %	32.68 %	88	A	66.95 %	30.12 %
4	A	61.67 %	33.95 %	21	B	80.29 %	14.72 %	38	D	82.57 %	16.71 %	55	C	57.9 %	35.67 %	72	C	56.23 %	39.77 %	89	A	85.58 %	14.14 %
5	D	19.8 %	75.86 %	22	A	48.32 %	50.73 %	39	D	87.98 %	11.86 %	56	C	45.83 %	41.94 %	73	D	30.08 %	67.85 %	90	A	20.1 %	75.41 %
6	B	43.9 %	53.62 %	23	A	41.88 %	53.36 %	40	A	62.99 %	34.02 %	57	A	51.73 %	30.6 %	74	A	83.74 %	10.78 %	91	D	49.17 %	40.97 %
7	A	46.59 %	34.97 %	24	C	68.79 %	30.06 %	41	A	59.33 %	36.17 %	58	A	63.98 %	34.85 %	75	A	77.46 %	11.76 %	92	B	61.4 %	36.89 %
8	C	24.77 %	69.12 %	25	C	40.38 %	47.15 %	42	A	53.07 %	37.27 %	59	C	24.52 %	67.65 %	76	D	30.35 %	68.67 %	93	A	45.59 %	36.39 %
9	D	66.03 %	30.3 %	26	A	58.33 %	34.73 %	43	A	53.44 %	40.18 %	60	A	44.69 %	30.69 %	77	D	66.42 %	31.85 %	94	A	57.84 %	30.1 %
10	D	40.04 %	37.74 %	27	A	68.47 %	30.21 %	44	C	21.13 %	67.99 %	61	A	68.92 %	30.8 %	78	D	57.57 %	36.6 %	95	D	64.3 %	30.16 %
11	A	30.47 %	67.6 %	28	C	59.64 %	39.11 %	45	A	50.12 %	44.38 %	62	C	68.32 %	30.17 %	79	B	27.52 %	69.52 %	96	A	56.99 %	42.5 %
12	A	12.25 %	71.69 %	29	D	55.18 %	30.02 %	46	C	21.15 %	78.56 %	63	A	83.16 %	13.26 %	80	C	54.2 %	44.65 %	97	D	40.91 %	30.03 %
13	D	64.24 %	34.99 %	30	A	30.67 %	67.92 %	47	D	69.68 %	30.21 %	64	C	14.9 %	83.78 %	81	C	47.17 %	46.75 %	98	C	15.91 %	81.69 %
14	B	63.74 %	32.06 %	31	A	81.49 %	11.1 %	48	C	58.22 %	36.65 %	65	D	58.3 %	31.63 %	82	B	47.97 %	32.11 %	99	D	55.68 %	38.51 %
15	D	50.44 %	41.2 %	32	B	16.35 %	70.08 %	49	B	53.72 %	37.99 %	66	D	58.58 %	36.56 %	83	A	58.35 %	31.38 %	100	B	68.68 %	31.11 %
16	D	56.35 %	31.42 %	33	B	42.99 %	34.14 %	50	A	48.37 %	38.36 %	67	C	65.92 %	30.16 %	84	B	52.6 %	45.23 %				
17	B	64.97 %	30.24 %	34	C	16.67 %	83.12 %	51	C	52.47 %	45.79 %	68	B	53.44 %	42.58 %	85	A	49.06 %	36.59 %				

//Hints and Solutions//

1. A few key points based on Huffman Encoding:

(1) It is a lossless data compressing technique generating variable-length codes for different symbols.

(2) It is based on the greedy approach which considers the frequency/probability of alphabets for generating codes.

(3) It has the complexity of n log n where n is the number of unique characters.

(4) The length of the code for a character is inversely proportional to the frequency of its occurrence.

(5) No code is a prefix of another code due to which a sequence of code can be unambiguously decoded to characters.

According to the question we get,

Character	Frequency	Huffman Code
a	2	1101
b	5	10
c	1	1100
d	4	111
e	8	0

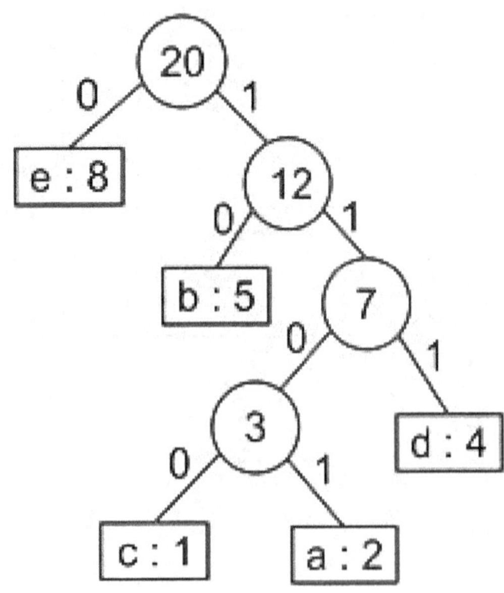

Huffman code for 'ace' $\Rightarrow 110111000$.

Hence, the correct option is (D).

2. According to the question, we get

Items	1	2	3	4
Profit (P)	120	60	60	100
Weight (W)	30	60	20	50
$\frac{P}{W}$	4	1	3	2

Sort according to $\frac{P}{W}$ ratio.

Items	2	4	3	1
Profit (P)	60	100	60	120
Weight (W)	60	50	20	30
$\frac{P}{W}$	1	2	3	4

Choose item 1 i.e. 30

Choose item 3 i.e. 20

Choose fraction of 4 i.e. $80 - \dfrac{50}{50}$

Total weight $= 50 + 50 \times 80 - \dfrac{50}{50}$

$= 80$

Total profit $= 120 + 60 + 100 \times \dfrac{30}{50}$

$= 240$

Hence, the correct option is (C).

3. Let's consider Kruskal's algorithm for Minimum spanning tree construction.

First, (h, g) edge will be selected as its edge weight is minimum.

$1.$ Then, (i, c) edge will be selected.

$2.$ Then, (g, f) edge will be selected.

$3.$ Then, (c, f) edge will be selected.

$4.$ Then, (a, b) edge will be selected. (i, g will be discarded as it creates a cycle in the MST).

$5.$ Then, (c, d) edge will be selected.

$6.$ Then, (b, c) edge will be selected.

$7.$ Then, (d, e) edge will be selected.

So, total weight will be:

$(= 1 + 2 + 2 + 4 + 4 + 7 + 8 + 9)$

$= 37$

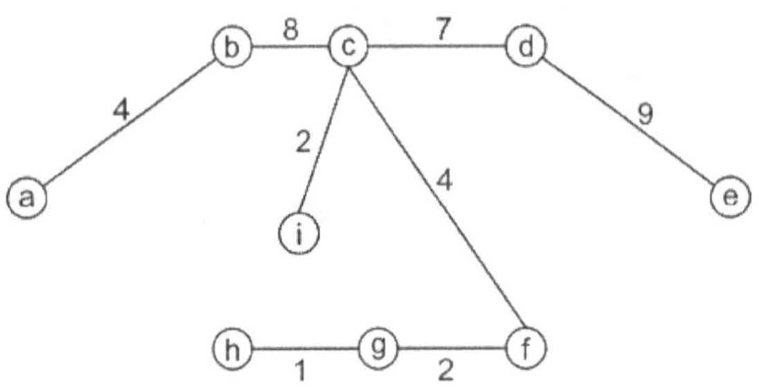

Hence, the correct option is (A).

4. The basic principle employed in the Rabin-Karp algorithm is hashing. In the given text every substring is converted to a hash value and compared with the hash value of the pattern. Rabin-Karp algorithm is an algorithm used for searching/matching patterns in the text using a hash function. Unlike the Naive string matching algorithm, it does not travel through every character in the initial phase rather it filters the characters that do not match and then perform the comparison.

Hence, the correct option is (A).

5. The pre-processing algorithm runs m (the length of pattern) times. This algorithm is used to compute p as the value of P[1 .... m] mod q and t_0 as the value of T[1 .... m]mod q. The pre-processing phase generally converts a string into a decimal number.

RABIN-KARP-MATCHER (T, P, d, q)

1. n ← length [T]
2. m ← length [P]
3. h ← dm-1 mod q
4. p ← 0
5. t0 ← 0
6. for i ← 1 to m
7. do p ← (dp + P[i]) mod q
8. t_0 ← (dt_0+T [i]) mod q
9. for s ← 0 to n-m
10. do if p = ts
11. then if P [1.....m] = T [s+1.....s + m]
12. then "Pattern occurs with shift" s
13. If s < n-m
14. then ts+1 ← (d (ts-T [s+1]h)+T [s+m+1])mod q

Once a match is found, a brute-force approach is implemented to verify the result of matching.

Hence, the correct option is (D).

6. The following steps explain the solution to the above problem:

Step- 1:

Construct min heap for all n elements using bottom up construction.

Construction cost in worst case comparisons exactly $O(n)$.

Step- 2:

Using heap:

Delete three element from top $= 3 \log n$.

Therefore, total time complexity $n + 3\log n = n + O(\log n)$ comparison.

Hence, the correct option is (B).

7. Graph of the given adjacency list is:

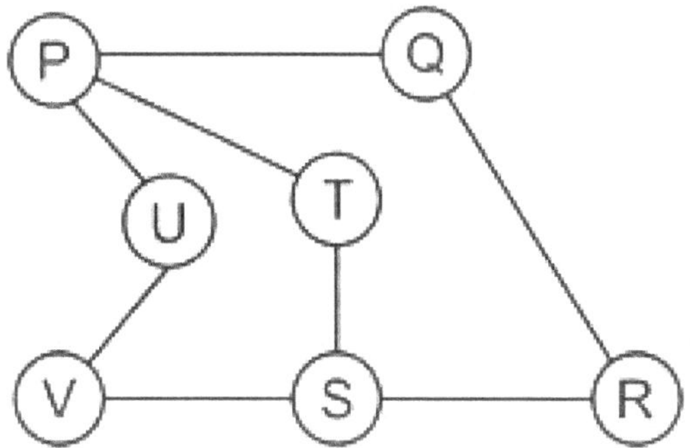

A DFS is started at node P. Push ' P' into the stack and, mark it as visited. $Q, T,$ and U are the adjacent unvisited nodes of P.

Push ' Q' into the stack and, mark it as visited. R is the adjacent unvisited node of Q. Push ' R' into the stack and, mark it as visited. S is the adjacent unvisited node of R. Push ' S' into the stack and, mark it as visited. T and V are the adjacent unvisited nodes of S.

Push ' T' into the stack and, mark it as visited. There is no adjacent unvisited node of T. So, pop ' T'. Now, node S is at top of the stack. V is the adjacent unvisited node of S.

Push ' V' into the stack and, mark it as visited. U is the adjacent unvisited nodes of V. Push ' U' into the stack and mark it as visited.

There is no adjacent unvisited node of U. So, pop ' U'. There is no unvisited node in the graph, pop all the elements from the stack. Order of visiting node is $P\ Q\ R\ S\ T\ V\ U$.

Hence, the correct option is (A).

8. Given,

$$T(n) = 1 \times 2^1 + 2 \times 2^2 + 3 \times 2^3 + 4 \times 2^4 + 5 \times 2^5 + 6 \times 2^6 + 7 \times 2^7 + \ldots n \times 2^n$$

Above series is bot $A.P$ and $G.P$ series.

Convert it into $G.P.$ series by method given below:

$$T(n) = 1 \times 2^2 + 2 \times 2^3 + 3 \times 2^4 + 4 \times 2^5 + 5 \times 2^6 + 6 \times 2^7 + 7 \times 2^8 + \times n \times 2^{n+1}$$

$$T(n) - 2 \times T(n) = 1 \times 2^1 + (2 - 1) \times 2^2 + (3 - 2) \times 2^3 + (4 - 3) \times 2^4 + \times - n \times 2^{n+1}$$

$$T(n) = 2^1 + 2^2 + 2^3 + 2^4 + 2^5 + 2^6 + 2^7 + \ldots + 2^n - n \times 2^{n+1}$$

Now, we get the $G.P$ series.

$$T(n) = 2 \times \left(\frac{(2^n-1)}{(2-1)}\right) - n \times 2^{n+1}$$

$$T(n) = 2 + n \times 2^{n+1} - 2^{n+1}$$

$$T(n) = O(n \times 2^n)$$

Hence, the correct option is (C).

9. Given postfix expression is:

$$2\ 3 + 4\ 5\ 6 - -*$$

Infix expression we get:

$$= (2 + 3)4(5 - 6) - *$$

$$= (2 + 3) * 4 - (5 - 6)$$

So, value $= (2 + 3) * \left(4 - (5 - 6)\right)$

$$= 5 * \left(4 - (-1)\right)$$

$$= 5 * 5$$

$$= 25$$

Hence, the correct option is (D).

10. Given,

Postfix expression is:

AB+CD-*

To convert from postfix to prefix, we first convert it to the infix and then to prefix.

Infix expression:

$$= (A+B) * (C-D)$$

So, prefix expression is:

$$= +AB*-CD$$

$$= *+AB-CD$$

Therefore, the prefix expression is *+AB-CD.

Hence, the correct option is (D).

11. To perform operations such as Dequeue using stack operation you need to empty all the elements from the current stack and push it into the next stack, resulting in a O(number of elements) complexity whereas the time complexity of dequeue operation itself is O(1). And there is a need of a extra stack. Therefore, more memory is needed.

Hence, the correct option is (A).

12. The operations that needed to be performed are:

- By performing push(pop()) on all elements on the current stack to the next stack you get 2 3 4 5 << top.
- Then, by performing Push(6) and perform push(pop()) you'll get back 6 5 4 3 2 << top.
- You have actually performed the enQueue operation using push and pop.
- So, all the operations are Push(pop()), push(6), push(pop()).

Hence, the correct option is (A).

13. When while loop completes its execution, node 'p' refers to the last node whereas the 'q' node refers to the node before 'p' in the linked list. q->next=NULL makes q as the last node. p->next=head places p as the first node. The head must be modified to 'p' as 'p' is the starting node of the list (head=p).

Thus, the sequence of steps are q->next=NULL; p->next=head; head=p.

Hence, the correct option is (D).

14. In OSI network architecture, the routing is performed by the network layer. Layer 3, the network layer, is most commonly known as the layer where routing takes place. A router's main job is to get packets from one network to another. The network layer is responsible for routing packets from the source to the destination.

Hence, the correct option is (B).

15. The session layer controls the conversations between different computers. Session layer services also include authentication and reconnections. The session layer (Layer 5) is responsible for establishing, managing, synchronizing and terminating sessions between end-user application processes. It works as a dialog controller. It allows the systems to communicate in either half-duplex or full-duplex mode of communication.

Hence, the correct option is (D).

16. A salesman telephoning orders to the office is not an example of data communication. It is because data communications is a computer connected to the Internet via a Wi-Fi connection, which uses a wireless medium to send and receive data from one or more remote servers. With half-duplex communications, information can go both ways, but not at the same time.

Hence, the correct option is (D).

17. ASCII abbreviated from American Standard Code for Information Interchange, is a character encoding standard for electronic communication. ASCII codes represent text in computers, telecommunications equipment, and other devices. Most modern character-encoding schemes are based on ASCII, although they support many additional characters.

The standard ASCII has 128 characters, including 32 control characters. Originally based on the English alphabet, ASCII encodes 128 specified characters into seven-bit integers. Ninety-five of the encoded characters are printable: these include the digits 0 to 9, lowercase letters a to z, uppercase letters A to Z, and punctuation symbols.

Hence, the correct option is (B).

18. The optical fiber is made of glass or plastic. In this cable, the transmission of data occurs in the form of light rather than the electric current, so this cable provides a higher data transfer speed than other cables. They are widely used in lighting, both in the interior and exterior of vehicles. Because of its ability to conserve space and provide superior lighting, fiber optics are used in more vehicles every day.

Hence, the correct option is (B).

19. Modem is required for the Internet connection. A modem is a hardware device that converts data so that it can be transmitted from computer to computer over telephone wires. A network interface card (NIC) is a circuit board or card that is installed in a computer so that it can be connected to a network.

Hence, the correct option is (B).

20. DHCP client and servers on the same subnet communicate via UDP broadcast. DHCP actually employs a connectionless service, which is provided by UDP, since TCP is connection oriented. It is implemented with two UDP port numbers 67 and 68 for its operations.

Hence, the correct option is (A).

21. The location of a resource on the internet is given by its URL. A URL (Uniform Resource Locator) is a database connection that describes the database's location on a computer network and the retrieval process. A URL is a different form of URI (Uniform Resource Identifier) although the two words are used interchangeably by many people.

Hence, the correct option is (B).

22. A proxy server is used as the computer with external access. A proxy server is a computer that acts as a gateway between a user's computer and the Internet. The proxy server is also called an application-level gateway. By this, the client computer can establish an indirect network connection to another network. It is used as a computer with external access.

Hence, the correct option is (A).

23. The special communication used in RAMBUS are RAMBUS channel. The special communication link is used to provide the necessary design and required hardware for the transmission. RAMBUS was a high-speed interface technology development and marketing company that invented 600 MHz interface technology, which solved memory bottleneck issues faced by system designers.

Hence, the correct option is (A).

24. The RAMBUS requires specially designed memory chips similar to DRAM. The special memory chip should be able to transmit data on both the edges and is called a DRAM. RAMBUS technology was based on a very high-speed, chip-to-chip interface that was incorporated on dynamic random-access-memory (DRAM) components, processors and controllers, which achieved performance rates over ten times faster than conventional DRAM.

Hence, the correct option is (C).

25. Because of the efficient paging mechanism, 80286 is one of the processors which allows the memory management unit. 8086 and 8088 does not allow paging mechanism. 8051 is a microcontroller which have an in-built memory and does not possess a paging mechanism.

Hence, the correct option is (C).

26. The situation wherein the data of operands are not available is called a data hazard. Data hazards are generally caused when the data is not ready on the destination side. Data hazards occur when instructions that exhibit data dependence modify data in different stages of a pipeline. Ignoring potential data hazards can result in race conditions (also termed race hazards).

Hence, the correct option is (A).

27. The stalling of the processor due to the unavailability of the instructions is called a control hazard. The control hazard also called an instruction hazard is usually caused by a cache miss. Control hazard occurs when the pipeline makes wrong decisions on branch prediction and therefore brings instructions into the pipeline that must subsequently be discarded. The term branch hazard also refers to a control hazard.

Hence, the correct option is (A).

28. The time lost due to the branch instruction is often referred to as branch penalty. This time also retards the performance speed of the processor. The branch penalty is analyzed as a function of the relative number of branch instructions executed and the probability that a branch is taken.

Hence, the correct option is (C).

29. The original design of the RAMBUS required for 9 data lines. Out of the 9 data lines, 8 were used for data transmission and the one left was used for parity checking. The direct RAMBUS is used to transmit 2 bytes of data at a time. Rambus Inline Memory Module (RIMM) technology, which is installed in pairs, transfers data from rising and falling clock signal edges and doubles physical clock rates. RIMM data travels on a 16-bit bus that is similar to a packet network with transmitted data groups.

Hence, the correct option is (D).

30. When we multiply a number by 2 this means a binary representation of this number is shifted left shifting depending upon how many times the number is multiplied by 2:

Given a hexadecimal number in 2's complement and required in (2)'s complement.

So, nothing want to change it.

$$P = (F87B)_{16} = (1111 \quad 1000 \quad 0111 \quad 1011)_2$$
$$8P = 2^3 * P$$

$2^3 * P$ this means that the binary number that is represented by P is shifted 3 times left.

So, it becomes:

$$(1111 \quad 1000 \quad 0111 \quad 1011)_2$$
$$= (1100 \quad 0011 \quad 1101 \quad 1000)_2$$
$$= (C3D8)_{16}$$

Hence, the correct option is (A).

31. The device which is allowed to initiate data transfers on the BUS at any time is called BUS master. It is used for currently accessing the BUS. BUS Arbitration refers to the process by which the current bus master accesses and then leaves the control of the bus and passes it to another bus requesting processor unit. The controller that has access to a bus at an instance is known as BUS master.

Hence, the correct option is (A).

32. Knox integrates with prevalent identity management and SSO systems. Knox allows identities from those enterprise systems to be used for seamless, secure access to Hadoop clusters. Knox SSO provides web UI SSO (Single Sign-on) capabilities to your cluster. Knox SSO enables your users to log in once and gain access to cluster resources. To set up Knox SSO, you will configure an identity provider, enable SSO using the Ambari CLI, and then manually configure various component settings.

Hence, the correct option is (B).

33. The easiest way to have an HDP cluster is to download the sandbox. The Apache Knox Gateway is a system that provides a single point of authentication and access for Apache Hadoop services. The Hortonworks HDP Sandbox is a straightforward, pre-configured, learning environment that contains the latest developments from Apache Hadoop, specifically the Hortonworks Data Platform (HDP). It allows you to learn and explore HDP on your own.

Hence, the correct option is (B).

34. A generalization is a bottom-up approach in which multiple lower-level entities are combined to form a single higher-level entity. Generalization is usually used to find common attributes among entities to form a generalized entity. As defined in the question the attributes of the Instructor Entity Set and the Secretary Entity Set.

Hence, the correct option is (C).

35. Functional dependencies are a generalization of key dependencies. A functional dependency is a generalization of the notion of a key. It requires the value for a certain set of attributes to determine uniquely the value for another set of attributes. Functional dependency is a relationship that exists between two attributes. It typically exists between the primary key and non-key attribute within a table.

Hence, the correct option is (A).

36. Name is a key.

Student:

Name	Marks
A	10
B	20
C	30

ID is a key

Teacher:

ID	Name	Salary
1	A	80K
2	B	50K

$$\text{Student} \bowtie \text{teacher} \equiv \sigma_{\text{student.name=teacher.name}} (\text{Student} \times \text{teacher})$$

Name	Marks	ID	Salary
A	10	1	80K
B	20	2	50K

Maximum tuple possible $=\mid \text{teacher} \mid = 2$

From above example:

Since $\mid \text{student} \mid = 300$ and $\mid \text{teacher} \mid = 100$

$\therefore$ Maximum tuple possible $= 100$

Hence, the correct option is (B).

37. Data abstraction means displaying or sharing only the data that is needed and hiding from all other data until it is necessary to share it. However, the data abstraction level that describes how the data was actually stored in the user's machine (or system) is known as the physical level.

Hence, the correct option is (B).

38. Data redundancy generally occurs whenever more than one copy of the exact same data exists in several different places. Sometimes it may cause data inconsistency, which can result in an unreliable source of data or information that is not good for anyone.

Hence, the correct option is (D).

39. Whenever we have some related data, information or records, we collect all those related data (or records), put them together, store them in one place, and give that collection a name that is known as a file. You can think of a traditional database as an electronic filing system, organized by fields, records, and files. A field is a single piece of information; a record is one complete set of fields; and a file is a collection of records. For example, a telephone book is analogous to a file.

Hence, the correct option is (D).

40. Apache Sqoop is an open-source tool designed for efficiently transferring bulk data between Apache Hadoop and structured data stores such as relational databases. Microsoft uses a Sqoop-based connector to help transfer data from Microsoft SQL Server databases to Hadoop. Sqoop is a tool designed to transfer data between Hadoop and relational database servers.

Hence, the correct option is (A).

41. A set of overlapping divisions in the main memory are called partitions. A partition is a logical division of a hard disk that is treated as a separate unit by operating systems (OSes) and file systems. The OSes and file systems can manage information on each partition as if it were a distinct hard drive.

Blocks: In computing, a block is also called a physical record, and it is a sequence of bytes or bits, usually containing some whole number of records, having a maximum length, a block size. Data thus structured are said to be blocked.

Modules:

1. The OS module in Python provides functions for interacting with the operating system.

2. OS comes under Python's standard utility modules.

3. This module provides a portable way of using operating system dependent functionality.

4. The *os* and *os. path* modules include many functions to interact with the file system.

Hence, the correct option is (A).

42. As we know,

Resource allocation graph helps in tracking which resource is taken up by which process, and which process is waiting for a resource of a particular type. It is a simple tool to illustrate how interacting processes can deadlock.

Now,

- The resource allocation graph is the pictorial representation of the state of a system. As its name suggests, the resource allocation graph is the complete information about all the processes which are holding some resources or waiting for some resources.

- It also contains the information about all the instances of all the resources whether they are available or being used by the processes.

- In Resource allocation graph, the process is represented by a Circle while the Resource is represented by a rectangle.

Hence, the correct option is (A).

43. The dispatcher actually schedules the tasks into the processor. The dispatcher is the module that gives process control over the CPU after it has been selected by the short-term scheduler.

This function involves the following:

Switching context. Switching to user mode.

Hence, the correct option is (A).

44. Throughput:

Throughput is the amount of work completed in a unit of time. In other words, throughput is the processes executed to the number of jobs completed in a unit of time. The scheduling algorithm must look to maximize the number of jobs processed per time unit.

$$\text{Throughput} = \mu = \frac{\text{number of process}}{\text{shedule length}}$$

$$= \frac{n}{l}$$

Given,

The number of processes $= n$ process

Completion time of all process (or) schedule length $= t$ seconds

$$\text{Throughput} = \frac{n}{t} \text{ processes per second.}$$

Hence, the correct option is (C).

45. A deadlock in OS is a situation where two or more processes are blocked. Conditions for Deadlock- Mutual Exclusion, Hold and Wait, No preemption, Circular wait. These 4 conditions must hold simultaneously for the occurrence of deadlock.

- **Mutual Exclusion:** At least one process must be held in a non-sharable mode.

- **Hold and Wait:** There must be a process holding one resource and waiting for another.

- **No preemption:** Resources cannot be preempted.

- **Circular wait:** There must exist a set of processes.

Hence, the correct option is (A).

46. In computing, VER is a command in various DOS, FlexOS, OS/2, and Microsoft Windows command-line interpreters such as COMMAND.COM, cmd.exe, and 4DOS/ 4NT. It prints the name and version of the operating system or the command shell or in some implementations the version of other commands. It is roughly equivalent to the Unix command name.

Hence, the correct option is (C).

47. The critical section problem needs a solution to synchronize the different processes. The solution to the critical section problem must satisfy the following conditions.

Mutual Exclusion:

Mutual exclusion implies that only one process can be inside the critical section at any time. If any other processes require the critical section, they must wait until it is free.

Progress:

Progress means that if a process is not using the critical section, then it should not stop any other process from accessing it. In other words, any process can enter a critical section if it is free.

Bounded Waiting:

Bounded waiting means that each process must have a limited waiting time. It should not wait endlessly to access the critical section.

Hence, the correct option is (D).

48. Page-map table is used for address translation. A page table is the data structure used by a virtual memory system in a computer operating system to store the mapping between virtual addresses and physical addresses. Virtual addresses are used by the program executed by the accessing process, while physical addresses are used by the hardware, or more specifically, by the RAM subsystem. The page table is a key component of virtual address translation which is necessary to access data in memory.

Hence, the correct option is (C).

49. The main function of the dispatcher is assigning the ready processes to the CPU. CPU scheduler selects a process among the processes that are ready to execute and allocates CPU to one of them. Short-term schedulers, also known as dispatchers, make the decision of which process to execute next.

Hence, the correct option is (B).

50. To convert a decimal number system to hexadecimal, we follow the successive division approach i.e. we divide the decimal number by 16 and note down the remainder. Each remainder is then expressed in hexadecimal.

Now,

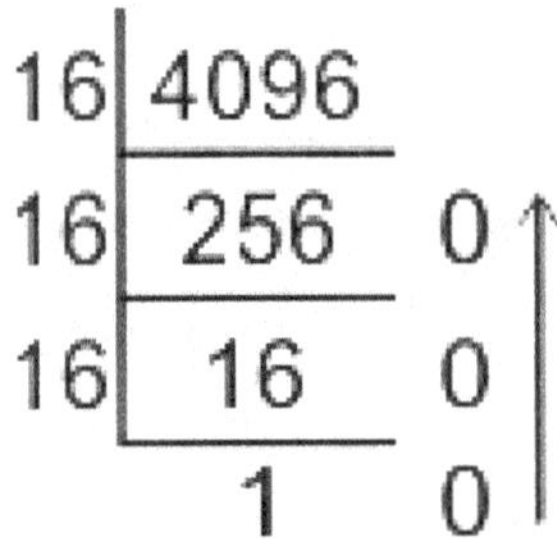

So, the hexadecimal equivalent of decimal number 4096 is 1000.

Hence, the correct option is (A).

51. The way to find: 2's complement:

Start reading the bits from LSB (right-hand side) and write it unless first 1 is encountered, leave the first 1 as it is and complement the remaining bits.

2	28	
2	14	0
2	7	0
2	3	1
2	1	1
	0	1

$\Rightarrow 28_{10} = (11100)_2 = (0000000000011100)_2$

$\Rightarrow -28_{10} = 2\text{'s complement of } 0000000000011100$

$\Rightarrow 2\text{'s complement of } 0000000000011100$

$= 1111111111100100$

Hence, the correct option is (C).

52. Decimal value:

$(3 \times 4096 + 15 \times 256 + 5 \times 16 + 3)$

It can be written as:

$3 \times 16^3 + 15 \times 16^2 + 5 \times 16^1 + 3 \times 16^0$

Hexadecimal representation:

$= (3F53)_{16}$

$= (0011111101010011)_2$

$= 2 + 4 + 2 + 2 = 10 \ (1's) \text{ complement}$

The number of 1's is 10.

Hence, the correct option is (C).

53. Practically, we don't get toggling in sequential circuits. Since clock pulse is more than the propagation delay, within one clock pulse the output will keep on toggling again and again and it may become indeterminate. This is known as the race-around condition.

Race around condition occurs because of the feedback connection.

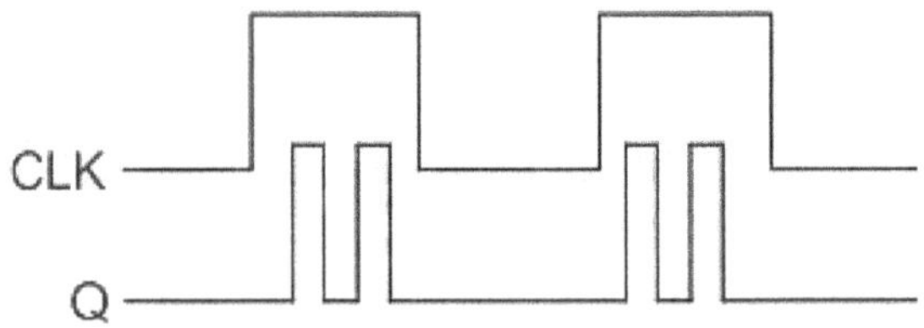

Race around condition (RAC):

- Race around condition occurs only in level-triggered flip flop
- Level triggered is transparent.
- Even though input is constant, output continuously toggles. Changes for some time continuously.

$t_p = 10\text{ms}$, J, K, F_f, Q $\quad 0 \to 1 \to 0 \to 1 \to 0 \to 1 \to 0 \to 1 \to 0 \to 1 \to 0$
toggles 10 times

- (RAC) is when $J = 1$ and $(K = 1)$ [flip flop in toggling mode] and $t_p > t_{\text{ff}}$.
- Output toggles many times instead of once in one clock pulse. It is undesirable and called as " (RAC) Around Condition".

Race around condition can further be explained with (SR) latch example:

A clocked latch is shown below.

- When $S = R = CLK = 1$.
- The outputs Q and Q' are maintained at logic 0.
- There is no race-around condition.

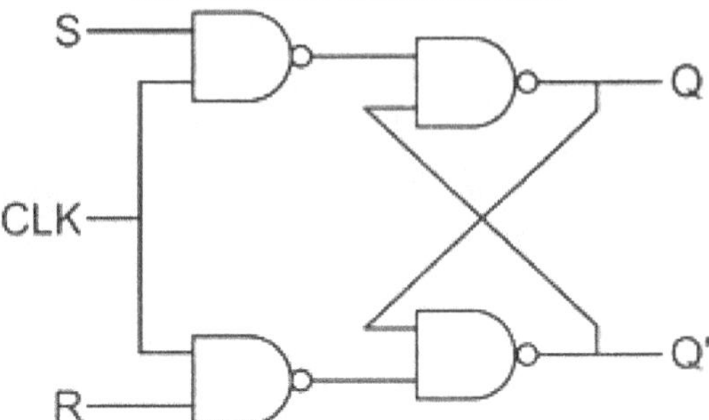

However, when clocked SR latch is converted to JK flip flop by providing feedback as shown below:

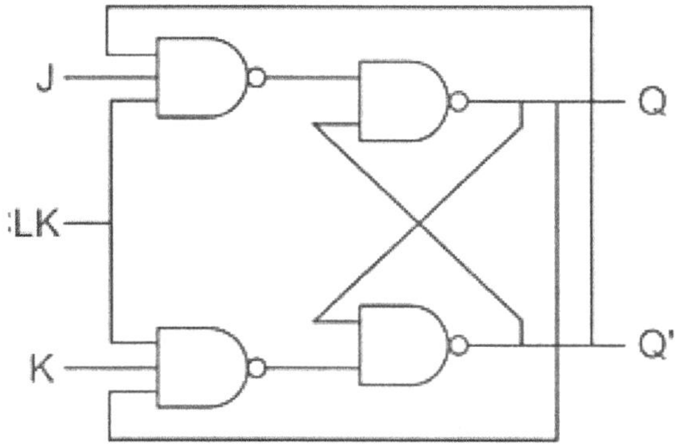

Then when $J = K = CLK = 1$, then the output Q and Q' keeps toggling between 0 and 1, thus, there is a race around condition there.

So, we can conclude that racing condition occurs in sequential circuits with the level-triggered clock.

Hence, the correct option is (B).

54. The truth table for a JK flip-flop is as shown:

Input J	Input K	CLK	Output
0	0	↑	Q_n (no change)
0	1	↑	0
1	0	↑	1
1	1	↑	$\overline{Q_n}$ (Toggle)

When both the inputs are 1, it operates in the toggle mode, i.e. the output will switch from $0 \rightarrow 1 \rightarrow 0 \rightarrow 1$ ... and so on.

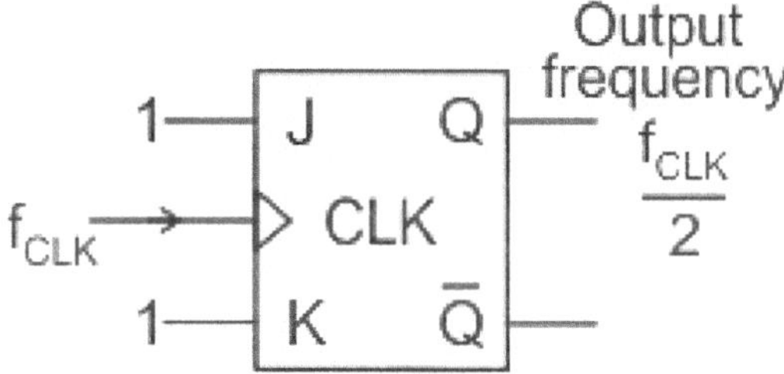

Since the input clock is a square pulse as shown, the waveform representation of the input and the output pulse is represented below:

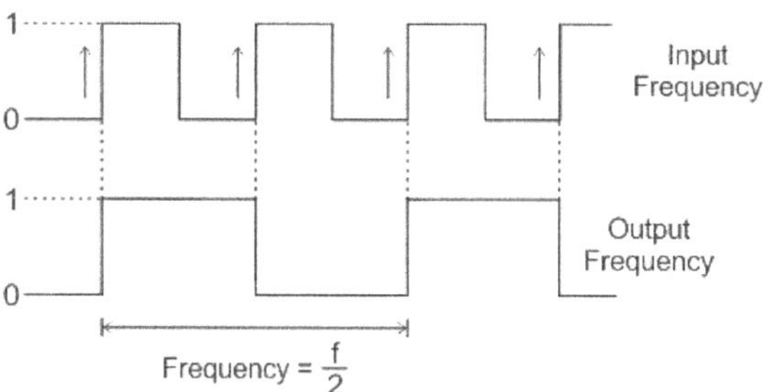

We observe that the output frequency is half of the input frequency for a JK operating in toggle mode, i.e.

$$f_{\text{out}} = \frac{\text{Input Frequency}}{2}$$

Given,

Clock frequency $(f_{clk}) = 1\ MHz$

$$f_{\text{out}} = \frac{f_{clk}}{2} = 0.5\ MHz$$

$$f_{\text{out}} = 500\ kHz$$

Hence, the correct option is (B).

55. In OR gate we need atleast one bit to be equal to 1 to generate the output as 1 because OR means any of the condition out of two is equal to 1 which means if atleast one input is 1 then it shows output as 1. Number of 1's in input may be more than one but the output will always be 1 in OR gate.

Hence, the correct option is (C).

56. The time required for a gate or inverter to change its state is called propagation time. The time required for a signal or wave to travel from one point of a transmission medium to another. There are two main components to the uncertainty of signal propagation time. The first is a static component that is due to differences in process technologies, process variations, electrical loading of an unknown number of memory modules, etc. The second is a dynamic component that is typically due to temperature or voltage fluctuations. Some fluctuations change too fast to be handled effectively, but most of the fluctuations in voltage and temperature change over a relatively long time period.

Hence, the correct option is (C).

57. The time required for a pulse to change from 10 to 90 percent of its maximum value is called rise time. Rise time is the time taken for a signal to cross a specified lower voltage threshold followed by a specified upper voltage threshold. This is an important parameter in both digital and analog systems. In digital systems, it describes how long a signal spends in the intermediate state between two valid logic levels.

Hence, the correct option is (A).

58. The maximum frequency at which digital data can be applied to the gate is called operating speed. The speed of operation of the logic gate is the time that elapses between giving input and getting output. The switching speed describes how long it takes a logic output to change from true to false or vice versa. Faster logic can accomplish more operations in less time. Modern electronic digital logic routinely switches at $5\ GHz$, and some laboratory systems switch at more than $1\ THz$.

Hence, the correct option is (A).

59. Suppose we have,

$$Y = A + B.$$

This is the equation of OR gate. We require three NAND gates to create OR gate. We can also write after 1st NAND operation:

$Y = (A\ \text{AND}\ B)'Y = A + B'$ (Demorgan's Law)

After 2nd NAND operation $Y = (A' + B')Y = A.B$ (Demorgan's Law)

After 3rd NAND operation

$Y = (A.B)'Y = A + B'$ (Demorgan's Law)

So, we need three NAND gates.

Hence, the correct option is (C).

60. Like any other value, only one object can be returned at once. The only possible way to return more than one object is to return the address of an object array. But that again comes under returning object pointer. Even though a function can return only one value but that value can be of pointer type.

Hence, the correct option is (A).

61. SmallTalk the language was developed as the first purely object programming language. This programming language was invented as the first pure OOPS (object-oriented) language. This language was designed by Alan Kay in the early 1970. It is a tool to support live programming and advanced debugging techniques such as on-the-fly inspection and code changes during execution in a very user-friendly format.

Hence, the correct option is (A).

62. A web browser is used to retrieve the information through URL (e.g. http://XYZ.com) on the world wide web. A web browser is a software application for accessing information on the World Wide Web. URL is an acronym for Uniform Resource Locator. It is a reference to the resource on the internet.

Hence, the correct option is (C).

63. Each C program has at least one function, and even the most trivial programs can specify additional functions. A function is a piece of code. In other words, it works like a sub-program. C programs are structured from 'functions'. Program execution starts with this function and the program is contained within it.

Hence, the correct option is (A).

64. While the machine runs on some input string, if it has the choice to split, it goes in all possible way and each one is different copy of the machine. The machine takes subsequent choice to split further giving rise to more copies of the machine

getting each copy run parallel. If any one copy of the machine accepts the strings, then NFA accepts, otherwise it rejects.

Hence, the correct option is (C).

65. While constructing DFA B, we need to take care of the following points:

1. The same set of states.

2. The same start state.

3. The same final state.

4. Input alphabet = the symbols to which homomorphism (h) applies.

Hence, the correct option is (D).

66. Homomorphism on an alphabet is a function that gives a string for each symbol in that alphabet.

Example: h(0)=ab, etc.

Closure properties on regular languages are defined as certain operations on regular language which are guaranteed to produce regular language. Closure refers to some operation on a language, resulting in a new language that is of the same "type" as originally operated on i.e., regular.

Hence, the correct option is (D).

67. Given,

The regular expression:

abe*+e(ab)*

Now,

Using the identity:

e=e*

We get,

abe+e(ab)

Now, again using identity:

Re=eR=R

So, we get

abe*+e(ab)*

Therefore, ab will contain inside (ab)*,

= (ab)*

Hence, the correct option is (C).

68. A language over an alphabet R is a set of strings over A which is uncountable and infinite. In automata theory, a formal language is a set of strings of symbols drawn from a finite alphabet. A formal language can be specified either by a set of rules (such as regular expressions or context-free grammar) that generates the language or by a formal machine that accepts (recognizes) the language.

Hence, the correct option is (B).

69. For NFA or extended transition function NFA, the tuple of elements remains the same i.e. 5. Since all the tuples in DFA and NFA are the same except for one of the tuples, which is Transition Function (δ). These are:

1. Q: The set of all states.
2. Σ: The set of input symbols (Symbols which machine takes as input).
3. q: Initial state (Starting state of a machine).
4. F: The set of the final state.
5. δ: Transition Function $Q \times (\Sigma \cup \varepsilon) \to 2^Q$.

Hence, the correct option is (A).

70. First, convert the given regular expression into an NFA and then find out the DFA from NFA.

Nowe,

Regular expression is $(0 + 1)^*0(0 + 1)1$

NFA for this expression is given here as:

Diagram: NFA

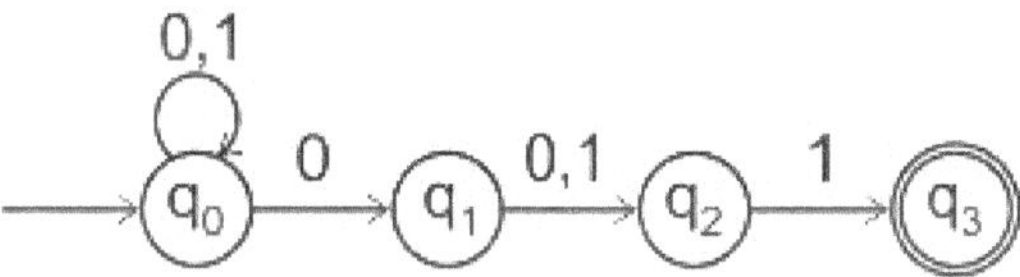

NFA Table:

States	0	1
$\to q_0$	$\{q_0, q_1\}$	q_0
q_1	q_2	q_2
q_2	ϕ	q_3
$* q_3$	ϕ	ϕ

DFA Table from the above NFA:

States	0	1
$\to q_0$	$\{q_0, q_1\}$	q_0
$\{q_0, q_1\}$	$\{q_0, q_1, q_2\}$	$\{q_0, q_2\}$
$\{q_0, q_2\}$	$\{q_0, q_1\}$	$\{q_0, q_3\}$
$*\{q_0, q_3\}$	$\{q_0, q_1\}$	q_0
$\{q_0, q_1, q_2\}$	$\{q_0, q_1, q_2\}$	$\{q_0, q_2, q_3\}$
$*\{q_0, q_2, q_3\}$	$\{q_0, q_1\}$	$\{q_0, q_3\}$

The minimum number of states in the DFA is 6.

Hence, the correct option is (A).

71. The transition from a state is to a single particular next state for each input symbol. So, it is called deterministic which allows backtracking. Backtracking is an algorithmic technique for solving problems recursively by trying to build a solution incrementally, one piece at a time, removing those solutions that fail to satisfy the constraints of the problem at any point of time (by time, here, is referred to the time elapsed till reaching any level of the search tree).

Hence, the correct option is (B).

72. NFA-I or e-NFA is an extension of Non-detrministic Finite Automata which are usually called NFA with epsilon moves or lambda transitions. In the automata theory, a nondeterministic finite automaton with ε-moves (NFA-ε)(also known as NFA-λ) is an extension of a non-deterministic finite automaton(NFA), which allows a transformation to a new state without consuming any input symbols.

Hence, the correct option is (C).

73. Software design encompasses Set of principles, Design Concepts and practices, Development of a high-quality system or product. Design principles establish design work. Design practices themselves lead to the creation of various representations of the software. Software design is a mechanism to transform user requirements into some suitable form, which helps the programmer in software coding and implementation.

Hence, the correct option is (D).

74. Unlike requirements modeling, design modeling produces a representation or model of software. Design modeling includes a detail description about the software architecture as well as data structures, interfaces, and other components that are required to implement in the system.

Hence, the correct option is (A).

75. In Software engineering, software designs are done by software engineers. Software design is a process to transform user requirements into some suitable form, which helps the programmer in software coding and implementation. Software design is the first step in SDLC (Software Design Life Cycle), which moves the concentration from the problem domain to the solution domain.

Hence, the correct option is (A).

76. The key significances of software designs are; design allows us to build the blue print of the system or product, the model gives clarity of the proposed system and can be improved before code is generated and tests can be carried out, and end-users involve during the process. As software design is performed by creating modules, it makes the task easier to maintain. Tasks like finding bugs, debugging, restructuring, and changing the functionality of specific elements in the software application become quite easy due to software design.

Hence, the correct option is (D).

77. The architecture of the system or product must be represented; the interfaces that connect to the software to end users, to other systems and the software components that are used to construct the system are designed are the key steps of software designs.

Hence, the correct option is (D).

78. The primary work products produced during software design are architectural design, Interface design and creation of components and deployment. A work product is a general abstraction that represents something obtained from the software development process. A work product may have many work product kinds.

Hence, the correct option is (D).

79. The software team evaluates the design model to identify whether there are any flaws, inconsistencies, or omissions; whether there are any alternatives; and whether the model can be implemented within the restrictions, schedule, and budget that have been specified.

Hence, the correct option is (B).

80. The key aspects of interface design are to keep smooth communication between the system and the users who use it. An Interface design implies a flow of information. Interface elements include but are not limited to:

- Input Controls: buttons, text fields, checkboxes, radio buttons, dropdown lists, list boxes, toggles, date field.

- Navigational Components: breadcrumb, slider, search field, pagination, slider, tags, icons.

Hence, the correct option is (C).

81. The information gathered from the class-based models and behavioral models are used to make the component design. During the design phase, we make decisions that will have an impact on the overall success of the software creation process. To "design" is to create, fashion, execute or construct according to plan. In successful systems design, three main components must be considered and managed effectively. These are quality, timeliness and cost-effectiveness.

Hence, the correct option is (C).

82. Given,

A basket contains 2 white, 3 red and 4 black balls, two balls are drawn at random.

Total number of balls $= 2 + 3 + 4 = 9$

We know that:

$$\text{Probability} = \frac{\text{Favorable Outcome}}{\text{Total Outcome}}$$

$$P(E) = \frac{n(E)}{n(S)}$$

Let S be the sample space.

Let $E =$ Event of drawing 2 balls, none of them is black

Number of all combinations of n things, taken r at a time is given by $^nC_r = \dfrac{n!}{(r)!(n-r)!}$

Total number of ways of drawing 2 balls out of 9 balls $n(S) = {}^9C_2$.

There are four black balls in the total nine balls.

Total number of non-black balls $= 9 - 4 = 5$

Number of ways of drawing 2 balls out of 5 balls, if none of them is black.

$$n(E) = {}^5C_2$$

$$\Rightarrow P(E) = \frac{n(E)}{n(S)} = \frac{{}^5C_2}{{}^9C_2}$$

$$= \frac{\frac{5!}{2!\,7!}}{\frac{9!}{2!\,7!}}$$

$$= \frac{\frac{5\times4\times3\times2\times1}{2\times1\times3\times2\times1}}{\frac{9\times8\times7\times6\times5\times4\times3\times2\times1}{2\times1\times7\times6\times5\times4\times3\times2\times1}}$$

$$= \frac{\left\{\frac{(5\times4)}{(2\times1)}\right\}}{\left\{\frac{(9\times8)}{(2\times1)}\right\}}$$

$$= \frac{10}{36}$$

$$= \frac{5}{18}$$

$\therefore$ The probability of not any ball being drawn is black is $\dfrac{5}{18}$.

Hence, the correct option is (B).

83. Let A be the event that both numbers are odd.

Let B be the event that the sum is even.

Then,

Odd $+$ odd $=$ even

Odd $+$ even $=$ odd

Even $+$ even $=$ even

On using:

$$P\left(\frac{A}{B}\right) = \frac{P(A\cap B)}{P(B)}$$

$$P(A \cap B) = \frac{{}^5C_2}{{}^{10}C_2}$$

$$= \frac{\frac{5!}{2!\,3!}}{\frac{10!}{2!\,8!}}$$

$$= \frac{\frac{5\times4\times3\times2\times1}{2\times1\times3\times2\times1}}{\frac{10\times9\times8\times7\times6\times5\times4\times3\times2\times1}{2\times1\times8\times7\times6\times5\times4\times3\times2\times1}}$$

$$= \frac{2}{9}$$

$$P(B) = \frac{\left({}^5C_2 + {}^5C_2\right)}{{}^{10}C_2}$$

$$= \frac{{}^5C_2}{{}^{10}C_2} + \frac{{}^5C_2}{{}^{10}C_2}$$

$$= \frac{2}{9} + \frac{2}{9}$$

$$= \frac{4}{9}$$

$$\therefore P\left(\frac{A}{B}\right) = \frac{\frac{2}{9}}{\frac{4}{9}}$$

$$= \frac{1}{2}$$

Hence, the correct option is (A).

84. Given,

$$f(x) = A\cos\left(\frac{2\pi x}{5}\right) + C$$

Now,

$$f(x) = A\cos\left(\frac{2\pi x}{5}\right) + C$$

$$\Rightarrow f'(x) = -A\sin\left(\frac{2\pi x}{5}\right) \times \frac{2\pi}{5}$$

$$\Rightarrow f'\left(\frac{15}{4}\right) = -A\sin\left(\frac{2\pi\left(\frac{15}{4}\right)}{5}\right) \times \frac{2\pi}{5}$$

$$\Rightarrow f'\left(\frac{15}{4}\right) = -A(-1)\left(\frac{2\pi}{5}\right) = \frac{1}{2}$$

$$\therefore A = \frac{5}{4\pi}$$

$$\Rightarrow \int_0^5 f(x)dx = \frac{A\pi}{2}$$

$$\Rightarrow f(x) = A\cos\left(\frac{2\pi x}{5}\right) + C$$

$$\Rightarrow \int_0^5 \left(\frac{5}{4\pi}\cos\left(\frac{2\pi x}{5}\right) + C\right)dx = \frac{\left(\frac{5}{4\pi}\right)\pi}{2}$$

$$\Rightarrow \left[\frac{5}{4\pi}\left\{\sin\left(\frac{2\pi x}{5}\right) \times \frac{5}{2\pi}\right\} + Cx\right]_0^5 = \frac{5}{8}$$

$$\Rightarrow 5C = \frac{5}{8}$$

$$\therefore C = \frac{1}{8}$$

Hence, the correct option is (B).

85. Given,

$$\frac{dy}{dx} + y = 1$$

Comparing given differential equation with first order linear equation,

$$\frac{dy}{dx} + Py = Q$$

$P = 1$ and $Q = 1$

Therefore, integrating factor, I.F. $= e^{\int 1dx} = e^x$

So, solution is given by, $y \cdot I \cdot F = \int q \cdot I \cdot F \cdot dx$

$$\Rightarrow ye^x = \int e^x dx = e^x + C$$

$$\Rightarrow y = 1 + Ce^{-x}$$

On seprating the variables we get,

$$\frac{dy}{1-y} = dx$$

On integrating we get,

$$\int \frac{dy}{1-y} = \int dx$$

$$\Rightarrow -\log(1 - y) = x + C$$

$$\Rightarrow \log(1 - y)^{-1} = x + C \quad [m\log n = \log n^m]$$

$$= \log\left|\frac{1}{1-y}\right| = x + C$$

Hence, the correct option is (A).

86. Given,

$$Y(s) = L\big(y(t)\big) = \frac{5}{2(s-1)} - \frac{2}{s-2} + \frac{1}{2(s-3)}$$

Now,

Apply inverse Laplace transform,

$$\Rightarrow y(t) = \frac{5}{2}e^t - 2e^{2t} + \frac{1}{2}e^{3t}$$

Differentiate with respect to ' t'.

$$\Rightarrow y'(t) = \frac{5}{2}e^t - 4e^{2t} + \frac{3}{2}e^{3t}$$

$$\Rightarrow y(0) = \frac{5}{2} - 2 + \frac{1}{2} = 1$$

$$\Rightarrow y'(0) = \frac{5}{2} - 4 + \frac{3}{2} = 0$$

$$\Rightarrow y(0) + y'(0)$$

$$= 1$$

Hence, the correct option is (B).

87. Laplace Transforms:

$$L(e^{at}) = \frac{1}{s-a}$$

$$L(e^{-at}) = \frac{1}{s+a}$$

Given,

$$L[f(t)] = \frac{s+3}{(s+1)(s+2)}$$

The above equation through partial fractions can be written as:

$$\Rightarrow \frac{s+3}{(s+1)(s+2)} = \frac{A}{(s+1)} + \frac{B}{(s+2)}$$

$$\Rightarrow s + 3 = A(s + 2) + B(s + 1)$$

$$\Rightarrow s + 3 = (A + B)s + 2A + B$$

Comparing co-efficients on both sides, we get

$A + B = 1$ and $2A + B = 3$

We get, $A = 2, B = -1$

So, $\frac{s+3}{(s+1)(s+2)} = \frac{2}{(s+1)} - \frac{1}{(s+2)}$

$$\Rightarrow f(t) = L^{-1}\left(\frac{2}{s+1}\right) - L^{-1}\left(\frac{1}{s+2}\right)$$

$$\Rightarrow (f(t) = 2e^{-t} - e^{-2t}$$

So, $f(0) = 2e^{-0} - e^{-0} = 2 - 1$

$$= 1$$

Hence, the correct option is (D).

88. Given,

$$\begin{bmatrix} 2 & 6 & 0 \\ 4 & 12 & 8 \\ -2 & 0 & 4 \end{bmatrix}$$

According to question,

$$\begin{vmatrix} 1 & 3 & 0 \\ 2 & 6 & 4 \\ -1 & 0 & 2 \end{vmatrix} = -12$$

Take 2 common from all the rows.

$$\begin{vmatrix} 2 & 6 & 0 \\ 4 & 12 & 8 \\ -2 & 0 & 4 \end{vmatrix} = (2)^3 \begin{vmatrix} 1 & 3 & 0 \\ 2 & 6 & 4 \\ -1 & 0 & 2 \end{vmatrix}$$

$$= 8 \times (-12) = -96$$

Hence, the correct option is (A).

89. Given,

$$A = \begin{bmatrix} 2 & 1 \\ 1 & k \end{bmatrix}$$

Let λ_1 and λ_2 be the Eigen value of matrix A.

$$|A| = \lambda_1 \lambda_2$$

$$|A| = 2k - 1$$

$\because \lambda_1$ and λ_2 are positive,

i.e., $\lambda_1 \lambda_2 > 0$

$$(2k - 1) > 0$$

$$\therefore k > \frac{1}{2}$$

Product of the Eigenvalues of any matrix gives determinant of that matrix.

Hence, the correct option is (A).

90. Given,

$$y = \log x^{\cos x}$$

Taking log on both sides, we get

$$\Rightarrow \log y = \log(\log x^{\cos x})$$

$$\Rightarrow \log y = \cos x \times [\log(\log x)]$$

Differentiate with respect to x, we get

$$\Rightarrow \frac{1}{y}\frac{dy}{dx} = \cos x \frac{d}{dx}[\log(\log x)] + [\log(\log x)]\frac{d}{dx}\cos x$$

$$\Rightarrow \frac{1}{y}\frac{dy}{dx} = \cos x \times \frac{1}{\log x}\frac{d}{dx}(\log x) - [\log(\log x)]\sin x$$

$$\Rightarrow \frac{dy}{dx} = y\left[\cos x \times \frac{1}{x\log x} - [\log(\log x)]\sin x\right]$$

$$\therefore \frac{dy}{dx} = \log x^{\cos x}\left[\cos x \times \frac{1}{x\log x} - [\log(\log x)]\sin x\right]$$

Hence, the correct option is (A).

91. Given,

$$I = \int \frac{dx}{\sec x + \tan x}$$

By rationalizing the denominator of the integrand we get:

$$I = \int \frac{(\sec x - \tan x)}{(\sec x + \tan x)\cdot(\sec x - \tan x)}dx$$

$$\Rightarrow I = \int \frac{(\sec x - \tan x)}{(\sec^2 x - \tan^2 x)}dx$$

As we know that, $\sec^2 x - \tan^2 x = 1$, therefore:

$$\Rightarrow I = \int (\sec x - \tan x)dx$$

$$\Rightarrow I = \int \sec x dx - \int \tan x dx$$

$\left[\because \int \tan x dx = \ln|\sec x| + C \text{ and } \int \sec x dx = \ln|\sec x + \tan x| + C\right]$

So,

$$I = \ln|\sec x + \tan x| - \ln|\sec x| + C$$

Hence, the correct option is (D).

92. Given,

$$\exists x, y, z \neg P(x, y) \wedge \neg P(x, z) \wedge \neg P(y, z)$$

Here means that G has at least three connected components.

Let us consider, 4 different vertex a, x, y, x.

Since no path exists between $(x, y), (x, z)$ and (y, z).

If a is connected to any of the vertices we have 3 connected component.

If a is not connected to any of the vertices we have 4 connected component.

From this, it can be said that G has at least three connected components.

Hence, the correct option is (B).

93. In an anti-symmetric relation: Symmetric pair, that is, (a, b) and (b, a) where $a \neq b$ should not be present.

$$\Rightarrow S = \{a, b, c, d\}$$

$$\Rightarrow S \times S = \{(a, a), (a, b), (a, c), (a, d), (b, a), (b, b), (b, c), (b, d), (c, a), (c, b), (c, c), (c, d), (d, a), (d, b), (d, c), (d, d)\}$$

$$\vec{\vec{R}} = \{(a,a),(b,b),(c,c),(d,d),(a,b),(a,c),(a,d),\ (b,c),(b,d),(c,d)\}$$

Since, we cannot add any other relation,

Maximum cardinality $= |R| = 10$

Important Points:

Maximum cardinality $= n + \dfrac{n^2 - n}{2}$

$|S| = 4$

Maximum cardinality $= 4 + \dfrac{4^2 - 4}{2}$

$= 4 + \dfrac{16 - 4}{2}$

$= 10$

Hence, the correct option is (A).

94. Given,

H be a group with 42 elements

K be a subgroup of H

The size of K is at least 15

Lagrange's theorem specifies: Order of subgroup divides the order of a group.

Order of a group $=$ Number of elements in a group $= 42$.

K is a subgroup,

$K \leq H$ and $K \neq H$

Divisor of $42 = 1,2,3,6,7,14,21,42$

K is at least 15, that is $K \geq 15$.

The size of K is 21.

Hence, the correct option is (A).

95. A graph G is Eulerian Circuit, if and only if it has at most one non-trivial component and its vertices all have even degree.

A bipartite graph is a graph whose vertices can be divided into two disjoint and independent sets U and V such that every edge connects a vertex in U to one in V.

A self-complementary graph is a graph that is isomorphic to its complement.

An n-vertex self-complementary graph has exactly half the number of edges of the complete graph.

For the complete graph (K_n):

Every vertex has $(n-1)$ degree, $d = 50 - 1 = 49$

Since degree is odd then Euler graph is not possible.

Option (A) is false:

For Cycle graph (C_n):

Every vertex has 2 degrees, therefore it always has Euler Circuit.

Therefore, even cycles are bipartite.

Diagonal elements can be put into a different set.

Option (B) is true.

For n-dimensional cube (Q_n):

Degree $= n$

Vertex $= 2^n$

$\Rightarrow \sum d_i = 2 \times e$

$\Rightarrow 2 \times e = n \times 2^n$

$\therefore e = n \times 2^{n-1}$

Option (C) is true.

Hence, the correct option is (D).

96. According to the question,

Number of people $(N) = 150$.

We have 12 months in a year. Therefore, according to pigeonhole principle, there are 150 objects to be placed in 12 boxes.

Pigeonhole principle states that "If N objects are placed into k boxes, then there is at least one box containing at least ceil $\left(\dfrac{N}{k}\right)$ objects".

So, there are atleast ceil $\left(\dfrac{150}{12}\right) = 13$ people who were born in the same month.

Hence, the correct option is (A).

97. Given,

There are 15 people in a committee.

The number of ways to choose 3 people out of 15 is $^{15}C_3$.

Then, number of ways to choose 5 people out of $15 =$ $(15 - 3) = 12$ is $^{12}C_5$.

Finally, the number of ways to choose 4 people out of $(12 - 4) = 8$ is $^8C_4$.

So, by the rule of product we get,

$$^{15}C_3 + {}^{12}C_5 + {}^8C_4 = 1317.$$

Hence, the correct option is (D).

98. A lattice is complete if every subset of partial order set has a supremum and infimum element.

For example, here we are given a partial order set R.

Now,

It will be a complete lattice if whatever be the subset we choose, it has a supremum and infimum element.

Here relation given is set containment, so supremum element will be just union of all sets in the subset we choose.

Similarly,

The infimum element will be just an intersection of all the sets in the subset we choose.

As R now is not complete lattice, because although it has a supremum for every subset we choose, but some subsets have no infimum.

For example, if we take subset $\{\{1,3,5\}, \{1,2,4\}\}$, then intersection of sets in this is $\{1\}$, which is not present in R.

So clearly, if we add set $\{1\}$ in R, we will solve the problem.

So, adding $\{1\}$ is necessary and sufficient condition for R to be a complete lattice.

Hence, the correct option is (C).

99. A lattice $(L, \vee, \wedge)$ is modular if for all elements a, b, c of L,

The following identity holds $\rightarrow$ modular identity: $(a \wedge c) \vee (b \wedge c) = [(a \wedge c) \vee b] \wedge c$.

This condition is equivalent to the following axiom $\rightarrow$ modular law: $a \leq c$ implies $a \vee (b \wedge c) = (a \vee b) \wedge c$.

A lattice is modular if and only if it does not have a sublattice isomorphic to N_5.

Hence, the correct option is (D).

100. Here we are given a forest with 54 vertices and 17 components.

A component is itself a tree and since there are 17 components means that every component has a root, therefore we have 17 roots.

Each new vertex of the forest contributes to a single edge to a forest.

So, for remaining $54 - 17 = 37$ vertices we can have $m - n = 37$ edges.

Hence, the correct option is (B).

Q.1 What is the product of following matrix using Strassen's matrix multiplication algorithm?

$$A = \begin{bmatrix} 1 & 3 \\ 5 & 7 \end{bmatrix}$$

$$B = \begin{bmatrix} 8 & 4 \\ 6 & 2 \end{bmatrix}$$

A. $C_{11} = 80; C_{12} = 07; C_{21} = 15; C_{22} = 34$
B. $C_{11} = 82; C_{12} = 26; C_{21} = 10; C_{22} = 34$
C. $C_{11} = 15; C_{12} = 07; C_{21} = 80; C_{22} = 34$
D. $C_{11} = 26; C_{12} = 10; C_{21} = 82; C_{22} = 34$

Q.2 Consider the minimum weight path problem on a directed graph where, instead of edges, vertices have weights. The weight of a path is the sum of the weights of the vertices on the path excluding the endpoints. The input is a directed graph with n vertices and m edges, weights W_v (not necessarily positive) for every vertex v, and a starting vertex S.

Which of the following is/are correct regarding finding the minimum weighted path on the given vertex weighted graph?

A. Dijkstra's algorithm can be used to find the shortest path.
B. The Time complexity of the above computation will be $O(E + v\log v)$.
C. If the graph is converted into an edge-weighted graph with some modification the shortest path will remain the same.
D. Both (B) and (C)

Q.3 A text is made up of the characters A, B, C, D, E, each occurring with the probability 0.11, $0.4, 0.16, 0.09$ and 0.24 respectively. The optimal Huffman coding technique will have an average length of:

A. 2.40   **B.** 2.16   **C.** 2.26   **D.** 2.15

Q.4 Consider the following two sequences:

$$X \to < B, C, D, C, A, B, C >$$
$$Y \to < C, A, D, B, C, B >$$

The length of the longest common subsequence of X and Y is:

A. 5   **B.** 3   **C.** 4   **D.** 2

Q.5 Which of the following is the correct mathematical application of Euclid's algorithm?

A. Determination of prime numbers
B. Lagrange's four square theorem
C. Cauchy-Euler theorem
D. Residue theorem

Q.6 Which time that depends on the input an already sorted sequence that is easier to sort?

A. Process   **B.** Evaluation
C. Running   **D.** Input

Q.7 What is the space complexity of quick search algorithm?

A. $O(n)$ **B.** $O(\log n)$
C. $O(m + n)$ **D.** $O(mn)$

Q.8 What character shift tables does Boyer-Moore's search algorithm use?

A. Good-character shift tables
B. Bad-character shift tables
C. Next-character shift tables
D. Both (A) and (B)

Q.9 Euclid's algorithm is used for finding __________.

A. GCD of two numbers.
B. GCD of more than three numbers.
C. LCM of two numbers.
D. LCM of more than two numbers.

Q.10 Which of the following class is known as the generic class?

A. Final class   **B.** Template class
C. Abstract class   **D.** Efficient code

Q.11 The programming language, which does not support all types of inheritance is:

A. Smalltalk   **B.** Kotlin
C. Java   **D.** C++

Q.12 In CSS, what is the correct syntax to add a background color for the body?

A. <body style ="background-color:lightgreen;">
B. <body style="bg-color:lightgreen;">
C. <body bg-color ="lightgreen;">
D. <body ="background-color:lightgreen;">

Q.13 What is the correct HTML code for inserting an image?

A. <img> image.gif </img>
B. <img href="image.gif"/>
C. <img src="image.gif">
D. None of these

Q.14 Which among the following is a high-level language used to develop software applications in compact, efficient code that can be run on different types of computers with minimal change?

A. FORTRAN   **B.** C
C. C++   **D.** COBOL

Q.15 A self-balancing binary search tree can be used to implement ______.

A. Priority queue
B. Hash table
C. Heap sort
D. Priority queue and Heap sort

Q.16 You are given pointers to first and last nodes of a singly linked list, which of the following operations are dependent on the length of the linked list?

A. Delete the first element.

B. Insert a new element as a first element.

C. Delete the last element of the list.

D. Add a new element at the end of the list.

Q.17 Why is implementation of stack operations on queues not feasible for a large dataset (Asssume the number of elements in the stack to be n)?

A. Because of its time complexity O(n).

B. Because of its time complexity O(log(n)).

C. Extra memory is not required.

D. There are no problems.

Q.18 Consider the postfix expression $456ab78ac$, where a, b, c are operators. Operator a has higher precedence over operators b and c. Operators b and c are right associative. Then, equivalent infix expression is:

A. $4a56b78ac$

B. $4a5c6b7a8$

C. $4b5a6c7a8$

D. $4a5b6c7a8$

Q.19 Which of the following cannot be used as a medium for 802.3 ethernet?

A. A thin coaxial cable

B. A twisted pair cable

C. A microwave link

D. A fiber optical cable

Q.20 Which of the following algorithms is not used in asymmetric-key cryptography?

A. RSA algorithm

B. Diffie-Hellman algorithm

C. Electronic code book algorithm

D. None of these

Q.21 The maximum throughput of the slotted aloha network is:

A. 50%   **B.** 35%   **C.** 36%   **D.** 18%

Q.22 The vast network of computers that connects millions of people all over the world is called:

A. Hypertext

B. LAN

C. Web

D. Internet

Q.23 What is DHCP snooping?

A. Techniques applied to ensure the security of an existing DHCP infrastructure

B. Encryption of the DHCP server requests

C. Algorithm for DHCP

D. None of these

Q.24 DNS translates ________.

A. Domain name into IP

B. IP into domain name

C. Domain name into physical address

D. None of these

Q.25 In a bus topology, the nodes do nothing to move the data along with the network, making it __________ topology.

A. Client/server

B. Active

C. Passive

D. Terminated

Q.26 The primary difference between a LAN and a WAN is the:

A. Distance that the network spans

B. Size of the servers

C. Difference in the variety and number of output devices

D. Power of the terminals

Q.27 When the microcontroller executes some arithmetic operations, then the flag bits of which register are affected?

A. PSW   **B.** SP   **C.** DPTR   **D.** PC

Q.28 When 8051 wakes up then $0x00$ is loaded to which register?

A. PSW

B. SP

C. PC

D. None of these

Q.29 8051 microcontrollers are manufactured by which of the following companies?

A. Atmel

B. Philips

C. Intel

D. All of these

Q.30 How are the status of the carry, auxiliary carry and parity flag affected if the write instruction:

$$\text{MOV A,\#9C}$$
$$\text{ADD A,\#64H}$$

A. CY = 0, AC = 0, P = 0

B. CY = 1, AC = 1, P = 0

C. CY = 0, AC = 1, P = 0

D. CY = 1, AC = 1, P = 1

Q.31 Which one of the following is the successor of 8086 and 8088 processor?

A. 80286   **B.** 80387   **C.** 8051   **D.** 8087

Q.32 Which are the two modes of 80286?

A. Real mode and protected mode

B. Mode 1 and mode 2

C. Alternate and main

D. Both (A) and (B)

Q.33 Which are the 4 general-purposes 16-bit registers in Intel 80286?

A. CS, DS, SS, ES

B. AX, BX, CX, DX

C. IP, FL, DI, SI

D. DI, SI, BP, SP

Q.34 The size of each MMX (Multimedia Extension) register is:

A. 32 bits   **B.** 64 bits   **C.** 128 bits   **D.** 256 bits

Q.35 After a sequence of MMX instructions is executed, the MMX registers should be cleared by an instruction:

A. CLEAR   **B.** RESET   **C.** EMM   **D.** EMMS

Q.36 Apache Knox eliminates ________ edge node risks.

A. SSL

B. SSO

C. SSH

D. All of these

Q.37 Which of the following is not an example of DBMS?

A. MySQL

B. Microsoft Acess

C. IBM DB 2

D. Google

Q.38 Apache Knox provides _________ REST API Access Point.

A. Single   **B.** Double   **C.** Multiple   **D.** Zero

Q.39 The term "Data" refers to:

A. The electronic representation of the information (or data)

B. Basic information

C. Row facts and figures

D. Row information

Q.40 Which of the following is a top-down approach in which the entity's higher level can be divided into two lower sub-entities?

A. Aggregation   **B.** Generalization

C. Specialization   **D.** Relation

Q.41 Rows of a relation are known as the ______.

A. Degree   **B.** Tuples   **C.** Entity   **D.** Column

Q.42 Which of the following refers to the number of tuples in a relation?

A. Entity   **B.** Column

C. Cardinality   **D.** Aggregation

Q.43 Which one of the following is a type of Data Manipulation Command?

A. Create   **B.** Alter   **C.** Delete   **D.** Drop

Q.44 _________ tool can list all the available database schemas.

A. Sqoop-list-tables

B. Sqoop-list-databases

C. Sqoop-list-schema

D. Sqoop-list-columns

Q.45 Which of the following algorithms is used to avoid deadlock?

A. Dynamic Programming algorithm

B. Primality algorithms

C. Banker's algorithm

D. Deadlock algorithm

Q.46 If all processes are I/O bound, the ready queue will almost always be _____ and the short-term scheduler will have a _____ to do.

A. full, little   **B.** full, lot

C. empty, little   **D.** empty, lot

Q.47 Let the page fault service time be $10\ ms$ in a computer with average memory access time being $20\ ns$. If one page fault is generated for every 10^6 memory accesses, what is the effective access time for the memory?

A. $21.4\ ns$ **B.** $29.9\ ns$ **C.** $23.5\ ns$ **D.** $35.1\ ns$

Q.48 The main objective in building the multi-microprocessor is:

A. Greater throughput

B. Enhanced fault tolerance

C. Both (A) and (B)

D. None of these

Q.49 When a computer is first turned on or restarted, a special type of absolute loader is executed, called a:

A. "Compile and Go" loader

B. Boot loader

C. Bootstrap loader

D. Relating loader

Q.50 Which of the following scheduling algorithms is preemptive scheduling?

A. FCFS Scheduling

B. SJF Scheduling

C. Network Scheduling

D. SRTF Scheduling

Q.51 The technique, for sharing the time of a computer among several jobs. Which switches jobs so rapidly such that each job appears to have the computer to itself:

A. Time-sharing   **B.** Time out

C. Time domain   **D.** FIFO

Q.52 Which of the following is an example of a real-time operating system?

A. MAC   **B.** MS-DOS

C. Windows 10   **D.** Process control

Q.53 In MS-DOS, relocatable object files and load modules have extensions:

A. .OBJ and .COM or .EXE, respectively

B. .COM and .OBJ, respectively

C. .EXE and .OBJ, respectively

D. .DAS and .EXE, respectively

Q.54 D flip flop can be made from a $J-K$ flip flop by making:

A. $J = K$ **B.** $J = K = 1$

C. $J = 0, K = 1$ **D.** $J = \bar{K}$

Q.55 Which gate is called the anti-coincidence and coincidence gate respectively?

A. XNOR and XOR   **B.** AND and OR

C. OR and AND   **D.** XOR and XNOR

Q.56 In a $J-K$ flip flop, when $J = 1$ and $K = 1$ then it will be considered as:

A. Set condition   **B.** Reset condition

C. No change   **D.** Toggle condition

Q.57 Which of the following logic circuits do not have no-change condition?

A. D-FF   **B.** T-FF

C. JK-FF   **D.** SR-Latch

Q.58 How many Flip flops circuits are needed to divide by 16?

A. 2   **B.** 4   **C.** 8   **D.** 16

Q.59 If input to T flip flop is $200\ Hz$ signal, then what will be the output signal frequency if four T flip flops are connected in cascade:

A. $200\ Hz$ **B.** $50\ Hz$

C. 800 Hz **D.** None of these

Q.60 A new flipflop with inputs X and X, has the following property:

Inputs		Current state	Next state
X	Y		
0	0	Q	1
0	1	Q	$\bar{Q}$
1	1	Q	0
1	0	Q	Q

Which of the following expresses the next state in terms of X, Y current state?

A. $\left(\bar{X} \wedge \bar{Q}\right) \vee \left(\bar{Y} \wedge Q\right)$

B. $\left(\bar{X} \wedge Q\right) \vee \left(\bar{Y} \wedge \bar{Q}\right)$

C. $\left(X \wedge \bar{Q}\right) \vee (Y \wedge Q)$

D. $\left(X \wedge \bar{Q}\right) \vee \left(\bar{Y} \wedge Q\right)$

Q.61 The one input RS flip flop is the _________ flip flop.

A. T **B.** D **C.** R **D.** Latch

Q.62 A Flip Flop is a oscillator:

A. four stable **B.** bi-stable
C. mono stable **D.** three stable

Q.63 Definition of a language L with alphabet $\{a\}$ is given as following:

$L = \{a\, n\, k \mid k > 0,$ and n is a positive integer constant $\}$

What is the minimum number of states needed in a DFA to recognize L?

A. $k + 1$ **B.** $n + 1$ **C.** $2n + 1$ **D.** $2k + 1$

Q.64 Given the language L = {ab, aa, baa}, which of the following strings are in L*?

1. abaabaaabaa
2. aaaabaaa
3. baaaaabaaaab
4. baaaaabaa

A. 1,2 and 3 **B.** 2,3 and 4
C. 1,2 and 4 **D.** 1,3 and 4

Q.65 Which of the following does the given Mealy machine represents?

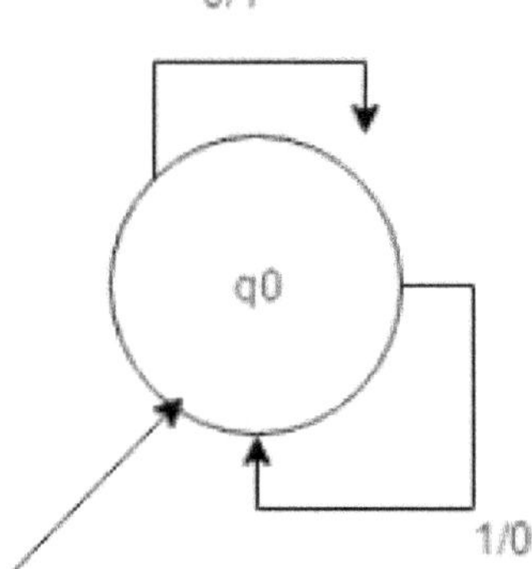

A. 9's Complement **B.** 2's Complement
C. 1's Complement **D.** 10's Complement

Q.66 Regular expression for all strings starts with ab and ends with ba is:

A. aba*b*ba **B.** ab(ab)*ba
C. ab (a+b)*ba **D.** All of these

Q.67 L is a regular language if and only If the set of _________ classes of L is finite.

A. Equivalence **B.** Reflexive
C. Myhill **D.** Nerode

Q.68 Which of the following is true for operator precedence parsing?

A. For all pair of non-terminal
B. To delimit the handle
C. Both (A) and (B)
D. None of these

Q.69 The process of assigning load addresses to the various parts of the program and adjusting the code and data in the program to reflect the assigned addresses is called?

A. Assembly **B.** Parsing
C. Relocation **D.** Symbol resolute

Q.70 Which of the following statements is false?

A. Left as well as right most derivations can be in unambiguous grammar.
B. An LL (1) parser is a top-down parser.
C. LALR is more powerful than SLR.
D. Ambiguous grammar can't be LR (k).

Q.71 YACC is a computer program for _________ operation system.

A. Windows **B.** DOS
C. Unix **D.** openSUSE

Q.72 YACC is an acronym for:

A. Yes Another Compile Compiler
B. Yet Another Compile Compiler
C. Yet Another Compiler Compiler
D. Yes Another Compiler Compiler

Q.73 Which one of the following options is correct given three positive integers x, y and z, and a predicate?

$$P(x) = -(x = 1) \land \forall y$$
$$(\exists z \, (x = y^*z) \Rightarrow (y = x) \lor (y = 1))$$

A. $P(x)$ being true means that x is a prime number.
B. $P(x)$ being true means that x is a number other than 1.
C. $P(x)$ is always true irrespective of the value of x.
D. $P(x)$ being true means that x has exactly two factors other than 1 and x.

Q.74 Consider the following statements regarding function f and g.

A. If go f is injective, then g is injective but f need not be.

B. If go f is surjective then both g and f are surjective.

A. A is true, B is false.
B. B is true, A is false.
C. Both are true.
D. Both are false.

Q.75 Let G and H be two groups. The groups $G \oplus H$ is abelian:

A. For any G and any H.
B. Only if one of them is cyclic.
C. Only if one of them is abelian.
D. Only if G and H are abelian.

Q.76 A number of ways to properly color (using just sufficient colors) a connected graph without any cycle using five colors such that no two adjacent nodes have the same color?

A. 20   **B.** 22   **C.** 24   **D.** 28

Q.77 How many binary sequences of length 10 are possible with exactly four 0's and no two 0's are consecutive?

A. 35   **B.** 40   **C.** 45   **D.** 50

Q.78 There are six movie parts numbered from 1 to 6. Find the number of ways in which they are arranged so that part- 1 and part- 3 are never together:

A. 876   **B.** 480   **C.** 654   **D.** 237

Q.79 Consider the ordering relation $a|b \subseteq N \times N$ over natural numbers N such that $a|b$ if there exists c belong to N such that $a * c = b$. Then _________.

A. | is an equivalence relation.
B. It is a total order.
C. Every subset of N has an upper bound under |.
D. $(N, |)$ is a lattice but not a complete lattice.

Q.80 Consider the set N* of finite sequences of natural numbers with a denoting that sequence a is a prefix of sequence b. Then, which of the following is true?

A. Every non-empty subset of has a greatest lower bound.
B. It is uncountable.
C. Every non-empty finite subset of has a least upper bound.
D. Every non-empty subset of has a least upper bound.

Q.81 A free semi-lattice has the _______ property.

A. intersection
B. commutative and associative
C. identity
D. universal

Q.82 Agile Software Development is based on:

A. Incremental Development
B. Iterative Development
C. Linear Development
D. Both (A) and (B)

Q.83 How is plan driven development different from agile development?

A. Outputs are decided through a process of negotiation during the software development process.
B. Specification, design, implementation and testing are interleaved.
C. Iteration occurs within activities.
D. All of these

Q.84 How many phases are there in Scrum?

A. 2   **B.** 5   **C.** 4   **D.** 0

Q.85 What is agile scrum methodology?

A. Project management that emphasizes incremental progress.
B. Project management that emphasizes decremental progress.
C. Project management that emphasizes neutral progress.
D. Project management that emphasizes no progress.

Q.86 Which type of DFD concentrates on the system process, and flow of data in the system?

A. Physical DFD   **B.** Logical DFD
C. Flowchart DFD   **D.** System DFD

Q.87 Which one of the following is not a step of requirement engineering?

A. Elicitation   **B.** Design
C. Analysis   **D.** Documentation

Q.88 Which testing has the highest-level modules are tested first and progressively, lower-level modules are tested there after?

A. Bottom-up integration
B. Top-down integration
C. Up-down integration
D. Both (A) and (B)

Q.89 _______ involves testing a software in order to identify any flaws and gaps from security and vulnerability point of view.

A. Portability Testing   **B.** Usability Testing
C. Load Testing   **D.** Security Testing

Q.90 Which of the following is not a Software Configuration Management Activity?

A. Configuration item identification
B. Risk management
C. Release management
D. Branch management

Q.91 The probability of guessing the correct answer to a certain test questions is $\dfrac{x}{12}$. If the probability of not guessing the correct answer to this question is $\dfrac{2}{3}$, then $x =$?

A. 2 **B.** 3 **C.** 4 **D.** 6

Q.92 Two letters were randomly chosen from the word GUITARIST. Find the probability that the letters are R and T:

A. $\dfrac{1}{18}$ **B.** $\dfrac{1}{9}$ **C.** $\dfrac{2}{9}$ **D.** $\dfrac{1}{3}$

Q.93 The solution of $x^2 \dfrac{dy}{dx} = x^2 + xy + y^2$ will be:

A. $\log x = \tan^{-1}\dfrac{y}{x} + c$

B. $\log x = \tan^{-1}\dfrac{x}{y} + c$

C. $\log y = \tan^{-1}\dfrac{x}{y} + c$

D. $\log y = \tan^{-1}\dfrac{y}{x} + c$

Q.94 The solution of the differential equation $dy = \sqrt{1 - y^2}\, dx$ is:

A. $y = \sin x + c$ **B.** $y = \sin(x + c)$
C. $\sin^{-1}(y + x) = c$ **D.** $\sin^{-1}(y + c) = x$

Q.95 The inverse Laplace transform of $H(s) = \dfrac{s+3}{s^2+2s+1}$ for $t \geq 0$ is:

A. $3te^{-t} + e^{-t}$ **B.** $3e^{-t}$
C. $2te^{-t} + e^{-t}$ **D.** $4te^{-t} + e^{-t}$

Q.96 Laplace transform of $3t^4$ is:

A. $\dfrac{18}{s^4}$ **B.** $\dfrac{24}{s^4}$ **C.** $\dfrac{72}{s^5}$ **D.** $\dfrac{12}{s^5}$

Q.97 The number of solutions of the simultaneous algebraic equations $y = 3x + 3$ and $y = 3x + 5$ is:

A. 0 **B.** 1 **C.** 2 **D.** Infinite

Q.98 Eigenvector of the matrix $\begin{bmatrix} 1 & 2 \\ 0 & 2 \end{bmatrix}$ be written in the form $\begin{bmatrix} 1 \\ a \end{bmatrix}$ and $\begin{bmatrix} 1 \\ b \end{bmatrix}$. What is the value of $(a + b)$?

A. 0 **B.** $\dfrac{1}{2}$ **C.** 1 **D.** 2

Q.99 $\displaystyle\int_0^{\frac{\pi}{2}} \dfrac{\tan^7 x}{\cot^7 x + \tan^7 x}\, dx$ is equal to:

A. $\dfrac{\pi}{2}$ **B.** $\dfrac{\pi}{4}$ **C.** $\dfrac{\pi}{6}$ **D.** $\dfrac{\pi}{3}$

Q.100 $\displaystyle\int \dfrac{\cot x}{1+\sin^2 x}\, dx =$?

A. $\ln\dfrac{\sec x}{\sqrt{1+\sin^2 x}} + c$ **B.** $\ln\dfrac{\tan x}{\sqrt{1+\sin^7 x}} + c$
C. $\ln\dfrac{\sin x}{\sqrt{1+\sin^2 x}} + c$ **D.** $\ln\dfrac{\cos x}{\sqrt{1+\sin^4 x}} + c$

// Smart Answer Sheet //

Correct Percentage of students who answered correctly. **Skipped** Percentage of students who skipped.

Q.	Ans.	Correct / Skipped	Q.	Ans.	Correct / Skipped	Q.	Ans.	Correct / Skipped	Q.	Ans.	Correct / Skipped	Q.	Ans.	Correct / Skipped	Q.	Ans.	Correct / Skipped
1	D	48.93 % / 35.65 %	18	C	59.63 % / 37.49 %	35	D	31.59 % / 67.78 %	52	D	50.01 % / 30.71 %	69	C	45.51 % / 37.24 %	86	B	67.42 % / 31.81 %
2	D	56.66 % / 36.93 %	19	C	65.23 % / 30.13 %	36	C	43.74 % / 42.15 %	53	A	78.52 % / 21.38 %	70	A	23.76 % / 75.78 %	87	B	51.7 % / 47.95 %
3	B	11.35 % / 77.09 %	20	C	87.65 % / 11.25 %	37	D	66.43 % / 33.23 %	54	D	86.23 % / 10.18 %	71	C	42.34 % / 39.24 %	88	B	14.04 % / 69.15 %
4	C	10.22 % / 74.42 %	21	C	67.96 % / 31.53 %	38	A	42.28 % / 51.05 %	55	D	56.08 % / 34.52 %	72	C	52.93 % / 36.22 %	89	D	67.52 % / 32.22 %
5	B	48.36 % / 45.41 %	22	D	87.64 % / 12.07 %	39	C	76.46 % / 10.27 %	56	D	42.8 % / 49.44 %	73	A	69.13 % / 30.11 %	90	B	54.8 % / 39.41 %
6	C	85.45 % / 14.1 %	23	A	25.45 % / 68.32 %	40	C	45.56 % / 33.88 %	57	A	78.3 % / 11.4 %	74	D	31.18 % / 68.11 %	91	C	67.46 % / 32.47 %
7	A	89.06 % / 10.06 %	24	A	47.97 % / 30.39 %	41	B	82.35 % / 15.87 %	58	B	62.23 % / 37.15 %	75	D	56.29 % / 35.04 %	92	A	24.42 % / 68.04 %
8	D	47.31 % / 36.82 %	25	C	52.62 % / 33.41 %	42	C	56.62 % / 30.49 %	59	D	11.63 % / 72.43 %	76	A	65.89 % / 31.15 %	93	A	44.3 % / 42.09 %
9	A	41.8 % / 38.68 %	26	A	51.23 % / 43.59 %	43	C	46.86 % / 48.06 %	60	A	57.26 % / 35.9 %	77	A	40.14 % / 40.32 %	94	B	66.51 % / 32.16 %
10	B	52.39 % / 43.54 %	27	A	66.58 % / 32.55 %	44	B	63.27 % / 36.57 %	61	B	57.14 % / 31.26 %	78	B	28.09 % / 67.19 %	95	C	58.59 % / 40.03 %
11	C	43.46 % / 38.03 %	28	C	65.46 % / 30.8 %	45	C	51.55 % / 30.8 %	62	B	48.8 % / 45.14 %	79	D	65.85 % / 30.18 %	96	C	68.92 % / 30.19 %
12	A	65.24 % / 34.03 %	29	D	24.92 % / 68.53 %	46	C	52.07 % / 44.51 %	63	B	21.33 % / 69.51 %	80	A	22.2 % / 71.8 %	97	A	13.91 % / 70.93 %
13	C	61.8 % / 33.18 %	30	B	17.49 % / 77.23 %	47	B	40.82 % / 35.28 %	64	C	20.6 % / 74.42 %	81	D	60.32 % / 33.02 %	98	B	44.51 % / 54.01 %
14	D	63.43 % / 30.37 %	31	A	58.67 % / 39.57 %	48	C	48.59 % / 42.22 %	65	C	22.71 % / 72.75 %	82	D	41.79 % / 51.96 %	99	B	48.66 % / 43.65 %
15	A	85.41 % / 14.02 %	32	A	67.46 % / 32.03 %	49	C	27.48 % / 68.76 %	66	C	67.19 % / 31.79 %	83	C	29.31 % / 67.51 %	100	C	66.48 % / 30.1 %
16	C	10.08 % / 81.25 %	33	B	43.51 % / 37.55 %	50	D	18.07 % / 68.27 %	67	A	61.96 % / 34.73 %	84	B	58.31 % / 30.41 %			
17	A	14.38 % / 77.29 %	34	B	47.8 % / 40.22 %	51	A	51.48 % / 32.46 %	68	A	78.79 % / 14.14 %	85	A	51.12 % / 42.9 %			

//Hints and Solutions//

1. As we know,

Strassen's matrix multiplication uses the divide and conquers approach. Divide both the matrices in 4 sub-matrices of size $\frac{n}{2} \times \frac{n}{2}$.

Perform 8 multiplications for matrices of size $\frac{n}{2} \times \frac{n}{2}$ and 4additions. The addition of two matrices takes $O(n^2)$ time.

So, recurrence relation is $T(n) = 8T\left(\frac{n}{2}\right) + O(n^2)$

Given,

$$A = \begin{bmatrix} 1 & 3 \\ 5 & 7 \end{bmatrix}$$

$$B = \begin{bmatrix} 8 & 4 \\ 6 & 2 \end{bmatrix}$$

Now,

$$AB = \begin{bmatrix} 1 & 3 \\ 5 & 7 \end{bmatrix} \begin{bmatrix} 8 & 4 \\ 6 & 2 \end{bmatrix} = \begin{bmatrix} 1 \times 8 + 3 \times 6 & 1 \times 4 + 3 \times 2 \\ 5 \times 8 + 7 \times 6 & 5 \times 4 + 7 \times 2 \end{bmatrix}$$

$$AB = \begin{bmatrix} 26 & 10 \\ 82 & 34 \end{bmatrix}$$

So, we have $C_{11} = 26; C_{12} = 10; C_{21} = 82; C_{22} = 34$.

Hence, the correct option is (D).

2. For the minimum weighted path on the given vertex weighted graph, we will covert this vertex-weighted graph to an edge-weighted graph by the following rule and converting vertex weighted graph to edge-weighted graph is not going to change the minimum weighted path.

For each out edge from vertex u to v, edge weight will be the weight of vertex u, i.e W_v.

The idea behind it is using an edge cost as the weight of the edge, and the cost of reaching the target vertices. The cost of the source was already paid, so you disregard it.

Now, the graph is an edge-weighted graph so apply Dijkstra's algorithm to find the minimum weighted path from S to all other vertices.

Reduce the problem to normal Dijkstra, which assumes no weights on the vertices. For this, you will need to define $W': E >> R$, a new weight function for edges.

$$W'(u, v) = W(u, v) + \text{vertex-weight } (v)$$

The time complexity of Dijkstra's algorithm is $O(E + v\log v)$

Hence, the correct option is (D).

3. Huffman coding is a data compression technique. It constructs a tree by selecting the minimum frequency of available nodes. And assign the weights 1 for the left child and 0 for the right child or 0 for the left child and 1 for the right-left.

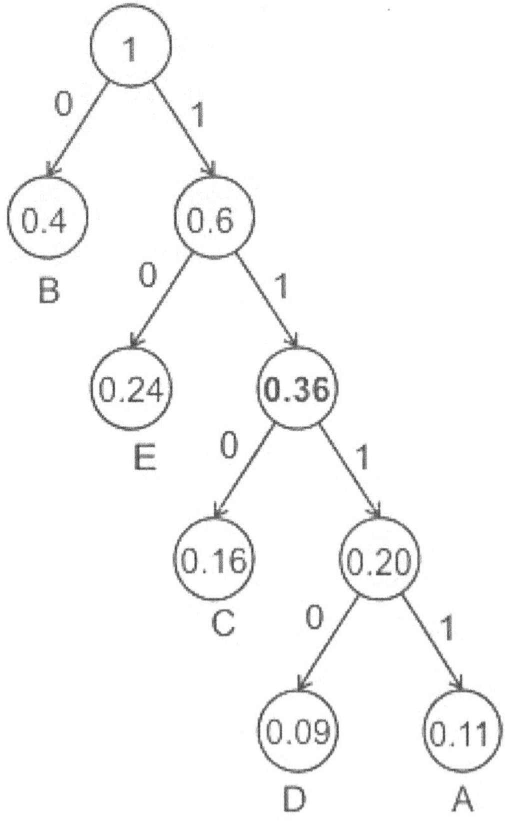

Now, add all the internal nodes of the tree.

Average length $= 1 + 0.6 + 0.36 + 0.20 = 2.16$

So, the optimal Huffman coding technique will have an average length of 2.16.

Hence, the correct option is (B).

4. Given,

$$X \to <B, C, D, C, A, B, C>$$

$$Y \to <C, A, D, B, C, B>$$

If there is a match in these sequences, $A[i, j] = A[i - 1, j - 1] + 1$

If there is not a match in these sequences, then max $(A[i - 1, j], A[i, j - 1])$

Now,

Let $M = $ length of X and $N = $ length of Y.

int $dp[N + 1][M + 1]$

Table of longest common subsequence:

	X	B	C	D	C	A	B	C
Y	0	0	0	0	0	0	0	0
C	0	0	1	1	1	1	1	1
A	0	0	1	1	1	2	2	2
D	0	0	1	2	2	2	2	2
B	0	1	1	2	2	2	3	3
C	0	1	2	2	3	3	3	3
B	0	1	2	2	3	3	4	4

The length of longest common subsequence of X and $Y =$ $A[N][M] = 4$.

Hence, the correct option is (C).

5. Lagrange's four square theorem is one of the mathematical applications of Euclid's algorithm and it is the basic tool for proving theorems in number theory. It can be generalized into other types of numbers like the Gaussian integers.

Hence, the correct option is (B).

6. The running time depends on the input an already sorted sequence is easier to sort. The running time is given by the size of the input, since short sequences are easier to sort than the longer ones. Generally, we seek upper bounds on the running time, because it is reliable.

Hence, the correct option is (C).

7. The space complexity of the quick search algorithm is mathematically found to be $O(n)$ where n represents the input size. The quick search algorithm uses only the bad-character shift table (see chapter Boyer-Moore algorithm). During the searching phase, the comparisons between pattern and text characters during each attempt can be done in any order. Search algorithms work to retrieve information stored within some data structure, or calculated in the search space of a problem domain, either with discrete or continuous values.

Hence, the correct option is (A).

8. Boyer-Moore's search algorithm uses both good and bad character shift tables whereas the quick search algorithm uses only bad character shift tables. Boyer-Moore-Horspool is an algorithm for finding substrings into strings. This algorithm compares each character of the substring to find a word or the same characters into the string.

Hence, the correct option is (D).

9. Euclid's algorithm is basically used to find the GCD of two numbers. It cannot be directly applied to three or more numbers at a time. Euclid's method is faster than this naive method, so lets us follow the Euclidean method to find out the GCD of 4598 and 3211. We represent the two numbers in the following way, the dividend should be the large number and the divisor is another number. At this point, the remainder is 0 and we get the GCD 19.

$$\text{GCD } (a,b) = \frac{(a \times b)}{LCM(a,b)}$$

Hence, the correct option is (A).

10. Template classes are those classes which can be used for any value of data type. So, these are known as a generic class. Template classes help in making the genetic classes and generate the objects of classes based on the parameters. This type of class also saves system memory.

Hence, the correct option is (B).

11. The programming language, which does not support all types of inheritance is Java. Java is a programming language that disapproves of the concept of 'multiple inheritances'. So, it does not support all types of inheritance. But, we can implement 'multiple inheritances' in Java language using the interface concept. This increases complexities and ambiguity in the relationship among classes.

Hence, the correct option is (C).

12. The CSS background-color property defines the background color for an HTML element

```
<html>
<body style ="background-color: lightgreen;">
<h1>Edugorilla Dashboard</h1>
<p>TESTSERIES</p>
</body>
</html>
```

Hence, the correct option is (A).

13. HTML code for inserting an image is `<img src="image.gif">`.

The `<img>` tag defines an image in an HTML page.

The `<img>` tag has two required attributes: src and alt.

src specifies the URL of an image and alt specifies an alternate text for an image.

Hence, the correct option is (C).

14. COBOL is a high-level language used to develop software applications in compact, efficient code that can be run on different types of computers with minimal change. It is compiled English-like computer programming language designed for business use. It object-oriented since 2002.

Hence, the correct option is (D).

15. Self-balancing binary search trees can be used to construct and maintain ordered lists, to achieve the optimal worst case performance. So, self-balancing binary search tree can be used to implement a priority queue, which is ordered list.

Hence, the correct option is (A).

16. Deletion of the first element of the list is done in O(1) time by deleting memory and changing the first pointer.

Insertion of an element as a first element can be done in O(1) time. We will create a node that holds data and points to the head of the given linked list. The head pointer was changed to a newly created node.

Deletion of the last element requires a pointer to the previous node of last, which can only be obtained by traversing the list. This requires the length of the linked list.

Adding a new element at the end of the list can be done in O(1) by changing the pointer of the last node to the newly created node and last is changed to a newly created node.

Hence, the correct option is (C).

17. To perform queue operations such as enqueue and dequeue there is a need of emptying all the elements of a current stack and pushing elements into the next stack and vice versa. Therefore, it has a time complexity of O(n) and the need of extra stack as well, may not be feasible for a large dataset.

Hence, the correct option is (A).

18. Given, postfix expression: $456ab78ac$

Infix expression:

$$\Rightarrow 4(5a6)b(7a8)c$$

$$\Rightarrow \left(4\ b(5a6)\right)(7a8)c$$

$$\Rightarrow \left(4\ b(5a6)\right)c(7a8)$$

$$= 4b5a6c7a8$$

So, the required infix expression is $4b5a6c7a8$.

Hence, the correct option is (C).

19. A microwave link cannot be used as a medium for 802.3 ethernets, because a microwave link is a transmission network that utilizes a beam of radio waves in the microwave frequency spectrum to relay video, audio, or data between two places.

Hence, the correct option is (C).

20. An electronic code book algorithm is a mode of operation for a block cipher, where each frame of text in an encrypted document refers to a data field. In other terms, the same plaintext value would also give the same value for ciphertext.

Hence, the correct option is (C).

21. We know that,

In slotted aloha, there are time slots for the stations to transmit the data. Stations can transmit data in time slots. Stations have to wait for their time slots to transmit the data.

Formula:

Throughput of slotted aloha $\left(F(G)\right) = G \times e^{-G}$

Now,

$$\Rightarrow F(G) = G \times e^{-G}$$

$$\Rightarrow F'(G) = -G \times e^{-G} + e^{-G}(1)$$

To get maximum value,

$$\Rightarrow F'(G) = e^{-G}(1 - G) = 0$$

$$\Rightarrow e^{-G} \neq 0$$

$$\therefore G = 1$$

Maximum throughput:

$$= G \times e^{-G}$$

$$= 1 \times e^{-1}$$

$$= 0.3678 \approx 0.36$$

Maximum throughput in percentage,

$$= 0.36 \times 100$$

$$= 36$$

Hence, the correct option is (C).

22. The vast network of computers that connect millions of people around the world is called the Internet. A global computer network that provides a variety of information and communication facilities, including interconnected networks using standardized communication protocols, is called the Internet.

Hence, the correct option is (D).

23. DHCP snooping is a security feature used in layer 2 of the network's OS. This technology prevents unauthorized DHCP servers from assigning IP addresses to DHCP clients. DHCP snooping can be configured on LAN switches to exclude rogue DHCP servers and remove malicious or malformed DHCP traffic. These techniques are applied to ensure the security of an existing DHCP infrastructure.

Hence, the correct option is (A).

24. DNS is an Internet service that translates domain names to IP addresses (forward DNS) and IP addresses to their associated domain names (Reverse DNS) with the help of a DNS server. DNS is a directory service that provides a mapping between the name of a host on the network and its numerical address. This allows the users of networks to utilize user-friendly names when looking for other hosts instead of remembering the IP addresses.

Hence, the correct option is (A).

25. In a bus topology, the nodes do nothing to move the data along with the network, making it a passive topology. A bus is a passive topology, which means that the workstations on the bus are not responsible for regenerating the signal as it passes by them. Since the workstations do not play an active role, the workstations are not a requirement of a functioning bus, which means that if a workstation fails, the bus does not fail.

Hence, the correct option is (C).

26. The primary difference between a LAN and a WAN is the distance that the network spans. LANs are for smaller, more localized networking in a home, business, school, etc. while WANs cover larger areas, such as cities, and even allow computers in different nations to connect.

Hence, the correct option is (A).

27. When the microcontroller executes some arithmetic operations, then the flag bits of PSW register are affected. It stands for program status word. It consists of carry, auxiliary carry, overflow, parity, register bank select bits etc. which are affected during such operations.

Hence, the correct option is (A).

28. When 8051 wakes up, Program Counter (PC) is loaded with 0000H. Because of this in 8051 first opcode is stored in ROM address at 0000H. A program counter (PC) is a CPU register in the computer processor which has the address of the next instruction to be executed from memory. It is a digital counter needed for faster execution of tasks as well as for tracking the current execution point. PC, is a special-purpose register that is used by the processor to hold the address of the next instruction to be executed. The PLA automatically updates the PC to point to the next instruction during the op-code decode cycle.

Hence, the correct option is (C).

29. 8051 microcontrollers are manufactured by Intel, Atmel, Philips/Signetics, Infineon, Dallas Semi/Maxim Intel MCS- 51. The Intel MCS- 51 (commonly termed 8051) is a single-chip microcontroller (MCU) series developed by Intel in 1980 for use in embedded systems. In addition, Atmel still makes microcontrollers that use the 8051 architecture, albeit improved to do single-cycle instructions. Philips semiconductor-signets microcontroller training foils features of the $8051 - 8$ bit data path and ALU. Easy interfacing 12 to 30 MHz versions are available.

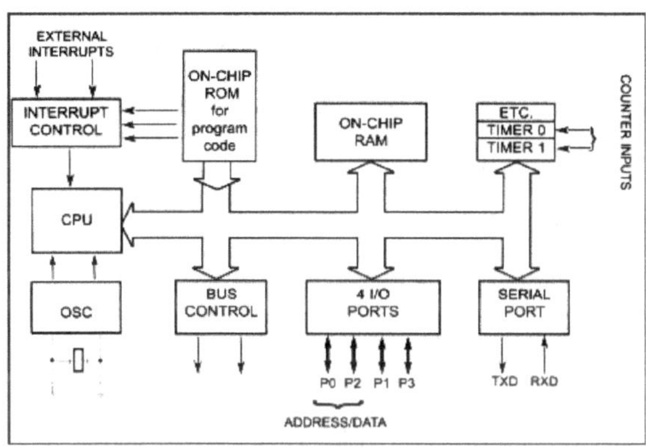

Hence, the correct option is (D).

30. For 8051 Microcontroller:

$$CY = \begin{cases} 0 \text{ [When no carry from MSB i.e. } D_7] \\ 1 \text{[When carry from MSB i.e. } D_7] \end{cases}$$

$$AC = \begin{cases} 0 \text{[When no carry from } D_3 \text{ to } D_4] \\ 1 \text{[When carry from } D_3 \text{ to } D_4] \end{cases}$$

$$P = \begin{cases} 1 \text{[When odd no. of } 1's \text{ present]} \\ 0 \text{[When even no. of } 1's \text{ present]} \end{cases}$$

$MOV A, \#9CH \Rightarrow A = 9C \{$Accumulator loaded with Data $9C\}$

$ADD A, \#64H \Rightarrow ADD\ 64H \{$with accumulator and store the result into accumulator $\rightarrow$ Taking Hexadecimal no. into Binary format $\}$

$9C\ H \Rightarrow 1001\ 1100$

$64\ H \Rightarrow 0110\ 0100$

$\Rightarrow$ Perform ADDITION OPERATION

		(1)	(1)	(1)	(1)	(1)	all are carry $\leftarrow$
0	1	0	0	1	1	1	0
0	0	1	1	0	0	1	0
D_0	D_7	D_6	D_5	D_4	D_3	D_2	D_1

Carry $\rightarrow$

1	0	0	0	0	0	0	0	0

$\therefore CY = 1, AC = 1, P = 0$ [From above result]

Hence, the correct option is (B).

31. 80286 is the successor of 8086 and 8088 because it possess a CPU based on 8086 and 8088. 8051 is a microcontroller designed by Intel which is commonly known as Intel MCS-5 1. 8087 is the first floating point coprocessor of 8086.

Hence, the correct option is (A).

32. 80286 possesses two modes which are called real and protected modes. In real modes, it adds some additional register in order to access a size greater than 16 MB but still preserving its compatibility with 8086 and 8088. The protected mode can directly execute 16-bit 80286 protected mode programs.

Hence, the correct option is (A).

33. Intel 80286 possesses 4 general-purpose registers and these are 16-bit in size. In addition to the general-purpose register, there are four segmented registers, two index registers and a base pointer register. The general registers AX, BX, CX, and DX are 16-bit. However, they are composed of two smaller registers. For example:

- **AX:** The high 8-bit is called AH, and the low 8-bit is called AL.
- **BX:** Base register, typically used to hold the address of a procedure or variable.
- **CX:** Count register, typically used for looping.
- **DX:** Data register, typically used for multiplication and division.

Hence, the correct option is (B).

34. The MMX registers use only the 64-bit mantissa portion of the general purpose floating point registers, to store MMX operands. Thus, the MMX programmers virtually get eight new MMX registers, each of 64 bits.

Hence, the correct option is (B).

35. After a sequence of MMX instructions is executed, the MMX registers should be cleared by an instruction, EMMS, which implies Empty the MMX Stack. Using EMMS is like emptying a container to accommodate new content. The EMMS instruction clears the MMX registers and sets the value of the floating-point tag word to empty.

Hence, the correct option is (D).

36. Apache Knox eliminates SSH edge node risks. Knox hides Network Topology. The use of a centralised front service also provides security advantages in that it hides the topology of your network and Hadoop services that are behind it, and provides security against SSH edge node risks (ssh tunnelling were tunnels on the external side of your firewall forward ssh into your internal network).

Hence, the correct option is (C).

37. MySQL, Microsoft Access, IBM DB 2 are database management systems while Google is a search engine. MySQL is a Linux-based database management system, Microsoft Access is a tool that is a part of Microsoft Office used to store data, IBM DB 2 is a database management system developed by IBM. Google's Bigtable is the database that runs Google's Internet search, Google Maps, YouTube, Gmail, and other products.

Hence, the correct option is (D).

38. The Apache Knox Gateway is a system that provides a single point of authentication and access for Apache. Knox also intercepts REST/HTTP calls and provides authentication, authorization, audit, URL rewriting, web vulnerability removal and other security services through a series of extensible interceptor pipelines. Knox supports LDAP/AD Authentication and Service Authorization.

Hence, the correct option is (A).

39. In general, the term "data" refers to the row facts and figures, whereas the information is referred to as the data, which is really important for someone or a particular person. Data, in the context of databases, refers to all the single items that are stored in a database, either individually or as a set. Data in a database is primarily stored in database tables, which are organized into columns that dictate the data types stored therein.

Hence, the correct option is (C).

40. In specialization, the top-down approach is used, and it is opposite to the generalization.

In specialization, the higher-level entity can be divided into sub-lower entities. It is generally used for identifying the subset of an entity set which shares the distinguishing characteristics.

To understand it more clearly, consider the following example:

Suppose you have an entity, e.g., A vehicle. So, through the specialization, you can be divided further into sub-entities like two-wheelers and four-wheelers.

Hence, the correct option is (C).

41. In SQL, the relation is represented by a table, and a table is a collection of rows and columns. Therefore the collection of rows and columns is called the table, whereas a table is known as the relation in the SQL. So in a relation (or we can say table), rows are called the tuples.

Hence, the correct option is (B).

42. Cardinality refers to the number of tuples of relation because cardinality represents the number of tuples in a relation.

To understand it in more detail, consider the following given example:

Suppose we have a relation (or table) that contains 30 tuples (or Rows) and four columns, so, the cardinality of our relationship will be 30.

Hence, the correct option is (C).

43. Delete is a type of Data Manipulation Command. In data manipulation language, command like select, insert, update, and delete is used to manipulate the information (or data, records), for example, insert a table, update table delete table, etc. While the commands create, alter and drop are DDL (Data Definition Language) commands.

Hence, the correct option is (C).

44. Sqoop also includes a primitive SQL execution shell (the sqoop-eval tool). A Sqoop-list-database is a tool that executes and parses the "SHOW DATABASES" query against the database server. This lists out the entire database present in the database server. The primary purpose of this tool is to list the database schemas present on the server.

Hence, the correct option is (B).

45. The Banker's algorithm, sometimes referred to as the detection algorithm, is a resource allocation and deadlock avoidance algorithm developed by Edsger Dijkstra that tests for safety by simulating the allocation of predetermined maximum possible amounts of all resources, and then makes an "s-state" check to test for possible deadlock conditions for all other pending activities, before deciding whether allocation should be allowed to continue.

Hence, the correct option is (C).

46. If all processes are I/O bound, the ready queue will almost always be empty and the short-term scheduler will have a little to do. I/O bound processes spend more time doing I/O than computation. A short-term scheduler selects a process that has to be executed next and allocates the CPU. CPU scheduler selects a process among the processes that are ready to execute and allocates CPU to one of them.

Hence, the correct option is (C).

47. Given,

Page fault service time $(S) = 10\ ms$

$= 10^7\ ns$

Page fault rate $(p) = \dfrac{1}{10^6}$

Memory access time $(m) = 20\ ns$

As we know,

Effective access time for memory (EMAT) $= p \times S + (1 - p) \times m$

Now,

$$\text{EMAT} = \dfrac{1}{10^6} \times 10\ ms + \left(1 - \dfrac{1}{10^6}\right) \times 20\ ns$$

$$= 29.99998\ ns$$

$$\approx 30\ ns$$

Hence, the correct option is (B).

48. Greater throughput and enhanced fault tolerance are the main objectives of the multi-microprocessor system. These systems incorporate a multiplicity of hardware and software, for the purpose. Throughput is the amount of a product or service that a company can produce and deliver to a client within a specified period of time. Fault tolerance is a process that enables an operating system to respond to a failure in hardware or software. This fault-tolerance definition refers to the system's ability to continue operating despite failures or malfunctions.

Hence, the correct option is (C).

49. A bootstrap loader is a program that resides in the computer's EPROM, ROM, or other non-volatile memory. It is automatically executed by the processor when turning on the computer. A bootloader, also known as a boot program or bootstrap loader, is special operating system software that loads into the working memory of a computer after start-up.

Hence, the correct option is (C).

50. Shortest Remaining Time First (SRTF) scheduling is preemptive scheduling. In this scheduling, the process that has the shortest processing time left is executed first. Since the currently executing process is the one with the shortest amount of time remaining by definition, and since that time should only reduce as execution progresses, the process will either run until it completes or get preempted if a new process is added that requires a smaller amount of time.

Hence, the correct option is (D).

51. The technique of sharing computer time between multiple jobs, which switches jobs so rapidly that each job appears to have its own computer, is called time-sharing. Time-sharing refers to the allocation of computer resources in time slots to several programs simultaneously. For example, a mainframe computer that has many users logged on to it. Each user uses the resources of the mainframe i.e. memory, CPU, etc.

Hence, the correct option is (A).

52. Process control is the best example of a real-time operating system. The function of the real time operation system is to control resources in the system shared by application tasks including input/output devices, computer memory, and the CPU itself.

Hence, the correct option is (D).

53. In MS-DOS, relocatable object files and load modules have extensions is .OBJ and .COM or .EXE, respectively.

.OBJ: OBJ is a geometry definition file format first developed by Wavefront Technologies for its Advanced Visualizer animation package.

.COM: The domain name com is a top-level domain in the Domain Name System of the Internet. Its name is derived from the word commercial, indicating its original intended purpose for domains registered by commercial organizations.

.EXE: EXE is a file extension for an executable file format. An executable is a file that contains a program - that is, a particular kind of file that is capable of being executed or run as a program in the computer. An executable file can be run by a program in Microsoft DOS or Windows through a command or a double click.

Hence, the correct option is (A).

54. D flip flop:

D flip flop has only one input terminal. The output of the D flip flop will be the same as the input. So, it is used in delay circuits.

The circuit is as shown below.

Logic symbol:

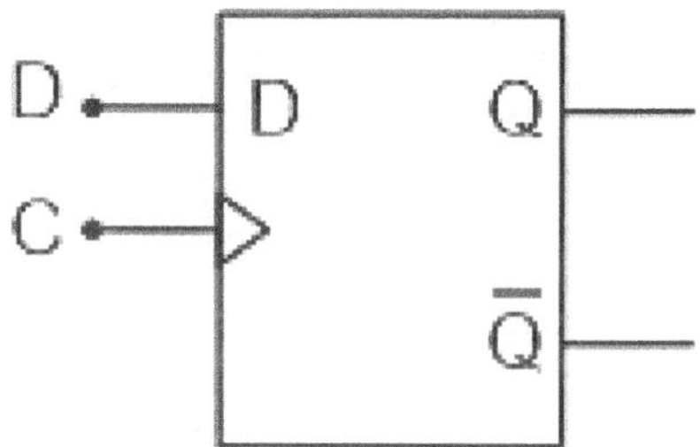

Truth table:

D	Q_n (Present state)	Q_{n+1} (Next state)
0	0	0
0	1	0
1	0	1
1	1	1

Characteristic equation: $Q_{n+1} = D$

The D flip flop may be obtained from an $S - R$ flip flop by just putting one inverter between the S and R as shown in the figure below.

$$S = \overline{R}$$

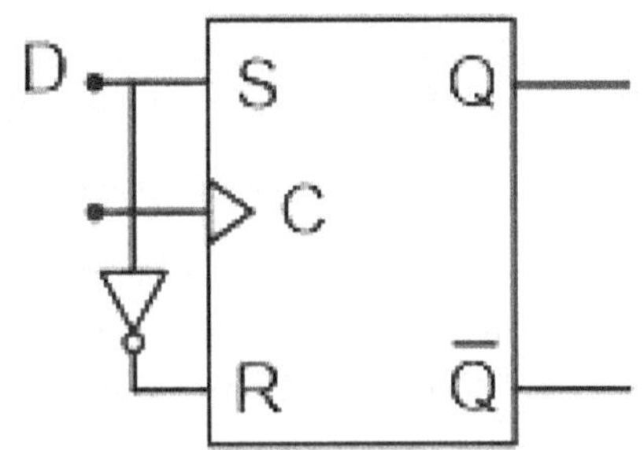

The D flip flop may be obtained from a $J - K$ flip flop by just putting one inverter between the J and K as shown in the figure below.

$$K = \overline{J}$$

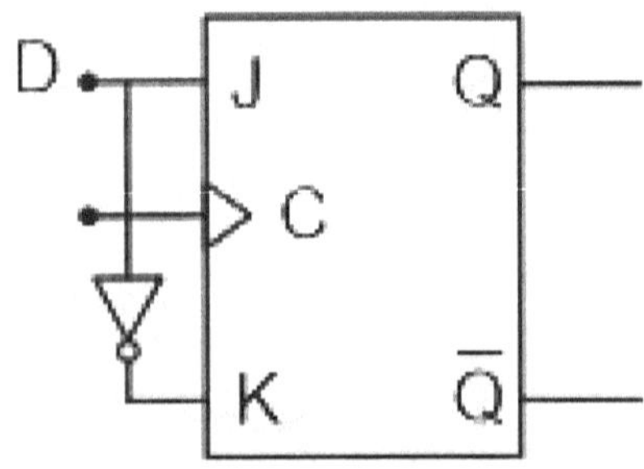

T flip flop:

T flip flop has only one input terminal. The output of the T flip flop will be toggled when the input is high on every new clock pulse. The output will be the same as the previous state when the input is low.

The circuit is as shown below.

Logic symbol:

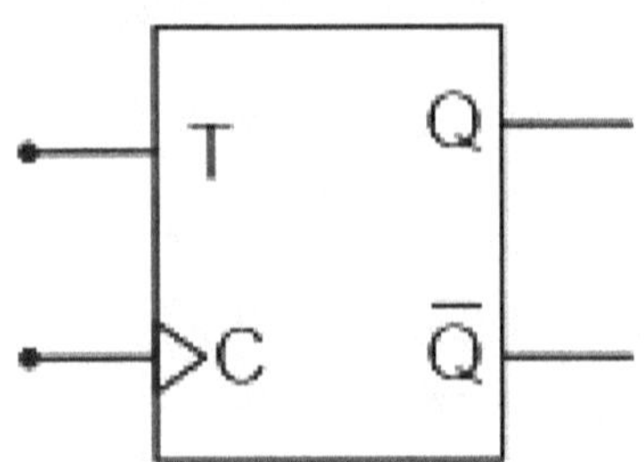

Truth table:

T	Q_n (Present state)	Q_{n+1} (Next state)
0	0	0
0	1	0
1	0	1
1	1	1

Characteristic equation: $Q_{n+1} = T\overline{Q}_n + \overline{T}Q_n$

The T flip flop may be obtained from a $J - K$ flip flop by making both the inputs are the same i.e. $J = K$.

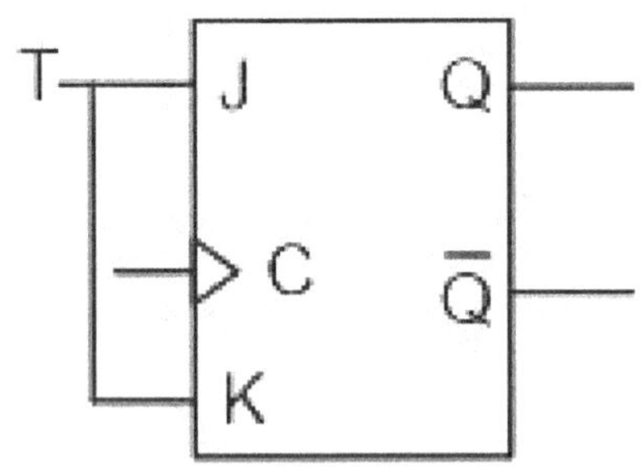

Hence, the correct option is (D).

55. XNOR gate is called coincidence gate and gives 1 if similar inputs are given to the gate and output is 0 if different inputs are given to the gate. XOR gate is called anti-coincidence gate and gives 0 if similar inputs are given to the gate and output is 1 if different inputs are given to the gate.

Hence, the correct option is (D).

56. JK flip flop:

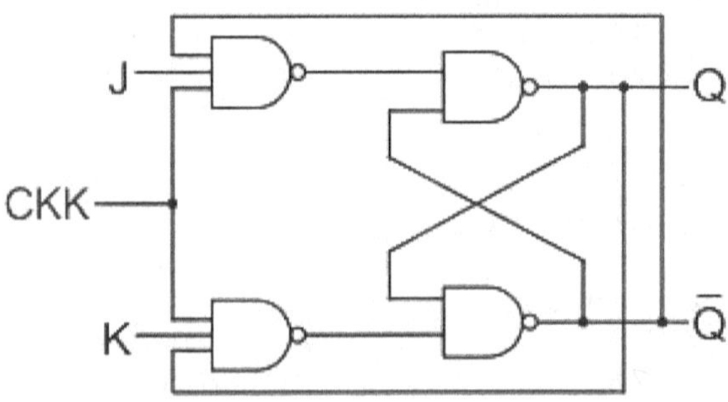

The truth table of JK flipflop:

J	K	Q	$\overline{Q}$
0	0	0	0
0	0	1	1
0	1	0	0
0	1	1	0
1	0	0	1
1	0	1	1
1	1	0	1
1	1	1	0

T flip-flop is formed by combining both J and K inputs of the JK-flipflop.

In the above truth table when $J = K = 1$, its output is toggled.

Characteristic Table of JK flip flop:

J	K	Q_n	Q_{n+1}
0	0	0	0
0	0	1	1
0	1	0	0
0	1	1	0
1	0	0	1
1	0	1	1
1	1	0	1
1	1	1	0

$$Q_{n+1} = J\bar{Q}_n + \bar{K}Q_n$$

Hence, the correct option is (D).

57. All flipflops except D-FF have input conditions that drive them in the Hold state.

However D-FF does not have such an input condition. Output always follows the input.

D	$Q(n+1) =$ D	State
0	0	Reset
1	1	Set

All flipflop truth tables are defined below:

SR flipflop:

S	R	$Q(n+1)$	State
0	0	$Q(n)$	Hold
0	1	0	Reset
1	0	1	Set
1	1	Undesirable if NOR gates used.	XX

JK flipflop:

J	K	$Q(n+1)$	State
0	0	$Q(n)$	Hold
0	1	0	Reset
1	0	1	Set
1	1	$\bar{Q}_n$	Toggle

T flipflop:

T	$Q(n+1)$	State
0	$Q(n)$	Hold
1	$\bar{Q}_n$	Toggle

Hence, the correct option is (A).

58. For a counter with 'n' flip flops:

- The total number of states $= 2^n (0$ to $2^n - 1)$
- The largest number that can be stored in the counter $= 2^n - 1$

To construct a counter with any MOD number, the minimum number flip flops required must satisfy:

Modulus $\leq 2^n$

Where, n is the number of flip - flops and is the minimum value satisfying the above condition.

Note: A MOD- n counter is also called a divide by n counter as the input frequency is divided by the number of states of the counter.

Number no. of flip – flops are required to construct mod -16 counter, must satisfy:

$$2^n \geq 16$$

The minimum value of n satisfying the above is:

$n = 4$ bits.

Hence, the correct option is (B).

59. If we pass the input signal to a single T-flip flop, we will get half of the frequency at the output.

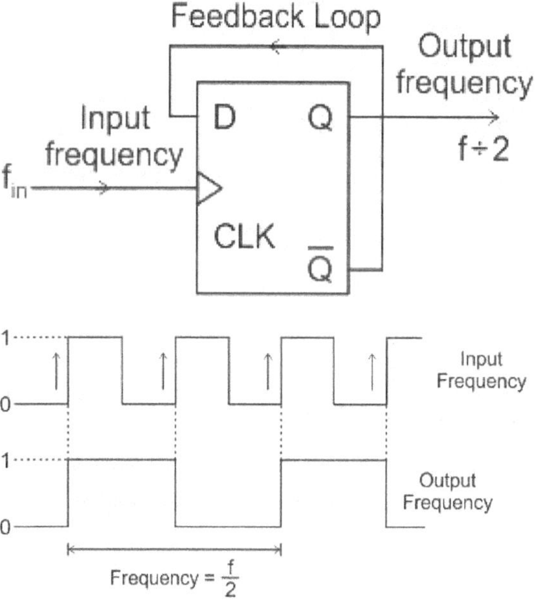

Similarly, when we pass the input signal into an n-bit flip flop counter, the output frequency (f_{out}) will be:

$$f_{out} = \frac{\text{Input Frequency}}{2^n}$$

Given Input frequency $f = 200 \, Hz$

Four T flip flops connected in cascade mode $(n=4)$

$$f_{\text{out}} = \frac{\text{Input frequency}}{2^n} = \frac{200 \, Hz}{2^4}$$

$$f_{\text{out}} = 12.5 \, Hz$$

Hence, the correct option is (D).

60. For finding the expression of Next state, a truth table needs to be constructed.

	Current State			Next State
	X	X	Q	Q_{n+1}
0	0	0	0	1
1	0	0	1	1
2	0	1	0	1
3	0	1	1	0
4	1	0	0	0
5	1	0	1	1
6	1	1	0	0
7	1	1	1	0

Equation for Q_{n+1} is made by writing all values of X, Y, Q for which $Q_{n+1} = 1$

$$Q_{n+1} = \bar{X}\bar{Y}\bar{Q} + \bar{X}\bar{Y}Q + \bar{X}Y\bar{Q} + X\bar{Y}Q$$

$$Q_{n+1} = \bar{X}\bar{Y}\left(\bar{Q} + Q\right) + \bar{X}Y\bar{Q} + X\bar{Y}Q$$

$$Q_{n+1} = \mathbf{\bar{X}\bar{Y}} + \bar{X}Y\bar{Q} + \mathbf{X\bar{Y}Q}$$

$$Q_{n+1} = \bar{Y}\left(\bar{X} + XQ\right) + \bar{X}\bar{Q}$$

$$Q_{n+1} = \bar{Y}\bar{X} + \bar{Y}Q + \bar{X}Y\bar{Q}$$

$$Q_{n+1} = \bar{X}.\bar{Y} + \bar{X}\cdot\bar{Q} + \bar{Y}Q$$

Consensus theorem: $ab + \bar{a}c + ac = ab + \bar{a}c$

In $a = \bar{Q}, b = \bar{Y}, c = \bar{Z}$

$$Q_{n+1} = \bar{X}\bar{Q} + \bar{Y}Q$$

$$Q_{n+1} = \left(\bar{X} \wedge \bar{Q}\right) \vee \left(\bar{Y} \wedge Q\right)$$

Important Point:

$\rightarrow$ AND $\rightarrow \wedge$

$+ \rightarrow$ OR $\rightarrow \vee$

Minimization could have been done using K-Map.

Hence, the correct option is (A).

61. D **flip flop:**

D flip flop has only one input terminal. The output of the D flip flop will be the same as the input. So, it is used in delay circuits.

The circuit is as shown below.

Logic symbol:

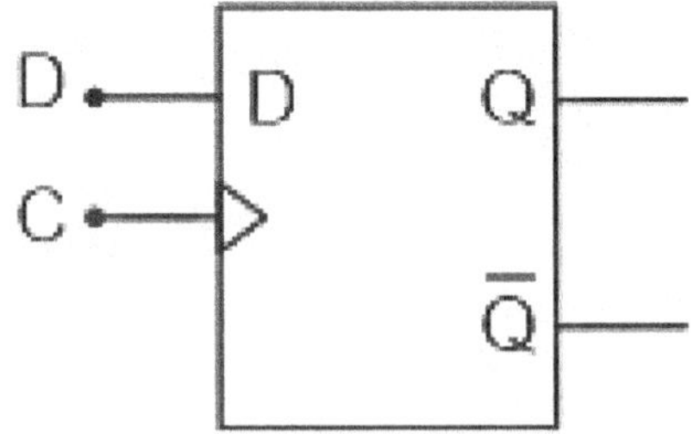

Truth table:

D	Q_n (Present state)	Q_{n+1} (Next state)
0	0	0
0	1	0
1	0	1
1	1	1

The D flip flop may be obtained from an $S - R$ flip flop by just putting one inverter between the S and R as shown in the figure below.

$$S = \bar{R}$$

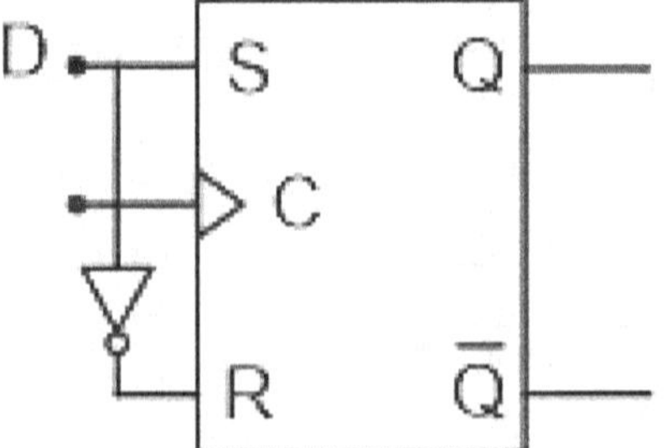

$\therefore$ The one input RS flip flop is the D flip flop.

Hence, the correct option is (B).

62. Flip-Flop:

- Flip-Flop is a data storage element. Its content changes only either at the rising or falling edge of the enabled signal (controlling clock signal). It has 2 stable states and threfore, sometimes it is referred to as a bistable-multivibrator.

- Flips-Flops are synchronous bistable devices, also known as bistable multivibrators.

- Synchronous means, output changes state only at a specified point on a triggering input called clock (CLK), which is designated as a control input.

Types:

1. S-R Flip Flop

2.   J-K Flip Flop

3.   D Flip Flop

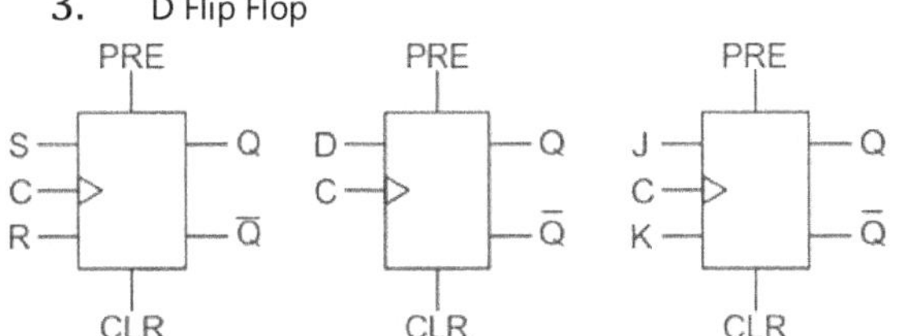

Hence, the correct option is (B).

63. Given,

A language L with alphabet $\{a\}$:

$$L = \{a\,n\,k \mid k > 0, \text{ and } n \text{ is a positive integer constant } \}$$

As we know that n is a constant and k is any positive integer. For example, if n is given as 3, then the DFA must be able to accept $3a, 6a, 9a, 12a, \dots$

To build such a DFA, we need 4 states.

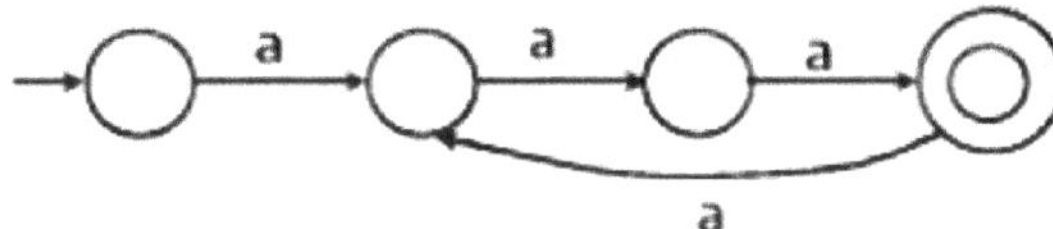

Hence, the correct option is (B).

64. Given,

L = {ab, aa, baa}

Any combination of strings in set {ab, aa, baa} will be in L*.

$1.$ "abaabaaabaa" can be partitioned as a combination of strings in set {ab, aa, baa}. The partitions are "ab aa baa ab aa".

$2.$ "aaaabaaaa" can be partitioned as a combination of strings in set {ab, aa, baa}. The partitions are "aa ab aa aa".

$3.$ "baaaaabaaaab" cannot be partitioned as a combination of strings in set {ab, aa, baa}.

$4.$ "baaaaabaa" can be partitioned as a combination of strings in set {ab, aa, baa}. The partitions are "baa aa ab aa".

Hence, the correct option is (C).

65. Inputs can be taken and can be verified. A Mealy machine is an FSM whose output depends on the present state as well as the present input. Σ is a finite set of symbols called the input alphabet. O is a finite set of symbols called the output alphabet. The output of the mealy type FSM is asynchronous it can change in response to any change in the input regardless of the clock.

So, the given Mealy machine represents 1's complement.

Hence, the correct option is (C).

66. The option (C) string ab (a+b)*ba starts with ab and ends with ba. Regular expressions are equal if and only if they correspond to the same language. Thus for example (a + b)* = (a*b*)*, because they both represent the language of all strings over the

alphabet {a, b}. A regular expression is a string representing a pattern used for matching some portion(s) of a target string. Regular expressions are very general and as a consequence, very complex with many different types of operations represented as special characters, or meta-characters.

Hence, the correct option is (C).

67. A language is regular if and only if it can be accepted by a finite automaton. This is according to the Myhill Nerode theorem, the corollary proves the given statement correct for equivalence classes. Another thing about the equivalence class is that, if x and y are two strings of the same class(here reaching the same state), and we append some strings z to then i.e, xz and yz, that will also reach to same equivalence class (either same or any other).

Hence, the correct option is (A).

68. There are two important properties for these operator precedence parsers is that it does not appear on the right side of any production and no production has two adjacent non-terminals. Implying that no production right side is empty or has two adjacent non-terminals.

Hence, the correct option is (A).

69. Relocation is the process of assigning load addresses for position-dependent code and data of a program and adjusting the code and data to reflect the assigned addresses. Some architectures avoid relocation entirely by deferring address assignment to run time; this is known as zero address arithmetic. Relocation is the process of replacing symbolic references or names of libraries with actual usable addresses in memory before running a program. Linker performs it during compilation.

Hence, the correct option is (C).

70. If a grammar has more than one leftmost (or rightmost) derivation the grammar is ambiguous. Sometimes in unambiguous grammar, the rightmost derivation and leftmost derivations may differ. A context-free grammar is called unambiguous grammar if there exists one and only one derivation tree or parse tree. In ambiguous grammar, the leftmost and rightmost derivations are not same. In unambiguous grammar, the leftmost and rightmost derivations are same.

Hence, the correct option is (A).

71. YACC technique is a computer code for the Unix operating system. It is a LALR parser generator, generating a parser, the part of a compiler that tries to make syntactic sense of the source code. YACC (yet another compiler compiler) is a grammar parser and parser generator. That is, it is a program that reads a grammar specification and generates code that is able to organize input tokens in a syntactic tree in accordance with the grammar.

Hence, the correct option is (C).

72. YACC stands for 'Yet another compiler compiler' and it was developed by Stephen Johnson in B programming language later translated to C. A YACC program consists of three sections: Declarations, Rules and Auxiliary functions. YACC can produce several output files.

Hence, the correct option is (C).

73.

Precedence of logical operators	
Operators	**Precedence**
¬ NOT	1
∧ AND	2
∨ OR	3
⇒ conditional	4
⇔ bi-conditional	5

The given predicate is,

$$P(x) = -(x = 1) \wedge \forall y$$
$$(\exists z \, (x = y^*z) \Rightarrow (y = x) \vee (y = 1))$$

If x is a prime number then $(x \neq 1$ and the only divisors of x are x and $1)$.

∴ $P(x)$ is true means x is a prime number.

Hence, the correct option is (A).

74. Given statements regarding functions f and g,

A. If go f is injective, then g is injective but f need not be.

B. If go f is surjective then both g and f are surjective.

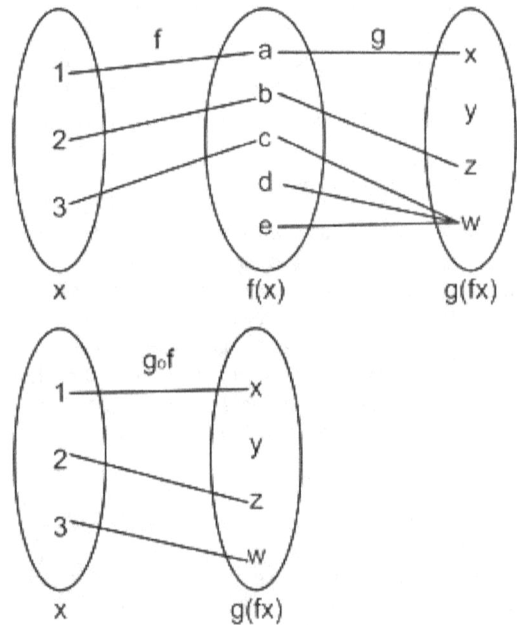

So, if go f is injective then f is injective but g need not be.

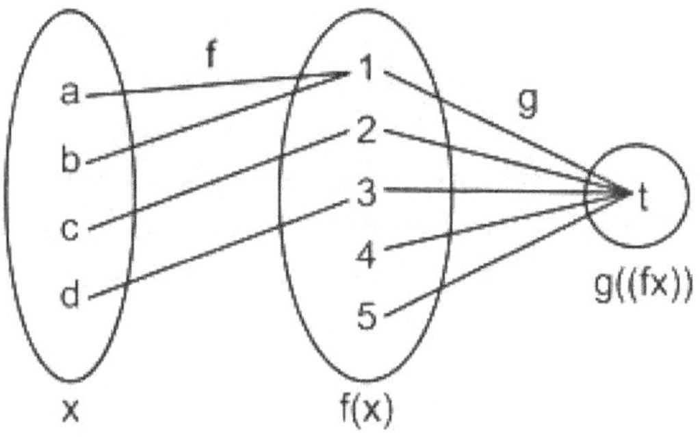

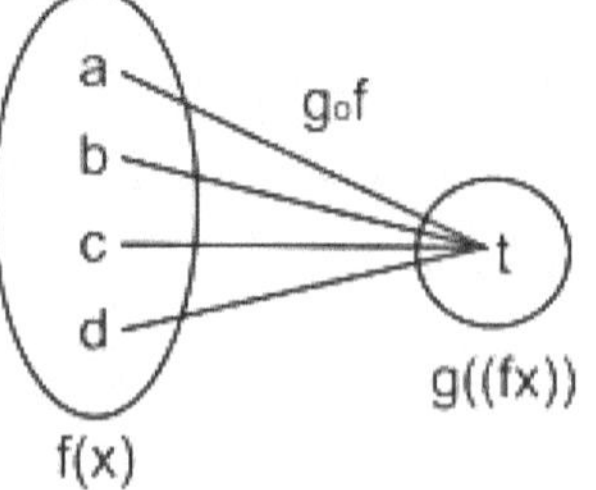

So, if go f is surjective then g has to be onto but f need not be.

Hence, the correct option is (D).

75. Given,

Let G and H be two groups.

Suppose that G and H are abelian, and that refers to:

$$(g_1, \, h_1), (g_2, \, h_2) \in G \oplus H.$$

Then, $(g_1, h_1)(g_2, h_2) = (g_1 g_2, h_1 h_2)$

$= (g_2 g_1, h_2 h_1)$ since G and H are abelian,

$= (g2, h2)(g1, h1).$

Therefore, $G \oplus H$ is abelian.

Conversely, suppose $G \oplus H$ is abelian and let $g_1, \, g_2 \in G, h_1, \, h_2 \in H.$

Then, $(g_1 g_2, h_1 h_2) = (g_1, h_1)(g_2, h_2)$

$= (g_2, h_2)(g_1, h_1)$ since $G \oplus H$ is abelian.

$= (g_2 g_1, h_2 h_1)$

Therefore, $g_1 g_2 = g_2 g_1$, and G is abelian, and $h_1 h_2 = h_2 h_1$, so H is abelian.

Hence, the correct option is (D).

76. The connected graph without cycle means it's a tree which is a bipartite graph. Every tree we can divide into two groups such that no two vertices in a group share an edge. Suppose we have done that and we have two groups-A and B.

Now, from 5 colors we can select 2 different colors in $^5C_2$ ways. Suppose we selected Red and Blue.

We have two ways to assign R and B to these 2 groups.

A-Red, B-Blue

A-Blue, B-Red

A tree is a bipartite graph, which is two colorable:

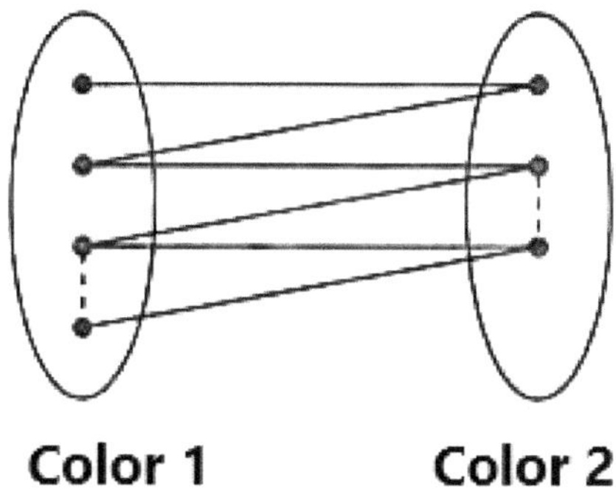

Total ways $= 5_{C_2} \times 2 = 20$

Hence, the correct option is (A).

77. It is given exactly 4 zero it means we have 6 1's which can be arranged in any order, therefore, $1!$ (since all 1 are identical).

First place all the 1's as given below:

1- 1- 1- 1- 1- 1-

After placing the six 1's, we have 7 places to arrange four 0's such that no two 0's are consecutive.

Now, we can choose four places out of seven for putting 0's.

Therefore total binary string $= 1! \times {}^7C_4 = 35$

Hence, the correct option is (A).

78. Given,

There are six movie parts numbered from 1 to 6.

The total number of ways in which 6-part can be arranged $= 6!$

$= 6 \times 5 \times 4 \times 3 \times 2 \times 1$

$= 720$

The total number of ways in which part- 1 and part- 3 are always together:

$= 5! \times 2!$.

$= 240$

Therefore, the total number of arrangements, in which they are not together is $= 720 - 240$

$= 480$

Hence, the correct option is (B).

79. A set is called lattice if every finite subset has a least upper bound and greatest lower bound. It is termed as a complete lattice if every subset has a least upper bound and greatest lower bound. As every subset of this will not have LUB and GLB so $(N, |)$ is a lattice but not a complete lattice.

Hence, the correct option is (D).

80. Consider any sequence like a " $45,8,7,2$", it can have many (infinite) least upper bounds like " $45,8,7,2,5$," " $45,8,7,2,1$" and so on but it can have only 1 greatest lower bound " $45,8,7$" because we are using the prefix relation. So, every non-empty subset has a greatest lower bound.

Hence, the correct option is (A).

81. The free semi-lattice is defined to consist of all of the finite subsets of X, with the semi-lattice operation given by ordinary set union. The free semi-lattice has the **universal property.**

The universal morphism is:

(FX, η)

Where η is the unit map η: X → FX which takes x ∈ X to the singleton set {x}.

Any set X may be used to generate the free semi-lattice FX.

Hence, the correct option is (D).

82. Agile software development is based on incremental development and iterative development. Scrum and agile are incremental development and iterative development. They are iterative in that they plan for the work of one iteration to be improved upon in subsequent iterations. They are incremental because completed work is delivered throughout the project.

Hence, the correct option is (D).

83. A plan-driven approach to software engineering is based around separate development stages with the outputs to be produced at each of these stages planned in advance. The process involves translating user needs into software requirements, transforming the software requirements into design, implementing the design in code, testing the code, and sometimes installing and checking out the software for operational use.

Hence, the correct option is (C).

84. The scrum models have 5 steps also called phases in the scrum.

$1.$ **Initiate:** This phase includes the processes related to the initiation of a project: Create Project Vision, Identify Scrum Master and Stakeholder(s), Form Scrum Team, Develop Epic(s), Create Prioritized Product Backlog, and Conduct Release Planning.

$2.$ **Plan and Estimate:** This phase consists of processes related to planning and estimating tasks, which include Create User Stories, Approve, Estimate, and Commit User Stories, Create Tasks, Estimate Tasks, and Create Sprint Backlog.

3. Implement: This phase is related to the execution of the tasks and activities to create a project's product. These activities include creating the various deliverables, conducting Daily Standup Meetings, and grooming (i.e., reviewing, fine-tuning, and regularly updating) the Product Backlog at regular intervals.

4. Review and Retrospect: This phase is concerned with reviewing the deliverables and the work that has been done and determining ways to improve the practices and methods used to do project work.

5. Release: This phase emphasizes on delivering the Accepted Deliverables to the customer and identifying, documenting, and internalizing the lessons learned during the project.

Hence, the correct option is (B).

85. Agile scrum methodology is a style of project management that emphasizes incremental progress. Each iteration is divided into two to four-week sprints, with the goal of completing the most important features first and delivering a possibly deliverable product at the end of each sprint.

Hence, the correct option is (A).

86. Logical data flow diagram (Logical DFD) mainly focuses on the system process. It illustrates how data flows in the system. Logical DFD is used in various organizations for the smooth running of system. Like in a Banking software system, it is used to describe how data is moved from one entity to another.

Hence, the correct option is (B).

87. Requirement elicitation, Requirement analysis, Requirement documentation and Requirement review are the four crucial process steps of requirement engineering. Design is in itself a different phase of software engineering.

Hence, the correct option is (B).

88. Top-down integration is a type of incremental integration testing approach in which testing is done by integrating or joining two or more modules by moving down from top to bottom through control flow of architecture structure. In these, high-level modules are tested first, and then low-level modules are tested.

Hence, the correct option is (B).

89. Security testing involves testing a software in order to identify any flaws and gaps from security and vulnerability point of view. Security testing is a type of software testing that uncovers vulnerabilities of the system and determines that the data and resources of the system are protected from possible intruders. It ensures that the software system and application are free from any threats or risks that can cause a loss.

Hence, the correct option is (D).

90. Risk management is an entirely different domain. These potential issues might harm cost, schedule or technical success of the project and the quality of our software device, or project team morale. Risk Management is the system of identifying addressing and eliminating these problems before they can damage the project. It is not a Software Configuration Management Activity.

Hence, the correct option is (B).

91. Given,

Probability of guessing the correct answer $= \dfrac{x}{12}$

Probability of not guessing the correct answer $= \dfrac{2}{3}$

We know that,

Probability of occurrence of an event $= 1 -$ Probability of not happening of the same event.

$$\Rightarrow \frac{x}{12} = 1 - \frac{2}{3}$$

$$\Rightarrow \frac{x}{12} = \frac{1}{3}$$

$$\Rightarrow x = \frac{12}{3}$$

$$\Rightarrow x = 4$$

$$\therefore x = 4$$

Hence, the correct option is (C).

92. Total number of letters in word GUITARIST $= 9$

Number of all combinations of n things, taken r at a time, is given by $^nC_r = \dfrac{n!}{(r)!(n-r)!}$

Total ways of two letters at randomly chosen $n(S) = {}^9C_2$

$$= \frac{9!}{2!7!}$$

$$= \frac{9 \times 8}{2 \times 1}$$

$$= 36$$

Possible opportunities in which one letter is T and one is R,

$$\Rightarrow n(E) = {}^2C_1 \times {}^1C_1$$

$$= \frac{2!}{1!1!} \times \frac{1!}{1!0!}$$

$$= 2 \times 1$$

$$= 2$$

$$\Rightarrow n(E) = 2$$

Required probability $(P(E)) = \dfrac{n(E)}{n(S)}$

$$= \frac{2}{36}$$

$$= \frac{1}{18}$$

Hence, the correct option is (A).

93. Given,

$$x^2 \frac{dy}{dx} = x^2 + xy + y^2$$

$$\Rightarrow \frac{dy}{dx} = 1 + \frac{y}{x} + \left(\frac{y}{x}\right)^2 \ldots (i)$$

Substituting, $\frac{y}{x} = v$

$$\Rightarrow y = vx$$

Then,

Differentiate with respect to x, we get,

$$\frac{dy}{dx} = v \times x \frac{dv}{dx} + x \times v \frac{d}{dx}$$

$$\Rightarrow \frac{dy}{dx} = v + x \frac{dv}{dx}$$

Now, putting these values in equation (i),

We get,

$$\Rightarrow v + x \frac{dv}{dx} = 1 + v + v^2$$

$$\Rightarrow x \frac{dv}{dx} = 1 + v^2$$

$$\Rightarrow \frac{dx}{x} = \frac{dv}{1+v^2}$$

On integrating both sides we get,

$$\Rightarrow \int \frac{dx}{x} = \int \frac{dv}{1+v^2}$$

$$\Rightarrow \log x = \tan^{-1} v + c, c = \text{constant of integration}$$

Putting the value of v we get,

$$\therefore \log x = \tan^{-1} \frac{y}{x} + c$$

Hence, the correct option is (A).

94. We know that,

$$\int \frac{dx}{\sqrt{a^2 - x^2}} = \sin^{-1} \frac{x}{a}$$

Now,

$$dy = \sqrt{1 - y^2}\, dx$$

$$\Rightarrow \frac{dy}{\sqrt{1^2 - y^2}} = dx$$

Integrating both sides, we get

$$\Rightarrow \int \frac{dy}{\sqrt{1^2 - y^2}} = \int dx$$

$$\Rightarrow \sin^{-1}(y) = x + c$$

$$= y = \sin(x + c)$$

Hence, the correct option is (B).

95. Some pairs of Laplace transforms are given below.

$$e^{-at} \leftrightarrow \frac{1}{s+a}$$

$$t^n e^{-at} \leftrightarrow \frac{n!}{(s+a)^{n+1}}$$

Given,

$$H(s) = \frac{s+3}{s^2 + 2s + 1}$$

$$\Rightarrow \frac{s+3}{(s+1)^2} = \frac{s+1}{(s+1)^2} + \frac{2}{(s+1)^2}$$

$$\Rightarrow \frac{1}{(s+1)} + \frac{2}{(s+1)^2}$$

By applying inverse Laplace transform:

$$= H(t) = e^{-t} + 2te^{-t}$$

Hence, the correct option is (C).

96. $L\{f(t)\} = F(s) = \int_0^\infty f(t) \cdot e^{-st} dt$

According to the property of Laplace,

$$L\{t^n \cdot f(t)\} = (-1)^n \times \frac{d^n}{ds^n} \{F(s)\} f(t) = 3t^4 = t^4 \cdot 3$$

$$L(3) = 3 \int_0^\infty e^{-st} dt = \frac{3}{s} [e^{-st}]_0^\infty = \frac{3}{s}$$

Now,

$$L\{t^4 . 3\} = (-1)^4 \times \frac{d^4}{ds^4} \left(\frac{3}{s}\right)$$

$$L\{t^4 . 3\} = 3 \times \frac{4!}{s^5} = \frac{72}{s^5}$$

You can also solve it directly by using:

$$L(t^n) = \frac{n!}{s^{n+1}}$$

Hence, the correct option is (C).

97. System of equations,

$$a_1 x + b_1 y = c_1$$

$$a_2 x + b_2 y = c_2$$

For unique solution,

$$\frac{a_1}{a_2} \neq \frac{b_1}{b_2}$$

For Infinite solution,

$$\frac{a_1}{a_2} = \frac{b_1}{b_2} = \frac{c_1}{c_2}$$

For no solution,

$$\frac{a_1}{a_2} = \frac{b_1}{b_2} \neq \frac{c_1}{c_2}$$

Given,

$$3x - y = -3$$

$$3x - y = -5$$

$a_1 = 3, b_1 = -1$ and $c_1 = -3$

$a_2 = 3, b_2 = -1$ and $c_2 = -5$

$$\frac{3}{3} = \frac{-1}{-1} \neq \frac{-3}{-5}$$

So, this shows that the number of solutions for given simultaneous algebraic equations is 0.

Hence, the correct option is (A).

98. If A is any square matrix of order n, we can form the matrix $[A - \lambda]$, where I is the nth order unit matrix. The determinant of this matrix equated to zero i.e. $|A - \lambda I| = 0$ is called the characteristic equation of A.

The roots of the characteristic equation are called Eigenvalues or latent roots or characteristic roots of matrix A.

Eigenvector (X) that corresponding to Eigenvalue (λ) satisfies the equation $AX = \lambda X$.

Properties of Eigenvalues:

The sum of Eigenvalues of a matrix A is equal to the trace of that matrix A.

The product of Eigenvalues of a matrix A is equal to the determinant of that matrix A.

Let $A = \begin{bmatrix} 1 & 2 \\ 0 & 2 \end{bmatrix}$

$|A - \lambda I| = 0$

$\Rightarrow \begin{vmatrix} 1 - \lambda & 2 \\ 0 & 2 - \lambda \end{vmatrix} = 0$

$\Rightarrow (1 - \lambda)(2 - \lambda) = 0$

$\Rightarrow \lambda = 1, 2$

Given,

Eigenvectors are: $\begin{bmatrix} 1 \\ a \end{bmatrix}$ and $\begin{bmatrix} 1 \\ b \end{bmatrix}$

For $\lambda = 1$, let the Eigenvector is $\begin{bmatrix} 1 \\ a \end{bmatrix}$

$\Rightarrow \begin{bmatrix} 1 & 2 \\ 0 & 2 \end{bmatrix} \begin{bmatrix} 1 \\ a \end{bmatrix} = 1 \begin{bmatrix} 1 \\ a \end{bmatrix}$

$\Rightarrow \begin{bmatrix} 1 + 2a \\ 2a \end{bmatrix} = \begin{bmatrix} 1 \\ a \end{bmatrix}$

$\Rightarrow a = 0$

For $\lambda = 2$, let the Eigenvector is $\begin{bmatrix} 1 \\ b \end{bmatrix}$

$\begin{bmatrix} 1 & 2 \\ 0 & 2 \end{bmatrix} \begin{bmatrix} 1 \\ b \end{bmatrix} = 2 \begin{bmatrix} 1 \\ b \end{bmatrix}$

$\Rightarrow \begin{bmatrix} 1 + 2b \\ 2b \end{bmatrix} = \begin{bmatrix} 2 \\ 2b \end{bmatrix}$

$\Rightarrow b = \frac{1}{2}$

Now, $a + b = \frac{1}{2}$

Hence, the correct option is (B).

99. Let, $I = \int_0^{\frac{\pi}{2}} \frac{\tan^7 x}{\cot^7 x + \tan^7 x} dx \dots (1)$

As we know,

$$\int_0^a f(x) dx = \int_0^a f(a - x) dx$$

$$\tan\left(\frac{\pi}{2} - x\right) = \cot x$$

$$\cot\left(\frac{\pi}{2} - x\right) = \tan x$$

So, similarly

$$I = \int_0^{\frac{\pi}{2}} \frac{\tan^7\left(\frac{\pi}{2} - x\right)}{\cot^7\left(\frac{\pi}{2} - x\right) + \tan^7\left(\frac{\pi}{2} - x\right)}$$

$$I = \int_0^{\frac{\pi}{2}} \frac{\cot^7 x}{\cot^7 x + \tan^7 x} dx \dots (2)$$

Thus equation (1) and equation (2), we get

$$I = \int_0^{\frac{\pi}{2}} \frac{\tan^7 x + \cot^7 x}{\cot^7 x + \tan^7 x} dx$$

$$\Rightarrow 2I = \int_0^{\frac{\pi}{2}} dx$$

$$\Rightarrow 2I = \int_0^{\frac{\pi}{2}} dx$$

$$\Rightarrow 2I = [x]_0^{\frac{\pi}{2}}$$

$$\Rightarrow 2I = \frac{\pi}{2} - 0$$

$$\therefore I = \frac{\pi}{4}$$

Hence, the correct option is (B).

100. Given:

$$\int \frac{\cot x}{1 + \sin^2 x} dx$$

$$\int \frac{\cos x}{\sin x (1 + \sin^2 x)} dx \dots \text{(i)}$$

$$\sin x = t, \cos x \, dx = dt$$

Put the values in (i),

$$\int \frac{dt}{t(1 + t^2)} dt$$

$$\because \frac{1}{t(1 + t^2)} = \frac{1}{t} - \frac{t}{1 + t^2}$$

$$\int \left(\frac{1}{t} - \frac{t}{1+t^2}\right) dt$$

$$\int \frac{dt}{t} - \frac{1}{2}\int 2\frac{t\,dt}{1+t^2}$$

$$\ln t + \frac{1}{2}\ln(1+t^2) + c \text{ ... (ii)}$$

Put the values of t in (ii),

$$\ln \sin x - \ln(1 + \sin^2 x)^{\frac{1}{1}} + c$$

$$\ln \frac{\sin x}{\sqrt{1+\sin^2 x}} + c$$

Hence, the correct option is (C).

Q.1 How many bits are needed to encode a string containing $14\ a's, 3\ b's, 6\ c's$ and $10\ d's$ using Huffman coding?

A. 61   **B.** 45   **C.** 59   **D.** 62

Q.2 Consider the following undirected graph with edge weights as shown:

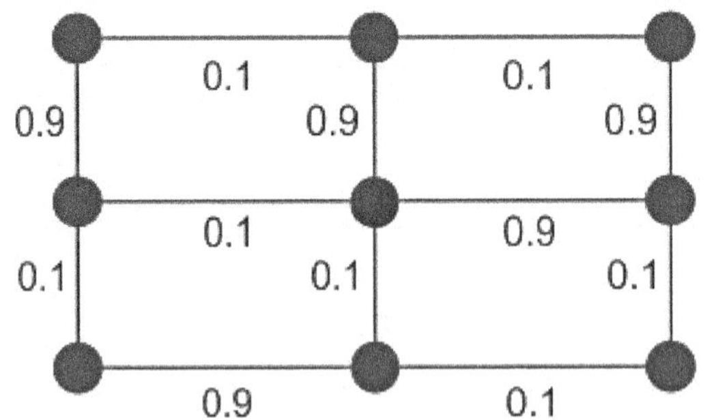

The number of minimum-weight spanning trees of the graph is _________.

A. 3   **B.** 4   **C.** 5   **D.** 2

Q.3 Let $f(n) = n$ and $g(n) = n^{(1+\sin n)}$, where n is a positive integer. Which of the following statements is/are correct?

I. $f(n) = O\big(g(n)\big)$

II. $f(n) = \Omega\big(g(n)\big)$

A. Only I   **B.** Only II

C. Both I and II   **D.** Neither I nor II

Q.4 What is the time complexity of the following code snippet? Assume "Statement" takes O(1) time:

```
int x=0;
int A(n)
{
Statement;
if(n==1){return(1);
}
else
{
x+=4A(n/2)+n²
return(x);
}
}
```

A. $\theta(n^2 \cdot \log n)$ **B.** $\theta(\log n)$

C. $\theta(n^2)$ **D.** $\theta(n \log n)$

Q.5 Assuming P ≠ NP, which of the following is true?

A. NP-complete = NP

B. NP-complete ∩ P = Φ

C. NP-hard = NP

D. P = NP- complete

Q.6 If 4 is the GCD of 16 and 12. What is the GCD of 12 and 4?

A. 12   **B.** 6   **C.** 4   **D.** 2

Q.7 Which of the following is not an application of Euclid's algorithm?

A. Simplification of fractions

B. Performing divisions in modular arithmetic

C. Solving quadratic equations

D. Solving diophantine equations

Q.8 Consider an algorithm that takes $O(N)$ time in the initialization part and in the main part for each input; a function will be called whose time complexity is $O(N\log N)$. What will be the overall time complexity of the above algorithm?

A. $N^2\log N + N$ **B.** $N\log N + N$

C. $N\log N$ **D.** N^2

Q.9 Let $M1, M2,$ and $M3$ be three matrices of dimensions $12 \times 9, 9 \times 15, 15 \times 10$ respectively. The minimum number of scalar multiplications required to find the product $M1, M2, M3$ using the basic matrix multiplication method is _________.

A. 2430   **B.** 2435   **C.** 2530   **D.** 2630

Q.10 If there is an abstract method in a class then, _____________.

A. Class must be abstract class

B. Class may or may not be abstract class

C. Class is generic

D. Class must be public

Q.11 Which two features of object-oriented programming are the same?

A. Abstraction and Polymorphism features are the same.

B. Inheritance and Encapsulation features are the same.

C. Encapsulation and Polymorphism features are the same.

D. Encapsulation and Abstraction.

Q.12 While working on a JavaScript project, in your JavaScript application, which function would you use to send messages to users requesting for text input?

A. display()   **B.** prompt()

C. alert()   **D.** getInput()

Q.13 The number of rotations required to insert a sequence of elements $9,6,5,8,7,10$ into an empty AVL tree is?

A. 0   **B.** 1   **C.** 2   **D.** 3

Q.14 A Borland Turbo Assembler is ________.

A. Nasm   **B.** Tasm   **C.** Gas   **D.** Asm

Q.15 In the worst case, the number of comparisons needed to search a singly linked list of length n for a given element is?

A. $\log 2n$ **B.** $\frac{n}{2}$

C. $\log 2n - 1$ **D.** n

Q.16 Consider yourself to be on a planet where the computational power of chips is slow. You have an array of size 10. You want to perform enqueue some elements into this array. But you can perform only push and pop operations. Push and pop operations both take 1 second respectively. The total time required to perform enqueue operation is:

A. 20   **B.** 40   **C.** 42   **D.** 43

Q.17 You have two jars, one jar which has 10 rings and the other has none. They are placed one above the other. You want to remove the last ring in the jar. And the second jar is weak and cannot be used to store rings for a long time.

A. Empty the first jar by removing it one by one from the first jar and placing it into the second jar.

B. Empty the first jar by removing it one by one from the first jar and placing it into the second jar and empty the second jar by placing all the rings into the first jar one by one.

C. There exists no possible way to do this.

D. Break the jar and remove the last one.

Q.18 The result of the postfix expression $53 * 9 + 6/84/+$ is ______.

A. 8   **B.** 6   **C.** 10   **D.** 9

Q.19 Many cables have "RS-232" connectors with some wires crossed or connected to each other because ______.

A. There are various RS-232 standards.

B. Many computers and peripherals use RS-232 serial interfaces, but not as DTE-to-DCE.

C. Asynchronous modem reverses the direction of transmitted and received data from the standar.

D. None of these

Q.20 Extended command sets supported by modern modems:

A. Are standardized.

B. Are prefixed with the letter E.

C. Use different commands to control many advanced modem features.

D. Can be counted on to provide a high-speed data transfer capability without requiring flow control.

Q.21 In CRC if the data unit is 100111001 and the divisor is 1011 then what is dividend at the receiver?

A. 100111001101   **B.** 100111001011

C. 100111001   **D.** 100111001110

Q.22 Mostly ______ is used in wireless LAN.

A. Time division multiplexing

B. Orthogonal frequency division multiplexing

C. Space division multiplexing

D. None of these

Q.23 What is required in the wireless ad-hoc network?

A. Access point is not required

B. The access point is a must

C. Nodes are not required

D. None of these

Q.24 The _________ is a collection of protocols designed by the Internet Engineering Task Force (IETF) to provide security for a packet at the Network level.

A. IPsec   **B.** Netsec

C. Packetsec   **D.** Protocolsec

Q.25 Loopback address __________ of IPv 6 address is equivalent to the IPv 4 loopback address $127.0.0.1$.

A. $(::1)$ **B.** $(::)$ **C.** $(::0)$ **D.** $(1::)$

Q.26 HBA stands for:

A. Host bus adapters

B. Host base adapters

C. Hedged base adapters

D. None of these

Q.27 In OSI network architecture, dialogue control and token management are the responsibility of:

A. Session layer   **B.** Network layer

C. Transport layer   **D.** Data link layer

Q.28 In semantic nets, to find relationships among objects are determined by spreading activation out from each of 2 nodes and identifying where the activation meets. This process is called:

A. Associative Search   **B.** Object Search

C. Knowledge Search   **D.** Intersection Search

Q.29 How are the bits of the register PSW affected if we select bank 2 of 8051?

A. $PSW.5 = 0$ and $PSW.4 = 1$

B. $PSW.2 = 0$ and $PSW.3 = 1$

C. $PSW.3 = 1$ and $PSW.4 = 1$

D. $PSW.3 = 0$ and $PSW.4 = 1$

Q.30 If we push data onto the stack then the stack pointer:

A. Increases with every push

B. Decreases with every push

C. Both (A) and (B)

D. None of these

Q.31 A non-pipelined CPU has 12 general purpose registers $(R0, R1, R2, \ldots, R12)$. Following operations are supported:

ADD Ra, Rb, Rr	Add Ra to Rb and store the result in Rr
MUL Ra, Rb, Rr	Multiply Ra to Rb and store the result in Rr

MUL operations takes two clock cycles, ADD takes one clock cycle.

Calculate a minimum number of clock cycles required to compute the value of the expression $XY + XYZ + YZ$. The variables X, Y, Z are initially available in registers $R0, R1$ and $R2$ and contents of these registers must not be modified.

A. 5   **B.** 6   **C.** 7   **D.** 8

Q.32 Which of the following is an application of RISC architecture by adding more instructions?

A. Multimedia applications

B. Telecommunication encoding

C. Image conversion

D. All of these

Q.33 How is expanded memory accessed in 80286?

A. Paging

B. Interleaving

C. RAM

D. External storage

Q.34 In $X = \dfrac{(M+N \times O)}{(P \times Q)}$, how many one-address instructions are required to evaluate it?

A. 4　　**B.** 6　　**C.** 8　　**D.** 10

Q.35 The number of clockcycles that take to wait until the length of the instruction is known in order to start decoding is __________.

A. 0　　**B.** 1　　**C.** 2　　**D.** 3

Q.36 The disadvantage of CISC design processors is:

A. It has a low burden on compiler developers.

B. It has a wide availability of existing software.

C. It is complex in nature.

D. None of these

Q.37 The errors that can be pointed out by the compiler are:

A. Syntax errors

B. Internal errors

C. Sematic errors

D. Logical errors

Q.38 In which one of the following, the multiple lower entities are grouped (or combined) together to form a single higher-level entity?

A. Specialization

B. Generalization

C. Aggregation

D. Transaction

Q.39 In a relation database, every tuples divided into the fields are known as the __________.

A. Queries

B. Domains

C. Relations

D. Commit

Q.40 The term "TCL" stands for __________.

A. Ternary Control Language

B. Transmission Control Language

C. Transaction Central Language

D. Transaction Control Language

Q.41 In the relational table, which of the following can also be represented by the term "attribute"?

A. Entity　　**B.** Row　　**C.** Column　　**D.** Degree

Q.42 In the relation model, the relation are generally termed as __________.

A. Tuples

B. Attributes

C. Rows

D. Tables

Q.43 Which of the following is an explicit numeric, character, string, or boolean value not represented by an identifier?

A. Delimiters

B. Literals

C. Comments

D. None of these

Q.44 How to select all data from student table starting the name from letter 'r'?

A. SELECT * FROM student WHERE name LIKE 'r%';

B. SELECT * FROM student WHERE name LIKE '%r%';

C. SELECT * FROM student WHERE name LIKE '%r';

D. SELECT * FROM student WHERE name LIKE '_r%';

Q.45 What operator tests column for the absence of data?

A. EXISTS operator

B. NOT operator

C. IS NULL operator

D. None of these

Q.46 What is true about Apache Flume?

A. Apache Flume is a reliable and distributed system for collecting, aggregating and moving massive quantities of log data.

B. It has a simple yet flexible architecture based on streaming data flows.

C. Apache Flume is used to collect log data present in log files from web servers and aggregating it into HDFS for analysis.

D. All of these

Q.47 What is multiprogramming?

A. Is a method of memory allocation by which the program is subdivided into equal portions, or pages and core is subdivided into equal portions or blocks.

B. Consists of those addresses that may be generated by a processor during execution of a computation.

C. Is a method of allocating processor time.

D. Allows multiple programs to reside in separate areas of the core at the time.

Q.48 If a process fails, most operating system write the error information to a __________.

A. New file

B. Another running process

C. Log file

D. None of these

Q.49 In operating system, each process has its own __________.

A. Open files

B. Pending alarms, signals, and signal handlers

C. Address space and global variables

D. All of these

Q.50 The state transition initiated by the user process itself in an operating system is:

A. Block

B. Dispatch

C. Wake up

D. Timer run out

Q.51 Which of the following operating system runs on the server?

A. Batch operating system

B. Distributed operating system

C. Real-time operating system

D. Network operating system

Q.52 SSTF stands for __________.

A. Shortest Signal Time First

B. Shortest Seek Time First
C. System Seek Time First
D. System Shortest Time First

Q.53 What type of memory stores data in a swap file on a hard drive?

A. Secondary memory   **B.** Virtual memory
C. Low memory   **D.** RAM

Q.54 Which one of the following is false?

A. Kernel remains in the memory during the entire computer session.

B. Kernel is made of various modules which can not be loaded in running operating system.

C. Kernel is the first part of the operating system to load into memory during booting.

D. Kernel is the program that constitutes the central core of the operating system.

Q.55 The process is in a "Blocked" state waiting for some I/O service. Then, the service is completed, it goes to the _________.

A. Terminated state   **B.** Suspended state
C. Running state   **D.** Ready state

Q.56 How many strings of length less than 4 contains the language described by the regular expression

$(x + y)^*y(a + ab)^*?$

A. 7   **B.** 10   **C.** 12   **D.** 11

Q.57 Backtracking is allowed in:

A. NDFA   **B.** DFA
C. Both (A) and (B)   **D.** None of these

Q.58 Given,

$S \rightarrow aSb$

$S \rightarrow e$

$S \rightarrow A$

$A \rightarrow aA$

$C \rightarrow D$

The ratio of number of useless variables to number of useless production is:

A. 1   **B.** $\frac{3}{4}$ **C.** $\frac{2}{3}$ **D.** 0

Q.59 Let $L = L_1 \cap L_2$, where L_1 and L_2 are languages as defined below:

$L_1 = \{a^m b^m c a^n b^n \mid m, n >= 0\}$

$L_2 = \{a^i b^j c^k \mid i, j, k >= 0\}$

Then L is:

A. Not recursive
B. Regular
C. Context free but not regular
D. Recursively enumerable but not context free

Q.60 Which of the following grammar rules violate the requirements of an operator grammar?

(i) $P \rightarrow QR$

(ii) $P \rightarrow QsR$

(iii) $P \rightarrow \varepsilon$

(iv) $P \rightarrow QtRr$

A. (i) only   **B.** (i) and (iii) only
C. (ii) and (iii) only   **D.** (iii) and (iv) only

Q.61 Consider a program P that consists of two source modules $M1$(contains reference to a function defined in $M2$) and $M2$ contained in two different files:

A. Edit time   **B.** Compile time
C. Link time   **D.** Load time

Q.62 The ______ table is created by YACC.

A. LALR parsing   **B.** LL parsing
C. GLR parsing   **D.** None of these

Q.63 Which of the following is false for B programming language?

A. Typeless
B. Influenced by PL/I
C. Designed by Dennis Ritchie
D. None of these

Q.64 The cable connecting a DB- 9 connector at one end to a DB- 25 connector at the other end must cross-connect pin 8 at the BD- 9 side to which pin at the DB- 25 side:

A. 4   **B.** 22   **C.** 5   **D.** 2

Q.65 What are the types of requirement in Quality Function Deployment (QFD)?

A. Known, Unknown, Undreamed
B. User, Developer
C. Functional, Non-Functional
D. Normal, Expected, Exciting

Q.66 Why is Requirements Elicitation a difficult task?

A. Problem of scope
B. Problem of understanding
C. Problem of volatility
D. All of these

Q.67 What is the major drawback of CORE?

A. Requirements are comprehensive
B. NFRs are not given enough importance
C. Role of analyst is passive
D. All of these

Q.68 How many type of cohesion are there in software design?

A. Five   **B.** Six   **C.** Seven   **D.** Eight

Q.69 Which of the following tool is used for structured designing?

A. Program Chart   **B.** Structure chart
C. Module Chart   **D.** All of these

Q.70 The activity that distributes estimated effort across the planned project duration by allocating the effort to specific software developing tasks is _________.

A. Project scheduling
B. Detailed schedule
C. Macroscopic schedule
D. None of these

Q.71 Where does the Case tool is used?
A. Project management
B. Schema generation
C. Data modeling
D. All of these

Q.72 Which of the following model in system modelling depicts the dynamic behaviour of the system?
A. Behavioral Model
B. Context Model
C. Structural Model
D. Object Model

Q.73 What is the defect rate for Six Sigma?
A. 1.0 defect per million lines of code.
B. 1.4 defect per million lines of code.
C. 3.0 defect per million lines of code.
D. 3.4 defect per million lines of code.

Q.74 A box contains 10 reds, 9 green and some blue balls. Find the probability of getting three different coloured balls when 3 balls are drawn from box at random if total number of balls in the box is 36:
A. $\frac{1}{15}$
B. $\frac{5}{27}$
C. $\frac{9}{14}$
D. $\frac{3}{14}$

Q.75 A box contains 100 round discs, 50 square - shaped discs and 30 triangular discs. All the discs are made up of iron and have an equal probability of getting attracted by a magnet. If a magnet which can attract only one disc in one pass and the disc is passed over them twice. What is the probability that both times a triangular disc is attracted? The disc attracted in one pass does not fall into box again, however each time a square shaped disc is kept into the box:
A. $\frac{29}{180}$
B. $\frac{29}{1074}$
C. $\frac{1}{36}$
D. $\frac{29}{1080}$

Q.76 Consider the following differential equation: $\frac{dy}{dt} = -5y;$

Initial condition: $y = 2$ at $t = 0$

The value of y at $t = 3$ is:
A. $-5e^{-10}$
B. $2e^{-10}$
C. $2e^{-15}$
D. $-15e^2$

Q.77 General solution of $(x^2 + y^2)dx - 2xy\,dy = 0$ is:
A. $y^2 + x^2 = cx^2$
B. $x^2 - y^2 = cx$
C. $x^2 = cx(x^2 - y^2)$
D. None of these

Q.78 The inverse Laplace transform of $\frac{1}{(s+1)(s-2)}$ is:
A. $\frac{e^{2t}+e^t}{3}$
B. $\frac{e^{2t}+e^{-t}}{3}$
C. $\frac{e^{2t}-e^t}{3}$
D. $e^{-2t} - e^t$

Q.79 If $f(t)$ is a function defined for all $t \geq 0$, its Laplace transform $F(s)$ is defined as:
A. $\int_0^\infty e^{st} f(t)dt$
B. $\int_0^\infty e^{-st} f(t)dt$
C. $\int_0^\infty e^{ist} f(t)dt$
D. $\int_0^\infty e^{-ist} f(t)dt$

Q.80 Find the eigenvalues of the 2×2 matrix $A = \begin{bmatrix} 0 & -2 \\ 3 & 4 \end{bmatrix}$:
A. $\begin{bmatrix} -1 \\ 1 \end{bmatrix}$
B. $\begin{bmatrix} -2 \\ 9 \end{bmatrix}$
C. $\begin{bmatrix} 2 \\ -1 \end{bmatrix}$
D. $\begin{bmatrix} 0 \\ 4 \end{bmatrix}$

Q.81 If $A = \begin{bmatrix} 2 & -0.1 \\ 0 & 3 \end{bmatrix} A^{-1} = \begin{bmatrix} \frac{1}{2} & a \\ 0 & b \end{bmatrix}$ then find $a + b$:
A. $\frac{6}{20}$
B. $\frac{7}{20}$
C. $\frac{8}{20}$
D. $\frac{5}{20}$

Q.82 Expand $\int \left(x^2 - \frac{1}{x^2}\right)^3 dx$:
A. $\frac{x^7}{7} + \frac{1}{5x^5} - x^3 - \frac{3}{x} + c$
B. $\frac{x^2}{7} + \frac{1}{5x^3} + x^3 + \frac{3}{x} + c$
C. $\frac{x^2}{7} + \frac{1}{5x^3} - x^3 - \frac{3}{x} - c$
D. $\frac{x^2}{7} - \frac{1}{5x^3} - x^3 - \frac{3}{x} - c$

Q.83 Evaluate: $\int \frac{dx}{(x-2)(x-1)}$
A. $\log\left|\frac{(x-2)}{(x+1)}\right| + c$
B. $\log\left|\frac{(x-2)}{(x-1)}\right| + c$
C. $\log\left|\frac{(x-1)}{(x-2)}\right| + c$
D. $\log\left|\frac{(x+2)}{(x-1)}\right| + c$

Q.84 If a JK flip=flop toggles more than once during one clock cycle, it is called ______.
A. Bouncing
B. Racing
C. Pinging
D. Spiking

Q.85

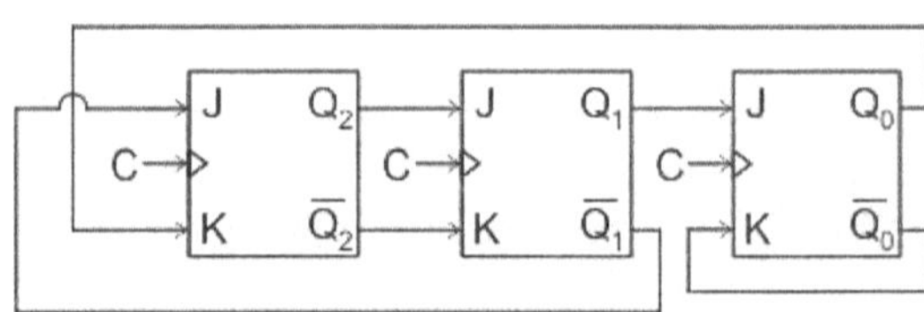

The above synchronous sequential circuit built using JK flip-flops is initialized with $Q_2Q_1Q_0 = 000$. The state sequence for this circuit for the next 3 clock cycles is:
A. 001,010,011
B. 111,110,101
C. 100,110,111
D. 100,011,001

Q.86 In a D flip-flop the output state Q is related with D input in what way?
A. Q is same as D
B. Q is complement of D
C. Q is independent of D
D. Q is dependent of D

Q.87 Which of the following is false about the logic gate?
A. It is an electronic device that implements a boolean function.
B. It is a digital circuit that has one or more inputs but only one output.

C. There is no logical relationship between input and output voltages.

D. It follows a logical relationship between input and output voltages.

Q.88 In a $J - K$ flip-flop, when $J_n = 0$ and $K_n = 1$, the output Q_{n+1} will have a value:

A. 1 **B.** 0 **C.** Q_n **D.** $\overline{Q_n}$

Q.89 Consider the sequential circuit shown in the figure, where both flip-flops used are positive edge-triggered D flip-flops.

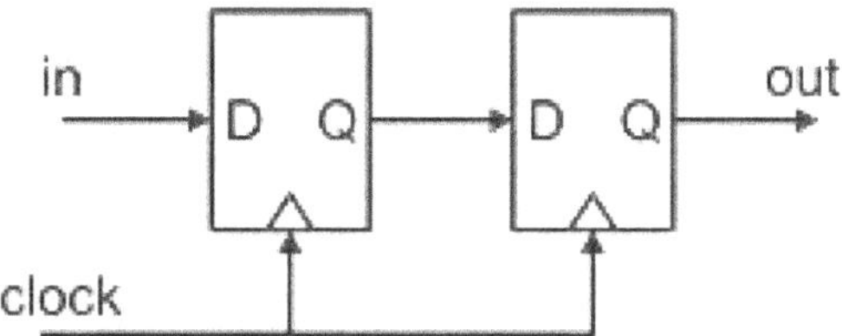

The number of states in the state transition diagram of this circuit that have a transition back to the same state on some value of "in" is ________.

A. 2 **B.** 3 **C.** 4 **D.** 6

Q.90 Which of the following flip-flops has a single control input?

A. The edge-triggered $J - K$ flip-flop.

B. The gated D-latch.

C. The edge-triggered T flip-flop.

D. The edge-triggered $S - R$ flip-flop.

Q.91 How many flip-flops are needed to divide the input frequency by 40?

A. 4 **B.** 5 **C.** 6 **D.** 40

Q.92 What does the following flip flop configuration does?

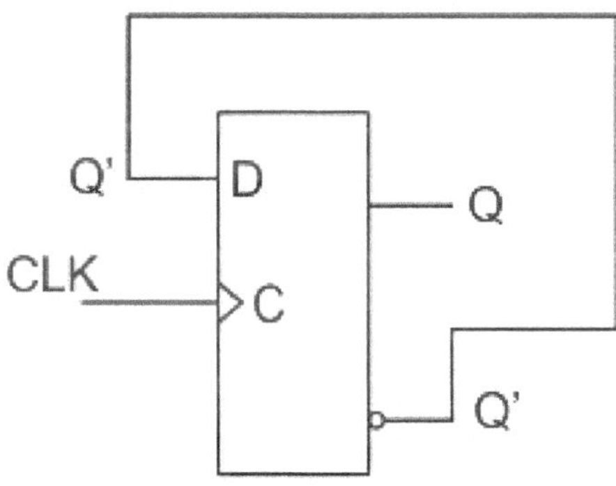

A. $Q = 1$ always

B. $Q = 0$ always

C. Acts as 1-bit counter

D. Act as 1-bit memory

Q.93 The number of integers between 1 and 350 (both are inclusive) that are not divisible by 2 or 5 or 9 is ________.

A. 125 **B.** 130 **C.** 135 **D.** 140

Q.94 Consider the following Hasse diagram of a partial ordered set:

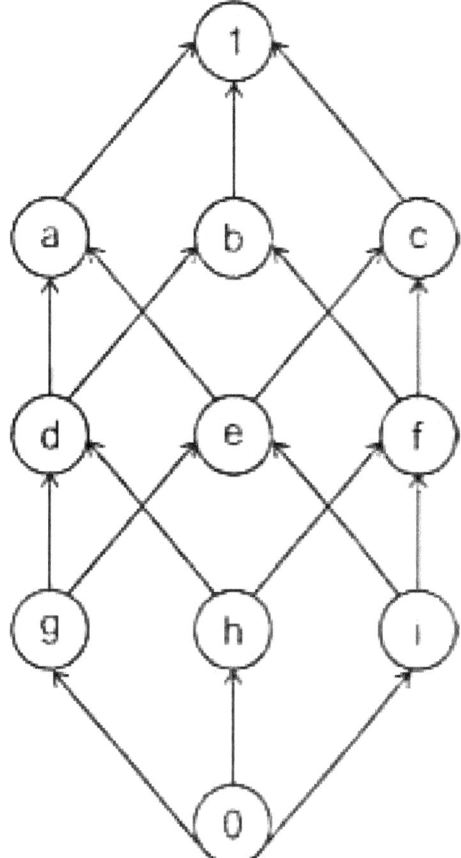

Assume lower bounds of $\{a, b\}$ are represented L and lower bounds of $\{b, c\}$ all represented by R.

$L \cap R = ?$

A. $\{0, g, h, i\}$ **B.** $\{0, h, s\}$

C. $\{d, e, f, g, h, i, 0\}$ **D.** $\{0, h, e\}$

Q.95 The chromatic number of the graph shown below is:

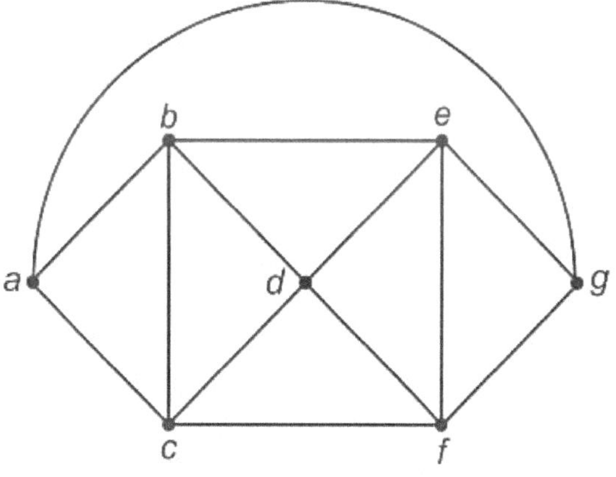

A. 2 **B.** 3 **C.** 4 **D.** 5

Q.96 How many ways are there to divide 4 Indian countries and 4 China countries into 4 groups of 2 each such that at least one group must have only Indian countries?

A. 6 **B.** 45 **C.** 12 **D.** 76

Q.97 A partial order $\leq$ is defined on the set $S = \{x, b_1, b_2, \dots b_n, y\}$ as $x \leq b_i$ for all and $b_i \leq y$ for all i, where $n \geq 1$. The number of total orders on the set S which contain the partial order $\leq$ is __________.

A. $n + 4$ **B.** n^2 **C.** $n!$ **D.** 3

Q.98 Let $(A, \leq)$ be a partial order with two minimal elements a, b and a maximum element c. Let $P: A \to$ {True, False} be a predicate defined on A. Suppose that $P(a) =$ True, $P(b) =$ False and $P(a) \Rightarrow P(b)$ for all satisfying $a \leq b$, where $\Rightarrow$ stands for logical implication. Which of the following statements cannot be true?

A. $P(x) =$ True for all $x \in S$ such that $x \neq b$
B. $P(x) =$ False for all $x \in S$ such that $b \leq x$ and $x \neq c$
C. $P(x) =$ False for all $x \in S$ such that $x \neq a$ and $x \neq c$
D. $P(x) =$ False for all $x \in S$ such that $a \leq x$ and $b \leq x$

Q.99 What is the generating function of the sequence $\{1,1,3,1,1,1,1 \dots\}$?

A. $(1 - x)^{-2}$ **B.** $\dfrac{(1+2x^2-2x^3)}{(1-x)}$

C. $\dfrac{(x^2+x)}{(1-x)^3}$ **D.** $\dfrac{2}{(1-x)^3}$

Q.100 Let G be a connected planar graph with 16 vertices. If the number of edges on each face is three, then the number of edges in G is ________.

A. 42   **B.** 45   **C.** 46   **D.** 48

// Smart Answer Sheet //

Correct Percentage of students who answered correctly.   **Skipped** Percentage of students who skipped.

Q.	Ans.	Correct / Skipped	Q.	Ans.	Correct / Skipped	Q.	Ans.	Correct / Skipped	Q.	Ans.	Correct / Skipped	Q.	Ans.	Correct / Skipped	Q.	Ans.	Correct / Skipped
1	A	14.94 % / 77.18 %	18	B	47.38 % / 51.05 %	35	A	43.99 % / 32.14 %	52	B	84.66 % / 11.31 %	69	B	49.28 % / 34.38 %	86	A	69.54 % / 30.14 %
2	A	50.51 % / 33.79 %	19	B	67.6 % / 30.34 %	36	C	30.88 % / 68.45 %	53	B	52.6 % / 44.74 %	70	A	64.62 % / 32.71 %	87	C	31.82 % / 67.84 %
3	D	56.99 % / 39.7 %	20	C	43.92 % / 53.5 %	37	A	64.17 % / 30.73 %	54	B	17.57 % / 70.07 %	71	D	84.78 % / 14.09 %	88	B	53.72 % / 34.52 %
4	A	69.13 % / 30.32 %	21	B	17.34 % / 78.35 %	38	B	48.16 % / 40.69 %	55	D	51.7 % / 32.18 %	72	A	48.51 % / 30.02 %	89	A	47.35 % / 47.09 %
5	B	66.86 % / 30.97 %	22	B	19.13 % / 71.74 %	39	B	48.53 % / 44.08 %	56	C	63.14 % / 33.52 %	73	D	46.31 % / 43.31 %	90	C	25.88 % / 71.69 %
6	C	53.46 % / 30.24 %	23	A	67.19 % / 30.54 %	40	D	88.22 % / 10.25 %	57	B	86.51 % / 12.4 %	74	D	42.29 % / 47.65 %	91	C	58.34 % / 33.0 %
7	C	42.58 % / 42.05 %	24	A	69.78 % / 30.13 %	41	C	42.02 % / 57.53 %	58	A	69.8 % / 30.18 %	75	D	10.72 % / 68.27 %	92	C	26.76 % / 72.42 %
8	A	24.83 % / 72.13 %	25	A	13.21 % / 73.4 %	42	D	62.98 % / 35.96 %	59	C	56.69 % / 41.71 %	76	C	43.67 % / 48.11 %	93	A	24.63 % / 73.0 %
9	A	30.38 % / 68.84 %	26	A	76.24 % / 23.6 %	43	B	53.92 % / 30.01 %	60	B	65.02 % / 31.17 %	77	C	26.57 % / 72.92 %	94	A	88.31 % / 10.61 %
10	A	65.85 % / 31.68 %	27	A	45.38 % / 52.75 %	44	A	57.42 % / 34.22 %	61	C	67.23 % / 30.26 %	78	C	61.7 % / 37.81 %	95	C	52.27 % / 42.75 %
11	D	79.68 % / 17.69 %	28	D	62.54 % / 32.58 %	45	C	67.09 % / 30.63 %	62	A	67.54 % / 30.38 %	79	B	54.02 % / 34.93 %	96	A	68.51 % / 31.31 %
12	B	59.52 % / 37.16 %	29	D	67.2 % / 32.45 %	46	D	26.96 % / 71.68 %	63	D	25.62 % / 71.03 %	80	D	53.38 % / 30.44 %	97	C	57.71 % / 37.51 %
13	D	57.74 % / 41.24 %	30	A	79.84 % / 11.54 %	47	D	40.58 % / 37.97 %	64	C	32.94 % / 67.01 %	81	B	55.07 % / 30.45 %	98	D	26.23 % / 67.3 %
14	B	59.82 % / 36.47 %	31	B	60.78 % / 32.2 %	48	C	49.47 % / 30.45 %	65	D	25.14 % / 70.25 %	82	A	47.4 % / 48.24 %	99	B	62.42 % / 33.15 %
15	D	69.9 % / 30.01 %	32	D	22.22 % / 72.6 %	49	D	69.43 % / 30.13 %	66	D	67.15 % / 30.62 %	83	B	40.09 % / 59.35 %	100	A	60.06 % / 36.56 %
16	D	19.95 % / 75.46 %	33	A	41.4 % / 53.5 %	50	A	43.96 % / 38.16 %	67	C	57.84 % / 30.72 %	84	B	60.03 % / 39.78 %			
17	B	15.93 % / 70.12 %	34	C	29.62 % / 68.23 %	51	D	65.04 % / 34.88 %	68	C	62.12 % / 35.42 %	85	C	22.46 % / 71.3 %			

//Hints and Solutions//

1.

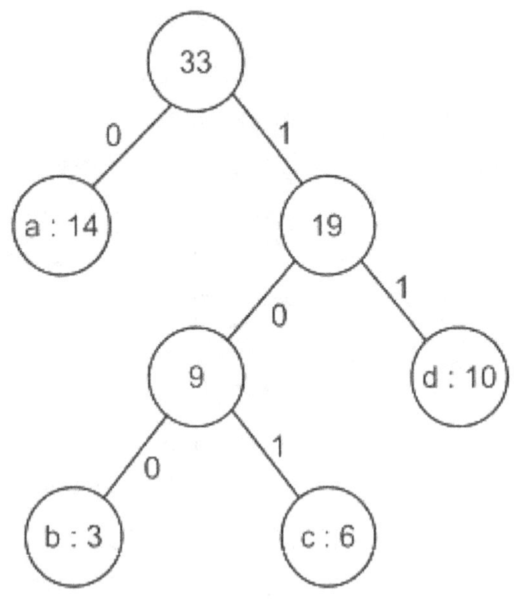

$a = 0$ (takes 1 bits), $b = 100$ (takes 3 bits)

$c = 101$ (takes 3 bits), $d = 11$ (takes 2 bits)

$14\ a's + 3\ b's + 6\ c's + 10\ d's$

$= 14 \times 1 + 3 \times 3 + 6 \times 3 + 10 \times 2$

$= 61$ bits.

Hence, the correct option is (A).

2. We know that,

A minimum spanning tree (MST) or minimum weight spanning tree is a subset of the edges $(V - 1)$ of a connected, edge-weighted undirected graph $G(V, E)$ that connects all the vertices together, without any cycles and with the minimum possible total edge weight.

Now,

The minimum weight in the graph is 0.1 choosing this we get.

Suppose we get two trees T_1 and T_2.

To connect to those two trees we got 3 possible edges of weight 0.9.

So, we can choose any one of those 3 edges.

The number of minimum-weight spanning trees of the graph is 3.

Hence, the correct option is (A).

3. We know that,

The sin function value ranges from -1 to $+1. (-1, 0, 1)$

Now,

Statement 1: When $\sin(n)$ is -1.

$$g(n) = n^{(1-1)} = n^0 = 1$$

Therefore, for this case $f(n) > g(n)$ i.e. $g(n) = 0(f(n))$

So, statement 1 is incorrect.

Statement 2: When $\sin(n)$ is $+1$.

$$g(n) = n^{(1+1)} = n^2$$

So, for this case $f(n) < g(n)$ i.e. $f(n) = 0(g(n))$

But for this, second statement i.e. $f(n) = \Omega(g(n))$ is incorrect.

Both statements are incorrect for all values of $\sin(n)$.

Hence, the correct option is (D).

4. As the value of n is divided by 2 at every recursive call, so after logn function calls the value of n will become 1.

Here master theorem concept is used:

The recurrence relation of the above code is,

$$T(n) = 4T\left(\frac{n}{2}\right) + n^2$$

By substitution method:

$$T(n) = n^2 + 4\left[4T\left(\frac{n}{2}\right) + \frac{n^2}{4}\right]$$

$$= 2n^2 + 16 + \left(\frac{n}{4}\right) \dots \dots$$

$$= k \cdot n^2 + 4^k T\left(\frac{n}{2^k}\right)$$

The process stops when 2^k reaches n.

$$k = \log n_2 n$$

$$T(n) = 0(n^2 \log n)$$

We can also solve this through the master theorem concept.

Extended Master Theorem,

Equation of the form:

$$T(n) = aT\left(\frac{n}{b}\right) + \theta\left(n^k \log^p n\right)$$

Will have the following solution:

1. If $a > b^k$, then $T(n) = \theta\left(n^{\log_b^a}\right)$

2. If $a = b^k$

a. If $p > -1$, then $T(n) = \theta\left(n^{\log_b^a} \log^{p+1} n\right)$

b. If $p = -1$, then $T(n) = \theta\left(n^{\log_b^a} \log\log n\right)$

c. If $p < -1$, then $T(n) = \theta\left(n^{\log_b^a}\right)$

3. If $a < b^k$

a. If $p \geq 0$, then $T(n) = \theta\left(n^k \log^p n\right)$

b. If $p < 0$, then $T(n) = O\left(n^k\right)$

Here $a = 4, b = 2, k = 2, p = 0$

Since $a = b^k$

We are in case 2 of extended master theorem.

Since $p = 0$

We are in sub case a.

By substituting values we get,

$$T(n) = \theta\left(n^{\log_2^4} \log^{0+1} n\right)$$

Therefore,

$$T(n) = \theta(n^2 \log n)$$

Hence, the correct option is (A).

5. We know that,

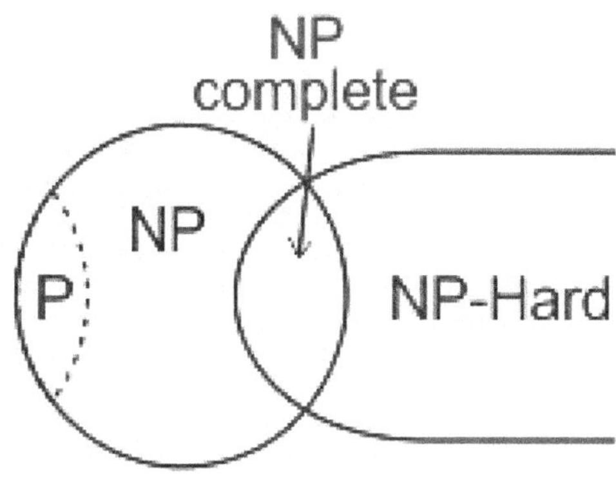

From the above diagram we get:

NP-complete ∩ P = φ

NP-complete problems:

They are those for which no polynomial-time algorithm exists. We can say a problem is NP-complete if it is NP and belongs to NP-hard.

NP problems:

A problem is a member of the NP class if there exists a non-deterministic machine that can solve it in polynomial time.

NP-Hard:

A problem is called NP-hard if all the NP class problems are polynomial-time reducible to that and as hard as any problem of NP class.

- Every problem in P is also in NP.
- Given that P ≠ NP, this means there exists a problem that is in NP but not in P.

Hence, the correct option is (B).

6. Euclid's algorithm states that the GCD of two numbers does not change even if the bigger number is replaced by a difference of two numbers.

So, GCD of 16 and 12

$$= (16 - 12)$$

$$= 4$$

It is the same. There are 3 common factors of 12 and 16, which are $1, 2$ and 4.

Therefore, the greatest common factor of 12 and 16 is 4.

Hence, the correct option is (C).

7. The Euclidean algorithm may be used to solve Diophantine equations, such as finding numbers that satisfy multiple congruences according to the Chinese remainder theorem, to construct continued fractions, and to find accurate rational approximations to real numbers. Solving quadratic equations is not an application of Euclid's algorithm whereas the rest of the options are mathematical applications of Euclid's algorithm.

Hence, the correct option is (C).

8. The time complexity is the number of operations an algorithm performs to complete its task with respect to input size (considering that each operation takes the same amount of time). The algorithm that performs the task in the smallest number of operations is considered the most efficient one.

The time is taken by an algorithm also depends on the computing speed of the system that you are using, but we ignore those external factors and we are only concerned on the number of times a particular statement is being executed with respect to the input size.

It is given that Initialization takes $O(N)$ time.

Then for each input (N), a function call will be made whose time complexity is $O(N \log N)$.

So, the total time required for the main part is:

$$N \times N\log N = N^2\log N$$

So,

Total time $= N + N^2\log N$

Hence, the correct option is (A).

9. Given,

$(M1, M2)M3$:

$12 \times 9 \times 9 \times 15 \rightarrow$ resultant matrix

$= 12 \times 15 \rightarrow$ number of multiplications

$= 12 \times 9 \times 15$

$= 1620$

$12 \times 15 \times 15 \times 10 \rightarrow$ resultant matrix

$= 12 \times 10 \rightarrow$ number of multiplications

$= 12 \times 15 \times 10$

$= 1800$

The total number of multiplication:

$= 1620 + 1800$

$= 3420$

Now,

$M1(M2, M3)$:

$9 \times 15 \times 15 \times 10 \rightarrow$ resultant matrix

$= 9 \times 10 \rightarrow$ number of multiplications

$= 9 \times 15 \times 10$

$= 1350$

$12 \times 9 \times 9 \times 10 \rightarrow$ resultant matrix

$= 12 \times 10 \rightarrow$ number of multiplications

$= 12 \times 9 \times 10$

$= 1080$

The total number of multiplication:

$= 1350 + 1080$

$= 2430$

Hence, the correct option is (A).

10. If there is an abstract method in a class then, the class must be an abstract class. It is a rule that if a class has even one abstract method, it must be an abstract class. If this rule was not made, the abstract methods would have got skipped to get defined in some places which are undesirable with the idea of an abstract class.

Hence, the correct option is (A).

11. Encapsulation and Abstraction are the same OOPS concepts. Encapsulation hides the features of the object and binds all the properties inside a single class. And abstraction is a feature that shows the required data to the user. For an example of encapsulation, I can think of the interaction between a user and a mobile phone. The user does not need to know the internal working of the mobile phone to operate, so this is called abstraction.

Hence, the correct option is (D).

12. The prompt() method displays a dialogue box that prompts the visitor for input.

The below statement will ask the user to input his/her test series and the default value is EduGorilla.

Code:

```
var favDrink = prompt("Which test series you are taking?", "EduGorilla");
```

Hence, the correct option is (B).

13. After inserting $9,6,5$:

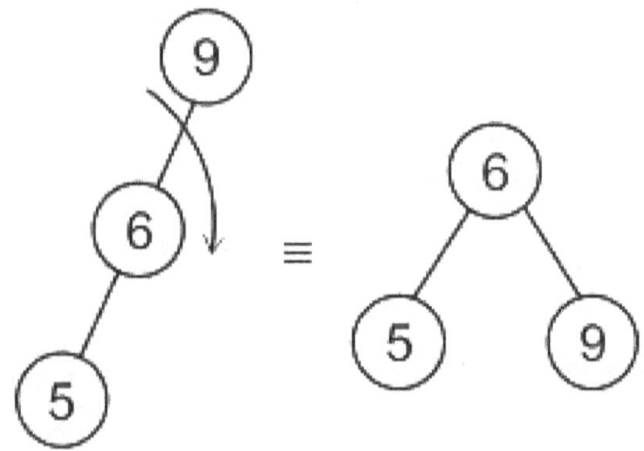

1 Rotation.

Insert 8:

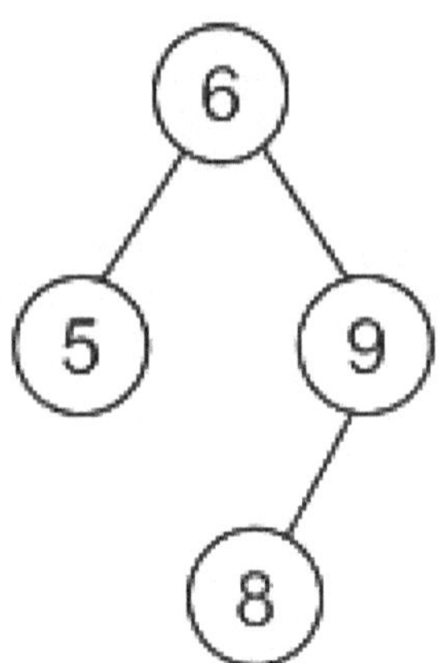

Insert 7:

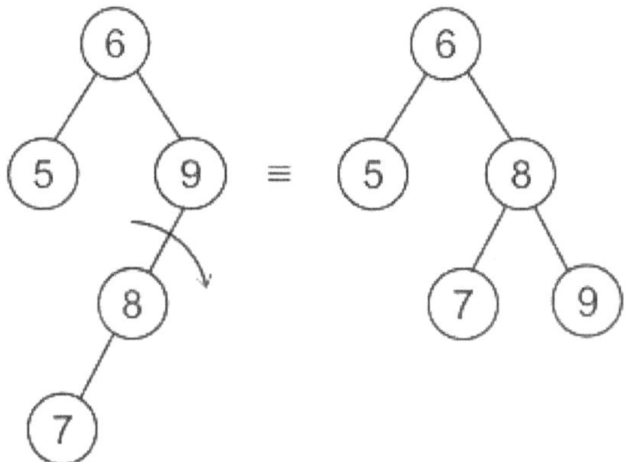

2 Rotation.

Insert 10:

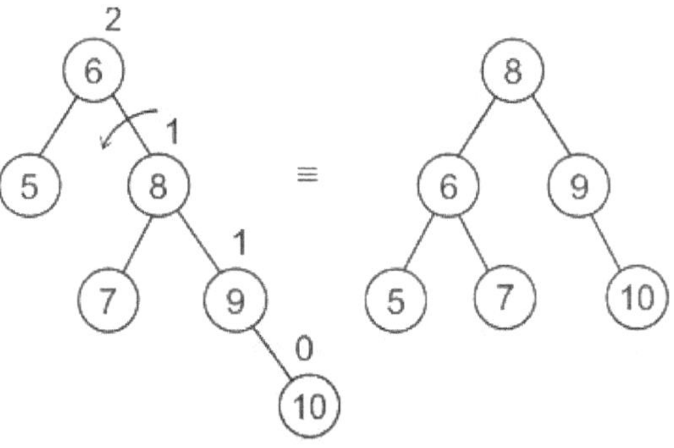

3 Rotation.

So, a total of 3 Rotations is required.

Hence, the correct option is (D).

14. Tasm is the borland turbo assembler. Tasm is an assembler for software development published by Borland in 1989. It runs on and produces code for 16 or 32-bit $x86$ MS-DOS and compatibles or Microsoft Windows. It can be used with Borland's other language products: Turbo Pascal, Turbo Basic, Turbo C, and Turbo C++.

Hence, the correct option is (B).

15. The worst-case happens if the required element is at last or the element is absent in the list. For this, we need to compare every element in the linked list. If n elements are there, n comparisons will happen in the worst case.

Hence, the correct option is (D).

16. The time complexity of a queue is implemented with a linked list data structure. We can the implement a queue in O (1) time by:

- Enqueueing at the back
- Dequeueing at the head

First, you have to empty all the elements of the current stack into the temporary stack, push the required element and empty the elements of the temporary stack into the original stack.

Therefore, taking $10 + 10 + 1 + 11 + 11 = 43$ seconds.

Hence, the correct option is (D).

17. This is similar to performing dequeue operation using push and pop only. Elements in the first jar are taken out and placed in the second jar. After removing the last element from the first jar, remove all the elements in the second jar and place them in the first jar. In this way, we can remove the last ring in the jar. Empty the first jar by removing it one by one from the first jar and placing it into the second jar and empty the second jar by placing all the rings into the first jar one by one.

Hence, the correct option is (B).

18. Given,

Postfix expression:

$$= 53 * 9 + 6/84/+$$

Result:

$$= 53 * 9 + 6/84/+$$
$$= (5{*}3)9 + 6/(8/4) +$$
$$= ((5 * 3) + 9)/6 + (8/4)$$
$$= (24/6) + 2$$
$$= 4 + 2$$
$$= 6$$

Hence, the correct option is (B).

19. Many cables have "RS- 232" connectors with some wires crossed or connected to each other because many computers and peripherals use RS- 232 serial interfaces, but not as DTE-to-DCE. RS- 232 was the first milestone reached in this journey. It was a standard for electromechanical typewriters and modems for digital data exchange introduced in 1962 by the Radio Sector of EIA. It made the data exchange more reliable over an analog channel. The standard-defined voltage levels made it immune to noise disturbances and reduced the error in data exchange.

Hence, the correct option is (B).

20. Extended command sets supported by modern modems use different commands to control many advanced modem features. Command and Data modes refer to the two modes in which a computer modem may operate. These modes are defined in the Hayes command set, which is the de facto standard for all modems. These modes exist because there is only one channel of communication between the modem and the computer, which must carry both the computer's commands to the modem, as well as the data that the modem is enlisted to transmit to the remote party over the telephone line. When a modem is in command mode, any characters sent to it are interpreted as commands for the modem to execute, per the Hayes command set.

Hence, the correct option is (C).

21. CRC stands for Cyclic Redundancy Check, which is an error-detecting code used to detect errors in the frame received.

CRC is used to detect errors in the Data link layer.

Steps to perform CRC on the sender side:

1. String of n 0's is appended to the data unit to be transmitted.

2. Where, $n \rightarrow$ number of bits in CRC divisor -1.

3. The binary division is performed of the data unit with the CRC divisor.

4. The remainder obtained after division is called CRC.

5. Append CRC at the last of data units.

Now,

Step 1:

No. of bits in divisor is 4 bits, append 3 0's to data bits.

Data bits after appending 0's is 100111001000.

Step 2:

Binary division of 100111001000 with 1011.

$$1011)\overline{100111001000}(101000001$$
$$\oplus\ 1011$$
$$\overline{01011}$$
$$\oplus\ 1011$$
$$\overline{1000}$$
$$\oplus\ 1011$$
$$\overline{011}$$

Step 3:

Append CRC 011 at last of data unit 100111001011.

Hence, the correct option is (B).

22. Mostly orthogonal frequency division multiplexing is used in wireless LAN. In telecommunications, orthogonal frequency-division multiplexing is a method of encoding digital data on multiple carrier frequencies. OFDM has developed into a popular scheme for wideband digital communication, used in applications such as digital television and audio broadcasting, DSL internet access, wireless networks, power line networks, and 4G mobile communications.

Hence, the correct option is (B).

23. In wireless ad-hoc network access point is not required. An ad-hoc network uses a connection between two or more devices without using a wireless access point. The devices communicate directly when in range. Because setup is easy and does not require an access point, an ad-hoc network is used in situations such as quick data exchange or a multiplayer video game.

Hence, the correct option is (A).

24. The IP security (IPsec) is an Internet Engineering Task Force (IETF) standard suite of protocols between 2 communication points across the IP network that provide data authentication, integrity, and confidentiality. It also defines the encrypted, decrypted and authenticated packets.

Hence, the correct option is (A).

25. Loopback address $(::1)$ of IPv 6 address is equivalent to the IPV 4 loopback address $127.0.0.1$. In IPv 6 the loopback address is written as $(::1)$. This is a 128-bit number, with the first 127 bits being ' 0' and the 128th bit being ' 1'. It's just a single address, so could also be written as $::\dfrac{1}{128}$. It is equivalent to the IPv 4 loopback address $127.0.0.1$.

Hence, the correct option is (A).

26. HBA stands for Host Bus Adapters. In computer hardware, a host controller, host adapter, or host bus adapter (HBA) connects a computer, which acts as the host system, to other network and storage devices.

Hence, the correct option is (A).

27. In OSI network architecture, dialogue control and token management are the responsibility of the session layer. The session layer establishes, manages and terminates connections between applications. The session layer sets up, coordinates, and terminates conversations, exchanges, and dialogues between the applications at each end. It deals with session and connection coordination.

Hence, the correct option is (A).

28. In semantic nets, finding relationships among objects is determined by spreading activation out from each of 2 nodes and identifying where the activation meets. This process is called Intersection Search. Neural Network (NN) and Adaptive Neuro-Fuzzy Inference System (ANFIS) are two intelligent controllers implemented in this study. For the sake of comparison, we also implement Q-learning and fixed-time controllers as benchmarks. Comprehensive simulation scenarios are designed and executed for a traffic network composed of nine four-way intersections.

Hence, the correct option is (D).

29. Bits of PSW register are $CY, AC, F0, RS1, RS0, OV, -, P$ so for selecting bank $2\ RS1 = 1$ and $RS0 = 0$ which are the fourth and third bit of the register respectively. Register bank 0 is the default when the 8051 is powered up. We can switch to the other banks using PSW register. $D4$ and $D3$ bits of the PSW are used to select the desired register bank, since they can be accessed by the bit addressable instructions $SETB$ and CLR.

Hence, the correct option is (D).

30. If we push elements onto the stack then the stack pointer increases with every push of the element. A stack pointer is a small register that stores the address of the last program request in a stack. When a new data item is entered or "pushed" onto the top of a stack, the stack pointer increments to the next physical memory address, and the new item is copied to that address.

Hence, the correct option is (A).

31. Given,

$$XY + XYZ + YZ$$

As we know,

$$XY + XYZ + YZ = (X \times Y) + (X \times Y \times Z) + (Y \times Z)$$

$$= (X \times Y) + (X \times Y + Y) \times Z$$

The instructions are non-pipelined and cycles for each instruction is shown. Therefore,

- $X \times Y$ takes 2 cycles.
- $X \times Y + Y$ takes 1 cycle $(X \times Y$ already done $)$.
- $(X \times Y + Y) \times Z$ takes 2 cycles.
- $(X \times Y) + (X \times Y + Y) \times Z$ takes 1 cycle.

So, total cycles $= 2 + 1 + 2 + 1$

$$= 6$$

Now,

$$XY + XYZ + YZ$$

$$X \times Y + (X \times Y + Y) \times Z$$

2 cycle 0 $cycle$

$1 cycle$

$2 cycle$

$1 cycle$

Hence, the correct option is (B).

32. By adding more instructions to the RISC architecture, some applications can be run much faster like multimedia applications, telecommunication encoding/decoding, image conversion and video processing. A Reduced Instruction Set Computer is a type of microprocessor architecture that utilizes a small, highly-optimized set of instructions rather than the highly-specialized set of instructions typically found in other architectures.

Hence, the correct option is (D).

33. The 80286 processor can access beyond 1 MB by paging and special hardware to stimulate the missing address lines. This is called expanded memory. Paging uses fixed-size pages to move between main memory and secondary storage. Paging uses page tables to map the logical addresses to physical addresses.

Hence, the correct option is (A).

34. So, to obtain operand value from memory, the address field of an instruction is used by the CPU. In single address instruction, one of the operands is stored in the accumulator and the other operand may be either in register or memory.

Now,

All the operations will be performed in the accumulator register (AC). The load operation is used to fetch the value from the register or memory to the accumulator. The store operation is used to store the value from the accumulator to the register or memory.

The one address instructions for the given equations are:

Load/Store/Operation	One-address Instruction
LOAD N	$AC \leftarrow M[N]$
MUL O	$AC \leftarrow AC \times M[N]$
ADD M	$AC \leftarrow AC + M[M]$
STORE T	$M[T] \leftarrow AC$
LOAD P	$AC \leftarrow M[P]$
MUL Q	$AC \leftarrow AC \times M[Q]$
DIV T	$AC \leftarrow \dfrac{AC}{M[T]}$
STORE X	$M[X] \leftarrow AC$

The one-address instructions are required is 8.

Hence, the correct option is (C).

35. The number of clockcycles that take to wait until the length of the instruction is known in order to start decoding is 0. The loading and decoding the instructions in a RISC processor is simple and fast. It is not needed to wait until the length of the instruction is known in order to start the decoding.

Hence, the correct option is (A).

36. Some computers are used in preference to CISC design due to its low burden on compiler developers and wide availability of existing software. But they are complex in nature. Therefore, chip hardware and instruction set became complex with each generation of the processor. The overall performance of the machine is reduced because of the slower clock speed. The complexity of hardware and on-chip software included in CISC design to perform many functions.

Hence, the correct option is (C).

37. A syntax error is an error in the source code of a program. Since computer programs must follow strict syntax to compile correctly, any aspects of the code that do not conform to the syntax of the programming language will produce a syntax error. Unlike logic errors, which are errors in the flow or logic of a program, syntax errors are small grammatical mistakes, sometimes limited to a single character. For example, a missing semicolon at the end of a line or an extra bracket at the end of a function may produce a syntax error.

Internal errors are due to faulty logic or coding in the program.

- Common types of internal errors include Bounds errors, Inserting a null pointer into a collection, Attempting to use a bad date.

A semantic error is a violation of the rules of the meaning of a natural language or a programming language.

- Semantic errors are the hardest to debug because the interpreter provides no information about what is wrong.

A logic error (or logical error) is a mistake in a program's source code that results in incorrect or unexpected behavior.

- It is a type of runtime error that may simply produce the wrong output or may cause a program to crash while running.

Hence, the correct option is (A).

38. The bottom-up approach is used in the generalization. The several lower-level sub-entities are grouped together to make an individual higher-level entity. In short, we can say that it is totally the opposite of specialization.

To understand it more clearly, consider the following example:

Suppose you have several lower entities like bus, car, motorbike etc. So, in order to make a more generalize (or higher level) entity, you can combine them under a new higher-level entity such as a vehicle.

Hence, the correct option is (B).

39. In a relation database, the number of rows inside a table is known as tuples, and if we further divide those tuples (or rows) into those fields, they become the domains. A domain is a set of allowable values for one or more attributes. Attribute domains are rules that describe the legal values of a field type. They are used to constrain the values allowed in any particular attribute for a table or feature class.

Hence, the correct option is (B).

40. The term "TCL" refers to the Transaction Control Language, which is another language just like the "DDL" and "DML". The commands like commit, save point, rollback come under the TCL used to control the transactions. Transaction Control Language commands are used to manage transactions in the database. These are used to manage the changes made by DML statements. It also allows statements to be grouped together into logical transactions. It is also used with the savepoint command to jump to a save point in a transaction.

Hence, the correct option is (D).

41. In the database, the number of rows inside a table is called the tuples, and the numbers of columns are known as the attributes. Attributes are the describing characteristics or properties that define all items pertaining to a certain category applied to all cells of a column.

Hence, the correct option is (C).

42. In the relation model, the relations are also referred to as the tables because the relations are considered as the technical name of the table. Tables are database objects that contain all the data in a database. In tables, data is logically organized in a row-and-column format similar to a spreadsheet. Each row represents a unique record, and each column represents a field in the record.

Hence, the correct option is (D).

43. The terms literal and constant value are synonymous and refer to a fixed data value. For example, 'JACK', 'BLUE ISLAND', and ' 101 ' are all character literals; 5001 is a numeric literal. Character literals are enclosed in single quotation marks so that Oracle can distinguish them from schema object names.

Literals are similar to the constants. There are 4 types of literal:

1. Text literals
2. Integer literals
3. Number
4. Date/Time literals

Hence, the correct option is (B).

44. By using LIKE query we can match part of the full data present in a column. Here our search word need not exactly match.

Using LIKE Query with wildcard in different combinations, we can match our keyword with the pattern of the data present in columns.

The best way to use LIKE command is to apply it against a text or varchar field along with wildcard (%or_).

Hence, the correct option is (A).

45. Always use IS NULL to look for NULL values. The NULL operator is the operator checking the column for the absence of data. The explanation for this response is that the NULL operator is being used in the database to show that a certain region is blank.

Syntax:
SELECT "column_name"
FROM "table_name"
WHERE "column_name" IS NULL

Hence, the correct option is (C).

46. Apache Flume is a reliable and distributed system for collecting, aggregating and moving massive quantities of log data. It has a simple yet flexible architecture based on streaming data flows. Apache Flume is used to collect log data present in log files from web servers and aggregating it into HDFS for analysis.

Hence, the correct option is (D).

47. Multiprogramming allows multiple programs to reside in separate areas of the core at the time. Multiprogramming is a rudimentary form of parallel processing in which several programs are run at the same time on a uniprocessor. Instead, the operating system executes part of one program, then part of another, and so on. To the user, it appears that all programs are executing at the same time.

Hence, the correct option is (D).

48. If a process fails, most operating systems write the error information to a log file. Log file is examined by the debugger, to find out what is the actual cause of that particular problem. Log file is useful for system programmers for correcting errors.

Hence, the correct option is (C).

49. In operating systems, each process has its own address space which contains code, data, stack, and heap segments or sections. Each process also has a list of files that is opened by the process as well as all pending alarms, signals, and various signal handlers.

Hence, the correct option is (D).

50. The state transition initiated by the user process itself in an operating system is block. A block is a contiguous set of bits or bytes that forms an identifiable unit of data. The term is used in database management, word processing, and network communication. It is a multiple of an operating system block, which is the smallest amount of data that can be retrieved from storage or memory.

Hence, the correct option is (A).

51. The network operating system runs on a server. This operating system has some functions that work to connect local area networks and computers. A network operating system (NOS) is an operating system that manages network resources: essentially, an operating system that includes special functions for connecting computers and devices into a local area network (LAN). The NOS manages multiple requests (inputs) concurrently and provides the security necessary in a multiuser environment.

Hence, the correct option is (D).

52. SSTF stands for Shortest Seek Time First. In the SSTF algorithm, that request is executed first, whose seek time is the shortest. Shortest seek time first is a secondary storage scheduling algorithm to determine the motion of the disk's arm and head in servicing read and write requests.

Hence, the correct option is (B).

53. A swap file is a space on a hard disk used as the virtual memory extension of a computer's real memory (RAM). Having a swap file allows your computer's operating system to pretend that you have more RAM than you actually do. The least recently used files in RAM can be "swapped out" to your hard disk until they are needed later so that new files can be "swapped in" to RAM.

Hence, the correct option is (B).

54. Kernel is the first program that is loaded in memory when operating system is loading as well as it remains in memory till operating system is running. Kernel is the core part of the operating system which is responsible for managing resources, allowing multiple processes to use the resources and provide services to various processes. Kernel modules can be loaded and unloaded in run-time i.e. in running operating system.

Hence, the correct option is (B).

55. The process is in a "Blocked" state waiting for some I/O service. When the service is completed, it goes to the ready state. The process never goes directly to the running state from the

waiting state. Only processes which are in the ready state go to the running state whenever the CPU is allocated by the operating system.

Hence, the correct option is (D).

56. Given,

$(x + y)^* y (a + ab)^*$ and length of strings be less than 4.

Now,

String of length $0 = $ Not possible (because y is always present).

String of length $1 = 1$ (y)

String of length $2 = 3 (xy, yy, ya)$

String of length $3 = $
$8 (xxy, xyy, yxy, yyy, yaa, yab, xya, yya)$

Total strings $= 1 + 3 + 8 = 12$

Hence, the correct option is (C).

57. The transition from a state is to a single particular next state for each input symbol. So, it is called deterministic which allows backtracking. DFA rejects the string in case it terminates in a state that is different from the accepting state. NFA rejects the string in the event of all branches dying or refusing the string. It is possible to use backtracking in DFA.

Hence, the correct option is (B).

58. A, B, C, D are the useless symbols in the given grammar as they never tend to lead to a terminal. The productions $S \rightarrow A, A \rightarrow aA, B \rightarrow C, C \rightarrow D$ are also termed as useless production as they will never produce a string to the grammar.

So, the ratio of the number of useless variables to the number of useless production is 1.

Hence, the correct option is (A).

59. The language L_1 accept strings $\{c, abc, abcab, aabbcab, aabbcaabb, \dots\}$ and L_2 accept strings $\{a, b, c, ab, abc, abc, aabbc, \dots\}$. Intersection of these two languages is $L_1 \cap L_2 = \{a^k b^k c \mid k \geq 0\}$ which is context free, but not regular.

Hence, the correct option is (C).

60. An operator precedence parser is a bottom-up parser that interprets an operator-precedence grammar.

Consider the grammar with the following translation rules and E as the start symbol.

$A \rightarrow A1 \# B \{A.\text{value} = A1.\text{value} * B.\text{value} \}$

$IB \{A.\text{value} = B.\text{value} \}$

$B \rightarrow B1 \& F \{B.\text{value} = B1.\text{value} + C.\text{value} \}$

$IC \{B.\text{value} = C.\text{value} \}$

$C \to$ num $\{C.\text{value} = \text{num value} \}$.

Hence, the correct option is (B).

61. Compiler transforms source code into the machine language which is in binary.

Kinds of object codes:

i. Defined symbols, which allow it to be called by other modules,

ii. Undefined symbols, which call the other modules where these symbols are defined, and

iii. Symbols which are used internally within object file for relocation.

Link time occurs after compile-time and before runtime (when a program is executed). It is common to speak of link time operations (the operations performed by a linker) or link time requirements (programming language requirements that must be met by compiled source code for it to be successfully linked).

Hence, the correct option is (C).

62. The LALR parsing table is created by YACC. LALR parser generator is software tool that reads a BNF grammar and creates a LALR parser which is capable of parsing files written in programming language identified by BNF grammar. LALR refers to the lookahead LR. To construct the LALR (1) parsing table, we use the canonical collection of LR (1) items. LALR (1) parsing is same as the CLR (1) parsing, only difference in the parsing table.

Hence, the correct option is (A).

63. B was a programming language designed by Dennis Ritchie and Ken Thompson for recursive, non-numeric, system and language software. It was a typeless language, everything is a word. B was derived from BCPL, and its name may possibly be a contraction of BCPL. Thompson's co-worker Dennis Ritchie speculated that the name might be based on Bon, an earlier, but unrelated, programming language that Thompson designed for use on Multics.

Hence, the correct option is (D).

64. The cable connecting a DB- 9 connector at one end to a DB- 25 connector at the other end must cross-connect pin 8 at the BD- 9 side to 5 pin at the DB- 25 side.

DB 9 to DB 9	DB 25 to DB 25	DB 9 to DB 25	Connection description
Pin 2 to Pin 2	Pin 3 to Pin 3	Pin 2 to Pin 3	DTE RD to DCE TD
Pin 3 to Pin 3	Pin 2 to Pin 2	Pin 3 to Pin 2	DTE TD to DCE RD
Pin 5 to Pin 5	Pin 7 to Pin 7	Pin 5 to Pin 7	SG to SG

Hence, the correct option is (C).

65. According to Quality Function Deployment (QFD), Normal, Expected and Exciting requirements maximize customer satisfaction from the Software Engineering Process. Quality Function Deployment (QFD) is a process and set of tools used to effectively define customer requirements and convert them into detailed engineering specifications and plans to produce the products that fulfill those requirements.

Hence, the correct option is (D).

66. Users specify unnecessary technical detail that may confuse, rather than clarify overall system objectives. Also, the customers/users are not completely sure of what is needed, have a poor understanding of the capabilities and limitations of their computing environment and they do not understand that the requirements change over time.

Hence, the correct option is (D).

67. In CORE the requirement specification is put together by all users, customers and analysts, so a passive analyst will not get the requirements properly. The first software program or set of software programs started by the central processing hardware of a computing device, which program(s) is/are responsible for initializing and managing the resources of such device including, but not limited to coordinating the memory, processors.

Hence, the correct option is (C).

68. Cohesion is a measure of the degree to which the elements of the module are functionally related. It is the degree to which all elements directed towards performing a single task are contained in the component. Basically, cohesion is the internal glue that keeps the module together. A good software design will have high cohesion.

There are seven types of cohesion are:

1. Coincidental cohesion
2. Logical cohesion
3. Temporal Cohesion
4. Procedural cohesion
5. Communicational cohesion
6. Sequential cohesion
7. Functional cohesion

Hence, the correct option is (C).

69. A structure chart is a tool is used for structured designing. A Structure Chart (SC) in software engineering and organizational theory, is a chart that shows the breakdown of a system to its lowest manageable levels.

Hence, the correct option is (B).

70. The activity that distributes estimated effort across the planned project duration by allocating the effort to specific software developing tasks is project scheduling. Software project scheduling is the process of allocating anticipated effort to specific software developing activities and distributing it across the project's intended length. A macroscopic schedule is created in the early phases of project planning.

Hence, the correct option is (A).

71. Case tool: Case tools are set of software application programs, which are used to automate SDLC activities. Case tools are used by software project managers, analysts and engineers to develop software system.

There are number of case tools available to simplify various stages of software development Life cycle such as analysis tools, Design tools, Project management tools, Database management tools, Documentation tools are to name a few.

Various uses of case tools: Project management, Creation of data dictionary, Design user interface, Code generation, Schema generation, Software testing, Project scheduling, Cost and benefit analysis, Data modeling, Analysis and Design for documentation.

Hence, the correct option is (D).

72. Behavioral models are used to describe the dynamic behavior of an executing system. This can be modeled from the perspective of the data processed by the system or by the events that stimulate responses from a system. Behavioral Model is specially designed to make us understand behavior and factors that influence behavior of a System. Behavior of a system is explained and represented with the help of a diagram. This diagram is known as State Transition Diagram. It is a collection of states and events.

Hence, the correct option is (A).

73. Six Sigma is a statistical term used to measure the number of defects that processes create.

The term implies high-quality performance because a process performing at a Six Sigma level allows only 3.4 defects per one million opportunities.

Different sigma levels of quality would lead to the following number of defects.

$1.$ **Three Sigma quality:** This level of performance produces a defect-free product 93.32% of the time. 770 applications would be processed incorrectly and would require rework every day.

$2.$ **Four Sigma quality:** This level of performance yields a defect-free product 99.349% of the time. With four sigma quality, 73 applications would need to be corrected every day.

$3.$ **Five Sigma quality:** Five Sigma performance produces defect-free products and services 99.977% of the time. Every week the bank would need to correct 13 application errors.

$4.$ **Six Sigma quality:** Six Sigma performance produces a defect-free product 99.99966% of the time; allowing only 3.4 errors per one million opportunities. 10 applications would need to be corrected during the entire year.

As we know,

Four sigma and six sigma levels of performance both have an error free rate over 99% of the time. However, the large volume of applications in this example makes all of the difference. With numbers this big, it turned out that the four-sigma process made $18,710$ more errors than the six sigma process.

Hence, the correct option is (D).

74. Given,

The total number of balls in the box $= 36$

The number of green balls is $= 9$

The number of red balls is $= 10$

$\therefore$ The number of blue balls $= 36 - 10 - 9 = 17$

As we know,

Number of all combinations of n things, taken r at a time is given by,

$$= {}^{n}C_{r} = \frac{n!}{(r)!(n-r)!}$$

The number of ways selecting three different coloured balls,

$$= {}^{10}C_{1} \times {}^{9}C_{1} \times {}^{17}C_{1}$$

$$= \frac{10!}{1!9!} \times \frac{9!}{1!8!} \times \frac{17!}{1!16!}$$

$$= 10 \times 9 \times 17$$

$$= 1530$$

The total number of ways of selecting balls $= {}^{36}C_{3}$

$$= \frac{36!}{3!33!}$$

$$= \frac{36 \times 35 \times 34 \times 33!}{3 \times 2 \times 1 \times 33!}$$

$$= 7140$$

$$\text{Probability} = \frac{\text{Number of observation}}{\text{Total number of observation}}$$

$$= \frac{1530}{7140}$$

$$= \frac{3}{14}$$

$\therefore$ Required probability $= \dfrac{3}{14}$.

Hence, the correct option is (D).

75. Given,

A box contains 100 round discs, 50 square-shaped discs and 30 triangular discs.

$$\text{Probability} = \frac{\text{Number of observation}}{\text{Total number of observation}}$$

Total number of discs $= 180$

Total number of triangular discs $= 30$

The probability that in first pass a triangular disc is attracted $= \dfrac{30}{180}$

$$= \frac{1}{6}$$

The first disc is kept aside and one square disc is kept inside.

The probability that in second pass a triangular disc is attracted

$$= \frac{29}{180}$$

Required Probability $= \frac{1}{6} \times \frac{29}{180}$

$$= \frac{29}{1080}$$

$\therefore$ Required Probability is $\frac{29}{1080}$.

Hence, the correct option is (D).

76. $\frac{dy}{dt} = -5y$

$\Rightarrow \frac{dy}{y} = -5dt$ (variables separable form)

Integrating both side we get,

$$\ln y = -5t + c \quad ......(1)$$

Initial condition: $y = 2$ at $t = 0$

From equation (1),

$$\ln 2 = -5 \times 0 + c$$

$$c = \ln 2$$

$$\ln y = -5t + \ln 2$$

$$\ln\left(\frac{y}{2}\right) = -5t$$

$$y = 2e^{-5t}$$

Now at,

$$t = 3, y = 2e^{-15}$$

Hence, the correct option is (C).

77. Given,

$$(x^2 + y^2)dx = 2xy dy$$

$\frac{dy}{dx} = \frac{(x^2+y^2)}{2xy}$ is homogeneous.

Put, $y = vx$

$$\frac{dy}{dx} = v + \frac{xdv}{dx}$$

$$\Rightarrow v + x\frac{dv}{dx} = \frac{x^2+v^2x^2}{2vx^2} = \frac{x^2(1+v^2)}{2vx^2}$$

$$\Rightarrow x\frac{dv}{dx} = \frac{1+v^2}{2v} - v = \frac{1-v^2}{2v}$$

$$\Rightarrow \frac{2v}{1-v^2}dv = \frac{1}{x}dx$$

By integrating both sides we get,

$$\int \frac{2v}{1-v^2}dv = \int \frac{1}{x}dx ......(1)$$

Now, we integrate $\int \frac{2v}{1-v^2}dv$

Let, $1 - v^2 = a$

On differentiating both sides w.r.t. v, we get

$$\frac{d}{dv}(1 - v^2) = \frac{d}{dv}a$$

$$-2v = \frac{da}{dv}$$

$$dv = -\frac{da}{2v}$$

Now, putting these values on equation (1), we get

$$\int \frac{2v}{a} \times -\frac{da}{2v} = \int \frac{1}{x}dx$$

$$\Rightarrow \int -\frac{da}{a} = \int \frac{1}{x}dx$$

We know that,

$$\int \frac{1}{x}dx = \log x$$

Now,

$$-\log(1 - v^2) = \log x + \log c$$

$$\Rightarrow \log\left[\frac{1}{(1-v^2)}\right] = \log x + \log c$$

$$\Rightarrow \left[\frac{1}{(1-v^2)}\right] = cx$$

$$\Rightarrow \left[\frac{1}{\left(1-\frac{y^2}{x^2}\right)}\right] = cx$$

$$\Rightarrow \left[\frac{x^2}{(x^2-y^2)}\right] = cx$$

$\therefore x^2 = cx(x^2 - y^2)$ is the general solution of the differential equation.

Hence, the correct option is (C).

78. We know that,

The Laplace transform of a general exponential signal is given by:

$$L[e^{-at}] \leftrightarrow \frac{1}{s+a}$$

Where 'a' is any positive integer.

Given,

$$\frac{1}{(s+1)(s-2)}$$

$$\Rightarrow \frac{1}{(s+1)(s-2)} = \frac{A}{(s-2)} + \frac{B}{(s+1)} = \frac{1}{3}\left\{\frac{1}{s-2} + \frac{-1}{s-1}\right\}$$

$$\Rightarrow L^{-1}\left(\frac{1}{(s+1)(s-2)}\right) = L^{-1}\left\{\frac{1}{3}\left(\frac{1}{s-2} - \frac{1}{s-1}\right)\right\}$$

$$= \frac{e^{2t}-e^t}{3}$$

Hence, the correct option is (C).

79. We know that,

This is a definition of Laplace transform.

$$L\{f(t)\} = \int_0^\infty e^{-st} f(t)dt = f(s)$$

Some important Laplace transforms are:

$$L(t^n) = \frac{n!}{s^{n+1}}$$

$$L(t^n) = \frac{n!}{s^{n+1}}$$

$$L(t^n e^{at}) = \frac{n!}{(s-a)^{n+1}}$$

Hence, the correct option is (B).

80. Given,

$$A = \begin{bmatrix} 0 & -2 \\ 3 & 4 \end{bmatrix}$$

Let $I = \begin{bmatrix} 1 & 0 \\ 0 & 1 \end{bmatrix}$ be the 2×2 identity matrix.

Let $I = \begin{bmatrix} 1 & 0 \\ 0 & 1 \end{bmatrix}$ be the 2×2 identity matrix.

$$|A - \lambda| = 0$$

$$\left| \begin{bmatrix} 0 & -2 \\ 3 & 4 \end{bmatrix} - \lambda \begin{bmatrix} 1 & 0 \\ 0 & 1 \end{bmatrix} \right| = 0$$

$$\left| \begin{bmatrix} 0 & -2 \\ 3 & 4 \end{bmatrix} - \begin{bmatrix} \lambda & 0 \\ 0 & \lambda \end{bmatrix} \right| = 0$$

$$\begin{vmatrix} -\lambda & -2 \\ 0 & 4 - \lambda \end{vmatrix} = 0$$

$$-\lambda(4 - \lambda) - (-2)(0) = 0$$

$$-4\lambda + \lambda^2 = 0$$

$$\lambda(\lambda - 4) = 0$$

$$\lambda = 0, \lambda - 4 = 0$$

Thus, $\lambda = 0$ and $\lambda = 4$

So, the two eigenvalues of the given matrix are $\lambda = 0$ and $\lambda = 4$.

Hence, the correct option is (D).

81. Given,

$$A = \begin{bmatrix} 2 & -0.1 \\ 0 & 3 \end{bmatrix}$$

$$A^{-1} = \begin{bmatrix} \frac{1}{2} & a \\ 0 & b \end{bmatrix}$$

Using the formula,

$$AA^{-1} = I$$

$$\Rightarrow \begin{bmatrix} 2 & -0.1 \\ 0 & 3 \end{bmatrix} \begin{bmatrix} \frac{1}{2} & a \\ 0 & b \end{bmatrix} = \begin{bmatrix} 1 & 0 \\ 0 & 1 \end{bmatrix}$$

$$\Rightarrow \begin{bmatrix} 1 & 2a - 0.1b \\ 0 & 3b \end{bmatrix} = \begin{bmatrix} 1 & 0 \\ 0 & 1 \end{bmatrix}$$

On comparing both matrix,

$$\Rightarrow 3b = 1$$

$$\Rightarrow b = \frac{1}{3}$$

$$\Rightarrow 2a - 0.1b = 0$$

$$\Rightarrow 2a = 0.1b$$

$$\Rightarrow a = \frac{0.1b}{2} \quad \ldots \ldots \text{(i)}$$

Putting value of b in equation (i), we get

$$a = \frac{1}{60}$$

Therefore, $a = \frac{1}{60}, b = \frac{1}{3}$

$$\Rightarrow a + b = \frac{1}{60} + \frac{1}{3}$$

$$\Rightarrow a + b = \frac{7}{20}$$

Hence, the correct option is (B).

82. Given,

$$I = \int \left(x^2 - \frac{1}{x^2} \right)^3 dx$$

As we know,

$$(a - b)^3 = a^3 - b^3 - 3a^2b + 3ab^2$$

$$= \int \left\{ (x^2)^3 - \left(\frac{1}{x^2} \right)^3 - 3(x^2)^2 \frac{1}{x^2} + \left(\frac{1}{x^2} \right)^2 x^2 \right\} dx$$

$$I = \int x^6 dx - \int x^{-6} dx - 3 \int x^2 dx + 3 \int x^{-2} dx$$

As we know,

$$\int x^n dx = x^{n+1}(n + 1) + c$$

$$I = \frac{x^7}{7} - \frac{x^{-5}}{-5} - 3\frac{3x^3}{3} + 3\frac{x^{-1}}{-1} + c$$

$$= \frac{x^7}{7} + \frac{1}{5x^5} - x^3 - \frac{3}{x} + c$$

Hence, the correct option is (A).

83. Given,

$$I = \int \frac{dx}{(x-2)(x-1)}$$

Using partial fraction method:

$$\frac{1}{(x-a) \cdot (x-b)} = \frac{A}{(x-a)} + \frac{B}{(x-b)}$$

$$\Rightarrow \frac{1}{(x-2)\cdot(x-1)} = \frac{A}{(x-2)} + \frac{B}{(x-1)} \;\ldots\text{(i)} \Rightarrow 1 = A(x-1) + B(x-2)$$

Compair cofficient both sides.

Cofficient of x is $A + B = 0$...(ii)

Coffiecient of constant $1 = -A - 2B$ ... (iii)

Solving the equation (ii) and (iii) we get,

$$A = 1, B = -1$$

Put the values of A and B in (i),

$$\frac{1}{(x-2)\cdot(x-1)} = \frac{1}{(x-2)} + \frac{-1}{(x-1)}$$

On integrating the above equation,

$$\int \frac{dx}{(x-2)(x-1)} = \int \frac{dx}{(x-2)} - \int \frac{dx}{(x-1)}$$

$$\Rightarrow \log|x-2| - \log|x-1| + c$$

$$= \log\left|\frac{(x-2)}{(x-1)}\right| + c$$

Hence, the correct option is (B).

84. If a JK flip-flop toggles more than once during one clock cycle, it is called racing.

Race-around condition (RAC):

- The race-around condition occurs only in level-triggered flip-flops.

- Level triggered is transparent.

- Even though input is constant, output continuously toggles. Changes for some time continuously.

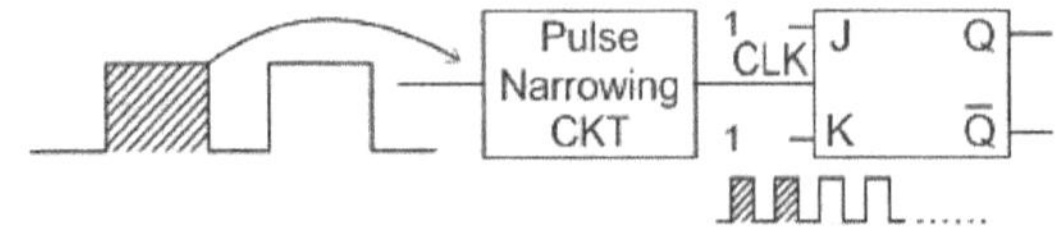

RAC is when $J = 1$ and $K = 1$ [flip-flop in toggling mode] and $t_p > t_{ff}$.

Steps to avoid Race-around condition are:

Before the next clock pulse comes conversion should be complete, if we use an edge-triggered flip-flop then cost increases.

1. Choose flip-flop propagation delay such that $t_p \leq t_{ff} \leq T$. Where t_p, t_{ff}, T are pulse width, flip-flop propagation delay and time duration of flip-flop.

2. We can use pulse narrowing circuits.

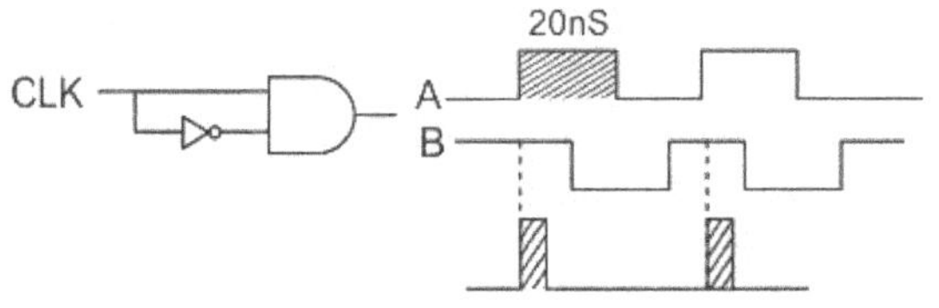

Hence, the correct option is (B).

85. JK **flip-flops:**

J	K	Output(Q new)
0	0	Q (no change or Latch)
1	1	Q' (Toggled)
1	0	1 (Set)
0	1	0 (Reset)

Now,

Q_2	Q_1	Q_0	$J_2 = Q_1$	$K_2 = Q_0$	$J_1 = Q_2$	$K_1 = Q_2$	$J_0 = Q_1$	$K_0 = Q_0$	Q_{2n}	Q_{1n}	Q_{0n}
0	0	0	1	0	0	1	0	1	1	0	0
1	0	0	1	0	1	0	0	1	1	1	0
1	1	0	0	0	1	0	1	1	1	1	1

The state sequence for this circuit for the next 3 clock cycles is $100, 110, 111$.

Hence, the correct option is (C).

86. We know that,

If input is 0 in D flip-flop, then reset mode (0).

If input is 1 in D flip-flop, then set mode (1).

$D \rightarrow$ input

$Q_n \rightarrow$ previous state Q

$Q_{n+1} \rightarrow$ output state Q

Function Table for D.

Flip-flops:

D	Q_n	Q_{n+1}
0	0	0
0	1	0
1	0	1
1	1	1

$$Q_{n+1} = D\overline{Q}_n + DQ_n = D\left(\overline{Q}_n + Q_n\right) = D$$

In D flip-flops, input is same as output.

Hence, the correct option is (A).

87. Logic gate: The digital circuit that can be analyzed with the help of boolean algebra is called a logic gate or logic circuit. A logic gate has two or more inputs but only one output. There are primarily three logic gates namely the OR gate, the AND gate, and the NOT gate.

- A logic gate has one or more inputs but only one output. Thus, option (B) is true.
- It is an electronic device that implements a Boolean function. Thus option (A) is true.
- A logic gate follows a logical relationship between input and output voltages. Thus option (C) is false.

Hence, the correct option is (C).

88. Given,

$$J_n = 0$$

$$K_n = 1$$

Now,

The truth table of $J - K$ flip-flops is:

JK	Q_n	Q_{n+1}
00	0	0
00	1	1
01	0	0
01	1	0
10	0	1
10	1	1
11	0	1
11	1	0

From the truth table when $J = 0$, $K = 1$ the output is reset, i.e. $Q_{n+1} = 0$.

Hence, the correct option is (B).

89.

Present state		Input x	F.F. inputs		Next state		Output $= Q1$
$Q1$	$Q0$		$D1 = x$	$D0 = Q1$	$Q1$	$Q0$	
0	0	0	0	0	0	0	0
0	0	1	1	0	1	0	0
0	1	0	0	0	0	0	0
0	1	1	1	0	1	0	0
1	0	0	0	1	0	1	1
1	0	1	1	1	1	1	1
1		0	0	1	0	1	1

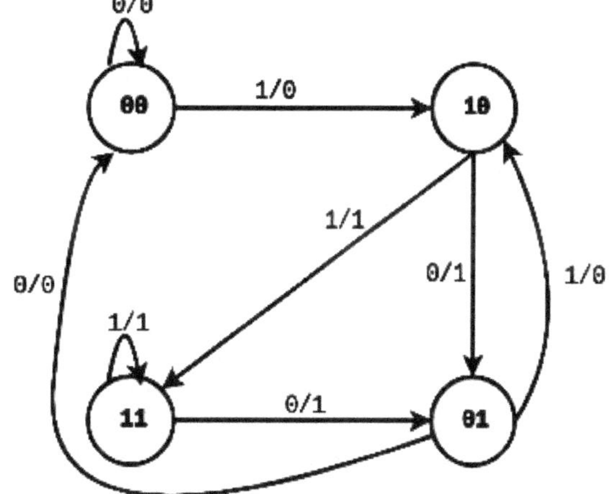

Here inputs 0 and 1 in the State " 00" and " 11" causes self loops, i.e. transaction back to itself.
Hence, the correct option is (A).

90. The edge-triggered T flip-flop has a single control input. Latches and flip-flops are the basic elements to store 1 bit of data.

Latches change the output continuously when there is a change in the input, i.e. they are level triggered. Flip-flop is a combination of latch and clock. It changes the output that is adjusted by the clock.

The main difference between a latch and a flip-flop is that a flip-flop has a clock signal, whereas a latch does not.

So, we can say that a flip-flop without a clock is a latch.

Latches are asynchronous which means that the output of a latch depends on its input.

Basically, there are 4 types of latches:

1. $S - R$ latch
2. $J - K$ latch
3. D latch
4. T latch

For different values of input T, the truth table of the below circuit diagram is:

T	Q_n	Q_{n+1}
0	0	0
0	1	1
1	0	1
1	1	0

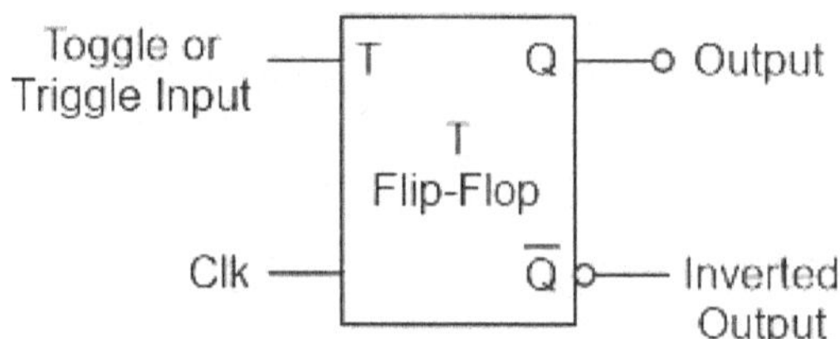

Hence, the correct option is (C).

91. A MOD- n counter is also called a divide by n counter as the input frequency is divided by the number of states of the counter.

For a counter with ' n ' flip flops:

The total number of states $= 2^n (0$ to $2^n - 1)$

The largest number that can be stored in the counter $= 2^n - 1$

To construct a counter with any MOD number, the minimum number flip flops required must satisfy:

Modulus $\leq 2^n$

Where n is the number of flip-flops and is the minimum value satisfying the above condition.

Now,

We are required to construct a counter which divides the input frequency by 40, i.e. we require a MOD- 40 counter.

Number no. of flip-flops are required to construct mod- 40 counter, must satisfy:

$2^n \geq 40$

The minimum value of n satisfying the above is:

$n = 6$ bits.

Hence, the correct option is (C).

92. D Flip-flop:

The truth table of the D flip-flop is given by:

D	$Q(t+1)$	Remarks
0	0	Reset
1	1	Set

The characteristic equation of the D flip-flop is:

$Q(t+1) = D$

From the given configuration the input of the flip-flop is:

$D = Q'$

The below table shows the outputs for the corresponding inputs to the flip-flop.

Let the initial input be 0, that is $D = 0$ then $Q = 0$ and $Q' = 1$.

Clock	$D = Q'$	Q	Q'
Initial	0	0	1
1	1	1	0
2	0	0	1
3	1	1	0
4	0	0	1

The output sequence is $010101 \ldots$

The output sequence is repeating after every two clock pulses. So, the counter value is 2.

The given configuration of the flip-flop represents the 1- bit counter.

Hence, the correct option is (C).

93. As we know,

$n(A \cup B \cup C) = n(A) + n(B) + n(C) - n(A \cap B) - n(A \cap C) - n(B \cap C) + n(A \cap B \cap C)$

$n(2 \cup 5 \cup 9) = n(2) + n(5) + n(9) - n(2 \cap 5) - n(2 \cap 9) - n(5 \cap 9) + n(2 \cap 5 \cap 9)$

$n(2) =$ total count of numbers divisible by $2 = \dfrac{350}{2} = 175$

$n(5) =$ total count of numbers divisible by $5 = \dfrac{350}{5} = 70$

$n(9) =$ total count of numbers divisible by $9 = \dfrac{350}{9} = 38$

Now,

$n(2 \cap 5) \geq$ L.C.M. of 2 and $5 = 10$

$\Rightarrow n(10) =$ total count of numbers divisible by 10.

$= \dfrac{350}{10}$

$= 35$

$n(5 \cap 9) \geq$ L.C.M. of 5 and $9 = 45$

$\Rightarrow n(45)$

Total count of numbers divisible by 45.

$= \dfrac{350}{45}$

$= 7$

$n(2 \cap 9) \geq$ L.C.M. of 2 and $9 = 18$

$\Rightarrow n(18)$

Total count of numbers divisible by 18.

$= \dfrac{350}{18}$

$= 19$

$n(2 \cap 5 \cap 9) \geq$ L.C.M. of $2, 5$ and $9 = 90$

$\Rightarrow n(90)$

Total count of numbers divisible by 90.

$= \dfrac{350}{90}$

$= 3$

$n(2 \cup 5 \cup 9) = 175 + 70 + 38 - 35 - 7 - 19 + 3$

$= 225$

So, there are 225 integers between 1 to 350 that are divisible by 2 or 5 or 9.

Therefore, $350 - 225 = 125$ integers are not divisible by 2 or 5 or 9.

Hence, the correct option is (A).

94. It is given that,

Lower bounds of $\{a, b\}$ are represented L.

Lower bounds of $\{b, c\}$ all represented by R.

Now,

$LB =$ Lower Bound

$LB(a, b) = \{d, g, h, 0, i\}$

$LB(b, c) = \{g, h, i, 0, f\}$

$\therefore L \cap R = \{g, h, i, 0\}$

Hence, the correct option is (A).

95. We know that,

The chromatic number of a graph:

It is the least number of colours required to colour the graph, such that no two adjacent vertices are assigned the same colour.

Diagram:

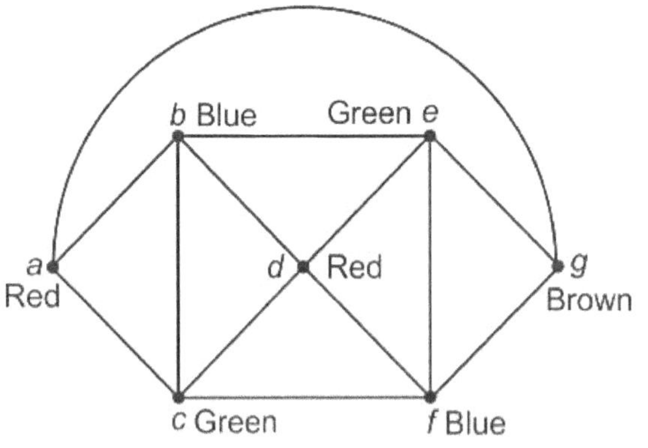

The minimum number of colours needed for the above graph is 4 (Red, Blue, Green, Brown).

Therefore, the chromatic number of a given graph is 4.

Hence, the correct option is (C).

96. The number of ways to divide is:

$4 + 4 = 8$

Countries into 4 groups of 2 each is as follows:

$\dfrac{\left({}^{10}C_2 \times {}^{10}C_2 \times {}^{10}C_2 \times {}^{10}C_2 \right)}{4!} = 30$

Since it is required that at least one group must have only Indian countries, we need to subtract 30 from the number of possible groupings where all 4 groups have 1 Indian country and 1 China country each.

This is equivalent to the number of ways to match each of the 4 Indian countries with one China country:

$= 4!$

$= 4 \times 3 \times 2 \times 1$

$= 24$

Therefore, the total ways are $30 - 24 = 6$.

Hence, the correct option is (A).

97. Given,

$S = \{x, b_1, b_2, \ldots b_n, y\}$

$x \leq b_i$ for all.

$b_i \leq y$ for all i

Where $n \geq 1$

Now,

To make this partial order a total order, we need the relation to hold for every two elements of the partial order.

Currently, there is no relation between any b_i and b_j.

Therefore, for every b_i and b_j, we have to add either $\left(b_i, b_j \right)$ or $\left(b_j, b_i \right)$ in total order.

So, this translates to giving an ordering for n elements between x and y, which can be done in $n!$ ways.

Hence, the correct option is (C).

98. Given,

Here, maximum element is c and so c is of a higher order than any other element in A. Minimal elements are a and b.

No other element in A is of lower order than either a or b.

We are given $P(a) =$ True.

So, for all x such that $a \le x$, $P(x)$ must be true. We do have at least one such x, which is c as it is the maximum element.

So, $P(x)$ = False for all $x \in S$ such that $a \le x$ and $b \le x \to$ cannot be true.

$P(x)$ = True for all $x \in S$ such that $x \ne b \to$ can be true as all elements mapped to true doesn't violate the given implication.

$P(x)$ = False for all $x \in S$ such that $x \ne a$ and $x \ne c$, $>$ can be true if a is related only to c.

$P(x)$ = False for all $x \in S$ such that $b \le x$ and $x \ne c >$ can be true as $b \le x$ ensures $x \ne a$ and for all other elements $P(x)$ can be false without violating the given implication.

Hence, the correct option is (D).

99. We know that,

For a sequence $\{a_0, a_1, a_2, a_3, \dots \dots \dots \dots, a_n\}$ of real numbers, the generating function will be defined as:

$$F(x) = a_0 + a_1 x + a_2 x^2 + a_3 x^3 + \cdots \dots \dots + a_n x^n$$

Then for this we take the binomial expansion, such as this generating function is a binomial expansion of $(1+x)^n$.

Now,

Here, sequence is:

$$\{1,1,3,1,1,1,1 \dots \dots \dots \dots \dots\}$$

$$F(x) = 1 + x + 3x^2 + x^3 + x^4 + \cdots \dots \dots + x^n$$

$$= (1 + x + x^2 + x^3 + \cdots \dots) + 2x^2$$

$$= (1-x)^{-1} + 2x^2$$

We can also write it as:

$$F(x) = \frac{(1 + 2x^2 - 2x^3)}{(1-x)}$$

Hence, the correct option is (B).

100. Number of faces $= |F|$

Number of vertices $= |V| = 16$

Edges covering each face $= 3$

Now,

According to Euler's formula:

$$|V| - |E| + |F| = 2$$

Edges on each face is three,

$$2|E| = 3|F| \quad \text{(every edge is shared by 2 faces)}$$

$$= |F| = \frac{2}{3}|E|$$

$$= 16 - E + \frac{2}{3} | E$$

$$= 16 - E + \frac{2}{3}|E| = 2$$

$$\therefore |E| = 42$$

The number of edges in G is 42.

Hence, the correct option is (A).

// Notes //

// Notes //